D0010699

PAULLIN'S HISTORY OF
NAVAL ADMINISTRATION

BOOKS BY CHARLES OSCAR PAULLIN

THE NAVY OF THE AMERICAN REVOLUTION

COMMODORE JOHN RODGERS

DIPLOMATIC NEGOTIATIONS OF AMERICAN NAVAL OFFICERS

GUIDE TO MATERIALS FOR UNITED STATES HISTORY SINCE 1783 IN
LONDON ARCHIVES (WITH F. L. PAXON)

ATLAS OF THE HISTORICAL GEOGRAPHY OF THE UNITED STATES

OUT-LETTERS OF THE CONTINENTAL MARINE COMMITTEE AND BOARD
OF ADMIRALTY, 2 VOLUMES (EDITOR)

DOCUMENTS RELATING TO THE BATTLE OF LAKE ERIE (EDITOR)

EUROPEAN TREATIES BEARING ON THE HISTORY OF THE UNITED
STATES AND ITS DEPENDENCIES 1716-1815 (EDITOR)

PAULLIN'S
HISTORY
OF
NAVAL
ADMINISTRATION
1775-1911

A COLLECTION OF ARTICLES FROM THE
U. S. NAVAL INSTITUTE *PROCEEDINGS*

BY

CHARLES OSCAR PAULLIN

ST. JOSEPH'S UNIVERSITY   STX
VB23.P32 1968
Paullin's history of naval administratio

3 9353 00007 6354

109627

VB
23
P32
1968

U.S. NAVAL INSTITUTE, ANNAPOLIS, MD.

Copyright © 1968
by
United States Naval Institute
Annapolis, Maryland

Library of Congress Catalogue Card No. 68-57010

PUBLISHER'S PREFACE

Naval history, as it is usually written, concentrates on the ultimate aim of all naval operations—battle. The tactical situation may be described, the strategic preliminaries may be touched on, but all too frequently the subjects of operational planning, logistics, training, procurement, recruiting and shipbuilding are overlooked. The multitudinous details involved in bringing a navy to the point of battle, which may be considered as administration for convenience, never result in stirring prose by naval historians or medals for the administrators.

Yet the history of the U. S. Navy is not complete without an understanding of the administrative processes under which it was created and developed. Fortunately—because that history commenced nearly two centuries ago—the details of early naval administration were searched out and preserved before they were buried in the vast accumulation of records resulting from two world wars. Charles Oscar Paullin, who produced the material contained in this book, commenced his work early in the twentieth century and the last chapter was published just prior to World War I.

Over the last half century, Paullin's sprightly accounts of early naval administration have become well known to historians, students and researchers. His detailed knowledge of the politics and personalities involved in managing the Navy, from the Revolutionary War through the Spanish-American War, give an insight into the times not available in any other work. "See Paullin" has become a standard answer to questions concerning much early naval history, but the student or researcher so instructed found that this was not a simple matter, as only some three dozen libraries throughout the United States maintained complete files of the U. S. Naval Institute *Proceedings* in which Paullin's history of naval administration appeared.

Accordingly, to make the material readily available, the U. S. Naval Institute has produced this single volume collection of the fifteen Paullin articles on early naval administration.

The titles under which these articles were originally published, and the dates, are as follows:

The Administration of the Continental Navy of the American Revolution (September, 1905)

The Administration of the Massachusetts and Virginia Navies of the American Revolution (March, 1906)

Early Naval Administration under the Constitution (September, 1906)

Naval Administration Under Secretaries of the Navy Smith, Hamilton, and Jones, 1801-1814 (December, 1906)

Naval Administration Under the Navy Commissioners, 1816-1842 (June, 1907)

Naval Administration, 1842-1861 (December, 1907)

A Half Century of Naval Administration in America, 1861-1911 (December, 1912; March, 1913; June, 1913; September, 1913; December, 1913; January-February, 1914; May-June, 1914; and July-August, 1914)

U.S. Naval Institute

CONTENTS

PAULLIN'S HISTORY OF
NAVAL ADMINISTRATION

CHAPTER ONE: THE AMERICAN REVOLUTION, 1775-1785

The history of the Continental navy covers a period of ten years extending from 1775 to 1785. During this time various organs of naval administration were employed by the Continental Congress and its successor, the Congress of the Confederation; these two bodies successively constituted the federal government of the Revolution, and their chief duties consisted of the providing, organizing, and maintaining of an army and a navy. The first armed vessels that sailed under Continental pay and control were a little fleet fitted out by Washington in the ports of Massachusetts in the fall of 1775. These vessels were manned by soldiers and commanded by army officers, and were designed to weaken the army of the enemy by capturing his transports which were carrying supplies and troops into Boston. Washington derived his authority for procuring and fitting out the fleet from his commission as commander-in-chief of the Continental army. On the evacuation of Boston by the British in March, 1776, Washington removed his army to New York, and here in April he began to equip a fleet similar to the one he had fitted out at Boston. Altogether these two fleets numbered a dozen vessels. They were abandoned in 1777.

Another "army fleet" was that which was collected and built on Lake Champlain in 1775 and 1776. Its building yard was at Skenesborough at the head of Lake Champlain. In the summer of 1776, this place was the scene of much naval activity. Naval stores, munitions of war, and seamen were collected, and several

3

small naval craft were constructed. The fleet was commanded by Brigadier-General Benedict Arnold. It reached its maximum size in October, 1776, when it consisted of fifteen small vessels mounting 94 cannon and carrying about 700 officers and men. The engagement of Arnold's fleet with that of the British under General Carleton was probably the most important naval battle of the Revolution, since it decided the military campaigns of 1776 and 1777.

Our naval affairs on the Mississippi during the Revolution were conducted by Oliver Pollock, originally a Pennsylvanian, and a man of great ability, integrity, and patriotism. He was the commercial agent at New Orleans of the federal government, and was responsible to the Commercial Committee of Congress. Pollock at different times fitted out three small vessels. One of these captured an armed sloop on Lake Ponchartrain called the *West Florida,* which became the third vessel of Pollock's fleet. He was also granted authority to commission privateers. His naval services came to an end in 1780.

The American Commissioners at Paris and their successor, the American Minister to the French Court, transacted a considerable naval business under the direction of the Committee of Foreign Affairs of Congress. They rented, purchased, and built naval vessels; and officered, manned, and fitted them for sea. They purchased naval supplies, paid officers and crews, and disposed of prizes. They devised plans of naval operations, commissioned privateers, and cared for the naval prisoners. The celebrated cruises in the waters of the British Isles of Conyngham, Wickes, and John Paul Jones were made under their direction. The vesting of these duties in the American representatives in France virtually constituted the establishment of a Branch Naval Office of the American Government at Paris. Benjamin Franklin, who was first one of the American Commissioners and later the American Minister, had more to do with the work of the navy than did his fellow commissioners, Silas Deane, Arthur Lee, and John Adams. Franklin's naval duties in 1779 and 1780 constituted a considerable part of this work at the French Court.

The naval services of Washington, Arnold, Pollock, and the American representatives at Paris, in their entirety by no means insignificant, nevertheless constituted the odds and ends of the naval business of the Continental navy. The far greater and far more important part of naval administration naturally fell to the regularly authorized naval executive of the federal Congress. This body, as is well known, experimented considerably in executive machinery. It established and tried in succession four different organs of naval administration, the Naval Committee, Marine Committee, Board of Admiralty, and Agent of Marine. The organization and work of each of these four naval executives will be now separately considered.

Early in October, 1775, Congress decided to fit out two armed vessels to intercept two British transports loaded with arms, powder, and other stores, and bound from England to Halifax. A committee consisting of Silas Deane of Connecticut, John Langdon of New Hampshire, and Christopher Gadsden of South Carolina was appointed to estimate the expense that would be incurred in fitting out the two vessels. On October 30, when Congress voted to prepare for sea two more vessels, it added four additional members to the committee, Stephen Hopkins of Rhode Island, Joseph Hewes of North Carolina, R. H. Lee of Virginia, and John Adams of Massachusetts. This reconstituted committee composed of seven members was sometimes called " the committee for fitting out armed vessels," but most frequently the " Naval Committee." It obtained for its use a room in a public house in Philadelphia, and in order that there should be no conflict between its meetings and those of Congress, it fixed its hours from six in the evening until the close of its business. Its sessions were sometimes pleasantly continued even until midnight, by conservational diversions marked by a rich flow of soul, history, poetry, wine, and Jamaica rum.

John Adams, who always wrote pungently, has left us a lively picture of the Naval Committee. His description makes it clear that the deliberations of this Committee were not always marked by that exalted seriousness and impassive dignity, which we too often ascribe to the Revolutionary Fathers. " The pleasantest part of my labors for the four years I spent in Congress from 1774 to 1778," he said, " was in the Naval Committee. Mr. Lee, Mr. Gadsden, were sensible men, and very cheerful, and Governor Hopkins of Rhode Island, above seventy years of age, kept us all alive. Upon business his experience and judgment were very useful. But when the business of the evening was over, he kept us in conversation until eleven, and sometimes twelve o'clock.

His custom was to drink nothing all day, nor till eight o'clock in the evening, and then his beverage was Jamaica spirit and water. It gave him wit, humor, anecdotes, science, and learning. He read Greek, Roman, and British history, and was familiar with English poetry, particularly, Pope, Thomson, and Milton, and the flow of his soul made all of his reading our own, and seemed to bring to recollection in all of us all we had ever read. I could neither eat nor drink in those days. The other gentlemen were very temperate. Hopkins never drank to excess, but all he drank was immediately not only converted into wit, sense, knowledge, and good humor, but inspired us with similar qualities."

The active life of the Naval Committee lasted from October, 1775, until January, 1776, during which time it laid the foundation of the navy. Its chairman in January, 1776, was Stephen Hopkins; whether he was the first to fill the position is not known. His knowledge of the business of shipping made him particularly useful to the Committee. The accounts of the Naval Committee were kept by Joseph Hewes, the member from North Carolina and close friend of John Paul Jones. Early in December, 1775, John Adams returned home, and by January only four members of the Committee were left to transact its business.

The Naval Committee prepared the naval legislation of Congress organizing the Continental navy. One of its most important pieces of work of this sort was the drafting of the first rules and regulations of the navy. These were in force throughout the Revolution and were re-adopted for the government of the new navy under the Constitution. They were largely the work of John Adams and are often referred to as Adams's rules. He drew liberally from the naval statutes and regulations in force in the British navy in 1775. Adams's rules, eight or ten pages in length, are brevity itself compared with the present voluminous Rules and Regulations of the United States Navy. The Committee also drafted the legislation that was adopted by Congress fixing the shares of the proceeds of prizes.

Under the authorizations of Congress of October 13 and October 30, 1775, the Naval Committee purchased four vessels, the *Alfred, Columbus, Cabot,* and *Andrew Doria;* named respectively for the founder of the English navy, the discoverer of America, the first English explorer of America, and the great Genoese Admiral. The first vessel to be bought, and the first vessel in the

American navy, was the *Alfred,* a ship of 220 tons burden. She was originally the *Black Prince* and was owned by John Nixon, the well-known Philadelphia merchant of Revolutionary times. By the end of January, 1776, the Committee had added four other small vessels to the navy, the sloops *Providence* and *Hornet,* and the schooners *Wasp* and *Fly.* The *Providence* had been the *Katy* of the Rhode Island navy. The *Hornet* and *Wasp* were obtained in Baltimore. These eight vessels were the nucleus of the Continental navy.

Meanwhile the Committee had been officering its fleet. On November 5, 1775, it appointed Esek Hopkins of Rhode Island, a brother of the chairman of the Committee, to be commander-in-chief of the fleet. On December 7, it gave a commission of lieutenant to John Paul Jones, an energetic and capable young man, twenty-eight years old, whose brilliant career was still unforeseen. On December 22, the Committee laid before Congress a "list of officers by them appointed." In addition to Hopkins and Jones the list included the names of four captains, four first lieutenants, five second lieutenants, and three third lieutenants. The little roll of captains was headed by Dudley Saltonstall, a brother-in-law of Silas Deane the Connecticut member of the Committee, and was ended by John Burroughs Hopkins, a son of the commander-in-chief. Immediately above J. B. Hopkins in rank was Nicholas Biddle, a young Philadelphian of great promise who had served in the British navy on board the same ship with Nelson. The fourth captain was Abraham Whipple, the commodore of the Rhode Island navy. In these appointments of the Committee it takes no eagle eye to discern the workings of nepotism and sectional influences.

In December, the Committee was preparing its fleet for sea. The Pennsylvania government contributed arms, ammunition, and sailors. Commodore Hopkins enlisted more than one hundred seamen in Rhode Island. On December 3, Lieutenant John Paul Jones hoisted the Continental flag on board the *Alfred,* the flagship of the fleet and the first Continental vessel to fly the colors of the new nation. In February, 1776, the fleet assembled at Cape Henlopen. On January 5, the Naval Committee issued sailing orders to the commander-in-chief. He was directed, if winds and weather admitted of it, to proceed directly to Chesapeake Bay and strike the enemy's fleet under Lord Dunmore, from thence to

sail southward and master the British forces off the coast of the
Carolinas, and from thence to proceed to Rhode Island and " attack, take, and destroy all the enemy's naval force that you may
find there." This program of the Committee seems rather ambitious when one considers the motley assemblage of officers, seamen, and cruisers that composed this fleet of made-over merchantmen. The first naval essay of the new government met with
rather indifferent success. Hopkins, having concluded that his
Armada might prove vincible on the stormy coasts of Virginia,
gave orders to his captains to sail for Nassau, New Providence,
on leaving the Delaware Capes. Meeting with but slight resistance, he early in March captured this town. He next sailed
for Rhode Island, and off the eastern end of Long Island met and
engaged His Majesty's ship *Glasgow*. The fleet permitted the
British ship to escape under circumstances that were regarded as
discreditable to the naval skill of the American commanders.
This expedition of Hopkins was the sole naval enterprise of the
navy while it was in charge of the Naval Committee. Early in
1776, this Committee, reduced in membership, yielded its control
of marine affairs to a new committee with a fuller complement of
members, whose organization and work will be next considered.

While the Naval Committee was purchasing, in the fall of 1775,
a few small merchantmen and fitting them out as naval vessels.
Congress was earnestly discussing a much larger and more important project, the building of a fleet of frigates adequately
adapted to the purposes of war. Several members who favored
the first undertaking were loth to embark on the more ambitious
and more warlike enterprise of constructing a navy. It was not
until December 13, 1775, that Congress decided to enter upon a
program of naval construction. It this day voted to build
thirteen frigates, five of 32, five of 28, and three of 24 guns,
to be distributed, as regards the place of their construction,
among the states as follows: New Hampshire ,one; Massachusetts, two; Rhode Island, two; Connecticut, one; New York, two;
Pennsylvania, four; and Maryland, one. It was estimated that
these ships would cost on the average, $66,666.67 each, and that
their whole cost would amount to $866,666.67. All the materials
for fitting them for sea, except canvas and gun powder, could be
procured in America.

On December 14, a committee consisting of one member from

each colony was chosen by ballot to take charge of the building and fitting out of these vessels. The members chosen with their states were as follows: Josiah Bartlett, New Hampshire; John Hancock, Massachusetts; Stephen Hopkins, Rhode Island; Silas Deane, Connecticut; Francis Lewis, New York; Stephen Crane, New Jersey; Robert Morris, Pennsylvania; George Read, Delaware; Samuel Chase, Maryland; R. H. Lee, Virginia; Joseph Hewes, North Carolina; Christopher Gadsden, South Carolina; and John Houston, Georgia. The committee was a very able one, comprising several of the foremost men of the Revolution. Hancock, Morris, Hopkins, and Hewes were especially interested in naval and maritime affairs. The absence of the name of John Adams is probably accounted for by his return home early in December.

This new committee was soon designated as the "Marine Committee," by which name it was referred to throughout the Revolution. Larger and with its engrossing work of building and fitting out the thirteen frigates more active than the Naval Committee, it soon overshadowed and finally absorbed its colleague. This absorbtion was facilitated no doubt by the fact that the four members of the Naval Committee remaining in January, 1776, also belonged to the new committee. On January 25, 1776, Congress placed with the Marine Committee the direction of the fleet that the Naval Committee had prepared and sent to sea. The Marine Committee now acquired a firm grasp of the naval business of the colonies and from this time until December, 1779, it was the recognized and responsible head of the Naval Department, and as such, during the period that saw the rise and partial decline of the Continental navy, its history is of prime importance.

The Marine Committee like the Naval Committee had an office of its own, in Philadelphia, and held its sessions in the evening. Its officers consisted of a chairman or president, a vice-president, and a secretary. Its clerical force comprised one or more clerks. On June 6, 1777, Congress resolved that five of its members— which number thereafter constituted a quorum—should form a "board" for the transaction of business. Each of the thirteen states had one member on the Committee. Rarely did more than one-half of the Committee's members attend its meetings. Its personnel was continually changing. This was in part necessitated by a similar change in the membership of Congress, whose old members retired and new ones filled their places. The members of the Marine Committee received no pay for their naval services as such. Each state of course paid its member of the Committee for his services as a delegate to the federal Congress. The wages of the secretary and of the clerks of the Committee varied. On June 16, 1778, the Committee was permitted to raise the wages of its clerks to $100 a month. After November 2, 1778, the secretary was paid at the rate of $8000 a year. During 1778 and 1779 Congress, owing to the depreciation of the currency, raised the salaries of it employees. The secretary of the Marine Committee was John Brown.

The most responsible duties of the Committee naturally fell to the four or five members eldest in its service. From this class it drew its chairman. Three of the five men who are known to have filled this office were on the first list of the Committee's members. During probably all of 1776 and for a part of 1777 courtly John Hancock presided over the Marine Committee, while at the same time he dignified the chair of the President of Congress. In December, 1777, Henry Laurens of South Carolina had succeeded to both of Hancock's positions. In 1778 and 1779 the mantles of these first leaders in naval administration, whether they exactly fitted or not, were worn by Richard Henry Lee, "one of the fine fellows from Virginia" as John Adams called him; Samuel Adams, the radical democrat and man of the Boston town meeting; and William Whipple of New Hampshire. Lee was chairman of the Committee in the summer of 1778. In December, 1778, Adams had succeeded him. Adams in turn yielded in June, 1779, to Whipple, who continued to fill the office until the Committee was superseded by the Board of Admiralty in December, 1779.

There were other members besides the chairmen upon whose shoulders rested the burden of the naval business. Morris, Hewes, and Hopkins have been previously mentioned as members who were deeply interested in naval affairs. Morris was for a time vice-president of the Committee. During the winter of 1776-77, while Congress was at Baltimore, he remained in Philadelphia and for a time, practically without assistance from the Committee, administered the naval affairs of the colonies. William Ellery of Rhode Island, who on October 13, 1776, succeeded Hopkins on the Committee, showed zeal in the business of the navy. The work of Francis Lewis of New York deserves mention. No doubt there were other members whose naval services were considerable. Unfortunately, time has been careless with many of the records of the Committee.

In carrying out the resolutions of Congress of December 13, 1775, authorizing the building of thirteen frigates, the Marine Committee employed agents to superintend the work. These men, who were variously designated, were residents of the colonies in which they were employed, and their selection was usually determined by local advice and influence. The New Hampshire frigate, the *Raleigh*, 32, was built at Portsmouth under the direction of John Langdon, formerly a member of the Naval Committee, but now Continental Agent at Portsmouth. He employed three master-builders who completed the frigate within less than sixty days after raising it. The Massachusetts frigates, *Hancock*, 32, and *Boston*, 24, were built at Salisbury and Newburyport under the direction of an agent.

The Rhode Island vessels, *Warren*, 32, and *Providence*, 28, were constructed at Providence under the superintendence of a committee of twelve influential men of that city, who were appointed by Stephen Hopkins, the Rhode Island member of the Marine Committee. Certain complaints were lodged with the Marine Committee against the committee at Providence. One of these was made by Commodore Esek Hopkins, who charged that the *Providence* and *Warren* had cost twice as much as their contract price, " owing to some of the very committee that built the ships taking the workmen and the stock agreed for off to work and fit their privateers, and even threatening the workmen if they did not work for them." When in the fall of 1776, the Marine Committee wrote to the Providence committee blaming them for some of their proceedings, they relinquished their authority over the two vessels to Stephen Hopkins.

The *Trumbull*, 28, was built under the direction of agents at Chatham on the Connecticut river. Two other frigates were begun in Connecticut in 1777, the *Confederacy*, 36, on the Thames river between Norwich and New London; and the *Bourbon*, 28, at Chatham. Each of these two frigates were constructed by a superintendent responsible to Governor Jonathan Trumbull and the Connecticut Council of Safety. Two commissioners at Poughkeepsie, New York, had charge of the work on the *Montgomery*.

28, and *Congress,* 24.   The Marine Committee kept well in their
own hands the direction of the building at Philadelphia of the
Pennsylvania frigates, the *Randolph,* 32, *Washington,* 32, *Effing-
ham,* 28, and *Delaware,* 24.   The *Virginia,* 28, was built at Baltimore with the assistance of the Baltimore Committee of Observation.   When under the resolves of Congress of November 20,
1776, two frigates were begun at the Gosport navy yard in
Virginia, the work was placed in charge of two commissioners and
a master-builder.   Richard Henry Lee, the Virginia member of
the Marine Committee, made the contract with the master-builder.

The need of some one to receive and dispose of prizes soon led
to the appointment of " agents for prizes " in the leading seaports
of the colonies.   On April 23, 1776, Congress on the recommendation of the Marine Committee appointed prize agents as follows :
one at Boston ; one at Providence ; one at New London, Connecticut ; one at New York ; two at Philadelphia ; one at Baltimore ; one at Williamsburg, Virginia ; and one each at Wilmington, Newbern, and Edenton, North Carolina.   On June 25, 1776,
Congress appointed an agent at Portsmouth, New Hampshire.
In November, 1776, the Marine Committee selected two prize
agents for South Carolina and one for Georgia.   This list was
not completed until September 1, 1779, when Congress appointed
a prize agent for New Jersey.   These agents had charge of the
Continental prizes sent into their respective states..   By far the
most important agency was that of John Bradford at Boston.   It
may be estimated that one-half of all the prizes captured by the
Continental vessels in American waters were ordered to Boston.
The naval port second in importance was Philadelphia.

The duties of the prize agents were to libel all of the Continental prizes sent into their jurisdiction, to see that they were
tried by the proper admiralty court ; and after they had been
legally condemned, to sell them, and make an equitable distribution of the proceeds in accordance with the resolutions of Congress governing the sharing of prizes.   The prize agents were
directed by the Marine Committee to render to it a quarterly statement showing the prizes received, sales effected, and distributions
of the proceeds made.

The same men who were prize agents were also as a rule " Continental agents," in which capacity they served the various administrative organs of Congress, including the Marine Committee.

They assisted the Committee, and the commander-in-chief of the
fleet in purchasing, refitting, provisioning, and manning the armed
vessels. The naval services of some of these men, both as prize
agents and as Continental agents, were so considerable as to
render their names worthy of mention. Most conspicuous among
the several naval agents were John Bradford of Boston, John
Nixon and John Maxwell Nesbitt of Philadelphia, John Langdon
of Portsmouth, New Hampshire, Nathaniel Shaw, Jr., of New
London, and Daniel Tillinghast of Providence.

The governors and legislatures of the colonies and the municipal
and local authorities often aided the Committee in its work. The
work of Governor Trumbull and the Connecticut Council of Safety
has already been mentioned. In the latter part of 1776 the New
York Convention attempted to secure the two Continental frigates
at Poughkeepsie from the British when they occupied the lower
Hudson. Such illustration could be multiplied.

In two services so closely connected as the army and navy, the
officers and agents of one were naturally called upon now and then
to serve the other. They borrowed and lent to each other cannon,
ammunition, and military stores.· The Commissaries of one and
the Navy Boards of the other had mutual dealings. The Commissary-General of Prisoners of the Army had much to do with
the care of the marine prisoners.

Towards the close of 1776, the unsatisfactory state of the naval
business, together with its increase, and its growing complexity,
forced home upon the Committee the necessity of providing some
permanent force to take charge of the details of naval administration. Accordingly on November 6, 1776, Congress at the instance of the Marine Committee resolved " that three persons,
well skilled in maritime affairs, be immediately appointed to execute the business of the navy, under the direction of the Marine
Committee." Later in the same month John Nixon, John Wharton, and Francis Hopkinson were selected as suitable persons for
this work. The three men lived within or near Philadelphia.

Nixon with his experience as a shipping merchant was probably
best fitted for his task. Fancy may discern a poetic fitness in his
choice, since he had been the owner of the *Alfred,* the first vessel
of the American navy. Nixon had also the distinction of being
the first man to read publicly the Declaration of Independence.
Wharton belonged to the distinguished Philadelphia family of

that name.   Of the three men Hopkinson probably had the widest culture.   At the outbreak of the Revolution he was practising law at Bordentown, New Jersey.   He was one of the signers of the Declaration of Independence.   From 1779 to 1789 he was judge of the admiralty court of Pennsylvania.   He is best known, however, not for his substantial services, but as the author of the humorous ballad, the Battle of the Kegs.

On April 19, 1777, Congress on the motion of John Adams decided to form a similar board for the four New England states, the members of which were to " reside at or in the neighborhood of Boston, in the state of Massachusetts Bay, with a power to adjourn to any part of New England; who shall have the super-intendence of all naval and marine affairs of these United States within the four Eastern states, under the direction of the Marine Committee."   Owing to the indifference of Congress to its estab-lishment, Adams obtained the filling of this board with some difficulty.   Finally, nine men were nominated and on May 6, three of these were chosen commissioners, James Warren of Plymouth, Massachusetts; William Vernon of Providence, Rhode Island; and John Deshon of New London, Connecticut.

Foremost of the three commissioners was Warren, an eminent patriot who had been President of the Massachusetts Provincial Congress and also of the Massachusetts Board of War.   He was an intimate friend of John and Samuel Adams, and it is said that he much resembled the latter in character.   Vernon, who was made President of the Navy Board, was one of the most dis-tinguished of the Newport merchants and one of the most self-sacrificing of patriots.   During the Revolution he advanced large sums of money to the federal government which were only in part repaid.   Before the war his trade extended to all the mari-time nations of Europe, and to the West Indies and Africa.   Deshon was of Huguenot descent.   He was conspicuous in the Revolutionary party of New London, and was a captain in the military forces of Connecticut.   He rendered much assistance in fitting out the Connecticut navy.

These two boards were variously designated in the official docu-ments of the time.   The one was most frequently called the Navy Board of the Middle Department or District, or the Navy Board at Philadelphia, Bordentown, or Baltimore, according to its loca-tion; and the other, the Navy Board of the Eastern Department or District, or the Navy Board at Boston. The Navy Board at Philadelphia was first referred to as the Continental Navy Board, or the Board of Assistants. These two names indicate that when the Board at Philadelphia was formed the establishing of a second board was not in contemplation. The Navy Board at Philadelphia seems to have taken little or no part in the naval affairs in New England. It was hardly settled in its work before the Navy Board at Boston was created. Attention should be called to the fact that the offices of Navy Board and of Commissioners of the Navy had long been established in the British navy, and that these British models were in the minds of the members of the Marine Committee and of Congress.

Each board had a secretary, treasurer, and paymaster, but one person sometimes served in two, or even the three capacities. Each board had one, and sometimes two clerks. A clerkship was at times joined with one of the other offices. The boards as a rule selected their own employees. Any two members of the Navy Board at Boston were empowered by Congress on October 23, 1777, to form a quorum.

The personnel of the Navy Board at Boston remained the same throughout its history, as did also its headquarters. On the other hand, the membership of the Board at Philadelphia made several changes. On May 9, 1778, William Smith of Baltimore was elected in the place of John Nixon, who had resigned. On August 19, since Hopkinson and Smith had given up their offices, Captain Nathaniel Falconer and James Searle, both of Pennsylvania, were appointed commissioners. Falconer declined the appointment; Searle accepted, but resigned on September 26. Meanwhile Wharton had resigned, and the three commissionerships were vacant. On November 4, 1778, the vacancies were filled by the reappointment of Wharton, and the selection of James Read of Delaware, the clerk and paymaster of the Board, and William Winder, a captain in the military forces of Maryland and a judge of the court of appeals of Somerset county in that state. When in December, 1776, Philadelphia seemed to be in danger from the enemy, Congress and the Board retreated to Baltimore, where they spent the winter of 1776-77. The fortunes of war compelled the Board in the fall of 1777 to retreat to Bordentown, New Jersey, and after the American fleet in the Delaware was destroyed, the Marine Committee early in 1778 ordered it to again meet in Baltimore. In the summer of 1778 after the British evacuated Philadelphia, the Navy Board permanently returned to the Quaker city.

The salary of a commissioner of the navy was first fixed at $1500 a year. On October 31, 1778, " in consideration of the extensive business of their departments," this salary was raised to $3000 ; and on November 12, 1779, by reason of the depreciation of the currency, to $12,000. It was reduced on September 25, 1780, to $1500, and was ordered to be paid quarterly in specie or its equivalent. The salaries of the employees of the navy boards underwent like variations. Beginning with $500, they advanced in some instances to as high as $2000 a year. On August 4, 1778, the clerk of the Navy Board at Boston was made a special allowance of $500 " in consideration of the great and constant business " in which he had been engaged.

The duties of the navy boards were of a varied character. Each board superintended the building, manning, fitting, provisioning, and repairing of the armed vessels in its district. It kept a register of the vessels which it built, showing the name, dimensions, burden, number of guns, tackle, apparel, and furniture of each vessel. Each board kept records of all the officers, sailors, and marines in its district, and required the commanders to make returns of these items upon the termination of their cruises. It was the duty of the boards to notify the Marine Committee of the arrivals and departures of the Continental vessels. They were required to settle the naval accounts and to " keep fair books of all expenditures of public moneys." The records of their transactions were to be open to the inspection of Congress and the Marine Committee. They rendered to the Committee annually, or oftener when required, an account of their disbursements. The boards paid the salaries of the officers and seamen and audited the accounts of the prize agents.

In the appointment of officers the Navy Board at Boston was given a freer rein than its colleague at Philadelphia. The share of the navy boards in selecting officers and in enlisting seamen was about as follows. The boards superintended the appointing of petty officers and the enlisting of seamen, both of which duties were chiefly performed by the commanders of vessels and by recruiting agents. The boards generally selected the warrant officers, very frequently on the recommendation of the command-

ers. Disregarding the one appointment to the office of commander-in-chief, there were in the Continental navy but two
classes of commissioned officers, captains, and lieutenants. The
boards often chose lieutenants; and they recommended captains to
the Marine Committee. The Committee furnished the boards
with blank warrants and commissions properly signed by the
President of Congress. When one of such forms was properly
filled out by a navy board for an officer, the validity of his title to
his position and rank could not be questioned.

The boards were empowered, under certain circumstances and
in accordance with the rules and regulations of the navy and the
resolutions of Congress, to order courts of enquiry and courts
martial. They could administer oaths to the judges and officials
of these courts. A board could suspend an officer of the navy
who treated it with "indecency and disrespect." On October 23,
1777, the Navy Board at Boston was given power to suspend a
naval officer "until the pleasure of Congress shall be known."
Not always did the kindliest relations exist between the navy
boards and the commanders of vessels. Officers, who but yesterday tramped the decks of their own merchantmen giving commands but not receiving them, chafed under the subordination
that their position in the navy exacted.

The navy boards made public the resolutions of Congress on
naval affairs, copies of which they lodged with the prize agents,
the commanders of vessels, and all interested persons. They
distributed among the naval captains the rules and regulations
of the navy, the sea-books, and the naval signals. The boards
acted in an advisory capacity to the Marine Committee, which
frequently called upon them for information or opinions; when a
revision of the rules and regulations was under consideration,
their assistance in the work was requested. Sometimes they
volunteered important suggestions looking to the betterment of
the navy. They communicated frequently with the Committee
giving in detail the state of the naval business in their respective
districts.

In the hiring, purchasing, and building of vessels the boards
had to do with craft of all sorts, freight-boats, fire-ships, galleys,
half-galleys, packets, brigs, schooners, sloops, ships, frigates, and
men-of-war. Measured by the standards of the time the building
of one of the larger vessels was a work of some magnitude. A

notion of the men and materials requisite for such an undertaking
may be gained from an estimate, made early in 1780, of the
sundries needed to complete the 74-gun ship *America,* the largest
of the Continental vessels constructed during the Revolution.
The construction of this ship had been begun at Portsmouth,
New Hampshire, in 1777. It was computed that there would be
required one hundred and fifty artisans and workmen for an
average period of eight months. Fifty carpenters, twenty ordinary laborers, twenty caulkers, ten riggers, ten sailors, two
master-builders, and an uncertain number of blacksmiths, sail-
makers, coopers, plumbers, painters, glaziers, carvers, boat-build-
ers, ship-copperers, tinners, cabinet-makers, and tanners were
demanded. Materials and provisions were needed as follows:
seven hundred tons of timbers, one hundred casks of naval stores,
forty tons of iron, one thousand water-casks, masts and spars of
all sorts, sheets of lead, train oil, and oakum; provisions for most
of the above workmen, and lastly an indispensable lubricant for all
naval services at this time, " rum one-half pint per day, including
extra hands, say for 150 hands, 8 months, 12 hhds., 1310 gallons."
In the building of the armed vessels the boards were greatly
hampered by the difficulty of obtaining artisans, owing to their
being called out for military service or to their engaging in
privateering. In providing armament and equipment they were
embarrassed by the inexperience of the colonists in casting
cannon, and by the obstacles that they encountered in importing
canvas, cables, arms, and ammunition.

For the future use of the fleet the navy boards collected in due
season provisions and naval stores. In their work as purveyors
for the navy a knowledge of the baking of bread and the curing
of meats might not prove amiss. The kinds and quantities of
provisions which they bought may be seen from an estimate of
the supplies that were requisite to equip for sea for a single cruise
the 36-gun frigate *Confederacy.* The names and quantities of
the articles needed were as follows: bread, 35,700 lbs.; beef, 15,300
lbs.; pork, 15,300 lbs.; flour, 5100 lbs.; potatoes, 10,000 lbs.;
peas, 80 bus.; mutton, 2500 lbs.; butter, 637 lbs.; rice, 2550 lbs.;
vinegar, 160 gals.; and rum, 2791 gals. The boards' supplies
of naval stores consisted chiefly of canvas, sails, cordage, cables,
tar, turpentine, and ship chandlery.

The commissioners of each district made some division of their work among themselves. For instance the special task of Wharton of the Philadelphia Board was the superintending of the accounting and the naval finances of the Middle District. During 1778 Deshon of the Boston Board, spent much time in Connecticut attending to the naval business in that state. This had to do chiefly with freeing the *Trumbull* frigate from a sand-bar upon which she had grounded. During the same year Vernon was for a time at Providence endeavoring to get to sea the Continental ships that the British had blockaded in that port. For part of the year Warren alone attended to the business of the board at its headquarters at Boston. On August 4, 1778, Congress appropriated $365 to each of the commissioners of the Navy Board at Boston to pay their travelling expenses during the past year, since in the right discharge of their office they were obliged " frequently to visit the different parts of their extensive district."

In the extent of its powers and the amount of its business the Boston Board exceeded the one at Philadelphia. This was largely owing to the centering of naval affairs in New England after the occupation of Philadelphia by the British in September, 1777, and to the capture or destruction in that year of a large part of the fleet to the southward of New England. After 1776 all the new vessels added in America to the navy, with the exception of two or three, were either purchased or built in New England. The distance of the Boston Board from the Marine Committee, with the consequent difficulties and delays in communicating with it, made it necessary for the Committee to grant to it larger powers than to the Philadelphia Board.

The most important work of a Naval Office is the directing of the movement of the fleet, or in other words the determining of the cruises of the armed vessels. This power the Marine Committee jealously guarded and was loath to yield any part of it. The Committee was forced at times, however, to give the Boston Board a considerable discretion in the directing of the cruises of the vessels in its district. In July, 1777, it ordered the Board to send out the cruisers as fast as they could be got ready, " directing the Commanders to such Latitudes as you shall think there will be the greatest chance of success of intercepting the enemy's Transports and Merchant Ships." In November, 1778, it wrote to the Board to send the vessels " either collectively, or singly, as you shall judge proper, using your discretion as to the time for

which their Cruises shall continue, and your best judgment in
directing the commanders to such places and on such stations as
you shall think will be for the general benefit of the United
States, and to annoy and distress the Enemy." Such general
orders were always subject to the particular plans and directions
of the Committee, which were by no means few. The Committee
itself determined the service of all the vessels that refitted at
Philadelphia. As a consequence the duties of the Navy Board
at Philadelphia had to do chiefly with the minor details of administration. The Committee and Congress reserved the right
to detail captains to vessels.

Turning now from the work of the navy boards to that of the
Marine Committee, one finds the significant fact to be the two-
fold relation that the Committee bore to the federal Congress.
By reason of the union in Congress of both legislative and
executive functions, the Committee was at one and the same time
an administrative organ of Congress charged with executing the
business of its Naval Department, and its legislative committee
on naval affairs. Naturally, there was at points no line of
demarcation between these two functions; and it is therefore not
always easy to determine in which capacity the Committee is
acting. The Committee's administrative duties *par excellence*
were the enforcing and the carrying out by means of its agents
of the various resolutions of Congress on naval affairs. Already
much light has been thrown upon this phase of the Committee's
work in the treatment of the navy boards and the navy agents.

It was the duty of the Committee to see that the resolutions on
naval affairs were brought to the attention of the proper persons,
officers, agents, and authorities. As the head of the Naval Department it issued its commands and orders to the navy boards,
the naval agents, and the commanders of vessels. This was done
both verbally and by letters. The Navy Board of the Middle
Department, the naval agents at Philadelphia, and often the naval
officers in that port received orders by word of mouth. In the
prosecution of its work outside of Philadelphia the Committee
conducted a large correspondence chiefly with the Navy Board
at Boston, the naval agents at Portsmouth, Boston, New London,
and Baltimore, and the leading naval captains. It addressed
letters to the governors of most of the states and to many of the
local governments within the states; to the commander-in-chief

of the navy, Washington, General Heath, General Schuyler, the Commissary-General of Prisoners, the Commissary-General of Purchases, the merchants of Baltimore, Count D'Estaing, the Commissioners in Paris, and most of the captains of the navy. This list of correspondents well represents the range of the business of the Committee.

Through its recommendations to Congress the Committee virtually selected most of the captains and lieutenants of the navy and marine corps, the commissioners of the navy, the prize agents, and the advocates for trying maritime causes. Appointments to these offices were rarely made by Congress contrary to the recommendations of the Committee, or on its own initiative independent of the Committee. A few captains and lieutenants of the navy were appointed by representatives of the United States in France. Oliver Pollock, the commercial agent at New Orleans, chose one of the Continental captains, William Pickles.

As is well known, all executive offices are called upon to establish certain forms, rules, and regulations for the guidance of their agents. Of this character was the fixing by the Marine Committee of the naval signals, the forms for sea-books, and the uniform of naval officers. The Committee's regulations on uniform were dated, September 5, 1776. For captains they prescribed a blue coat, " with red lappels, slash cuff, stand up collar, flat yellow buttons, blue britches, red waistcoat with narrow lace." The uniform of the officers of marines was equally resplendent in colors. It included a green coat with white cuffs, a silver epaulet on the shoulder, white waistcoat and breeches edged with green, and black gaiters with garters. Green was the distinctive color of the marines. The privates were to display this badge in the form of green shirts, " if they can be procured." Not enough information is accessible to determine what influence the regulations prescribing the uniform of British officers had on those adopted by the Marine Committee. Both required in the uniform of captains, blue coats, standing up collars, and flat buttons; neither required epaulets, the wearing of which, as is well known, originated in France. It is probable that the prescribed uniform was little worn by the Continental naval officers. Grim necessity forced each officer to ransack whatever wardrobe Providence offered, and it is somewhat inaccurate to call their miscellaneous garbs, " uniforms."

As the Naval Office at Philadelphia developed, letters, memorials, and petitions poured in upon it in increasing numbers. Many of these communications were addressed to the President of Congress, were read in Congress, and were formally referred to the Marine Committee to be acted or reported upon. It was only infrequently that Congress offered any suggestions as to their proper disposition. These complaints and requests were of a varied character and came from many sources; not a few originated with that obsequious crowd with axes to grind that always attend upon official bodies. The wide range of these communications may be judged from the following subjects selected at random.

New Hampshire and Massachusetts request that the frigates building in those states be ordered to defend the New England coast. Governor Livingston of New Jersey asks for a naval office for a relative, Musco Livingston. Gerard, the minister of France to the United States, wishes to know "the opinion of Congress respecting his offering a premium to the owners of privateers that shall intercept masts and spars belonging to the enemy, coming from Halifax to New York and Rhode Island." John Macpherson asserts that the position of commander-in-chief in the navy was promised to him by Messrs. Randolph, Hopkins, and Rutledge, to whom he communicated an important secret. An affront has been offered several French captains in Boston by the commander of the Continental frigate *Warren*. Twelve lieutenants who have been dismissed from the navy for combining in order to extort an increase of pay ask to be reinstated. The ambassador of Naples at the court of France, whose king has opened his ports to American vessels, wishes to " know the colours of the flag and the form of the sea-papers of the United States." Captain Biddle writes concerning the cruel treatment inflicted by Lord Howe upon Lieutenant Josiah of the Continental navy. Captain Skimmer has been killed in an action with the *Montague* and has left eleven children, nine of whom are unable to earn a livelihood. His widow asks for a pension.

In the course of its business the Marine Committee made frequent reports to Congress, both in response to previous orders therefrom, and of its own accord. Occasionally parts of its reports were recommitted by Congress to a limited number of the Committee's members, doubtless for the purpose of obtaining prompt and expert action. The Committee sometimes assigned special business to sub-committees, or to single members. The subjects that the Committee considered, discussed, and reported upon ran the whole gamut of naval activities and interests. The substance of many of its reports may be found in the Journals of the Continental Congress for the years, 1776, 1777, 1778, and 1779. During this period the Marine Committee prepared and reported the larger part of the naval legislation of Congress. It is true that special committees contributed sometimes to this work, but these were composed in part of members of the Marine Committee. Congress, as a body, originated little, although occasionally it was moved to the passage of resolutions on naval affairs by some real or supposed emergency, the importunities of the self-seeking, or the whims of individual members. It of course amended the reports of its committees.

The Marine Committee reviewed the findings of courts martial. These with its recommendations it laid before Congress for final action. During its incumbency of the Naval Office several interesting and important naval trials were held. Captain Thomas Thompson in 1778, and Captain Dudley Saltonstall in 1779, were broken by courts martial. Other captains who lost their vessels were tried but escaped so severe a punishment. The cases growing out of Commodore Hopkins's expedition to New Providence, his engagement with the *Glasgow,* and the immediately succeeding events of his fleet in the spring of 1776, deserve more extended notice. During the summer of 1776, the Marine Committee ordered Commodore Hopkins and Captains Dudley Saltonstall and Abraham Whipple to leave the fleet, which was then stationed in Rhode Island, and to come to Philadelphia for trial. After calling before it the inferior officers of the *Alfred* and *Columbus* and hearing their complaints against the two captains, the Committee reported to Congress that the charge against Captain Saltonstall was not well founded, and that the charge against Captain Whipple " amounts to nothing more than a rough indelicate mode of behaviour to his marine officers." Congress ordered the two captains to repair to their commands, and recommended Captain Whipple " to cultivate harmony with his officers."

Commodore Hopkins was not to get off so easily. His whole conduct since he left Philadelphia early in January, 1776, was investigated. The principal charge against him was disobeying

the instructions of the Naval Committee of January 5, 1776, to
attack the forces of the enemy in the region of Virginia and the
Carolinas. Hopkins based his defence on the statement that the
enemy in that region had become too strong to attack by February
17, when his fleet sailed; and also on a certain clause in his instructions granting him discretionary powers. After the Marine
Committee had investigated his case and reported upon it, Congress on August 12 took into consideration " the instructions
given to Commodore Hopkins, his examination and answers to
the Marine Committee, and the report of the Marine Committee
thereupon; also the farther defence by him made, and the testi-
mony of the witnesses." On the 15th Congress came to the
resolution, " That the said commodore Hopkins, during his cruise
to the southward, did not pay due regard to the tenor of his
instructions . . . . . . and that his reasons for not going from
Próvidence immediately to the Carolinas are by no means satisfactory." The next day Congress resolved, " That the conduct
of Commodore Hopkins deserves the censure of this house, and
this house does accordingly censure him."

This action seems more severe than the facts justify. John
Adams who defended Hopkins had with difficulty prevented
Congress from cashiering the commodore. According to Adams's
view, Hopkins was " pursued and persecuted by that anti-New
England spirit which haunted Congress in many other of their
proceedings, as well as in this case." The action of Congress
may be interpreted differently. Hopkins had not met the expectations of Congress or the Marine Committee. As the head
of the fleet, blame naturally fell upon him whether he deserved
it or not. He had his shortcomings as a naval officer, and failure
magnified them. By placing the blame upon him, the skirts of
Congress, of the Marine Committee, and of other naval officers
were cleared, and the hopes of a few self-interested men were
brightened.

Commodore Hopkins's failure to carry out the plans of the
Marine Committee during the fall of 1776, together with the
partial inaction of the fleet under his command, increased his
disfavor with the federal authorities at Philadelphia. His praiseworthy endeavors to man and prepare his fleet for sea won for him
the enmity of the owners of privateers at Providence, for his
success would have meant the taking of men and materials sorely

needed by the privateersmen. Hopkins's intemperate language, lack of tact, and naval misfortune bred a spirit of discontent and gave an excuse for insubordination among his inferior officers. Encouraged by the discontented privateersmen of Providence, ten of the inferior officers of the *Warren,* the Commodore's flagship, signed a petition and certain letters containing complaints and charges against Hopkins and sent their documents to the Marine Committee. They were taken to Philadelphia by the chief "conspirator," Captain John Grannis of the marines. These documents asserted, that Hopkins had called the members of the Marine Committee and of Congress "ignorant fellows—lawyers clerks—persons who don't know how to govern men;" that he was "remarkably addicted to profane swearing;" that he had "treated prisoners in a most inhuman and barbarous manner;" that he "was a hindrance to the proper manning of the fleet;" and that "his conversation is at times so wild and unsteady that I have sometimes thought he was not in his right mind." Besides these accusations there were a few others of even less substantial character.

On March 25, 1777, the Marine Committee laid before Congress the complaints and charges against Commodore Hopkins, and on the next day Congress took them into consideration; whereupon it resolved that "Esek Hopkins be immediately, and he is hereby, suspended from his command in the American navy." Hopkins remained suspended until January 2, 1778. The Journals of Congress for this date contain the following entry: "Congress having no farther occasion for the services of Esek Hopkins, esq. who, on the 23d of December, 1776, was appointed commander-in-chief of the fleet fitted out by the Naval Committee, Resolved, That the said Esek Hopkins, esq. be dismissed from the service of the United States."

Hopkins's suspension and removal did not improve the navy. Indeed it was far less fortunate in 1777 than it had been in 1776. That its chief officer should have been suspended without a hearing, on flimsy charges, offered by a small number of inferior officers, whose leader was guilty of insubordination, convicts Congress of acting with undue haste, and of doing a possible injustice; and arouses the suspicion that it was not actuated wholly by a calm and unbiased judgment. The wording of Hopkins's dismissal seems needlessly curt and harsh. Since he had lost the confidence of Congress, the Marine Committee, and many of his countrymen, his removal from the office of commander-in-chief to that of a captain might have been justified.

The Marine Committee both built and purchased vessels. In addition to the thirteen frigates ordered by Congress in December, 1775, it built the *Alliance,* 36, and *General Gates,* 18, in Massachusetts; and the *Confederacy,* 32, in Connecticut. It placed several other vessels upon the stocks. Of these the *Saratoga, Bourbon,* and *America,* were eventually launched and completed. The construction of the others was abandoned. The Committee added several small craft by purchase to the fleet of extemporized merchantmen fitted out by the Naval Committee. One of the best known of these was the ship *Ranger,* which under the command of Captain John Paul Jones rendered such effective service in British waters. The navy reached its maximum size in 1776 when it numbered 27 vessels. Owing to the losses inflicted by the enemy, and notwithstanding the additions that were made to it, the navy early in 1779 consisted of only thirteen vessels. In 1776 the number of seamen in the navy was about 3000 men; in later years it was considerably less. The total number of enlisted officers in the Continental navy in each of the commissioned grades was about as follows: in the navy proper, commander-in-chief, 1; captains, 46; and lieutenants, 132; in the marine corps, major, 1; captains, 31; and lieutenants, 91. In 1776 and 1777 the total numbers of commissioned officers in the navy and marine corps were about half of the totals of the above figures. In other years they were considerably less.

With its pygmy fleet the Marine Committee was able to inflict but little injury upon the British navy, which at the close of the war numbered 468 vessels, many of them powerful frigates and ships of the line. The Committee was compelled to confine the military movements of its ships almost entirely to operations against British merchantmen, transports, and small naval craft. It sometimes specifically instructed its captains to avoid the large vessels of the enemy. The American ships cruised either separately, or in small fleets of two, three, or four vessels. Such were the insuperable impediments to manning and equipping the Continental fleet that at no time during the Revolution were there as many as twelve armed vessels at sea, and the actual number cruising against the enemy even during the favorable season was usually less than six. Owing to the superior inducements offered to sailors by privateersmen, the Continental captains were often unable to man their ships. The blockade of the American ports maintained by the British greatly interfered with the movements of the Continental vessels. The year 1779, the last during which the fleet was controled by the Marine Committee, was the most successful one in the history of the Continental navy. The year 1776 had been a rather successful one, but both 1777 and 1778 were lean and empty years and many ships were taken by the enemy. The navy in 1779 captured more than fifty prizes. Almost all of these reached safe ports. Twenty-six arrived in Massachusetts, principally at Boston. The average burden of these twenty-six prizes was 190 tons. They were all insignificant craft as compared with present standards, but they were quite large as compared with the prizes made by the Continental fleet during other years or by the privateers of the Revolution. The value of the prizes taken in 1779 greatly exceeded that of other years. The proceeds of the prizes captured during two of the cruises of 1779 were more than two million dollars.

The foregoing attempt to define the duties of the Marine Committee and its several agents probably draws the lines of division somewhat too clear and definite. Such lines were not hard and fast, for there was a painful lack of system in the business methods of the federal government of the Revolution. Then, official routine was not settled as at present. Usage had had no opportunity to establish fixed and orderly forms of procedure, and amid the distractions of war, when some real or supposed emergency was continually inviting one authority or another to disregard regularity and order, usage could obtain but scant permission to begin its work. Wars are famous for breaking through, not for forming, a crust of official precedent. The administrative machinery of armies and navies tends to adapt itself to the conditions of peace—now the normal state of nations. During long periods of partial stagnation this machinery becomes complicated; its tension is weakened; and many of its axles grow rusty from disuse. When war breaks out the conditions of administration are greatly changed. A thousand extra calls for work to be done at once are loud and inexorable. Expedition must be had at all hazards. Rapid action of the administrative machinery must be obtained, its tension screwed down, extra cog wheels discarded, and efficient

machinists substituted for the dotards of peace. It is obvious
that with this sort of difficulty those who managed the naval affairs
of the Revolution did not have to contend, for the organ of naval
administration was then created from its foundation. Their
difficulties sprang not from the age, but from the newness of this
organ. It lacked a nice correlation of parts, the smooth action
that comes from long service, and the system that immemorial
routine establishes.

The absence of system in the Naval Department was most conspicuous in the appointment of naval officers, from the captain to
the coxswain. This work was shared by Congress, the Marine
Committee, the navy boards, the Continental agents, the commander-in-chief of the navy, the commanders of vessels, the
Commissioners at Paris, and the commercial agents in foreign
countries. Appointments were sometimes actually determined by
the governors of states, " conspicuous citizens," and local governments in the states. A good illustration of the way in which
convenience was sometimes consulted is found in the resolution
of Congress of June 14, 1777, designating William Whipple the
New Hampshire member of the Marine Committee, John Langdon
the Continental agent at Portsmouth, and John Paul Jones the
commander of the ship *Ranger,* to select the commissioned and
warrant officers of the *Ranger* then at Portsmouth. In a new
navy without *esprit de corps,* it no doubt made for proper subordination to permit a commander to have a voice in choosing his
officers.

It was a source of annoyance and confusion to the navy boards
to find through accidental sources of information, as they sometimes did, that the Marine Committee had given orders to naval
agents to transact business, the immediate control of which was
vested in the boards. Naval agents sometimes discovered that
they were serving in a single task two or three naval masters.
Irregularities were chargeable not alone to the Naval Department.
The governor of a state was known on his own authority and to
the vexation of the rightful executive to take part in the direction
of the cruises of the Continental ships. Naval commanders were
now and then guilty of breaches of their orders. Congress had
its share in the confusing of business. On one occasion, making
a display of its ignorance, it suspended Captain John Roach from
a command to which he had not been appointed. Roach in fact

was not an officer in the Continental navy. It sometimes made impracticable details of the armed vessels. It also exerted its privilege of refering bits of business to special committees that logically belonged to the Marine Committee.

These irregularities, notwithstanding their number, were after all exceptions. The very nature of business forces it to follow some system, however imperfectly. Where a number of agents are employed there must be some division of labor. Without such arrangements chaos would exist. The Naval Department of the Revolution divided its duties among its different agents, but it broke through its routine of business much more frequently than would be now permitted in the present Department of the Navy.

The Marine Committee was not a satisfactory executive. It proved to be slow, cumbrous, inexpert, and irresponsible. The wiser members of Congress had long seen that it was a prime defect in governmental practice to add to the duties of a legislative committee those of an executive office; for it threw upon the same men too much work of too diverse kinds, and it removed from the administrative organ its most essential attributes of permanency, technical skill, and responsibility. In December, 1776, Robert Morris had urged the employment of a corps of executives chosen outside the membership of Congress as a requisite to a proper and orderly management of the business of the Revolutionary government.

As early as February, 1776, William Ellery, a member of the Marine Committee from Rhode Island, wrote to William Vernon at Providence that a proper board of admiralty was very much wanted. "The members of Congress," he said, "are unacquainted with this Department. As one of the Marine Committee I sensibly feel my ignorance in this respect. Under a mortifying Sense of this I wrote to you for Information in this Matter. Books cannot be had here; and I should have been glad to have been pointed to proper Authors on this subject." Early in 1779 when Congress was groping in search of a more efficient naval executive, Ellery again expressed regret at the lack of technical skill in the management of the navy. He said that the marine affairs would never be " well conducted so long as the supreme direction of them is in the hands of Judges, Lawyers, Planters, etc." Even before Morris and Ellery had declared for better executives, John Paul Jones, while distressed by a loss of naval

rank caused by the appointing and placing above him of certain
" political skippers," wrote that efficient naval officers could never
be obtained, until Congress " in their wisdom see proper to appoint
a Board of Admiralty competent to determine the respective merits
and abilities of their officers, and to superintend, regulate, and
point out all the motions and operations of the navy."

During 1778 and 1779 Congress hit upon a system of executive
departments that did little violence to its lust for power and at
the same time obtained a permanent body of administrators and
advisors. This was the system of executive boards, composed
jointly of commissioners selected outside the membership of
Congress and of members of Congress. Congress and the Marine
Committee probably derived their knowledge of executive boards
from ,the practice of the English government and of the states.
" Board of Admiralty " was the name during the Revolution,
as now, of the British Naval Office. Pennsylvania, Virginia, and
South Carolina had early in the Revolution established " Navy
Boards." In October, 1777, Congress had formed a Board of
War composed of five commissioners. In October, 1778, Con-
gress attempted to clip the wings of this Board and bring it under
Congressional control by substituting two members of Congress
for two of its five commissioners. On July 30, 1779, a Board of
Treasury was constituted on exactly this plan, being composed
of three commissioners and two members of Congress.

In the spring of 1779 the feeling was general that some change
must be made in the management of the navy. Both 1777 and
1778 had been lean, empty, and disastrous years for the Continental fleet. The blame for this failure was placed upon the
Marine Committee and the naval commanders. It was in April,
1777, that Washington wrote to John Jay asking questions and
making suggestions about the management of the navy, which
may be briefly summarized as follows: What are the reasons for
keeping the Continental vessels in port? Had not Congress
better lend them to " commanders of known bravery and capacity "
for a limited term? If additional encouragement is necessary in
order to induce seamen to enlist, why not give them the whole of
their captures? Great advantage might result from placing the
whole fleet under a " man of ability and authority commissioned
to act as commodore or admiral." Under the present system the
Continental ships are not only very expensive and totally useless,
but sometime they require a land force to protect them.

This arraignment of the navy is somewhat severe. The last clause in the above paragraph refers to an incident that took place at New London in the spring of 1776. The reader may recollect that Commodore Hopkins put into this port on his return from New Providence, and just after his unfortunate engagement with the *Glasgow*. He then received a temporary loan from Washington of one hundred and seventy troops, with whom for the time being he replenished his depleted crews. He kept the troops less than six weeks.

In his reply to Washington's letter Jay ascribed the naval inefficiency to a defective Naval Department. He said: " while the maritime affairs of the continent continue under the direction of a committee, they will be exposed to all the consequences of want of system, attention, and knowledge. The Marine Committee consists of a delegate from each state; it fluctuates, new members constantly coming and old ones going out; three or four, indeed, have remained in it from the beginning; and few members understand even the state of our naval affairs, or have time or inclination to attend them. But why is not this system changed? It is in my opinion inconvenient to the family compact." The " family compact " is supposed to refer to the Lees. During the Revolution the Lees and the Adamses formed the nucleus of a faction, which was generally opposed to constructive legislation in the field of administration.

When this letter of Jay was written a new naval system was forming. On June 9, Congress resolved to vest in " commissioners all business relating to the marine of these United States." Apparently this resolution meant that the naval affairs were to be given over to a board chosen outside the membership of Congress; if so, Congress soon retracted it. On October 1, 1779, Congress discharged the Committee that had had the new project in hand and directed the Marine Committee " to prepare and report a plan of regulations for conducting the naval affairs of the United States." The Marine Committee reported on October 28, 1779; thereupon Congress passed resolutions making provisions for a Board of Admiralty " to be subject in all cases to Congress." In important respects these resolutions were based upon those of October 17 and November 24, 1777, establishing a Board of War. This was natural, as the work of war and a naval office are quite similar. In the composition of the two boards, however, there was a vital difference. The Board of War, as has been said, consisted of five commissioners; the Board of Admiralty consisted of three commissioners and two members of Congress, being modeled after the Board of Treasury. Any three members of the Board of Admiralty were empowered to form a quorum. No two members could come from the same state. The Board must have its office in the same town in which Congress was sitting. It selected its clerks, but Congress chose its secretary.

The powers and duties of the Board of Admiralty was practically the same as those of the Marine Committee. The Board was to order and direct all ships and vessels of war. It was to superintend and direct the navy boards and see that they kept fair entries and proper accounts of all the business transacted by them. It was to keep a complete and accurate register of the officers of the navy, giving their rank and date of their commissions; which commissions were to be signed by the President of Congress and countersigned by the secretary of the Board. The Board was to have the care and direction of the marine prisoners. It was to obtain regular and exact returns of all warlike stores, clothing, provisions, and miscellaneous articles belonging to the marine department. Lastly, the Board of Admiralty was to " execute all such matters as shall be directed, and give their opinion on all such subjects as shall be referred to them by Congress, or as they may think necessary for the better regulation and improvement of the navy of the United States; and in general to superintend and direct all the branches of the marine department."

The officers of the navy were enjoined to obey the directions of the Board of Admiralty. The proceedings, records, and papers of the Board were to be open at all times to the inspection of the members of Congress. The Board of Admiralty was ordered to examine at once the unsettled accounts of the navy boards and naval agents and report thereon to Congress. It was further directed to form proper plans for increasing the naval force of the United States, and for the better regulation of the same.

The salary of each commissioner was fixed at $14,000, and of the secretary of the Board at $8000 a year. On September 13, 1780, these salaries were decreased to $1850 and to $1100 a year, respectively, to be now paid quarterly in specie or its equivalent.

When Congress increased the salary of the Commissioners of the Treasury from $1850 to $2000, the Commissioners of the Admiralty, exhibiting that delicate sense of the fitness of more pay that characterizes the employees of governments, petitioned for a similar increase in their salaries. Congress now established a precedent that was long followed by its successor, the Congress under the Constitution. It refused a favor to the navy that it granted to a more popular branch of the public service. The salary of the Commissioners of the Admiralty was not increased. The Congressional members received no pay for their services on the Board.

When Congress came to select Commissioners of Admiralty it found no easy task. Men who were eager for distinction and honor felt that they were cultivating a surer field in their home governments or in the army. The prestige of the Continental government was now declining. The dilution of salaries caused by the depreciation of the currency lessened the attractiveness of the Continental offices. Employees of Congress found it hard to support their families on their pay. Then too, the navy business had become a thankless and disheartening task. The class of men who will accept a disagreeable office with little pay and no glory is a small one at any time.

The first three commissioners elected by Congress were William Whipple of New Hampshire, chairman of the Marine Committee, Thomas Waring of South Carolina, and George Bryan of Pennsylvania. Each declined the position. On December 7, 1779, Francis Lewis of New York was chosen commissioner and on the next day accepted the office. Congress on the 3d had named the two Congressional members of the Board, William Floyd of New York, and James Forbes of Maryland. The appointment of Lewis resulted in the vacation of the position of Floyd, since two members could not come from the same state. William Ellery of Rhode Island was now elected as the second Congressional member. Congress had already chosen John Brown, the secretary of the Marine Committee to be secretary of the Board of Admiralty. Lewis, Forbes, and Ellery were sufficient to organize the Board. Accordingly on December 8, 1779, Congress resolved "that all matters heretofore referred to the Marine Committee be transmitted to the Board of Admiralty." On December 10, the Board of Admiralty wrote to the Navy Board at Boston informing it of the dissolution of the Marine Committee and directing it to address in the future all letters and applications relating to the navy to the "Commissioners of the Admiralty of the United States."

Upon the organization of the Board of Admiralty its difficulties in obtaining quorums began, and the troubles of Congress in its search for additional commissioners continued. On January 22, 1780, Congress gave Brigadier-General Thomas Mifflin of Pennsylvania an opportunity to decline a commissionership. On March 21 Lewis was complaining to Congress that Forbes was sick and that consequently there had been no Board since the 4th instant. He hoped that Congress would fill up the vacancy and prevent the navy business from being longer suspended. On the death of Forbes on March 25, Congress elected James Madison to fill his place. Madison had but recently arrived at Philadelphia as a delegate from Virginia.

In June, 1780, Lewis was again in trouble and was writing to Congress. He conceived that the addition of members of Congress to the Board of Admiralty was principally intended to lay such information before Congress from time to time as the Board desired to give, to explain its reports, and in the absence or during the sickness of a commissioner to make a quorum. He said that notwithstanding the attention that Madison and Ellery had been disposed to give, their necessary attendance on Congress did not admit of their being daily and constantly present at the sessions of the Board; that Ellery had been superseded in Congress; and that at present there was, therefore, no Board for lack of a quorum. Congress once more came to the rescue of Lewis and his Board by appointing Ellery and Thomas Woodford as commissioners. Ellery at once accepted but Woodford for some reason declined the appointment. Congress never obtained a third commissioner. In the fall of 1780 Daniel Huntington of Connecticut and Whitmill Hill of North Carolina were the Congressional members of the Board. On their being supplanted in November of that year by new delegates to Congress from their respective states, it took the earnest solicitations of Lewis to get Congress to fill their places. When the Board was discontinued in July, 1781, it had but one Congressional member, Daniel of St. Thomas Jenifer of Maryland.

To all intents and purposes Lewis and Ellery were the Board

of Admiralty; and in many respects they were well qualified for
their positions. Both were able men, though not brilliant. Both
had passed the meridian of life; Lewis was in his sixty-seventh,
and Ellery in his fifty-second year. Both had taken prominent
parts in the Revolutionary counsels in their respective states;
both had been members of the Continental Congress and of the
Marine Committee. Both were among the immortal signers of
the Declaration of Independence. Lewis had amassed a fortune
as an importing merchant in New York, and he had served in the
French and Indian war. Ellery had been a merchant and later a
lawyer in Newport, Rhode Island. Both were interested in
naval affairs, and had rendered good service on the Marine Committee.

From the first the Board of Admiralty was more dependent on
Congress than the Marine Committee had been. Congress, always jealous of its prerogative, naturally permitted a freer exercise of power to a committee of its own members than to a mixed
board whose work was almost entirely that of commissioners
selected outside the membership of Congress. To the Board's
dependence on Congress for its organization was added that for
means to carry out its naval program. The frequency with which
it went to Congress asking for quorums and money indicates its
helplessness and weakness.

The work of the Board of Admiralty was, generally speaking,
that of the Marine Committee under a change of name. It managed the dwindling business of the navy from December, 1779,
until July, 1781. It was served by the navy boards and naval
agents of its predecessor. Immediately after its organization the
Board of Admiralty, in compliance with the resolutions of Congress, urged the navy boards and naval agents to transmit to it
accurate accounts of their transactions up to December 31, 1779.
Owing to the loose methods of business that obtained during the
Revolution, the agents of the Board found it impossible in most
cases to make such statements.

The failure of the agents to properly report their accounts, together with a diminution in the naval business of Congress, now
led to some decrease in the naval machinery. In August, 1780,
the Board recommended that the two Philadelphia prize agents be
discharged, since it had not been able to induce them by means of
its repeated written and verbal requests to exhibit their accounts.

Congress discontinued their office and gave their work to the Board of Admiralty. In the winter of 1780-81 the resignations of Winder and Wharton of the Navy Board at Philadelphia were accepted by Congress and the duties of this Board were vested in its remaining member, James Read. On May 7, 1781, Congress accepted the resignation of Deshon of the Navy Board at Boston. The work of the navy boards and naval agents had now greatly diminished. Already the settling of accounts was becoming one of their principal tasks. After 1779 there were few Continental prizes to libel. Upon the resignation of the naval agents at Philadelphia, those at Boston, Portsmouth, and New London, were the only ones of consequence.

The Board of Admiralty was called upon to act upon divers letters, petitions, and memorials, differing little from similar communications which Congress referred to the Marine Committee. It also fell to its lot to prepare and report not a little important legislation. The reports of the Board, which were in writing, were chiefly the work of Lewis and Ellery, and were presented to Congress by the Congressional members of the Board. Congress usually referred these reports to a committee before it discussed them or took final action on them. Not a few of the reports of the Board were pigeon-holed by Congress and no action was taken on them. The naval legislation of Congress during the incumbency of the Board of Admiralty was in part rendered necessary by the decline of the navy. Certain other legislation was caused by the change made in the federal government on March 1, 1781, when the Articles of Confederation were put into effect. A few Congressional resolutions on naval affairs may be attributed to the legislative activity and enterprise of the Board of Admiralty.

On the recommendation of the Board, Congress in January, 1780, passed a resolution that was no doubt in harmony with administrative thrift and economy, but which pressed hard upon the naval officers. The pay of all officers not in actual service was at once to cease. Their commissions were to be deposited with the nearest navy board until the officers should be again called into service; each officer was to retain his rank. This was merely a courteous way of disestablishing the larger part of the navy. Owing to the capture and destruction of many Continental vessels, most of the naval officers were not in actual service. The number of commissioned officers in actual service at this time in both the navy proper and the marine corps was about twenty. The only naval captain cashiered by a court martial held under the direction of the Board of Admiralty was the eccentric Peter Landais, a jealous rival of John Paul Jones.

On May 4, 1780, the Board of Admiralty reported and Congress adopted the following device for a seal: " The arms, thirteen bars mutually supporting each other, alternate red and white, in a blue field, and surmounted by an anchor proper. The crest a ship under sail. The motto sustentans sustentatus. Legend, U. S. A. Sigil, Naval." The anchor and ship under sail are still a part of the seal of the Department of the Navy. Instead of the arms, motto, and former legend, there now appear an eagle with outstretched wings, and the words, " Navy Department, United States of America." On April 20, 1780, Congress adopted a new form of commission for naval officers, which the Board of Admiralty had prepared. This varied but little from the one that had been in use since the beginning of the Revolution. This new form, with slight changes in its phraseology made to adapt it to the government under the Constitution, is still used in the Department of the Navy.

The Board of Admiralty directed the movements of the armed vessels from December, 1779, until July, 1781. Its fleet in commission consisted of nine vessels. Two ships, the *America* and *Bourbon,* still remained on the stocks. Both in refitting the vessels in commission and in building those that had been placed upon the stocks, the Board was greatly hampered by a lack of money. All the difficulties which the Marine Committee had encountered were now intensified by the prostration of the nation's finances and credit. The Board resorted to all means within reason in its attempts to obtain the requisites for prosecuting its work. Thus embarrassed it was able to accomplish very little with its fleet. During its incumbency some half dozen cruises were made by the Continental vessels. Twenty prizes were captured, but only one-half of them reached safe ports. Of the nine vessels in commission, five were captured by the British and one foundered at sea. When the Board of Admiralty was discontinued in July, 1781, only three ships were in commission.

The Board of Admiralty was not a satisfactory executive. It was at all times dependent on its Congressional members for quorums. It proved to be slower, more cumbersome, and less responsible than the Marine Committee. The management of the navy still lacked unity and concentration. The members of the Board had had no training in the naval profession. However, had the Board not been superseded, its members would no doubt in time have developed greater expertness and technical skill than did the members of the Marine Committee. It should also be said that under more favorable auspices the Board would have shown a higher administrative efficiency than it did; for its lines had indeed fallen in unpleasant places, and a bankrupt federal treasury denied it the means so requisite to the successful prosecution of its work. Its inefficiency, however, was only one of the causes that led to its discontinuance.

On the question of the proper organization of the executive departments, the leaders of the Revolution were divided into two factions. Moved by their love of liberty, their distrust of governments, and their jealousy of delegated and concentrated powers, the members of one faction favored the vesting of the executive business in Congressional committees. The members of the other faction, who stood for authority and control on the part of the government, for constructive legislation in the field of administration, and for the application of the principles of business to the affairs of state, declared for a system of permanent and single-headed executives chosen outside of the membership of Congress. The issue that was here joined in the special field of administration was of course a part of that perennial and perpetual conflict between the freedom of the individual and social control. In this case, as everywhere and always, the political doctrinaires, the iconoclasts and radicals, and the men of heart rather than head, lined up on the side of liberty; while the practical and conservative men, the representatives of vested interests, and the cold logical thinkers, stood together on the side of governmental control.

The faction that distrusted power and wished to keep it scattered may be called the " dispersive school;" and the faction that wished to gather up the power and lodge it with a few men may be called the "concentrative school." To the "dispersive school" belonged Samuel Adams, the Lees, Patrick Henry, and William Whipple; to the "concentrative school," Hamilton, Washington, the Morrises, and Jay. Early in the Revolution the advantage lay with the "dispersive school." Its executive plan of Congressional committees needed little work to put it into operation; it was more flexible than the scheme of permanent single-headed executives; and it was more in harmony with the ultra anti-monarchical spirit of the times. The Revolutionary government originated as a congress of delegates, and organized itself after the manner of congresses by means of committees of its own members. When the Congress became a government and had trusted to it a multiplicity of executive duties, it naturally continued and adapted the old organization for the transaction of the new business. The executive system of Congressional committees in this way becoming set could not be easily changed.

By 1780 the "concentrative school" was winning its way. Indeed, the adoption in 1779 of mixed boards composed of men both in and out of Congress was a compromise between the two schools, in which the "concentrative school" gave up its contention for simplicity in the executive organs in order to obtain, in part at least, another of its objectives, permanency in the tenure of the administrators. But now both committees and boards had been tried and found wanting. Then too in 1780 there was greater need for a change in executive system than in the first years of the war. As Congress became imbecile, the quality of its committees and their work deteriorated; and as the country wearied of the war and its finances tightened, the necessity for greater economy and efficiency in administration increased. In 1780 the feeling among the leaders was general that a crisis in the army, in the finances, and in the business of the government, which could be met only by some thorough and far-reaching reform, was approaching. The leaders of the "concentrative school" proposed a complete change in the administrative system of Congress as a solution of the serious problems that confronted the country. By the end of 1780 a movement for a reform of this sort was in progress. It was diligently furthered by one school and zealously opposed by the other.

"If Congress," Washington wrote in December, 1780, " suppose that Boards composed of their own body, and always fluctuating, are competent to the great business of the war (which requires not only close application, but a constant and uniform train of thinking and acting), they will most assuredly deceive themselves. Many, many instances might be adduced in proof of this." Washington was convinced that extravagant and improper expenditures of the public money, inexpertness in the transacting of business, and needless delays resulted from vesting all or a part of the duties of an executive office in Congress.

Hamilton declared specifically for the substitution of single executives for plural ones, and he named three men whom he considered especially qualified for departmental posts, General Schuyler for Minister of War, General McDougall for Minister of Marine, and Robert Morris for Minister of Finance. He conceived that there were always more knowledge, energy, responsibility, decision, despatch, zeal, and attraction for first rate ability " where single men, than where bodies are concerned." Gouverneur Morris contributed to the agitation in behalf of better executives an enumeration of the qualifications requisite in the men who were to become heads of the leading departments. He held, as do still some of the writers on naval administration, that a Minister of Marine should possess a practical and technical knowledge of naval affairs ; and he presented a unique list of his qualities in the following words :

" A minister of the marine should be a man of plain good sense, and a good economist, firm but not harsh ; well acquainted with sea affairs, such as the construction, fitting, and victualling of ships, the conduct and manœuvre on a cruise and in action, the nautical face of the earth, and maritime phenomenon. He should know the temper, manner, and disposition of sailors ; for all which purposes it is proper that he should have been bred to that business, and have followed it, in peace and war, in a military and commercial capacity. His principles and manners should be absolutely republican, and his circumstances not indigent."

The debate in Congress over the change in the executive system was long and was marked by the workings of party spirit, the self interest of some members, and the doubts, fears, and divided opinions of others. Samuel Adams placed himself at the head of the advocates of the old system. He strongly opposed the new system, and on its adoption he had forebodings of coming disaster to his country. On January 10, 1781, the friends of the new system gained their first decisive victory ; for on this day Congress resolved to established a Department of Foreign Affairs. On February 7, Congress " resumed the consideration of the plan for the arrangement of the civil executive departments," and resolved that there should be a Superintendent of Finance, a Secretary of War, and a Secretary of Marine. It summed up the duties of the Secretary of the Marine in the following brief paragraph:

" It shall be the duty of the secretary of marine to examine into and report to Congress the present state of the navy, a register of the officers in and out of command, and the dates of their respective commissions; and an account of all the naval and other stores belonging to that department; to form estimates of all pay, equipments, and supplies necessary for the navy; and from time to time to report such estimates to the superintendent of finance, that he may take measures as may best suit the condition of the public treasury; to superintend and direct the execution of all resolutions of Congress respecting naval preparations; to make out, seal, and countersign all marine commissions, keep registers thereof, and publish annually a list of appointments; to report to Congress the officers and agents necessary to assist him in the business of his department; and in general to execute all the duties and powers specified in the act of Congress constituting a board of admiralty."

Speaking generally, the Secretary of Marine was to succeed to the powers and duties of the Board of Admiralty. It is, however, significant that the Secretary is not specifically charged with the ordering and directing of the vessels of war, as was the Board. The specified duties of the new office are largely ministerial. Congress was disposed to be less liberal in granting powers to a Secretary chosen outside its membership than to a Board partly composed of Congressmen. The salary of the Secretary was fixed at $5000 a year.

On February 27, 1781, Congress with a promptness that was exceptional elected Major-General Alexander McDougall of New York to be Secretary of Marine, for which position he had been recommended by Alexander Hamilton. McDougall's qualifications for the office, although by no means perfect, were above the average. In the French and Indian war he had been a commander of privateers. Later he became a merchant in New York city, where he was a leader in the Revolution. He had risen to the rank of major-general in the Continental army. He now declined to accept the position proffered him unless permitted to hold his rank in the army, and to retain the privilege of returning to the field when his services were required. He based this partial refusal on patriotic grounds. Congress did not wish a secretary on these conditions; and it therefore voted that it did not expect the acceptance of Major-General McDougall and that it had a due sense of his zeal " for the safety and honour of America and applaud his magnanimity in declining ' to retire from the toils and perils of the field in the present critical condition of the United States in general and that of New York in particular.'" Congress made no other choice of a Secretary of Marine.

In June, 1781, the plan of appointing an Agent of Marine and vesting in him the duties of the Board of Admiralty, pending the selection of a Secretary of Marine, was brought forward in Congress. The Commissioners of Admiralty were able to forecast the result of this agitation for a new navy system. On July 9, 1781, Ellery informed Congress "that his family affairs pressed his return home, and therefore requested leave of absence." As there was at this time but one Congressional member serving on the Board, on the absence of Ellery, no quorum could be obtained. Lewis now prayed Congress to permit him to resign, or to give him such further direction " as they in their wisdom shall deem meet." On July 17, Congress accepted his resignation. On July 18, Congress put the marine prisoners in charge of the Commissary of Prisoners of the Army, and ordered the seal of the Admiralty to be deposited with the Secretary of Congress until a Secretary of Marine should be appointed. The Revolutionary Naval Department was without a head.

During the summer of 1781, the control of naval affairs gravitated towards Robert Morris. Soon after assuming the office of Suprintendent of Finance in May, 1781, he was brought into close relation with the navy. He was invited to take upon himself more or less of the naval business by the urgent need of sending the cruisers on important errands, the helplessness of the Board of Admiralty, the inertia of Congress, and the interregnum in the headship of the Naval Department, which lasted from the discontinuance of the Board of Admiralty early in July, 1781, until the appointment of an Agent of Marine on September 7. The figure that Morris presents at this time is that of the strong and confident man of affairs, sagacious, expeditious, and painstaking, who is surrounded by weaker men, hesitating, vacillating, and procrastinating in their administrative attempts.

In June, 1781, Morris wrote to the President of Congress re-

commending the appointment of a captain for the 74-gun ship
America, and explaining how money for completing her might
be obtained.   He said that he was aware that John Jay had liberty
to sell this ship at the Court of Madrid ; that he thought and hoped
that he would not succeed, for the sale of the *America* would be
injurious to the United States ; and that it would be " more consistent with economy and with the dignity of Congress to have her
finished than to let her perish."   On the receipt of this letter
Congress authorized Morris to take measures for launching the
America and fitting her for sea.   Morris now hinted to the Board
of Admiralty that the frigate *Trumbull* could perform an essential
public service if put under his direction, and pursuing his plan he
obtained a resolution of Congress giving him control of this vessel.
During the summer of 1781 while the reorganization of the Naval
Department was in suspense, Morris on his own initiative directed
the fitting out of the *Alliance* and *Deane,* and ordered them to
sea, being " convinced that while they lay in port an useless expense must necessarily be incurred."

Meanwhile a movement to place the Naval Department under
the control of Morris had been set on foot in Congress.   On June
26, Meriwether Smith of Virginia reported a series of resolutions
providing for the reorganization of the Naval Department, a work
which he considered necessary because the present naval system
was " inefficient and expensive."   The most important of these
resolutions was one that dissolved the offices of the Board of
Admiralty, the navy boards, and the naval agents ; and another
which empowered the Superintendent of Finance to appoint some
discreet agent to manage the navy under the order and inspection
of the said Superintendent, until a Secretary of Marine should
be appointed, or until the further pleasure of Congress.   On the
day of their introduction these resolutions were referred to a committee of three of whom Smith was chairman.   This committee
on July 2, after having made a slight change in the phraseology
of the resolutions, reported them to Congress ; and on July 6, it
again reported them, having added a few additional resolutions.
One of the new resolutions was to the effect that the election of a
Secretary of Marine should be postponed until November.   After
voting this resolution down, Congress referred the remaining
resolutions to a new committe of which Thomas McKean of
Delaware was chairman.

On July 18, the new committee reported a series of resolutions differing little from those that had been referred to it, with the exception of one important change; the Agent of Marine was now not to be appointed by Morris, but by Congress. On this day Congress passed two of the committee's resolutions. One of these transferred the care of the marine prisoners from the Board of Admiralty to the Commissary of Prisoners of the Army; and the other ordered the seal of the Admiralty to be deposited with the Secretary of Congress and empowered him to use it in counter-signing commissions. The remaining resolutions again went over. Congress was able to agree on the discontinuance of the Board of Admiralty, but not on the arrangements for its successor.

Finally, the whole business of the reorganization of the Naval Department was referred to a third committee of three members of whom Theodoric Bland of Virginia was chairman. On the report of this committee on August 29, Congress agreed " that for the present an agent of marine be appointed with authority to direct, fit out, equip, and employ the ships and vessels of war belonging to the United States, according to such instructions as he shall from time to time receive from Congress." The Agent of Marine was to direct the selling of all prizes. He was to settle and pay the naval accounts, and keep a record of his work. As soon as he entered into the execution of his office, " the functions and appointments of the Board of Admiralty, the several navy boards, and all civil officers appointed under them shall cease and be determined." The salary of the new head of the Naval Department was fixed at $1500 a year, and that of his clerk at $500. Both the Agent of Marine and his clerk were required to take an oath " well and faithfully to execute the trust reposed in them according to the best of their skill and judgment; " and to give good and sufficient bond.

These resolutions of August 29 were to be only temporary, for they did not displace those of February 7, 1781, which provided for a Secretary of Marine. A second temporary expedient was resorted to on September 7, when Congress resolved: " That until an agent of marine shall be appointed by Congress, all the duties, powers, and authority assigned to the said agent, be devolved upon and executed by the said superintendent of finance." In other words Congress appointed Morris Agent of Marine.

The reason why Congress appointed an Agent of Marine instead of a Secretary of Marine is not at all points clear. Having failed to obtain the acceptance of McDougall as Secretary of Marine, Congress may have decided that the small and disheartening business of the navy would not attract first-rate talent; or that for the transaction of this business a full-fledged executive department was not necessary. It is more probable that the appointment of an Agent of Marine, under the circumstances of a disagreeing Congress, the breaking down of the Board of Admiralty, and the failure to obtain a Secretary of Marine, was merely a temporary and feasible expedient for conducting the affairs of the navy. There are obvious reasons why the proposal to give the Superintendent of Finance the power to appoint the Agent of Marine, or the selection of Morris as Agent, should have aroused vigorous opposition. Men of Samuel Adams's way of thinking would oppose it, among other reasons, because it placed too much power in the hands of one man. The friends of the navy would dislike to see the Naval Department swallowed up by the Department of Finance. But on the other hand many considerations recommended the step that was finally taken. It was the most economical disposition of the naval business that could have been made. Morris had superior qualifications for the office and he was at once available. Indeed, he was the only man in sight that promised to be equal to the task of straightening out the tangle of marine accounts, of financing a bankrupt navy, and of wielding effectively this arm of the military service. He was admirably qualified for the headship of the Naval Department by his experience as a man of business familiar with accounts and the selection of employees, as the owner of a fleet of merchantmen, and as one of two or three of the most influential members of the Marine Committee during the years 1776 and 1777 when the navy was founded. Whatever may have been the shortcomings of the navy while Morris was directing it, they did not spring from the lack of an efficient executive. For the first time during the Revolution its management was marked by despatch, decision, and an expert and adequate understanding of its problems.

On September 8, 1781, Morris wrote to the President of Congress accepting in words of modesty and reluctance his appointment. "There are many Reasons," he said, "why I would have wished that this burthen had been laid on other shoulders, or that at least I might have been permitted to appoint a temporary Agent until the further Pleasure of Congress. As it is I shall undertake the Task however contrary to my Inclinations and inconsistent with the many duties which press heavily upon me, because it will at least save Money to the Public." He then added in a characteristic way some observations on his new task. "True economy in the public business," he declared, "consists in employing a sufficient number of proper persons to perform the public business." He wished the accounts of the marine department to be speedily settled.

Morris filled the office of Agent of Marine from September 7, 1781, until November 1, 1784. It is believed that he received no salary as Agent of Marine. In addition to Morris the personnel of the Marine Office consisted of James Read, secretary to the Agent of Marine at a salary of $1000 a year; Joseph Pennell, paymaster at $1000; and George Turner, commissary of naval prisoners at $1200. Read who had been one of the commissaries of the Philadelphia Navy Board was of great service to Morris in conducting the Marine Office. The clerical work of the Office was performed by the clerks of the Office of the Superintendent of Finance, an instance of Morris's economies. According to the resolution of September 7, the positions of commissioner of the navy boards, and of prize agent were abolished. The Navy Board at Boston, however, continued to fit out vessels until March, 1782. It was not until sometime later that the commissioners delivered over the books and papers of the Board to John Brown, the former secretary of the Board of Admiralty, whom Morris had appointed naval agent for settling the business of the navy in New England. In the four New England States, North and South Carolina, and Georgia, Morris either reappointed the prize agents of the Board of Admiralty or appointed new ones. In the other states he served in this capacity himself.

The Agent of Marine like the Board of Admiralty communicated with Congress by means of written reports, which that body referred to committees of its own members. Accordingly when naval business was discussed in Congress, it usually came up in the form of a "report of a committee on the report of the Agent of Marine." The subjects upon which the Agent of Marine reported were similar to those dealt with by is predecessors in naval administration. Not a few of his reports were concerned with the settling of marine accounts and the satisfying of claimants against the government, which business was now insistent. During his tenure of the office of Agent of Marine, Morris prepared the greater part of the naval legislation of Congress. The changes or additions to his work which were made by committees of Congress were unimportant.

When Morris became Agent of Marine the direction of the movements of the Continental vessels was vested in him, but with a serious limitation; he was authorized to employ the armed cruisers " according to such instructions as he shall from time to time receive from Congress." Morris could never abide indefinite grants of power which confused authority; and he therefore by means of a cleverly written letter elicited a resolution from Congress giving him full power " to fit out and employ the ships of war belonging to these United States in such manner as shall appear to him best calculated to promote the interests of these United States."

When Morris fell heir to the duties of the Naval Department in the summer of 1781, the Continental navy was reduced to small numbers. There were in active service only five captains and seven lieutenants in the navy proper, and three captains and three lieutenants in the marine corps. Including with these, those officers who were unemployed, were in private service, were prisoners, or were on parole, there were twenty-two captains and thirty-nine lieutenants in the navy proper, and twelve captains and twelve lieutenants in the marine corps. Only three vessels were now in commission; the frigate *Trumbull,* 28, at Philadelphia, and the *Alliance,* 36, and *Deane,* 32, at Boston. The *America* and *Bourbon* were still on the stocks. About the first of September, 1782, Morris purchased the ship *Washington,* 20, and in October he took over into the Continental service in payment for a debt the ship *Duc de Lauzun,* 20.

The movements of the fleet under Morris's directions were marked as formerly by bits of good and bad fortune, encounters with naval craft, privateers, and merchantmen, and voyages to France and the West Indies. From the summer of 1781 until the end of the war the little fleet captured twenty prizes, some fifteen of which reached safe ports. The last of His Majesty's vessels to surrender to a Continental ship was the schooner *Jackall,* 20, Commander Logie, which was taken in the spring of 1782, by Cap-

tain Samuel Nicholson when in command of the *Deane,* or the
Hague as she was now called. By a singular coincidence the
first and the last valuable prize captured by a Continental ship during the Revolution were taken by Captain John Manly. On
one of the last days of November, 1775, he received the surrender
of the brig *Nancy,* a transport; and in January, 1783, while in
command of the *Hague* he captured the ship *Baille* of 340 tons
burden with a cargo consisting of sixteen hundred barrels of provisions. The last vessel captured by the British was the *Trumbull,* taken in August, 1781, and commanded by Captain James
Nicholson, the senior captain of the navy. In the fall of 1782,
Captain John Barry carried into L'Orient four Jamaicamen with
rich cargoes of rum and sugar. The proceeds from these four
prizes were £620,610, the largest sum realized on any cruise of the
Revolution.

The attempts of Morris in 1782, to obtain an increase in the
naval force of Congress form one of the most interesting and
characteristic parts of his naval work. The surrender of Cornwallis on October 19, 1781, was not considered by many con-
temporaneous Americans as an event that must necessarily end
the Revolution. Indeed the final outcome of the war was felt to
be in doubt for more than a year. The Agent of Marine was too
cautious and conservative to count on peace before its actual ac-
complishment had been sealed by a formal treaty. After the
surrender of Cornwallis he not only continued to send the Continental cruisers against the enemy, but whenever an occasion presented itself he vigorously urged on Congress the necessity of a
naval increase. To the mind of Morris the need of a navy in
1782 was greater than it had been at any previous time during the
Revolution. He conceived that up to this time Britain had attempted to conquer the colonies on land by means of her army;
having been defeated in this, it was now her purpose to starve
the colonies into submission by means of her navy and superior
sea-power. The United States must meet the enemy's change of
tactics by building a navy.

In April, 1782, Morris took steps to have the frigate *Bourbon*
completed. Congress was not convinced of the expediency of this,
and was inclined to sell the frigate in its unfinished state. Morris
wrote reprovingly to Congress that the most economical thing to
do was to complete the vessel; and that " there is also a degree of

Dignity in carrying through such measures as Congress have once adopted, unless some change of circumstances render the execution improper." He then added: " The present circumstances of the United States I apprehend to be such as should induce our attention to the reestablishment of a Naval Force, and altho' former attempts have proved unfortunate, we must not take it for granted that future Essays will prove unsuccessful. Altho' the Naval Force of our enemy is powerful and their ships numerous, yet that Force is opposed by equal Numbers so as to give them much more employment than at the time when our infant Fleet was crushed."

On May 10, 1782, in response to a request of Congress, Morris submitted an exhaustive report on the state of American commerce. Referring to the intentions of the British, he declared that their " avowed design was to annihilate the American commerce," having been compelled to abandon the idea of conquest. The plans of the enemy could be frustrated and the American trade protected by so small a fleet as two ships of the line and ten frigates. The ships of the line should be stationed in the Chesapeake to cruise as occasion might require. The frigates should be divided into two equal squadrons, each of which should serve as a convoy of the American trade between the United States and France. By each squadron making two round trips a year, a quarterly communication both ways between the two countries would be established. The United States of course could not provide this service, but the ten frigates which the plan required might be detailed from the French or Spanish fleet. " It is to be hoped," Morris said, " that if the war continues much longer, the United States will be able to provide the necessary force for themselves, which at present they are not, tho' if the above arrangements take place, they might now provide for the trade from America to the West Indies." Congress authorized Morris to apply to both Spain and France for the needed vessels. Nothing came of Morris's suggestion.

But a still more extensive naval plan than this was in Morris's mind, and one which could be undertaken independent of foreign ships. On July 30, 1782, he submitted to Congress an estimate for the public service of the United States for the year 1783, amounting to eleven millions of dollars. More than one-fifth of tis sum was to be spent on the navy. " Congress will observe," he said, " that the estimates for the Marine Department amount to two Millions and a half, whereas there was no Estimate made for that Service in the last year any more than the civil list." Morris based this most remarkable estimate for a naval increase on his belief that the enemy had changed his mode of warfare, and that it was now his purpose to annihilate the commerce of America, and thus starve her into submission. With this sort of campaign conducted by the enemy, an American army without a navy would be burdensome without being able to accomplish anything. With a navy, we could prevent the enemy from making predatory excursions, ruining our commerce, and capturing our supplies; he would either be compelled to keep a superior naval force in this country, which would give our allies a superiority elsewhere; or else he must permit the balance of naval strength in America to be on our side; in which latter case we could protect our trade, annoy his commerce, and cut off the supplies which he would be sending to his posts in America. Then, concluded Morris in words which remind one of the Annual Report of some recent Secretary of the Navy asking for his yearly quota of battleships: " By economizing our Funds and constructing six Ships annually we should advance so rapidly to Maritime importance that our enemy would be convinced not only of the Impossibility of subduing us, but also of the Certainty that his forces in this Country must eventually be lost without being able to produce him any possible Advantage," and we should in this way regain the " full Possession of our country without the Expense of Blood, or treasure, which must attend and other Mode of Operations, and while we are pursuing those Steps which lead to the Possession of our natural Strength and Defence."

The signing on November 30, 1782, of the Provisional Articles of Peace between the United States and Great Britain, news of which reached America early in the Spring of 1783, removed the necessity of a naval increase, and in the minds of many the need of a navy at all. Morris did not at once give up the notion that the government on a peace footing should maintain a respectable marine. In May, 1783, he asked Congress to relieve him of is naval duties. " The affairs of the Marine Department," he said, " ocupy more time and attention than I can easily spare. This Department will now become important, and I hope extensive. I must therefore request that Congress will be pleased to appoint an agent of marine as soon as their convenience will admit." He became convinced, however, that not much could be done for the navy until the finances of Congress were placed upon a better and more permanent basis. In July, 1783, Morris made a report on a proposition of Virginia offering to sell her naval ship *Cormorant* to the United States. Congress agreed to his report which was as follows: " That although it is an object highly desirable to establish a respectable marine, yet the situation of the public treasury renders it not advisable to purchase ships for the present, nor until the several states shall grant such funds for the construction of ships, docks, naval arsenals, and for the support of the naval service, as shall enable the United States to establish their marine upon a permanent and respectable footing."

Meanwhile Congress had been rapidly going out of the naval business by formally ending the war at sea, by providing for the settlement of the marine accounts, and by disposing of her naval stock. On March 24, 1783, it ordered the Agent of Marine to recall all armed vessels cruising under the American colors. On April 11 it issued a " Proclamation, Declaring the cessation of arms, as well by sea as by land, agreed upon between the United States and His Britannic Majesty; and enjoining the observance thereof." On April 15 it ordered the Agent of Marine to set free all the naval prisoners of the enemy.

During the last year of the Revolution and for several years after its close, one of the principal tasks of the federal government was the settling of the outstanding accounts of the several executive departments. This was a work fraught with extraordinary difficulties. The administration of a government founded and conducted amid the distractions of war was necessarily marked by irregularities in official procedure, the lack of system in accounting, and in general by haphazard ways of business. On February 27, 1782, Congress acting on the recommendation of Morris authorized him to appoint five commissioners with full power and authority to liquidate and finally settle the Revolutionary accounts. Each commissioner was to be paid $1500 a year, and was permitted to employ a clerk. Each commissioner was given charge of a certain class of accounts, and to one of the five men fell the settling of the accounts of the Marine Department. Owing to Morris's caution in making appointments and

to the obstacles that stood in the way of a wise choice, the " commissioner for settling the accounts of the marine department"
was not selected until June, 1783, when Joseph Pennell, the paymaster of the Marine Office was named for the place.   Offices for
settling the naval accounts were opened in Philadelphia, New
York, and Boston.   On the retirement of Morris, Pennell became responsible to the new Board of Treasury.

In the last year of the war Congress began to dispose of its
naval craft.   On September 3, 1782, the 74-gun ship *America,*
now at last ready for launching, was on the recommendation of
the Agent of Marine given to France to replace the ship of the
line *Magnifique,* 74, which the French fleet had recently lost
in Boston harbor.   Congress, " desirous of testifying on this
occasion to his Majesty, the sense they entertain on his generous
exertions in behalf of the United States," directed the Agent of
Marine to present the *America* to Luzerne, the French minister at Philadelphia, for the service of His Most Christian Majesty.
It was a gracious act of international friendship.   In April, 1783,
the *Duc de Lauzun* was lent to the French minister to carry
home some French troops, after which service she was to be sold.
In July Morris ordered the *Hague* to be sold, and recommended
to Congress a like disposition of the *Bourbon,* which latter ship
in all probability had been recently launched.   In March, 1784,
Morris recommended the sale of the Alliance, as she was " now
a mere bill of costs;" and also of the *Washington,* because
much money would be required to repair her, and there was
no need to employ her as a packet since the French and English
had established a mail service.   Lieutenant Joshua Barney, acting
as agent for the Naval Department, sold the *Washington* in Baltimore in the summer of 1784.

The members of Congress were not unanimous on the question
of the proper disposition of the *Alliance.*   On January 15,
1784, a committee of three reported " That the honour of the Flag
of the United States and the protection of its trade and coasts
from the insults of pirates require that the frigate *Alliance* should
be repaired."   A committee in March, 1784, and another in May,
1785, recommended her sale.   Finally on June 3, 1785, Congress directed the Board of Treasury " to sell for specie or public
securities, at public or private sale, the frigate *Alliance,* with tackle
and appurtenances."   In August, 1785, the Board of Treasury sold

this vessel for £2887, to be paid in United States certificates of public debt. The purchasers afterwards sold her at a great profit to Robert Morris. In June, 1787, she sailed for Canton, China, as a merchantman. The *Alliance* was the last vessel in the Navy of the Revolution. From her sale until the establishment of a new navy under the Constitution, it was left to the stars and stripes floating from American merchantmen to familiarize foreign ports and seas with the symbol of the new nation.

Congress did not formally end the naval establishment by act or resolution. It is recalled, however, that the resolution of January 25, 1780, provided that the pay of all naval officers except those in actual service should cease. After this date it would seem that as the vessels were captured, sold, or thrown out of commission, the names of the officers were taken from the pay roll. In September, 1783, an unsuccessful attempt was made in Congress to discontinue the Agent of Marine. Morris continued to fill this office until November 1, 1784, when he retired from public service. Congress made no move to fill his place as Agent of Marine, since there was little need for such an official. Certain unimportant naval business, however, chiefly concerned with naval accounts, remained to be transacted. This for the most part naturally fell to the Board of Treasury, organized in the spring of 1785. This Board, aided by the commissioner for settling the marine accounts, and by James Read, the efficient secretary to the Agent of Marine with whom Morris on retiring left the books and papers of the Naval Department, wound up the small, unimportant, and dwindling business of the navy.

CHAPTER TWO: STATE NAVAL FORCES, 1775-1783

With the exception of New Jersey and Delaware each of the thirteen original states during the Revolution owned one or more armed vessels. Massachusetts, Connecticut, Pennsylvania, Maryland, Virginia, and South Carolina had the largest fleets. New Hampshire with its one ship and Georgia with its four galleys just escaped being in the same class with New Jersey and Delaware. The navies of Rhode Island, New York, and North Carolina were small. The navy of no one state was so large as that of Congress. The total number of state craft, however, greatly exceeded the number of vessels in the Continental navy. The state vessels on the average were smaller and not so well armed as the Continental vessels. The states generally had less means for naval purposes at their disposal than had Congress, and were therefore not so well able to build large vessels. Then, too, the chief need of each state for a navy was to defend its seaports, coasts, and trade. For such services small craft adapted for running in and out of shallow harbors, rivers, and bays, were demanded. The states, therefore, provided themselves with armed boats of various sizes, galleys with and without sails, half-galleys, floating batteries, barges, and fire-ships. Besides such vessels as these most of the states had a few larger and stouter sailing craft, mounting generally from ten to twenty guns and fairly well fitted for deep-sea navigation. The one state whose deep-sea exceeded its inshore craft was Massachusetts.

The history of naval administration in the several states possesses some common features. It will be recalled that in most of the states the provincial government about the year 1775 was superseded by a revolutionary government, and this in turn about a year later was succeeded by a permanent state government. The revolutionary government consisted of a legislative body, or Provincial Congress, and of an executive body, or Committee of Safety. The permanent state government consisted of a Legislature of one or two Houses and an Executive, which was either a Council, or a Governor and Council. The initial naval administration in the states usually fell to the Committee of Safety, or Revolutionary Executive, which upon the change to a permanent state government bequeathed its naval duties to the Council or to the Governor and Council. In most of the states the details of naval administration were at some time during the Revolution lodged with an Executive Board. In some states there were separate boards for naval and military affairs; in others, one board performed both functions.

The history of naval administration in the states falls into two periods, one embracing the years from 1775 to 1778, the other the years from 1779 to 1783. In the first period each state procured a naval armament, as a rule for the general purpose of providing a naval defence, and not to meet some specific call for armed vessels. By 1779 the first naval craft had been largely captured, destroyed, or sold; and often the first machinery of naval administration had been in large part removed. In response to special needs for armed vessels, calls for which came most often from those who were suffering from the ravages of the British fleets, the states now procured additional vessels, and often devised new administrative machinery to manage them.

In defensive warfare the problem in each state was to provide for the defence of its ports, trade, coasts, and shipping. The offensive warfare of the state navies, which was quite secondary in importance, consisted chiefly of commerce-destroying, conducted along the great ocean-paths of British trade. The principal problem here was for the American vessels in leaving home ports and in returning with their prizes to elude the British vessels, which hovered along the American coast, especially at the mouths of the Chesapeake, Delaware, and Narragansett bays. It is always to be remembered that in all the states the privateers

exceeded the state craft, which were often insignificant in comparison.

The reader will recall that in June, 1775, the battle of Bunker
Hill was fought, a British army occupied Boston, and British vessels sailed the New England seas with little or no opposition.
These vessels had already committed depredations and " piracies "
upon the coasts and trade of Massachusetts, and were obstructing
the importation of ammunition and provisions for the Continental army. It was under these circumstances that Massachusetts
took her first step towards procuring a naval armament. On
June 7, her Third Provincial Congress appointed a committee of
nine " to consider the expediency of establishing a number of
small armed vessels, to cruise on our seacoasts, for the protection
of our trade, and the annoyance of our enemies." The Provincial Congress, which moved very cautiously, enjoined secrecy on
the committee. On June 10, three additional members were
added to the committee; but later in the day a new committee
consisting of seven members was apparently substituted for the
old one. On June 12, the committee " appointed to consider the
expediency of establishing a number of armed vessels " made a
report which provided for the fitting out of not less than six vessels, to mount eight to fourteen carriage guns, and to cruise under
the orders of the Committee of Safety—the chief executive organ
of the Provincial Congress, consisting of nine members, three of
whom were from Boston. This report came up several times
between June 12 and June 20. Finally on the latter date " the
matter was ordered to subside." [1] The Battle of Bunker Hill,
which was fought on June 17, may have had something to do with
this action of the Provincial Congress.

On July 19, 1775, the Revolutionary Government in Massachusetts was superseded by a permanent government consisting of a
House of Representatives and a Council of eighteen members
elected by the House; the two houses were called the General
Court. The continued depredations of the British now caused
several endangered ports to ask the General Court to provide

---

[1] Journals of Third Provincial Congress of Massachusetts, June 7, June
10, June 11, June 12, June 13, June 16, June 19, and June 20, 1775. All
references to the state records of Massachusetts refer to the manuscripts
or early printed copies to be found in the State Library or State Archives
at Boston.

them with a naval defence. The part of Massachusetts which during the Revolution was most exposed to the attacks of the British, and which was most troublesome to defend, was the coast of Maine, then often referred to as the Eastern Coast. In August, 1775, a petition came to the General Court from Machias, a town situated on the Maine coast a few miles west of the present Eastport, asking that commissions be granted to officers and men on board two armed vessels which citizens of Machias had fitted out for the defence of their town. In response the General Court took into the service of the state the sloop *Machias Liberty* and the schooner *Diligent.*[2] Jeremiah O'Brian, one of the men who had signed the petition, was commissioned by the Council commander-in-chief of the two vessels, and he was directed to enlist a number of men, not to exceed thirty, for each vessel. The *Machias Liberty* and the *Diligent* were in the service of the state until October, 1776, when they were discharged. About the first of October, 1775, Salem and Newburyport each asked the General Court for naval aid similar to that granted to Machias, but did not receive it.[3]

The General Court of Massachusetts next turned its attention to privateering. The acts of the states on this head fall into two general classes; those which in terms established state privateering, and those which adopted Continental privateering or accommodated state laws to the same. After the first half of 1776 all the states used Continental commissions and bonds. Massachusetts, moving in this matter before Congress, necessarily established state privateering. On September 28, 1775, her House of Representatives, having such establishment in view, appointed a committee of seven to consider the " Expediency of fitting out a Number of Armed Vessels." On October 9, this committee reported in favor of instituting privateering and a prize court to try cases of capture. On October 14 a bill embodying the committee's recommendations was introduced. It now passed slowly through the legislative mill, and on November 1, it became a law.[4]

---

[2] Journals of Massachusetts House of Representatives, August 21, 1775. O'Brian's name is found spelled in various ways.

[3] Journals of Massachusetts House of Representatives, September 29, October 2, October 4, 1775; Records of General Court of Massachusetts, October 4, 1775.

[4] Journals of Massachusetts House of Representatives, September 28, October 6, 9, 14, 17, 18, 19, 27, November 1, 1775.

John Adams once referred to this statute of Massachusetts as one of the most important documents in the history of the Revolution. Its preamble was the work of Elbridge Gerry, and the body of the law was drafted by James Sullivan, many years later Governor of Massachusetts.[5] Gerry stated the sanctions for the law. These he found in the arbitrary and sanguinary acts of Great Britain, in the charter of Massachusetts granted by King William and Queen Mary, and lastly in the resolution of the Continental Congress of July 18, 1775, recommending each colony to provide by armed vessels or otherwise for the protection of its harbors and navigation.

The Massachusetts law provided that all vessels convicted of making unlawful invasions or attacks on the seacoasts or navigation of any part of America should be forfeited. The Council was authorized to grant letters of marque and reprisal to masters and owners of vessels upon their entering into bond to faithfully discharge the duties of their office and to observe the naval laws of the colony. Three admiralty districts embracing the counties on the Massachusetts seacoast were established. The Southern district, with the seat of its court at Plymouth, embraced Plymouth county and the counties to the southward; the Middle district, with the seat of its court at Ipswich, embraced the counties of Suffolk, Middlesex and Essex and extended from Plymouth county to New Hampshire; and the Eastern district, with the seat of its court at North Yarmouth, embraced the seacoast counties of Maine. The form of procedure in these courts was fixed for both captured and recaptured vessels. In the latter case salvage was to be from one-third to one-fourth of the selling price of the vessel. The facts in prize cases were to be tried by twelve good and lawful men. At this time the people of Massachusetts were so enraged at the judges of the former Provincial admiralty court that they would have universally condemned the trying of facts in prize cases by judges.[6]

The Council soon appointed three judges of admiralty, Nathan Cushing for the Southern district, Timothy Pickering for the Middle district, and James Sullivan for the Eastern district. Elbridge Gerry declined the judgeship for the Middle district.

[5] Austin's Gerry, I, 94-95; Works of John Adams, X, 37.
[6] Amory's Sullivan, II, 378-79, James Sullivan to Gerry, December 25, 1779.

After trying about one hundred and fifty prize cases Pickering, in June, 1777, resigned and was succeeded by Nathan Cushing, who now served as judge in both the Southern and Middle districts.[7] Comparatively few cases were tried in the Southern and Eastern districts. Timothy Langdon was for a long time judge of the Eastern district.

During the fall of 1775 the General Court took no steps towards establishing a state navy. It was at this time assisting Washington in obtaining and arming vessels for the Continental military service around Boston. Early in December the House of Representatives, acting on a recommendation contained in a letter from John Adams at Philadelphia, resolved to obtain statistics on the number of officers, seamen, and vessels, suitable for naval purposes, in the seaports of Massachusetts. On December 29 the Council declared for a navy by passing the following resolution: "Whereas several of the United Colonies have of late thought it expedient and necessary to fit out armed Vessels for the Defence of American Liberty, and it appears to this Court necessary that Measures be taken by this Colony for our further Protection by Sea: Therefore, Resolved, that John Adams and Joseph Palmer, Esqurs. with such as the Hon. House shall join be a committee for fitting out one or more Vessels for the Defence of American Liberty."[8]

The House at once appointed its members of the committee, which on January 12, 1776, made a report favorable to the establishment of a navy.[9] Accordingly, on February 7, a resolution passed the General Court to build ten sloops of war, of 110 or 115 tons burden, each, suitable for carrying fourteen to sixteen carriage guns, 6-pounders and 4-pounders. A joint committee of the two houses was appointed to build the vessels, and £10,000 was voted for this purpose.[10] On the 16th the committee was

---

[7] Records of Massachusetts Council, November 14, December 9, December 12, 1775; Pickering's Pickering, I, 79-80; Amory's Sullivan, I, 63.

[8] Records of General Court of Massachusetts, December 29, 1775.

[9] Journals of Massachusetts House of Representatives, January 12, 1776. On January 11 the Council resolved that two ships, one of 36, and the other of 32 guns, should be built. On the same day both House and Council voted to recommit the resolution in order that the committee which prepared it might report on the expense to be incurred in building and fitting the two ships. It does not appear that further action was taken.— Records of Massachusetts Council, January 11, 1776.

[10] Ibid., February 6, 1776; Journals of Council, February 7, 1776.

authorized to contract for the building of only five vessels, until there was a prospect of procuring materials for ten; it was authorized to buy five vessels if it thought it best.[11] By July, 1776, the sloop *Tyrannicide* built at Salisbury, the brigantine *Rising Empire* built at Dartmouth, and the brigantine *Independence* built at Kingston were ready for sea; and by September the sloops *Republic* and *Freedom* built at Swanzey, and the *Massachusetts* built at Salisbury were completed.

Meanwhile the General Court had prepared and adopted the legislation necessary to establish a navy. It had drafted proper naval forms; and it had appointed a number of naval officers. A partial pay-table was established on February 8.[12] This on April 12 was succeeded by a new one, which generally raised wages, and which provided for a number of new offices. A captain was now to receive a monthly wage of £8; a first lieutenant, £5 8s.; a second lieutenant, £5; a master, £4; a mate, £3; a surgeon, £7; and an ordinary seaman, £2. Each vessel was to be provided with 115 officers and seamen. No better proof of the rawness of the naval service is needed than the regulation that recruits, whether officers, seamen, or marines should furnish themselves with "a good effective Fire Arm, Cartouch-Box, Cutlass, and Blanket." The captains were ordered to recommend to the Council a list of inferior officers and to enlist the proposed number of seamen and marines. Captors were given one-third of the proceeds of prizes.[13]

On April 27, 1776, the General Court fixed the respective shares of the proceeds of prizes for officers and seamen: a captain was to receive six shares, and "all the Cabbin Furniture;" a first lieutenant, five shares; a drummer, one and one-fourth shares; a seaman, one share; and a boy, one-half a share.[14] On April 29, in order to encourage enlistment, an advance of one month's wages was voted to recruits. On the same day it was decided that "the Uniform of Officers be Green and White, and that the Colours be a white Flagg, with a green Pine Tree, and an Inscription, 'Appeal to Heaven.'"[15] On July 26 the Council appointed a

---

[11] Journals of Massachusetts House of Representatives, February 16, 1776.

[12] Ibid., February 7, 1776; Records of Massachusetts Council, February 8, 1776.

[13] Journals of Massachusetts House of Representatives, April 12, 1776.

[14] Ibid., April 27, 1776.

[15] Ibid., April 29, 1776; Records of Massachusetts Council, April 29, 1776.

prize agent in each of the three admiralty districts, whose duty
it was to represent the state in receiving, trying, and selling
prizes.[16] At times the prize agents assisted in fitting out vessels.

During the first half of 1776 the law of November 1, 1775,
establishing privateering was three times amended and re-mod-
elled.[17] The law was thereby accommodated to the resolutions
of the Continental Congress fixing the kinds of property subject
to capture, and the respective shares of captors and recaptors.
Doubts which had arisen as to the proper construction of the original act were now removed. The procedure before admiralty
courts was made more specific. In cases of captures made by
Continental vessels, appeals were permitted from state admiralty
courts to the Continental Congress; in all other cases appeals
were allowed to the superior state courts. In each of the three
admiralty districts in Massachusetts additional towns were named
where court might be held. The towns named for the Middle
district were Boston, Salem, Ipswich, and Newburyport.

During the summer and fall of 1776 the instructions and orders
to the captains of the armed vessels were issued to them by the
Council, having been previously prepared by a committee. The
following instructions which were drafted by Thomas Cushing
and Daniel Hopkins were given to Captain John Fisk, and will
suffice as a sample of such documents:

" The Brigantine *Tyrannicide* under your Command being
properly Armed and Man'd and in other respects fitted for a
Cruize you are hereby Ordered and directed immediately to proceed to Sea and Use your utmost Endeavours to protect the Sea
Coast and Trade of the United States and you are also directed to
exert yourself in making Captures of all Ships and other Vessels
Goods Wares and Merchandise belonging to the King of Great
Britain or any of his subjects wherever residing excepting only
the Ships and Goods of the Inhabitants of Bermuda and the Ba-
hama Islands—You are directed not to Cruize further Southward
than Latitude Twelve North nor farther East than Longitude
Nine Degrees West from London nor farther West than the
Shoals of Nantucket. At all times using necessary precautions
to prevent your Vessel from falling into the hands of the Enemy."

[16] Records of Massachusetts Council, July 26, 1776.
[17] Laws of Massachusetts, February 14, April 13, May 8, 1776.

" And Whereas you have received a Commission authorizing
you to make Captures aforesaid and a set of Instructions have
been delivered you for regulating your Conduct in that matter;
these Instructions you are Hereby directed diligently to attend to,
and if you are so fortunate as to make any Captures you are to
Order them to make the first safe Harbor within the United
States.—and you are furthered Ordered not to expend your Ammunition unnecessarily and only in time of Action or firing Alarm
or Signal guns." [18]

Until October, 1776, the Massachusetts navy was administered
by the General Court, committees of its members, the Council,
and naval agents. The General Court for the period of its recess in May, 1776, placed the armed vessels in the charge of " the
committee for fortifying the harbor of Boston." By the fall of
1776 it realized that " secrecy, dispatch, and economy in conducting the war" demanded a special executive department.
Accordingly, on October 26 it established a Board of War consisting of nine members, any five of whom constituted a quorum.
The Board of War was " empowered to Order and Direct the
Operations of the Forces in the Pay of this State, both by sea
and land, by giving the Commanders of the Troops, Garrisons,
and Vessels of War, such Orders for their Conduct and Cruizes
from time to time as they shall think proper." [19] It organized by
electing a president and secretary; and it rented permanent quarters near the State House in Boston. In December, 1776, James
Warren, later Commissioner for the Continental Navy Board at
Boston, was president of the Board of War. Philip Henry Savage was for a long time its president. Savage presided at the
meeting in 1773 at Old South Church which decided that the tea
should not be landed.[20] The Board of War entered upon its work
with vigor in November, 1776. It was yearly renewed, until it
was dissolved in February, 1781.

The principal business of the Board of War was the administration of the naval, commercial, and military affairs of the state.
Its naval and commercial duties were quite engrossing. The

[18] Records of Massachusetts Council, October 29, 1776. The naval documents introduced into the narrative on the Massachusetts navy are typical
of similar ones in other states.
[19] Resolves of Massachusetts, October 26, 1776.
[20] Winsor's Memorial History of Boston, II, 543.

Board kept fairly distinct the activities of its " armed " and " trading " vessels.   It is true that the armed vessels were now and then
sent on commercial errands, or combined in a single voyage naval
and trading duties.   The sloop *Republic* used for a short time
as a naval vessel was taken into the commercial service.   The
Massachusetts Archives contain a list of thirty-two trading vessels owned or chartered by the Board of War.[21]   These vessels
visited Nantes, Bilbao, Martinique, Guadaloupe, St. Eustatius,
Cape Francois, Baltimore, and the ports of North and South Carolina.   They carried as staple exports, fish, lumber, and New
England rum.   As a rule the work of the Board of War in looking after its trading vessels exceeded its naval work.   At times,
as in the case of the Penobscot expedition, the naval duties were
the important ones.   A week's work of the Board in behalf of its
armed vessels shows a curious mixture of orders on the commissary-general for clothing and provisions, and on the state store
keeper for naval stores; and of directions to the prize agents, the
agents for building armed vessels, and the naval captains.   The
General Court permitted the Board a fairly free hand in its management of the navy.   The Board carried on a considerable correspondence with the commanders of the armed vessels.   The
following letter written to the Board by Captain John Clouston
of the armed sloop *Freedom* on May 23, 1777, from Paimboeuf,
France, will illustrate this correspondence from the Captain's
side.   Clouston's disregard of orthography and punctuation is
exceptional even for a Revolutionary officer.

[21] Massachusetts Revolutionary Archives, XL, 110-111. The influence of
the friendly relations existing between the United States and France during
the Revolution in the naming of vessels early manifested itself.   On December 27, 1776, the Massachusetts Board of War changed the names of a
number of its trading vessels as follows: Ships *Julius Caesar* to *Bourbon,
Venus* to *Versailles,* and *Friend* to *Paris;* brigantines *Charming Sally* to
Penet, and *Isabella* to *Count D'Estaing.* The brigantine *Penet,* which was
named for a French merchant at Nantes, a member of the firm of Pliarne,
Penet & Co., agents for the United States, has been sometimes confused
with the brigantine *Perch,* which was obtained by Massachusetts in the
fall of 1777 for the sole purpose of conveying the news of Burgoyne's
surrender to the American Commissioners at Paris.   The letters and dispatches were intrusted with Jonathan Loring Austin, secretary to the
Board of War, who after a passage of thirty days reached the Commissioners at Passy on December 4, 1777.—Board of War Minutes, December
27, 1776; Hale's Franklin in France, I, 155.

" Gentlemen :

I have the pleasure of Informing your Honours by Capt. Fisk of the Massachusetts That on the first Instant I arrived safe in this Port after taking twelve Sail of Englis Vessels Seven of which I despatched for Boston Burnt three gave one smal Brigg to our Prisners and one Retaken by the Futereange which Chast us fore Glasses and finding she Could not Cume ·up with us she gave Chase to our Prize and toock her in our sight—I have Cleaned & Refited my Vessel and Taken in forty Tons of War like Stores and have bin waiting for a wind to go this fore days— Capt. Fisk being short of Provisions I have supplied him with foreteen Barels of Pork and Eleven of Beef and have Suffi- santse for my Vessel left." [22]

In January, 1777, a new sea establishment was effected. Wages were generally raised, no doubt chiefly to meet their de- crease caused by the depreciation of the currency. A captain was now to receive a monthly wage of £14 8s.; a lieutenant or a master, £7 4s.; a seaman, £2 8s.; and a boy, £1 4s. The offices established in the Massachusetts navy, while not quite so many, were in general the same as those in the Continental navy. The Massachusetts navy however had the offices of prizemaster, pilot, and boy, which did not occur in the Continental list. Following the regulations of Congress the General Court now gave captors one-half of their captures. The rations for seamen were modelled on the Continental bill of fare.[23] On March 21, 1777, the General Court adopted rules and regulations for its ships of war; and it ordered that they should be read by the commanding officer of a vessel at least once a week. These rules, while briefer than the Continental rules, naturally followed the same general lines. They show either the influence of the Continental rules or of the English rules upon which the Continental rules were based. The following curious rule in part parallels one of the Continental rules.

" And if any Person belonging to either of such Vessels shall be convicted of Theft, Drunkenness, profane Cursing, or Swear-

---

[22] Board of War Letters, Massachusetts Revolutionary Archives, May 23, 1777.

[23] Massachusetts Resolves, January 8, January 24, 1777. On December 6, 1776, six naval offices were established, which included a captain's clerk, prizemaster, and sergeant of marines.

ing, disregarding the Sabbath, or using the Name of God lightly, or profanely, or shall be guilty of quarrelling or fighting, or of any reproachful or provoking Language tending to make Quarrels, or of any turbulent or mutinous Behavior, or if any Person shall sleep upon his Watch, or forsake his Station, or shall in any wise neglect to perform the Duty enjoined him, he shall be punished for any of the said Offences at the Discretion of the commissioned Officers of such Vessel, or the Major Part of them, according to the Nature and Aggravation of the Offence, by sitting in the Stocks, or wearing a wooden Collar about his Neck, not exceeding 4 Hours, nor less than one, or by whipping, not exceeding 12 Lashes, or by being put in Irons for so long Time as the said Officers shall judge the Safety and well being of the Ship and Crew requires, or otherwise shall forfeit to the State not more than six, nor less than two Days Pay for each offence." [24]

During every year of the Revolution attempts were made to increase the Massachusetts navy. In the fall of 1777 the brigantine *Hazard* was added. On August 6, 1777, the General Court resolved that, since the armed vessels at the lowest computation had netted the state £55,000, the Board of War should purchase or build two vessels mounting 28 and 32 guns respectively. In January, 1778, it reduced the sizes of these vessels almost one-half; and finally it gave up building them. [25] In the spring of 1779 a prize of the *Hazard,* the brigantine *Active,* taken in April off the island of St. Thomas in the West Indies, was purchased. [26] In April, 1778, the General Court resolved to build a

[24] Massachusetts Resolves, March 21, 1777.

[25] Ibid., August 6, 1777; January 17, 1778.

[26] The following is an extract from the enlisting contract of the armed brig *Active,* which was signed by officers, seamen, and marines: "And we hereby bind ourselves to Submit to all orders and regulations of the Navy of the United States of North America and this State and faithfully to observe and obey all such orders, and Commands as we shall receive from time to time from our Superior Officers on board or belonging to the said Brig, *Active,* and on board any Such Boats or Vessel or Vessels as foresaid.

"And it is on the part of the State that such persons as by Land or sea shall Loose a Limb in any Engagement with the Enemies of these United States of America or be otherwise so disabled as to be rendered incapable of getting a Lively Hood Shall be entitled to the same Provisions as the disabled Persons in the Continental Service."—Massachusetts Revolutionary Archives, XL, 20.

frigate of 28 guns which would carry two hundred officers and men.[27] This vessel was built at Newburyport and was named the *Protector*. In the fall of 1779 it was nearing completion. The launching of the *Protector,* which was the largest ship in the Massachusetts navy, was a matter of more than usual local interest. Stephen Cross who was in charge of the construction of the frigate wrote a letter to the Board of War in July, 1779, which throws light upon the minor naval duties of the Board. Cross's language is a bit involved, but his meaning is clear; it is hardly necessary to say that the " souring " refers to lemons.

" Gentlemen :

it being customary for the owners of Vessels when they are Launched to give the Workmen something Better than New England Rum to drink & Likewise something to Eat and also all those Persons who attend the Launching Expect to be asked to Drink and Eat something and Especially Publick Vessells it will be Expected that something be Provided and it is my opinion about sixty Galls of West India Rum & sugars for the same & souring if it be had and one Quarter Cask of Wine and A Hamper of ale or Beer together with a Tierce hams Néet Tongs or Corn Beef will be necessary to comply with the Customs in these Cases." [28]

After August, 1779, when the disaster on the Penobscot occurred the naval duties of the Board of War were slight. For a time the *Protector* was the only vessel in the navy. With the coming in of a new government under a Constitution on October 25, 1780, there was no longer much need for a Board of War. According to the provisions of the new Constitution the Governor was commander-in-chief of the navy; and he was authorized to " train, instruct, exercise, and govern it," and to call it into service in time of war. On February 8, 1781, the Board of War was discontinued, and Caleb Davis, who was appointed Agent of the Commonwealth, succeeded to its ministerial duties.[29] The Governor and the Agent now shared the naval duties. The Governor commissioned officers, issued orders to the naval commanders, and was responsible to the General Court; the Agent had

---

[27] Massachusetts Resolves, April 21, 1778.
[28] Massachusetts Revolutionary Archives, XLIV, 279.
[29] Massachusetts Resolves, February 8, 1781. Three members of the Board of War and two clerks were continued for a few months to settle the accounts of the Board.

direct oversight of the fitting out of vessels, the selling of prizes, and was responsible to the Governor. As the Revolution spent itself the simplification of the administrative machinery of the state continued. On January 1, 1783, the Agent was discontinued. His naval duties fell to the Commissary-General.[30]

During each year from 1780 to 1783 the General Court made one or more attempts to increase the naval force of the state. It was spurred to action by the ravages of the British cruisers on the Eastern Coast. On March 21, 1780, two armed vessels mounting not less than ten or more than fourteen 4's or 6's were ordered. The expense incurred was to be met by the sale of the "Rising Empire" and of the confiscated estates of Loyalists, and from rents of the property of absentees. On March 6, 1781, the Agent was directed to obtain a small vessel of eight to twelve guns to serve as a tender for the *Mars;* and on April 23 he was ordered to procure by hire or purchase two small craft to be employed as "guarda coasta." On November 12, 1782, a committee was appointed to purchase a vessel of twelve or sixteen guns to be used in protecting the coast. On March 26, 1783, the Commissary-General was ordered to obtain a small vessel and a whaleboat to cruise against the enemy in Casco Bay and along the Eastern Shore.[31] As the result of these resolutions four armed vessels were added to the navy; in the spring of 1780 the *Mars;* in the summer of 1781, the *Defence;* in the winter of 1781-1782, the *Tartar,* which was built by the state; and in the spring of 1782, the *Winthrop.*

Private naval enterprise throughout the Revolution was exceedingly active in Massachusetts. In 1775, some months before the General Court granted letters of marque, Massachusetts citizens unauthorized were capturing the vessels of the enemy. Scarcely a fortnight after the battles of Lexington and Concord men from New Bedford and Dartmouth fitted out a vessel and attacked and cut out from a harbor in Martha's Vineyard a prize of the British sloop-of-war *Falcon,* 16. This act was called forth by the captures which the *Falcon* had made from the people of Buzzard's Bay. On June 12, 1775, the inhabitants of Machias, Maine, had captured the King's sloop *Margaretta,* Lieutenant Moore, after mortally wounding the commander and inflicting a

---

[30] Ibid., October 4, 1782.
[31] Massachusetts Resolves, March 21, 1780; February 19, March 6, April 23, 1781; November 12, 1782; March 26, 1783.

loss of fourteen men. Still other British vessels were captured off the coast of Maine during the summer of 1775.[32]

With the act of November 1, 1775, granting the Council the power to issue letters of marque and reprisal, all such private enterprises as the above when done under the authority of a commission were legal. It does not appear however that Massachusetts granted many commissions until the second half of 1776. In 1777 she granted 96 commissions. The best year was 1779 when she issued 222 commissions; the year 1781 with 216 commissions was not far behind. The total number of commissions issued by Massachusetts for the years 1777 to 1783 was 998.[33] In 1779 one hundred and eighty-four prizes captured by privateers were libelled in the Massachusetts prize courts.[34] The privateering industry in this year was very active. The following is an extract from a letter dated May 16, 1779, written from a Massachusetts seaport:

" Privateering was never more in vogue than at present; two or three privateers sail every week from this port, and men seem as plenty as grasshoppers in the field; no vessel being detained an hour for want of them. We have near 1,000 prisoners on board the guard-ships in Boston, and a great balance due us from the enemy. Cruisers from New York, &c are daily brought in, and often by vessels of inferior force; our privateers-men being as confident of victory, when upon an equal footing with the English, as these were of gaining it of the French in the last war." [35]

The rivalry between the state service and privateers for seamen was exceedingly active. In 1779 the Council recommended that some effectual measures be taken to prevent the owners of private ships of war and merchantmen from seducing seamen away that were engaged in the public service. It declared that proper encouragement must be given to state officers and seamen, and that commanders must have the aid of the government in manning their vessels, " or they will lie by the Walls and so be of little or

---

[32] Winsor, Narrative and Critical History, VI, 564; Maclay, History of American Privateering, 52-60.

[33] Massachusetts Revolutionary Archives. The total number of privateering commissions always exceeds the total number of vessels, as the same vessels were often commissioned two or more times.

[34] Boston Gazette for 1779.

[35] Virginia Gazette, June 19, 1779.

no service." [36]   In 1778 the General Court found some difficulty
in securing commanders.

The movements of the armed vessels of the Massachusetts navy
were quite similar to the movements of the naval vessels of Congress.[37]   The smaller fleet like the larger cruised in European
waters, in the region of the West Indies, and to the eastward of
the Bermudas in the path of the richly-laden West Indiamen.
The Massachusetts vessels, however, cruised more frequently
nearer home.   About the first of June, 1779, the *Hazard* and
Tyrannicide were in the region of Nantucket.   After 1779 the
vessels were frequently ordered to protect the Eastern Coast.   In
the spring of 1777 the *Tyrannicide,* Captain Jonathan Haraden,
Massachusetts, Captain John Fisk, and *Freedom,* Captain John
Clouston, cruised eastward as far as the coasts of France and
Spain, capturing some twenty-five prizes, many of which however
were recaptured by the British.[38]   This was a most fortunate ven-

----

[36] Journals of House of Representatives, January 6, 1779.

[37] The vessels in the Massachusets navy with the approximate periods of
their service was as follows: Sloop, *Machias Liberty,* 1775-1776; schooner,
Diligent, 1775-1776; brigantine (at first a sloop), *Tyrannicide,* 1776-1779;
brigantine, *Rising Empire,* 1776-1777; brigantine, *Independence,* 1776-1777;
sloop, *Republic,* 1776-1777; sloop, *Freedom,* 1776-1777; brigantine, *Massachusetts,* 1776-1778; brigantine, *Hazard,* 1777-1779; brigantine, *Active,*
1779; frigate, *Protector,* 1779-1781; ship, *Mars,* 1780-1781; sloop, *Defence,*
1781; ship, *Tartar,* 1782-1783; sloop, *Winthrop,* 1782-1783; and galley,
Lincoln, 1779-1781. Most of these vessels mounted from ten to twenty
guns, 4's and 6's. The only larger vessel was the *Protector,* 26. Vessels
such as the *Tyrannicide, Hazard,* and *Winthrop* carried about 125 officers
and men. The following captains were the chief officers in the Massachusetts navy: Jeremiah O'Brian, John Lambert, John Fisk, John Foster
Williams, John Clouston, Jonathan Haraden, Daniel Souther, Simeon
Samson, Richard Welden, Allen Hallet, James Nevens, John Cathcart,
and George Little. Massachusetts did not establish the rank of commodore.

[38] These three vessels captured the four prizes mentioned in the following advertisement which appeared in the Continental Journal and Weekly
Advertiser for July 3, 1777, a paper published at Boston. The advertisement is introduced here to illustrate the final disposition of prize vessels:

To be sold by Public Auction at eleven o'clock on Wednesday the 23d
of July instant at Mr. Tileston's wharf in Boston, the following prizes with
their appurtenances.

The Ship *Lonsdale,* about 250 tons.   Brig *Penelope,* about 130 tons.
    Brig *Britannia,* about 140 tons.   Scow *Sally,* about 180 tons.

The above prizes lay at Tileston's wharf. They are all good vessels
and well found. Inventories to be seen at the sheriff's office Cornhill, and
at the place of sale.   W. GREENLEAF, Sheriff.

ture, for all told one can not now count more than seventy prizes captured by the Massachusetts navy. In the summer of 1780 the Board of War turned over the *Mars,* Captain Simeon Samson, to the Massachusetts Committee for Foreign Affairs which sent her to France and Holland for supplies.

The state vessels were at times joined in cruises with privateers or with Continental vessels; and enterprises were concerted with all three classes of armed craft. In April, 1777, the state took into its service for a month nine privateers, mounting 130 guns, and carrying 1,030 men, to cruise with the Continental frigates *Hancock* and *Boston* after the British frigate *Milford* which had been especially annoying and destructive to the trade of the state.[39] In February, 1781, the *Protector* was cruising with the Continental frigate *Deane* thirty leagues windward of Antigua. In March, 1781, the Admiral of the French fleet at Newport was requested to send two French ships to cruise with the *Mars* on the Eastern Shore; and a bounty was offered to privateers who would cruise against the " worthless banditti " in that region.[40]

The capture of a prize often amounted to little more than the chasing of a merchantman and the firing of a few shots as a signal for surrender. At times, however, when the merchantman was armed or when the enemy's vessel happened to be a privateer the action was more serious. One of the most severe single engagements in which a Massachusetts vessel was concerned was that between the *Protector* 26, Captain John Foster Williams, and the privateer frigate *Admiral Duff* 32, Captain Stranger. It took place on June 9, 1780, in latitude 42° N. and longitude 47° W. The engagement was heavy for an hour and a half when the *Admiral Duff,* having caught fire, blew up, all on board being lost except fifty-five men who were picked up by the *Protector.* The American vessel lost six men.[41] The following brief account of one of these minor engagements told in the simple and direct language of the Massachusetts captain who took part in it is taken from a letter of Captain Allen Hallet to the Board of War, which is dated at sea on board the *Tyrannicide,* latitude 28° N., longitude 68° W., March 31, 1779. This graphic account shows with

[39] Massachusetts Resolves, April 26, 1777; Massachusetts Revolutionary Archives, XL, 29, 55.

[40] Massachusets Resolves, March 2, 1781.

[41] Massachusetts Gazette, July 24, 1780.

clearness the character of the minor engagements of the Revolution.

" I have the pleasure of sending this to you by Mr. John Blanch who goes prizemaster of my Prize, the Privateer Brig *Revenge,* lately commanded by Capt. Robert Fendall belonging to Grenada, but last from Jamaica, mounting 14 Carriage Guns, 6 & 4 pounders, 4 swivels & 2 Cohorns, & sixty ablebodied Men, which I took after a very smart & Bloody Engagement, in which they had 8 men killed & fourteen wounded, the Vessell cut very much to pieces by my Shott, so that they had no command of her at all— amongst the killed was the 1st Lieut. & one Quarter Mr.— amongst the wounded is the Capt. 2nd. Lieut. & Gunner—I captured her as follows: on the 29 Inst. at 4 PM. I made her about 4 leagues to windward coming down upon us, upon which I cleared the Ship and got all hands to Quarter, ready for an Engagement, I stood close upon the Wind waiting for her, about half past six PM. she came up with me, and hailed me, ask'd me where I was from, I told them I was from Boston & asked where they were from, they said from Jamaica & that they were a British Cruizer, I immediately told them I was an American Cruizer, upon which they ordered me to Strike, & seeing I did not intend to gratify their desires, they rang'd up under my Lee & gave me a Broadside, I immediately return'd the Compliment & dropping a Stern, I got under their Lee and then pour'd out Broadsides into her from below and out of the Tops, so fast & so well directed that in one hour & a Quarter we dismantled two of her Guns & drove them from their Quarter & compell'd them to Strike their Colors, during the whole Engagement we were not at any one time more than half Pistol Shott distant & some part of the Time our Yards were lock'd with theirs—I had Eight men wounded only two of which are Bad—amongst the wounded are my first Lieut. & Master, I intended to man her and keep her as a Consort during the Cruize, but having twenty wounded Men on board, of my own men & prisoners I thought it Best to send her home, with all the wounded men on board under the Care of the Surgeons Mate." [42]

By far the largest naval undertaking of the Revolution made by the Americans was the Penobscot Expedition. Until 1779

[42] Massachusetts Revolutionary Archives, XLIV, 408.

the general policy of those who managed the fleet of Massachusetts was to send its vessels cruising against the British transports, merchantmen, and small privateers, leaving the coast to be
defended by the seacoast establishment and by local forces. In
August, 1777, the Council agreed with this policy for it then spoke
of the Continental vessels, the state vessels, and the privateers
as "imporper" to be employed in clearing the coasts of these
"vermin." [43] In April, 1779, it disapproved this policy. It now
in a message to the House submitted whether, instead of sending
the armed vessels of the state on long cruises after prizes, it
would not have been vastly more to the advantage and profit of
the state to have employed them cruising on the coast of Massachusetts for the protection of trade and the defence of harbors
and seacoasts, "which have been left in such an unguarded and
defenceless Situation that where we have taken one Vessel of the
Enemy their small privateers out of New York have taken ten
from us." [44] It would seem that the Board of War was right in
employing its fleet in prize-getting rather than in defensive warfare. The capturing of small privateers and merchantmen were
the only enterprises for which the Revolutionary fleets were
adapted. Those vessels that cruised continually near the American coast sooner or later fell foul of the stouter and better armed
ships of the enemy. The Board of War, had it not responded
to the commercial spirit of the times, would have been compelled to adopt the methods of the privateers, did it wish to succeed in its competition with them for seamen.

During the first half of 1779 the British vessels were very destructive to the trade and shipping of Massachusetts and New
Hampshire. On June 9, 1779, eight hundred of the enemy, encouraged by certain Tories in Maine, effected a lodgement on the
Maine coast at a place called Bagaduce, now Castine, near the
mouth of the Penobscot river. [45] This made a fine vantage-point

[43] Ibid., 268.

[44] Journals of Massachusetts House of Representatives, April 7, 1779.

[45] Amory's Sullivan, II, 376-78, James Sullivan to John Sullivan, August
30, 1779. James Sullivan says that the occupation of Bagaduce by the
British greatly alarmed Boston and neighboring seaports at the prospect
of a scarcity of wood; and that men who had made their fortunes by war,
for once and for a moment, felt a public spirit, and freely offered their
ships to the government. They were careful to have their ships appraised
and insured by the state, which of course suffered the loss on the failure
of the expedition.

as a base for naval operations. The appeal for naval protection which the inhabitants of Massachusetts now made upon her was a strong one. Towards the close of June the Massachusetts government began concerting with the Continental Navy Board at Boston and with the government of New Hampshire an expedition to capture and destroy this British station. Samuel Adams, who had recently retired from the chairmanship of the Marine Committee of Congress and had returned to Boston furthered the enterprise. To the fleet which was now formed, New Hampshire contributed the *Hampden,* 22; the Navy Board at Boston, the Continental vessels, *Warren,* 32, *Providence,* 12, and *Diligent,* 12; and Massachusetts, the three state brigantines, *Tyrannicide,* 16, *Hazard,* 14, and *Active,* 14, together with thirteen privateers, which were temporarily taken into the state service. These twenty armed vessels mounted in all 324 guns, and were manned by more than 2,000 men. Besides the armed fleet there were twenty transports which carried upwards of 1,000 state militia. The naval forces were under the command of Captain Dudley Saltonstall of the Continental navy; and the troops were commanded by Brigadier-General Solomon Lovell of the state military forces of Massachusetts. Paul Revere was Chief of Artillery with the rank of Lieutenant Colonel.

The assembling, manning, provisioning, and fitting of so many vessels greatly taxed the resources of Massachusetts. The fleet left Boston on July 19, and during the last days of the month it appeared off the Penobscot and attacked Bagaduce with only partial success, failing to take the main fort. Before a second attempt was made a British fleet from New York under the command of Sir George Collier, who had received news of the expedition, appeared in the Penobscot. The British fleet consisted of the *Raisonnable,* 64; *Blonde* and *Virginia,* 32's; *Greyhound, Camilla,* and *Gallatea,* 20's; and *Otter,* 14; together with three small vessels at the garrison, the *Nautilus,* 16, *Albany,* 14, and *North,* 14. It mounted 248 guns and carried more than 1600 men. In number of guns and men the advantage lay with the Americans, but in weight of metal and tonnage it was probably with the British. On the morning of August 14 the British fleet came in sight of the American. The two fleets were barely in range of each others guns when the Americans were seized with a panic, and fled with their vessels helter skelter up

the river, pursued by the British. The Americans offered almost
no resistance whatever, but ran their ships ashore, set fire to them,
and escaped afoot, when not too closely pursued. With the exception of two or three vessels which were captured, the American fleet was annihilated. The British lost 13; the American
loss has been placed at 474. The larger part of the American
sailors and soldiers returned by woods to New Hampshire and
Massachusetts.

The total cost of this expedition to Massachusetts as calculated
by the Board of War was £1,739,175. The larger part of this
sum £1,390,200 was charged to the account of the navy. It suffered the loss of three state armed vessels and a victualer, nine
privateers, and twenty transports. Among the twenty transports, with possibly one exception, was the whole trading fleet
of the state. Soon after the disaster a joint committee of the
Massachusetts House of Representatives and Council with Arte-
mas Ward as president, held an inquiry and made a report on
the causes of the failure of the expedition. In answer to the question, " what appears the principal reason of the failure," the committee decided unanimously, " want of proper Spirit and Energy
on the part of the Commodore." A court-martial which was
held on the frigate *Deane* in Boston harbor about the first of
October found against Captain Saltonstall, and dismissed him
from the navy. Rarely has a more ignominious military operation been made by Americans than the Penobscot Expedition. A
New Englander with some justice has likened it to Hull's surrender at Detroit. Had it been successful, it would not have
been worth the effort it cost. Its object had no national significance; it was an eccentric operation. " Bad in conception, bad
in preparation, bad in execution, it naturally ended in disaster
and disgrace." [46]

Besides the *Tyrannicide, Hazard,* and *Active* the Massachusetts navy lost to the enemy at least three other vessels. Towards
the close of 1777 the British captured the *Freedom* and *Inde-*

---

[46] Massachusetts Revolutionary Archives, CXLV, 199-203, 350; Wey-
mouth Historical Journal, chapters VII-X, gives the best account of the
Penobscot expedition, also contains the Original Journal of General Solomon Lovell kept on the expedition; Massachusetts Historical Society Collections 7th, II, 430; Proceedings of Massachusetts Historical Society 2d,
XII, 201-202; Clowes' Royal Navy, IV, 28-29.

pendence. On May 5, 1781, His Majesty's ships *Roebuck,* 44, and *Medea,* 28, captured the *Protector,* 26, with more than one hundred and thirty men on board.[47] She was added to the Royal Navy as the *Hussar.* In the latter half of 1782 Captain George Little in the *Winthrop* cruised on the Eastern Coast and captured and sent into Boston "nearly the whole of the arm'd force they possessed at Penobscot," thus in part retrieving the naval honor of his state.[48] Acting under orders of Governor Hancock, Little in the *Winthrop* made the last cruise of the Massachusetts navy when in the winter of 1782-1783 he visited Martinique. On his return, he was fitting for a cruise on the Eastern Coast when about April 1, news of permanent peace arrived. On June 4, 1783, the Commissary-General was directed to sell the *Winthrop,* the last vessel in the navy. The *Tartar* had been sold during the past winter.[49] Captain Little's accounts were being settled in March, 1785.

In July, 1775, Virginia began to raise and officer an army of more than one thousand men. By the fall of that year Lord Dunmore, the Provincial Governor of Virginia, who in June had retreated to His Majesty's ship *Fowey* at Yorktown, had collected a small flotilla, and had begun a series of desultory attacks upon the river banks of Virginia. On October 25 he was repulsed at Hampton; on December 9 he was beaten by the Virginia patriots at Great Bridge; and on January 1 he burned Norfolk. His movements excited so much alarm that the leading patriot families on the James, York, Rappahannock, and Potomac rivers retreated inland for safety. In order to prevent the depredations of Lord Dunmore, and to provide effectually for the general defence of the state, the Virginia Provincial Convention in December authorized the Committee of Safety of the state to "provide from time to time such and so many armed vessels as they may judge necessary for the protection of the several rivers in this colony, in the best manner the circumstances of the country will admit." The Committee of Safety was further directed to raise a sufficient

[47] Massachusetts Revolutionary Archives, XXXIX, 45.
[48] Ibid., CLVIII, 274, Message of Governor Hancock to House of Representatives, February 6, 1783.
[49] Massachusetts Resolves, June 4, 1783. Those naval vessels which were not captured, destroyed, or sold, were either returned to their owners, when rented, or thrown out of commission and employed in other services.

number of officers, sailors, and marines; and settle their pay, provided certain specified rates were not exceeded. The maximum wage of " the chief commander of the whole as commodore " was fixed at fifteen shillings a day.[50]

Between December, 1775, and July, 1776, the Committee of Safety procured and established a small navy. On April 1 it fixed the naval pay, generally at the maximum rates permitted. Captains in the navy were to receive a daily wage of 8s.; captains of marines, 6s.; midshipmen, 3s.; marines, 1s. 6d. The Committee resolved that two years ought to be a maximum period of service. It appointed a number of the most prominent officers in the Virginia navy, among whom were Captains James Barron, Richard Barron, Richard Taylor, Thomas Lilly, and Edward Travis. It fixed the relative rank between army and navy officers. It purchased the boats *Liberty* and *Patriot,* the brigs *Liberty* and *Adventure,* and the schooner *Adventure.* It contracted for the construction of a number of galleys on the different rivers of the state.[51]

George Mason and John Dalton were appointed a committee to build two row-galleys, and buy three cutters for the defence of the Potomac. In April, 1776, Mason wrote that the galleys were well under way, and that three small vessels had been purchased, of which the largest was a fine stout craft of about 110 tons burden, mounting fourteen 8's and 4's, carrying ninety-six men, and named the *American Congress.* A company of marines for this vessel, he said, were being exercised in the use of the great guns.[52] The Committee of Safety chose a " Lieutenant of Marines in the Potomac river Department."

The Provincial Convention of Virginia, which met at Williamsburg on May 6, 1776, being convinced that the naval preparations would be conducted more expeditiously and successfully if proper persons were appointed to superintend and direct the same, chose a Board of Naval Commissioners consisting of five per-

[50] Hening, Statutes of Virginia, IX, 83.

[51] Calendar of Virginia State Papers, VIII, 75-240, Journal of Committee of Safety of Virginia, February 7 to July 5, 1776. Virginia had a class of vessels which she referred to as armed boats. They were smart craft, and appear to have been schooner-rigged.

[52] Miss Rowland's George Mason, I, 214, 218.

sons.[53] The Board was authorized to appoint a clerk and assistants, and to elect from its membership a First Commissioner of the Navy, the title of a well-known officer in the English naval service. No member of the Board could sit in the legislature or hold a military office. Each Commissioner was to receive twenty shillings a day, when employed. On the depreciation of the currency this was doubled.[54] A majority of the Board constituted a quorum. Thomas Whiting served as First Commissioner of the Board throughout its existence.

In general the business of the Navy Board was to " superintend and direct all matters and things to the navy relating." It had charge of the building, purchase, fitting, arming, provisioning, and repairing of all armed vessels and transports. It had charge of the shipyards and the public rope-walk. In case of vacancies in the navy or the marines it recommended officers to the Governor and Council. It could suspend an officer for neglect of duty or for misbehavior. It was to keep itself informed on the state of the navy through reports from the naval officers. It was authorized to draw warrants on the treasury for money expended in the naval department, and to audit the naval accounts.

The Navy Board had charge of naval affairs in Virginia for three years, from the summer of 1776 until the summer of 1779. During 1776 and 1777 vessels were built on the Eastern Shore of Virginia, on the Potomac, Rappahannock, Mattapony, Chickahominy, and James rivers, and at Portsmouth, Gosport, and South Quay. After 1777 vessels were chiefly built at the Chickahominy and Gosport shipyards. No other state owned so much land, property, and manufactories, devoted to naval purposes as Virginia. In April, 1777, the Navy Board purchased 115 acres of land, for £595, on the Chickahominy twelve miles from its confluence with the James.[55] Virginia's ships found here a safer retreat than at Gosport, which lay convenient for the enemy's

[53] Hening, Statutes of Virginia, IX, 149-51. The Provincial Convention which met May 6, 1776, adopted a Constitution which provided for a Legislature of two houses, and an Executive consisting of a Governor and a Privy Council of eight members.

[54] Ibid., 521-22, October session of General Assembly in 1778.

[55] Southern Literary Messenger, 1857, 14. The references to this magazine refer to a series of valuable articles entitled the " Virginia Navy of the Revolution."

ships. It is said that before the Revolution the British had established a marine-yard at Gosport, and named it for Gosport, England, where they had an important dockyard. In some way Virginia came into possession of the shipyard at this place.[56] Two ships were built for the defence of Ocracoke Inlet, the chief entrance to Albemarle Sound, at South Quay on the Blackwater a few miles north of the North Carolina line.

At Warwick on the James a few miles below Richmond the state built and operated a rope-walk. The state owned a manufactory of sail-duck and a foundry. In July, 1776, four naval magazines were established, one each for the James, York, Rappahannock, and Potomac rivers. For each magazine one or two agents were appointed to collect and issue provisions, ship-supplies, and naval stores.[57] For the location of the magazine on the Potomac the General Assembly authorized the Navy Board to purchase an acre of land at the head of " Potomack Creek."[58] In January, 1777, the Navy Board appointed James Maxwell, Naval Agent, to superintend the shipyards, and the building, rigging, equipping, and repairing of the naval vessels. He was to follow the instructions of the Board and keep it informed on the state of the navy.[59] Maxwell's annual salary was £300, payable quarterly. He lived at the Chickahominy shipyard.

Virginia had a naval staff consisting of pay masters, muster masters, surgeons, and chaplains. The captains and recruiting officers enlisted seamen. Their task was rendered difficult not so much on account of the superior attractions of privateering, as in New England, as because of the small number of seamen resident in the state. The first commodore of the Virginia navy was John Henry Boucher. He was serving as lieutenant in the Maryland navy when in March, 1776, Virginia called him to the command of her Potomac fleet, and soon promoted him to the head of her navy.[60] He served as commodore for only a few months, resigning in November, 1776. Walter Brooke was commodore from April, 1777, until September, 1778. Brooke's

[56] E. P. Lull, History of U. S. Navy Yard at Gosport, Virginia, 8-11.
[57] Journals of Virginia Navy Board, Virginia State Archives, June 25, June 26, 1776.
[58] Hening, Statutes of Virginia, IX, 235-36.
[59] Journals of Virginia Navy Board, January 7, 1777.
[60] Maryland Archives, XI, 293-94.

successor, James Barron, was not appointed until July, 1780; he
served until the end of the war. The commodore of the navy
made his headquarters regularly at or about Hampton, and superintended the armed vessels in that part of the state.[61]

In Virginia, as in other states and in the Continental Congress,
naval enthusiasm and interest was at its height in 1776. In the
fall of that year the Navy Board contracted for the building of
twenty-four small transports.[62] The General Assembly in its October session authorized the Navy Board to construct two frigates of thirty-two guns each, and four large galleys adapted " for
river or sea service." For manning these galleys and those
already building the Navy Board was empowered to raise thirteen
hundred men, exclusive of officers, to serve three years from
March 3, 1777. It was to recommend proper officers to the Governor and Council. Having been commissioned by the Governor,
the officers were to enlist the crews of their respective galleys. As
it would be impossible to secure a sufficient number of experienced
seamen, it was provided that each crew should consist of three
classes of men: able seamen, at a daily wage of 3s.; ordinary seamen, at 2s.; and common landsmen, at 1s. 6d. As the men in the
second and third classes became proficient, they were to be promoted. Every recruit was given a bounty of $20.[63]

The Provincial Convention in its December session in 1775
erected a Court of Admiralty consisting of three judges to enforce the Continental Association against trading with England.
In its May session in 1776 it gave this court jurisdiction over all
captures of the enemy's vessels. The General Assembly at its
October session in 1776 superseded all previous admiralty legislation by an " Act for Establishing a Court of Admiralty." Such
court was to consist of three judges elected by joint ballot of the
two houses of the General Assembly. They were to hold their
offices " for so long a time as they shall demean themselves well
therein." The court, which was to be held at some place to be
fixed by the General Assembly, was to have cognizance of " all

[61] Journals of Virginia Navy; State Navy Papers, I; Southern Literary
Messenger, 1857, 3.
[62] Journal of Virginia Navy Board, September-October, 1776.
[63] Hening, Statutes of Virginia, IX, 196-97. In August, 1776, the Navy
Board drew up a list of naval rules which were endorsed by the Governor
and Council. Journals of Virginia Navy Board, August 2, 1776.

causes heretofore of admiralty jurisdiction in this country." Its
proceedings and decisions were to be governed by the regulations
of the Continental Congress, the acts of the General Assembly of
Virginia, the English Statutes prior to the fourth year of the
reign of James; and by the laws of Oleron and the Rhodian and
Imperial laws, so far as they have been heretofore observed in the
English courts of admiralty. In cases relating to captures from
a public enemy with whom the United States should be at war,
and in which a conflict should arise between the regulations of
Congress and the acts of the General Assembly, the regulations
of Congress should take precedence; in all other cases of conflict
the acts of Virginia were to prevail. This provision is of particular interest. It is one of the first instances in which a state
recognized the superiority of federal law when in conflict with
state law. Virginia was liberal in granting appeals to Congress,
as she permitted them in all cases of capture of the enemy's
vessels.[64]

The Admiralty Court of Virginia had few prize cases. Governor Thomas Jefferson in writing to the President of Congress
in June, 1779, no doubt understates the truth when he says that
" a British prize would be a more rare phenomenon here than a
comet, because one has been seen, but the other never was." His
state, he said, had long suffered from a lack of blank letters of
marque, and he wished fifty to be sent to him.[65] Virginia did not
establish state privateering, but followed the regulations of Congress on this subject. Because of the lack of seamen and the
continual presence of the enemy's vessels at the mouths of the
Virginia rivers, the privateering interest was not important in this
state.

The Navy Board superintended both the trading and armed
vessels of the state until April, 1777, when the trading vessels
were placed in charge of William Aylett.[66] Writers on the Virginia navy have not as a rule distinguished one class of vessels
from the other, nor is it always easy to do so. During 1776
seven vessels were employed chiefly in commerce.[67] In the fall

[64] Hening, Statutes of Virginia, IX, 103, 131-32, 202-08.
[65] Ford, Writings of Thomas Jefferson, II, 241-43.
[66] Journals of Virginia Navy Board, April 8, 1777.
[67] These vessels were the brig *Adventure,* the schooners *Hornet, Peace*
and *Plenty, Revenge,* and *Speedwell,* sloop *Agatha,* and armed boat
Molly. The lists of vessels here given were compiled from the Virginia
naval archives.

most of them were ordered to the West Indies with cargoes of flour and tobacco; one, the brig *Adventure,* was directed to proceed to Dunkirk, France. The armed fleet for 1776 consisted of sixteen small craft adapted chiefly for service in the rivers of Virginia and in Chesapeake Bay.[68] In 1777 the galleys *Accomac* and *Diligence* were built and stationed on the Eastern Shore; and the ships *Caswell* and *Washington* were built at South Quay on the Blackwater for the defence of Ocracoke Inlet, which Virginia was undertaking jointly with North Carolina. Besides these four vessels, two brigs, one armed boat, and the ships *Gloucester, Protector, Dragon,* and *Tartar* were this year added to the navy. In 1778 an armed boat and the ships *Tempest* and *Thetis* were built; and in 1779 two armed boats, the brig *Jefferson,* and the ship *Virginia* were added.[69]

This fleet is formidable only in its enumeration. It was poorly armed, incompletely manned, and in almost every respect illfitted for service. But few of its vessels went beyond Chesapeake Bay. It showed most activity during 1776 and the spring of 1777. From 1775 until 1779 fifteen small prizes were captured. In May, 1776, Captain Taylor seized four small merchantmen; in June one of the Barrons brought up to Jamestown the transport *Oxford* with 220 Highlanders on board; in the spring of 1777 the *Mosquito,* Captain Harris, carried into St. Pierre the ship *Noble* valued at 75,000 livres; and a few months earlier the brig *Liberty* captured the ship *Jane* whose cargo of West India goods were valued at £6,000. These were the most fortunate captures made by the Virginia navy.[70]

[68] These vessels were the galleys *Henry, Hero, Lewis, Manly, Norfolk Revenge, Page,* and *Safeguard;* the brigs *Liberty, Mosquito, Northampton,* and *Raleigh;* the schooners *Liberty* and *Adventure;* the sloop *Scorpion,* and the armed boats *Liberty* and *Patriot.* The schooner *Liberty* was taken into the trading fleet as the *Hornet.* It is believed that this list does not contain the vessels in Mason's Potomac fleet.

[69] The names of the vessels not mentioned in the text which were added during 1777, 1778, and 1779 were the brigs *Greyhound* and *Hampton,* and the armed boats *Nicholson, Experiment, Dolphin,* and *Fly.* The names of several other vessels, which were probably used in trade, occur during this period. Some of the ships are at times referred to as galleys.

[70] Files of Virginia Gazette; Journals of Virginia Convention, May 8, 1776; Virginia Historical Register, I, 77; Calendar of Virginia State Papers, III, 365.

Virginia's naval craft met with the usual misfortunes. During the first half of 1777 His Majesty's ship *Ariadne* captured the *Mosquito*. About the same time the frigate *Phoenix* took the *Raleigh*. The British made two raids into Virginia which were destructive to both the shipping of the state and private individuals. The first was ordered by Clinton in the spring of 1779, the troops being under the command of Matthews and Collier. At the Gosport shipyard they destroyed five uncompleted vessels, three of which were frigates, besides a large quantity of masts, yards, timber, plank, iron, and other ship's stores. The shipyards on the Nansemond were looted; and twenty-two vessels with a considerable quantity of powder were taken or destroyed on the " South Branch of the Navy." Suffolk was burned and upwards of two thousand barrels of Continental Pork and fifteen hundred barrels of flour were destroyed. In all one hundred and thirty vessels were burned.[71] The raid of Arnold and Phillips will be considered later.

The General Assembly at its May session, 1779, discontinued the Navy Board and vested its strictly naval duties with a newly created Board of War consisting of five members. The Board of War was empowered to appoint a Naval Commissioner. A Board of Trade was now given charge of the trading vessels of the state and of the state manufactories of military supplies.[72]

The General Assembly in its May session, 1780, " for the purpose of introducing economy into all the various departments of government, and for conducting the publick business with the greatest expedition " abolished the Boards of War and Trade, and authorized the Governor to appoint a Commissioner of the War, a Commercial Agent, and coordinate with these two a Commissioner of the Navy. This act is properly regarded as the outgrowth of the same movement for economy and efficiency in administration, which resulted in the establishment in January and February, 1781, of single-headed departments of the Continental Congress. The salary of the Commissioner of the Navy was fixed at thirty thousand pounds of tobacco a year, and that of his clerk at ten thousand pounds.[73] The Commissioner was

[71] Almon's Remembrancer, 1779, 289-95, account given by British officers; Records of State of North Carolina, XIV, 85-86, 94-95. Some of the vessels destroyed at Gosport probably belonged to Congress.
[72] Hening, Statutes of Virginia, X, 15-18, 123.
[73] Ibid., 278, 291-92.

to be under the "controul and direction of the governour and council." Governor Jefferson appointed James Maxwell, the naval agent under the Navy Board, Commissioner of the Navy.

At the October session of this year, moved by its need for money and the impossibility of fitting out the whole fleet, the General Assembly, ordered the governor to sell nine of the armed vessels and to equip and man the remaining six with all diligence. For some reason the governor did not carry out the order. There was probably little market for the vessels.

The General Assembly in the May session of 1779, as an inducement to enlistment, granted seamen and marines additional bounties and pensions. Recruits entering for the rest of the war were now to receive $750 and one hundred acres of land. They were to be furnished upon enlistment, and once a year thereafterwards, with a complete suit of clothes. Naval officers were entitled to a " grant of the like quantity of lands as is allowed officers of the same rank in the Virginia regiments on continental establishment." Disabled sailors and the widows of the slain were entitled to immediate relief and an annual pension.[74]

The years 1780 and 1781 were marked by a renewed naval activity in Virginia. It is recalled that the theater of war had now shifted to the Southern states. Savannah was in the hands of the enemy. Charleston surrendered in May, 1780. By the fall of 1780 the lowlands of the states to the south of Virginia were generally in the possession of the British. Apparently Virginia would be the next to feel the rough hand of the conquering enemy. British privateers and naval craft lay off the mouths of the Virginia rivers and captured all the vessels that ventured towards the Bay or the sea. Early in 1780 it was apprehended that the enemy meditated an invasion of the coasts of the state.

When the General Assembly met in May, 1780, it at once took measures for the protection of the coasts. It passed " an act for putting the eastern frontier of this commonwealth into a posture of defence." This act after providing for calling out the militia in the seaport counties, ordered the Governor and Council to direct the Commissioner of the Navy to immediately make ready for service in the Bay and on the seacoast the ships *Thetis, Tempest,* and *Dragon,* the brig *Jeffer-*

[74] Hening, IX, 537; X, 23-24, 217.

son, and the galleys *Henry, Accomac,* and *Diligence.* Three hundred marines to be commanded by five captains and fifteen lieutenants were to be recruited. Marines and sailors who enlisted for three years were to receive a bounty of $1,000. Naval officers were put on the same footing in regard to pay, rations, and privileges as officers of the same rank in the land service.[75]

When the Legislature came together in October, 1780, the situation being still more critical, it was moved to pass an additional act for the defence of the seacoast. This act shows that the navy was in sore need for seamen and money and it provided drastic measures to secure both. Naval officers were now authorized, under certain restrictions and limitations, to impress seamen. The eastern counties of the state were directed to bind to the sea " under the most prudent captains that can be procured to take them " one-half of all orphans of certain descriptions living below the falls of the Virginia rivers. A hospital for seamen was established at Hampton to be maintained by a tax of nine pence a month on the salaries of all mariners and seamen in either the navy or the merchant service of the state. Officers and seamen were given the whole of their captures; and still other inducements to enlistment, by way of pay and clothing, were held out. Two new galleys of the same construction as those built by Congress in 1776 carrying two 32's at the bow and at the stern, and 6's at the sides, were ordered for the defence of the Chesapeake. Five vessels of the state fleet were to be immediately made ready for service; and all the other naval vessels were to be sold and the proceeds devoted to naval purposes. For the use of the navy import duties were laid upon rum, gin, brandy, and other spirits; on wine, molasses and sugar; and on all imported dry goods, except salt, munitions of war, and iron from Maryland. Tonnage was laid upon merchant vessels. Despite these efforts few seamen and little money were raised, and the fleet during 1780, accomplished almost nothing.[76]

The salient event in the history of the Virginia navy in 1781 was the invasion of Arnold and Phillips during the first half of the year. Arnold was first reported on the coast of Virginia on December 29, 1780, when his fleet consisting of twenty-seven sail

[75] Hening, X, 296-99.   [76] Hening, X, 379-86.

was seen at Willoughby Point.[77] Governor Jefferson began at
once to make strenuous efforts to get the Virginia fleet in condition to oppose Arnold. The rôle of Admiral was an odd one for
Jefferson. In February, he sent Benjamin Harrison, Speaker of
the Virginia House of Delegates to Philadelphia to obtain from
the French minister the aid of the French fleet.[78] A half dozen
or more privateers were taken into the service of the state.
Twelve vessels of the state fleet of 1776-1779 still remained.
Most if not all of these vessels were either at the Chickahominy
shipyard and nearby on the James, or else at the mouth of the
James. Few of these vessels were sufficiently manned to render
much service. On April 26, Maxwell reported 78 men on board
seven vessels, whose complement was 520. Other vessels had
neither arms nor men.[79]

In April, 1781, Arnold and Phillips made their raid up the
James, penetrating as far as Richmond. On April 21 and 22 a
detachment under Lieutenant-Colonel Abercrombie destroyed the
shipyard on the Chickahominy, including a number of naval craft
and the warehouses. On April 27 at Osbornes, on the James a
few miles below Richmond the Virginia fleet supported by two or
three hundred militia upon the shore opposite the British army,
drew up to oppose the enemy. It consisted of six ships, eight
brigs, five sloops, two schooners, and a number of smaller craft.
Its chief vessels were the *Tempest*, 16; *Renown*, 16; and *Jefferson*, 14. The British sent a flag of truce to the Commodore of
the Virginia fleet proposing to treat with him for its surrender. He sent back the spirited reply that " he was determined to defend it to the last extremity." A few cannon
planted on the shore soon gave the enemy a command of the situation. After a short engagement the Virginians scuttled or set
fire to a number of their vessels and fled to the opposite shore.
None of the fleet escaped. The British captured twelve vessels,
which the Virginians had been unable to destroy. The British
burnt the state rope-walk at Warwick. After the raid of Phillips,
but one vessel remained in the Virginia navy, the armed boat
Liberty.[80]

[77] Ford, Writings of Jefferson, II, 392.
[78] Ibid., 443-44.
[79] Virginia Calendar of State Papers, I, 588; II, 74.
[80] Almon's Remembrancer, 1781, II, 62-63. Arnold to Clinton, Petersburg, May 12, 1781.

The officers and seamen of the Virginia navy, thrown out of employment by the loss of their fleet, aided the allied forces at the siege of Yorktown in collecting supplies and transporting troops. The boat *Liberty* was used as a transport; and also the ships *Cormorant, Loyalist,* and *Oliver Cromwell,* which three vessels is it believed Virginia purchased for this purpose. Soon after the surrender of Cornwallis, the Virginia General Assembly, recognizing that " during the continuance of the present expensive war it is necessary to husband the resources of the state with the utmost economy," dismissed almost all of the officers and seamen, the Commissioner of the Navy, the chaplains, surgeons, paymasters, and all others on the naval staff.[81]

A number of times during the Revolution and now for the last time in 1782, Virginia and Maryland undertook to concert a naval defence of their trade in the Chesapeake. The General Assembly of Virginia, which met in May, 1782, appointed three commissioners to superintend the work of protecting the Bay. The *Cormorant* and *Liberty* were to be immediately prepared for this service. Two galleys and two barges or whaleboats were to be built. For this work the state appropriated the proceeds arising from the sale of the *Loyalist,* £1000, and certain tonnage and import duties. The Commissioners were to fix the pay and subsistence of the seamen; the fleet was not to be sent outside of the Capes.[82]

The Commissioners managed a small naval force during 1782 and 1783 until the war came to an end. Commodore Barron, stationed at Hampton, was chiefly occupied with the exchanging of prisoners. Beyond the building of a few naval craft, it does not appear that this final naval enterprise of Virginia was attended with fruitful results. When peace was declared in the spring of 1783 the Commissioners had in different stages of construction, the schooners, *Harrison, Fly,* and *Patriot* and the barges *York* and *Richmond.* Virginia now disposed of all of her fleet except the *Liberty* and *Patriot,* which she retained as revenue cutters.[83] In order to keep these two armed vessels in time of peace Vir-

---

[81] Hening, Statutes of Virginia, X, 450; Virginia Navy Papers, I and II.

[82] Hening, Statutes of Virginia, XI, 42-44. In March, 1783, the three Commissioners were Paul Loyall, Thomas Brown, and Thomas Newton, Jr.—Virginia Calendar of State Papers, III, 456.

[83] Virginia Navy Papers, II.

ginia in accordance with a provision in the Articles of Confederation, obtained permission from Congress.[84] These two boats
were still in the employ of the state in 1787. The *Liberty* saw
more service than any other state or Continental vessel of the
Revolution. She was in the employ of Virginia from 1775 until
1787.

[84] Journals of Continental Congress, October 3, 1783.

CHAPTER THREE: UNDER THE CONSTITUTION, 1789-1800

The Navy under the Department of War, 1789-1798.

The Constitution of the United States, which went into effect in 1789, contained several provisions in respect to a navy. It gave Congress power to " provide and maintain a navy," to make rules for the government and regulation of the naval forces, and to exercise exclusive legislation over all places purchased for dock-yards. It made the President " commander-in-chief of the navy," and it forbade the states to own ships of war in time of peace. The Constitution did not specifically establish the executive departments. It, nevertheless, implied that such departments were to be established, and that each of them was to have a " principal officer." Inasmuch as the framers of the Constitution were accustomed during the American Revolution to transact the naval business of the country by means of a naval department, distinct from the other executive departments, it is likely that those who thought upon the subject contemplated the organization of a naval department under the Constitution.

When, in 1789, the first executive departments were organized, the United States had no navy, and there was no pressing need for one. A naval department at this time would have been a piece of unnecessary machinery. However, in anticipation of the time when a navy should be established, it seemed wise to Congress that the control of the naval affairs should. be definitely lodged in one of the executive departments. Congress, therefore, vested it in the secretary of war. This was a natural disposition, as the office of the secretary of war is analogous to that of the secretary of the navy. According to the act of August 7,

[1] Constitution of the United States, Art. I, Sec. 8, 10; Art. II, Sec. 2.

1789, establishing the Department of War, the Secretary of War was directed to perform and execute all duties relating to " military commissions, or to the land or naval forces, ships, or warlike stores of the United States, or to such other matters respecting the military or naval affairs, as the President of the United States shall assign to the said department." [2]

It was not until the beginning of Washington's second administration that an occasion arose, which led to the procuring of an armed fleet. The relations between the United States and the Barbary Powers had been more or less unsettled and unsatisfactory since 1783. These countries claimed the right to exact tribute from the United States, to disregard their treaties, to prey upon American commerce, and to demand a ransom for the American prisoners in their hands. It is noteworthy that in 1786, some months after the last vessel of the navy of the Revolution had been sold, a committee of the Congress of the Confederation favored the reestablishment of a navy in order to bring to terms these corsairs of the Mediterranean. It reported that " it is proper and expedient for the federal government to turn their earliest attention to the Marine Department, and that a committee be appointed to frame and report an ordinance for organizing the same." [3] Nothing came of this recommendation.

The difficulties with these corsairs may have led the Secretary of War in the fall of 1790 and again in the fall of 1791 to turn his attention towards procuring an armed fleet. In November, of the latter year, he submitted to a committee of the Senate several estimates, showing the cost of maintaining ships of different types. As early as the fall of 1790 the Secretary had obtained two estimates of the cost of building frigates, one from a naval constructor of Philadelphia, and the other from John Foster Williams, of Massachusetts, the well-known captain of the frigate *Protector,* the largest vessel in the Massachusetts navy of the Revolution. Williams's letter, dated Boston, October 30, 1790, is the first letter relating to naval affairs, as far as is known, that was received by the War Department. It read as follows:

" Agreeably to your request, I enclose you an estimate of a frigate of nine hundred tons, and believe it to be not far wide of what will be the real cost, but as the circumstances would not

[2] U. S. Statutes at Large, I, 50.
[3] Records and Papers of the Continental Congress, No. 25, II, 459.

admit of my being too open in my enquiries, it may vary a little. The cost of the guns and warlike stores you can form a better judgment of than myself. The timber, etc., should be cut in the fall of the year, as that would add much to its duration. Should any further inquiries be necessary, or any services that I can render be acceptable, shall be happy in being favored with your commands." [4]

The earliest attempts to procure some armed vessels for the purpose of sending them against the corsairs were unsuccessful. Late in 1793 the attempts were renewed. In December of that year, Washington brought the matter to the attention of Congress by laying before it a report of the Secretary of State on the measures which the United States had taken for the purpose " of obtaining a recognition of our treaty with Morocco and for the ransom of our citizens and the establishment of peace with Algiers." [5] The relations of the United States with the Barbary Powers, and especially with Algiers, were now thoroughly discussed in Congress, and it was finally decided to try the efficacy of an armed force. On March 27, 1794, a bill " to provide a Naval Armament," which had been passed by Congress, was signed by the President. Its purpose, according to its preamble, was to protect the commerce of the United States from the depredations of the Algerine corsairs.

The navy under the Constitution began with this act. It provided for the purchase or construction of four ships of 44 guns each, and of two ships of 36 guns each. For service on board of these six ships, it authorized the President to employ and commission 6 captains, 22 lieutenants, 6 lieutenants of marines, 6 surgeons, 4 chaplains, and 10 surgeon's mates; a total of 54 commissioned officers. The President was to appoint for each ship, a sailing master, purser, boatswain, gunner, sailmaker, carpenter, and 8 midshipmen; the total number of warrant officers was 84. The petty officers, seamen, and marines were to number 1922. The entire naval establishment, according to this act, would consist of 2060 men. To each of the 44-gun ships there were allowed 150 able seamen, 103 " midshipmen " and ordinary seamen, 1 corporal, 1 sergeant, 1 " drum," 1 " fife," and 50 marines. The

[4] Naval Correspondence in the War Department, Navy Department Archives, 1-16.
[5] Richardson's Messages and Papers of the Presidents, I, 148-49.

salary of a captain was $75 a month, and of a lieutenant, $40.
The subsistence of a captain was six rations a day. The President was to fix the pay of the petty officers, seamen, and marines.[6]

A synopsis of the debate in the House on this measure has been preserved. Its supporters were for the most part Northerners and Federalists. Thomas Fitzsimmons, of Pennsylvania; Zephaniah Swift, of Connecticut; William Vans Murray, of Maryland; Benjamin Goodhue, of Massachusetts; and William Smith, of South Carolina, argued in behalf of the measure; and James Madison, John Nicholas, and William B. Giles, of Virginia, and John Smilie, of Pennsylvania, spoke against it. The procuring of the proposed ships was argued chiefly with a view to its competency to settle the difficulties with Algiers. It was plain to all, however, that the passage of the measure might lead to the permanent establishment of a navy, and some of the arguments for and against it were based upon this possibility. Giles objected to the " certainty and enormity " of the expense which would attend the procuring of a fleet. He " viewed the establishment of a navy as a complete dereliction of the policy of discharging the principal of the public debt. History does not afford an instance of a nation which continued to increase their navy and decreased their debt at the same time. It is an operation escaping the ability of any nation. The naval competition of the Powers of Europe has produced oppression to their subjects and ruin to themselves. The ruin of the French monarchy, he believed, might be ascribed very much to that cause. A navy is the most expensive of all means of defence, and the tyranny of governments consists in the expensiveness of their machinery. The expensiveness of the French monarchy is the true cause of its destruction. The navy of France furnished the principal item of expense." [7]

William Smith, who represented the " Pinckney district " of South Carolina, was one of the most ardent and persistent of the friends of the early navy. " This country," he declared, " is peculiarly fitted for a navy; abounding in all kinds of naval resources, we have within ourselves those means which other maritime nations were [are?] obliged to obtain from abroad. The nature of our situation, and the navigating disposition of a consid-

---

[6] U. S. Statutes at Large, I, 350-51.
[7] Annals of Congress, IV, 438-41, 485-98.

erable proportion of our citizens, evince still more the propriety of some Naval Establishment. Perhaps the country is not yet mature for such an establishment, to any great extent; but he believed the period was not far distant when it would [be]. Sweden, with a population not greater than that of the United States, and with more slender resources, maintained a large navy. He saw no reason why the United States, with an increasing population, much individual wealth, and considerable national resources, might not without ruin, do as much; or why the equipment of a squadron, inferior to that of any of the petty nations of Italy, should involve us in an insupportable expense."

From March 27, 1794, when the measure for building the six ships became a law, until April 30, 1798, when the Navy Department was created, the War Department transacted not a little naval business. During this period, a little more than four years, three different secretaries presided over the War Department. The initial work of providing a naval armament fell to Henry Knox, who continued in office until January 1, 1795. On January 2 the Senate confirmed the nomination of Timothy Pickering as Secretary of War. On January 27, 1796, he was succeeded by James McHenry, who had charge of naval affairs until the founding of the Navy Department. Knox superintended the navy for a little less than a year; Pickering for a little more than a year; and McHenry for a little more than two years.[8]

At this time the War Department consisted of two offices, the office of the Secretary of War, and the office of the accountant of the War Department. Some half dozen clerks were employed in the secretary's office, for which the appropriation for salaries in 1794 was $7050. Of this sum $3000 was paid to the secretary. In 1798 this appropriation had increased to $8100. A sum of almost equal amount was the same year appropriated for salaries in the office of the accountant.[9] The accountant's duties were similar to those of the present auditor for the War Department.

Secretary Knox's work in building the six ships consisted of making plans for their construction, procuring materials of various sorts, and selecting officers, naval agents, and constructors. Joshua Humphreys, a skilled ship-builder of Philadelphia; John Hackett, of Salisbury, Massachusetts, who had during the Revo-

---

[8] Executive Journals of Congress, I, 168, 198.
[9] U. S. Statutes at Large, I, 343, 543.

lution built the celebrated frigate *Alliance;* and other constructors, were consulted upon " the best properties to be adopted as a general plan for the vessels now to be built," and upon other details of their construction. The models submitted by Humphreys, after much consultation and consideration, were adopted. Humphreys' drafts were similar to certain French plans, and his ships were nearly of the same dimensions as some French seventy-fours which had been cut down to make heavy frigates. Humphreys said that one of his ships would be a match for any vessel carrying less than 64 guns. Josiah Fox assisted Humphreys in preparing the " draughts and molds " for the six ships. Washington increased their displacement above that intended by Congress. The measurements of the 44-gun frigates were as follows: length of gun-deck, 174 feet 10½ inches; length of keel, 145 feet; and breadth of beam, 43 feet 6 inches.[10]

The frigates were to be built of live oak and red cedar in all the parts where these durable woods could be used to advantage. It was thought that the live oak and red cedar would last five times as long as white oak. They could be obtained only on the Georgia and Carolina coasts. A master shipwright was sent to Charleston from Boston to superintend the cutting and shipping of the timber. Captain John Barry went to Georgia to expedite the work. Woodcutters and carpenters were sent south from Connecticut, Rhode Island and Massachusetts. A Boston company supplied the ships with sail-cloth; a Maryland company and a Rhode Island company, with cannon; and two New Jersey companies, with cannon balls. The Treasury Department, which at this time greatly exceeded the other departments of the government in importance, bought most of the articles of equipment for the secretary of war. Home industries were patronized to the fullest extent possible. It was found necessary, however, to import " composition metal, sheathing copper, bolts, nails, bunting, and iron kitchens." [11] Not until many years later did the United States supply the bunting for its own flags.

On June 3, 1794, Washington appointed John Barry, Samuel Nicholson, Silas Talbot, Joshua Barney, Richard Dale, and Thomas Truxtun to be captains in the navy. The assistance of these officers in building the ships was desired. Other officers

---

[10] Goldsborough's Naval Chronicle, 57; State Papers, Naval Affairs, I, 8, 10-11, 19.

[11] State Papers, Naval Affairs, I, 6-10.

were not at this time appointed since their services would not be required until the ships were completed. Each one of the captains was made superintendent of a ship. He had a general oversight of its construction, and he inspected the various materials to see that they were durable and in good condition. Barry, Nicholson, and Talbot had been captains in the Continental Navy; Barney and Dale had been lieutenants; and Truxtun, during the Revolution, had commanded privateers. All had served with distinction. Barry had commanded the *Alliance* during some of her most famous cruises. Talbot's naval exploits were gallant and brilliant. Dale was the senior lieutenant under Jones on board the *Bon Homme Richard* in her memorable engagement with the *Serapis*. Barney, who had greatly distinguished himself in his fight with the *Hyder Ally,* declined his appointment because it placed him below Talbot in rank. He declared, contrary to fact, that Talbot's naval rank during the Revolution was only honorary. On July 18, 1794, James Sever was appointed to fill the vacancy caused by Barney's declination.

In order to construct the ships to the best advantage and to distribute the benefits arising locally from their construction, Washington decided to build the six vessels at as many different ports. The 44-gun ships were to be built at Boston, New York, Philadelphia, and Norfolk; and the 36-gun ships at Portsmouth, N. H., and Baltimore. Whether to build the vessels by contract, or by means of agents of the government, was thoroughly considered by the Secretary of War and the President; and they finally decided to employ agents. In Philadelphia it was feared that if the ship was let to a contractor the unsuccessful bidders would, because of their ill-will and jealousy, raise the price of labor and ruin the successful one. The government obtained building yards at each of the six ports. At Portsmouth the yard was on Langdon's island. At Boston Edmund Hart's shipyard was rented. At New York a building yard was rented from " Marinus Willet, called Corler's Hook on East River." At Philadelphia the yard was located at Southwark. At Norfolk the Gosport navy-yard, at which Virginia built some of her naval craft during the Revolution, was rented from the State.

At each of the six yards a superintendent, naval constructor, navy agent, and clerk of the yard was established. The superintendent had general charge, and the constructor immediate charge.

of the building of the vessel. Joshua Humphreys, the naval constructor in charge of the Philadelphia ship, and the " Principal Constructor of the Navy," was paid a salary of $2000 a year. The navy agent bought all the materials not purchased by the Treasury Department, and was allowed a commission of two and a half per cent on the sums that he expended. He paid the artisans and laborers. His office was modeled on that of the Continental agents of the Revolution. The clerk received, issued, and accounted for all the public property in the yard. He was paid $750 a year.[12]

The following table gives the names of the first superintendents, naval constructors, and naval agents, together with the ports at which they were employed:[13]

Port.	Superintendent.	Naval Constructor.	Naval Agent.
Boston........	Samuel Nicholson.	George Claghorne.	Henry Jackson.
New York	Silas Talbot.	Forman Cheeseman,	John Blagge.
Philadelphia .	John Barry.	Joshua Humphreys.	Gurney and Smith.
Norfolk..	Richard Dale.	Josiah Fox.	William Pennock.
Portsmouth ..	James Sever.	James Hackett.	Jacob Sheafe.
Baltimore	Thomas Truxtun.	David Stodder.	Samuel and Joseph Sterett.

During the administration of Timothy Pickering the keels of the six vessels were completed and laid upon the blocks, their frames were in part constructed, and much ship-building material was collected at the six yards. Pickering was instrumental in selecting the names of the first ships of the new navy, names which now suggest so many memorable achievements. The actual naming of the several vessels was probably the work of Washington. On March 14, 1795, Pickering laid before the President a list of ten names, " such as have occurred in my conversations with gentlemen on the subject."[14] Five of Pickering's list were selected, the *Constitution, United States, President, Constellation,* and *Congress*. The sixth frigate, the *Chesapeake,* was probably so called because she was built at Norfolk at the southern end of the Chesapeake Bay.

Soon after McHenry became head of the War Department a treaty of peace was signed with Algiers, and in accordance with the act of March 27, 1794, providing for the construction of the six frigates, it was incumbent upon the President to suspend their construction. Washington, who was strongly in favor of creating

[12] State Papers, Nav. Aff., I, 6-8.
[13] State Papers, Nav. Aff., I, 17-21.
[14] Upham's Timothy Pickering, III, 154.

a navy, delayed the carrying out of this provision on the ground that to suddenly stop the work of building the frigates would not comport with the public interest.[15]   Many members of Congress, however, wished to abandon the navy and dispose of the ships and the naval materials.   It was with difficulty that the Federalists prevented this from being done.   A compromise was effected. Three of the ships were ordered to be completed, and the work on the other three was directed to be stopped and their perishable materials to be sold.   The three ships whose construction was continued were the *Constitution,* 44, building at Boston; *United States,* 44, building at Philadelphia; and *Constellation,* 36, building at Baltimore.   When the Navy Department was established on April 30, 1798, these vessels were almost completed.   The *United States* was launched on May 10, the *Constellation* on September 7, and the *Constitution* on October 21, 1797.   The average cost of the three vessels was $305,420.   This was considered an extravagant price.

In the summer of 1797 work upon these ships was pushed rapidly forward because of the strained relations between the United States and France.   A war between the two countries became more and more imminent.   In May, 1797, President Adams pointed out the necessity of a fleet for the defense of the nation.   On July 1, 1797, Congress passed an act empowering the President to man and employ the three frigates, and in other respects committing the country to the establishment of a navy, a project that had the hearty support of President Adams.   This act ordered that the new navy should be governed by the rules and regulations of the Continental Navy, which, it is recollected, were drafted by John Adams in 1775.   McHenry, during the last months of his control of the navy was officering, manning, and preparing for sea the *United States, Constellation,* and *Constitution.*   In March and April, 1798, Adams sent to the Senate a list of the commissioned officers of these three vessels.   McHenry, in one of his last reports, made in April, recommended the building of 20 vessels, of from 16 to 22 guns; and, in case of a war with France, the procuring of six ships of the line.[16]

---

[15] U. S. Statutes at Large, I, 453-54; Richardson's Messages and Papers of the Presidents, I, 192-93.

[16] Richardson's Messages and Papers of the Presidents, I, 236-37; U. S. Statutes at Large, I, 523-25; Executive Journals of Congress, I, 264, 268; State Papers, Nav. Aff., I, 34.

One frigate was built by the War Department by contract. After the treaty of peace with Algiers of September 5, 1795, had been concluded, the Dey continued to make demands of the United States. Barlow, the American Peace Commissioner, promised him a frigate. This was built for the War Department by James Hackett at Portsmouth, N. H., who launched her on June 29, 1797. She was a 36-gun ship and was named the *Crescent*. She sailed for Algiers in January, 1798, loaded with naval stores for the Dey.[17]

THE FOUNDING OF THE NAVY DEPARTMENT, 1798-1801.

In the spring of 1798 a war with France was imminent. In such a struggle a navy must necessarily play a large part, and the urgency of increasing the small American fleet was great. Armed vessels were immediately needed to protect American commerce, which had already suffered severely from the depredations of the French. Now, an increase in the navy meant much additional work of the War Department. Besides, its administration of naval affairs had been adversely criticised. It was charged with slowness and extravagance. Under these circumstances it was inevitable that men who were familiar with the Naval Department of the Revolution, and with the practice of foreign governments of separating the administration of the navy from that of the army, should demand the establishment of a Navy Department. Moreover, the creation of a strong navy and of a department to administer it were favorite measures with the Federalists. They formed a part of the Federalist plan of strengthening the central government. In President Adams and his Secretary of the Navy, Benjamin Stoddert, the navy found two of its most ardent advocates.

A recommendation concerning the defense of the country and the protection of its commerce in President Adams's First Annual Speech of November, 1797, was the occasion of a proposal to erect a marine office in the War Department. On March 8, 1798, a committee of the House of Representatives which was considering this recommendation reported in favor of establishing a Commissioner of Marine in the War Department, " who shall have charge of the construction, equipment, and supplies of the public

[17] Allen's Navy and Barbary Corsairs, 61; Naval Correspondence of War Dept., Nav. Dept. Arch., 184, 201.

vessels of the United States, and all other matters relating to their naval concerns, which shall be entrusted to him according to law." The committee observed that apparently enormous expenses and unaccountable delays had attended the naval administration of the War Department. It was of the opinion that a Commissioner of Marine would effect important economies. On March 22, Secretary of War McHenry went a step further than the committee. In making suggestions for the betterment of naval administration he proposed, as one alternative, the separation of the marine business from the War Department.[18]

The particular movement in Congress that resulted in the establishment of the Navy Department began on April 2, 1798, when William Bingham, of Pennsylvania, moved in the Senate to appoint a committee " to take into consideration the propriety of instituting a separate Executive department for the purpose of superintending and regulating the various objects connected with the Naval Establishment of the United States." The committee contemplated by Bingham's motion was appointed on the next day, and consisted of Bingham, Henry Tazewell, of Virginia, and Benjamin Goodhue, of Massachusetts. On April 11, Bingham, the chairman of the committee, introduced a bill in the Senate " to establish an Executive Department to be denominated the Department of the Navy." The bill had its three readings on the 11th, 12th, and 16th, and on the latter day it passed the Senate. Before its passage on the 16th an attempt was made by the opponents of the bill to virtually kill it by limiting the period of its operation. Humphrey Marshall, of Kentucky, moved to limit the life of the act to one year, and from thence to the end of the next session of Congress. He, however, accepted the amendment of Elijah Paine, of Vermont, to substitute four years for one. It is significant that both Marshall and Paine came from inland States, where the navy at this time found little favor. The amendment of Marshall was lost; yeas, 10; nays, 15. The vote on the passage of the bill was, yeas, 19; nays, 6. Five of the six negative votes came from the South.[19]

On April 23, the bill received its first and second readings in the House, and on April 26 it was read the third time and was passed. The division of opinion in the House is best disclosed by

[18] Richardson's Messages and Papers of the Presidents, I, 251; Annals of Congress, VIII, 1246; State Papers, Nav. Aff., I, 39.

[19] Annals of Congress, VII, 534, 535, 539-41.

the vote on the reading of the bill for the third time. This vote was, yeas, 47; nays, 41. Of the yeas, 39 votes came from the States north of the Potomac, and 8 from those south.[20] Of the nays, 14 votes came from the States north of the Potomac, and 27 from those south. At this time the members of Congress from the North generally favored, and those from the South generally opposed, naval expenditures of all kinds. It should, however, be remembered that certain South Carolina members were enthusiastic advocates of a navy, and that no man in Congress during the decade of 1794-1803 was so persistent in opposition to a naval armament as Albert Gallatin, of Pennsylvania. He argued in season and out of season that a navy was expensive and useless; indeed, worse than useless, for it caused more evils than it prevented.

No account of the debate in the Senate on the bill establishing the Navy Department has been preserved. A synopsis of the debate of April 25 in the House is recorded in the Annals of Congress. Edward Livingston and John Williams, of New York; Albert Gallatin, of Pennsylvania; Thomas Claiborne, of Virginia; and Nathaniel Macon, Joseph McDowell, and Robert Williams, of North Carolina, spoke in opposition to the measure; while Samuel Sewall and Harrison Gray Otis, of Massachusetts; Samuel Smith, of Maryland; and Robert Goodloe Harper, of South Carolina, defended it.

The friends of the measure argued that in the long run it would result in important economies, and that one department of the government could not efficiently administer the business of both the army and the navy. Samuel Smith said that an expenditure of two million dollars for naval purposes would be authorized this session, and that a secretary of the navy knowing something of naval architecture would be able to save more in the present year than his office would cost in ten. He supposed that the great expense attending the building of the three frigates which composed the present fleet had been chiefly owing to the want of a naval department. Robert Goodloe Harper called attention to the European practice of two military departments, one each for the army and the navy. Harrison Gray Otis made a somewhat novel argument. He said that " it was necessary, even for the sake of appearances, to establish an office of this kind. We ought not

---

[20] Annals of Congress, VIII, 1426, 1522, 3553-54.

only to prepare measures of defense by sea and land, but, in doing this, we ought to do it in conformity to the opinion of the European world. He thought $5000 a year would be well expended in purchasing the good opinion of the European nations in this respect, and particularly that of France."

Talk like that of Otis has never failed to bring forth a spirited reply in the House of Representatives. On this occasion Robert Williams declared that the policy of Otis was the " most fatal of any other to this country. He believed that the less we had to do with European politics, and their mode of administration, the better." Those countries that have established large navies are " involved in debt which they never can, and never will, pay." Gallatin argued that the proposed measure would cause an additional expense and that the War Department was quite competent to manage the naval business. Livingston, however, conceded that the secretary of war could not be supposed to be acquainted with both army and navy affairs. But, it would not do to appoint a ship-builder secretary of the navy, for such a person was not " fit to be one of the great council of the nation ; and it must be recollected that the person who holds this office will become one of the councillors of the President on all great concerns." The principle that no person in the government was to have business under his direction which he did not understand, was of limited application. Otherwise, there must be in the War Department " commissioners of gun-barrels and ramrods." John Williams and Thomas McDowell opposed the measure because it involved the establishment of a large and permanent naval force.[21]

The bill creating the Navy Department became a law on April 30, 1798, being on that day signed by President Adams. This law comprises five sections and is quite brief. It provides that " there shall be an executive department under the denomination of the Department of the Navy, the chief officer of which shall be called the Secretary of the Navy." The duty of this officer " shall be to execute such orders as he shall receive from the President of the United States, relative to the procurement of naval stores and materials, and the construction, armament, equipment, and employment of vessels of war, as well as all other matters connected with the naval establishment of the United States." The law authorized the secretary of the navy to appoint a principal

[21] Annals of Congress, VIII, 1545-54.

clerk and such other clerks as he should think necessary. The secretary was to receive a salary of $3000 a year, payable quarterly; the clerks were to receive the same salaries as the clerks of the other executive departments. He was directed to take possession of all the records pertaining to the navy, which were deposited in the War Department. In case of a vacancy in the secretaryship, the principal clerk was authorized to take possession of the records and documents of the Navy Department.[22]

The day after President Adams signed the bill he nominated George Cabot, of Massachusetts, to be Secretary of the Navy. Adams considered Cabot " eminently qualified " to fill the position.[23] On May 3, the Senate confirmed the nomination. Timothy Pickering, the Secretary of State, seems to have had doubts of Cabot's accepting the proffered station, for, when he sent Cabot his commission, Pickering wrote to him a personal letter, urging him to make sacrifices for the public advantage and to accept the appointment. On May 11, Cabot wrote to Pickering, declining the office on the ground that he did not have the mental or physical qualifications demanded of a secretary of the navy. Cabot's belief in his own unfitness seems to have been honest, but no doubt his dislike of publicity and his love of indolence and repose were influential in causing his declination. It is well known that at this time the Federal offices had few attractions for first-rate talent.

Some of the qualifications for a secretary of the navy which Cabot considered requisite he may not have possessed. Indeed, measured by Cabot's standard, there have been but few secretaries of the navy who have not fallen short. Had the President applied it, the office might have remained vacant indefinitely. Cabot conceived that the head of the Naval Department should possess " considerable knowledge of maritime affairs; but this should be elementary as well as practical, including the principles of naval architecture and naval tactics." Above all, he should possess the " inestimable secret of rendering a naval force invincible by any equal force of the enemy. Thus a knowledge of the human heart will constitute an essential ingredient in the character of this officer, that he may be able to convert every incident to the elevation of the spirit of the American seamen.

[22] U. S. Statutes at Large, I, 553-54.
[23] Works of John Adams, I, 553-54.

Suffer me to ask how a man who has led a life of indolence for twenty years can be rendered physically capable of these various exertions." [24]

Although Cabot never acted as secretary of the navy, he legally held this office from the date of his confirmation until his declination was accepted. His "term of office" was not longer than fifteen days, for, on May 18, the President nominated Benjamin Stoddert, of Georgetown, District of Columbia, to fill the vacancy. Stoddert's nomination was confirmed on the 21st. It was some days before he reached Philadelphia from Georgetown, and not until the 18th of June did he enter upon the business of his office. On this day the Secretary wrote three letters, one to the Treasury Department asking for a statement in respect to the purchase of the twelve ships authorized by Congress, and the other two to Captain Jeremiah Yellott, navy agent at Baltimore. These letters were the first that were written by the American Navy Department. The second letter to Yellott is of general interest and is worth transcribing:

" I mentioned to you in a Letter of to Day that I had not before entered upon the duties of my Office, in fact I have not yet taken the oath of office, this I shall do Tomorrow, and by the next Post shall write you officially; my opinion is that the *Montezuma* ought to be purchased. I shall Tomorrow consult the President on the subject, in the meantime I wish Mr. Taylor would suspend her loading.

" Mr. McHenry [25] has been absent ever since my arrival here— now Mr. Wolcot [26] is gone to New York, these circumstances have kept back the Business of my Department. I hope it will be better attended to in the future, and with the assistance of Gentlemen of your knowledge and worth can be obtained, I shall not despair of discharging the duties of my Office with promptness and economy, two things highly essential to be observed in the present crisis of our affairs." [27]

Stoddert remained at the head of the Navy Department until April 1, 1801. Stoddert was a native of Maryland, and a merchant by profession. He served with distinction in the Continental Army, rising to the rank of major. Owing to a severe wound

---

[24] Lodge's George Cabot, 144, 155-57.
[25] James McHenry, Secretary of War.
[26] Roger Wolcott, Secretary of the Treasury.
[27] General Letters, Nav. Dept. Arch., I, 4.

which he received at the battle of Brandywine, he was compelled to leave the active service. For several years he served as secretary of the Continental Board of War. His term of service in the department amounted to not quite three years. This period, when the foundation of the American Navy was being laid, is one of the most important in its history. Every part of the naval service underwent a most rapid development. Stoddert, who was an ardent friend of the navy, was a worthy and efficient administrator. In his own words, which are just and accurate, he discharged his " duty to the Public with zeal and diligence, and not without judgment." [28] While other members of the Cabinet intrigued against the President, he remained true to his chief. His task seems to have been as uncongenial to him as possibly it would have been to Cabot, but, against his own inclination, he manfully stayed with it. A few months after entering upon the duties of his office he wrote: " In truth my determination has always been, and will continue to be, to quit it the moment when it will not be dishonorable to quit the public service." [29] Charles W. Goldsborough, who, beginning with 1798, served the department almost continuously for more than forty years, said that the selection of Stoddert was the most fortunate that could have been made, and that " to the most ardent patriotism he united an inflexible integrity, a discriminating mind, great capacity for business, and the most persevering industry." [30] While Goldsborough's characterization sounds somewhat epitaphic, it is just.

The Navy Department under Stoddert consisted of two offices, the secretary's office and the office of the accountant of the navy. In addition to the secretary of the navy, the secretary's office comprised the principal clerk, four or five subordinate clerks, and a messenger. In 1800, the pay-roll of the secretary's office amounted to $9152. Almost one-half of this sum went to the secretary, for, in 1799, his yearly salary was increased to $4500. The principal clerk, or chief clerk of the department as he was soon called, was paid $1200 a year. The first to fill this position was Garrett Cottringer.[31] In the latter part of 1799 he was succeeded by Abishai Thomas, who held the office until early in Jefferson's administra-

---

[28] General Letters, Nav. Dept. Arch., III, 496.
[29] General Letters, Nav. Dept. Arch., I, 334.
[30] Goldsborough's Naval Chronicle, 86.
[31] U. S. Statutes at Large, I, 730; II, 64; Congress Letters, Nav. Dept. Arch., I, 17-18.

tion. Employed in Philadelphia, outside of the secretary's office proper, was Robert Gill, navy storekeeper, at a salary of $1000; and Joshua Humphreys, " Principal Naval Constructor of the United States," at a salary of $2000. During the early history of the department Humphreys was one of its most important officials. He was the chief technical adviser of the secretary of the navy. He was a man of marked ability and skill in his profession.

The office of the accountant of the navy was established by a statute, dated July 16, 1798. The accountant was appointed by the President and confirmed by the Senate. He was the auditor for the Navy Department. He was charged with the settlement of all accounts for moneys advanced and stores issued and distributed by or under the direction of the secretary of the navy. His salary, which was first fixed at $1600 a year, was, in 1799, raised to $2000. The accountant employed some six or seven clerks. The pay-roll of the office in 1800 amounted to $9250.[32] The first accountant of the navy was William Winder, of Maryland, who entered upon his duties in September, 1798. Winder, during the Revolutionary War, had served as a commissioner of the Navy Board of the Middle Department. In January, 1800, he was succeeded by Thomas Turner, of Georgetown, District of Columbia, who was the accountant of the navy until his death in 1816.

Stoddert continued the naval agencies which the War Department had established at Portsmouth, Boston, New York, Baltimore, and Norfolk. The navy agent at Philadelphia had resigned in June, 1795, and the Secretary of War had vested his duties in the Public Purveyor of Supplies and in the Principal Naval Constructor. On entering upon the work of his office, Stoddert found the building and purchasing of vessels to be among his chief duties. To aid him in this work he appointed navy agents at several of the less important Atlantic ports. In 1798 he chose agents for Newburyport, Massachusetts; Newport, Rhode Island; Middletown, Connecticut; Wilmington, North Carolina; Charleston, South Carolina; and Savannah, Georgia. In 1799 navy agents were appointed for Salem, Massachusetts; Norwich, Connecticut; and the District of Columbia.[33] The usual commission of the navy agents was two per cent on the moneys that

[32] U. S. Statutes at Large, I, 610, 730; II, 64.
[33] General Letters, Nav. Dept. Arch., I, 342-43, 530; II, 24, 122.

they expended.   Their principal duty was to purchase naval supplies of all sorts—timber, hemp, copper, powder, cannon, canvas,
pork, beef, and bread.   The first navy agent for the District of
Columbia was William Marbury, who later attained notoriety in
the famous case of Marbury *versus* Madison.   He had resided at
Annapolis, and was appointed navy agent to purchase materials
for a 74-gun ship, which was to be constructed at Washington.
In May, 1800, when the department was preparing to remove from
Philadelphia to Washington, Stoddert appointed George Harrison navy agent at Philadelphia.   Harrison's name is worth re-
calling, for he performed his duties most creditably for many
years.   Stephen Higginson was the Federalist navy agent at
Boston.

The naval war with France was almost coincident with Stoddert's term of office.   During this irregular and desultory conflict
the little navy did itself much credit.   Commodore Thomas
Truxtun achieved the most notable successes.   In the *Constellation,* 38 guns, he captured the two French ships, the *Insurgente,*
40 guns, and the *Vengeance,* 44 guns, after two hard-fought
engagements.   The American fleet operated chiefly in the West
Indies.   It was usually divided into four squadrons.   These were
the St. Kitts or Guadaloupe squadron, Santo Domingo squadron,
Havana squadron, and Surinam squadron.   The St. Kitts and
Santa Domingo squadrons were the largest and most important.
At Basseterre and Cape Francois the Navy Department had navy
agents who received provisions sent from the United States for the
fleet, purchased other necessary supplies, and provided for the
maintenance of the French prisoners.   These agents also negotiated
for the exchange of prisoners, and when they accumulated
shipped them to the United States.   For the supply of the Havana squadron the department for a time in 1799 employed an
agent at Havana.   In December, of that year, he was discharged
and his duties were vested in the American consul at Havana.
The consul at Surinam assisted in supplying the Surinam squadron.   The navy agents in the West Indies were paid a commission of five per cent on all moneys expended.   Sometimes their
commissions were supplemented by a fixed salary.[34]

During Stoddert's administration, the Navy Department was
somewhat peripatetic.   For the first two years it was regularly

[34] General Letters, Nav. Dept. Arch., II, 26, 53, 68; IV, 55-57.

located at Philadelphia. During the autumn of 1798 and 1799, however, it was temporarily situated at Trenton, leaving Philadelphia on account of an epidemic of yellow fever. The Secretary of the Navy was not pleased with the temporary capital at Trenton. He wrote that the town was an indifferent place for the officials of the government, but that they would, however, have " leisure to think, and that may prove an advantage." For its quarters in Philadelphia the department paid an annual rental of $800.[35] In the autumn of 1798 Stoddert was absent from the department for a month. He made a visit to Georgetown, and after the frosts had checked the fever at Philadelphia returned to that city with his family. This incident assumes interest, since the department was for the first time left without its regular head. Timothy Pickering, the Secretary of State, was placed in charge of the Navy Department, and became " Acting Secretary of the Navy." He, however, signed only a part of the correspondence, since Cottringer, the chief clerk, and Goldsborough, a subordinate clerk, shared in this work.

The Navy Department made a third move in June, 1800, and this time from Philadelphia to the " City of Washington," then a city only in name and plan. On May 30, Stoddert issued to his clerks, " Orders for the Removal of the Department to the City of Washington." This document is of interest, since it throws light upon the details of the moving of the capital which have been greatly obscured by the fancy of ingenious writers. The document seems to indicate that the reputed impecuniosity of government clerks was at this time a reality. It read as follows:

" The President having directed the offices to be opened at the City of Washington on the 15th of June, the Gentlemen belonging to the offices of the Secry. and Accountant of the Navy will regulate their affairs accordingly. There will be an advance of as much money to each person as is due at the time for salary—perhaps a little more, but this cannot at present be counted upon.

" Vessels are daily preparing and carrying the furniture of the Gentlemen in the other offices. Such things as can be spared may be sent as soon as the owners please in such vessels at the Public Expence. But Mr. Whelan, the Purveyor, must be consulted in every instance—he having directions from the Treasury

[35] General Letters, Nav. Dept. Arch., I, 155; V, 137.

particularly on this subject. It is intended to close the offices here on Saturday the 7th Inst." [36]

The records and original papers of the department were either considered too valuable to be moved on board the vessels, or it was thought that a quicker trip could be made overland. They were loaded into a wagon, and George Sutherland, a clerk of the department was detailed by the Secretary of the Navy to accompany the wagon from Philadelphia to Washington to guard its contents. Sutherland rode behind the wagon on horseback. The furniture and printed books of the department were loaded on board vessels, which sailed down the Delaware and up the Chesapeake into the Potomac. All the clerks of the secretary's office, except one whose private interests forbade and who therefore resigned, removed to Washington. Stoddert arrived in Washington on June 15 and opened his office on the 18th. Sutherland and the records had not yet come, and the Secretary of the Navy was compelled to transact the naval business for a few days under serious difficulties. On the arrival of the heavy articles which had been shipped on board the vessels, they were stored in Tobias Lear's warehouse in Georgetown, where they remained until temporary quarters were obtained.[37]

When the removal to Washington was first contemplated, Stoddert had counted on having " six rooms in the Treasury House for my office." Finding that these could not be spared he wrote to Marbury, the naval agent in Georgetown, to have two of " the six houses of Forrest and Templeman," one for the Navy Department, and the other for the State Department, so far completed as to answer for offices during the summer. The " Six Buildings," as they were for a long time called, were situated between the White House and Georgetown on Pennsylvania Avenue. The Six Buildings were not ready for occupancy when the departments moved to Washington in June. The State Departmen obtained temporary quarters and did not move into one of the Six Buildings until August. The exact location of the Navy Department during the summer of 1800 has not been ascertained, but its movements most probably corresponded with those of the State Department. About the first of May, 1801, the Navy Department moved into permanent quarters in the " Old

[36] General Letters, Nav. Dept. Arch., III, 423.

[37] General Letters, Nav. Dept. Arch., III, 439, 442, 469; Records of the Columbia Historical Society, III, 143 .

War Office," which was situated near the White House. The southern end of the present State, War, and Navy Building is on or near the site of the Old War Office. In 1800, Washington could boast of little else than magnificent views and distances. Here and there were a few dwelling houses, often wide apart, and separated by " slashes," which were covered with scrub oaks and alders. The construction of four government buildings had been begun—the capitol, President's house, treasury office, and war office. Only the treasury office was ready for occupancy. In the spring of 1800 the work of expediting the construction of the President's house fell to the Secretary of the Navy. The building of the first foot-ways in Washington also was superintended chiefly by Stoddert. In these rude and narrow walks which connected the President's house with the capitol and with Georgetown, one may discover the beginning of the present superior system of paved streets in Washington.[38]

Although the country was at war with France until nearly the close of Stoddert's administration, yet practically the whole naval increase in ships was made in 1798 and 1799. During these two years the building and purchasing of ships were among the chief activities of the department. At the close of 1797 three ships were in service; at the close of 1798, twenty; and at the close of 1799, thirty-three. Of these thirty-three vessels, five were 44's; four, 36's; seven, 32's; three, 24's; seven, 20's; four, 18's; and three, 14's. Nine galleys were built for the protection of the Southern ports, and eight revenue cutters were obtained from the Treasury Department. These fifty vessels, large and small, comprised the naval force during the war with France. Some of them, the department built at the navy-yards, which had been rented by the War Department; others, it had built under contract; and still others, it purchased. Several were built by the patriotic citizens of the chief seaports, who raised the necessary money by subscription. Vessels were built in this way by the citizens of Newburyport, Salem, Boston, New York, Philadelphia, Baltimore, Norfolk, and Charleston. The department completed the construction of the *President, Chesapeake,* and *Congress,* which had been commenced in 1796.[39].

[38] General Letters, Nav. Dept. Arch., III, 94, 157, 305, 311, 366, 372, 390; IV, 62, 85, 332, 336.
[39] State Papers, Nav. Aff., I, 58-59; General Letters, Nav. Dept. Arch., II, 123-24.

In selecting officers for his fleet Stoddert received aid from many sources. They were usually chosen from the locality in which the ship was built. The captains often chose their lieutenants and warrant officers. For the highest positions the requests and recommendations of influential friends and relatives had much weight. Congressional influence was not so pervasive or powerful as now. The applicants were numerous and persistent. President Adams took with him to Quincy, Massachusetts, where he spent his summers, both blank commissions and warrants, which he filled out whenever he wished to make appointments. Owing to the haste and the exigency of the service, officers frequently did not receive their commissions or warrants until after their first cruise.

Under Stoddert the list of captains in the navy was increased from 3 to 28. According to Goldsborough's Naval Chronicle, there were in the navy on March 3, 1801, 7 masters commandant, 110 lieutenants, and 354 midshipmen. Many of the famous names of the Old Navy first appeared in the navy list during the administration of Stoddert—Preble, Bainbridge, Decatur, Chauncey, Stewart, Barron, John Rodgers, James Biddle, and O. H. Perry. In response to the importunities of his friends and his country's friends, Stoddert swelled the number of midshipmen until he confessed that he was ashamed of himself. Many of the most celebrated officers of the Old Navy served their apprenticeship in it as midshipmen. The most suitable age for a young man to enter the grade of midshipman was from twelve to eighteen years. It was possible in the early years of the navy for an intelligent young officer, fortunate and skilful in his profession, to pass through the grades of midshipman, lieutenant, and master commandant, and become a captain, the highest grade in the navy, at the age of thirty or thirty-five. Stoddert appointed many youths who knew little of the sea to be midshipmen. He insisted, however, that they should be " sprightly well-educated young men of good principles and spirit." [40] Chaplains and schoolmasters were provided to teach these lusty youths the rudiments of navigation and mathematics.

In striking contrast with the experiences of the Navy Department in both the Revolutionary War and the War of 1812 was the little difficulty that was encountered during the war with

---

[40] General Letters, Nav. Dept. Arch., II, 142

France in enlisting seamen. Enough men to man a frigate could usually be enlisted in a week's time. One reason why the seamen entered more readily was because the enemy had few vessels afloat superior to those of the Americans.[41] At this time seamen enlisted for a year, or for a year and thence until the end of their cruise. A captain serving in the West Indies usually returned with his vessel at the end of a year's cruise, dismissed his men, and while his vessel was repairing and refitting enlisted another crew. This practice makes it difficult to ascertain the number of the enlisted force of the navy. The number of seamen was not fixed by statute but by the President, and the records of enlistment seem to have disappeared. To fully officer and man the fifty vessels that composed the American Navy in 1800 required 8400 men.[42] If we assume that two-thirds of these vessels were completely officered and manned at one time, the total number of men in the navy may be estimated at 5600. The maximum strength of the Marine Corps as fixed by law was 1085 officers and men.

Difficulties in respect to rank early arose in our navy. During Stoddert's administration Captains Truxtun and Talbot had a long and bitter contention over their relative standing. The Secretary of the Navy and the President disagreed upon the points at issue, and the dispute was not ended until Talbot withdrew from the navy. " This avarice of rank in the infancy of our Service is the Devil," Stoddert wrote in 1799.[43]

For many years an agitation in behalf of higher naval ranks was conducted in the Navy Department, in the navy, and in Congress. This subject was earnestly considered by Secretary Stoddert. In March, 1800, he asked Congress to authorize the President to appoint two admirals, two vice-admirals, and two rear-admirals. He said that he was " well aware of the ridicule that may attach to the idea of making Admirals before we have such ships as Admirals usually command, and when our whole Naval force amounts to no more than eleven Frigates, or fifteen if we call every ship carrying 32 Guns a Frigate, and twenty smaller vessels." He believed, however, " that Justice and Policy require that the brave and experienced officer should be rewarded, and the Young stimulated, by conferring upon long extraordinary skill and valor the usual Naval

[41] Congress Letters, Nav. Dept. Arch., II, 124.

[42] State Papers, Nav. Aff., I, 59-63.

[43] General Letters, Nav. Dept. Arch., II, 254.

Honors and Distinctions." In response to Stoddert's recommendation the Naval Committee of the House in April introduced a bill which provided for one vice-admiral and four rear-admirals. It did not pass the House. The captains of the navy in all probability brought their views on the subject of higher rank to bear on the secretary. Stoddert wrote in 1799 that Captain Barry " is old and infirm, and not satisfied that he is not made an Admiral." [44]

Various tasks which fell to the Secretary of the Navy were incident to a new and rapidly developing naval service. He revised the Rules and Regulations of the Navy. He was instrumental in having revised in 1800 the penal code of the navy, which Congress had adopted in 1799. He drafted a bill for the government of the Marine Corps. He established six navy-yards, and began the work of locating naval docks. In papers addressed to Congress he vigorously pointed out the need of these institutions. He began the construction at Newport, Rhode Island, of the first naval hospital. It was to be a small building and its cost was not to exceed $4000.[45] In 1801 the Republicans stopped the work upon it. In respect to naval construction or to the location of navy-yards and docks, the secretary sought the advice of his chief naval constructor, Joshua Humphreys. The captains of the navy sometimes assisted him with those duties which lay particularly within the field of their professional knowledge. The work of the Navy Department was much simpler and much less technical in the first years of its existence, than is its work at the present time. A civilian secretary, such as Stoddert, was therefore able to master most of the department's problems.

No work of Stoddert was more important or far-reaching than that which had to do with the establishment of navy-yards. Here, he set his seal, which remains to this day. The navy-yards are the manufactories, repair-shops, and storehouses of the navy; the Navy Department, in one of its most important functions, is the central office that superintends the activities of the navy-yards. In the work of the navy, especially in providing, repairing, and improving the naval *materiel,* these establishments are of the greatest importance. They must of course be situated at seaports or at ports convenient to the sea. Several attempts to obtain

[44] Congress Letters, Nav. Dept. Arch., I, 55-56; Annals of Cong., X, 676; General Letters, I, 515.
[45] General Letters, Nav. Dept. Arch., IV, 31.

permanent navy-yards, that were made, were unsuccessful. A plan for the navy, which was prepared by John Paul Jones in 1777, provided for three navy-yards. In January, 1797, Secretary of War McHenry recommended to Congress the purchase of a navy-yard. In February, upon the request of the Committee of the House on Naval Equipment, he reported an estimate of the " probable cost of a Scite for a Navy Yard and the Buildings necessary thereto." [46] He thought that one hundred acres of land located within fifteen or twenty miles of a large city would be needed. In July, 1798, Robert Goodloe Harper, of South Carolina, introduced in the House a resolution " that it is expedient to enable the President to establish one or more dock-yards for the use of the United States, with suitable buildings for marine stores, arsenals, and magazines." [47] In December, Stoddert, in a communication to the House, pointed out the need of the navy for ample building yards.

On several important occasions when Congress has refused the Navy Department specific authority to make needed improvements, the department has obtained the authority desired by a liberal construction of the statutes. Stoddert was the first secretary of the navy to resort to this expedient. On February 25, 1799, Congress passed an act appropriating money for the construction of six 74-gun ships. With the exception of the *America,* which was constructed during the Revolution, Congress had not previously undertaken to build vessels as large as these. The yards, which had been rented, had already proved to be too small for the construction of the 44's; considerable additional expense had been incurred in moving and removing the timbers in them, necessitated by their restricted quarters. The inconvenience and expense of building the 74's in these yards would be still greater; and, moreover, considerable improvements, such as the building of wharves, slips, and sheds, would have to be made. It did not appear economical for the government to improve private property. The President and the Secretary of the Navy, therefore, determined to purchase permanent building grounds for the navy. They derived their authority for making the purchases from the act of Congress, directing the building of the six 74-gun ships. [48] In order to properly carry out this act, they argued that ample

[46] State Papers, Nav. Aff., I, 26-27.
[47] Annals of Congress, VIII, 2083.
[48] State Papers, Nav. Aff., I, 74, 84.

building grounds were necessary. It must be said, however, that
the incidental effect of these purchases, the acquisition of six
permanent navy-yards, strongly appealed to the President and
the Secretary of the Navy, ardent Federalists, and open advocates
of a large and efficient navy.

Stoddert decided to build the six ships in as many different
places, although he thought that ultimately three building yards
would be found sufficient for the needs of the navy; one in New
Hampshire or Massachusetts, one on the Hudson River, and one
on the Chesapeake Bay.[49] By May, 1799, he had decided to build
one of the ships at Washington, on ground already owned by the
Federal government. In August, he sent Humphreys from Philadelphia to the new capital to locate the site. After this had been
determined, Humphreys, in October, made another trip to Washington to fix upon the proper place for wharves. Stoddert at
first hoped to have the land transferred to the Navy Department
without expense; but finally, in order to obtain a good title and
to prevent the carrying of the business to Congress, he consented
to pay $4000 for the ground selected. On March 17, 1800, the
transfer was made and the Navy Department came into possession
of its first navy-yard. It contained 47.7 acres, and was situated
on the Eastern Branch of the Potomac, within the city of Washington, about one-half mile from the capitol. In January, 1800,
Stoddert ordered Captain Thomas Tingey to proceed to Washington and superintend the construction of the 74-gun ship and the
improvements to be made in the yard. Tingey was well qualified for this position. He had at one time visited the chief navy-
yards of England.[50]

The yard at Gosport, Virginia, which the United States had
been renting since 1794 from the State of Virginia, next received Stoddert's attention. He first obtained an act of the
Virginia Legislature authorizing the transfer of the property.
Stoddert thought that Virginia ought to give the land to the
United States, but she was disposed to make as good a bargain as
possible. The act of the legislature called for the appointment
of two appraisers to value the land. The Governor of Virginia
selected Thomas Nelson, Jr.; and the Secretary of the Navy,
William Pennock, the navy agent at Norfolk. These two men

[49] General Letters, Nav. Dept. Arch., II, 43.
[50] General Letters, Nav. Dept. Arch., II, 268-69, 426-27; III, 1, 3, 34-35,
119.

decided that the 16 acres comprising the yard were worth $12,000. Stoddert willingly paid this sum, since he greatly desired to obtain a navy-yard at this place, and he knew that Congress would not consent to its purchase if the business was referred to that body. As some misunderstanding arose about paying over the money, the deed was not signed until June 15, 1801.[51]

A yard at Portsmouth, New Hampshire, was acquired from William and Sarah Dennett on June 12, 1800, for $5500. It consisted of an island, known as Fernald's or Dennett's Island, and contained 58 acres. The navy agent at Portsmouth acted in behalf of the department in making the purchase. The various sites for a navy-yard around Boston were viewed by Joshua Humphreys, who selected a location at Charlestown. Dr. Aaron Putnam was authorized by the department to purchase the land. He bought from various persons for $37,348 ten adjacent lots, amounting in the aggregate to 34 acres. The deed for the first lot purchased was dated August 26, 1800; and for the last, April 2, 1801.[52]

Stoddert first wished to locate the Philadelphia navy-yard on the Delaware, a short distance below Philadelphia; and in June, 1800, he had an army engineer examine the river at this point with a view to its fortification. Later, he sent Humphreys to inspect the eligible sites around the city. Humphreys reported in favor of a situation north of Philadelphia, but in November, the Secretary of the Navy decided to buy the grounds in the District of Southwark in Philadelphia, which the department had been renting. These grounds could be obtained immediately, while those which Humphreys had selected could not be. The site at Southwark was purchased by Humphreys for the department on January 20, and February 20, 1801. It embraced 11 acres, and cost $37,000. On February 23, 1801, James and Ebenezer Watson, navy agents at New York, purchased a navy-yard situated on Wallabout Bay in Brooklyn, Long Island. It comprised a tract of 40 acres, known as Martynes Hook. It cost the department $40,000.[53]

[51] General Letters Nav. Dept. Arch., III, 116-17, 302, 516; IV, 193-95; Hening's Statutes of Virginia New Ser., II, 246-47.
[52] Archives of the Bureau of Yards and Docks, Nav. Dept., Deeds to Portsmouth and Boston navy-yards.
[53] General Letters, Nav. Dept. Arch., III, 412-13; IV, 4, 116-17; Archives of the Bureau of Yards and Docks, Nav. Dept., Deeds to the Philadelphia and New York navy-yards.

During the last weeks of Adams' administration, which ended on March 4, 1801, the purchases of the yards at Boston, New York, Philadelphia, and Norfolk were being made. Stoddert urgently pressed each of the four agents, who were commissioned to buy these yards, to complete their work at once. It was plain that the Secretary of the Navy feared that his work might be undone by the incoming Republican administration, and was determined, if possible, to have the whole business consummated before he turned the keys of the department over to his successor.[54] When he retired on April 1, 1801, the purchasing of the six navy-yards was virtually completed.

On February 25, 1799, three important Federalist measures were passed.[55] The act which provided for the building of six 74-gun ships has already been referred to. The second act appropriated $50,000 for the establishment of two docks for the purpose of repairing naval vessels. In December, 1798, Stoddert had reported to the Committee of the House on the Naval Establishment that " docks will be highly necessary in repairing our ships, to avoid the tedious, expensive, and sometimes dangerous operation of heaving down. They can undoubtedly be made in the Eastern States, where the tides rise very considerably; probably in New Hampshire, Massachusetts, and Rhode Island." He said that, if they could be made to equal advantage to the southward, it would be well to have a dock near the entrance of the Chesapeake Bay. It was in pursuance of this recommendation that Congress passed the act of February 25, 1799, providing for two docks. Various interested persons now recommended sites for docks to the Secretary of the Navy. In August, 1799, he appointed Stephen Sayre, who had seen all the principal docks in Europe, to visit the chief ports of New England and report on the advantages which they offered. In January, 1800, he sent Humphreys to New England for the same purpose. Humphreys visited all the principal ports to the eastward of New York, and made an elaborate report on various eligible sites for docks. He considered a site at Newport as the most superior place for a dock, and the Secretary of the Navy agreed with him. Adams' administration came to a close before this business was concluded. Moreover, the appropriation was too small to have done more

---

[54] General Letters Nav, Dept. Arch., IV, 116-17, 166, 183, 193-95, 203, 206, 209-11, 214, 228.

[55] U. S. Statutes at Large, I, 62.

than purchase the sites. It was certainly not the fault of the Secretary of the Navy or of his plans that docks were not erected. When Humphreys was about to leave for New England on his tour of inspection, Stoddert instructed him that it was proper that a dock " should be begun, and at a place, and on a plan capable of great extension. Although a Dock sufficient to contain not more than one Ship will be attempted in the first instance, it ought to be foreseen that it may be necessary to annex to it hereafter Docks to contain 20 Ships of the line, and that the works now to be erected should constitute a permanent part of the whole establishment." Many years, however, were to elapse before the American Navy was to have a single dock; and even at the present time its docking facilities are hardly so extensive as those planned by the first Secretary of the Navy.[56]

The third act of February 25, 1799, appropriated $200,000 for the purchase of timber, or land upon which timber was growing. This measure, which contemplated the purchase of live oak and live-oak lands for the future use of the navy, was a favorite one with the Federalists, and had more than once been defeated by the Republicans. In carrying out the latter part of the act, the purchase of timber lands, the Secretary of the Navy bought for $22,500 Grover's Island and Blackbeard's Island, which lay off the coast of Georgia.[57] These islands belonged to the Navy Department until about 1890, when they were turned over to the Interior Department.

Stoddert showed a wise foresight in providing for the future needs of the navy. He believed that every material used in the construction and repair of a ship could be made in America, if the manufacturers were given the proper encouragement. He advanced to Samuel Lyman, of Springfield, Massachusetts, $1000 to aid him in the manufacture of canvas. Paul Revere, of Boston, more famous for his ride to Concord than as a manufacturer of copper, was advanced $10,000 to assist him in purchasing a mill and apparatus for making dry-rolled sheathing copper for the navy.[58] Stoddert believed that if the growers of hemp were encouraged, a sufficient quantity for the needs of the navy could be

---

[56] State Papers, Nav. Aff., I, 66, 89-102; General Letters, Nav. Dept. Arch., II, 300-01; III, 136-44.

[57] Goldsborough's Naval Chronicles, 351.

[58] General Letters, Nav. Dept. Arch., II, 49; V, 166; Miscellaneous Letters, II, 14, 32.

grown in the river valleys of the Ohio, Mississippi, Susquehanna, Potomac, and James.

The ratifying of the treaty of peace with France early in 1801 brought to an end the naval war, and necessitated the placing of the navy upon a peace footing. One of the last acts of the expiring Federalist government, which was passed on March 3, 1801, provided for a naval peace establishment. This act authorized the President to sell all the vessels of the navy except thirteen, whose names were given, and of these to keep six in commission in time of peace and to lay up the remaining seven in ordinary. All the officers except those needed were to be discharged. Of the officers of the higher grades, 9 captains, 36 lieutenants, and 150 midshipmen were to be retained; the rank of master commandant was abolished. Charles W. Goldsborough, in his Naval Chronicle, says that this act originated with the avowed friends of the navy, " who were impressed with the conviction, that the existence of the establishment could be preserved by no other means, than by reducing it to the lowest possible scale." This does not seem to be the whole truth. The necessity of reducing the naval establishment in 1801 to a peace footing was fully recognized by the Federalists. On January 12, 1801, the Secretary of the Navy made a report to a committee of the House in which he recommended reductions in the navy similar to those made by the act of March 3. The thirteen frigates which were reserved by this act were those recommended to be reserved by Stoddert. He said that it would be good economy to sell the rest of the public vessels, because they were built of materials that did not promise to last, and in addition they were too small to form a part of the national defense. In the place of these he recommended that the government should build twelve 74's and thirteen frigates. Stoddert wished to retire all the higher officers not needed for the naval service in time of peace on half-pay. These were to remain subject to the call of Congress. The original bill in Congress contained provisions in line with Stoddert's wishes. The Republicans, however, carried an amendment dismissing from the navy all the officers not required on a peace footing, after giving them four months' extra pay.[59]

[59] U. S. Statutes at Large, II, 110-11; Goldsborough's Naval Chronicle, 181; State Papers, Nav. Aff., I, 74-78; Annals of Congress, X, 1056-59.

CHAPTER FOUR: BUILDING THE NAVY, 1801-1814

ROBERT SMITH, 1801-1809.

The administration of Thomas Jefferson, which came into power on March 4, 1801, differed definitely on naval questions from that of John Adams. The one wished to reduce the naval expenditures to the lowest terms; the other to appropriate most generously for officers, seamen, ships, docks, and navy-yards. The one favored a defensive navy; the other, an offensive navy. The one would build, if vessels must be built, sloops of war, gunboats, and barges, for the defence of the coasts and harbors; the other would add to the existing fleet of ships of the line and stout frigates, equal or superior to the best seagoing vessels of the European navies. In 1799 Jefferson had written to Elbridge Gerry that he was " for such a naval force only as may protect our coasts and harbors from such depredations as we have experienced." But he was not " for a navy, which, by its own expenses and the eternal wars in which it will implicate us, will grind us with public burthens, and sink us under them." In 1800 he declared that the country was running " navy 'mad." [1]

Jefferson's secretary of the treasury, Albert Gallatin, who in Congress in past years had vigorously opposed every measure for the increase or encouragement of the navy, now outdid his chief in proposals for retrenchment in naval expenditures. In 1802 he recommended that the cost of the navy for that year be reduced to $600,000. He considered one frigate and two or three small vessels " amply sufficient." [2] All the members of the Re-

---

[1] Ford, Jefferson, VII, 328, 406.
[2] Adams, History of the United States, II, 136.

119

publican party were not as strongly opposed to naval expenditures
as Jefferson and Gallatin. On the other hand, the opposition of
a few members went even farther. In 1802 Michael Leib, a
member of Congress from Pennsylvania, moved in the House for
a committee to consider the question of abolishing the navy.[3] In
1805 John Randolph said that he should not " be surprised to
see the Navy Department abolished, or, in more appropriate
phrase, swept by the board, at the next session of Congress." [4]

Randolph's wish may have been father to his expectation, for
it is well known that he bore a lively antipathy to Jefferson's secretary of the navy, not a man of national note when chosen to
the headship of the department. That Jefferson's chief naval
adviser was of importance on account of his kin rather than on
account of his weight in the public counsels, was not the fault of
the President, for he made numerous attempts to obtain a national
character to manage the navy. As early as December, 1800, before he knew certainly that he and not Aaron Burr was to be
president, he offered the naval portfolio to Robert R. Livingston,
of New York. Jefferson had the notion, which was common
during the early history of the department, that a secretary of
the navy should have some knowledge of maritime, naval, and
commercial affairs. He keenly felt his need of a secretary of
this sort, for he confessed that he knew less of the Navy Department than of any other branch of the government. Few Republicans, however, who had been bred to the sea or to commerce,
possessed at the same time all the political and intellectual qualifications that were considered essential to a member of the cabinet.
Livingston fell short in his knowledge of seafaring pursuits.
When urging him to accept the secretaryship, Jefferson wrote to
him as follows: " Tho' you are not nautical by profession, yet
your residence and your mechanical science qualify you as well
as gentlemen can possibly be, and sufficiently to enable you to
choose under-agents perfectly qualified, and to superintend their
conduct." [5] Livingston refused the tender.

In February, 1801, Jefferson offered the position to General
Samuel Smith, a Baltimore merchant, and one of the most influential men in the Republican party. When Smith declined to

[3] Adams, History of the United States, I, 296-99.
[4] Adams, Randolph, 160-61.
[5] Ford, Jefferson, VII, 465.

abandon his business for the service of the government, the President decided on John Langdon, of New Hampshire, a Republican of national fame. On Langdon's refusal, he again turned to Smith, but without success. William Jones, a Republican member of Congress from Philadelphia, was now given an opportunity to decline the secretaryship. Meanwhile, Adams's secretary of the navy, Benjamin Stoddert, who in February had tendered his resignation to take effect in March, became tired of waiting. A temporary arrangement was therefore effected. Samuel Dearborn was made acting secretary of the navy; and Samuel Smith agreed to perform, nominally under Dearborn, the actual duties of the office.[6] The Republicans took possession of the Navy Department on April 1, 1801.

In May Jefferson wrote jestingly to Gouverneur Morris that he believed that he would have to advertise for a secretary of the navy. In June he once more offered the position to John Langdon, and for a time it was thought in Washington that Langdon would accept. In the same month General Smith returned to Baltimore and left the department in charge of Dearborn and Abishai Thomas, the chief clerk of the department.[7] On Langdon's second refusal Jefferson became discouraged in his search for national characters, and accepted Robert Smith, the brother of General Samuel Smith. It has been said that Robert's chief recommendations were the advice and aid which his brother Samuel was expected to give him. In its political aspect the appointment was a good one, for the family of the Smiths was well connected and influential in Maryland and Virginia. Robert Smith was a "Baltimore gentleman, easy and cordial, glad to oblige and fond of power and show, popular in the navy, yielding in the Cabinet, but as little fitted as Jefferson himself for the task of administering with severe economy an unpopular service."[8] After graduating from Princeton, Smith had practised law, and had served several terms in the Maryland legislature. In 1789 he was one of the presidential electors. He became the last survivor of the first electoral college, dying in 1842. For a time he

[6] Ford, Jefferson, VII, 484; VIII, 13-14, 28; Adams, History of the United States, I, 219-20.
[7] Ford, Jefferson, VIII, 49; General Letters, Navy Department Archives, IV, 409-10.
[8] Adams, History of the United States, I, 222.

was secretary of state under Madison. While Smith lacked the driving power of the statesman, he possessed in considerable measure the lubricating qualities of the politician, which by reducing the friction may greatly accelerate the speed of the administrative machine.

On July 15, 1801, Smith received a temporary commission, as the Senate was not then in session. He was confirmed by the Senate and recommissioned on January 26, 1802. On July 27, 1801, he relieved Dearborn and Thomas, and took charge of the department. He served continuously as secretary of the navy until March 7, 1809. Only two other naval secretaries, Gideon Welles, 1861-1869, and George M. Robeson, 1869-1877, have had longer terms of office. During Jefferson's second administration the official status of Robert Smith was an anomalous one. In January, 1805, Smith asked to be transferred from the Navy Department to the Department of Justice. Jefferson consented, and selected Jacob Crowninshield, a member of Congress from Massachusetts, to take the place of Smith in the Navy Department. Crowninshield declined the offer, as his wife did not wish to leave her kin and friends in Massachusetts and live in Washington. Nevertheless, on March 2, the President sent the nomination of Crowninshield to the Senate, along with that of Robert Smith, " now Secretary of the Navy to be Attorney-General of the United States "; and on the same day the two nominations were confirmed. Crowninshield still persisted in declining the secretaryship, and Smith continued to fill it throughout Jefferson's second term. According to the records of the State Department, Crowninshield during this period was secretary of the navy, although he died on April 15, 1808. From March 3, 1805, until March 7, 1809, Smith acted by no known authority except the verbal request or permission of the President.[9]

On July 31, 1801, two days after entering upon the duties of his office, Smith dismissed Thomas French, one of the clerks of the secretary's office, and appointed Thomas T. Anderson to the place made vacant. This appointment bears the ear-marks of a personal or political one, and seems to be the first application of the spoils system to the Navy Department proper—several Federalist navy agents had been removed before this. The two letters of Smith,

[9] Adams, History of the United States, III, 10-12.

one dismissing French, and the other appointing Anderson, are interesting; both were written on the same day. In one letter Smith denies the responsibility that he assumes in the other. To French he wrote: " An arrangement having been made and a Gentleman appointed to succeed you as a Clerk in the Office of the Secretary of the Navy, previous to my taking upon myself the functions of that office, it remains for me only to notify you of the Circumstance, and to assure you that since my arrival at this place I have observed with Satisfaction your prompt and cheerful Attention to your official Duties." The letter to Anderson read as follows: " Confiding in your Capacity and Integrity from the very respectable Manner in which you have been recommended to me, I have appointed you a Clerk in the Navy Office. You will therefore be pleased to come to this place as early as conveniently may be. Your Services are immediately necessary." [10]

A more important change in the force of the secretary's office was made on April 1, 1802, when Charles W. Goldsborough succeeded Abishai Thomas as chief clerk of the department. Goldsborough was promoted from the position of a subordinate clerk, which he had held since 1798. Some of his duties were prescribed in his letter of appointment: As chief clerk he was to have " under the superintending control of the Secretary, the custody and charge of all the Books, Papers, and Documents of every description belonging to the Department." He was to be responsible for the accuracy of the records of the department. " He must see that the Business of each day be brought up during that day, and that all the books and papers of the Office are arranged in the most regular order." He was to apportion the duties of the subordinate clerks, and to have charge of the appropriation for the contingent expenses of the secretary's office. In the future the secretary of the navy was to communicate only with the chief clerk, who was expected to " be duly prepared at all times when called upon." [11]

Goldsborough was one of the most important officials of the Navy Department during the first half-century of its existence. With the exception of a period of some two years during the War of 1812, he was connected with the department from 1798 to 1843.

[10] General Letters, Navy Dept. Arch., IV, 476-77.
[11] General Letters, Navy Dept. Arch., V, 273-74.

Although not a profound man, yet his knowledge of naval affairs, by virtue of his long service, was large and accurate. He was thus able to be of great assistance to the secretaries of the navy and to the board of navy commissioners, of which he was for a long time secretary. Students of the American navy are under many obligations to him for his Naval Chronicle, published in 1824, a narrative and documentary history of the early navy. He came of good Maryland stock. One of his sons was Rear-Admiral Louis M. Goldsborough, who rendered gallant service to the Union during the Civil War, and the other, Commodore John Rodgers Goldsborough, also a naval officer of this war.

For several years Smith employed but one other clerk in addition to Goldsborough and Anderson, but in 1806 a fourth clerk was added. The pay of the clerks were considerably higher under Smith than under Stoddert. The salary of the chief clerk was raised from $1200 to $1800 a year. In 1806 Congress limited the total compensation of the clerks of the secretary's office to $4900, and of the accountant's office to $8000. The office hours of the department began at nine o'clock in the morning, as at present, and closed at three in the afternoon, an hour and a half earlier than is now the rule. In 1803 Smith informed Congress that his clerks were frequently compelled to work over-time.[12]

The eccentric John Randolph, who was a most unfriendly critic of the Secretary of the Navy, has described an interview which he had with Smith and Goldsborough in 1807 at the Navy Office in Washington. There is plainly much caricature, as well as some truth, in Randolph's amusing picture. He had called to ask Smith for an explanation of certain items in the navy estimate for 1807: " The Secretary called up his chief clerk, who knew very little more of the business than his master. I propounded a question to the head of the department; he turned to the clerk like a boy who cannot say his lesson, and with imploring countenance beseeches aid; the clerk with much assurance gabbled out some commonplace jargon, which I would not take for sterling; an explanation was required, and both were dumb. This pantomime was repeated at every item, until, disgusted, and ashamed for the degraded situation of the principal, I took leave without pursuing

[12] U. S. Statutes at Large, II, 396; Congress Letters, Navy Dept. Arch., I, 134-35.

the subject, seeing that my subject [object] could not be attained. There was not one single question relating to the department that the Secretary could answer." [13]

On April 1, 1801, the day upon which the Republicans took charge of the Navy Department, the official axe fell promptly and the official lives of Higginson & Co., navy agents at Boston; and of James and Ebenezer Watson, navy agents at New York, came to an end. Exactly one month later, the Federalist navy agent at Portsmouth, New Hampshire, was removed; and Woodbury Langdon, a prominent Republican, was appointed to fill the vacancy. Within less than a year after Smith became secretary of the navy, all the chief naval agencies in the United States, except the one at Philadelphia, had been filled with Republicans. At first Jefferson was disposed to get along with fewer agencies, and several of the smaller ones necessitated by the war with France were discontinued. The destroying of offices, however, proved to be an unpopular and little appreciated work, and the Republicans soon found themselves creating new agencies. In 1804 a detachment of marines was ordered to New Orleans, as this city was now in possession of the Americans. A naval station under the command of a naval officer was soon located here, and a naval agent for New Orleans was appointed. In 1805 Captain Henry Carbery was sent to Cincinnati to act as a navy agent for the construction of gunboats on the Western Waters. In 1807 a navy agent for Cuba was appointed, and in 1808 one was chosen for Madeira. In February, 1809, a naval agency was created for Portland, Maine.

During the Tripolitan war of 1801-1807 it was necessary to provide the fleet in the Mediterranean with money, provisions, and naval stores. At first the American consul at Gibraltar and the firm of Degen and Purviance at Leghorn, who acted as navy agents, were thought sufficient for the work of attending to the needs of the fleet. But later naval agencies were established at Naples, Syracuse, Malta, and one for the two cities of Marseilles and Toulon. In 1804 William Eaton was appointed navy agent for the " Barbary Regencies." The firm of McKenzie and Glennie, of London, was the financial agent of the Navy Department, and supplied the commanders of the vessels and the agents in the Mediterranean with money. Supply ships were regularly sent

[13] Adams, Randolph, 211.

out from America to these agents. They were loaded with provisions of all sorts, and with candles, cordage, canvas, twine, and slops. The naval vessels that were sent to relieve the vessels in the Mediterranean of course always carried supplies for that station. The maintenance of a fleet at so great a distance from home was very expensive . Towards the end of the war Smith came to suspect that some of the supplies were diverted from their proper uses. He concluded that the division of the business of purveying among so many navy agents was not economical, and in 1807 he decided to concentrate their work at Port Mahon on the island of Minorca.[14]

During the first year of their administration, the Republicans were quite suspicious and critical of the transactions of their predecessors. When the Messrs. Watson, navy agents at New York, delayed the turning over of the public property to their successors, Samuel Smith, who was then in charge of the Navy Department, declared that they feared an investigation of their accounts. A contract for making hemp into cordage entered into by Messrs. Higginson, navy agents at Boston, appeared to Smith " to be a job." The purchase price of the navy-yard on Long Island seemed to him to be " extravagantly high." In July, 1801, Dearborn, while acting secretary of the navy, appointed a commission of seven men to reconsider the locating of the Philadelphia navy-yard. The commission, two of whose members were Captains Barry and Decatur, reported in favor of another site, but Smith decided against its purchase since the sale of the old yard would cause delays and embarrassments. He also decided against removing the New York yard from its site on Wallabout Bay, when the propriety of its location was questioned.[15]

Could Gallatin have had his way, the number of navy-yards would have been reduced. Jefferson also was inclined to favor a reduction. In his first annual message to Congress, after expressing a doubt whether the Federalists had been authorized to purchase and improve the several yards, he said: " I have in certain cases suspended or slackened these expenditures, that the legislature might determine whether so many yards are necessary as

[14] Barbary Powers Letters, Navy Dept. Arch., 1-44; General Letters, VIII, 299.

[15] General Letters, Navy Dept. Arch., IV, 321, 362, 400, 458, 516, 518, 524.

have been contemplated." [16] Congress and the Secretary of the Navy investigated and reported upon the subject, but in the end the Federalist purchases were allowed to stand and no reduction in the number of yards was made.

The Republicans were able to effect important economies in the management of the navy-yards by reducing the forces employed in them and by refusing to improve them after the manner contemplated by Adams and Stoddert, who before March 4, 1801, had begun the construction of wharves, shops, and sheds. In October, 1801, the duties of Marbury, the navy agent at Georgetown, District of Columbia, who had been dismissed in July, were vested in Captain Thomas Tingey of the navy, and he was made both navy agent for the district and superintendent of the Washington navy-yard. At Portsmouth, New York, Philadelphia, and Norfolk the naval constructors, clerks of the yard, and naval storekeepers were dismissed, and the yards were placed in the hands of the navy agents, each of whom was permitted to employ an assistant at a salary of $600 a year. Only at Boston were there left in service both a superintendent and a navy agent. Captain Samuel Nicholson, of the navy, who filled the former position, was probably considered too incapacitated by sickness and age to competently act as navy agent; and his gallant Revolutionary services plead too eloquently for him to admit of his removal from the superintendency. In 1804 the four civilian navy agents who were also superintendents received, in addition to their commissions on their purchases, $1200 a year, and were allowed an assistant and a porter.[17]

One of the last naval acts of the Federalist Congress, passed March 3, 1801, appropriated $500,000 to continue the construction of the six 74-gun ships and to complete the navy-yards, docks, and wharves; and $20,000 for the erection of marine barracks. These were the first specific appropriations for navy-yards, docks, and barracks, made by Congress.[18] A considerable part of the $500,-000, the Republicans returned to the treasury unexpended, and but a very small part was devoted to the improvement of the yards. As early as June, 1801, Jefferson, however, ordered $4000 of the sum appropriated for barracks to be paid for " square No. 927 in Washington for the purpose of erecting thereon Barracks

[16] Ford, Jefferson, VIII, 122.
[17] General Letters, Navy Dept. Arch., V, 49, 53-58; VII, 19-23.
[18] U. S. Statutes at Large, II, 122-23.

for the Marine Corps." This lot, which constitutes a part of the present site of the Washington Marine Barracks, is situated near the navy-yard. It was purchased, and the construction of buildings was at once commenced.[19] The making of this expenditure accorded well with Jefferson's desire to promote the improvement of the capital city, and it therefore met his favor.

The navy-yard at Washington was the only one in which Jefferson manifested any particular interest. The seven ships, which the act of March 3, 1801, providing for a naval peace establishment, authorized to be laid up in ordinary, he directed to be brought to the Washington yard and to be laid up in the Eastern Branch, where they would require " but one set of plunderers to take care of them." He made this yard the chief depot of supplies and the repair shop of the navy. By February, 1806, the improvements in it made since its purchase had cost $177,000, a little more than had been spent on all the other yards. The Federalists in New England, and even in Virginia, raised the hue and cry over this diverting of the naval expenditures from home ports and the concentrating of them at a point so inconvenient to the sea as Washington. Jefferson defended his course on the ground that the navy and the naval establishment, which he thought would bear watching, were thus placed under the eye of the government. The inaccessibility and poverty of Washington and its lack of artisans, seamen, and ample naval resources, afforded an excellent opportunity for Randolph's stinging criticism. He declared that ship timbers and naval stores were repeatedly brought from Norfolk and were worked up by men obtained in Baltimore, Philadelphia, and other ports, in order that when worked up they might be returned to Norfolk. The mail coach, he said, carried to Washington for the navy-yard, workmen, live stock, " copper bolts, and such light articles." [20]

Jefferson's plan of erecting a " dry dock " at Washington for the preservation of ships formed a part of his policy of concentrating the navy at the capital. Among other characteristics of this singular and remarkable man was a taste for mechanical inventions, and especially those that promised to effect by a short cut some novel and striking economies or improvements. He

[19] General Letters, Navy Dept. Arch., IV, 343, 410. 425.
[20] State Papers, Naval Affairs, I, 150; Annals of Congress, XIV, 1009; XV, 324; XXI, 1971; Ford, Jefferson, VIII, 338.

doubtless derived the greatest satisfaction in conceiving and maturing the details and principles of his " dry dock." The primary purpose of his invention was not to facilitate the building or repairing of ships, although it was supposed that the dock would prove useful in these respects, but to preserve vessels during long periods of peace by preventing their decay from the action of water, sun, and weather. During peace Jefferson proposed to lay up nearly all the ships of the navy in the " dry dock," and discharge almost the whole force of officers and seamen. By November, 1802, he had worked out his plan with considerable detail. It provided for a lower basin, into which the vessels were to be floated by the tide. Adjoining this and twenty-four feet higher was an upper basin, 800 feet long, and 175 feet wide; and large enough to contain twelve frigates. These were to be raised from the lower to the upper basin by a lock or locks. On discharging the water in the upper basin, the frigates would be left high and dry. They were to be covered by a roof " like that of the *Halle du blé* at Paris, which, needing no Underworks to support it, will permit the Basin to be entirely open and free for the movements of the vessels." Jefferson thought that the water for the locks could be obtained either from the Potomac or from one of the three branches of that river in Washington, the Eastern Branch, Tiber Creek, or Rock Creek. If this dock proved to be successful, a second one was to be built.[21]

Jefferson obtained the services of Benjamin H. Latrobe, who later became one of the architects of the capitol, to make the preliminary surveys and to estimate the cost of the first " dry dock." Latrobe considered Jefferson's plan feasible, and recommended that the dock be constructed on the Eastern Branch. According to his estimate two such docks would cost nearly a million dollars. Beautiful and appropriate drawings, with estimates, which Latrobe prepared, were laid before Congress by the President. When these were considered in January, 1803, various objections were raised. Some members of Congress believed that the dock could not be economically constructed on the Eastern Branch; others thought that the ships would be strained and " wracked " by leaving them out of the water for a long time; and still others doubted whether they could be really preserved

---

[21] General Letters, Navy Dept. Arch., VI, 70-72.

in the dock. It was said that even under shelter, " septic vapors, with moisture, would exert their disorganizing powers " on the older vessels. It was asserted in favor of the dock that Sweden and Venice had constructed similar ones. Although the President considered his project one of great importance to the country and urged upon Congress its adoption, that body refused to follow him, and doubtless exhibited wisdom in its decision.[12]

In deciding all questions of naval policy, the views of Jefferson and Gallatin prevailed. When Robert Smith in the summer of 1801 entered upon the duties of his office, he showed a disposition to make considerable improvements in the navy-yards, somewhat after the manner of the Federalists, but he soon learned in this as well as in all larger naval problems readily to yield to the opinions of the President and his brilliant secretary of the treasury. In the routine work of purchasing naval supplies and of making minor naval appointments, he was given a freer hand. The secretary of the navy at this time attended to many minor details such as are now never brought to his attention, engrossed as he is in the more general and more important duties of his position.

Each winter Smith laid in for his fleet a supply of salt beef and pork. In order to distribute the profits, these provisions were purchased in different states of the Union. In the winter of 1801-1802 Connecticut, New York, Maryland, and North Carolina furnished them. In later years the states on the Western Waters provided some of the meats for the navy. Smith gave his agents in this business the following specific directions in regard to packing the beef: "All the Legs, shins, necks, shoulders, clods, and Leg-rounds must be excluded—the rest of the Beef must be cut in pieces of 10-lb. each, so that 20 pieces will make a barrel—there must be a sufficient quantity of salt petre and it must be inspected and branded agreeably to law. The barrels must be made of white oak heart, and well bound."[23]

A letter of Smith to E. Williams, Hagerstown, Washington County, Maryland, dated May 31, 1806, illustrates still better the petty details upon which the first secretaries of the navy spent their time. It is hardly necessary to say that the " Spirit " to which Smith refers is West India rum.

[22] State Papers, Nav. Aff., I, 104-08; Annals of Congress, XII, 401-410; Ford, Jefferson, VIII, 188.
[23] General Letters, Navy Dept. Arch., V, 96.

" We require for the use of the Navy Yard here and for our Ships in commission, considerable Supplies of beans or peas and butter, and we have heretofore very often experienced considerable difficulties in procuring them. Our present annual consumption is about 1600 bushels of beans or peas, and about 12,500 lbs. of butter. Cannot Washington County supply us? If she can, inform me on what terms. There is, I have understood, a process of putting up butter, known in Washington County, to last for one year, without becoming ranced. If so, I would engage to receive in the month of Novr. or Decr. the whole quantity wanted for the ensuing year.

" The articles of Whiskey and Linseed oil I should suppose Washn. [County] might supply of good qualities and upon reasonable terms. The Sailors are by law allowed Spirit, but being persuaded that Whiskey is a more wholesome drink as well as a much more oeconomical one, I am anxious to introduce the use of it into our Navy generally; but this cannot be immediately effected. I have therefore made experiment to introduce it, and the result has satisfied me that in time the Sailors will become perfectly reconciled to it, and probably prefer it to Spirit. Our annual consumption of Spirit is about 45,000 Gallons. I would for the ensuing year engage 20,000 Gallons of Whiskey, but it must be pure rye whiskey of 3rd or 2nd proof, and one year old, if to be had. This Whiskey I would receive early in the ensuing year." [24]

One of Smith's duties related to the appointment and promotion of midshipmen. This position was exceedingly attractive to ambitious and adventurous youths, who longed for the thrill and romance of a seafaring life, but who knew nothing of its monotonies, its hardships, and its tragedies. Many of the applicants for a midshipman's berth were disappointed in their struggles to attain it. The usual brief formula of the secretary of the navy by which he deferred their hopes read as follows: " Your application for an appointment as midshipman in the navy has been received and filed on the roll of applicants. When vacancies occur in the corps of midshipmen your application shall be considered." Smith insisted that all applications should be accompanied with recommendations from men of worth and note who were personally acquainted with the young men. He once

[24] General Letters, Navy Dept. Arch., VIII, 172.

wrote to the Right Reverend Bishop Carroll of Baltimore, who
had presented the claims of an applicant, that respectable connections, good education, and unexceptionable character, and especially the latter, were essential qualifications for the position. In
a letter to DeWitt Clinton, who had written in behalf of a youth,
and had enclosed a certificate stating that he had a " Good natural
temper," Smith explained that this possession might recommend
the applicant " in private life, but is not sufficient for a military
one." A young man, he said, may be " extremely amiable and
Respectable, yet unqualified for the Navy Service, which requires
a strong Constitution of Body and mind, a high love of Character, and passion for Glory." In appointing midshipmen Smith
tried to attend to the respective claims of the different states, and
in 1808 he wrote that Virginia had her full proportion. In promoting midshipmen he had regard not so much to the seniority of
the appointment, as to fitness, which he determined from the
communications of the commanding officers.[25]

When the Republicans took charge of the navy, the most congenial duty of reducing it to the numbers fixed by the act of
March 3, 1801, providing for a naval peace establishment, fell
to them. In December, Smith reported the sale of sixteen vessels
for $276,000, a sum scarcely sufficient for the purchase of one
first-class frigate. In July, 1801, Jefferson ordered the privates
of the marine corps to be reduced to 400 men. After the reduction, the number of commissioned officers of the corps was 31.
In the navy, the rank of master commandant was discontinued.
The captains were reduced from 28 to 15; the lieutenants, from
110 to 56; and the midshipmen, from 354 to 150. At times the
whole number of officers and men did not greatly exceed 1000.
In April, 1806, the number of able seamen, ordinary seamen,
and boys was fixed by law at 925. In 1801 the Republicans
expended $925,000 less than the Federalists had appropriated for
that year. In 1802 the navy cost but $946,000. Never again
were the expenditures of the United States navy to fall below the
million-dollar mark. In 1800 the Federalists had spent on the
navy $3,385,000.[26]

It was the irony of fate that a President devoted to peace and to retrenchment in naval expenditures should have had to conduct one naval war and to face the probability that others might break out at any time. The war with Tripoli lasted from 1801 to 1806. Its picturesque events, notably Decatur's burning of the *Philadelphia* and Preble's spirited attacks against Tripoli, are familiar to all students of American naval history. During Jefferson's second administration a war with Spain was a possibility; and early in 1809 it was thought that a war with Great Britain could not longer be deferred. These circumstances forced the President after 1802 to gradually increase the naval expenditures. Early in his second administration he began to consider the advisability of building ships of the line, and Gallatin recommended the spending for this purpose of a million dollars a year for several years. To meet the needs of the Tripolitan war seven small vessels, mounting 14 or 16 guns, were built or purchased. In 1806, the rank of master commandant was restored; 9 officers of this rank were authorized, and the number of lieutenants was increased to 72. In December, 1807, the total number of officers and seamen in the navy was 2304. Early in 1809 when a war with Great Britain seemed imminent Congress authorized the President to increase the navy by the addition of 300 midshipmen and 3600 seamen and boys, and to add to the marine corps 784 officers and privates. The appropriations for the navy for 1809 were $2,917,000, but the actual expenditures were considerable less. Since the war clouds soon disappeared, only a small part of the contemplated naval increase was made. Randolph, who was not above juggling with figures to suit his own argument, declared that Jefferson's navy cost in 1808 for each seaman almost twice as much as Adams's. It is true that Jefferson's navy cost for each seaman much more than did that of Adams, but manifestly this is an unfair basis of comparison, for the fixed expenses of the naval establishment vary little with the enlisting or discharging of additional seamen.[*]

The largest naval increase made by Jefferson was at the same time the most useless. The " gunboat policy " was another of his naval inventions. As would the " dry docks," so would the gunboats save the country vast sums of money. These vessels cost

---

[*] Gallatin's Writings, I. 252; Annals of Congress, XXI, 1979, 1993; U. S. Statutes at Large, II. 390, 514, 544, 546; State Papers, Nav. Aff., I, 171.

little to build, and during periods of peace could be hauled up on shore and placed under shelter safe from the ravages of wind, wave, and weather. He found sanction for their use and proof of their value in the naval experiences of Algiers, England, and Russia. The opinions of Generals Horatio Gates and James Wilkinson and Commodores Samuel Barron and Thomas Tingey as to the efficacy of these vessels fortified his own.[28] In 1803 Congress authorized the construction of 15 gunboats; in 1805, 25; in 1806, 50; and in 1807, 188. In 1807 Smith estimated that the defence of the Atlantic coast and of New Orleans would require 257 gunboats.[29] The number of these vessels actually built was 176. The cost of their construction was $1,584,000; the cost of maintaining 24 gunboats in service at New Orleans for one years was $250,-000. Gunboats were built at various ports on the Atlantic coast between Charleston, South Carolina, and Portland, Maine; on Lake Ontario; Lake Champlain; and the Western Waters; and at New Orleans. The first fifteen of them were authorized for the purposes of the Tripolitan war. All the later authorizations were for the protection of the harbors, coasts, and commerce of the United States.[30]

The construction of the first two gunboats was commenced in January, 1804. They were constructed "by way of Experiment and as models." One was built at the Washington navy-yard under the superintendence of Captain John Rodgers; and the other, at Hampton, Virginia, under the direction of Captain James Barron. In conducting their experiments in naval architecture, the two captains had the use of a plan of the gunboats of Messina and of a model of those of Naples.[31] To what extent the vessels that were later constructed followed the two experimental ones is not known. The gunboats varied in size; one of average dimensions was 60 feet long, 17 feet wide, and 6 feet deep. They were manned with twenty-five to forty-five men. They carried one or two large guns, 24-pounders or 36-pounders. They were not at all adapted to deep-sea navigation, nevertheless several of those first built actually made the trip across the Atlantic and took part in the Tripolitan war.

[28] State Papers, Nav. Aff., I, 163.
[29] U. S. Statutes at Large, II, 206, 330, 402, 451.
[30] State Papers, Nav. Aff., I, 194-200.
[31] Gunboat Letters, Navy Dept. Arch., 1-8.

Some of the gunboats were constructed of green timber and soon rotted. Others decayed through disuse and neglect. It took much money to keep them in repair. They could be built in time of war without much difficulty, and whole fleets of them have been so constructed in a few weeks; on the other hand, frigates and ships of the line could be built during a war only at the cost of much time, money, and effort. The service on board these vessels was very unpopular with both officers and seamen, nor did it fit them for duty at sea. It is true that many of Jefferson's gunboats were used in the War of 1812, and that other craft of this type were then built. But the actual protection that they afforded was small. All things considered, the construction of these vessels during 1804-1807 was a blunder and a misdirection of the national resources. As usual, Randolph was the most pungent critic of the administration. " Children must have toys and baubles," he said, " and we must indulge ourselves in an expense of many millions on this ridiculous plaything."[32] Jefferson was loth to learn that his versatile mind was not competent to master naval problems, whose solution belonged to men versed in the naval profession. It is fortunate for his fame that it does not depend upon his work as a naval administrator. In this capacity the only lustre that he acquired sprang from the successful prosecution of the war with Tripoli.

PAUL HAMILTON, 1809-1812, AND WILLIAM JONES, 1813-1814.

On March 4, 1809, James Madison, member of the Virginia line of Republican presidents, and heir to the policy and principles of Jefferson, entered upon his eight years of office. Three days later Paul Hamilton was nominated, confirmed, and commissioned as secretary of the navy. Why Madison should have chosen Hamilton for this position rather than a man of national renown is not known. Hamilton's public service had been confined largely to his own state. Before he was of age he took part in the Revolutionary war. From 1799 to 1806 he served his State first as comptroller and later as governor. This South Carolina gentleman and planter naturally brought to his task in the Navy Department no special knowledge of naval affairs. At this time such a deficiency was regarded as a considerable disqualification, although later it came to be not so considered.

[32] Annals of Congress, XXI, 1972.

The limited and provincial experiences of Hamilton made his outlook upon naval affairs somewhat narrow. Many of his standards, which had been established by a life of great simplicity and integrity, had, however, a wholesome influence upon the navy. The habits of thought, the customs, and the economies, which obtained upon a South Carolina plantation, were far from being amiss when applied to the administration of naval affairs. As secretary of the navy, Hamilton naturally insisted upon economy in naval expenditures, a scrupulous regard for the letter of the law, a conscientious attention to duty on the part of the higher naval officers, and correct habits for the midshipmen. This sober and dignified gentleman took a paternal interest in the young men of the navy. His praiseworthy attempts to form, or reform, their characters must have been often unsuccessful. Once he ordered Captain Tingey to tell several midshipmen, who frequented a public house in Washington and engaged in drinking spirits and playing billiards, " that the eye of the Department is upon them—that such practices will not be permitted—that a perseverance in them will make it my duty to dismiss them—and that I shall not fail to perform my duty on the occasion." [33]

The kindly heart, high sense of duty, and honesty of purpose, of Hamilton are well shown in the following communication, addressed to " Charles W. Goldsborough, First and confidential Clerk." The latter part of the letter is interesting for the light that it throws upon the current work of the department. The letter was dated August 12, 1809, about three months after Hamilton took charge of the Naval Office. The occasion of its writing appears from the context.

" In leaving only for a short time, as I contemplate, my office, I confess that I am not entirely easy, for certainly there are duties and trusts which can consistently with law be under the performance and guidance only of the Head of the Departments. In indulgences similar to that which I mean to take, I am informed have been usual, but they are not the less wrong—the prevalence of error, even universally, cannot constitute it as right.

" Under the influence of these Sentiments, in transferring duties, which properly I alone ought to perform, I am to be excused only by the necessity, which exists of my going to Carolina, for

[33] Navy-yard Letters, Navy Dept. Arch., I, 298.

the purpose of conducting my family to Washington, without whose presence I cannot longer consent to serve the United States; and while I think myself thus to be excused, my mind derives consolation only from the belief that in leaving my responsibility in your hands, I am safe.

" I have not long had the Satisfaction of a knowledge of you, but it has been sufficient to convince me that we are alike actuated by a desire to promote our Country's good, and the honor and dignity of the Department in which we act. This belief is strengthened by not only your faithful coöperations with me in official duties, but by the reputation which has been ascribed to you as a gentleman on whom every reliance may be placed. You know well my ideas as to the grand outlines of our duty, and as the first of these you are apprized that a wholesome oeconomy is to be observed as to disbursements, and that in no instance is an appropriation to be exceeded unless under Sanction of the President, who by Law is authorized to supply the deficiency of one fund from the Surplusage of another. . . . You know my Sentiments as to the equipment for Service of our Ships of War; refuse nothing which may conduce to their efficiency, and watch well the behaviour of our officers; attend also to the Navy Yard at Washington; 'tis a sink of all that needs correction, and if God spares me it shall be rectified; make advances according to your best judgment for a Steam Engine in the Navy Yard here, for a Shed in front of the Blockmaker's Shop, and a Coal oven in this yard; attend to the erection of a Magazine or Powder House here and at Gosport on Latrobe's plan; attend to the Subjects required by Congress at its annual Session, of which are reports of all the Contracts which we have made, and beyond which, but not the less to be attended to, is the requisiton of Mr. Randolph, as the Chairman of the Committee of Enquiry, I have only to add my firm persuasion that you will do your duty for your own sake and our Country's, and that thus you will gratify your mind, and effectually serve and oblige your friend—Paul Hamilton." [84]

In time of peace, with a president who looked at the naval affairs through Jefferson's spectacles, and with a Republican Congress in power that threatened to reduce the fleet to six small ships, Hamilton did not prove unequal to his post. But when the

[84] General Letters, Navy Dept. Arch., X, 71.

War of 1812 began, and there was demanded of the naval secretary decision, initiative, activity, expert knowledge, and skill in the handling of details, Hamilton fell short of the requirements of his position. Certain members of his own party were among his severest critics. In the summer of 1812 James Monroe, Madison's secretary of state, and Ex-president Jefferson agreed that, while the secretary of the navy possessed some merits, a change in the headship of the Navy Department was indispensable.[35] Nathaniel Macon, a Congressman from North Carolina, and a prominent Republican, considered Hamilton " about as fit for his place as the Indian Prophet would be for Emperor of Europe "; and William H. Crawford, a Senator from Georgia, declared that the secretary of the navy was incompetent, and complained that he diverted the naval officers from their proper duties in order to supply the heads of the departments with pineapples and other tropical fruits.[36] One must, however, properly discount criticism of a member of the cabinet, which is made during the heat of a war, when sentiment and self-interest are often more influential than calm reason and unbiased judgment. Nor must it be forgotten that in the winter of 1812-1813 Madison's discredited administration sorely needed some scapegoats in order to appease the clamorous public and to shift the burden of blame. It still remains true that Hamilton did not measure up to the high stature of a successful war secretary.

Hamilton, who contemplated retiring from the cabinet at the end of Madison's first administration, or sooner if peace should be declared, was towards the close of 1812 urged to hasten his departure; and accordingly on December 31 he resigned.[37] On January 8, 1813, Madison nominated William Jones of Philadelphia to the vacant secretaryship. On the 12th Jones was confirmed by the Senate, and on the 25th he entered upon the duties of his office. It is recollected that Jones had been offered the same position by Jefferson in 1801, and had declined it. His appointment was probably as good as his party could supply. Niles' Register in announcing his choice referred to him as Captain William Jones, " an old and experienced seaman." [38] He had had

[35] S. M. Hamilton, Monroe, V, 260.
[36] Adams, History of the United States, VI, 290, 395.
[37] National Intelligencer, January 11, 1813.
[38] Niles' Register, III (1813), 320.

considerable experience at sea, first during the American Revolution on board a privateer with Truxtun, and later in the merchant service. His career for many years as a merchant in Philadelphia was calculated to prepare him for his duties in the Navy Department. He was credited with having a considerable knowledge of gunboats and the arts of naval defence. He possessed information on the subject of shipbuilding, and regarded himself competent to criticise Robert Fulton's plans for a steam frigate. In 1814 he wrote to Fulton that the "principles and practice of Naval Architecture, having been a favourite study and pursuit, may apologize for these criticisms upon a subject on which you have bestowed so much thought." [39] Jones was a member of the American Philosophical Society. He was the author of a pamphlet on the Winter Navigation of the Delaware. Upon resigning from the Navy Department he served without distinction as the first president of the Second National Bank.

The organization of the Navy Department underwent no change under Secretaries Hamilton and Jones. The department still consisted of only two administrative divisions, the secretary's office and the accountant's office. The extra work necessitated by the war caused the force of clerks in the secretary's office to be increased to nine, and in the accountant's office to eleven. Hamilton continued Goldsborough as chief clerk; but Jones soon after entering upon his duties early in 1813 appointed Benjamin Homans, of Massachusetts, to this position. Goldsborough was not connected with the department for the next two years. Thomas Turner, who had been appointed accountant in 1800, continued in service under both secretaries.

The simplicity of the organization and work of the secretary's office is well shown by the duties of Hamilton's four clerks in 1810. The following information is derived from a statement of the secretary of the navy for the use of Congress. C. W. Goldsborough, who was paid a salary of $1900 a year, prepared, from minutes and under the immediate direction of the secretary of the navy, answers to letters received by the department; he made out the exhibits and estimates of the department for the use and information of Congress; and he performed various miscellaneous duties not within the regular routine of the office. Nathaniel

[39] General Letters, Navy Dept. Arch., XII, 158.

G. Maxwell, who was paid an annual salary of $1300, was the "office of detail." He kept the roll of officers, and prepared for signatures and recorded all the naval commissions and warrants of appointments; he also kept a record of all the letters of the department to the officers of the navy; and he endorsed and filed all the letters received, except those relating to the expenditure of money. These latter were in charge of Samuel P. Todd, who for an annual salary of $1300, served as a sort of "bureau of supplies and accounts." He prepared for signature and recorded all warrants for money, endorsed and filed all requisitions, and recorded the estimates and financial statements of the department. The fourth clerk, Conrad Schwartz, for the sum of $800 a year, did numerous odd jobs after copying the letters of the department into the "general letter books." He made copies, drafts, and charts; and translated foreign letters written in German or other European language into English. Hamilton said that the duties of these clerks were at times "extremely arduous and oppressive." [40]

Hamilton is to be credited with obtaining the passage of a most important law relating to the establishment of naval hospitals. In 1799 a law had been enacted authorizing the secretary of the navy to deduct twenty cents a month from the pay of each officer, seaman, and marine of the navy, and to pay the money thus received to the secretary of the treasury. In accordance with an act passed in 1798 a like deduction was made from the wages of each seaman in the merchant service. The whole fund thus realized was applicable to the relief of the sick and disabled officers, seamen, and marines of the navy, and the seamen of the merchant service. The money was expended under the direction of the secretary of the treasury. The navy and the merchant service received the benefits of the fund without discrimination. Their seamen were treated in the same hospitals, by the same doctors, and under the same regulations. The naval hospital service was not at this time separated from the marine hospital service.

In 1810 sick and disabled seamen were relieved at twenty-four of the chief seaports of the Atlantic and Gulf coasts. Only at Norfolk and Boston had marine hospitals been erected. In New York, Philadelphia, Savannah, and New Orleans provision was

[40] Congress Letters, Navy Dept. Arch., I, Dec. 17, 1810.

made for seamen at the city hospitals. At several ports they were boarded at private houses at the expense of the government. At Baltimore the seamen were supplied " under contract with doctor Tobias Watkins with every necessary thing, except cloathing and funeral expenses, at the rate of 55 cents a day for each seaman." At Alexandria, Virginia, they were in part cared for at the alms-house at the rate of $5 a week for each patient.[41]

With such inadequate facilities, no naval officer, and compara-tively few seamen and marines of the navy, took advantage of their right to free medical service. In 1810 at the Marine Hos-pital at Boston the number of inmates during the year averaged twenty-four, one-fifth of whom were seamen of the navy; at Nor-folk only one-ninth of the inmates were from the navy. Where the enlisted men did avail themselves of their rights, incon-veniences and embarrassments arose from placing them, subject as they were to naval law and discipline, in institutions where no such law and discipline were enforced. It was difficult for the department to obtain reports from the officials and doctors of the hospitals, and when the seamen became convalescent they usually deserted. In order better to meet the needs of the navy, the de-partment had permitted the use of several temporary naval hos-pitals. The one at New York was a rude structure situated in the navy-yard. It was proof against neither wind nor water, and was ill-adapted to even the needs of the well. " To give you some faint idea of what is called the hospital on this station," Captain Isaac Chauncey wrote in 1810, " imagine to yourself an old mill, situated upon the margin of a mill pond, where every high tide flows from twelve to fifteen inches upon the lower floor, and there deposits a quantity of mud and sediment, and which has no other covering to protect the sick from the inclemency of the season than a common clap-board outside, without lining or ceiling on the inside. If, sir, you can figure to yourself such a place, you will have some idea of the situation of the sick on this station."[42]

Such was the provision made for the relief of the sick and dis-abled of the American navy when Hamilton in February, 1810, recommended to Congress the separation of the naval and marine hospital services. On February 26, 1811, Congress passed an act

---

[41] Report of the Secretary of the Treasury, 12th Congress, 1st Session, Statement of Expenditures for Sick and Disabled Seamen.

[42] State Papers, Nav. Aff., I, 227-28, 233-34.

establishing naval hospitals. The money raised by deducting twenty cents from the monthly pay of the officers, seamen, and marines of the navy was now to be separated from the money similarly obtained from the seamen of the merchant service, and was to constitute the Naval Hospital Fund. This fund was to be controlled by a board of commissioners composed of the secretary of the navy, secretary of the treasury, and secretary of war. This board was authorized to purchase sites and erect buildings thereon. The secretary of the navy was directed to draft rules and regulations for the government of the naval hospitals.[43] These were in due time prepared by a commission of four naval surgeons, of which Dr. Edward Cutbush was the head. More than twenty years, however, elapsed before any naval hospitals were erected. In the meantime the temporary facilities within or near the navy-yards were extended.

Until early in 1812, when a war with Great Britain became imminent, Hamilton's administration of the navy was more or less uneventful. With the exception of the act establishing naval hospitals, no important naval legislation was enacted. In the spring of 1810 a significant bill was introduced into the House. In April of that year the House voted by a large majority to reduce the naval establishment—yeas 60, nays 31. Accordingly, a bill was reported by John Randolph to reduce the number of vessels in the navy to three frigates and three small craft; to discharge all the officers and seamen except such number as was necessary to man these six vessels; to discontinue the Portsmouth, Philadelphia, and Washington navy-yards, and to decrease the marine corps to two companies. The House spent much time in debating the provisions of this bill, but in the end it was unable to agree upon the reductions, which it had in the beginning voted to make; and the bill was dropped. The fact that a measure of this sort was seriously considered by the House on the eve of a war, and so soon after it had in 1809 voted to increase the navy considerably, convicts that body of marked incapacity of government.[44]

It was in the debate on the above measure that the management of the Washington navy-yard was attacked. Macon of North Carolina wished to continue the yard in order that Congress might

[43] U. S. Statutes at Large, II. 650-51.
[44] Annals of Congress, XXI, 1933.

have in plain sight an object lesson of the evils of a navy. " Sir," exclaimed John Randolph, " as long as a single chip remains in that navy-yard, you will never see anything like reform ; as long as you have a chip of public property—one chip of live oak belonging to the United States—you will have a man riding in his carriage, with a long retinue and deputies and clerks to take care of it." [45] Randolph called the marine barracks in Washington the " Praetorian Camp." So unpopular was the Washington navy-yard, that even Hamilton declared that it was " a sink of all that needs correction, and if God spares me it shall be rectified.". As a part of his work of reform, he considerably reduced the force of men employed there, which had at times been as large as 225 men. He established a naval school at this yard under the esteemed Doctor Andrew Hunter, a chaplain in the navy. He permitted the commandant to employ " twenty good Slaves belonging to the Neighbourhood." [46]

During the War of 1812, not only the six navy-yards which had been purchased by the Federalists, but also several naval stations, were used for the building and repairing of ships, the recruiting of seamen, and the storage of naval supplies. At New Orleans the Government had erected an armory, marine barracks, and some storehouses; and it maintained there a flotilla of gunboats and small armed craft. At Charleston, South Carolina, the department had been renting, for several years prior to the war, certain grounds, which it used for a naval station. In 1813 Secretary Jones was drawn into a considerable altercation over an alleged contract to buy this land. Its owner, Charles B. Cochran, maintained that Hamilton had in 1812 agreed to purchase it for a navy-yard. Jones refused to carry out the alleged contract on the ground that it was unauthorized by law, that the site was utterly unfit for a navy-yard, and that the price stated was at least four times the value of the land.[47] During the war the department had a naval station at Baltimore. From 1798 to 1816 when many naval vessels were built by contract, it is said that Baltimore constructed more ships for the navy than any other city in the Union. In 1810 Hamilton replied favorably to a memorial from the offi-

[45] Annals of Congress, XXI, 1953, 1970.

[46] General Letters, Navy Dept. Arch., X, 72, 301; Navy-yard Letters, I, 98.

[47] General Letters, Navy Dept. Arch., XI, 269.

cials of Annapolis in behalf of a navy-yard for that city, but he explained that nothing could be done at present since the navy was unpopular with Congress.[48]

The naval war on the Lakes during 1812-14 caused the Navy Department to obtain building yards and naval depots on Lakes Ontario, Erie, and Champlain. The most important of these were the grounds at or near Sacketts Harbor on Lake Ontario, consisting of three small lots. They were purchased for the government by Commodore Isaac Chauncey at a cost of $4425.[49] Sacketts Harbor was an exceedingly important naval station throughout the war. It was the rendezvous and headquarters of the American fleet on Lake Ontario. A naval hospital, naval school, and rope-walk were located there. Ten vessels, mounting from 16 to 74 guns, were built at Sacketts Harbor by Chauncey. Here, late in the war, the *New Orleans,* pierced for 100 guns, was placed upon the stocks, but she was never launched. Large quantities of naval supplies were sent to this station from New York city. The construction, manning, and equipping of the fleets on Lakes Ontario and Erie were quite the most brilliant work of its kind performed during the War of 1812. This work fell largely to Chauncey, one of the most efficient officers of the navy. His energy and activity is well shown by the following extract taken from a letter which he wrote to Hamilton from New York. It was dated September 26, 1812, twenty-three days after he received his appointment to the command of the fleet on the Lakes. He gives an account of the artisans, seamen, and naval stores, that were being sent from New York to Sacketts Harbor: " I have sent from this place 140 carpenters, about 700 sailors and marines (every man of which I am proud to say are volunteers), and more than 100 pieces of Cannon, the greater part of which are of a large calibre, with muskets, shot, carriages, etc., etc., and the carriages have nearly all been made and the shot cast since that time [September 3] ; nay, I may say that nearly every article that has been sent forward has been made." [50]

The ship-yard for Lake Erie was early in the war located at Black Rock, on the Niagara river; but Chauncey soon removed it to Erie, on Lake Erie. Many ship carpenters, seamen, and naval

[48] General Letters, Navy Dept. Arch., X, 328-29.
[49] Congress Letters, Navy Dept. Arch., IV, 249.
[50] Captains' Letters, Navy Dept. Arch., 1812, III, 79.

supplies were sent from Philadelphia to Erie. Naval stores of all sorts were also purchased in Pittsburg. George Harrison, the navy agent at Philadelphia, who had general charge of the forwarding of men and supplies to Erie, employed a sub-agent at Pittsburg. Commodore Perry's two famous vessels, the *Niagara* and *Lawrence,* were built at the ship-yard at Erie. The building yard on Lake Champlain was situated at Vergennes, Vermont.

The regular navy agents employed at the chief Atlantic ports and at New Orleans were of course continued in service. At the beginning of the war additional agents became necessary, and they were appointed for several of the smaller Atlantic ports, and one for Niagara, New York. In 1812 an agent was chosen for Tennessee to purchase flour, hemp, and whiskey for the New Orleans naval station. The work of the navy agents, which consisted chiefly of the purchasing of naval supplies of all sorts, was greatly increased by the war.

It is recollected that in 1801 the navy-yards at Portsmouth, New York, Philadelphia, and Norfolk were placed under the superintendence of the navy agents at those ports, and that the Boston and Washington yards were permitted to remain in charge of naval officers. Gradually the civilian control of the four former yards was superseded by a naval one. The head of each navy-yard came to be called the " commandant," instead of the " superintendent "; and naval law and discipline was enforced in all the yards. In 1807 the New York yard received its first naval commandant in the person of Captain Isaac Chauncey. In 1810 Captain Samuel Barron took charge of the Norfolk yard, succeeding the Norfolk navy agent; and in 1813 the Portsmouth and Philadelphia yards were placed under naval captains. No civilian has served in the capacity of superintendent of a navy-yard since 1813. The New York yard greatly increased in importance during the war. The Washington yard lost its primacy among the establishments of the navy. After it was burned by the British in 1814, it never regained its former rank. The disaffection of New England towards the war and the Union rather decreased the value of the Boston and Portsmouth yards to the federal government. The relative importance of the several navy-yards is roughly indicated by the number of employees at work in them. In November, 1814, the number of officers and men employed at the Portsmouth yard was 18; at the Boston yard, 20; at the New York yard, 102; at the Philadelphia yard, 13; at the Washington yard, 36; and at the Norfolk yard, 33.[31]

The imminence of a war with Great Britain naturally revived the consideration of the subject of dry docks. During peace, under the naval régime of Jefferson, dry docks could be dispensed with; but in time of war, when expedition was important and the fleet was greatly augmented, they were almost indispensable. In December, 1811, Hamilton informed Congress of the navy's deficiency. He wrote as if conveying a piece of news: "The United States do not own a dock. To repair our vessels we are compelled to heave them down—a process attended with great labor, considerable risk, and loss of time; and upon a ship thus hove down, the carpenters cannot work without much inconvenience. Hence the Department is subjected to much expense, which might be avoided by the construction of one or more suitable docks." [32]

Finally, on March 3, 1813, Congress appropriated $100,000 to establish a dock yard at some central and convenient place on the seaboard.[33] After making a general inquiry as to the best site, Secretary Jones decided in favor of the right bank of the Hudson above the Highlands. He said that "the motives to this decision were from considering the contemplated dock yard as the nucleus around which a great naval establishment may be formed, comprising wet and dry docks, forges, foundries, boring, rolling, saw, and block mills, blast and smelting furnaces, an armory, hydraulic engines, rope walks, manufactories of sail duck, and work shops of all kinds, which will require a copious head of water, readily commanded in this vicinity. Here also will be the main arsenal, and depot of timber and materials of all kinds, and the principal dock yard for constructing and repairing ships of war. Such an establishment in any of our seaports, accessible to ships of the line, would form so great a temptation to a powerful enemy as to render destruction certain, unless protected by forts and garrisons of the most formidable and expensive nature." [34] The blockade of the Atlantic coast, which the British had by this time effected, admonished Jones to locate his contemplated establishment at a safe distance from the coast. Occurring in the midst of a war,

---

[31] State Papers, Nav. Aff., I, 325-45.
[32] State Papers, Nav. aff., I, 249.
[33] U. S. Statutes at Large, II, 821.
[34] State Papers, Nav. Aff., I, 306.

nothing naturally came from this agitation in behalf of dry docks. It was no time to build them, to do the work that ought to have been done in time of peace. The failure of the Republicans to establish and construct dry docks during the ten years preceding the War of 1812 may be set down as another instance of their incapacity of government.

In the winter of 1811-1812 on the eve of the war with Great Britain, the Navy Department was unprepared in every essential means, instrument, and material of naval warfare. It had no dry docks. It had few ships. With the exception of the naval establishment at Washington, the navy-yards were in a state of neglect and decay. The navy had few conveniences for building, repairing, and laying up ships. In December, 1811, Secretary Hamilton informed Congress that the present stock of cannon ball, shot of every description, carronades, muskets, pistols, rifles, blunderbusses, and gunpowder was inconsiderable. The blame for this unfortunate state of affairs rests upon Presidents Jefferson and Madison and Congress, rather than upon the two Republican Secretaries of the Navy, Smith and Hamilton, who moderately favored the strengthening of the navy. Early in 1811 Hamilton had said that many measures of vast importance for the defence of the country might be effected, were the navy not unpopular with Congress. In November, 1811, he made his first preparations for war by buying a little saltpetre and sulphur. But for want of money, he could do little. He therefore appealed to Congress. On December 10 he asked for $400,000 to purchase arms and ammunition; and on January 14, 1812, Congress gave it to him.[55] Almost the only timber in the navy-yards was that which had been purchased by the department under Stoddert. On March 30 Congress therefore appropriated $200,000 annually for three years to buy timber for the repairing and building of ships. On the same day it voted $300,000 to repair and equip the frigates *Chesapeake, Constellation, and Adams*. On July 5 it appropriated $829,000 for purchasing and equipping vessels captured from the enemy, and for repairing vessels damaged by war. This Congress also voted to spend $1,000,000 on fortifying the maritime frontier.[56]

---

[55] Congress Letters, Navy Dept. Arch., II, 63; U. S. Statutes at Large, II, 675.

[56] U. S. Statutes at Large, II, 675, 692, 699, 776.

It is noteworthy that the war Congress, which was in session from November, 1811, until July, 1812, did not authorize the building of ships. It was not able to pass so radical a measure. Soon, however, the shock of actual war, the pressure of military necessity, the rebound of public opinion, and the patriotism aroused by glorious victories on the sea, effected a revolution in naval sentiment in and out of Congress. In the winter of 1812-13 conservative members continued to oppose energetic measures of naval defense, but they were not able to prevent the passage of the law of January 2, 1813, which appropriated $2,500,-000 to build four ships of the line and six frigates.[57] From this time until the end of the war various other measures designed to increase and strengthen the navy were passed by Congress. The last act was that of November 15, 1814, which appropriated $600,-000 for the construction or purchase of twenty small vessels of from 8 to 16 guns each.[58] The war caused the expenditures of the navy to increase as follows: from $1,970,000 in 1811 to $3,960,000 in 1812; to $6,450,000 in 1813; to $7,310,000 in 1814; to $8,660,-000 in 1815. In 1816 the expenditures fell to $3,910,000.[59]

At the beginning of 1812 the navy consisted of eighteen vessels. Three of these were frigates, which had been built by the Federalists, and needed much repairing. The remaining fifteen were ready for sea. Seven of the fifteen, chiefly frigates, and mounting 254 guns, had belonged to the Federalist navy of 1798-1801; and eight, chiefly brigs, mounting 122 guns, had been built or purchased by Jefferson or Madison. The larger and the effective part of the navy of 1812 the Republicans inherited from the Federalists. In addition to the above fleet, there were 165 gunboats, which had been constructed by Jefferson. Of these, at the beginning of 1812, 63 were in commission, and 102 were in ordinary or undergoing repairs. The gunboats were stationed at the chief Atlantic ports from St. Mary's, Georgia, to Portland, Maine, and at New Orleans. Fifty-four of them were at New York, 26 at New Orleans, 20 at Philadelphia, and lesser numbers at other ports. Such was the naval force with which Madison began a war with the chief European naval power.[60]

[57] U. S. Statutes at Large, II, 789.
[58] U. S. Statutes at Large, III, 144.
[59] Senate Ex. Docs. 45th Long. 1st Sess., No. 3, 156.
[60] State Papers, Nav. Aff., I, 249, 250, 252.

When the war ended the navy comprised about 75 armed vessels of from 10 to 74 guns each, and about 240 gunboats, barges, and other small naval craft. The additions to the navy were made by construction, purchase, or capture. Of the vessels authorized under the act of January 2, 1813, three 74's and three 44's were built at the principal navy-yards, but they were not completed in time to be of use during the war. The 74-gun ship *Columbia*, when almost ready to be launched, was burned, at the Washington navy-yard, to prevent its being captured by the enemy. When the treaty of peace was signed, two 74's and two 44's were on the stocks at Sackett's Harbor. Some 60 vessels, largely insignificant craft, comprised the fleet on the Lakes. More than 200 gunboats, barges, and small craft were stationed at the chief Atlantic ports and at New Orleans.[61]

During the War of 1812 the repairing of vessels was an important activity of the Navy Department. Such work, in a few instances, was comparable to that of building a new vessel. One of the old frigates, which required a complete overhauling was the *Adams*. Apropos of the repairing of this ship is the following account of " A Launch," which was printed in the National Intelligencer of December 29, 1812, published at Washington: " On Thursday last, about half past 11 o'clock was launched from the Navy Yard at this City, the frigate *Adams,* which had been hauled up, divided in the middle, lengthened fifteen feet, and almost rebuilt. She proudly swam into her destined element at the appointed time, amid the acclamations of hundreds, and under a salute of artillery. After the launch many of the ladies and gentlemen assembled in a sail-loft, which had been cleaned for the occasion, and spent a pleasant hour. The *Adams* is to be commanded by capt. Morris." In the above account the Intelligencer, according to present standards, omitted a valuable piece of news, the presence on this interesting occasion of the President and members of Congress. This fact is proved by the following anecdote: When the frigate *Adams* glided off the stocks a Federalist member of Congress opposed to the administration, abruptly said to President Madison, with whom he was standing, " What a pity it is, sir, that the vessel of state won't glide as smoothly in her course as this vessel does." " It would, sir," Madison replied, " if the crew would do their duty as well." [62]

[61] State Papers, Nav. Aff., I, 305-09, 379-80.
[62] National Intelligencer, December 29, 1812; January 18, 1813.

Some historians of the War of 1812 have greatly overestimated the numbers of the personnel of the American navy. The total number of officers, seamen, and marines at the close of the war was about twice the number at its commencement. In December, 1811, the number of seamen and boys in the navy was 4010; and the number of marines, exclusive of commissioned officers, was 1823. The navy was probably as large in October, 1814, as at any time during the war. Secretary Jones then estimated the total force, exclusive of a few stationary marines, at 10,617. The Navy Lists for 1812 and 1815 show the increase in the numbers of officers caused by the war. The captains increased from 12 to 30; the masters commandant, from 9 to 17; the lieutenants, from 70 to 146; and the midshipmen, from 403 to 436. The number of commissioned officers in the marine corps in 1812 was 38; and in 1815, 59. In April, 1814, the number of marine was increased by 799. The number of seamen in the navy was throughout the war much below the needs of the service. In October, 1814, Secretary Jones estimated that 15,200 officers, seamen, and marines would be needed for the coming year.[63]

There was, however, no dearth of officers. The requests for offices in the navy were so many that, in order to preserve the time of the department for more important work, Jones established the rule that no applications for office should be answered. The applicants for the position of midshipman were especially numerous, and at the end of the war the files of the department showed that upwards of one thousand youths had been disappointed. Requests for employment were sometimes made by veterans of the Revolution. These always touched the kindly heart of Secretary Hamilton. For a veteran, Hamilton once wrote an order to Captain Tingey, commandant of the Washington navy-yard. The bearer, he informed Tingey, is " an old revolutionary officer for whom I wish to make some provision in the Navy Yard. He is too old to labor now, and he must not want. You will consider of some place in which his fidelity may be of use to the public, and report the same to me." [64]

A disproportionate share of the appointments of officers to the navy was made from Maryland, Virginia, and the District of

---

[63] State Papers, Nav. Aff., I, 255, 265; Private Letters, Navy Dept. Arch., 1813-1840, 196-202; U. S. Statutes at Large, 124-25.

[64] Navy-yard Letters, Navy Dept. Arch., I, 224.

Columbia. Of the 240 captains, masters commandant, lieutenants, and marine officers, whose names are printed in the Navy Register for 1816, 38 per cent were born in the above section. Of all the states of the Union, Maryland furnished the largest number, 46; and Virginia, the next largest number, 42.[65] The location of the Navy Department and the chief navy-yard in this section of the Union accounts in part for its large representation in the navy. Doubtless, too, Secretaries Stoddert and Smith and Presidents Jefferson and Madison were disposed to favor their own states in making appointment.

Jones cordially welcomed inventors of naval appliances and improvements, and gave them such financial encouragement as the limited resources of the department warranted. His knowledge of naval architecture made him an intelligent critic of some of these real or alleged inventions. He consulted his naval officers upon such subjects as came within their special knowledge, and at times had them report on the experiments and tests of the inventors. He ordered Captain Decatur to be present at the trial of an inflammable liquid, which was to be used in destroying the enemy's ships. He authorized a "multiplied repeating swivel, and a repeating musket and pistol" to be tried on board the vessels composing the flotilla on the Delaware. Jones approved of Uriah Brown's submarine boat. He gave Robert Fulton financial aid for three different inventions, a torpedo, a steam frigate, and a "bullet proof boat." Several of Fulton's torpedoes were manufactured at the Washington navy-yard. One of his steam frigates, *Fulton the First*, was built at New York; and another was begun at Baltimore. The department purchased one of his "bullet proof boats." These inventions, however, owing to their imperfections and the ending of the war when they were being brought into use, were of little value to the government.[66]

During the War of 1812 the Navy Department had constantly in view three main objects, the defending of the maritime frontier, the maintaining of the naval superiority on the Lakes, and the capturing of the enemy's small vessels of war and merchantmen at sea. Most American writers of the naval history of the War of 1812 have treated very briefly, or omitted altogether, the naval

[65] Roosevelt, Naval War of 1812, I, 55-56.
[66] General Letters, Navy Dept. Arch., XI, 265; XII, 158, 183, 258; Private Letters, 1813-1840, 39, 63; Miscellaneous Letters, 1814, VI, 72.

preparations and operations in defense of the Atlantic and Gulf coasts; and have confined their attention almost exclusively to the two latter objects enumerated above. The defense of the maritime frontier possesses few attractive features, and its study at most points is not conducive to national pride. Nevertheless, the fitting out and manning of vessels at the chief Atlantic ports and at New Orleans and the directing of their movements, for the purpose of defending the American seacoast, was a work of great importance and difficulty to the head of the Navy Department, and demanded much of his time and attention. At least one-half of the navy was employed in this way. Of the 10,617 men that constituted the entire naval force in October, 1814, 6512 were on the maritime frontier; 3260, on the Lakes; 450, at sea; and 405, in British prisons.[67]

The seamen on the maritime frontier were chiefly attached to the various flotillas, composed of gunboats, barges, and other small naval craft; some of them, however, were employed on board ships of war, and, owing to the close blockade which the British maintained during 1813-14, were much to their disgust detained in port and were compelled to assist in defending the coast. A flotilla was stationed at or near each of the following ports: New Orleans, St. Mary's in Georgia, Charleston, Wilmington, Norfolk, Baltimore, Philadelphia, New York, New London, Newport, Boston, and Portsmouth. Each flotilla was under the command of a naval officer, who sometimes reported to the commander of an adjacent naval station. The nucleui of these flotillas were collections of Jefferson's gunboats.

When the British blockaded the American coast and began to ravage it, a cry for naval protection was sent forth from Maine to Georgia. The same men who opposed naval expenditures during peace now blamed the government for not supplying naval ships that it did not have and could not get. Numerous requests for armed vessels were made of the secretary of the navy. He responded to as many of them as the limited resources of the department permitted. Early in 1812 Congress appropriated $1,000,000 for the defense of the maritime frontier. It also appropriated $750,000 for the construction of barges and floating batteries to be used for the same purpose.[68] Numerous small craft

[67] Private Letters, Navy Dept. Arch., 1813-1840, 196-202.
[68] U. S. Statutes at Large, III, 3, 104.

carrying a few heavy guns were added to the various flotillas. Each locality coöperated with the Federal government in the work of defense. This service on the seacoast was, however, unpopular with both officers and seamen, for it was not suited to their habits or comforts; nor was either glory or prizes to be obtained in it. To man the vessels was difficult, and often impossible. The log-book of a certain gunboat records the fact that after much diffi-culty two men only were enlisted—" from the jail, with a paren-thetical memorandum to the effect that they were both very drunk." [69] The usefulness of the flotillas was greatly impaired owing to the want of seamen. These little fleets, however, were able to supplement the land defenses, and to check to some extent the ravages of small British ships on the coast. But they offered little resistance to strong fleets. They did not prevent the enemy from making frequent depredations. No better proof of the inef-fectual character of their work is needed than that afforded by the raid of the British in August, 1814, when they destroyed Barney's flotilla and burned Washington.

The most uniformly successful work during the war of both the Navy Department and the navy was the obtaining and hold-ing of the naval superiority on Lakes Ontario, Erie, and Cham-plain. The martial deeds of Commodores Perry and Macdonough have been amply celebrated. But the achievements of the Navy Department and of Commodore Chauncey in providing the in-struments and sinews of war are equally noteworthy, although less dramatic. With much energy and expedition they con-structed fleets from the trees standing in the forests, hastened for-ward artisans, armament, and naval stores of all sorts from the seaports, and enlisted seamen wherever they could be obtained. At times both the service on the maritime frontier and at sea yielded to that on the Lakes. In 1814 in order to man the fleets of Commodores Chauncey and Macdonough, heavy drafts of men were made on the flotilla service, and rendezvous for recruits were opened in various seaports. Ships which had been destined for the sea were laid up in ordinary, and their armaments and crews were sent to the Lakes. The Lake service, however, was not liked. Secretary Jones wrote that it was " one of peculiar priva-tion, destitute of pecuniary stimulus, and unpopular both with the Officers and Men." While but 3250 sailors were employed

[69] Roosevelt, Naval War of 1812, 45.

on the Lakes during 1814, he estimated that 7000 would be needed in 1815. Many additional seamen were required to man the new ships. The contest on Lake Ontario, Jones said in October, 1814, had become a "warfare of Dockyards and Arsenals." [70]

The Muse of history, national pride, and popular tradition have vied with each other in perpetuating the fallacy that the American navy inflicted serious injury on the British navy in the War of 1812. During 1812-1815 the Americans captured 23 British naval vessels of from 10 to 38 guns each; and the British captured 17 American naval vessels of from 10 to 44 guns each—not including the ships burned at the Washington navy-yard. Of the 23 British ships captured by the Americans, four were taken by Perry on Lake Erie, four by Macdonough on Lake Champlain, and four were captured after the treaty of Ghent was signed. Of the eleven remaining vessels, the five principal ones were captured during the latter half of 1812.[71] In 1813 and 1814, owing to the British blockade of the American coast, the naval war on the ocean almost ceased; the little that existed was in favor of the British. No vessel captured from the enemy was so heavily armed as the *Serapis*, 44, the Revolutionary prize of John Paul Jones. In 1812 the Royal Navy consisted of 130 ships of the line, mounting from 60 to 120 guns, and 600 frigates and smaller vessels. The value of the twenty-three ships captured by the Americans was not equal to that of two of England's best ships of the line. Of course these figures do not depreciate the skill and courage of the American commanders, nor dim the glory and prestige that they won for the American navy. The striking success of the American ships in the engagements between the *Constitution* and *Guerriere,* the *Essex* and *Alert,* the *Wasp* and *Frolic,* the *United States* and *Macedonian,* and the *Constitution* and *Java* will ever make the latter half of 1812 a memorable time in our naval history. It is also true that the moral effect of the brilliant fighting of the American navy was greatly to the advantage of the government at Washington, and to the disadvantage of that at London.

The exact determination of the department early in 1812 in respect to sending the vessels to sea is still involved in obscurity. It has been asserted that the cabinet sometime during the first

[70] Private Letters, Navy Dept. Arch., 1813-1840, 196-202.
[71] Emmons, Navy of the United States, 6-11, 18-21, 56-59.

half of 1812, deeming it unwise to jeopardize our small ships in
a contest with the gigantic British navy, decided that the American fleet should be laid up in ordinary for the period of the war;
and that Captains Bainbridge and Stewart drew up a remon-
strance, which led the secretary of the navy to abandon this policy
of prudence and fear. Considerable doubt has now been cast on
the accuracy of this story. It is certain that on June 22, 1812,
Hamilton ordered the fleet to be divided into squadrons and to
cruise off the Atlantic coast for the protection of American commerce. In September the fleet was arranged in three squadrons
of three vessels each, and they were ordered to proceed to sea.
After 1812 the ships usually cruised singly, since the close blockade, which the British maintained off the chief American ports,
interfered with the sending out of squadrons.[72]

The movements of the secretary of the navy and the Navy Department during the raid of the British on Washington, in
August, 1814, are, in the annals of the department, wholly unique
and exceptional. It is appropriate that a brief account of them
should be here given. They form a part of a most interesting
melodrama, whose principal characters are the President of the
United States and the dignified members of his cabinet. The
destruction of the Washington navy-yard is one of the thrilling
features. Jones's report of his own movements, which were most
numerous, varied, and rapid, will be followed. By August 22
Commodore Joshua Barney, having burned his "American Flotilla" on the Patuxent in Maryland, had retreated with his seamen and marines towards Washington. He was closely followed
by a small detachment of British troops under General Ross. On
the night of the 22nd Barney and General Winder, who commanded the American troops, camped at Old Fields in Maryland,
seven miles from Washington. Jones writes in respect to his own
movements on the 22d as follows: " In the evening of that day
I accompanied the President to General Winder's Camp at the
Old Fields, and passed the night in Commodore Barney's tent—
the Army of the Enemy at Upper Marlborough eight miles
distant—on the morning of the 23rd reviewed the Seamen and
Marines, whose appearance and preparation for battle promised

[72] Harris, Commodore Bainbridge, 135-36; Gallatin's Writings, II,
611-22; Officers' Letters, Ships of War, Navy Dept. Arch., X, 66; Navy-
yard Letters, I, 329; John Rodgers Papers.

all that could be expected from cool intrepidity, and a high state of discipline." On the afternoon of the 23rd Jones and Madison returned to the capital. The army and the navy frightened by the advance of the British now made a sudden retreat and reached Washington not long after the arrival of the Secretary of the Navy and the President. The military and naval forces rested near the navy-yard and the adjacent bridge across the Eastern Branch of the Potomac.

On the 24th the battle of Bladensburg was fought, and the British entered the capital. Bladensburg is situated on the Eastern Branch, about five miles from Washington. Let us return again to Jones's narrative: "On the morning of the 24th I proceeded to General Winder's quarters at Doctor Hunter's house near the Eastern Branch Bridge, where the President and Secretaries of War, State, and Treasury soon after arrived. I found Commodore Barney employed by order of the General in planting his Battery on the hill near the head of the Bridge. He was charged to defend that pass and to destroy the Bridge on the appearance of the Enemy, for which purpose Scows and Boats with combustible materials were placed under the Bridge ready to explode. At this time the Enemy was apparently advancing on the road to the Bridge; but shortly after advice was received that he had turned off on the road towards Bladensburg." General Winder with his troops now hastily marched to Bladensburg in order, if possible, to head off the British, leaving Barney and his force of seamen and marines to guard the bridge. "It was soon observed that a very efficient part of the force had been left to destroy the Eastern Branch Bridge, which could as well be done by a half dozen men, as by five hundred. The subject was discussed by the President, Heads of Departments, and Commodore Barney, which resulted in the order for his immediate and rapid march to join the army near Bladensburg. Captain Creighton was left in charge of the Bridge to destroy it on the near approach of the Enemy." Jones now presented to the President and his cabinet the subject of the navy-yard; and it was agreed that, if the enemy should approach the city, the Secretary of the Navy should order all the buildings, naval stores, and ships in the yard, to be destroyed, rather than let them fall into the hands of the British.

At two o'clock in the afternoon Jones was to be again found at the Washington navy-yard. He ordered the commandant, Captain Tingey, to prepare trains of powder, and to touch them off on the approach of the enemy. The battle of Bladensburg resulted in the complete rout of the Americans, who, with the exception of Barney's seamen and marines, made an ill-conceived and half-hearted resistance. The British now advanced upon Washington. As they entered the city, Captain Tigney at half-past eight o'clock in the evening set fire to the navy-yard. The next day the British continued its destruction. The most valuable parts of the yard were destroyed. The whole loss was estimated at $418,000. The largest single item of loss was the 74-gun ship *Columbia,* valued at $106,000. Some days before the invasion the Secretary of the Navy had ordered the gunpowder, lighter stores, and smaller vessels to be removed to a point of safety northward of the city, but few materials were thus saved.

Soon after Jones retired from the navy-yard on the afternoon of the 24th, he heard that the enemy was moving towards Washington from Bladensburg; and a little later at the house of Charles Carroll he received a message from Madison requesting him to follow and join the party of the President, which had already crossed the Potomac at Georgetown. Jones and the Attorney-General followed the fortunes of their retreating chief. The party travelled until dark and spent the night on the Virginia side of the Potomac a few miles above the Lower Falls. The next day it reached a little Virginia tavern, situated in the midst of an apple orchard, sixteen miles from Washington, where it rested. On the evening of the 25th the British, having occupied the capital for twenty-four hours, left it. On the 28th the Secretary of the Navy returned to Washington; and his week of melodrama came to an end. The "old war office," which had housed the Navy Department since 1801, was among the public buildings destroyed by the British. Jones rented temporary quarters for the department.[73]

The movement of the Navy Department during these troublous times is best told in the words of Benjamin Homans, its chief clerk: "In obedience to instructions from the Secretary of the Navy to prepare for the removal and safety of the Public Documents and Archives of the Navy Department on Saturday, the 20th day of August, 1814, and anticipating a difficulty in pro-

[73] Congress Letters Navy Dept. Arch., II, 271-80, 294-98; Cutts, Dolly Madison, 99-118; Adams, History of the United States, VIII, 120-168.

curing Waggons, he sanctioned the transportation by Water in
Boats up the Potomac River. On Sunday three of the Clerks
were employed packing up in Boxes and Trunks, all the Books of
Record, Papers, Library, Maps, Charts, Plans, Stationery,
Trophies, various valuable Instruments, Paintings, Prints, etc.,
ready for removal on the next day. And in the evening of Sunday, the 21st August, two River Boats with their Crews were
engaged for the purpose at the ordinary Wages.

"On Monday, the 22nd August, two of the City Carts were
engaged, and all the Boxes and Articles in the Navy Department
(heavy Desks and furniture excepted) were put on board the
Boat at the nearest Wharf to the Offices, and at 4 P. M. proceeded
up the River as far as Georgetown. In the forenoon of Monday,
the 22nd, two large Waggons with drivers presented themselves
at the Department for employ, and on account of the previous
arrangements, to transport by Water, they were transferred to
the Accountant of the Navy Department, who loaded them with
the Effects of his Office.

"On Tuesday, the 23rd August, the Chief Clerk with one of
the Clerks of the Department proceeded up the River Potomac,
and passed through the Locks and Canal to a place of safety.
There was no difficulty in procuring more boats, and men enough
to navigate them up the River above the Falls." [74]

Secretary Jones found his duties arduous and confining; nor
did his management of the department escape adverse criticism.
By April, 1814, he had decided to retire from the cabinet, because
of the indispensable attention that his private affairs required.[75]
The position of secretary of the navy has always been vastly
more attractive to the candidate seeking it, than to the incumbent
performing its duties. Each of the first four secretaries, Stoddert, Smith, Hamilton, and Jones, longed for more congenial
work. Jones would not wait until the war was ended. On September 11, 1814, he tendered his resignation to take effect on
December 1. On the latter date he turned over the keys of the
department to its chief clerk.

[74] Congress Letters, Navy Dept. Arch., II, 299-300.
[75] Ingersoll, History of the Second War between Great Britain and
the United States, 2d ser., II, 326; Madison's Writings, ed. 1865, II,
581-82.

CHAPTER FIVE: THE NAVY COMMISSIONERS, 1816-1842

The Personnel of the Navy Department.

The American navy during the War of 1812 fought itself into public favor and convinced the nation at the cannon's mouth of its value and importance. During and immediately after this war the navy for the first time found itself popular with Congress and the people. The nascent spirit of nationalism now demanded a naval armament. The Republicans, admonished by both victories and defeats, faced right about, and seemed to admit, as did Robert Y. Hayne, several years later that the naval policy of Jefferson was a delusion.[1] They no longer argued, as they often did before 1812, that the addition of ships to a minor navy in effect added vessels to a superior one, for in case of a naval war, the vessels of the former must necessarily fall into the hands of the latter. The new arguments which were now upon their lips seemed as if drawn from the armory of the elder Adams. " The destinies of the nation," the Secretary of the Navy declared in February, 1815, " appear to be intimately connected with her maritime power and prosperity; and as the creation of a Navy is not a work to be quickly performed, it seems necessary not only to cherish our existing [naval] resources, but to augment them gradually and steadily." In December of that year he recommended that five ships be annually added to the national fleet. President Madison was in general accord with his Secretary of the Navy.[2] A new period in the history of the American navy had opened.

---

[1] Cong. Debates, IV, 350.
[2] Cong. Letters, Navy Dept. Arch., II, 367-369; State Papers, Nav. Aff., I, 365-366; Richardson, Messages and Papers of the Presidents, 566-567.

During the twenty-seven years extending from 1815 to 1842, nine men filled the office of Secretary of the Navy. Their average term was three years. Their names and periods of service were as follows: Benjamin W. Crowninshield, of Massachusetts, 1815-1818; Smith Thompson, of New York, 1819-1823; Samuel L. Southard, of New Jersey, 1823-1829; John Branch, of North Carolina, 1829-1831; Levi Woodbury, of New Hampshire, 1831-1834; Mahlon Dickerson, of New Jersey, 1834-1838; James K. Paulding, of New York, 1838-1841; George E. Badger, of North Carolina, 1841; and Abel P. Upshur, of Virginia, 1841-1843. Of these nine men, all except Crowninshield and Paulding were lawyers; and rather oddly, jurists, since they had served as judges in the courts of their respective States. Only four of the nine had served in Congress—Southard, Branch, Woodbury, and Dickerson. These lawyers and jurists, when first called upon to perform the unfamiliar duties of their office, sometimes made amusing blunders. Secretary Branch actually resolved to send a frigate into the Pacific Ocean to pass Cape Horn in the month of June in order that it might have the benefit of a summer passage; and once he gravely asked an officer of the navy on what part of the coast of South America the island of Barbadoes was situated.[3] At a dinner, given shortly after Southard received his appointment as Secretary of the Navy, Chief Justice Kirkpatrick of New Jersey, twitting this landsman on his ignorance of the sea, exclaimed, " Now, Mr. Southard, can you honestly assert that you know the bow from the stern of a frigate "?[4]

Not until after 1820 did political, personal, and geographical considerations become all-important in the selection of Secretaries of the Navy. The early presidents had a conviction that the head of the Navy Department should possess a knowledge of maritime or mercantile pursuits; and at least four of the first five secretaries had such a knowledge. It was supposed that men of this sort were better fitted to administer naval affairs than lawyers, judges, or statesmen. President Madison once offered the secretaryship to Commodore John Rodgers, one of the most skillful and efficient officers of the Old Navy, who at the time lacked but one number of being at the head of the navy list. When Crownin-

[3] J. Q. Adams, Memoirs, VIII, 354.
[4] Appleton's Cyclopedia, V, 613.

shield vacated the department in 1818, Rodgers was again offered the office, and he again declined it; naturally preferring his rank and permanent tenure in the navy. Before President Monroe finally chose Smith Thompson, John Quincy Adams, the Secretary of State, recommended Thomas Worthington, late governor of Ohio, as a suitable candidate from the Western States, and as " having once been a seafaring man."[5]

Benjamin W. Crowninshield, 1815-1818, was the last of the old line of secretaries. He and his brother Jacob, to whom Jefferson had offered the naval portfolio in 1805, were merchants of Salem, Massachusetts, when the sails of Salem's ships of trade whitened every sea. Early in life each of the two brothers had commanded East Indiamen. Crowninshield's successor, Smith Thompson, 1818-1823, first of the legal and juridical line of secretaries, found his position in the Navy Department a convenient stepping-stone from the Supreme Court of New York, which he left in 1818, to the Supreme Court of the United States, to which he was elevated in 1823. Levi Woodbury, 1831-1834, who had a most remarkable career as judge, senator, and cabinet officer, also reached the Supreme Bench, but in his case some years after he left the Navy Department.

That the two North Carolina lawyers and jurists, John Branch, 1829-1831, and George E. Badger, 1841, should have been invited to administer the navy, illustrates the fact that politics, and not a practical knowledge of the marine, had become the controlling factor in choosing naval secretaries. North Carolina was for many years unfriendly to the navy. Her lack of important seaports, and therefore of wide commercial and maritime interests, caused her to be behind her sister State, South Carolina, in naval sentiment. The services of Branch and Badger in the Navy Department are not especially important. Branch's naval policy was one of retrenchment and reform. The social dissensions of Jackson and his cabinet over Mrs. Eaton caused Branch to drag his anchor in the department, and he was expelled from the cabinet in 1831. Badger was in office only from March to September, 1841. Having been appointed by Harrison, he resigned on the separation of Tyler from the Whig party.

Neither Badger nor his successor, Abel P. Upshur, was, when

[5] J. Q. Adams, Memoirs, IV, 136, 144.

appointed, widely known outside of his own State, in which, however, they were highly regarded. When Badger was nominated by the President, more than one Congressman propounded the query, " Who is George E. Badger? " A similar question might have been appropriately asked on the nomination of Upshur. He was characterized in the public prints of the time as " an accomplished gentleman of the Virginia school; and in all the social relations of public and private life, he is dignified in manners, conciliatory in deportment, and accessible to friends, to neighbors, and to all others in the common intercourse of business." [6] The policy of the Badger-Upshur administration was one of naval increase and expansion. Before appointing Upshur, Tyler had offered the naval secretaryship to Captain R. F. Stockton, of the navy, who declined it.

The choosing of James K. Paulding, 1838-1841, was in a way an application of the principles of civil service. He had been connected with the department for twenty-three years, first as secretary to the Board of Navy Commissioners and later as navy agent at New York. This long experience was a valuable preparation for his more exacting duties as Secretary of the Navy. Until 1838 Paulding was, however, primarily a literary man, a writer chiefly of fiction and essays. Not until he became secretary, did the navy exact his best thought and exertions. Indeed, he owed his entrance into the department and his final promotion to its headship, to his eminence in literature quite as much as to his abilities as an administrator. His Jacksonian democracy of a pure type, his residence in New York, and his acquaintance and friendship with the leaders of his party, were also important factors in determining his political career. It is said that President Van Buren first offered the naval portfolio to Washington Irving, who upon declining it suggested Paulding, his literary friend and his collaborator in the writing of " Salmagundi." Had Van Buren been successful in the presidential election of 1840, Paulding would have doubtless remained in the cabinet. On November 11, 1840, just after the result of the election had been decided, he wrote to Irving that the " question being now settled, I am perfectly resigned to my fate, and cannot resist the inclination to rejoice at the prospect of getting rid of a laborious, vexatious, and

[6] Army and Navy Chronicle for 1841, 290.

thankless office, in which my duty has been almost always in direct opposition to my feelings, and I have been obliged to sacrifice private to public considerations."[7]

Of the nine naval secretaries of the period 1815-1842, Samuel L. Southard rendered the most efficient service. For one reason, his term of office was longer than that of either one of the other eight secretaries. It extended from September 16, 1823, to March 3, 1829. Beginning under Monroe, he served throughout the administration of John Quincy Adams. The younger Adams had imbibed the naval views of his father, who was for a long time one of the chief promoters of the American navy. He took the greatest interest in improving this arm of the military service. Southard and Adams were well-mated, and were vigorous and far-sighted naval administrators. Southard's ability as an executive consisted not so much in a knowledge of the details of the navy, as in his intelligent conception of the navy's needs and his steady exertions to satisfy them. He had the practice, which not every secretary has had, of looking beyond the limits of his desk and its daily load of routine business. In his reports, hardly a subject of naval betterment escaped him; he boxed the compass of naval reform and improvement. His recommendations were always practical, and were easily attainable could Congress have been moved to adopt them. Among other measures he recommended the establishment of a naval academy, the reorganization of the navy and the marine corps, a complete survey of the coasts of the United States, the sending out of an exploring expedition, higher ranks for the navy, a plan for the improvement of the navy yards, and the construction of dry docks. Some of these improvements Southard obtained, but others were postponed for many years. He vigorously maintained the discipline of the navy. This may have had something to do with making him rather unpopular with the service. Charles W. Goldsborough, the secretary of the navy board, is quoted as saying that the navy commissioners and all the navy " were extremely dissatisfied with Mr. Southard's administration of the Navy Department, and especially mortified at an intimation in a late report that few of the navy officers were profound astronomers."[8]

[7] Griffis, M. C. Perry, 157; Paulding's Paulding, 283.
[8] J. Q. Adams, Memoirs, VIII, 141.

Southard took his office rather more seriously than did his two predecessors. He was less generous to himself in fixing limits to his summer vacations. On March 25, 1819, John Quincy Adams wrote in his diary: " Mr. Thompson, the Secretary of the Navy, left the city this morning for a visit to New York. The office sits easy upon its holders. Mr. Crowninshield used to remain in Washington only when Congress was in session, and spent the remainder of his time at home. Mr. Thompson appears to be determined to follow his example. The chief clerk and the navy commissioners make the duties of that department comparatively light." [9] This visit of Thompson, which began on March 28, did not end until December 8. No subsequent secretary has been absent from the department for so long a time. That the navy did not suffer by reason of the long absences of Crowninshield and Thompson was because of the efficiency of the chief clerk, and more especially because the Secretary of the Navy had been relieved since 1815 of many details of administration by the Board of Navy Commissioners. The establishment of this board will be now considered.

Before the War of 1812 some of the naval officers had advocated the establishment of a naval board to assist the Secretary of the Navy in the performance of his duties. In 1798 Commodore John Barry recommended the vesting of the management of the navy in three naval commissioners. Benjamin Stoddert, the first Secretary of the Navy, in one of his last reports to Congress said that the business of the Navy Department embraced too many objects for the superintendence of one person; and he recommended the " establishment of a board to consist of three or five experienced navy officers, to superintend, in subordination to the Head of the Department, such parts of the duties as nautical men are best qualified to understand and to direct." [10] The first Republican Secretaries of the Navy were inclined to simplify the machinery of the department, rather than add to it. Since the navy was small and simple, they did not feel the need of technical advice in managing it.

The War of 1812 greatly increased the work of the Secretary of the Navy, and soon caused him to seek expert counsel and assist-

[9] J. Q. Adams, Memoirs, IV, 310-311.
[10] Griffin, Commodore John Barry, 336; State Papers, Nav. Aff., I, 75.

ance. It also directed the attention of Congress to those administrative abuses that had arisen under the existing system. In February, 1813, soon after he entered upon his duties Secretary of the Navy Jones complained that the minor details of the naval business diverted his attention from its larger and more important objects. He recommended the appointment by the President of a naval purveyor, and of several deputies to reside in the chief seaports. They were to purchase all the naval supplies, and were to be under the control of the Secretary. Jones's object was to systematize and expedite the purchase of supplies and to correct existing abuses.[11]

The beginning of the specific movement that resulted in the establishment of the Board of Navy Commissioners may be dated with a report of Jones, made in February, 1814, to the naval committee of the Senate, recommending the reorganization of the Navy Department. On March 18 the Senate ordered Jones to devise and digest a system for the better organization of the Navy Department.[12] Owing to the increased work caused by the war, Jones was unable to make a report until November 15. This contained a bill for the better organization of the department, which he discussed at some length. The bill provided for a board of inspectors of the navy, consisting of three naval officers and " two other judicious persons, skilled in naval affairs." The President of the United States was to designate the presiding officer of the board and to appoint its secretary. The latter was to keep a record of the proceedings of the board and transmit copies of them to the Secretary of the Navy " for the inspection and revision of the President of the United States." The board was not to sit at Washington, but at some convenient and central port. The Secretary of the Navy was to assign separate duties to each of its members. The five classes of duties were as follows: general correspondence and the preparation of reports, estimates, and statements; personnel of the navy and naval courts; ordnance and transportation; victualling, sustenance, and medicine; and equipment of vessels. The last two classes were to be in charge of the civilian members. The bill further provided, that for the faithful performance of their duties the " said inspectors shall, severally,

[11] State Papers, Nav. Aff., I, 285.
[12] Annals of Cong., XXVI, 672-673.

be held responsible, under the instruction, and subject to the revision of the board of inspectors, to which a statement of all the transactions of each inspector shall be submitted, for revision, at each stated meeting, and an abstract thereof transmitted monthly to the Secretary of the Navy." [13]

Jones's recommendation provided also for the appointment of a chief naval constructor, two assistant naval constructors, and a paymaster of the navy; and for the establishment of a naval academy. His plan for the reorganization of the department stripped the Secretary of the Navy of his principal duties and prerogatives. Exactly what powers would be left to him is not clear. Jones's experience in the department seems to have convinced him that a civilian was not able to manage a naval war without professional assistance.[14] With the President and the Secretary of the Navy at Washington, and with a board formed after Jones's plan at New York or Boston, the business of the navy must have become greatly confused. In short, his plan would not have worked. It was too complicated. Responsibility was too diffused. Jones evidently was a novice in political science. The chief officers of the navy quickly detected the deficiencies of his plan.

A committee of the House of Representatives on retrenchment and reform in the management of the naval establishment, which had been appointed in March, 1814, sent Jones's report to every captain in the navy with a request that he suggest such additions and alterations as appeared to him necessary. The captains invariably approved the recommendation for the appointment of a navy board. Captains Bainbridge, Stewart, Hull, Decatur, Evans, Morris, Shaw, and Tingey offered particular observations on the plan of Jones. A majority of the eight captains believed that the board should consist of three instead of five members, and that it should be chosen entirely from the navy. Several captains recommended that the senior officer of the board should preside. Captains Decatur and Shaw thought that the Secretary of the Navy should be the presiding officer. Decatur, Tingey, and Evans could see no advantage in placing the board at some central location, away from Washington. "One principal object of this arrangement," Decatur said, "ought to be to bring into the depart-

[13] State Papers, Nav. Aff., I, 322-324.
[14] Ex. Doc., 26C. 1S., No. 39, 1-2.

ment the experience and activity of a number of professional men, who should be at all times ready on the spot to furnish either Congress or the Secretary with such information as either might call for, and which their professional experience enables them to communicate." Captains Bainbridge and Stewart thought that the division of duties among the members of the board, with individual responsibility, would serve no good purpose, and that a collective responsibility and management would be much better. Captain Morris was of the opinion that the board itself should distribute the duties among its members.[15]

The suggestions of the captains tended to define and simplify Jones's plan. Their desire to exclude civilians from the board was a natural one. A board composed entirely of naval officers was likely to act more harmoniously. The captains were liberal in leaving to the Secretary of the Navy more power than he had left to himself. The wisdom of substituting collective for individual responsibility may be questioned in the light of future experience. Several years later the bureau system with individual responsibility was adopted. Congress followed many of the recommendations of the captains. In one particular, however, it departed from them; it made the board entirely subordinate to the Secretary of the Navy.

On January 9, 1815, the committee on reform and retrenchment reported to the House a plan for correcting abuses in the management of the navy and for improving the organization of the department. This they digested from Jones's plan and from the replies of the captains. The committee attributed the abuses in the department to three causes: the excessive and laborious duties of the Secretary of the Navy; the want of sufficient checks on subordinate agents; and the great latitude allowed the commanders in altering, repairing, and equipping their ships. As the principal corrective for the administrative abuses, it recommended a bill " to alter and amend the several acts establishing a Navy Department, by adding thereto a Board of Commissioners." On January 21 the House passed the bill, and on February 4 after amendment it passed the Senate. On the same day the House concurred with the Senate's amendments, and on February 7 it was signed by the President and became a law.[16]

---

[15] State Papers, Nav. Aff., I, 354-359.
[16] Annals of Cong., XXVIII, 223, 1047-1061, 1085, 1122-1123.

This act established the Board of Navy Commissioners. It was to be composed of three post-captains, who were to be appointed by the President and to be confirmed by the Senate. The board was attached to the office of the Secretary of the Navy. Nothing in the act was to be construed " to take from the Secretary of the Navy his control and direction of the naval forces of the United States, as now by law possessed." Under the superintendence of the secretary, the board was to " discharge all the ministerial duties of said office, relative to the procurement of naval stores and materials, and the construction, armament, equipment, and employment, of vessels of war, as well as all other matters connected with the naval establishment of the United States." It was empowered to adopt rules and regulations for the government of its meetings, and to appoint a secretary, " who shall keep a fair record of their proceedings, subject at all times to the inspection of the President of the United States and the Secretary of the Navy." The ranking officer of the board was to be its president. Each commissioner was to receive $3500 a year, in lieu of wages, rations, and other emoluments, as a naval officer; the secretary was given an annual salary of $2000. The board was authorized to employ two clerks at $1000 a year each.[17]

On February 15, 1815, President Madison nominated as navy commissioners Captains John Rodgers, Isaac Hull, and David Porter; and on the next day they were confirmed by the Senate. Rodgers, the president of the board, stood second in the navy list of 1815. The ranking officer of the navy, Alexander Murray, was not qualified for the position. Before the selection of commissioners was made Crowninshield asked Rodgers to characterize the captains on shore, with a view to aiding him in choosing the board. Rodgers responded in a paper dated February 11, 1815. He described the senior officer of the navy in the following words: " Commodore Murray, although an amiable old gentleman, has not been regularly bred to the profession of a seaman; his pretensions, therefore, as a navy officer are of a very limited description." Rodgers regarded Hull as a " man of most amiable disposition; and although he does not pretend to much science, he is an excellent seaman, and at the same time he unites all the most essential qualifications necessary for such a situation." Captain

[17] U. S. Statutes at Large, III, 202-203, 231.

Porter was characterized as a " man of far more than ordinary natural talents, indefatigable in whatever he undertakes; and added to these, his acquirements, professional as well as more immediately scientific, are respectable." Rodgers recommended as the most suitable for commissioners either Bainbridge, Hull, and Morris; or Hull, Porter, and Morris. Madison after substituting Rodgers for Morris, accepted the latter list.

The Board of Navy Commissioners, during the twenty-seven years of its existence, had five presidents: John Rodgers, 1815-1824 and 1827-1837; William Bainbridge, 1824-1827; Isaac Chauncey, 1837-1840; Charles Morris, 1840-1841; and Lewis Warrington, 1841-1842. In the paper referred to above Rodgers described three of the officers who served as presidents of the board. He said that Bainbridge was an " excellent officer, uniting much practice with considerable theory; he is also industrious, and if there is any objection to him, it is because he feels the importance of his own abilities too sensibly to qualify him as well as he otherwise would be for a subordinate situation." Rodgers thought that Chauncey was an excellent officer, but was best fitted for a command at sea. He described Captain Morris as a man of " strong discriminating mind, of considerable science, and unites perhaps as much, if not more, theoretical and practical knowledge than any man of his age in the service." [18]

By all odds the most influential member of the Board of Navy Commissioners during its existence was Commodore John Rodgers. He left his mark upon the administration of the Old Navy as did no other officer. For more than nineteen years he served as president of the navy board. He filled this office continuously from 1815 to 1837, with the exception of a period of about three years from 1824 to 1827, when he commanded the Mediterranean squadron. For a brief time in 1825 he served as Secretary of the Navy, *ad interim*, being the first naval officer to act in this capacity. Of the officers of his time, Rodgers was the type and exemplar. He won and maintained the regard of Presidents, Secretaries of the Navy, Senators, and Congressmen. He was much admired by Thomas H. Benton, the great Senator from Missouri, who wrote an appreciative sketch of the life and character of this typical and heroic sea-officer of the old school. The following extract is taken from Benton's Thirty Years' View:

[18] Proc. of Mass. His. Soc., 2d. ser., IV, 207-208.

" My idea of the perfect naval commander had been formed from history, and from the study of such characters as the Von Tromps and De Ruyters of Holland, the Blakes of England, and the De Tourvilles of France—men modest and virtuous, frank and sincere, brave and patriotic, gentle in peace, terrible in war; formed for high command by nature; and raising themselves to their proper sphere by their own exertions from low beginnings. When I first saw Commodore Rodgers, which was after I had reached senatorial age and station, he recalled to me the idea of those model admirals; and subsequent acquaintance confirmed the impression then made. He was to me the complete impersonation of my idea of the perfect naval commander—person, mind, and manners; with the qualities for command grafted on the groundwork of a good citizen and good father of a family; and all lodged in a frame to bespeak the seaman and officer.

" His very figure and face were those of the naval hero—such as we conceive from naval songs and ballads; and, from the course of life which the sea-officer leads—exposed to the double peril of waves and war, contending with the storms of the elements as well as with the storm of battle . . . . Commodore Rodgers needed no help from the creative imagination to endow him with the form which naval heroism might require. His person was of the middle height, stout, square, solid, compact, well-proportioned; and combining in the perfect degree the idea of strength and endurance with the reality of manly comeliness, the statue of Mars, in the rough state, before the conscious chisel had lent the last polish. His face, stern in outline, was relieved by a gentle and benign expression, grave, with the overshadowing of an ample and capacious forehead and eyebrows." [19]

The navy board held its first meeting on Tuesday, April 25, 1815. Its manuscript journals inform us that " on this day Captains Rodgers, Hull, and Porter met and read their commission as commissioners of the Navy of the United States." The commission of the president of the board, which was signed by Madison and Crowninshield, read as follows:

" To all who shall see these Presents, Greeting:

" Know ye, That in pursuance of an Act of Congress, entitled ' An act to alter and amend the several acts for establishing a

[19] Benton, Thirty Years' View, II, 144-145.

Navy Department, by adding thereto a board of Commissioners,' passed on the seventh day of February, one thousand eight hundred and fifteen, and of the special trust and confidence reposed in the patriotism, integrity, and abilities of John Rodgers, a post-captain in the navy of the United States, I have nominated, and by and with the advice and consent of the Senate, do appoint him a Commissioner of the board aforesaid, to have and to hold this appointment, with all the powers, privileges, and emoluments, thereunto legally appertaining, during the pleasure of the President of the United States, for the time being."

After the commissions had been read, " Captain Rodgers, holding the oldest commission as a Captain in the Navy, took his seat in conformity to law as President of the Board; which then went into an examination of the merits of the different candidates for the office of secretary and clerks to the board, and elected Lyttleton W. Tazewell for the former, and Charles W. Goldsborough and Charles G. DeWitt for the latter. The board then, being properly organized, reported themselves ready to receive such communications from the Hon. Secretary of the Navy as he might have to make to them, relative to the Navy Department of the United States; and adjourned to meet to-morrow at 10 o'clock a. m."

On the next day the board adopted rules for its government. It fixed its office hours from 10 a. m. to 3 p. m. No member of the board or person attached to it was to absent himself from the District of Columbia without its consent. So far as practicable all business was to be presented to the board in writing.[20]

Tazewell declined the appointment of secretary. The place was then offered to James K. Paulding, of New York, who accepted it, and held it until November, 1823. He was then succeeded by Charles W. Goldsborough, the principal clerk of the board, who held the secretaryship until the board was dissolved in 1842. The clerical force of the office of the navy commissioners was gradually increased. In 1818 it consisted of three clerks, in 1824 of six clerks and a draftsman, and in 1842 of eight clerks and a draftsman.

In May, 1815, immediately after the navy board was organized, a dispute, in which considerable heat was generated, arose be-

[20] Arch. of Bureau of Construction and Repair, Journal of Navy Board, I, 6-7.

tween Crowninshield and the commissioners over their respective spheres of duty. The questions at issue turned upon the interpretation of the act of February 7, 1815, establishing the board. Its terms were so general and ambiguous that differences of opinion as to their meaning easily arose. The dispute originated in a contention of the commissioners that the Secretary of the Navy was bound to communicate to them the "destination of a squadron." Crowninshield declared that the communicating of such information was in his own discretion.[21] The claims of the commissioners amounted to the assertion of the right, under the act of February 7, to exercise control over the movements of the fleet and the personnel of the navy. Crowninshield claimed that the act gave them no such right. The settlement of the dispute decided which should be supreme in the department, the Secretary of the Navy or the navy board.

From May 22 until June 14 the board did nothing but meet and adjourn from day to day. On the latter date it received from Crowninshield a copy of a letter of President Madison setting forth the relations existing between the President and the Secretary of the Navy, and between the Secretary of the Navy and the navy board. According to Madison, the Secretary of the Navy was the organ of the executive and was responsible only to the President. The board had no immediate relation to the President. It was attached to the secretary's office, and was responsible to the Secretary of the Navy. All "ministerial duties" heretofore transacted by the secretary were now vested in the board.[22]

The actual powers of the board were determined by the interpretation that Crowninshield gave to the words, "ministerial duties." He decided that they referred to the materiel of the navy; to the building, repairing, and equipping of ships, and the superintending of navy yards, naval stations, and dry docks. Respecting the personnel of the navy, the commissioners exercised merely advisory powers. All questions relating to appointments and the detailing of officers, the movements of vessels, and the discipline of the navy were decided by the secretary. The func-

---

[21] Arch. of Bureau of Construction and Repair, Secretary's Letters, I, 8-9.

[22] Ibid., 11; Journal of Navy Board, 14-18.

tions of the commissioners were of a civil, rather than of a
" naval " or military character. They were called upon, however,
to advise the secretary upon " naval " matters. The secretary and
the commissioners communicated with each other both orally and
in writing. In all important business the commissioners first
received the consent of the secretary before proceeding with it.
They were, however, allowed their own discretion as to the manner in which they performed their work. They kept the secretary
informed upon the work of their office.

A dispute also arose between the board and the chief clerk of
the department over their respective duties. This was decided in
favor of the latter. These inevitable disagreements were soon
settled, and the administrative machine ran for a long time with
much smoothness. When John Branch, Jackson's first naval secretary, came into the department some friction again occurred
between the secretary and the board. Branch wished to limit the
commissioners' powers, and to take upon himself the responsibility
for many details, which former secretaries had placed upon the
commissioners. This difficulty was removed with the resignation
of Branch. The succeeding secretaries followed the old routine.[23]

For a short time the Navy Department consisted of three administrative divisions, the office of the secretary of the navy, the
office of the navy commissioners, and the office of the accountant
of the navy. On March 3, 1817, the latter office, whose personnel
then comprised the accountant of the navy and thirteen clerks,
was abolished; and its duties were vested in the office of the fourth
auditor of the treasury, which was now established under the
Treasury Department.[24] The concentrating of the work of audit-
ing the accounts of the government in the Treasury Department
had been recommended by Albert Gallatin as early as 1802. Constant Freeman, who in March, 1816, had succeeded Thomas
Turner as the accountant of the navy, was now made fourth
auditor of the treasury.

The offices of the third and fourth auditors of the treasury were
for a long time in the building of the Navy Department, in Wash-

[23] Navy Comms. Letters, Navy Dept. Arch., 1831, I, 72; Commodore
Morris' Autobiography, 89-90.
[24] U. S. Statutes at Large, III, 366-368.

ington. After the British burned the capital in 1814, the department had obtained temporary quarters. By 1816 the " old war
office " had been reconstructed, and it was once more occupied by
the State, War, and Navy Departments. About January, 1820,
the State and War Departments moved into new buildings that
had been erected for them, leaving the Navy Department in full
possession of the old war office. This in time was called the " old
Navy Department building," or sometimes in official documents
the " Southwest Executive building." The navy commissioners,
who before 1820 had been renting a small house of five rooms for
their office, moved into the old war office. Both the secretary and
the commissioners occupied the second floor of this building. By
1842 the need of the department for additional quarters was very
great. Secretary Upshur said that owing to insufficient space the
records of the department could no longer be filed away or be
otherwise arranged, and were scattered here and there in confused piles. The chief naval constructor occupied a small inconvenient room in the garret, which was so dark on cloudy days
that he could not see to work, and which, when certain winds
prevailed, was " liable to smoke." [25]

The only Navy Department building was about two hundred
yards west of the White House. It was built of brick, and was
one hundred and sixty feet long and fifty-five feet wide. It was
originally two stories high, with a basement and an attic. It was
divided throughout its length by a broad passage ; and in the center of the building was a " spacious staircase." An observer who
walked through the offices of the government in 1830 was " impressed with favorable ideas of the system and order with which
the affairs of this great people are conducted. The heads of the
departments, with 250 clerks, occupy these buildings. They exhibit no sinecure places, but all are engaged in the business of
their employments, and with as little of relaxation as is compatible
with a due attention to health." [26] In 1842 the entire personnel of
the Navy Department in Washington, Secretary of the Navy,
commissioners, clerks, messengers, and all, numbered about
thirty men.

[25] Cong. Letters, Navy Dept. Arch., VIII, 428.
[26] Elliott, Ten Miles Square, 164.

The Naval Materiel.

During the period 1815-1842 the problems relating to the naval materiel were more successfully handled than those relating to the naval personnel. For this success the Board of Navy Commissioners deserves credit, for it was specifically charged with the administration of the materiel of the navy. It was easier to obtain legislation respecting ships, navy yards, and dry docks than legislation respecting officers and seamen, for the former was often to the advantage of local interests, while the latter was generally not. In legislating for the materiel Congress was, as a rule, liberal and intelligent. While on the other hand, many of the best recommendations of the department regarding the officers and seamen Congress refused to adopt. The influence and traditions of parties and politicians had their effect upon both classes of legislation.

The Republican party came out of the War of 1812 with a considerable momentum in the direction of naval expansion. By 1820, however, its enthusiasm for the navy had perceptibly cooled. Slavery had begun to localize its interests and to lessen its concern for national institutions. The Whig and Democratic parties, which were formed during the period 1825-1833, manifested certain differences in naval sentiment. The Whigs, inheritors in a way of Federalist principles, inclined towards a strong navy and large naval expenditures; and the Democrats, influenced by Republican traditions, favored a more moderate naval establishment. While this division of opinion is always perceptible it is not always sharply defined. The administrations of John Quincy Adams and of Harrison and Tyler were especially disposed to favor the navy; and made many attempts, more or less successful, to increase and better it. On the other hand, the intervening administrations of Jackson and Van Buren showed less zeal for the navy, although they were by no means indifferent to its needs. Jackson early in his administration wished to reduce the naval expenditures; and in his first annual message he recommended that the building of large ships be discontinued, and that the country look for its naval defense in the possession of ample materials ready to be made into ships in case of war. Later he became more liberal, and the naval expenditures towards the end of his administration exceeded those under Adams. Van Buren was friendly to the navy, but

much less so than Harrison and Tyler. During the period 1815-
1842, New England continued to be more interested in the national
marine than the Southern States, and likewise the Eastern States
more than the Western.[27]

From 1815 to 1835 the annual naval appropriations were usually
more than three and less than five million dollars. In 1821, 1823,
and 1824, owing to a reaction against the navy, they fell slightly
below three millions. In 1836, for the first time since 1815, they
exceeded five millions. From 1836 to 1842 they remained continuously above that sum. The high-water marks were reached
in 1837 and 1841, when the annual naval appropriations were respectively $7,465,000 and $7,420,000. The naval expenditures
were highest in 1842, when they were $8,275,000.[28] The increased
cost of the navy during 1836-1842 was caused by various circumstances: the expansion of the country and its commerce made
it necessary to keep more ships in commission; the building of a
steam navy was begun; the critical state of our foreign relations
seemed to demand the augmenting of the navy; an expensive exploring expedition was sent out in 1838; and an act of 1835 increased the annual salaries of the officers and seamen some eight
hundred thousand dollars. Levi Woodbury once ascribed the
beginning of the naval increase to an overflowing national
treasury.

The Republicans inaugurated their policy of naval expansion
in time of peace by the passage, on April 29, 1816, of an " act for
the gradual increase of the navy of the United States." This appropriated $1,000,000 annually for eight years, and authorized the
building of nine line of battle ships and twelve 44-gun frigates.[29]
This act was one of great importance and far-reaching influence.
It definitely committed the United States, now for the first time,
to the policy of building up a fleet in time of peace, and of establishing a navy comparable to those of the European nations. Its
program of naval construction was larger than any hitherto
planned by the department, even in time of war. The Secretary
of the Navy decided to build the new ships at the navy yards,

[27] Benton, Thirty Years' View, II, 452; Richardson, Messages and Papers
of the Presidents, II, 459.
[28] Ex. Doc., 45 C. 1S., No. 3, 156.
[29] U. S. Statutes at Large, III, 321.

since experience showed that better vessels could be built by the government than by private ship-builders.

The construction of the first of the nine 74-gun ships, the *Columbus,* was begun at the Washington navy yard in May, 1816; and she was launched in March, 1819. Work on the remaining vessels was commenced as follows: at Norfolk, the *Delaware* in 1817, and *New York* in 1820; at New York, the *Ohio* in 1817; at Philadelphia, the *North Carolina* in 1818, and *Pennsylvania* in 1821; at Boston, the *Vermont* in 1818, and *Virginia* in 1822; and at Portsmouth, the *Alabama* in 1819. Progress in the building of some of these vessels was very slow. The *Vermont, Virginia, New York,* and *Alabama* were still on the stocks in 1842. The *Virginia* and *New York* were never launched. The former was sold on the stocks in 1873, and the latter was burned by the Unionists on the evacuation of the Norfolk navy yard in 1861. Some notion of the size of these lines of battleships may be obtained from the dimensions of the *Ohio*. She was 198 feet long, 54 feet wide, and 15 feet deep. Her tonnage was 2170 tons. The *Pennsylvania,* at first intended to carry 74 guns, was finally built for 120 guns. She was the largest sailing ship in the Old Navy. In 1827 President John Quincy Adams, who went aboard her at Philadelphia, wrote that she " was said to be the largest ship that will float upon the ocean. She is built chiefly of live oak, and looks like a city in herself." From 1819 to 1826 the construction of nine 44's was begun. Work upon them proceeded very slowly, and several were still uncompleted in 1842. The first of them to be launched were the *Potomac,* in 1821; *Brandywine,* in 1825; and *Columbia,* in 1836. These three ships were built at the Washington navy yard. In size and architecture the ships of the line and the frigates built under the navy commissioners compared favorably with the ships of the European navies.[30]

Early in 1820 a movement in behalf of naval retrenchment developed in the House. The navy commissioners, being called upon to give their opinion upon the expediency of diminishing the annual expenditure of one million dollars for the increase of the navy, begged leave to " decline recommending a suspension, even for a limited time, of any portion of the appropriation for the

[30] Cong. Letters, Navy Dept. Arch., IV, 423-424; J. Q. Adams, Memoirs, VII, 331.

gradual increase of the navy "; and Secretary Thompson agreed
with them. Towards the end of the year the House again took
up the subject; and when the commissioners and the secretary
were again called upon for information, they yielded to the rising
opposition to the navy, and said that the time for building the
ships fixed by the act of April 29, 1816, might be extended three
years. Accordingly on March 3, 1821, this act was so changed
that instead of appropriating one million dollars for the remaining three years that the act had to run, five hundred thousand
dollars was appropriated annually for six years. In 1827 and
again in 1833 Congress voted five hundred thousand dollars
annually for six years for the improvement of the navy.[31]

Various other measures besides the above-mentioned ones were
passed by Congress, authorizing the construction or purchase of
ships. For instance, on March 3, 1825, five hundred thousand dollars was appropriated towards the construction of ten sloops of
war. Several small vessels, rigged as sloops or schooners were
added to the navy from time to time. About 1827 a 44-gun
frigate, the *Hudson*, was purchased. In 1816 the navy contained
41 vessels, carrying 1178 guns; and in 1842, 56 vessels, carrying
2002 guns. These figures disregard all small craft below ten guns.
The increase in the size of the ships was relatively greater than
that in their number. Counting vessels upon the stocks and those
in and out of commission, the navy in 1816 contained five 74's
and five 44's; and that of 1842, one 120, ten 74's, and fourteen 44's.
Only about one-half of the total naval force was placed in commission. In 1822, 27 vessels, mounting 358 guns were in
commission; and in 1842, 32 vessels, mounting 850 guns.[32]

For several years after the War of 1812 the *Fulton the First*
was the only steam vessel in the navy. She blew up in 1829. In
1822 the *Sea Gull,* a steam galliot of 100 tons, was bought. The
second steamship to be built was the *Fulton the Second*, whose
construction was begun at the New York navy yard in 1835. Her
length was 180 feet, beam 35 feet, and displacement 1200 tons.
Her first commander was Captain M. C. Perry, who was an early
advocate of steam naval vessels. He was a brother of Commodore

[31] State Papers, Nav. Aff., I, 651, 676; U. S. Statutes at Large, III, 642;
IV, 242, 646.
[32] Navy Registers for 1816, 1822, 1841, 1842.

O. H. Perry, the hero of the battle of Lake Erie, and is himself famous for his expedition to Japan. By the late thirties the European nations were using steam vessels in considerable numbers, and their knowledge of them was in advance of ours. In 1838 Secretary Dickerson therefore sent Perry abroad to collect information on the use and construction of steamships for naval purposes. For a long time it was generally believed that naval steamships were only valuable for the defense of coasts and harbors. As early as 1826 Secretary Southard had recommended their use for this purpose.

The introduction of steamships into our navy did not assume much importance until the administration of Secretary Paulding, 1838-1841. The letters of the secretary to his friends have many amusing references to the " steam fever," as he called the movement for steam naval ships. In June, 1839, he wrote that he was " steamed to death." Paulding, whose views were confirmed by those of many naval officers, believed that the utility of naval steamships for deep-sea operations had yet to be demonstrated. The use of these vessels aroused considerable opposition among the older naval officers, who were naturally prejudiced against so great an innovation.[33] Some of the younger officers, with the confidence in novelties born of youth, warmly favored the immediate construction of a small fleet of steam frigates. Paulding finally decided " to go with the wind," but not to carry full sail (a not very happy figure of speech), and " to keep the steam enthusiasts quiet by warily administering to the humor of the times." In other words, a compromise was effected between the advocates and opponents of the steam navy, and Congress voted to build three steamships. Paulding, however, with a touch of sentiment befitting a literary man, declared that he would " never consent to let our old ships perish, and transform our navy into a fleet of sea monsters." He wrote at this time that the United States " must have some mania to excite them, whether it be a merino, a *morus multicaulis*, a canal, a railroad, or a steam mania." [34]

In 1839 two naval boards, one composed of line officers and the other of naval constructors and a naval engineer, convened in Washington to consider methods of constructing the steamships

[33] Life of Commodore Stockton (1856), 80-81.
[34] Paulding's Paulding, 277-278.

that Congress had authorized. It was concerning these boards that Paulding wrote to a friend that " according to custom we have had boards to sit and cogitate, and disagree, and compromise, so that in the end nobody will be responsible for a failure if one should take place. If they don't settle the matter soon, I shall dissolve them into empty air, and take the whole matter on my own shoulders." Upon the completion of the work of these boards, the construction of two side-wheel steam frigates was begun. These vessels were the *Mississippi* and *Missouri*. They were twin ships. Their dimensions were as follows: extreme length, 229 feet; beam, 40 feet; draft, 19 feet. Their displacement was 3220 tons. They were completed in 1842. Since the two *Fultons* were little more than floating steam batteries, the construction of the two steam frigates *Mississippi* and *Missouri* properly marks the beginning of our steam navy. Their fates were tragic. " Both underwent the doom of fire, the *Missouri* at anchor on a peaceful morning in the friendly harbor of Gibraltar ; and her mate in the dead of night while attempting to pass the batteries of Vicksburg, with the din of war about her, and the fierce waters of the river whose name she bore clamoring for what the other element might spare." [35]

The first steamships were built of wood. In the winter of 1841-1842 Secretary Upshur made another innovation in our naval architecture by constructing an iron steam frigate. His reasons for selecting this material were to test its utility in shipbuilding and to encourage the development of the resources of iron in the United States. At this time but few iron steamships had been built. Upshur said that " with us the undertaking was altogether new, and we had no safe light to guide us furnished by the experience of others." The parts of the new iron steamship were made in Pittsburg, transported to Erie on Lake Erie, and there set up. This vessel was named the *Michigan*. She was launched in 1843. She was the first iron vessel that floated upon the Great Lakes. She is still in the navy. [36]

A new era in the history of the ordnance of our navy began in the fourth and fifth decades of the last century. It was marked by the application of modern science and a high order of intelli-

[35] Bennett, Steam Navy, 32-44; Paulding's Paulding, 278.
[36] Cong. Letters, Navy Dept. Arch., VIII, 438; Bennett, Steam Navy, 44-45.

gence to the designing, manufacture, and operation of guns.
Larger, higher-powered, and more destructive guns began to be
constructed. To protect the ships from these new cannon, armor
was invented. About 1840 the first shell guns and the first pivot
guns came into use in our navy. The former were Paixhans guns.
They were first made about 1822 by a French artillery officer, inventor, and author, of that name. He is said to have taken up
the idea of Colonel George Bomford, of the American army, who
during the War of 1812 invented the bomb-cannon. In 1839 and
1840 Commodore M. C. Perry conducted at Sandy Hook and on
board the *Fulton the Second* the first school of gun practice in our
navy. At this time Perry also established at Sandy Hook an experimental battery, and tested Paixhans guns, shells, and hollow
and solid shot. It was about 1840 that target practice on shipboard began. In 1841 Congress appropriated $550,000 for the
purchase of ordnance and ordnance stores, and $50,000 for the
testing of improvements in ordnance and in the construction of
steamers and other war vessels. As late as 1842 shells were still
a curiosity in the navy. Captain W. H. Parker writing of a voyage which he had made in that year from Madeira to Rio Janeiro
says that the " shells were a great bother to us; as they were kept
in the shell-room, and no one was allowed even to look at them;
it seemed to be a question with the division-officers whether the
fuse went in first or the sabot; or whether the fuse should be
ignited before putting the shell in the gun or not! However, we
used to fire them off, though I cannot say I ever saw them hit
anything." [37]

Under the younger Adams the six navy yards which the elder
Adams had purchased were increased to seven. Before 1819 New
Orleans was the most eligible port for a naval station or navy
yard on our Gulf coast. But after the purchase of Florida, Key
West and Pensacola were available sites and were more accessible
than New Orleans. In the days of sailing ships the two Florida
ports had the advantage over New Orleans more than now. In
August, 1824, Secretary Southard recommended the abandonment
of New Orleans as a naval station and the establishment of a
navy yard on the coast of Florida.

[37] Parker, Recollections of a Naval Officer, 20; Griffis, M. C. Perry, 146;
Captains' Letters, Nav Dept. Arch., June, 1839, 14.

Accordingly on March 3, 1825, Congress passed an act authorizing the establishment of a navy yard and naval depot on the coast of Florida, and appropriated $100,000 for the purchase of a site and the making of improvements thereon. Captains Bainbridge, Warrington, and Biddle were appointed by Southard to select the site of the yard at Pensacola. They sailed from Norfolk in October, 1825, and by December had completed their work. The land which they chose already belonged to the government, and was situated about six miles from Pensacola in the vicinity of Barancas to the northward and eastward of Tartar's Point.[38] Improvements of this yard were at once begun, but for many years they progressed very slowly. In 1828 additional land adjoining the Pensacola navy yard was purchased by Southard for a live oak plantation.

Before the administration of Secretary Southard the navy yards were improved by temporary expedients, and their buildings were erected without any regard to the future and growing wants of the navy. In his annual report for 1825 Southard recommended the preparation of a general plan for each yard, prescribing the various buildings that were to be eventually erected, and establishing their location. The navy commissioners also urged the adoption of such a plan. Finally, in 1827 Congress authorized the President to cause the navy yards to be thoroughly examined and plans for their improvement to be prepared. This work fell to a navy board consisting of Captains Bainbridge, Chauncey, and Morris. It was assisted by Loammi Baldwin, a skilled engineer. It performed its task with great thoroughness, and by the end of 1828 it had prepared detailed plans for all the yards except those at New York and Pensacola. The board decided that the New York yard was not well located, and therefore prepared no plan for it. It had expected to visit the Pensacola yard in the spring of 1829, but its work was cut short by Jackson and Branch. In 1837 a naval board, of which Commodore Charles Stewart was president, drew up a plan for the improvement of the Pensacola yard. For many years the navy yards were improved in accordance with the plans that were prepared during the period of the navy commissioners.[39]

[38] State Papers, Nav., Aff., I, 951; II, 99, 728.

[39] State Papers, Nav. Aff., II, 101-102, 763; III, 53-54, 212-213; U. S. Statutes at Large, IV, 242-243; Sen. Doc., 24C. 2S., No. 1, 466.

During the War of 1812 Congress authorized the establishment of a dockyard, but owing to the many imperative duties that at this time fell to the department nothing more than the making of surveys and reports was accomplished. After the war the subject came up again. In 1821 the navy commissioners reported to Secretary Thompson that the naval service called imperatively for the construction of dry docks. Finally, in January, 1825, Southard forcibly reviewed the whole subject, beginning with Secretary Stoddert's recommendation for the construction of docks, of December, 1798. "It is a remarkable circumstance," Southard wrote, "that, holding the naval rank which we do among the naval powers, we should not have one dock for the repairs of the vessels in which we take so much pride; and that we are in this respect behind every other nation, however inferior in naval strength." He recommended the building of two docks; one at Boston and the other at Norfolk.[40] On March 3, 1827, Congress provided for the erection of two docks, one to the north, and the other to the south of the Potomac. Southard at once engaged Loammi Baldwin to superintend the work of construction. For his services Baldwin was allowed a salary of four thousand dollars a year, eighty dollars a month for board, and fifteen cents a mile for travelling expenses. He was one of the most distinguished civil engineers of his time. His technical skill and knowledge found an ample field for their employment in the construction of the two docks, which was a work of considerable magnitude and difficulty, according to the prevailing standards.

The department decided to build one of the docks at Boston, and the other at Norfolk. Work upon them began in 1827, and was continued for seven years. The docks were first used in June, 1833, although they were not entirely completed until about a year later. They were of about the same size. The extreme length of the Boston dock was 341 feet, and its extreme breadth 100 feet. Its inner chamber, which ordinarily was the only one used in docking, was at the top 253 feet long and 86 feet wide. New England granite was used in constructing its main walls. Its stone floor was 5½ feet thick. It cost $677,000. The Norfolk dock cost $944,000. A variety of circumstances caused this differ-

[40] State Papers, Nav. Aff., I, 366, 434, 486, 735, 1032.

ence. The Norfolk dock was inconvenient to the quarries of granite, and the work of excavating was exceedingly difficult.[41]

The first vessel to enter a drydock in the United States was the line of battleship *Delaware*, which was received in the Norfolk dock on June 17, 1833, the anniversary of the battle of Bunker Hill. Exactly one week later the historic ship *Constitution,* under most impressive circumstances, entered the Boston dock. In accordance with the orders of the commandant, all the officers of the Boston yard assembled in full dress to witness the event. Vice-President Van Buren, Secretary of the Navy Woodbury, and Secretary of War Cass were present. President Jackson was expected, but he was detained at home by illness. A large crowd of people added life and color to the scene. Commodore Isaac Hull appeared once more upon the deck of the *Constitution*, the man and the vessel that " first broke the charm of British naval invincibility on the ocean." [42]

During the period of the navy commissioners the several navy yards grew in importance. From 1825 to 1842 the expense of running them increased forty per cent; and the number of commissioned and warrant officers attached to them, more than one hundred per cent—that is, from eighty officers to one hundred and seventy.[43] In 1836 a rope-walk was established at the Boston yard. Owing chiefly to their greater accessibility the Boston, New York, and Norfolk yards did most of the repairing and equipping of ships. The Pensacola yard took no part in the work of shipbuilding. After 1825 the Washington yard did little shipbuilding. As a naval rendezvous, depot, and repair shop, it never regained the rank among the yards, which it lost during the War of 1812. After the war, vessels were chiefly laid up and repaired at the yards convenient to the sea. The Washington yard came to engage largely in the manufacture of articles of naval equipment—cables, cambooses, anchors, blocks, castings, and laboratory stores.

Under the commissioners the administrations of the commandants of the yards were on the whole uneventful. Captain Thomas Tingey, who with two or three slight intermissions had

[41] State Papers, Nav. Aff., IV, 29, 370-371.
[42] Preble, Boston Navy Yard, MS., 212-226.
[43] Cong. Letters, Navy Dept. Arch., X, 188-189.

had charge of the Washington yard since its establishment in 1800, died in 1829, and was succeeded by Captain Isaac Hull. After having served for a few months as navy commissioner, Hull had in 1815 been appointed commandant of the Boston yard. He remained in this position until 1823. In 1822 his conduct was investigated by a court of enquiry, of which Commodore John Rodgers was president. He was accused of appropriating public property and the services of some of the employees of the yard. The court found some of his acts incorrect and indiscreet, but pronounced his conduct in general " correct and meritorious." With the coming of Jackson to the presidency, politics became an important factor in the selection of commandants, mechanics and laborers. In 1831 Secretary Branch summarily removed Captain William Bainbridge from the Philadelphia yard for writing a letter that was considered disrespectful to Amos Kendall, fourth auditor of the treasury, and a warm friend of Jackson. Bainbridge criticised Kendall for refusing him compensation for certain extra services. In 1833 Captain J. D. Elliott, who was an ardent and enthusiastic supporter of Jackson, was made commandant of the Boston yard. Elliott was a strict disciplinarian. He was arbitrary, and restlessly active. He instituted a series of changes in the regulations of the yard. His stormy administration was marked by collisions with his officers and the citizens of Boston, with both of whom he was very unpopular.[44]

The Naval Personnel.

From 1815 to 1842 the principal duty of the navy was the protection of American citizens and commerce in foreign ports and seas. Next in importance was its work in suppressing piracy. Indeed, its cruises against the West India pirates from 1821 to 1826 constitute the chief " naval war " of the period. The only other war was that against the Algerines in 1815-1816. For the most part, the period of the navy commissioners was a peaceful one, and the duties of the navy were such as fall to it in times of peace.

Under the commissioners the fleet was for the first time divided into squadrons. There was a fleet in the Mediterranean during the war with Tripoli in 1801-1806, nor was it entirely

[44] Preble, Boston Navy Yard, MS., 211-255.

withdrawn until a few years after the close of that war. From
1810 to 1814, however, American interests in these waters were
practically unguarded. In 1815 two fleets, one under Decatur
and the other under Bainbridge, were sent against the Algerines.
From this time onward our ships were regularly stationed in the
Mediterranean. Bainbridge's flagship was the *Independence,* 74,
the first line of battleship to show the American colors in
European waters. In 1816 Commodore Isaac Chauncey succeeded to the command of the fleet on the Mediterranean station.
His flagship was the *Washington,* 74. In 1818 he was superseded
by Commodore Charles Stewart, whose flagship was the *Franklin,*
74. These three vessels were the first American line of battleships
to be placed in commission.

The first ship of our navy to double Cape Horn and penetrate
into the Pacific was the *Essex,* Captain David Porter, in February,
1813. The *Essex* was then on her famous cruise in the Pacific
Ocean after English whalemen and merchantmen. In 1817 the
United States sloop-of-war *Ontario,* Captain James Biddle, was
sent to the Columbia River to assert peacefully the sovereignty
of our country over the adjacent territory. The next vessel to
visit the Pacific was the *Macedonian,* Captain John Downes. The
establishment of the Pacific station may be dated with the ordering
of Commodore Charles Stewart to the west coast of South America in 1821. The occasion of Stewart's mission was the revolt of
Spain's South American colonies and the consequent need of
protection of our whaling and commercial interests in the Pacific.
His flagship was the *Franklin.* Stewart returned in 1824. Being
accused of misconduct by the government of Peru, he was tried
by a court-martial shortly after his return to the United States.
The court acquitted him. Stewart was succeeded in the command of the Pacific station by Commodore Isaac Hull.

The first commander of the Brazil squadron, which was permanently established in 1826, was Commodore James Biddle. The
West India squadron properly dates from the suppression of
piracy in the West Indies in 1821-1826. As early as 1816, however, Commodore Charles Morris was placed in command of the
naval force on the New Orleans station, and ordered to protect
American commerce in the Gulf of Mexico. The three commanders of the West India squadron from 1822 to 1826 were,
respectively, James Biddle, David Porter, and Lewis Warrington.

The first American naval vessel to visit the East Indies was the *Essex*, Captain Edward Preble, in 1800. In 1829 and 1830 the *Vincennes*, Master Commandant W. B. Finch, visited the Society Islands, Sandwich Islands, Macao, Manila, and the Straits of Sunda. In 1831 the frigate *Potomac*, Captain John Downes, was sent to Sumatra to redress an injury that the natives had committed against American merchantmen. Not until 1835, however, was the East India squadron established. It then consisted of two vessels, the sloop *Peacock* and the schooner *Enterprise,* and was commanded by Commodore E. P. Kennedy. Under the act of March 3, 1819, establishing an agency for recaptured negroes on the west coast of Africa, the United States corvette *Cyane,* Captain Edward Trenchard, sailed in 1820 for Africa with the ship *Elizabeth,* which carried out eighty-nine colonists. From this time it was customary for our naval ships to visit the African coast and to engage in the suppression of the slave trade, but not until 1843 was the African squadron organized. Although our naval vessels often cruised along our coasts, a " home squadron " was not established until 1841. Provision was made for it in an act of Congress of August 1 of that year, according to which the squadron was to consist of eight vessels.

In addition to employing its ships on the several stations that have been enumerated, the department often detailed one or more vessels on special duties, such as surveying the coast of the United States, guarding the live oak reservations, protecting the Newfoundland fisheries, and conveying our diplomatic representatives abroad. The latter duty was for many years a very common one. For instance, in 1823, the frigate *Congress,* Captain James Biddle, carried Hugh Nelson to Spain, and Cæsar A. Rodney to Buenos Ayres, two newly-appointed American ministers. In 1825 the frigate *Brandywine,* Commodore Charles Stewart, was selected to make the voyage to France with Lafayette, who was returning home after his memorable visit to the United States. In 1838 an exploring expedition, under the command of Lieutenant Charles Wilkes, sailed for the Pacific Ocean. Both before and after the War of 1812 a few small vessels were kept upon the American Lakes. The arrangement of 1817-1818 between the United States and Great Britain limited the naval armament on these lakes of each of the two contracting countries to four small vessels—one on Lake Champlain, one on Lake Ontario, and two on the upper lakes.

The chief increase in naval ships during 1815-1842 was made in the first half of the period. On the other hand, the number of officers and seamen in the navy decreased during the first part of the period, but increased during the latter part. Immediately after the War of 1812 the policy of the government was to build ships for future wars, but not to provide them with officers and seamen. These were to be obtained when a war arose. In the latter part of the period, however, the needs of commerce, the fitting out of a costly exploring expedition, the uncertain foreign relations, and the policy of rapid naval expansion begun by the Harrison-Tyler administration, caused a considerable increase of the naval personnel.

The first estimate for the navy on a peace footing that was made after the war of 1812-1815 provided for 7386 officers and seamen. In 1816 the total naval force was 5540 men. In 1822 and 1823 it fell to about 4000 men—the low-water mark. From the latter date until 1837 it increased very slowly. From 1837 to 1842 it increased rapidly from 6250 to 11,250 men. The total number of line officers, from midshipman to captain, in 1818 was 645; in 1842, 951. The number of captains, the highest rank in the navy, varied as follows: 1818, 34; 1822, 31; 1835, 37; 1837, 40; 1841, 55; and 1842, 68. In March, 1817, the number of officers and privates in the marine corps was fixed by law at 915; and in June, 1834, this number was raised to 1287.[45]

During the period of the navy commissioners the number of officers and seamen in the navy was not definitely fixed by Congress. Of course, the amount of money that Congress appropriated for " naval pay " roughly limited this number. The Peace Establishment Act of 1801 had fixed the number of officers in each of the higher grades of the navy, but during the War of 1812 this restriction was removed and the fixing of numbers was left to the President and the Secretary of the Navy. Under the commissioners there was great need for a statute completely organizing the navy, and thus making certain and definite many points that remained uncertain and indefinite, and providing the department with established and uniform guides to its conduct. Various

[45] Cong. Letters, Navy Dept. Arch., II, 367, 373; III, 43-44; VIII, 376; X, 179; Navy Registers for 1818, 1822, 1835, 1837, 1841, 1842; U. S. Statutes at Large, III, 376-377; IV, 712-713.

plans for a naval peace establishment were proposed at different times. In January, 1824, Southard submitted a plan which authorized the employment of 5760 officers and seamen in the several grades that he prescribed; and in 1830 Branch proposed to diminish the personnel of the navy to the number actually required in the service.[46]

The frequency and time of appointments and promotions depended in large measure on the President and Secretary of the Navy. When an officer died, or when one was promoted, the President could either fill or leave unfilled the vacancy thus created; and he could at will add additional numbers to any grade. For these reasons appointments and promotions were very irregular. From 1818 to 1824 only one captain was appointed; but in 1825, nine. In 1836 five lieutenants were appointed; and in 1837, forty-nine. Adams in 1828 chose somewhat more than one hundred midshipmen; and Jackson in 1830, one-tenth as many. In February, 1829, Adams appointed more than fifty midshipmen, and gave grounds for Jackson's belief that he filled up this grade in order to cheat the Democrats of their spoils. This irregular method of making appointments and promotions disregarded completely the proper ratios that should exist between the numbers in the higher and the lower grades of the navy.[47]

In expanding the navy list no administration equalled that of Harrison and Tyler. This may be seen by comparing the list of 1841 with that of 1842. The captains increased from 55 to 68; commanders, 55 to 96; lieutenants, 288 to 328; pursers, 53 to 64; and chaplains, 13 to 24. The enlisted men of the navy were increased proportionately. Secretary Upshur was a warm advocate and promoter of naval reform and expansion. He set as the goal that the American navy should reach, " half the naval force of the strongest maritime power in the world." Upshur's policy aroused vigorous opposition in Congress, even among the Whig members. John Quincy Adams regarded the naval program of the Secretary of the Navy as absurdly extravagant. The opposition of the Democrats in the Senate was led by Thomas H. Benton and Ex-Secretary of the Navy Levi Woodbury. Alarmed at the use which the President had made of his discretionary power to increase the

[46] State Papers, Nav. Aff., I, 1906; III, 541.
[47] Navy Registers from 1818 to 1837.

navy, Congress decided to limit him in this respect. It therefore placed a proviso in the naval appropriation bill of 1842 fixing the maximum number of midshipmen at the number in that grade on January 1, 1841; and the maximum numbers of all other grades at their respective numbers on January 1, 1842.[48]

Throughout the period 1815-1842 the subject of higher ranks for the navy was agitated. In February, 1815, Secretary Crowninshield directed the attention of the House to a bill " for erecting the rank of admiral in our naval service." It appeared to him that this measure, which had already received the sanction of the Senate, was " necessary, not only as the means of furnishing commanders of proper rank for our squadrons; but as the means of bestowing professional distinction and reward upon the veterans of the navy." The recommendation of Crowninshield, as well as similar ones of subsequent secretaries, was disregarded by Congress. The favorable reports of the navy commissioners, the eloquent appeals of brilliant young officers, and the pointed arguments of journalists, were equally in vain. In 1824 Southard in his plan for a peace establishment provided for one vice-admiral, two rear-admirals, and three commodores. With many people, however, a large navy was unpopular, and many prejudices against the service still existed. To some the word " admiral " savored of royalty, and its use in the American navy was felt to be contrary to democratic principles. Moreover, questions of more importance than those of naval rank, such as the questions involved in the contest over slavery, were pressing for solution, and occupied the time and attention of Congress. Many members of that body did not appreciate the value to the navy of higher ranks, nor the evils that the withholding of them caused: the stagnation of promotions, the sapping of the officers' ambition, the impairing of discipline, and the indignities and embarrassments suffered in foreign countries.[49]

There were many drawbacks to service in the Old Navy. Regarding the bad effects of the infrequency of promotions, James Fenimore Cooper wrote in 1839 that " when young men, in particular, are condemned to pass fifteen or twenty years in the same

[48] Navy Registers for 1841 and 1842; Sen. Doc., 27C. 2S., No. 1, 381; Cong. Globe, XI, 630-634, 638-642; U. S. Statutes at Large, V, 500.

[49] Cong. Letters, Navy Dept. Arch., II, 367; State Papers, Nav. Aff., I, 910.

rank, the spirit grows weary, the character loses its elasticity, the ambition is deadened, and the duty that with a proper attention to these details might be rendered attractive becomes monotonous and discouraging." [50]   The navy was more or less rent by cliques. The Perry party hated the Elliott party; and the Barron faction was at swords' points with the anti-Barron faction. The inferior officers accused their superiors of applying or withholding the laws of the navy according to the dictates of convenience and prejudice. Lieutenant M. F. Maury wrote in his figurative and lucid style that the " laws of the navy are kept in two vials—one of which is closely sealed, and seldom permitted to be opened—the other, large-mouthed and convenient, ready at all times with its wrath to be emptied upon the younger, and therefore the weaker and more frail members of the corps." [51]   The attempts of the department to enforce discipline were at times counteracted by Congress; for, when an officer was cashiered, or passed over in making promotions, a party was organized in that body to " see him righted." Secretary Paulding clinched his fists and set his teeth in his determination to restore discipline in the navy and to bring about a proper naval subordination. He made this the chief object of his administration. In March, 1839, he wrote, with a show of spirit, that the " President stands by me manfully, and please God, if I live and Congress does not counteract me, I will make both high and low, young and old, know who is their master, before I have done with them." In spite of his forcible resolution Paulding left the navy much as he found it. [52]

The typical commodore of the Old Navy was a law unto himself. He was a most austere and august personage, bluff, proud, pompous, reserved, and self-willed. " The little tyrant," Commodore David Porter called him, " who struts his few fathoms of scoured plank." Wrapped up in his own notions of dignity, he associated but little with his officers, a " solitary being in the midst of the ocean." He was surrounded with all the pomp and circumstance of a royal court. His smallest movements were accompanied with great ceremony. Lieutenant A. S. Mackenzie, a writer of much charm, has described the departure of an American

[50] Cooper, History of the Navy, XXV.
[51] Southern Literary Messenger for 1841, 13.
[52] Paulding's Paulding, 274-275.

commodore from his ship at Gibraltar, about 1830: "The sailors were drawn up before the mainmast, looking with silent respect towards the hallowed region of the quarter-deck. Upon this spacious parade-ground, flanked by a double battery, a company of fine-looking soldiers, with burnished and well-brushed attire, were drawn up to salute the departure of the commander. A splendid band of music, dressed in Moorish garb, was stationed at the stern, and the officers were all collected for the same purpose upon the quarter-deck, in irregular groups of noble-looking young fellows, the present pride and future hope of our country. At length the Herculean form and martial figure of the veteran commodore was added to the number. Here was the master-spirit that gave impulse and soul to the machine; a thousand eyes were fixed upon him, a thousand hats were raised; and as he passed over the side, the soldiers presented arms, and the music sent forth a martial melody. I thought I had never seen any array so soul-inspiring, so imposing." [53]

Service in the Old Navy was by no means all dull sailing in the doldrums of monotony and routine. The spectacle of the old commodore leaving his ship illustrates its glamor and picturesqueness. One cannot but regret the loss of the beautiful ships with their clouds of snow-white canvas, the duel-loving officers gay and debonair in their bright uniforms, and all the elaborate ceremony and display that regulated the conduct of the members of the little sea-going monarchies. Our navy was seen at its best on the Mediterranean station, which was regarded as the choicest berth by both officers and seamen. Here naval life took on a sort of Oriental luxury and dissipation. It was all one whether the ships lay basking in the winter sunshine at sportive Mahon, or were visiting the gay capitals of the Riveria, Barbary, and the Levant. Its charm and color may still be seen from the fascinating pages of N. P. Willis's Pencillings by the Way. The reader who wishes to pursue the subject should read especially Willis's description of a ball on board the famous old frigate *United States,* at Trieste.

From 1815 to 1860 dueling was quite common in the navy. More duels were fought during these years than during all the

---

[53] Porter, Constantinople and Its Environs, II, 10; Mackenzie, A Year in Spain, II, 264.

others of the navy's history. Before 1815, however, the practice was common. Benjamin Franklin was of the opinion that he prevented a hostile meeting between Captains John Paul Jones and Peter Landais, in 1779. Lieutenant Richard Somers, who was a naval officer from 1798 to 1804, and who is described as "mild, amiable, and affectionate, both in disposition and deportment," fought three duels in one day.[54] These encounters usually originated in trivial and imaginary causes. The sense of personal honor among the officers of the Old Navy was so excessive and extravagant that it was often absurd. In 1840 a duel between D. D. Porter and S. C. Rowan, the former of whom later became admiral and the latter vice-admiral of the navy, was narrowly averted. They were engaged in work in the hydrographic office of the coast survey, and one day fell into a dispute over the rights of Porter to prod a table with the points of a pair of dividers, and the rights of Rowan to stop this diversion. Of the several grades of officers, the midshipmen fought duels most frequently. Niles' Register for October 1, 1825, briefly chronicles one of these encounters as follows: "Two boys, midshipmen attached to the frigate *Constellation,* amused themselves by shooting at one another, on the 22d ult., at Fort Nelson, by which one of them was killed, and the other has the pleasure to say that he has slain a brother." On the Mediterranean, Brazil, and Pacific stations our officers often fought with foreigners, and especially with foreign officers. At home they sometimes engaged in bouts with civilians. President Jackson dismissed three lieutenants for affairs with a young Philadelphia doctor, being determined to prevent dueling between officers and civilians. He remarked, however, that he would not interfere with duels "between officers whose profession was fighting, and who were trained to arms."[55]

A contributory cause of insubordination in the navy was the failure of the government to provide proper schools for the young officers. Again and again the department recommended the establishment of a naval academy. Able articles in the public prints pointed out its necessity, and many officers of the navy plead for it. But Congress was not convinced, nor even thoroughly interested in the project. John Quincy Adams and Southard urged it

---

[54] Cooper, Lives of Naval Officers, I, 119.
[55] Sands, From Reefer to Rear-Admiral, 40, 121.

year after year, and in 1827 had it not been for the opposition of
the House, a naval school would have been established. Meanwhile schoolmasters, chaplains, and professors, at sea and on
shore, by dint of discouraging efforts, under conditions that often
rendered their work largely futile, instructed the midshipmen in
the rudiments of navigation and mathematics. At best these
spasmodic attempts to inculcate bits of elementary information,
heroic on the part of the teachers as they sometimes were,
amounted to mere makeshifts.

One of the most beneficial services rendered by the present
Naval Academy is its weeding out of the physically, mentally, and
professionally unfit. In the Old Navy this was done not at all, or
else done imperfectly. The most important factor in the selection
of midshipmen was political and personal influence; and many
statesmen of the olden time left memorials of their families in the
navy list by making midshipmen of sundry sons, grandsons,
nephews, and cousins. The schooling required of applicants was
most meager. They were asked to " furnish evidence that they
could read and write well, that they understood the principles of
English grammar, and the elementary rules of arithmetic and
geography." Upon receiving an appointment a midshipman was
directed to bring with him a " Bowditch and a quadrant," two
articles equally indispensable in the Old Navy. Few of the young
gentlemen learned thoroughly the science of their profession, but
many of them became proficient in its art. At first a midshipman's
duties on board ship were most elementary—such as repeating the
orders of his superiors and keeping a journal of the cruise. But
exigency or chance, after he had been some years in the service,
might require him to perform the duties of almost any grade.
" To-day, the monarch of the peopled deck, and the dignified oc-
cupant of the captain's cabin; to-morrow, the puling middie
again, without authority, the mere walking echo to a trumpet of
tin on the quarter-deck."

One might suppose that the Old Navy with its many hardships,
its few promotions, and its poor rewards, went begging for officers. But such was not the case. The glamor and romance of
a naval and seafaring life, and the paternal care and neglect that
a benign and indifferent government bestows on naval officers,
possesses for many persons a strange fascination. On March 1,
1835, the number of applications on file at the Navy Department

for the position of midshipman was 2355; assistant surgeon, 406; teacher, schoolmaster, and professor, 50; chaplain, 131; and secretary and clerk, 170. At this time two hundred more midshipmen were employed in the navy than the service required.[56] Secretary Paulding greatly enjoyed the diverting incidents of his duties in the Navy Department, but none more so than those connected with the making of appointments. The following plea, in which the original punctuation and italics are preserved, was once sent to him by an applicant for any office whatever: " I have now been engaged ten years in editorial life; and the thirteen years which I spent in the vocation of a pedagogue, have not been spent entirely in vain. I commenced at sixteen, and am now thirty-nine, with good health, and good morals *considering my avocations.*"[57]

Beginning with the inauguration of Jackson in 1829, at each change of the federal administration, the mail of the department was flooded with the letters of new applicants for various naval positions hastening to be first to offer their services to the victors, and with the communications of former applicants taking fresh hopes of success at the prospects of the coming of a new Secretary of the Navy. In the spring of 1829 Jackson's followers besieged John Branch for naval jobs of all sorts. Several of the most enterprising expressed their desires before March 4. Some half dozen clergymen were among the first to feel a call to higher service, possibly opened to them by the victory of the Democrats; and they made known their merits for the position of naval chaplain. Branch signalized his entrance into the department by removing its chief clerk. In May two other clerks were displaced. The larger part of the clerical force of the department was, however, untouched. The naval establishment was protected by its permanent tenure, and no important changes were made in it.[58]

Although under the commissioners the condition of the naval personnel was discouraging and many valuable recommendations of the department were passed over by Congress, yet several important improvements were effected. In 1835 Congress increased the pay of the naval officers. Until this time the highest pay in the navy, that of a captain, was $100 a month. His allowance

[56] General Letters, Navy Dept. Arch., XXI, 308, 517.
[57] W. K. Paulding, ed., Tales of a Good Woman (1867), 13-14.
[58] General Letters, Navy Dept. Arch., XVII, 111-194.

for subsistence, however, raised his annual salary to a little more than $2000. The act of 1835 gave the senior captain $4500 a year; and all other captains, in command of squadrons $4000, and on shore $3500. The wages of the officers of the other grades were raised proportionately. In addition to his salary each officer was allowed one ration a day.[59]

Something was done by the department by way of schools and examinations to improve the character of the naval officer. From the establishment in 1821 on board the *Guerriere* at the Norfolk navy yard of a school for midshipmen, such schools became more common, and more regular in their sessions. In 1835 Congress fixed the salary of the schoolmaster, or professor of mathematics as he was now called, at $1200 a year. At one time four naval officers were studying at Yale college, and one midshipman at the Military Academy at West Point. In 1840 four naval surgeons were granted permission to attend the clinical lectures of the Philadelphia Hospital.

The system of examinations for entrance into the navy and for promotions from one grade to another, which is now so important a feature of the service, was introduced during the period of the commissioners. One of the first examinations for promotions was held in New York in 1819. Its purpose was to determine the fitness of some midshipmen for promotion. The board of examiners was composed of naval officers. Its president was Captain William Bainbridge. In November, 1824, in accordance with an order of Secretary Southard, the first entrance examination for surgeon's mates was held at Gadsby's hotel, in Washington. It was conducted by a board of surgeons, which was ordered to ascertain the moral character and the scientific and professional attainments of the candidates. Those doctors who wished to attend the examination had first to obtain the consent of the department. In 1828 the examining of candidates for assistant surgeons, and of assistant surgeons who were candidates for promotion, were prescribed by law. In 1835 the first examination of prospective professors of mathematics was held. It was conducted by a board composed of men distinguished for their literary and scientific attainments.[60]

[59] U. S. Statutes at Large, IV, 755-757.
[60] General Letters, Navy Dept. Arch., XV, 2; XXI, 359; U. S. Statutes at Large, IV, 313-314.

The advent of steam as a motive force of naval vessels caused the establishment of a new naval corps, that of steam engineers. On July 12, 1836, Secretary Dickerson appointed C. H. Haswell chief engineer of the steamship *Fulton the Second*, then building. He was the first engineer in the navy. In 1839 Paulding appointed a principal engineer. In February, 1842, Upshur informed Congress that he had no authority to enlist engineers " *eo nomine,* and of course they can be employed only under some other name. Their pay is unascertained and dependent on private contract, and their rank in the service, and their position in the ship, are equally undetermined." Accordingly, on August 31, 1842, Congress passed a statute organizing a corps of engineers. An engineer-in-chief was placed at the head of the corps, at a salary of $3000 a year; and a requisite number of chief and assistant engineers, not to exceed eight for each steamship, was authorized. On the day following the approval of this act, Gilbert L. Thompson was appointed engineer-in-chief of the navy. He was a lawyer, gentleman, scholar, and diplomatist; and the son of Ex-Secretary of the Navy Smith Thompson. " His engineering was purely nominal, and confined to a very prompt and efficient drawing of his salary." [61]

During the years from 1812 to 1836 when the principal sailing-ships of the Old Navy were built, the corps of naval constructors assumed greater importance than hitherto. The principal constructors during this period were Henry Eckford, Samuel Humphreys, William Doughty, Francis Hartt, and John Floyd. Eckford was an eminent naval architect, of New York city. During the War of 1812 he and Christian Bergh, another noted shipbuilder, had charge of the construction of naval vessels at Sackett's Harbor, on Lake Ontario. Eckford was the naval constructor at the New York yard from 1817 to 1820. One of his vessels was the line of battleship *Ohio*, a famous ship in her day. Owing to a disagreement with the commissioners, he left the navy. Later, he built a vessel for the sultan of the Ottoman empire, and established a navy yard in Turkey. Samuel Humphreys held the position of chief naval constructor from 1826 to 1846. He was a son of Joshua Humphreys, the chief

[61] Cong. Letters, Navy Dept. Arch., VIII, 354; U. S. Statutes at Large, V. 577; Bennett, Steam Navy, 40-41.

naval constructor under Washington and the elder Adams. Doughty was for a long time employed at the Washington yard; Grice, at the Norfolk yard; and Floyd, at the Portsmouth yard.

The Navy Department often had difficulty in obtaining enough seamen to man its ships. Few vessels went to sea in which the whole crew was enlisted for the maximum period of three years. Southard believed that the failure to procure seamen was caused by the higher wages and the stronger inducements of other sorts offered to them by the merchant service, and also by the temptations presented to them by other governments. As a remedy for the deficiency of seamen, he proposed to admit more boys into the service as apprentices, and to enter healthy and robust landsmen from the Western States, rating them as ordinary seamen. Under the commissioners it was customary to enlist foreigners of various nationalities. It was commonly said that they were more prone to insubordination than native seamen.

Captain M. C. Perry was an early advocate of the establishment of an apprentice system. He addressed a letter to the department on this subject as early as 1823, and in January of the succeeding year he drew up a plan for an apprentice system. It provided for the annual enlistment of one thousand boys to serve until of age, and to be clothed at the expense of the government. Perry believed that it would effect the reformation of many bad and idle boys and would bring into the navy native-born Americans, from whom warrant and petty officers might be drawn. In 1835 Perry addressed the department again on the same subject. In the same year John Goin, of New York city, proposed the establishment of nautical schools for boys who wished to follow the sea as a livelihood. His proposition was zealously advocated by the press, and about this time such schools were established at Baltimore and Charleston (South Carolina).[62]

In 1837 Congress passed an act establishing a naval apprentice system. According to its provisions boys between the ages of thirteen and eighteen were to be enlisted to serve until they were twenty-one. Under this law several hundred boys at once entered the navy. School-ships were established at the principal navy yards—the *Hudson* and *North Carolina* at New York, the *Colum-*

    [62] Griffis, M. C. Perry, 146-151, 435-439; Officers' Letters, Navy Dept. Arch., 1824, I, No. 13; Lossing, U. S. Navy, 375-378.

bus at Boston, and the *Java* at Norfolk. The boys were also instructed on board the regular cruising ships of the navy. A visitor to the *Java* at Norfolk describes the apprentices as " neatly attired in sailors' garb and good-looking." Most of the apprentices were recruited at Northern ports. The system lasted only some five or six years. Its failure has been ascribed to the extravagant expectations of promotion which were held out to the boys by the department. When these were not realized the boys became dissatisfied and left the navy.[63]

The scientific work of the navy began in the decade of the thirties, when a decided movement towards mental and professional improvement manifested itself among the naval officers. This awakening seems to have been connected with that great intellectual and reformatory " wave " that swept over Europe and America at this time. No social group apparently was left untouched by it. Near the close of 1833 the officers at the New York navy yard, under the leadership of Captain M. C. Perry, organized the United States Naval Lyceum " to promote the diffusion of useful knowledge, to foster a spirit of harmony and a community of interests in the service, and to cement the links which unite us as professional brethren." The organization soon obtained a library, museum, and ample rooms. Its motto was *tam Minerva quam Marte,* as well for Minerva as for Mars. Out of the lyceum grew in 1836 the Naval Magazine, the first periodical in the United States conducted by naval officers. Its editor was Rev. Charles S. Stewart, a chaplain in the navy. Although a highly creditable production, it had but a brief existence, of two years. About the first of January, 1836, the American Historical Society of Military and Naval Events was organized. The beginnings of the Naval Observatory and the Hydrographic Office were laid in 1830 by the establishment in Washington of the Depot of Charts and Instruments. Here the navy began its observational work in astronomy, magnetism, and meteorology; and Lieutenants Wilkes, Gilliss, and Maury commenced their scientific careers. From 1834 to 1836 the coast survey was under the direction of the Navy Department. The first naval exploring expedition was sent out in 1838 in charge of Lieutenant Wilkes.

[63] Naval Magazine, I, 176-182; U. S. Statutes at Large, V. 153; General Letters, Navy Dept. Arch., XXVIII, 160, XXIX, 510.

Lieutenant Matthew F. Maury was the first naval line officer to write a scientific book before 1840. His " New Theoretical and Practical Treatise on Navigation," a work of no great originality, appeared in 1835. The earliest scientific book by a naval officer is believed to be one entitled " Observations on the Means of Preserving the Health of Soldiers and Sailors and on the Duties of the Medical Department of the Army and Navy, with Remarks on Hospitals and their Internal Arrangement." It was written by a naval surgeon, Edward Cutbush, for many years the senior officer of his corps; and it was published at Philadelphia, in 1808. Between 1815 and 1830 another naval surgeon, W. P. C. Barton, wrote numerous volumes relating to botany and medicine. Barton was a graduate of Princeton, a scientist and botanist of distinction, and the organizer of the naval bureau of medicine and surgery.

To certain departments of general literature naval officers are specially qualified to make contributions. Their unique life on ship-board, their varied experiences in foreign lands, and their active work in time of war, afford them much highly valuable and entertaining information. When they have chosen to do so, they have produced some delightful voyages and travels, sketches of naval life, and naval biographies and autobiographies. The beginnings of this literature were made during the period of the navy commissioners.

In 1822 appeared Commodore David Porter's journal of a cruise made in the Pacific Ocean in the *Essex* in 1813-1814; and in 1835 his most entertaining letters respecting Constantinople and its environs were published. The most attractive writer among the naval officers of his time was Lieutenant A. S. Mackenzie, of unfortunate fame in connection with the brig *Somers*. His travels in Spain are still interesting reading, and at the time of their publication were much in vogue, even in London. In 1840 he issued a life of Commodore O. H. Perry; and in 1841 a life of John Paul Jones. In the late twenties and early thirties Naval Chaplains Walter Colton and C. S. Stewart and Naval School-masters George Jones (later chaplain) and E. C. Wines wrote several popular volumes describing their voyages and the life on board naval ships. In 1834 W. S. W. Ruschenberger's " Three Years in the Pacific " appeared. The author was a naval surgeon, and a prolific writer. A species of literature that fortunately or unfortunately stands alone is Midshipman William Leggett's

"Leisure Hours at Sea; Being a Few Miscellaneous Poems."
This volume was published in 1825. The navy may lay some
claim to the writings of James Fenimore Cooper, as he was at one
time a midshipman, and he found in his naval life inspiration and
information for his sea stories. His history of the navy, which
was first issued in 1839, is still the authority for the period
covered.

Soon after the establishment of the navy board in 1815, the
commissioners revised the regulations of the navy. The commissioners' edition of the regulations of 1818 was in force for more
than forty years. They also revised the regulations respecting
naval uniforms. They greatly improved the financial system of
the department, against which its critics fulminated from time
to time. The system of procuring supplies by contract was
adopted; and many valuable checks against frauds and misappli-
cations of the public money by navy agents, pursers, and contractors were instituted. Improvements were also effected in the
method of keeping the naval accounts and of making the naval
estimates. Some of the beneficial changes in the financial system
made by the commissioners were embodied in statutes by
Congress.[64]

During the last ten years of the existence of the Board of Navy
Commissioners, a growing feeling of dissatisfaction with it was
manifested both in and out of the navy. Some of the adverse
criticism of the board was just; but much of it fell wide of the
mark. The navy board was blamed for evils, for which the navy
system, Congress, or the office of the Secretary of the Navy were
censurable. It had no more unsparing critic among the older
naval officers than Commodore Charles Stewart. In March, 1842,
in a letter to Secretary Upshur, he declared that the board had
failed to meet the expectations of the navy and of the country.
He thought it lacked " individual responsibility." It vacillated;
and it was a fruitful source of many evils. The " absence of
economy in the construction, equipment, and repair of our vessels;
the diversity in their models, classes, and qualities; the incapacity
of some and the worthlessness of others; the excessive waste by
continual experiments, have never been surpassed, if ever equalled,
in any other naval establishment of the same limits." On the

[64] Commodore Morris's Autobiography, 90.

other hand, Secretary Southard had said in 1825 that the navy
board had managed its work in a way " deserving the highest
commendation," and that it had superintended the expenditure
of $15,500,000 without loss to the public.[65]

The public prints of the time often discussed naval reform and
the reorganization of the Navy Department. In January, 1842,
the Madisonian said concerning the department that "an *imperium
in imperio* exists, with all the evils concomitant on such an institution."[66] In 1840 and 1841 some remarkable articles on naval
reform appeared in the Southern Literary Messenger, a periodical published at Richmond, Virginia. They were entitled " Scraps
from the Lucky Bag," and were signed pseudonymously, under
the name of " Harry Bluff." They attracted much attention, were
widely read and discussed, and were in part reprinted for the use
of the members of Congress. Their author was Lieutenant
Matthew F. Maury, a young man of brilliant parts, who later
achieved renown for his studies and publications in meteorology
and hydrography. Maury was a facile writer. His style was
vivid, lucid, and vigorous. He marshalled his facts and details
in a most convincing way, and wrote with the zeal of a reformer.
Such notoriety did these articles gain the young lieutenant, that
he was mentioned as a proper character for Secretary of the
Navy.

A few quotations will give a notion of Maury's style and criticism: " The organization of the Navy Board is bad. The seeds
of disease were implanted in its system from the beginning. La-
boring thus under a constitutional malady, it has inflicted upon
the service first one and then another of its ills, until at last the
whole navy has got the *cachexia*. The friends of the patient have
become alarmed ; and in the consternation that prevails many and
various remedies are proposed. But let us, if possible, Mr. Editor,
retain our presence of mind, and attempt first to ascertain in what
stage of disease the patient really is ; then we may proceed to
prescribe remedies with a better grace, and to treat the case with
more chances of success." " Some will tell you that the Navy
Board is a power behind the Secretary greater than the Secretary
himself—that there is a Master-Spirit in that board, which rules

---

[65] Army and Navy Chronicle for 1844, 416.
[66] Army and Navy Chronicle for 1842, 24.

the Navy. Others will tell you that the evil genius of the Navy presides at that board." The navy is inflicted with an " organization quaint and *outre,* with a board of commissioners, and many a blunder and foolish notion."

Maury accused the commissioners of waste, extravagance, dilatoriness, and bad judgment, in building and repairing the public vessels ; of ruinous delays in fitting out ships ; of vacillation and lack of science in preserving timber ; of bad accounting and of misstatements in making reports ; and of attempting to abolish the marine corps. He said that no vessels had been built by the navy board comparable to those of Eckford and the elder Humphreys. The commissioners " had turned out upon the navy a nest of tubs and sent them to sea as men-of-war." [67]

Maury greatly overstated his case against the commissioners. His arguments were, of course, one-sided. They were brilliant and exaggerated. He proved too much. In common with all enthusiasts, he saw the evils of the system that he criticised, but failed to see those of the system he recommended. He overestimated the importance of an administrative system, whether it be good or bad. His papers furthered the cause of naval reform and strengthened the opposition to the navy board.

As an administrative organ the Board of Navy Commissioners was moderately successful. It displayed both the good and bad qualities of a plural-headed executive. Its acts were conservative and deliberate. The principles and information upon which it acted were well-considered. Its advice to the Secretary of the Navy when drawn from its professional knowledge was valuable and judicious. As its members were not specially trained in the art of shipbuilding, it sometimes blundered in naval construction. Its work often lacked expedition. Since each member had to reach a decision on all questions presented to it, it was sometimes slow in reaching a conclusion. When its members failed to agree, it gave forth discordant advice. Unfortunately, many of the problems that the board by reason of its professional information was best able to solve did not fall to it, but to the Secretary of the Navy.

[67] Southern Literary Messenger for 1840, 233-240, 305-320, 785-800; for 1841, 3-25, 345-379.

CHAPTER SIX: THE NAVAL BUREAUS, 1842-1861

THE NAVY DEPARTMENT.

The first period of the naval bureaus lasted almost two decades, from the organization of the bureaus on September 1, 1842, until March 5, 1861, when Lincoln's Secretary of the Navy, Gideon Welles, entered upon his duties. The principal work of the department during this period had to do with the construction of a steam fleet, the improvement of the naval personnel, naval voyages of exploration, the operations of the Mexican War, and the disturbed relations between the North and the South in the winter of 1860-1861. The list of naval secretaries for this period contains but few illustrious names. They were upon the whole men of less ability than were their predecessors under the navy commissioners. The succession of secretaries was as follows: Abel P. Upshur, of Virginia, 1842-1843; David Henshaw, of Massachusetts, 1843-1844; Thomas W. Gilmer, of Virginia, 1844; John Y. Mason, of Virginia, 1844-1845; George Bancroft, of Massachusetts, 1845-1846; John Y. Mason, of Virginia, 1846-1849; William B. Preston, of Virginia, 1849-1850; William A. Graham, of North Carolina, 1850-1852; John P. Kennedy, of Maryland, 1852-1853; James C. Dobbin, of North Carolina, 1853-1857; and Isaac Toucey, of Connecticut, 1857-1861.

During the twenty years preceding the Civil War, the naval affairs of the United States were largely under the influence of Southern men. In Congress, probably no one man so much determined naval legislation as Stephen R. Mallory, of Florida, who in 1861 became the Secretary of the Navy of the Southern Confederacy. For several years he was chairman of the Senate Committee on Naval Affairs. Of the eleven secretaries named

above, all except three, Henshaw, Bancroft, and Toucey, came
from States south of Mason and Dixon's line. The joint service
of Henshaw and Bancroft was only two years; and Toucey,
Buchanan's naval secretary, was a Southerner in his sympathies.
Of the eight Southern secretaries, three were from North Carolina, four from Virginia, and one from Maryland. They were all
lawyers, and most of them had served in Congress. They had
few practical or technical qualifications for the secretaryship.
Toucey also was a lawyer, and had been attorney-general and
later a senator of the United States. Bancroft was an historian;
and Henshaw, a sometime druggist, a promoter of railroads, and
a Massachusetts politician. Henshaw was commissioned during
the recess of the Senate on July 24, 1843. President Tyler sent
his nomination to the Senate on December 6, which body rejected
it on January 15, 1844, it is said, for political reasons. This is the
only instance in which the Senate refused to accept the President's
choice of a Secretary of the Navy.

Henshaw's successor, Thomas W. Gilmer, performed the duties
of his office for only ten days. Both he and Ex-Secretary of the
Navy Upshur were killed on February 28, 1844, by the explosion
of a gun on board the naval steamship *Princeton*. This vessel,
which had been just completed, was fitted with improved
machinery and guns. She was a screw-propeller, and her two
largest cannon fired balls weighing 225 pounds each—a great
weight of metal for that day. She was brought up the Potomac
to Washington in order that the officers of the government might
inspect her. On the morning of February 28 a large company of
invited guests, drawn chiefly from official life in Washington,
went on board the vessel. She proceeded down the Potomac
below Mount Vernon. The accident occurred on her return trip,
after she had made a most excellent showing of her machinery
and guns. The guests had just refreshed themselves with a
" sumptuous collation," and were seated around the table when
word was sent them that one of the guns was to be again fired.
The gentlemen of the company led by President Tyler immediately went on deck, but fortunately the President was called back
and escaped death. The gun burst, killing all that stood near it.
Among the dead were Gilmer, Upshur, Commodore Beverly
Kennon of the navy, and Mr. Virgil Maxey of the diplomatic
service.[1]

[1] Benton, Thirty Years' View, II, 567-569.

George Bancroft and John P. Kennedy may be classed among the literary Secretaries of the Navy. Bancroft's "History of the United States" is well known. Less familiar to most readers and doubtless less deserving to be remembered, is a slender volume of poems that he published in his youth. Bancroft has been tersely described as "learned, full of semi-poetic fire, something of a popular orator, and a sincere democrat."[2] In the midst of his legal and political duties, Kennedy found time to compose several volumes of pleasing fiction and a biography of William Wirt. No more genial, cultured, and sweet-spirited man than Kennedy has filled the secretaryship. Like Paulding, he was an intimate friend of Washington Irving, who in 1853, when collecting information for his "Life of Washington," was the guest of the Secretary at the capitol. Irving was quite taken with the Navy Department and discovered much poetry in its materials and incidents. Kennedy regarded it as much the most interesting department of the government.[3]

A friendly pen has written concerning Kennedy that the "versatility of his usefulness and his sympathies may be inferred from the many and widely distant associations that endear his memory. His name gracefully designates a channel of the lonely Arctic sea, and is identified with the initial experiment which established the electric telegraph; with the opening of Japan to the commerce of the world; with the exploration of the Amazon and the China sea; with the benefactions of Peabody and the loyalty of Maryland; with the cause of education and the old genial life of Virginia; with what is graceful and gracious in American letters and useful and honorable in American statesmanship; with the pleasures of society and the duties of patriotism; with the fondest recollections of friendship and the tenderest memories of domestic love."[4]

Literary men when called to participate in the affairs of state are supposed to bring to their work a high sense of duty and an elevated view and purpose. The services in the Navy Department of Bancroft and Kennedy bear out this supposition. Bancroft manifested great zeal for naval education and a thorough-going reform of the naval personnel; while Kennedy

[2] Trent, American Literature, 542.
[3] Tuckerman, Kennedy, 235.
[4] Tuckerman, Kennedy, 21-22.

was chiefly interested in the scientific work of the navy, and took much satisfaction in the aid which he was able to give to naval voyages of exploration.

The characters of Bancroft and Kennedy are more interesting than those of the other secretaries from 1842 to 1861. All showed a fair degree of zeal and industry in their work; but none, with the possible exception of Bancroft, achieved distinction. For one reason their terms of office were short. Only Dobbin, 1853-1857, and Toucey, 1857-1861, served for the full four years. The services of Mason, whose two terms were separated by that of Bancroft, amounted to three and a half years.

The lives of several secretaries after they resigned from the department are interesting. Gilmer left Fillmore's cabinet to become the candidate of the Whig party for Vice-president on the ticket with General Scott. During the Civil War he was a member of the Confederate Senate. Preston, President Taylor's naval secretary, also served in that body. Bancroft and Kennedy, one a Democrat and the other a Whig, ardently espoused the cause of the Union. When Toucey, Buchanan's secretary, yielded his office to Gideon Welles on March 5, 1861, he returned to Hartford, Connecticut, to the practice of law, where he remained during the war.

From 1842 to 1861 no settled policy was followed as respects the designation of an acting Secretary of the Navy, an officer appointed to take charge of the department during the absence of the secretary from Washington. The chief clerk of the department, the chiefs of bureaus, and the Secretary of War at different times served in this capacity. In June, 1853, Jefferson Davis, who was then Secretary of War, was also acting Secretary of the Navy. Twice a Secretary of the Navy *ad interim* was appointed. In 1844 Commodore Lewis Warrington, when chief of the Bureau of Navy-Yards and Docks, and again in 1859, when chief of the Bureau of Ordnance and Hydrography, was so designated. The chief clerks of the department were no longer chosen to act in this capacity.

In the fall of 1841 Secretary Upshur took up the subject of naval administration, and discussed it at some length in his annual report for that year. He believed that a reorganization of the department was indispensable, and that it could not longer be delayed without serious injury to the service. The following

extract from his report contains the gist of his criticism of the old
navy system:

"I have had but a short experience in this department, but a short experience is enough to display its defects, even to the most superficial observation. It is, in truth, not organized at all. The labor to be performed,
must, under any circumstances, be great and onerous, but it is rendered
doubly so by the want of a proper arrangement and distribution of duties.
At present a multitude of duties are imposed upon the head of the department, which any one of its clerks could discharge as well as himself, but
which from their pressing nature, he is not permitted to postpone. Hence,
his whole time is occupied in trifling details, rendering it impossible for
him to bestow the requisite attention upon more important subjects involving the great interests of the service. These details are, indeed, so numerous and multifarious, as to constitute in themselves an amount of duties
fully equal to the powers of any one man. In addition to this, the present
want of proper arrangement is extremely unfavorable to that individual
responsibility, which it is so necessary to impose upon every public officer.
The same cause occasions delays in the operations of the department by
rendering necessary a variety of tedious official forms, and consequently
preventing that promptness of action which is indispensable to its due efficiency. And it is not the least among the evils of this state of things that
the precise condition of the several branches of the service cannot be ascertained without much time and labor; thus adding to the cost of the department, while it diminishes its usefulness. These inconveniences and
embarrassments, and many others which are daily felt in the administration
of the department, would in some degree be removed by a mere rearrange-
ment and proper distribution of the labor now employed in it; but additional labor is absolutely necessary in order to enable it to discharge its
functions in the manner required by the interests of the service." [5]

These thoroughgoing criticisms reveal a secretary new to his
office and ardent for reform. Upshur's next step was to draft
and send to the House a rough sketch of a bill for the reorganization of the department. With this as a basis, the House by March,
1842, had prepared a bill, which provided for six naval bureaus;
navy-yards and docks; construction and repairs; equipment, provisions, and stores; ordnance; hydrography; and medicine and
surgery. Upshur recommended that the duties of the Bureau of
Equipment, Provisions, and Stores be vested in two bureaus
instead of one. Accordingly on June 17, 1842, William S. Archer,
of Virginia, introduced a bill in the Senate providing for seven
naval bureaus. This passed the Senate on August 6. After
being amended, it was passed by the House on August 30. Two
of the amendments of the House are important: one united

[5] Ann. Rept. of Sec. of N., 1841, p. 378.

the Bureau of Equipment with the Bureau of Construction and Repairs, and the Bureau of Hydrography with the Bureau of Ordnance; and the other vested the power of appointing the bureau chiefs in the President and Senate instead of in the Secretary of the Navy. This bill became a law on August 31, 1842.[6]

The most significant fact about this legislation for the reorganization of the Navy Department is that the act of August 31, 1842, contained no provision organizing the chiefs of the bureaus into a board and vesting it with corporate functions. The division of labor among the bureaus was complete. Each chief was individually responsible to the Secretary of the Navy; all collective responsibility was abolished. The only unifying factor in the department was the Secretary of the Navy. The new act specifically repealed the law establishing the Board of Navy Commissioners. In place of the board it substituted five naval bureaus, whose names are as follows:

1. Bureau of Navy-Yards and Docks.
2. Bureau of Construction, Equipment and Repairs.
3. Bureau of Provisions and Clothing.
4. Bureau of Ordnance and Hydrography.
5. Bureau of Medicine and Surgery.

The law prescribed that the chiefs of the Bureaus of Navy-Yards and Docks and Ordnance and Hydrography should be captains of the navy, and should receive an annual salary of $3500, in lieu of all compensation whatever as naval officers. The chief of the Bureau of Construction, Equipment and Repairs, who must be a skilful naval constructor, was to receive the same salary. The chief of the Bureau of Provisions and Clothing was given $3000 a year, and might be either a naval officer or a civilian. The chief of the Bureau of Medicine and Surgery, who was paid $2500 a year, was to be selected from the surgeons of the navy. The several chiefs were to be appointed by the President and confirmed by the Senate.

The naval bureaus were subordinated to the Secretary of the Navy by the enactment that " all the duties of the said bureaus shall be performed under the authority of the Secretary of the Navy, and their orders shall be considered as emanating from him, and shall have full force and effect as such." No change in

---

[6] Congress Letters, VIII, 362; Congressional Globe, 1841-1842, pp. 854, 970-973; U. S. Statutes at Large, V, 579-581.

the Secretary's office, except in its clerical force, was made. To it was assigned a chief clerk at $2000 a year, and nine other clerks with annual salaries ranging from $800 to $1500. The Bureau of Navy-Yards and Docks was allowed a civil engineer, a draftsman, and three clerks; the Bureau of Construction, Equipment and Repairs, a draftsman and four clerks; the Bureau of Provisions and Clothing, three clerks; the Bureau of Ordnance and Hydrography, one draftsman and three clerks; and the Bureau of Medicine and Surgery, an assistant surgeon and two clerks. The annual salaries of the clerks of the bureaus ranged from $800 to $1400. Officers in the navy might be appointed to clerkships. The books, records, and papers of the navy board were ordered to be distributed among the several bureaus.

The Secretary of the Navy was authorized to assign such duties to the five bureaus as he should judge expedient and proper. The names of the bureaus indicate the duties that were assigned them. The Bureau of Navy-Yards and Docks was vested with the construction and maintenance of the docks, wharves and buildings within the navy-yards. It was given a general control of the administration of the yards. The several commandants reported to the chief of this bureau. The Bureau of Construction, Equipment and Repairs was charged with the designing, building, fitting, and repairing of wood and iron hulls; and with the equipping of vessels with sails, anchors, cables, fuel, galleys, blocks, and yeomen's stores. The Bureau of Provisions and Clothing provided the navy with provisions, clothing, and small stores. On shore, its agents were the navy agents and storekeepers; and on shipboard, the pursers. The duties of the Bureau of Ordnance and Hydrography related to the maintenance of magazines, the manufacture and use of ordnance and ammunition, the issuing of naval charts, and the collection and dissemination of hydrographic information. The Bureau of Medicine and Surgery purchased medical supplies, and superintended the naval medical corps and the naval laboratories, hospitals, and dispensaries.

The bureau system was immediately put into operation. On August 31, 1842, President Tyler appointed Commodore Lewis Warrington, the president of the Board of Navy Commissioners, to be chief of the Bureau of Navy-Yards and Docks; Commodore William M. Crane, the second member of the board, to be chief of the Bureau of Ordnance and Hydrography; and Commodore David Conner, the third member of the board, to be chief of the Bureau of Construction, Equipment and Repairs. Dr. William P. C. Barton, who stood second on the list of navy surgeons, was made chief of the Bureau of Medicine and Surgery; and Charles W. Goldsborough, secretary of the navy board, became the first chief of the Bureau of Provisions and Clothing. On the same day, August 31, these appointments were confirmed by the Senate. On September 1 the bureaus were organized.

The act of August 31, 1842, required that the chief of the Bureau of Construction, Equipment and Repairs should be a " skilful naval constructor." This provision was disregarded by Secretary Upshur when he appointed Commodore David Conner, an officer of the line, to be the first chief of this bureau. Upshur explained in his annual report for 1842 that in selecting Conner, he had preferred a naval captain qualified to equip, to a naval constructor qualified to construct and repair. This violation of the law, which was in the interest of the officers of the line, continued until 1853 when a provision was inserted in the general appropriation bill for that year and retained after considerable opposition, directing that the chief of the Bureau of Construction, Equipment and Repairs should " be a ' skilful naval constructor,' as required by the act approved August thirty-first, eighteen hundred and forty-two, instead of a captain of the navy." [7]

Early in 1843 an attempt was made in Congress to modify the act reorganizing the Navy Department so as to render civilians ineligible for the position of chief of the Bureau of Provisions and Clothing. The success of this attempt would have necessitated the retirement of Goldsborough. In September, 1843, Goldsborough died, and in December President Tyler nominated a civilian to fill the vacancy—Isaac Hill, of New Hampshire. The Senate refused to confirm this nomination. On January 30, 1844, the President nominated and the Senate confirmed a naval officer, Commodore William B. Shubrick. Gideon Welles, Shubrick's successor, was the last civilian chief of the Bureau of Provisions and Clothing. Since Welles's resignation in 1849, members of the naval pay corps, in accordance with law, have been regularly appointed to the chiefship of this bureau. In these early contentions over appointments, one discovers evidences of the rivalry

[7] Ann. Rept. of Sec. of N., 1842, p. 538, U. S. Statutes at Large, X, 196.

and jealousy that then existed between the staff and the line on the one hand, and naval officers and civilians on the other.

The terms of office of several of the early chiefs of naval bureaus were of unusual length. Rear-Admiral Joseph Smith, a fine officer of the Old Navy, who in 1846 succeeded Commodore Warrington as chief of the Bureau of Navy-Yards and Docks, held this position for almost a quarter of a century. John Lenthall, who in 1853 succeeded Samuel Hartt as chief of the Construction Bureau, served for more than seventeen years. He was the most eminent shipbuilder of the corps of naval constructors during the first years of the steam navy. Hartt, who was in office only a few months, was the first naval constructor to become head of the Construction Bureau. His predecessor, the last line officer to fill the position, was Commodore William B. Shubrick. Horatio Bridge was chief of the Bureau of Provisions and Clothing from 1854 to 1869; and William Whelan presided over the Medical Bureau from 1853 to 1865. Commodore Charles Morris was at the head of the Construction Bureau from 1844 to 1847; and at the head of the Ordnance Bureau from 1851 to 1856. In the latter place he succeeded Commodore Warrington, who had had charge of ordnance since 1846.

For a time the most important bureau was that of Navy-Yards and Docks and its head was the ranking officer among the bureau chiefs. In 1845 the control of the timber agents in the Southern States was assigned to this bureau; and in 1849 it was given charge of the Naval Asylum at Philadelphia, much to the displeasure of the Bureau of Medicine and Surgery, to whose care the asylum had been previously committed. The Bureaus of Construction, Equipment, and Repairs, and Ordnance and Hydrography were next in importance. Their work rapidly increased. To the former fell the building of the new steam fleet; and to the latter, the construction and improvement of naval ordnance and the direction of the educational and scientific establishments of the navy. The Hydrographical Office and the Naval Observatory founded in 1842, the Naval Academy founded in 1845, and the Nautical Almanac Office founded in 1849, were at first a part of the Secretary's office and their activities were immediately directed by the Secretary of the Navy; but in time they were all subordinated to the Bureau of Ordnance and Hydrography.

Under the act of August 31, 1842, the Navy Department was

allowed twenty-nine clerks. Secretary Henshaw regarded this force as inadequate, and in his annual report for 1843 he asked for nine additional clerks. To one of these, he wished to assign the custody of all the books and papers of the late navy commissioners and the library of the department. By 1860 the clerical force had increased to forty-two men. At this time the highest paid clerks were the chief clerk of the department, who received an annual salary of $2200, and the disbursing clerk, who received $2000. On the establishment of the bureaus in 1842, three clerks in the navy commissioners' office and one in the Secretary's office were made chief clerks of bureaus. The employees of the department were generally industrious, painstaking, and methodical in their work. In 1843, however, a subordinate clerk was discharged for gross negligence, inattention to duty, and "unpardonable inaccuracy."

The department continued to occupy the old Navy Department building, which was now well-worn and somewhat dilapidated. On the establishment of the naval bureaus, some of them found accommodations outside of this building. In 1851 several rooms in the "Winder building" were being rented. In 1844 the Naval Observatory and Hydrographical Office occupied their permanent quarters in Washington, which had been constructed under the superintendence of Lieutenant James M. Gilliss. Already the government was planning the construction of a new building for the joint occupancy of the Navy and War Departments.

Under the bureaus, the system of making purchases through navy agencies was continued. When navy-yards were located at Memphis and Mare Island navy agents for Memphis and San Francisco were appointed. Temporary navy agents or navy store-keepers residing at various naval depots supplied the needs of the squadrons in foreign waters. The ships of the home squadron when in the West Indies could obtain stores at St. Thomas, Aspinwall, or Key West. The Brazil squadron replenished its stores at Rio de Janeiro. The China squadron had depots at Manila, Singapore, Shanghai, Hong Kong, and Macao. The Pacific squadron obtained supplies at San Francisco and Monterey, California; Mazatlan, Mexico; the Sandwich Islands; Panama, New Grenada; Lima, Peru; and Valparaiso, Chile. For the African squadron depots were maintained at Porto Praya, Cape Verde Islands, and at Monrovia and St. Paul de Loando, on the coast of Africa. Financial agencies were situated at London and Marseilles. At London the Baring Brothers had been acting as the agents of the department since about 1816. In 1846 Spain requested the removal of the American naval station from the island of Minorca, and the department acceded to the request. Mahon had become objectionable on account of the frequent disorders that occurred between the sailors of the American fleet and the soldiers and Mahonese rabble. Nor were the difficulties always confined to the sailors, for in 1842 Midshipman J. S. Anderson, when returning to his ship, was mortally stabbed through the heart. The department established the naval station for the Mediterranean squadron at Spezzia, Sardinia.

Grave charges of corruption and violations of law having been preferred against the Navy Department, the House in January, 1859, appointed a select committee to investigate the naval contracts and expenditures. The committee consisted of five members, three of whom were favorable to the administration, and two opposed to it. To the latter class belonged the committee's chairman, John Sherman, of Ohio. Many witnesses were examined and a voluminous report prepared containing about one thousand pages. The majority of the committee reported that some glaring abuses existed in the management of the New York navy-yard, and in the purchasing of anthracite coal, but that nothing had been proved impeaching the personal or official character of the Secretary of the Navy. The minority found Buchanan and Toucey guilty of corrupt practices and misdemeanors. The work of this committee was instrumental in bringing about reforms in the administration of the navy-yards.[8]

During the last months of Secretary Toucey's administration of the navy a state of incipient civil war existed. " The fact can not be disguised," President Buchanan wrote on January 8, 1861, " that we are in the midst of a great Revolution." [9] Under such circumstances he should have harked back to the memorable example set by one of the great founders of his party, Andrew Jackson, and have resolved to hold firmly and defend vigorously the public property of the United States. Instead, he adopted a weak and lukewarm policy of mild and innoxious defense, a policy of peace, conciliation, temporization, and avoidance of offense to the

[8] Sherman, Recollections, I, 158-161; House Rept., 35C. 2S., No. 184; House Rept., 36C. 1S., No. 621; Congress Letters XIII, 324.

[9] Richardson, Messages and Papers of the Presidents, V, 656-657.

South. Buchanan and his cabinet had their eyes set upon a compromise, and were continually smoothing the way to it. The failure of their passive plan was complete. The adherence of the Secretary of the Navy to it accounts for many of his acts that were denounced as traitorous by his Republican critics. His patriotism seems to have been sound.

The first indications in the Navy Department of the approach of the Civil War was the tendering by Southern officers of their resignations. From November 12, 1860, immediately after the election of Lincoln, until January 24, 1861, forty-seven naval officers from South Carolina, Florida, Georgia, Alabama, and Mississippi resigned. Toucey accepted each resignation as soon as tendered. In some instances this was of doubtful propriety. Those officers implicated in the surrender of the Pensacola navy-yard should have been first court-martialed, and only the innocent have been permitted to resign. Toucey might at least have hesitated to accept the resignation of an officer who declared that he wished to be released from his obligations to the United States in order that he might be free to act against the Union. Had the Secretary of the Navy showed deliberation, he would have been able to have strengthened his defense against the charges made in the following partisan resolution adopted by the House of Representatives on March 2, 1861: "Resolved, That the Secretary of the Navy, in accepting without delay or inquiry the resignations of officers of the Navy, who were in arms against the Government when tendering the same, and of those who sought to resign that they might be relieved from the restraint imposed upon them by their commissions on engaging in hostility to the constituted authorities of the nation, has committed a grave error, highly prejudicial to the discipline of the service and injurious to the honor and efficiency of the Navy; for which he deserves the censure of this House."

The charge that has been frequently made by high authorities that Toucey sent the naval ships abroad, or to inconvenient ports, in the interest of the South, is not true. He, however, administered the navy as if no war at home was threatening. He dispatched ships to the foreign squadrons in accordance with their needs. He failed to place the navy in a posture of defense. He made only the usual repairs of naval vessels, turning over to his successor a considerable part of the appropriation for repairs for the fiscal year of 1860-1861. All this was a part of the policy of the administration. Without a change in it, Toucey could not have acted differently. According to it, the South must not be offended; and the prospects for a peaceful solution of the difficulties must not be jeopardized. Any movement of the North, offensive or defensive, it was feared, would touch off the fuse and precipitate a civil war, and this must be avoided at all hazards. Toucey was a victim of the policy of the administration.

On January 14, 1861, four days after Florida seceded, the Secretary of the Navy received the following telegraphic despatch, dated January 12, from Captain James Armstrong, the commandant of the Pensacola navy-yard: "Commissioners appointed by the Governor of Florida with a regiment of armed men at the gate demanded surrender of the navy-yard, having previously taken possession of one of our magazines. I surrendered the place and struck my flag at half past one o'clock this day." Rumors of this movement had been current at the yard for some time. On January 3, Toucey had telegraphed to Armstrong "to be vigilant to protect the public property." He had also ordered several vessels to Pensacola, and had ordered one from Pensacola. He had been very sparing of instructions to the commandant. Under all the circumstances his acts did not indicate any settled determination to defend the yard at all hazards. Armstrong struck his flag without making any defense. He was old, without initiative, and aware of the desire of the administration to avoid a rupture with the South. Some of his officers and many of his men sympathized with the seceding states, and were opposed to defensive movements. His failure to take measures to protect the public property and to oppose to the full extent of his ability the Florida troops deserved the strong condemnation which they received in the North.

The commissioners of Florida, on the surrender of the yard, placed it under the command of Victor M. Randolph, of Alabama. At this time his name was borne on the pay-rolls of the United States navy. He had been on leave of absence on account of ill health. On January 10 he forwarded his resignation to Washington. Before noon of January 12 he appeared at the head of the Florida troops before the gates of the Pensacola yard. His resignation was accepted by Toucey on January 14. It thus appears that Randolph was receiving pay from the United States government at the time he was capturing its public property. Three officers of the yard next in rank to Armstrong, a commander and two lieutenants, soon after the surrender, resigned their commissions and took office under the new commandant. As a part of the policy of conciliation, the Secretary of the Navy on January 18 despatched Captain Samuel Barron to Pensacola, to patch up a truce between the Confederate forces at the navy-yard and the Unionists at Fort Pickens.[10]

It is greatly to be regretted that Buchanan and Toucey did not vigorously defend the Pensacola yard. Neither the states-rights nor the nationalist theory of our government was directly at issue here. This yard had never belonged to the State of Florida, and under either theory she had no legal right to it. The feelings of the Northern naval officers on its surrender may be seen from the following words of Captain S. F. DuPont to Captain A. H. Foote, written on January 25, 1861: "But if I feel sore at these resignations, what should a decent man feel at the doings in the Pensacola Navy-Yard? Here I can not trust myself to speak; and the Department accepting these resignations, not waiting for a single particular after hearing that the Yard had been surrendered! . . . . Oh, why was not some one like you at Pensacola? I pass no judgment on the old commodore; he was in a tight place, and if he had only ironed well the traitors under him before he gave up, I should have been thankful." [11]

NAVAL SHIPS AND STATIONS.

Owing to the Mexican War, the annual naval expenditures during the fiscal years 1848 and 1849 increased to about $9,150,-000, the highest since 1812-1815. This, however, was an increase of only $1,000,000 over the expenditures for 1842. The annual expenditures for 1844-1846 were about $6,300,000, considerably less than those for 1841-1843. This decrease marks a reaction against the policy of naval expansion of the Badger-Upshur administration. Secretary Bancroft, who entered the department in March, 1845, ardently furthered the counter-policy of

[10] House Rept., 36C. 2S., No. 87; Official Records, Ser. I, Vol. 14, 3-89; Congressional Globe, 1860-1861, pp. 1095-1097, 1423-1424; Sen. Rept. 37C. 2S., No. 37; Congress Letters, XIII, 340-347; Sands, From Reefer to Rear-Admiral 221; Naval Actions and History, 77-100; Chadwick, Causes of the Civil War, 248.

[11] Hoppin, Admiral Foote, 148.

naval retrenchment. For 1850, 1851, and 1852, the annual cost of the navy was about $7,750,000. In 1853 a period of increased naval expenditures set in, caused in large part by the acquisition of a steam fleet, the improvement of the navy-yards, and the augmenting of the number of naval officers. For the fiscal year 1859 the expenditures reached the wholly unprecedented sum of $14,-233,000. Owing chiefly to the stringency of the national treasury, the cost of the navy in 1860 was some $3,000,000 less.[12]

As respects naval ships, the significant fact during the twenty years preceding the Civil War was the building of a steam fleet. The Old Navy was passing away. A period of transition in naval construction had set in. From 1843 to 1860 the number of sailing ships decreased from 59 to 44; while the number of steamships increased from 6 to 38. Of the 44 sailing ships remaining in the navy in 1860 not a few were old and of little value. The ships of the line were now used chiefly as receiving ships. Three of them were still upon the stocks. The Secretaries of the Navy, especially Secretaries Dobbin and Toucey, would have increased the steam fleet more rapidly than they did, but Congress repeatedly moderated their recommendations. As usual, the naval policy of Congress was adversely affected by perturbations and aberrations in the naval opinions of its members. The principal additions to the steam fleet were made during the six years, 1854-1859, when thirty steam vessels were added to the navy. From 1835 to 1853 only eighteen steam vessels were acquired. In December, 1859, Toucey said that the fleet had been increased by twenty steamships since his term of office began in March, 1857.[13] Of these, thirteen were built and seven purchased, at a total cost of a little less than $5,000,000. Twelve of the vessels constructed in 1857 and 1858 were steam sloops. They were fitted with screw-propellers, and at the outbreak of the Civil War were the best vessels in the navy of the smaller types.

In 1854 Congress appropriated $3,000,000 for the construction of six first-class steam frigates, to be provided with screw-propellers. These ships were built at the navy-yards on the Atlantic coast, and were launched in 1855 and 1856. They were the *Merrimac, Wabash, Minnesota, Roanoke, Colorado,* and *Niagara*. Their dimensions varied but little; those of the

[12] Sen. Ex. Doc., 45C. 1S., No. 3, 156.
[13] Ann. Rept. of Sec. of N., 1859, p. 1139.

Merrimac, whose name became historic, were, length 257 feet
and beam 51 feet. Her displacement was 4636 tons. She cost
$752,000. These vessels represented the most advanced type
of construction in our navy before the Civil War. They were
"objects of admiration and envy to the naval architects of
Europe," who modeled some of their ships after them. Five of
them were frigate-built, and one sloop-built. They were constructed of seasoned live oak. They were propelled chiefly by
sails, having merely "auxiliary steam power." The engines were
to be used chiefly in calms and in leaving port, and as aids in
storms and in battle. At this time few naval experts foresaw that
steam was destined to supplant entirely sails on board naval
vessels.[14]

The earliest naval steamships, as might be expected, were only
moderately successful. There was much experimenting with their
boilers, paddle-wheels, smoke-stacks, and propellers. Some of
the devices that were tried were more or less absurd. The *Missouri* was at one time fitted with lateral, instead of the usual
perpendicular, smoke-stacks. The consumption of fuel on some
of the first steamships was so great, according to the standards
of the time, that they were placed out of commission to save
expense. They were all fitted with sails, since their steam power
was only an auxiliary means of propulsion. The *Fulton the
Second* originally carried but 75 tons of coal, an amount sufficient for three days' steaming; her maximum speed was 13 knots.
The *Mississippi* had a maximum speed of 9½ knots. She
carried 620 tons of fuel, and had a complement of 260 men. Her
horse-power was 498, and her tonnage 1693. Her armament
consisted of two 10-inch and eight 8-inch shell guns. Her cost
was $570,000. The first naval steamships were paddle-wheel
vessels. In 1842-1843 the first screw-propeller war-ship was
built. Its plans were furnished by the well-known mechanical
genius, John Ericsson. The chief promoter of the enterprise was
Captain R. F. Stockton, and the ship was named the *Princeton*
after his home-town in New Jersey.[15]

In 1842 Congress authorized the Secretary of the Navy to contract with Robert L. Stevens, a distinguished American mechanic,
for the construction of a war steamer, "shot and shell proof, to

[14] Bennett, Steam Navy, 141-153, app. B.
[15] Ex. Doc., 32C. 2S., No. 63.

be built principally of iron." This was the second ironclad ordered for the navy. The first was Robert Fulton's " bullet-proof boat," authorized in 1814; according to Fulton's plans, the boat was to be partly submerged, and its deck was to be plated with iron. After some delay Stevens laid down the keel of an ironclad, 250 feet long, 40 feet wide, and 28 feet deep. The plating was to be 4½ inches thick. In 1854 he abandoned his original plans and designed a much larger ship. The hull and machinery of the second vessel were practically completed when Stevens died in 1856. Work on the ironclad then ceased. In 1861 a naval board reported against completing the vessel, and the department's connection with it came to an end.[16]

In 1845 a " board of captains " was convened by the department to consider means of simplifying the naval ordnance. A uniform calibre throughout the fleet was now the ideal of naval officers in both this country and Europe. In 1829 this ideal had been in large part realized by France; and in 1839, by England. The board of captains, following the lead of these two countries, recommended the adoption of the long 32-pounder as the unit-calibre of the navy, and the use of only two kinds of cannon, the 32-pounder and the 8-inch shell gun. The department put in force the recommendations of the board. The simplification thus effected was, however, not so great as it may appear, for the 32-pounders were of six, and the 8-inch guns of two classes. Guns of larger calibres were shortly introduced into the navy. In 1854 the department adopted for the new steam frigates then building the Dahlgren 9-inch, 10-inch, and 11-inch guns; and by 1856 several of the larger ships were mounting 64-pounders. At the outbreak of the Civil War cannon of various sizes and kinds were in use.[17]

The Mexican War did not cause a large increase in the number of naval ships. During the war some 20 small craft were temporarily added to the navy. In 1846 the United States came into possession of the Texan navy. By the terms of annexation, Texas ceded to the Union her navy, navy-yards, and docks. On May 11, 1846, Hiram G. Runnels, acting as the agent of the federal government, received from the Texan authorities the sloop *Austin,* the brigs *Wharton* and *Archer,* and the schooner *San Bernard.* The *Austin* was sent to Pensacola to be rebuilt. The remaining vessels, since they were not worth repairing, were sold.

[16] Bennett, Steam Navy, 262; Thurston, Robert Fulton, 153.
[17] Dahlgren, Shells and Shell-Guns, 14, 23, 259-292.

The period of 1842-1861 was an exceedingly important one in the history of the navy-yards. Two new yards were established, one at Mare Island and the other at Vicksburg. In 1848 the area of the New York yard was increased. The Mexican War revealed the need of a first-class establishment at Pensacola, and during the war liberal appropriations for this yard were made for the first time. By 1861 it was in comparatively good condition. The disposition of Congress to give the South a larger share of the naval appropriations was of advantage to the Pensacola establishment. By the outbreak of the Civil War the navy-yards had taken on a somewhat modern appearance. New machinery adapted to the building and repair of steamships had been installed and various boiler shops, coal sheds, and other improvements had been constructed. The annual appropriation for the improvement and repair of the navy-yards increased from about $500,000 for 1842, to more than $2,100,000 for the fiscal year 1858, and to almost $1,600,000 for the fiscal year 1859.[18] In the latter year Congress changed its policy respecting the yards, and for two years appropriated nothing for their improvement. At the beginning of the Civil War the principal establishments were those at Boston, New York, Norfolk, Pensacola, and Mare Island; and the secondary or auxiliary ones, those at Portsmouth, Philadelphia, and Washington.

The need of a naval depot and rendezvous on the West coast was early recognized. In 1838 Secretary Paulding ordered the commander of the Pacific squadron to make a close and accurate survey of the straits of Juan de Fuca in order to ascertain their fitness for a rendezvous of the American navy in the Pacific. Paulding also ordered Lieutenant Charles Wilkes, partly with a view to the interests of the navy, to devote as much time as the objects of the United States Exploring Expedition would permit to an examination of the Columbia River, the coast between it and California, and most especially the Bay of San Francisco, " represented as one of the finest in the world." In 1841 Secretary Upshur recommended the establishment of a naval depot and rendezvous on the West coast. The settlement of the differences with Great Britain over Oregon, the acquisition of California and New Mexico, and the discovery of gold in California greatly enhanced the importance of the Pacific squadron and its need of

---

[18] U. S. Statutes at Large V, 500-501, XI, 244-245, 316.

a naval station. In 1847 a station was established at Monterey, California. In 1848 a joint board of army and navy officers was organized and sent to the Pacific coast to report on the location of fortifications, lighthouses, navy-yards, and dry docks. The principal naval officer on the board was Commander Louis M. Goldsborough. Secretary Mason in his annual report for 1848 recommended the establishment of a navy-yard and dry dock on the coast of California ; and the next year Secretary Graham made a similar recommendation.

In September, 1850, Congress authorized the Secretary of the Navy to enter into a contract for the construction of a sectional or a floating dock and a basin and railway at such harbor on the Pacific coast as he might select. Graham at once contracted with Eastern builders to construct a sectional dock for $610,000. The contractors were permitted to prepare their materials on the Atlantic coast. The permanent location of the dock could not, however, be fixed until the site for a navy-yard was determined. The central situation and excellent harbor of San Francisco bay permitted no question as to the general location of the yard. Its exact situation on the bay or its connecting waters was a matter of some difference of opinion. In 1852, in accordance with an authorization of Congress, the Secretary of the Navy appointed a board to choose a site. It selected Mare Island, which is situated some 30 miles northward of San Francisco, in the extensive sheet of waters connecting with San Francisco bay. The Mexican name of the island was *Isla de las Yeguas.*

In August, 1852, Congress appropriated $100,000 to buy Mare Island, to make surveys, and to begin improvements. The island was purchased on January 4, 1853, for $83,491. It contained 1066 acres. In making the transfer, certain difficulties arose in respect to the title. These were not removed until July, 1854. The first commandant of the yard was Commander David G. Farragut, who was appointed to this position in August, 1854. To Farragut fell the responsible duties of planning and building up the yard, under the general instructions of the department. When he arrived at the island, there were no improvements on it. He and his family were compelled to spend the first seven months on an old sloop of war anchored near by. The yard was rapidly improved during the four years that Farragut was commandant. A wharf, shops and sheds of various kinds, and dwelling houses for the officers, were erected. The grounds were graded and the streets paved. The sectional dock and the basin and railway were completed and were placed in position.[19]

The most important improvements made under the Bureau of Navy-Yards and Docks during 1842-1861 were the construction of several dry docks for the repairing of vessels. Mention has already been made of the floating sectional dock built for the Mare Island navy-yard. The construction of a dry dock for the New York yard was long delayed. In 1835, Congress appropriated $100,000 for this purpose, but owing to a disagreement over the location of the dock little of the money was expended. Finally the work of construction was begun on October 1, 1841; but on August 1, 1842, it was discontinued, after the expenditure of $35,000. It was resumed on April 1, 1845. These delays were caused chiefly by the questions that arose respecting the removal of the New York yard, and by doubts as to the proper materials of construction for the proposed improvement. In the end it was decided not to move the yard, and to build the dry dock of stone. The work was placed under the direction of W. P. S. Sanger, the civil engineer of the Bureau of Navy-Yards and Docks. The most serious obstacles which Sanger encountered were caused by numerous springs of water. So strong was the pressure from these springs, that vent had to be given them through the bottom of the completed structure. By January, 1850, the work had advanced far enough towards completion to admit of the docking of the U. S. ship *Dale*. On September 1, 1851, the dock was turned over to the commandant of the yard. Its total cost was $2,146,255. It was somewhat larger than the similar structures at Boston and Norfolk. The main chamber at the top was 307 feet long and 98 feet wide.

In 1847 Congress ordered the construction of a floating dry dock at each of the navy-yards at Portsmouth, Philadelphia, and Pensacola. At this time a floating dry dock was not so durable nor so well adapted to the docking of large ships as those constructed of stone, but it was much cheaper to build. In August, 1848, Congress, guided by the report of a board of officers, and by a report of the Bureau of Navy-Yards and Docks, specified with more detail the character of these three improvements. That

[19] Congress Letters, VII, 513, Ann. Rept. of Sec. of N. 1841 p. 369; 1848, p. 619; 1849, p. 436; 1851, p. 8; Bay of San Francisco, 325; Miscl. Data, Bureau of Yards and Docks 8; Mahan, Admiral Farragut, 99.

at Portsmouth was to be a " floating dry dock "; that at Philadelphia, a " sectional floating dry dock "; and that at Pensacola, a
" balance floating dry dock." Work upon them was at once begun
by the contractors. In 1852 the Portsmouth and Philadelphia
docks were accepted. A test of the Pensacola dock made in 1853
was not satisfactory, and it was not accepted until 1855. A notion
of the size of these structures may be gained from the dimensions
of the Portsmouth dock; it was 350 feet long and 105 feet broad.[20]

The specializing of the Washington yard in the manufacture of
ordnance may be dated with the appointment of Lieutenant John
A. Dahlgren as ordnance officer. Here in 1847 Dahlgren began
his great work of improving the naval ordnance. In 1848 his
department at the yard was placed under the direct charge of the
Navy Department. During this year he established an experimental battery, with ranges, on the Eastern branch of the Potomac.
In 1850 he submitted to the Secretary of the Navy plans for a
" Naval Ordnance Establishment," but they were not approved.
He of course expected to be made superintendent of the new
department. Like his friend, Lieutenant M. F. Maury of the
Naval Observatory, he was an ambitious genius and a steady
promoter of his own interests. He was the first ordnance expert
to design cannon proportioned to the " curve of pressures." His
most important invention was the " Dahlgren gun." The first
Dahlgren was a 9-inch shell gun, and weighed 9000 pounds. Later
he made 10-inch and 11-inch guns, some of which could throw
shells weighing 170 pounds. He improved several kinds of small
ordnance, and invented a navy howitzer that was much used. In
1859 he began the manufacture of rifled cannon. Dahlgren was
a man of conspicuous ability and indefatigable energy, and took
high rank among the ordnance experts of his time.[21]

NAVAL OFFICERS AND SEAMEN.

The work of the navy from 1842 to 1861 was similar to that
under the navy commissioners. The fleet was chiefly engaged in
the protection of American commerce and citizens in foreign ports
and waters, the suppression of the slave trade, and the making
of scientific explorations and surveys. It was regularly organized into six squadrons: the African, Mediterranean, Brazil,

[20] Ann. Rept. of Sec. of N., 1845, p. 666; 1851, pp. 168-169; Hamersly,
Naval Encyclopedia, 218; U. S. Statutes at Large, IX, 170-171, 270-271.

[21] Dahlgren, Dahlgren, 125-235.

Pacific, East Indian, and "home" squadrons. The cruising-grounds of the home squadron included the West Indies; and of the East India squadron, the China seas. Although the Mexican War was fought chiefly by the army, the navy nevertheless rendered some important services. It blockaded and occupied several Mexican ports, co-operated with the army in the capture of Vera Cruz, and seized and conquered the coast of California. Of the officers who took part in the war, Commodores Conner and Perry most distinguished themselves in Mexico; and Commodores Sloat and Stockton, in California. In 1847 Perry commanded the largest fleet, with possibly one exception, that up to this time had been assembled under the American flag.

Questions relating to the naval personnel now pressed for solution even more insistently than under the navy commissioners. These had to do chiefly with the education and improvement of officers and seamen, naval rank, a retired list for officers, and the government and discipline of the navy. All these questions received much attention from Congress and the Navy Department. Several noteworthy laws relating to them were passed, and they were made the subjects of not a few important departmental regulations.

During the first two decades under the naval bureaus reasonably adequate educational facilities for young line officers were established. From 1842 to 1845 the agitation in Congress for a naval academy was continued, but without success. The problem of naval education was at last solved by the Secretaries of the Navy without recourse to federal legislation. A long step towards its solution was taken by Secretary Bancroft in 1845 when he moved the Naval School at Philadelphia to Annapolis to a home-plot of its own, reorganized and enlarged it, and greatly improved its curriculum. A step of almost equal importance was taken in 1850-1851 when the school was named the "Naval Academy," was again reorganized, and a four years' course of study was adopted. During the decade preceding the Civil War, the Naval Academy grew steadily in numbers, educational facilities, and efficiency of instruction.

These improvements in naval education elevated the character of the naval officer and the moral tone of the service, and doubtless had their influence in bringing about a decline of dueling. Moreover, public sentiment both in and out of the navy was now setting strongly against this lamentable practice. The naval regulations prepared by a board of naval officers in 1857 made dueling punishable by dismissal from the navy or by such other penalty as a court-martial might inflict. As early as 1839, Congress, moved by the sentiment aroused by the unfortunate meeting between Congressmen Cilley and Graves in 1838, passed a law forbidding the giving or accepting of a challenge in the District of Columbia. The act for the better government of the navy of July 17, 1862, made the sending or accepting of a challenge, or the acting as a second, subject to such punishment as a court-martial might adjudge; and the naval regulations of 1865 contained this provision on the subject: " No person in the Navy will upbraid another person in the Navy for refusing a challenge to fight a duel. Every person is enjoined to assist in the honorable adjustment of any differences that may occur. No disgrace can attach to any one for refusing a challenge, as such a course would be in obedience to law." It is probable that a few duels among naval officers were fought during the Civil War, and at least one since that conflict.[22]

Under the naval bureaus the principle of testing the fitness of officers for appointment and promotion by means of examining boards received new applications. Admittance to the engineer corps was conditioned on the passing of a technical examination. In August, 1846, Secretary Bancroft issued a general order establishing an entrance examination for naval constructors, boatswains, gunners, carpenters, and sail-makers. He recommended that the fitness for promotion of all line officers should be determined either by examining boards or by the reports of commanders on the efficiency of their subordinates. He held strong views on this subject, declaring that the " doctrine that advancement is due to seniority alone, irrespective of capacity for duty, places personal interests before the public good and partakes of the very essence of the worst form of an aristocracy." [23]

In 1844, Congress, taking from the President a power which he had long exercised, fixed by statute the number of seamen in the navy. From 1844 to 1857, with the exception of the years of the Mexican War, the number of seamen thus established was 7500. In the latter year it was increased to 8500. During the Mexican

---

[22] U. S. Statutes at Large, V. 318, XII, 602; Ann. Rept. of Sec. of N., 1858, p. 234; Regulations of the Navy, 1865, p. 30.

[23] Navy Register 1859, pp. 131-132; Ex. Doc., 29C. 1S., No. 188, 7.

War Congress authorized a naval force of 10,000 men, and the addition of 1112 officers and men to the marine corps. Only about 8100 men, however, were enlisted in the navy. In 1854 the marine corps, all told, numbered only 1452 men. It had grown very little in the past fifty years.[24]

The apprentice system of 1837 lasted until 1843. In 1855 Secretary Dobbin put into operation a new system, and enlisted 500 boys between 14 and 18 years of age with a view to training them for a seafaring life. Dobbin also recommended the teaching of seamen the " management of heavy ordnance in storm and calm " on board an ordnance-ship. Accordingly, in 1857 the ordnance-ship *Plymouth,* under Commander John A. Dahlgren, went to sea for a six months' cruise. This was one of the first practice cruises of our navy for the instruction of seamen in gunnery. The apprentice system of 1855, like that of 1837, was soon abandoned.[25]

The crews of the ships of the Old Navy were divided into five classes; petty officers, seamen, ordinary seamen, landsmen, and boys. According to law, their pay was fixed by the President. In 1830 the petty officers received $18 a month; seamen $12; ordinary seamen $10; landsmen $8; and boys, $8 or $5. The petty officers were selected by the captain from the most experienced and trustworthy of the seamen. On board a frigate, they consisted of a master-at-arms, eight quarter-masters, four boatswain's mates, eight quarter-gunners, a boatswain's yeoman, gunner's yeoman, carpenter, sailmaker's mate, armorer, cooper, cook, and coxswain. The seamen had much pride of profession and entertained the greatest contempt for men who knew nothing of the seafaring life. The landsmen were as " green as a cucumber, having never smelt salt water." The boys were principally employed as servants to the commissioned officers. The crews were usually shipped for three years, at the end of which time they were discharged. In 1852 President Pierce and Secretary Kennedy recommended the establishment of a permanent corps of seamen.[26]

A too long and exclusive use of salty meats, hard bread, and bad drinking-water often caused scurvy, the scourge of the sailor of the olden time. Small-pox and in tropical latitudes cholera and yellow fever were not uncommon. In dealing with these and

[24] U. S. Statutes at Large, V, 699, IX, 100, 154-155; Ann. Rept. of Sec. of N., 1847, p. 945; 1850, p. 200; 1854, pp. 584-585.

[25] Ann. Rept. of Sec. of N., 1856, p. 411; 1857, p. 579.

[26] Wines, Two Years and a Half in the Navy, I, 38-41.

other diseases the early naval surgeons were less skilful and successful than those of the present day, since in the first half of the
last century modern medical and surgical science was in its
infancy. On some of the old ships the ventilation was bad beyond
belief. They were so overcrowded that the "men lived almost
like kenneled dogs." The excellent and abundant air aloft and on
deck had to compensate for its foulness in the sleeping apart-
ments. The berths on the berth-deck of the *Constellation* were 18
inches in width by 9 feet in length, and were practically without
ventilation. The living space on shipboard has been greatly
increased in recent years. While a modern battleship is more than
five times the size of an old 44-gun frigate, it carries practically
the same number of men. The ships of the Old Navy were models
of order and cleanliness, and careful captains were generally able
to keep their crews reasonably healthy.[27]

The man-of-war's men of the olden time were interesting and
picturesque characters, possessing many good and bad qualities
strangely intermingled. An ancient schoolmaster of our navy
wrote that "generosity, a sort of grumbling contentment, sus-
ceptibility to kindness, a mixture of credulity and scepticism, a
superstitious dread of imaginary and a contempt of real dangers,
a strong love of the marvellous, a rough open-hearted simplicity
of manners and language, gross sensuality, shocking profaneness,
imperturbable effrontery in lying, and an insatiable thirst for
strong drink, will generally be found to be the constituent parts of
a sailor's character when carefully analyzed. On the whole, the
bad qualities preponderate, and the character of our seamen as a
body is very low in the scale of moral excellence."[28]

Some notion of the temptations and impositions to which the
sailors were subjected may be obtained from the following extract
taken from the autobiography of Samuel F. Holbrook, a petty
officer of the navy. His vessel, the sloop-of-war *Ontario,* arrived
at New York on May 27, 1817, after a cruise in the
Mediterranean:

"Scarcely had our anchor gone from the bow, before the ship
was surrounded by land sharks and bad women; the latter, however, were not permitted to come on board; and only a few of the
former. They obtained permission only by urgently desiring to

[27] Hollis, The Frigate Constitution, 18-19.
[28] Wines, Two Years and a Half in the Navy, II, 112.

see some particular friend. As none of the crew were allowed
to go on shore, the landlords went off, but soon returned with any
quantity of good things, such as pies, puddings, roast beef,
chickens, and had also contrived to smuggle on board an ample
supply of good stuff to wash down the savory viands; notwithstanding they were strictly forbidden against bringing any intoxi-
cating liquor on board, the master-at-arms was placed in the gangway with the orders to search everything and everybody, and
'the Maine Liquor law in full force,' there were bottles of
brandy, gin, rum, and wine enough to supply a regular bacchana-
lian feast. Tailors and watch venders came alongside; and all,
knowing that the boys had between $300 and $400 a piece coming
to them, were very willing to trust them to any amount. Nothing
pleases this sort of sailors so much, as to show a willingness to
trust them; and what was very remarkable, nearly every one of
these skulking lubbers that had been in the sick bay during all
the bad weather and were so sick that they could not be turned
over in their hammocks without a crowbar, were the most lively
and vociferous among the whole crew; and with the rest were all
blind drunk before morning. Many of these fellows had bought
nice long-tailed coats, pantaloons, new hats, watches, and dandy
boots, and everything to constitute a fine go-ashore-rig; for
which, as it subsequently appeared, they were charged $100, and
some of them put on their new rig to see how they would look.
One fellow would try to haul a pair of dandy pantaloons over a
thick pair of blanket drawers and a great brawny leg, which would
tear them of course; and then off they go, and he must have
another pair, which with considerable trouble and with the assistance of the tailor he managed to get on; then his legs looked like
well-stuffed sausages. Another would try to get a narrow-backed
coat over a pair of broad shoulders, when, away goes the back,
and another $20 out of the fool's pocket, and in this way these
land pirates contrived to rob this crew." [29]

On board the larger ships the spiritual and moral welfare of the
sailors was doubtless improved by the ministrations of the naval
chaplains, who were generally, although not invariably, men of
piety and high character. Even this slight boon was denied to
the crews of the smaller vessels, to which no chaplains were
assigned. At the principal navy-yards Sunday-schools were estab-

[29] Holbrook, Autobiography, 190.

lished for the enlisted men; and numerous bibles, testaments, prayer-books, and religious tracts were distributed for their edification. A pious visitor to a Sunday-school held on board a man-of-war at the New York yard describes it as being "particularly solemn. Nearly 200 naval boys were present, and some of the officers, while many of the old tars leaned upon the heavy cannon, in serious attention to the religious services. The band aided in the sacred melodies; and the whole service was truly impressive. Nearby was moored the *Somers,* bringing forcibly to mind the awful consequences of sin among her crew; and below in irons were some of the actors in that terrible mutiny." [30] To another visitor the occasion of a religious exercise appeared less solemn, for he records that the old tars grew painfully restive as the time for the distribution of their grog approached and the service showed no signs of being brought to a close.

Beginning about the middle of the first half of the nineteenth century, a strong humanitarian sentiment arose in the North, and especially in New England. Many devout and kind-hearted men and women of this section manifested a warm sympathy for the slaves of the South, the American sailors, and the suffering and downtrodden of all lands. Before 1840 boarding-houses, schools, reading-rooms, savings-banks, and churches had been established for the seamen. In that year, with a view to enlightening the public as to the hardships of the merchant service, Richard H. Dana wrote his "Two Years Before the Mast," one of the world's classics of adventure. The zeal of some of the reformers often outran their knowledge of actual conditions. Their activities in behalf of man-of-war's men, while partly encouraged by the navy, was sometimes resented as an unwarranted interference. There can be no doubt, however, that ample room for improvement existed.

Two time-honored practices of the Old Navy were flogging and the issuing of grog. They had been long common in every navy of Christendom. Flogging was first established in our service by the Continental Congress in 1775. The act for the bettering government of the navy, passed on April 23, 1800, limited the number of lashes that might be inflicted by a captain to 12; and by a court-martial, to 100. An act of the previous year made the cat-o'-nine-tails the legal instrument of punishment, and per-

[30] Army and Navy Chronicle, 1843, p. 278.

mitted the use of " no other cat." The boys of the navy, however, were often punished with a smaller whip called the " boys' cat," or " kitten." In practice a lieutenant was allowed to give a dozen lashes with the " colt," a rope with a knot in the end of it. Rear-Admiral Foote says that when he was mate of the gun-deck of a frigate he always carried a colt in his cap ready for use. Rear-Admiral Thatcher, when first-lieutenant, kept one under his pillow for the disciplining of the ward-room boys. Among the common offenses punishable by means of the cat-o'-nine-tails were drunkenness, fighting, skulking, theft, cursing, disobedience of orders, sleeping on the lookout, and smuggling of liquor. The cat consisted of nine small hard-twisted pieces of cotton or flax cord, with three knots in each, fixed on a short thick rope as a handle. The lashes were administered on the bare back of the culprit, in the presence of his comrades, at the gangway of the ship. The cat was wielded by the boatswain's mate, whom the seamen regarded as a devil incarnate. The master-at-arms counted audibly the blows. In exceptional cases the cat was applied with horrible brutality. Captain Wolcott Chauncey once flogged two young men until the " flesh was fairly hanging in strips upon both backs; it was a sickening sight." Chaplain C. S. Stewart, writing in 1829, says that the " keenest emotions that I have known on board the *Gurriere* have come suddenly upon me in the sound of the lash and the cry of some wretch suffering at my side." He felt that there was an indignity and degradation in this mode of punishment.[81] The sailors, however, looked at flogging quite differently.

An interesting, though melancholy, anecdote was once told by Commodore J. H. Aulick in proof of his belief that " badges of disgrace " could not be effectively employed as substitutes for corporal punishment: " On my passage to the Mediterranean some 30 years ago, an old seaman was brought to the gangway, by order of the Captain, for some offence he had committed; when the Captain said to him, ' You are only an old woman unworthy of being punished as a man.' And he ordered the boatswain's mate to dress him in tarpaulins to represent a woman. The old man protested that he was a man, and was ready to receive the punishment of a man. ' Give me,' said he, ' my dozen, or as many lashes as you think proper, but I will not submit to being

[81] Holbrook, Autobiography, 98.

disgraced. I'll jump overboard rather than submit to it.' The dressing was completed. The man went forward, and immediately threw himself under the bows of the ship. We were sailing at a rapid rate, and though every effort was made to save him, he sank to rise no more." [32]

To the sailor of the Old Navy a much severer punishment than flogging was the "stopping of the grog." Both in the Continental navy and the early navy under the Constitution the regular daily allowance of spirits to each man was half a pint. In 1842 this was reduced to one-fourth of a pint, or a gill. The marines were given a half-pint of distilled spirits or one quart of beer daily. On Christmas the allowance was doubled. Until the administration of Secretary of the Navy Robert Smith rum was the spirits issued. Smith introduced the use of whiskey which in time became common. Efforts were made to substitute wine and beer for spirits, but they failed. The sailors refused to drink these mild beverages. The cargo of whiskey, which on a 44-gun frigate amounted to 100 barrels, was the largest single item of expense for the stores of a ship. Secretary of the Navy Woodbury, 1831-1834, who favored the gradual abolition of the spirit ration, promulgated an order permitting the sailors to commute their grog for money; and in 1842 a law was passed forbidding the issuing of spirits to all minors, whether officers or seamen. Some of the chaplains and naval surgeons were early advocates of temperance in the navy.

By 1845-1850 the feeling in the North in favor of the abolition of flogging and the grog had come to be exceedingly strong. In 1849 the legislature of Rhode Island adopted a resolution requesting the senators and representatives of that State in Congress "to use their best influence to have the supply of ardent spirits as rations, and the use of the lash, prohibited throughout our navy." Many memorials on these two subjects were sent to Congress. In 1845 the Naval Committee of the House recommended the abolition of the grog; and in 1849 the House voted to prohibit flogging. The deep interest manifested in these subjects led Secretary Preston in January, 1850, to address a circular letter to the leading officers of the navy asking for their views upon the abolition of corporal punishment and the spirit ration. Their replies reveal that the navy was almost a unit against doing

[32] Letters of Officers on the Abolition of Flogging, No. 22.

away with the cat, and that a strong sentiment existed in favor
of gratifying the sailors in their love of the grog. Even the
sailors were generally opposed to the abolition of flogging, and
some of them petitioned Congress to leave them this manly form
of punishment. In 1850, in direct opposition to the preponderance
of opinion in the navy, Congress abolished flogging. A provision
to this effect passed the House by a large majority, but it narrowly
escaped defeat in the Senate. The fight in the latter body was led
by John P. Hale, of New Hampshire.[83]

Immediately after the disuse of the cat numerous complaints
reached the Navy Department of insubordination and serious
irregularities among the seamen. Some 200 or 300 men left the
frigate *Brandywine* in willful violation of orders. The number
of desertions increased, and many good seamen refused to enlist.
In June, 1851, the department addressed another circular letter
to the leading officers of the navy asking for their views on the
effect of the recent law. The consensus of naval opinion was
that the effect was very bad. Frequent complaints against the
disuse of the cat were made by the seamen. In 1852 the
demoralization of the navy continued, and the officers still had
hopes that Congress would reconsider its decision. The evils
caused by the prohibition of flogging were greatly increased by
the failure of Congress to establish new punishments to take the
place of the old one. The Secretaries of the Navy for several
years recommended the revision of the penal code of the navy in
order to adapt it to the new conditions. Finally, Congress acceded
to their wishes, and in 1855 established summary courts-martial.
These courts could be ordered by the commanders of vessels,
and they could inflict various minor punishments, such as dishonorable discharge from the service, " solitary confinement in
irons, on bread and water or diminished rations," reduction in
rating, deprivation of liberty on shore, extra police duties, and
loss of pay. After their establishment, naval discipline was completely restored.[84]

The abolition of the spirit ration was delayed until 1861 and

[83] Ex. Doc., 23C. 1S., No. 486; U. S. Statutes at Large, V, 547; Sen.
Miscl. Doc., 30C. 2S., No 63; Letters of Officers on the Abolition of Flogging; Congressional Globe, 1848-1849, p. 506; 1849-1850, p. 2057.

[84] Sen. Ex. Doc., 31C. 2S., No. 12; Sen. Ex. Doc., 32C. 1S., No. 10;
Ann. Rept. of Sec. of N., 1850, p. 207; 1852, p. 312; 1853, p. 315; 1854, p.
394; U. S. Statutes at Large, X, 627.

1862. In the former year Congress forbade it to commissioned and warrant officers, and in the latter year it was enacted that the " spirit ration in the navy of the United States shall forever cease." Next to spirits, the chief articles of diet of the sailors of the Old Navy were bread, beef, pork, and beans. On certain days of each week, peas, cheese, rice, suet, butter, vinegar, and molasses were served. The quantities of these articles allowed are enumerated in the navy ration established by Congress in 1801. In 1842 a few luxuries were added—dried fruits, tea, coffee, sugar, cocoa, pickles, and cranberries. At sea the main reliance of the sailors was " salt junk and hard tack," that is, salted provisions and sea-biscuit. In port, for this fare, " fresh grub and soft tack," the sea-terms for fresh meats and bread, were substituted. The staple desert of the sailors was " duff," a heavy indigestible plum pudding. " Lobscowse," a hash consisting of salt beef and potatoes, was a favorite dish. The bread was often moldy, and the drinking-water offensive to the smell as well as to the taste. For convenience in serving the food the crew was divided into messes of 15 to 20 men each. Each member of a mess took turns in waiting on the table, receiving the title of " berth-deck cook." Sometimes a boy was given this duty. Although his fare was simple and monotonous and not always well-cooked, yet Jack ate it with an abundant appetite, highly sharpened by physical exercise and an out-of-door life. We are told that " princes do not sit down at their tables, groaning beneath a thousand delicacies, with greater contentment, or enjoy their luxurious viands with a higher relish, than those which the tempest-tost, weather-beaten sailor squats by the side of his greasy tarpaulin, and devours his humble dish of lobscowse or duff." [85]

The questions of naval rank that for a long time agitated the navy related to either " relative," " higher," or " assimilated " rank. The relative rank of army and navy officers was agreed upon in 1850 by a board composed of officers drawn from the two services. The report of the board was approved by the Navy Department. Congress, however, failed to act upon it, although its attention was directed to the subject by President Pierce in his annual message for 1851. [86]

The movement for higher ranks in the navy during the 20

[85] U. S. Statutes at Large, II, 110; V. 546; XII, 265, 565; Wines, Two Years and a Half in the Navy, I, 16-51.

[86] Richardson, Messages and Papers of the Presidents, V, 88.

years preceding the Civil War was well-nigh fruitless. Nothing less than a successful war with its train of naval heroes and its need of commodores and admirals to command its fleets in battle would obtain for the navy this boon. In 1857 Congress passed a law giving the commander of a squadron the designation of " flag-officer," a very awkward term. About this time the department directed that a captain of 20 years' standing when in command of a squadron should carry at the fore a square flag—the designation of a vice-admiral; and that a captain of less than 20 years' standing should carry at the mizzen a square flag—the designation of a rear-admiral. Captain W. B. Shubrick, who assembled a fleet at the mouth of the La Plata in 1858, was the first American officer to carry abroad a vice-admiral's flag. A short time previous, Captain E. A. F. La Valette for the first time in the American navy displayed the flag of a rear-admiral. A joint resolution of Congress of March 2, 1859, conferred on Captain Charles Stewart, in recognition of his distinguished and meritorious service, the rank of " senior flag officer of the United States navy on the active service list." [37]

The warm contentions between the line and the staff officers over assimilated rank caused much bitterness and jealousy on both sides. The " line " may be defined as those officers whose essential duty is to fight the enemy, and who have naval command. The line grades were those of captain, commander, lieutenant, master, and midshipman. The " staff " comprises those officers whose duties are auxiliary to the line, and who do not have naval command. The staff officers were the surgeons, pursers, engineers, chaplains, and professors of mathematics. Assimilated rank may be defined as the relative position of the staff officers to those of the line. In 1842 the staff did not have assimilated rank, but ardently desired it.

The civilian may have some difficulty in understanding the character and importance of assimilated rank. To the naval man the nature of this incorporeal hereditament is very clear and real. In naval and official life, and especially in the society aboard ship, rank confers precedence, social rights and privileges, and the esteem of your fellows. It determines the apartment in which an officer sleeps, the position of his chair at the table when eating,

---

[37] Cooper, Navy of United States, 1866, III, 108; U. S. Statutes at Large, XI, 442.

his relative position on entering or leaving the ship, his place of promenade on deck, and the fashion and decorations of his clothes. The official worth of a man on board ship is read by his fellow-officers from the buttons and gold bullion on his coat, and he is esteemed accordingly. To be without rank is to be penniless of the current coin of the naval realm. An officer with rank may demand privileges as his right; while without rank he may accept them, if offered, as a courtesy. If the staff officer in the days before he was granted assimilated rank was fortunate in his ship-mates, he might have no cause to complain; but if not, he would "break the bread of bitterness to the end of the cruise."

The surgeons were foremost in presenting their case and urging their claims. The pursers were scarcely less insistent; and soon the engineers had increased in numbers and began to make demands. The line naturally resisted the assignment of rank to the staff. An institution that has developed traditions and a cor-porate life, and that enjoys a monopoly of rights and privileges, is wont to resist strenuously its being cheapened or made common either by undue additions to its membership or by extension of its privileges to others. The line argued with reason that rank, owing to its very essence, belonged peculiarly to the "military corps" of the navy, and that it was incongruous to clothe the staff in the garb of the line. It urged that the granting of rank to the staff would injuriously affect the discipline, harmony, and general good of the service; that the wearing of epaulets by both classes of officers would cause confusion; and that to admit staff officers to seats on courts-martial was not "military." A respect-able lieutenant of this period is reported to have said: "I hold my rank dearer than life itself, and were any purser of the navy to sign an official report above me, I would cleave him to the chin with my cutlass. I could never suffer my rank to be outraged in that way; I would rather die."

In the end, the movement for assimilated rank proved to be too strong for the officers of the line; nor, indeed, did all of them oppose it. Secretaries Upshur, Henshaw, and Mason, each in turn, favored the claims of the staff. Finally, Secretary Ban-croft solved the problem so far as the surgeons were concerned by issuing the general order of August 31, 1846, according to which, surgeons of the fleet and surgeons of more than 12 years standing were to rank with commanders; surgeons of less than 12 years standing, with lieutenants; passed assistant surgeons, next after lieutenants; and assistant surgeons, next after masters. A similar order of Secretary Mason, issued in May, 1847, fixed the assimilated rank of the pursers. These orders were thoroughly disliked by the line, and many officers considered them illegal. Each side published pamphlets setting forth its own arguments. In 1848, 60 or 70 officers of the line met in Washington to concert action with a view to obtaining a revocation of the orders of Bancroft and Mason. The current, however, could not be turned. In 1854 Congress gave these orders the sanction of law. The engineers had a long struggle before they won the coveted prize. In January, 1859, they were granted assimilated rank by a general order of Secretary Toucey; and a little later in the same year Congress inserted the order in the naval appropriations act.[38]

Upon the construction of many new steamships during the decade preceding the Civil War, the engineer corps greatly increased in numbers and importance. In 1860 it contained 175 engineers. A most significant recommendation in respect to the engineers was made in 1854 by the board of visitors to the Naval Academy, and was repeated by the board for 1859: " In view of the great and growing importance of the steam engine as applied to ships of war, the board have given very mature consideration to this subject, and are satisfied that the union of the duties of the engineer with those of the sea officer, so far from being incompatible, will be found entirely practicable and of decided advantage. The watches may be so arranged as to give to each officer who leaves the academy his regular turn of duty at the engine and on deck, and thus an intimate knowledge of the duties of the engineer and sea officer may be kept up at the same time." [39] More than 40 years elapsed before this recommendation was realized in the amalgamation of the line and the engineers by the Naval Personnel Act of 1899.

On February 28, 1855, Congress passed " an Act to promote the Efficiency of the Navy." The enforcement of no other naval law has probably caused so much discussion, commotion, and ill-feeling. For some 15 years presidents, secretaries of the navy, naval officers, civilians, and newspapers had advocated the estab-

[38] Ruschenberger, Controversy on Assimilated Rank; Navy Register, 1849, p. 44; U. S. Statutes at Large, X, 587; XI, 407.
[39] Ann. Rept. of Sec. of N., 1859, p. 1161.

lishment of a retired or reserved list of naval officers. Many of
the annual reports of the secretaries of the navy between 1842 and
1854 treat the subject at considerable length. Bills providing for
a retired list were from time to time introduced in Congress.
For various reasons these all failed to pass: Congress was indifferent to the needs of the navy; some members believed that a
retired list was a pension list and was not consonant with a
democratic government; and the difficulty of drafting a law suitable to all the officers was very great. Secretary Bancroft was
ardent in behalf of this reform. In 1846 he wrote to the chairman
of the Naval Committee of the House that a " retired list, desirable in peace, was necessary in war. Why should you leave the
unavailable supernumeraries to stand in the way of the promotion
of young, active, and able men? I hope you are friendly to a
retired list, and to the young officers of the navy. The present
system puts upon the active all the hazard and toil, and gives promotions and emoluments to the idlers at home." [40]

The upper ranks of the navy had long been overstocked with
old and incapacitated men, who impeded the flow of promotions.
The younger officers urged that the quarter-deck was not the
proper place for the " lean and slippered pantaloon " of old age.
In 1854, of the 68 captains, the youngest was 56 years of age;
and of the 97 commanders, 74 were between 50 and 55 years;
the 327 lieutenants were from 30 to 50 years; and the 198
passed midshipmen, from 21 to 37 years. Under the then existing conditions, the lieutenants when promoted to be commanders
would be 53 years of age; and the commanders when promoted to
be captains would be 74 years. The incapacity for service was by
no means confined to the upper ranks. Bancroft considered some
of the masters " utterly ignorant of navigation." He said that in
one year more than 200 warrants for midshipmen had been issued
and had brought into the service " without much discrimination
young persons, some of whom were even physically and mentally
disqualified for duty." [41]

As a result of the incapacity of many naval officers and of the
excess in their numbers, the Secretary of the Navy had virtually,
without sanction of law, established a " retired list." He never
sent to sea those officers who had become incapacitated by age,

[40] Congress Letters, XI, 35.
[41] Congressional Globe, 1853-1854, p. 1459; Congress Letters, XI, 5-22.

disease, or the accidents of their profession; but gave them nominal shore-duty, or else no duty at all with leave-of-absence pay. One captain who had been in the service for 54 years had been unemployed 36 years. Another officer had been a captain for 30 years, but had spent only two of them at sea. In 1848 a certain commander had not been to sea for more than 41 years; and of 67 captains, 40 were on leave-of-absence pay. For various reasons certain lieutenants were regularly passed over in the making of promotions; one had not been promoted since 1832 owing to physical and mental incompetence; and others were regularly "overslaughed" for habitual intemperance or mental derangement.[42] Of the 28 masters, 18 had never performed a cruise. The exercise of favoritism on the part of the department may account for some of these anomalies. It was a common saying in the Old Navy, that "a cruise of a few months in Washington tells more in an officer's favor than a 3-years' cruise at sea."

The act of 1855 to promote the efficiency of the navy provided for a board of 15 naval officers, composed of five captains, five commanders, and five lieutenants.[43] Under such regulations as the Secretary of the Navy should prescribe, this board was to make a careful examination into the efficiency of the officers of the line, and report to the Secretary those officers who were "incapable of performing promptly and efficiently all their duties both ashore and afloat." The board was to ascertain the character and extent of the incompetency of each incapable officer, and place him accordingly into one of three classes. Those officers who were incompetent by reason of their own fault were to be discharged from the navy; certain other officers were to be retired on furlough pay; and still others on leave-of-absence pay. The scrutiny of the board was to extend only to the captains, commanders, lieutenants, masters, and passed midshipmen of the navy. No member of the board was to examine or report upon an officer who stood higher than himself in the Navy List.

President Pierce appointed the board on June 5, 1855. Its ranking officers were Commodores Shubrick, Perry, and McCauley. Commander Samuel F. DuPont was one of its most able and prominent members. It began its labors on June 20, and made its report on July 26. It found 201 officers incapacitated. Of

[42] Congressional Globe, 1853-1854, p. 2155; 1854-1855, p. 709.
[43] U. S. Statutes at Large, X, 616-617.

these, it recommended that 49 be dismissed from the navy; that 81 be retired on furlough pay; and that 71 be retired on leave-of-absence pay. President Pierce and Secretary Dobbin approved the findings of the board, and they were at once put into operation.[44]

This report, both in and out of the navy, attracted the most earnest attention and created a profound sensation. The feeling against the board and its action was strong throughout the country. A considerable part of the influential press took up the cause of the "degraded officers." The "Scientific American" declared that the board had struck down every officer who had distinguished himself by his scientific attainments. The legislature of New Jersey transmitted resolutions to Congress in behalf of the restoration to the active list of Commodore Charles Stewart, the ranking officer of the navy, whom the board had "reserved." The Virginia legislature resolved that the action of the retiring board "was not in accordance with the principles which our Government recognizes as the only guarantees of judicial fairness and impartiality." It found "on the list of dismissed Virginians names of men who have by their achievements in war and peace, in arms and in science, not only commanded the thanks and compliments of their own country, but had extorted, and whilst the board was in session, were extorting the homage and admiration of all the great commercial and naval powers of the world." An allusion is here found to the notable achievements in meteorology of Lieutenant M. F. Maury, who had been placed upon the "reserved list."

The dismissed and retired officers earnestly appealed to their representatives and senators to have their names restored to the active list; and when Congress assembled in December, 1855, various petitions and memorials to this effect were received by that body. Certain members of both houses warmly espoused the side of the dissatisfied officers. Senator Houston, of Texas, was a zealous, though indiscreet, champion of their cause. He declared that they were the victims of a conspiracy and that Commander S. F. DuPont was the prime mover in it. Indeed, the brunt of the opprobium fell upon DuPont. His zeal for naval reform, the excellence of his professional reputation, and his long and efficient service in the navy marked him out among the members of the board as the best target for criticism. In the Senate, Sena-

[44] Ann. Rept. of Sec. of N., 1855, pp. 10-13, 30-44.

tor Bayard, of Delaware, DuPont's State, came to his defense. That the board should have been sharply criticised was inevitable. Several of the "degraded officers" were able men and had influential friends. Moreover the cause of some of them was just. Many of the criticisms against the board, however, were most unreasonable. Its members were accused of conspiracy, favoritişm, gross impartiality, jealousy, and the promotion of their own interests. That the board was moved by improper motives was never proved. It probably made errors of judgment. The brief time allotted to its work did not admit of a thorough examination of the worth of the officers. The standard for testing an officer's incapacity was, however, provided by Congress and the Navy Department; and it may have been too rigid. The board applied it rigorously and with consummate fearlessness. It undoubtedly caused some injustice. At this time, the naval officers were not familiar with a retired list. Moreover, retirement under the act of 1855 seemed to discredit them professionally. They naturally opposed a reduction of their pay.[45]

The storm of opposition could not be wholly resisted. While Secretary Dobbin and President Pierce valiantly defended the board, they nevertheless expressed a willingness to remedy all errors of judgment committed by it. After much debating, marked by many intemperate assertions, Congress finally in January, 1857, passed a law giving to each officer who had been dismissed or retired the right to have his case re-examined before a court of enquiry. This court was empowered to recommend, in accordance with the evidence presented, the entire or partial restoration of an officer to his former status. In March, 1858, the President and Senate were authorized to restore such officers as were recommended by the courts of enquiry. As a result of these laws, many officers who had been dismissed or retired were wholly or partially rehabilitated. The effect on the active list of this rehabilitation is shown by the increase in the number of officers in the higher ranks. From 1856 to 1859 the number of captains on the active list increased from 68 to 81 ; commanders, from 97 to 116 ; and lieutenants, from 326 to 338.[46]

In the end, the objects of the naval efficiency act were only in

[45] Congressional Globe, 1855-1856, pp. 386-387, 711; app., 242-245; Corbin, Maury, 110.

[46] U. S. Statutes at Large, XI, 153-154, 367-368; Navy Register, 1856 and 1859.

part attained. Under it, several incapacitated officers were permanently dismissed or retired; the reserved list of 1860 contains
the names of 19 captains, 16 commanders, and 35 lieutenants.
Many young men obtained promotion. On the other hand, not a
few old and inefficient men still remained on the active list. The
excess of officers in the higher ranks was never so great as in
1859. The naval efficiency act was a rough pruning knife, whose
use caused much pain, ill-temper, and hard feelings. Had not the
bitter memories of it been obliterated by the events of the Civil
War, they must have long rankled in the minds of many officers.

The quarter of a century preceding the Civil War may be
appropriately called the golden age of science in the navy. That
wonderful movement of the last century which was marked by a
passion for natural science, exact research, and the inductive
method of reasoning, and which produced in England such illustrious names as Lyell, Darwin, Spencer, Huxley, and Tyndall,
was keenly felt in this country and especially in our navy. During the period of 1842-1861 three important scientific bureaus were
founded, several noteworthy exploring expeditions were undertaken, and more than one naval officer gained international fame
for his research and discoveries.

Under the guidance of Lieutenants Wilkes, Gilliss, and Maury,
the Depot of Charts and Instruments, established in Washington
in 1830, developed into two scientific bureaus, the Naval Observatory and the Hydrographical Office. At this time these two
offices were directed by a single superintendent. From 1844 to
1861 they were in charge of Lieutenant Matthew F. Maury, a man
of much industry, fervor, and genius. During these years he
accomplished his noted work in marine meteorology, and won the
esteem of the savants of Europe and the gaudy decorations of
numerous foreign governments. The name of Professor James
P. Espy is also justly celebrated for his meteorological researches.
Under the direction of the Secretary of the Navy, he made observations of the weather from stations on land and investigated the
law of storms.

In July, 1849, the Nautical Almanac Office was founded, and
the compilation of an American ephemeris was begun. The men
most active in obtaining the new establishment were Lieutenant
Charles H. Davis, the first superintendent of the office; Lieutenant M. F. Maury, superintendent of the Naval Observatory;

Alexander D. Bache, superintendent of the Coast Survey; and Joseph Henry, secretary of the Smithsonian Institution. Their prime objects were " to advance the scientific character and standing of the country by a publication of the highest order, to promote the cause of astronomy, and to render substantial services to navigation by producing a work on a higher plane than the British Nautical Almanac." In order that the new almanac might have the benefit of the scientists and libraries of the chief educational center of the United States, the Nautical Almanac Office was located at Cambridge, Massachusetts. At this time the poverty of Washington in these respects was very great. Some of the leading American astronomers and mathematicians, residing at Cambridge and elsewhere, assisted in making observations and calculations. Davis sought out and employed in his office young men of talent, without regard to political or personal influence. Several of these youths found the Nautical Almanac Office a pathway to scientific eminence. Among the famous men connected with the office during its first years, were Professor Benjamin F. Pierce, in his day the leading mathematician in America; Professor John D. Runkle, sometime president of the Massachusetts School of Technology; and Professors William Ferrel, Joseph Winlock, and Simon Newcomb, famous as mathematicians or astronomers.[47]

Of the many important exploring expeditions that were sent out in quest of scientific knowledge of all sorts, only the chief ones will be here mentioned. After four years of exploration the Wilkes expedition returned to the United States in 1842. Among other places, it visited the Madeira Islands, New South Wales, New Zealand, Friendly Islands, Samoa, Fiji Islands, Hawaii, Columbia River, Philippine Islands, and Saint Helena. It made two voyages to the Antarctic regions, where Wilkes, according to his claims, discovered an Antarctic continent. The expedition acquired much information and collected many materials relating to zoology, botany, geology, ethnography, philology, hydrography, and geography. From 1842 to 1861 several scientists and naval officers were employed in digesting and publishing this information. Commander Wilkes was still engaged in this task at the outbreak of the Civil War. The work of publication was never completed. Nineteen quarto volumes, however, were issued.

[47] Davis, Davis, 86-93; Newcomb, Reminiscences, 66.

The three volumes on zoology were prepared by James D. Dana, and one on botany by Asa Gray.

The surveying expedition of Ringgold and Rodgers, 1852-1855, consisting of five vessels, made a survey and reconnaisance of the China seas, Bering Strait, and North Pacific ocean; and collected a vast quantity of information relating to these hitherto little-known regions. In 1848 Commander W. F. Lynch explored the course of the river Jordan and the shores of the Dead Sea. In 1850-1851 Lieutenant Edwin J. De Haven conducted the Sir John Franklin relief expedition to the Arctic sea. In 1853 Dr. Elisha K. Kane, of the naval medical corps, made a similar expedition; and in 1855 Lieutenant Henry J. Hartstene went to the relief of Kane. From 1849 to 1852 Lieutenant James M. Gilliss was engaged in making astronomical observations at Santiago, Chile, with a view to the more accurate determination of the distance between the earth and the sun. In 1850-1851 Lieutenants W. L. Herndon and L. Gibbon explored the Amazon river; and in 1852-1856 Lieutenant T. J. Page made important surveys of the rivers of Uruguay, Paraguay, and the Argentine, and collected many valuable specimens of the birds, fishes, and reptiles of these countries. Commander W. F. Lynch made an exploring expedition, 1852-1853, to the West coast of Africa. In 1856 Lieutenant O. H. Berryman in the steamer *Arctic* demonstrated the possibility of laying a cable between the United States and Europe. In 1857-1858 Lieutenant T. A. M. Craven surveyed the Isthmus of Panama with a view to ascertaining the practicability of joining the two oceans by means of a ship canal. Lieutenant I. G. Strain in 1854 had made a similar expedition under extraordinary difficulties and hardships, resulting in his death.

The officers of the Old Navy were frequently called upon to settle, on their own responsibility, either through diplomacy or by the exercise of force, various troubles and disputes arising in foreign ports. These occasions now arise much less frequently than formerly. The cables and overland wires have placed our government in close communication with its naval officers and foreign representatives, and it therefore now leaves much less to their discretion. During the 20 years preceding the Civil War instances of their independent diplomatic or military action were frequent. In passing, one may refer to the palavers of Commodore M. C. Perry with the native chiefs ending in the

Berribee affair of 1843; the Nagaski incident of Commander James Glynn in 1849; Commander Duncan N. Ingraham's protection of the Hungarian refugee, Koszta, at Smyrna in 1853; and the storming and destruction of the Barrier Forts at Canton in 1856.[48]

Our greatest sailor-diplomat is Commodore M. C. Perry, whose famous expedition to Japan is well known. The command of the expedition was originally given to Commodore J. H. Aulick. In 1851 he was organizing a squadron in Hong Kong, when the department, apparently acting under a misapprehension, recalled him. He was superseded by Perry early in 1852. On November 24, Perry, after having made thorough preparations for his mission, sailed from Norfolk for the East on the U. S. S. *Mississippi*. He had been promised an imposing squadron, but the fleet which he finally brought to anchor in Yedo Bay on July 7, 1853, consisted only of his flag-ship *Susquehanna*, and three other vessels. By virtue of his tact, policy, and firmness, Perry succeeded in delivering the letter of the President of the United States addressed to the Emperor of Japan and setting forth the purposes of the mission. He then sailed for Hong Kong, having given notice that he would return in the spring. In February, 1854, he was again in Yedo Bay, this time with a larger and more imposing fleet. In March he made a treaty with the Japanese, according kind treatment to shipwrecked American sailors and permission for American vessels to anchor at certain ports and obtain supplies. Only in this limited way was trade and residence granted. The treaty was merely the entering wedge in the reopening of Japan. It was for this reason, however, none the less significant. Perry's glory consists not in originating the expedition, but in conducting it, without bloodshed, to a successful conclusion. His skill, tact, patience, and pertinacity surmounted every obstacle.[49]

A court-martial of great tragic interest was held at the New York navy-yard, beginning February 1, 1843, and lasting 40 days. The chief point which the court was called upon to decide was whether the execution of midshipman Philip Spencer, boatswain's mate Samuel Cromwell, and seaman Elisha Small, by Commander Alexander S. Mackenzie was directed and carried into effect with

---

[48] Naval Actions and History, 60-61.
[49] Griffis, M. C. Perry, 270-374; Narrative of the U. S. Japan Expedition.

justifiable cause. Mackenzie was the commander of the U. S. brig *Somers*. In November, 1842, when his vessel was bound from the coast of Africa for St. Thomas, he believed that he discovered a conspiracy to murder the officers and the faithful of the crew and to convert the brig into a piratical cruiser. He regarded Spencer, Cromwell, and Small as the principal conspirators, and they were placed under arrest. Certain officers of the ship, whom he directed to investigate the mutiny, advised the execution of the three ringleaders. Accordingly, on December 1, 1842, they were hung to the yard-arm of the *Somers*. The midshipman and the seaman confessed their guilt, but the boatswain's mate protested his innocence. This extreme act of discipline subdued the crew for the rest of the voyage. The court-martial, which tried Mackenzie, was presided over by Commodore John Downes, and included ten captains and two commanders. It acquitted the accused, as had also a previous court of enquiry. The public mind, however, was greatly excited over this melancholy event, and the feeling against the commander ran high. The case was aggravated by the fact that the executed midshipman was a nephew of John C. Spencer, the Secretary of War.[50]

[50] Cooper, Navy of the United States, 1866, III, 52; Defence of Mackenzie in the case of the *Somers* Mutiny; Benjamin, U. S. Naval Academy, 133.

CHAPTER SEVEN: THE CIVIL WAR, 1861-1865

Part I

THE NAVY DEPARTMENT

With the inauguration of Abraham Lincoln on March 4, 1861, there began at Washington a new administrative régime, destined to be long-lived, and to exercise a great influence upon the nation. New men, animated with fresh purposes and trained in a different political school from that of their predecessors, took up the work of Federal administration. The executive departments passed from the Democrats to the Republicans. With the exception of the Harrison-Tyler and Taylor-Fillmore administrations, the Democrats had been in power since the first inauguration of Andrew Jackson, on March 4, 1829. Disregarding Grover Cleveland's two administrations, the Republicans at the end of the administration of President Taft will have controlled the departments continuously since March 4, 1861—a period of fifty-two years.

On the coming of Lincoln, Southern influences, which for twenty years had predominated in the Navy Department, yielded to Northern. The Southern line of Secretaries of the Navy was succeeded by a new Northern line. The first Secretary under the Republicans was Gideon Welles, of Hartford, Connecticut. Welles served longer than any of his predecessors; and, up to the present time, than any of his successors. Two Secretaries, however, served almost as long—Robert Smith, 1801-1809, and George M. Robeson, 1869-1877. Welles's term extended from March 5, 1861, to March 3, 1869, and covered the administrations of

Abraham Lincoln and Andrew Johnson. This period of eight years forms an important and well-defined era in naval history, since it is marked by the rise and decline of the navy of the Civil War. The first four years saw the rise, and the second four the decline of the navy. The former period, that of Welles's first administration, is practically coincident with the Civil War, and is treated of in this and the succeeding chapter.

The task of Secretary Welles from 1861 to 1865 was of greater magnitude and diversity than that of any of his predecessors. For four momentous years it was his lot to work and suffer with Lincoln under the heat, burden and turmoil of civil conflict. Many new duties unknown to the piping times of peace fell to him, and the old and usual duties of the naval office were greatly complicated, and were rendered important and insistent by the needs of war. The rusty machinery of the Department had to be repaired, lubricated, and enlarged. The thunderbolts of war had to be forged. Officers, sailors, and ships—the staples of navies—had to be supplied in great numbers. From 1861 to 1865 the number of ships increased from 90 to 670; of officers, from 1300 to 6700; and of seamen, from 7500 to 51,500. The annual naval expenditures rose from $12,000,000 to $123,000,000. With Welles rested the final decision respecting all shipbuilding programs, the principal plans of naval operations, and the general lines of naval policy. He was held responsible for the blunders and failures of the Department and the navy.

Gideon Welles was descended from the best stock of Connecticut. The original emigrant of his family to that state, Thomas Welles, held many important public offices between 1639 and 1659, being twice elected governor of the infant colony. Gideon was educated at the Episcopal Academy, in Cheshire, Connecticut, and at the Norwich University. He read law, and at the age of twenty-three became editor and one of the proprietors of the *Hartford Times,* which he edited until 1837. From 1827 to 1835 he was a member of the Connecticut legislature. For several years he served his state as comptroller of public accounts, and for some five years was postmaster of Hartford. From 1846 to 1849 he was chief of the Bureau of Provisions and Clothing in the Navy Department, at Washington.

In politics, Welles was for many years a Jacksonian Democrat. His anti-slavery views, however, carried him into the Republican party, and in 1856 he was its candidate for Governor of Connecticut. He was a leading contributor to the *Hartford Evening Press,* the Republican organ of his state. For several years Welles was a member of the Republican National Committee. He was a delegate to the Republican National Conventions of 1856 and 1860, serving in the latter year as the chairman of the Connecticut delegation. During the presidential campaign of 1860 he labored earnestly for the election of Lincoln.[1]

In November, 1860, Lincoln began to consider various men for places in his cabinet. Welles's name was one of the first presented to him, and was the subject of a special consultation. Vice-President Hannibal .Hamlin urged Welles's appointment. Senator John P. Hale, a New Hampshire politician of unsavory repute, was rather earnestly pressed upon the President for Secretary of the Navy, and he was somewhat mortified that his pretensions for the place were not more seriously regarded. Other names may have been considered. Lincoln, however, was from the first convinced of Welles's fitness, availability and representative character, and decided to invite him to a seat in the cabinet.[2]

The assignment of Welles to the Navy Department instead of to some other secretaryship may be ascribed to his three years' experience as chief of the Bureau of Provisions and Clothing, and to his residence in New England, whose maritime interests have given her a claim upon the naval portfolio. In making up his cabinet, Lincoln apportioned its members according to their sectional residence and their party antecedents. Welles was chosen as the New England member, and as a representative of the Democratic element of the Republican party. The early Republicans, it is recollected, were recruited principally from the Whigs, Democrats, and Free Soilers. The Whig faction was not generally friendly to Lincoln's naval secretary. Within the cabinet no love was lost between Welles and the Secretary of State, William H. Seward. In December, 1860, Thurlow Weed, one of the leaders of the Whigs in New York, spoke to Lincoln against his choice of Welles for the naval portfolio. Weed, so the story goes, said to the President that if he would, on his way to his inaugu-

---

[1] Boynton, Navy during the Great Rebellion, I, 22-24.
[2] Manuscript Papers of Gideon Welles in the possession of Mr. Edgar T. Welles of New York City; Nicolay and Hay, Lincoln, III, 367; Diary of Gideon Welles, vol. I, p. xxi.

ration in Washington, stop long enough in New York, Philadelphia, or Baltimore, to select an attractive figurehead from the
prow of a ship, would adorn it with an elaborate wig and luxuriant whiskers, and would transfer it to the entrance of the Navy
Department, this figurehead would be quite as serviceable to the
navy as Welles, and much less expensive. " Oh," Mr. Lincoln
replied, " wooden midshipmen answer very well in novels, but we
must have a live Secretary of the Navy." [3]

Welles's " elaborate wig and luxuriant whiskers " gave him a
patriarchical appearance, which his age and vigor of mind belied.
When he entered the cabinet he was in his fifty-ninth year. Secretary of State Seward and Secretary of War Cameron were older
than the Secretary of the Navy, and Attorney-General Bates was
ten years his senior. Among the naval officers and sailors his
paternal and benevolent aspect won for him the familiar appellation
of " Father Welles," or " the Old Man of the Sea." Mr. Charles
A. Dana, for a time an Assistant Secretary of War to Edwin
M. Stanton, has left us one of the best characterizations of Lincoln's naval secretary. " Welles was a curious-looking man,"
Dana said, " he wore a wig which was parted in the middle, the
hair falling down on each side; and it was from his peculiar
appearance, I have always thought, that the idea that he was an
old fogy originated. I remember Governor Andrew, of Massachusetts, coming into my office at the War Department one day,
and asking where he could find ' that old Mormon deacon, the
Secretary of the Navy.' In spite of his peculiarities, I think Mr.
Welles was a very wise, strong man. There was nothing decor-
ative about him; there was no noise in the street when he went
along; but he understood his duty, and did it efficiently, continually, and unvaryingly. There was a good deal of opposition to
him, for we had no navy when the war began, and he had to create
one without much deliberation; but he was patient, laborious, and
intelligent at his task." [4]

Welles was sometimes unjustly regarded as a time-serving,
routine-loving secretary, a friend to red-tape. It is true that he
was not one of those dashing administrators, who reach conclusions by intuition, put their decisions into effect with great

[3] Weed, Autobiography, I, 606-607, 611.
[4] Dana, Recollections, 170.

strenuosity, and are at once the inspiration and the terror of their subordinates. Rather, he was the quiet, unswerving, fearless executive, who reasons carefully from the evidence, and draws temperately his conclusions therefrom, who enforces his judgments with firmness and uniformity, and who gains the esteem of his fellows by reason of his patience, integrity, and justice. His qualities were solid, and never showy. While he had his antipathies, he nevertheless administered the navy as a rule with great impartiality. That he distributed the honors and rewards at his disposal without prejudice and bias, did not always appear to be true to those officers who were disappointed in not receiving their share of distinctions, and there are always many such officers during a war. Could they have known the mind of the Secretary of the Navy, they would have found that his decisions were based upon just principles of administration and the information presented to him.

Welles applied the laws of the navy fearlessly and without favor, no matter what the rank of the offender. He stood, as few Secretaries have, for naval discipline and an impartial administration of the naval code. More than once he rebuked a naval court for bringing in a verdict contrary to the evidence presented to it. A court-martial, of which Farragut was president, found the captain of a certain ship guilty of failing to do his utmost to overtake and capture a certain Confederate vessel, an offense punishable with death. The court sentenced the offending officer to be suspended from the navy for two years on leave-of-absence pay—a mere nominal penalty. Welles in reviewing these absurd findings pointed out that the sentence of the court would be too mild for a trivial offense, and declared that such punishment as the court had prescribed " no officer could obtain from the Department as a favor." [5]

Welles was generous in his praise of gallant and meritorious conduct. His congratulatory messages to the victorious naval officers were warm and hearty, and felicitously phrased. As a newspaper writer, he had acquired considerable facility in composition, and his official reports are therefore more interesting reading than most documents of this sort, usually so dry, commonplace and dispiriting. Unlike some of the Naval Secretaries, Welles did not depute to his subordinates the composition of his annual reports, although he availed himself of their criticisms and suggestions. His writings reveal a faculty for lucid expression, clear thinking and the discernment of the gist of any subject. From the diary which he kept during and after the war, a recently published document of great historical value, one gathers that its author was methodical, painstaking and honest, and fearless in criticising his colleagues.[6]

In determining the policy of the government, Welles's advice was much valued by the President. His knowledge of public affairs was seasoned, and his judgment was sober and generally well balanced, but his counsel was not always politic. In the Mason and Slidell episode, he wrote a warmly congratulatory letter to Captain Wilkes, whose acts were finally disavowed by the President. That the Secretary of the Navy should have had a profound knowledge of international law was, however, hardly to be expected. Regarding the government's powers under the constitution, Welles took a middle ground, being neither a strict nor a broad constructionist. He and the Secretary of State were instinctively opposed to each other, and were usually on opposite sides of the questions that came before the cabinet. Welles regarded Seward as an intriguing and designing politician. He held, on plausible grounds, that Seward's conduct during the first weeks of Lincoln's administration was, if not traitorous, certainly highly unpatriotic. The Secretary of the Navy possessed none of those superb delusions that sometimes afflicted Lincoln's brilliant Secretary of State. On matters lying within the field of his information, his judgment was certainly as reliable as that of his colleague in the State Department.

Early in the war Welles and Seward did not get along well together, and some grave misunderstandings arose between them. At one time Welles and Secretary of War Stanton engaged in a serious altercation over the exchanging of prisoners. Several naval officers, notably Dupont, Wilkes, and Preble, had unpleasant differences with the Secretary. For all his controversies, it must be said, Welles had ample grounds. A fearless executive, intent upon the performance of his duties, is certain to have more or less trouble with his subordinates and colleagues. Some of Welles's critics, however, hold that his disputes reveal defects of character common to New Englanders—a lack of tact and sympathy, an

[6] See The Diary of Gideon Welles, 3 vols. (1911.)

arbitrary and inflexible mind, and an inability to understand an opponent's point of view.

To a technical and intimate knowledge of the navy, Welles made no pretensions. He, however, was better equipped for his duties than most Secretaries have been. His three years' service in one of the naval bureaus had given him a considerable acquaintance with the business of the Department. Fortunately, the limitations in Welles's naval knowledge were adequately compensated by the extensive professional information of his Assistant Secretary, Gustavus V. Fox, whose selection by President Lincoln as Welles's aid in the Navy Department was a most happy one.

At the beginning of the war Fox was in his fortieth year. He was born in Saugus, Essex County, Massachusetts. His father was a country physician, in moderate circumstances. At the age of sixteen young Fox was appointed midshipman in the navy, where he remained for eighteen years, and had a most varied naval career. He served in the Mediterranean, East Indian, Pacific, Brazil, and African squadrons, participated in the naval operations of the Mexican War, and for a time assisted in the work of the Coast Survey. In 1853-1854 he commanded a mail steamer, plying between New York and the Isthmus of Panama, and belonging to one of the subsidized steamship lines. In July, 1856, having reached the rank of lieutenant, he resigned from the navy and accepted the position of " agent " of the Bay State Woolen Mills, at Lawrence, Massachusetts. Early in 1861 he came to Washington with a plan for the relief of Fort Sumter, and in April President Lincoln permitted him to put it into operation. In planning, promoting and conducting this daring adventure, he displayed such energy, tact, and initiative, that the President was most favorably impressed with him. These qualities, together with the strong influence of his family connections, who stood close to Lincoln, soon brought him political preferment. On May 9, 1861, he was appointed chief clerk of the Navy Department, and on July 31 he was promoted to be Assistant Secretary of the Navy, a newly-created position.

Fox's career both in and out of the navy admirably fitted him for the assistant secretaryship. His long service in the navy gave him a wide acquaintance among the naval officers. He had acquired the habit of the navy and of the sea, and knew well the practice of the naval profession. On the other hand, his expe-

riences as a New England manufacturer had familiarized him
with the currents of thought and action outside of the navy, with
the methods of business, its economies and administration, and
the qualities of commercial men. In the science of the naval profession, in contradistinction to its art, Fox was not especially well
grounded. His knowledge of naval architecture was naturally
limited, and his naval strategy proved to be at times faulty. He
sometimes appeared more ready to plan, than laboriously to execute. Fox was decisive, quick of mind, and self-confident. No
matter how dark and gloomy were the prospects of the Unionists,
the buoyancy of his spirits never failed him. He was urbane and
suave, and had a most engaging personality. The amenities of
social life came easy to him. His father-in-law was Francis P.
Blair, one of the leaders at the National Republican Convention of
1860; and his brother-in-law was Lincoln's postmaster-general,
Montgomery Blair. During the war the Blairs were exceedingly
influential in national politics. Few men, who in the eventful
spring of 1861 came to the surface of that tempestuous political
sea at Washington, were as likely as Gustavus V. Fox to survive
in its rough waters and ride its waves to preferment and eminence.[7]

It is said that Fox was not Welles's first choice for the assistant
secretaryship.[8] This may well have been, for the two men differed
widely in professional training, habit of mind, and personal characteristics. Their official relations, however, were intimate, cordial, and unruffled by discords. Welles valued Fox's services
highly, although he discovered certain shortcomings in him.
Each gave to the other his confidence. As Assistant Secretary of
the Navy, Fox was Welles's " chief of staff," his professional and
confidential adviser. In choosing officers for important tasks, in
formulating plans of naval operations, and in the execution of the
technical business of the Secretary's office, Welles received the
counsel and suggestions of his assistant, and largely acted upon
them. In the work of the department, he gave Fox a remarkably
free hand. Fox corresponded with many of the naval officers,
sending them much valuable information, and often discussing
with them their plans of naval operations. Notwithstanding these
letters are personal, they assume a semi-official character by reason

[7] Nicolay and Hay, Lincoln, V, 4-5; Davis, Davis, 132-133.
[8] United Service, IV (1881), 36.

of the subjects discussed and the circumstances under which they were written. Respecting minor naval affairs, Fox gave official orders in his own name. Lincoln advised as freely with the Assistant Secretary as with the Secretary.

Both Welles and Fox had a great capacity for work, and each wrote with their own hands a vast number of letters. To their subordinates they often appeared fatigued and overworked. Night after night they toiled over their desks at the Department. In the course of his duties, Fox now and then visited the navy yards, or some of the principal seaports of the North. Infrequently, Welles and Fox went to the " front," the latter more often than the former. The Assistant Secretary of the Navy witnessed the fight at Hampton Roads between the *Monitor* and the *Merrimac*. In May, 1862, the Secretary of the Navy invited two or three members of the cabinet, the chief clerk of the Department, and several naval officers with the ladies of their families, to make a special cruise on the steamer *City of Baltimore*, and visit the Union fleets in the waters between Washington and Richmond. Such excursions must have brought to the Secretary and his Assistant a welcome relief from their arduous toil, and have given a brief diversion to their lives, so full of anxieties, vexations and discouragements.

It may be a little early, even yet, to apportion with nicety the respective shares of Welles and Fox in the management of the navy and the Department during the Civil War. It is plain that the Secretary of the Navy has not received sufficient credit for his services at the hands of historians. The brilliancy of Fox has somewhat obscured the deeper colors of Welles. To some writers it has appeared that the real power in the Department was the Assistant Secretary of the Navy, and that the Secretary was a sort of antiquated figurehead. While Admiral David D. Porter did not always write history with precision or impartiality, yet his estimate of Welles's services are worthy of consideration, coming as it does from a contemporary who was well situated for observation, fearless in the expression of his opinions, and not altogether friendly to the man about whom he was writing. In his naval history, Porter says that Gideon Welles was the responsible head of the Navy Department. " It was his judgment that decided almost all matters; it was his coolness and placidity of temper that controlled those around him and smoothed over the little asperities and jealousies which would spring up among his subordinates—with a smooth word he brought back to his proper position any one who attempted to assume more than his rightful authority—in this way making a unit of the Department." Welles was the " judicial, financial, and political head, under whose directions everything was done; all plans were submitted to him, and no movement was made without his consent, and he weighed every matter before coming to a conclusion." According to Porter, Fox was the " able assistant," by virtue of whose aid the Secretary of the Navy accomplished his great work.[9]

The creation of the new post of Assistant Secretary of the Navy was earnestly desired by Welles. During the first months of the war his labors were so increased that the employment of an assistant was rendered imperative. Before the war the need of the Department for an official of this sort had been pointed out. In 1841 Lieutenant Matthew F. Maury had recommended the appointment of an " Under-Secretary " from the post-captains of the navy. Maury said that the Secretary "usually comes into office uninformed as to the condition of the navy, ignorant of its wants and usages, and unacquainted with the official character and standing of most of its officers. Accordingly he goes to work in the dark, and of course blunders and mismanagement ensue. It is a postulate granted by common sense, that a knowledge of details is as essential to the proper management of the navy as to the proper management of every other business, whether public or private." Maury wished, therefore, to attach to the Secretary's office a permanent official who should take charge of the detailing of officers, the shipping of seamen, and the equipment of vessels for sea. It may be said in passing that the duties Maury assigned to an Under-Secretary are at the present time performed in large part by the Bureau of Navigation and not by the Assistant Secretary of the Navy, who bears little resemblance to Maury's official.[10]

The first act authorizing the appointment of an Assistant Secretary of the Navy was passed on July 31, 1861. It did not enter into details. In the absence of the head of the Department, the new official was to act as Secretary of the Navy, and he was to

[9] Porter, Naval History of the Civil War, 360.
[10] Congressional Globe, 1861, p. 177; Southern Literary Messenger, VII, 24.

perform all such duties, in the office of the Secretary, " as shall be prescribed by the Secretary of the Navy, or as may be required by law." The salary attached to the new post was $4000 a year."

During the first months of the war, the defects of the administrative system of the Navy Department were apparent. It was slow in adapting itself to the new conditions and in responding to the " executive touch." Indeed, early in the war the executive touch was not exercised with much confidence and precision. The weakness of the Secretary's office as a directing and unifying force was manifest. It was strengthened, as we have seen, by attaching to it an Assistant Secretary of the Navy. This may be regarded as a step towards unifying and correlating the work of the Department. The differentiating of the Department's functions, however, proceeded rapidly, and several new offices, bureaus and boards were created."

One of the most important of the new departmental organizations was the " office of detail " which the Secretary of the Navy, on his own initiative, established as a part of the Secretary's office. Unfamiliar with the respective abilities and merits of the several naval officers, Welles, in March, 1861, ordered Commodore Silas H. Stringham to report to the Secretary's office for the purpose of assisting in the detailing of officers. On the breaking out of the war Stringham was detached, and his duties were vested in a navy board, or " office of detail." Commodore Hiram Paulding was placed at its head, and Commanders Charles H. Davis and Maxwell Woodhull were selected as its other members. Owing to Paulding's advanced age, the duties of chief of the office fell largely to Davis, who performed them until he was detached in the fall of 1861. In addition to the assignment of officers to duty, the office of detail had charge of the appointment and instruction of the volunteer officers. During the war it formed a part of the Secretary's office; but on April 28, 1865, it was placed in charge of the chief of the Bureau of Navigation."

In his important reports of July 4 and December 2, 1861, Secretary Welles recommended, in general terms, a modification and

" U. S. Statutes at Large, XII, 282-283.
" Porter, Naval History of the Civil War, 20, 21; Church, Ericsson, II, 36; Davis, Davis, 146; Soley, Admiral Porter, 133.
" The Galaxy, X (1870), 624-626; Davis, Davis, 115-116, 121, 128, 133-134; Hamersly, List of Officers of the Navy, 1901, p. 4.

improvement of the organization of the Navy Department. He believed that the duties of the Department could be better distributed and classified. On January 24, 1862, Senator John Sherman, of Ohio, introduced in the Senate a bill providing for two new naval bureaus. In February there was substituted for Sherman's measure a " bill to reorganize the Navy Department of the United States," which provided for eight naval bureaus. One of these, among other duties, was to have the management of the Light House Service, but the friends of the Treasury Department prevented this innovation. The bill to reorganize the Navy Department became a law on July 5, 1862.[14] It established the following eight bureaus:

1. Bureau of Yards and Docks.
2. Bureau of Equipment and Recruiting.
3. Bureau of Navigation.
4. Bureau of Ordnance.
5. Bureau of Construction and Repair.
6. Bureau of Steam Engineering.
7. Bureau of Provisions and Clothing.
8. Bureau of Medicine and Surgery.

The act of July 5, 1862, which is still the basis of the organization of the Navy Department, increased the number of bureaus by three. The duties of the former Bureau of Equipment and Repairs were distributed among three new bureaus, Equipment and Recruiting, Construction and Repair, and Steam Engineering, and the duties of the former Bureau of Ordnance and Hydrography were divided between two new bureaus, Ordnance, and Navigation. Formerly, the chiefs of the several bureaus served during the pleasure of the President, but hereafter they were to be appointed for a term of four years. They were to receive $3500 a year, in lieu of all compensation as officers of the navy. The chiefs of the Bureaus of Yards and Docks, Equipment and Recruiting, Ordnance, and Navigation, were to be line officers, not below the grade of commander. The chiefs of the Bureaus of Construction and Repair, Steam Engineering, Medicine and Surgery, and Provisions and Clothing were to be, respectively, a

[14] Sen. Ex. Doc., 37 Cong., I sess., No. 1, 96; Ann. Rept. of Sec. of N., 1861, p. 22; Congressional Globe, 1861-1862, pp. 467, 761, 875-876, 1323, 1504, 2744-2745; U. S. Statutes at Large, XII, 510-512.

naval constructor, a chief engineer, a surgeon of the navy, and a naval paymaster, of not less than ten years' standing. The bureaus were to perform their duties " under the authority of the Secretary of the Navy, and their orders shall be considered as emanating from him, and shall have full force and effect as such "—a repetition of a provision of the act of August 31, 1842, instituting the bureau system. The new law provided for fifty clerks and draftsmen, which was a small increase in the clerical force of the Department. It further provided for an assistant chief in the Bureau of Ordnance, and a civil engineer in the Bureau of Yards and Docks.

The act of July 5, 1862, authorized the Secretary of the Navy to distribute the duties of the Department among the several bureaus as he should judge expedient and proper. The only important changes made in the distribution of duties were those necessitated by the establishment of the three additional bureaus. The duties of the Bureau of Equipment and Recruiting are sufficiently indicated by its name. The work of the Bureau of Steam Engineering related chiefly to the designing, construction and repairing of the steam machinery of ships. The Bureau of Navigation was made the scientific bureau of the Department. It owed its origin largely to Rear-Admiral Charles H. Davis, a progressive officer, who was much interested in promoting science within the navy. He was appropriately made its first permanent chief, entering upon his work in November, 1862, after the bureau had been organized by Captain James M. Gilliss. The Bureau of Navigation was given the supervision of the Naval Observatory and the Hydrographical Office, the Nautical Almanac Office, and the Naval Academy.

The chiefs of the naval bureaus during the Civil War were efficient and painstaking administrators, who were safe and conservative, rather than brilliant and aggressive. Several of them had been long in the service of the Department. Rear-Admiral Joseph Smith, the chief of the Bureau of Yards and Docks, entered the navy in 1809, and served with distinction in the War of 1812. He was chief of this bureau from 1846 to 1869. Paymaster Horatio Bridge, the life-long friend of Nathaniel Hawthorne, held the chiefship of the Bureau of Provisions and Clothing from 1854 to 1869. John Lenthall, of the Bureau of Construction and Repair, and William Whelan, of the Bureau of

Medicine and Surgery, each became head of his bureau in 1853, and served throughout the war. Lenthall did not retire from the chiefship until 1871. In 1865 Whelan was succeeded by his able assistant during the war, Surgeon P. J. Horwitz. Only a single bureau chief resigned to enter the Confederacy, Captain G. A. Magruder, of the Bureau of Ordnance. His successors were Captain A. A. Harwood, 1861-1862; Rear-Admiral John A. Dahlgren, 1862-1863; and Commander Henry A. Wise, 1863-1865. The work of these three chiefs was frequently commended for its promptness and efficiency. Dahlgren was the principal ordnance expert of the old navy, and during the war a close friend of President Lincoln. Davis, the first chief of the Bureau of Navigation, was succeeded in 1865 by Captain Thornton A. Jenkins. The first chief of the new Bureau of Equipment and Recruiting was an officer of the highest professional standing, Rear-Admiral Andrew H. Foote. During the war Davis and Foote rendered distinguished service on the Mississippi. The colonels-commandant of the marine corps were John Harris, 1861-1864, and Jacob Zeilin, 1864-1876.

The new Bureau of Steam Engineering was presided over from its organization in 1862 to 1869 by Engineer-in-Chief Benjamin F. Isherwood, a man of much originality, great independence of character and indefatigable industry. Unlike many of his colleagues, he was a comparatively young man. He was still living in 1912, the last survivor of the principal naval administrators of the Civil War. Before his appointment as chief of the new bureau, Isherwood was serving as engineer-in-chief of the Bureau of Construction, Equipment and Repairs. His work during the war, when a steam fleet was supplanting the old wooden one, was most exacting and important. It was sharply criticised, probably more so than that of any other chief of bureau. A recent writer seems to have completely vindicated Isherwood, who, he says, was the foremost man of the engineering corps in professional ability and zeal. Every demand made upon his bureau was promptly and efficiently met, and the standard of naval engineering during Isherwood's term of office was raised to an enviable height.[15]

At the very close of the war Congress created the office of naval judge-advocate general. Probably the first man to recommend the appointment of a permanent law officer, or officers, for the

---

[15] Bennett, Steam Navy, 202, 608-609.

navy was Secretary Crowninshield, in 1816. Many later secretaries made similar recommendations. On February 10, 1865, Secretary Welles wrote to the chairman of the House Naval Committee setting forth the need of the Department for a judge-advocate. He said that many " legal questions and suits growing out of the transactions of this Department are constantly arising. Some of them involve large pecuniary amounts, and frequently embrace great variety of detail. The cases of courts martial are numerous, and require scrutiny and careful preparation and revision. The forms and execution of contracts under the provisions of law demand deliberate and attentive care and consideration. Frauds and abuses on the part of contractors and employees call for investigation and prosecution, and the miscellaneous legal questions which arise are innumerable, involving often a vast extent and variety of detail." To take charge of these matters, and to advise the Department on them, a law officer was necessary. Welles enclosed the draft of a bill.[16]

Acting on the advice of the Secretary of the Navy, Congress, on March 2, 1865, authorized the appointment of a solicitor and naval judge-advocate general. He was to receive a yearly salary of $3500, and was to serve during the war and one year thereafter.[17] On March 6 President Lincoln appointed to the new post William E. Chandler, of New Hampshire, who many years later became Secretary of the Navy. On July 10, 1865, Chandler was succeeded by John A. Bolles, of Massachusetts, who served until 1870, when the office was discontinued and its duties transferred to the Department of Justice.

To assist him in his work, Welles created several temporary boards and agencies. The appointment of experts to advise and direct the Department or to perform some of its duties is a familiar device. By all odds the most important board instituted by Welles was the " Commission of Conference," the purpose of which was to determine the military and naval operations on the Atlantic and Gulf coasts, collect hydrographic, geographic, and topographic information, and to devise methods for rendering the blockade effective. It was especially to obtain such information as would be of value in capturing a naval base on the Atlantic coast of the Southern States. The notion of establishing this

---

[16] Congress Letters, II, 427; XIV, 236.
[17] U. S. Statutes at Large, XIII, 468.

commission origihated with Professor Alexander Dallas Bache, the eminent superintendent of the United States Coast Survey. Its members were Professor Bache, Captain Samuel F. Dupont, and Commander Charles H. Davis, of the navy, and Major J. G. Barnard, of the engineer corps of the army. Dupont was its senior member, and Davis its secretary.

The Commission of Conference was organized in the latter part of June, 1861, and held its sessions at various times in July, August and September. It embodied the results of its labors in six reports, three relating to the Atlantic and three to the Gulf coast. Its views were developed by discussion, and were later written out by its secretary. The hydrographic and geographic information contained in its reports, which exceeded in amount that of a purely naval or military character, was chiefly derived from the records of the Coast Survey. The reports of the commission, which were discussed by the cabinet and by General Winfield Scott, of the army, proved to be valuable in formulating and executing the plans of naval operations. The commission was a confidential one, and its reports were not intentionally made public. Early in July, 1861, however, accounts of its deliberations began to be printed in the newspapers. It was impossible at this time to keep secret the work of the government, so successful were the friends and agents of the Confederates in obtaining information.[18]

In the spring of 1861 Welles instituted another confidential board. It was composed of the chiefs of the several bureaus of the Navy Department, and was charged with the duty of " considering and acting upon such subjects connected with the naval service as may be submitted to [them] by the Department for their opinion at this important juncture of our national affairs." It was further charged to make " such suggestions regarding the naval service generally as may occur to the board." [19]   Commander C. H. Davis was its secretary.

In February, 1863, the Secretary of the Navy established the " Permanent Commission." Its original members were Davis, Bache and Joseph Henry, the secretary of the Smithsonian Institution. Its purpose was to report on all questions relating to

[18] Official Records, ser. I, vol. 12, 195-207; vol. 16, 618, 651, 680; Davis, Davis, 117-134; The Galaxy, XII (1871), 672.

[19] Davis, Davis, 117.

science and art upon which the Department wished advice, and it was authorized to call to its aid technical assistants. Many inventions, plans and devices, with which the government was flooded during the war, were referred to it for its opinion of their value. Until the end of the war it held frequent sessions, and transacted much business. The organization of this commission is of an additional interest, since it led to the founding of the National Academy of Sciences.[20]

Various other temporary boards, besides those above mentioned, were appointed by the Department during the war. There were, for instance, an "iron-clad board," a "harbor commission," a "board on steam expansion," a "board on plans and designs for new vessels," and a "board on parole of prisoners." The work and organization of the iron-clad board will be considered in another connection.

Since the construction and engineering bureaus in Washington were unfavorable to the building of vessels of the "monitor," or double-turretted iron-clad type, a sort of monitor bureau was created at New York. Rear-Admiral F. H. Gregory was placed at its head, and directly under him was Chief Engineer A. C. Stimers. This office had charge of the construction of all ships and engines of the navy, and especially of monitors and iron-clads built by private contract. Its staff of assistants, draftsmen and clerks was almost as large as the similar force of the Navy Department in Washington. It was sometimes called the "draftsmen's paradise," on account of the large number of employees of this class, and the large wages paid them, twenty dollars a day. Under Gregory were some forty-five or fifty naval officers, who were stationed at the various ports where the navy had work which was being performed under contract. "The New York section of the Navy Department" ran its affairs with a rather high hand. It was especially partial to the construction of monitors.[21]

Several agencies were established for the transaction of special duties. One of great importance was that of Mr. George D. Morgan for the purchase of vessels. The superintendence of the construction of certain light-draft monitors was intrusted to Chief Engineer A. C. Stimers. In March, 1863, Messrs. John M. Forbes

[20] Davis, Davis, 285-286, 289-290; Bureau Letters, IV, 153.
[21] Bennett, Steam Navy, 485; Buell, Charles H. Cramp, 79.

and Wm. H. Aspinwall were sent to England to prevent the sailing
of the iron-clads that were being built there for the Confederates,
but their mission was unsuccessful. At the outbreak of the war,
most of the navy agents of the Department in foreign countries
were discontinued, as there was little need of them, since from
1861 to 1865 but few vessels were maintained abroad. At London,
however, the Baring Brothers continued to act as the financial
agents of the Department. Navy storekeepers were employed at
Spezzia and Panama.

The chief clerk of the Navy Department was an important
official during the war. He had charge of the records, correspondence and personnel of the Secretary's office, and the finances
of the Department. Charles W. Welsh, Toucey's chief clerk, was
succeeded by Hobart Berrian on March 14, 1861; Berrian, by
Gustavus V. Fox, on May 9; and Fox, by William Faxon, on
July 31, who held the position until June 1, 1866. Faxon, like
Welles, was a resident of Hartford, Connecticut. For many
years he had been a friend of Welles, and had been associated with
him in the work of the *Hartford Evening Press*. Faxon entered
the Department on March 19, as a clerk of the second class in the
Secretary's office. His fitness for this position was determined by
a board of examiners appointed by the Secretary of the Navy—
an early application of the principles of civil service to the Navy
Department. Welles, Fox and Faxon were the New England
trio that presided over the Department during the darkest period
of its existence.

During the war the clerical work of the Department was considerably increased, though by no means to the extent one might
suppose. The number of regular clerks and draftsmen employed
in the Department at Washington in 1860 was 39, and in 1865,
66. The office hours, which were regularly from 9 a. m. to 3 p. m.,
were, for many clerks, greatly lengthened, and often extended into
the night. On certain afternoons, however, some of the employees
were dismissed at 2 o'clock, to engage in military drills and exercises. But few of them welcomed this relief from their desks,
since they generally preferred their writing and accounting to the
hauling about of brass howitzers in the hot sunshine. At the
beginning of the war all the clerks were required to take an oath
to support the constitution. In March and April, 1861, most of
the clerks who sympathized with the Confederacy, about one-

fourth of the clerical force, resigned; and some of them found positions in the Confederate Navy Department. There remained in the Department throughout the war several employees who were unfriendly to the North, and who, in the opinion of the Unionist clerks, were at heart disloyal. In July, 1861, President Lincoln removed the Democratic navy agents in the several Northern ports, and appointed Republicans in their places. Welles was disinclined to remove any employees for political reasons or " offensive partisanship," and much clamor was raised against him for his forbearance. His stand was in striking contrast to that of some of his colleagues in the cabinet, who discharged the Democrats from their department by the wholesale. In order that the policy and action of the government should be uniform, Lincoln requested the Secretary of the Navy to remove a few Democrats from the Navy Department.

To meet the demands of the bureaus for additional quarters, a new wing and a third story were added to the old Navy Department building. It was situated a stone's throw to the westward of the White House. The rooms of Welles, Fox and Faxon were on the second floor, in easy reach of each other. Here throughout the war President Lincoln often called and chatted in the most informal manner, and his gaunt form became a familiar figure to the employees of the Department. A clerk, who is still living, remembers seeing him appear in one of the bureaus wearing " carpet slippers." Occasionally he wore a shawl over his shoulders—a common article of dress for men at this time. It was in the Bureau of Ordnance, while watching a German regiment pass the window, that Lincoln propounded the conundrum, " Why is an Amsterdam Dutchman like any other damn Dutchman? " The diary of Rear-Admiral John A. Dahlgren abounds with references to Lincoln's visits to the Department, and to the Washington navy yard. The following characteristic entry for March 29, 1863, may be quoted: " I went to the Department. Found the President in the Chief Clerk's room with the Secretary and Fox. He looks thin and badly, and is very nervous. Complained of everything. They were doing nothing at Vicksburg and Charleston. Dupont was asking for one iron-clad after another, as fast as they were built. He said that the canal at Vicksburg was of no account, and wondered that a sensible man would do it. I tried my hand at consolation, without much avail.

He thought the favorable state of public expectation would pass away before anything was done. Then levelled a couple of jokes at the doings at Vicksburg and Charleston. Poor gentleman! " [22]

The details of the naval business were of course generally managed by the Navy Department. The President, however, kept in close touch with the navy. As a rule, the orders of the officers were issued by the Secretary of the Navy. But infrequently, when the need of action was very great, they were written by the President himself. Whenever the chief commanders were in Washington they always called upon Lincoln, and found him an eager listener to all they had to tell about their plans and operations. Farragut, Porter, Dahlgren, Dupont, Davis, Foote, and other leading naval men were often in conference at the White House. In the selection of officers for important commands, Lincoln generally followed the advice of the Department. Porter said that Lincoln seemed to be familiar with the name, character, and reputation of every officer of rank in the army and navy, and " appeared to understand them better than some whose business it was to do so." [23]

When Welles entered upon his duties on March 7, 1861, he found the Department and the navy in a deplorable condition. Many of the clerks were hostile to him. The disaffected officers of the Department maintained a rallying-point in the Bureau of Ordnance, whose chief, Captain George A. Magruder, and whose clerks, almost to a man, later allied themselves with the Confederacy. The Naval Observatory, under the command of Commander Matthew F. Maury, a warm friend of the South, was another center for the propagation of secessionist doctrines. The officers of the navy were more or less demoralized. Already several of them had resigned, and many others were suspected of disaffection to the Union. Captain Samuel Barron, one of the leaders of the clique of Southern officers favorable to the interests of the Confederacy, was exercising a considerable influence on naval affairs. It was impossible for the Secretary of the Navy to tell his friends from his foes. The Pensacola navy yard was in the hands of the Confederates. The situation at the Norfolk yard was by no means assuring. Among the officers of the Washington yard sentiments of disloyalty were common. All of the navy

[22] Dahlgren, Dahlgren, 390.
[23] Porter, Incidents and Anecdotes of the Civil War, 283.

yards were in bad repair, since no appropriations for their improvement had been made for several years. The national treasury was bankrupt. In pursuance of President Buchanan's policy, Secretary Toucey had failed to place the navy in a posture of defense. As was customary in peace, most of the vessels were on foreign stations. The home squadron in commission consisted of 12 vessels, carrying 187 guns and about 2000 men.

It was under these circumstances that Welles took charge of the Navy Department. A sharp turn in its policy might have been expected to signalize the advent of a Republican administration and Secretary of the Navy, but no sudden change of any sort took place. For the first three weeks Welles did almost nothing to increase or improve the naval defense of the country, and for the second three weeks he did but little. In the first days of April he prepared an expedition for the relief of Fort Sumter, and opened rendezvous for the enlistment of seamen at several Northern ports. Until the firing on Fort Sumter, the policy of Lincoln differed only slightly from that of Buchanan. It was one of conciliation and temporization; it was passive, hesitant, expectant, uncertain, cautious, and tentative. Lincoln and the members of his cabinet were not familiar with Federal administration, nor with each other, and at first they did not pull well together. They were strangely awkward at their new work, how awkward it is painful to tell. The attempts of the Secretary of State to manage the government and the President are well known.

Seward's interference with the affairs of the' Navy Department greatly added to the confusion of the first weeks of the new administration. On April 1, without consulting the Secretary of the Navy, he obtained the signature of President Lincoln to a most remarkable naval document. It was addressed to Welles, and was in the handwriting of Captain Montgomery C. Meigs, of the army—with the exception of the postscript, which was written by Lieutenant David D. Porter, of the navy. The document was an order of Lincoln to Welles to make certain details of naval officers and certain changes in the organization of the Navy Department. Of special significance was the direction to Welles to detach Commodore Silas H. Stringham from the Secretary's office, to order him to Pensacola, and to supersede him as detailing officer with Captain Samuel Barron. The postscript,

which related to the organization of the Department, read as
follows:

As it is very necessary at this time to have a perfect knowledge of
the personal of the navy, and to be able to detail such officers for special
purposes as the exigencies of the service may require, I request that you
will instruct Captain Barron to proceed and organize the Bureau of Detail
in the manner best adapted to meet the wants of the navy, taking cognizance of the discipline of the navy generally, detailing all officers for
duty, taking charge of the recruiting of seamen, supervising charges made
against officers, and all matters relating to duties which must be understood by a sea officer. You will please afford Captain Barron any facility
for accomplishing this duty, transferring to his department the clerical
force heretofore used for the purposes specified. It is to be understood
that this officer will act by authority of the Secretary of the Navy, who will
exercise such supervision as he may deem necessary.[24]

These orders went far towards superseding Welles as Secretary of the Navy by Barron. In the management of the Department, they made the naval officer the more important official.
Upon receiving them, Welles was greatly astonished, and he
immediately, on the night of April 1, carried them to the White
House for an explanation. Lincoln was much surprised to find
that he had signed a document of such import. He said that
Seward, with two or three young men, had been at the White
House during the day on a matter which the Secretary of State
had much at heart; and that he had signed the document without
reading it, or knowing what it was, supposing that it related to an
enterprise of Seward. Welles told Lincoln that he had no confidence in the fidelity of Barron, who was by the order forced into
an official and personal intimacy with him, and was virtually given
charge of the Department, that the establishment of a bureau by
an executive order was unlawful, and that the proposition to make
a naval officer Secretary *de facto* was illegal, and in his view
" monstrous." The President replied that he knew nothing of
Barron, that the document was not his, although he had signed it,
and that Welles should treat it as cancelled. He expressed regret
that he had blundered, and was wont afterwards to say that during the first weeks of his administration he and the members of his
cabinet were all new to their work, and naturally made mistakes.
Welles believed that the attempt of Seward and Porter to place
the principal business of the Department in the hands of Barron

[24] The Galaxy, X (1870), 624.

was a movement in behalf of the Confederacy and the Southern naval officers. Barron was shortly dismissed from the naval service. He entered the Confederate navy, taking rank as captain, from March 26, 1861, five days before the date of the executive order giving him charge of the Federal Navy Department.[25]

Seward's interference with the Department was not confined to measures for its reorganization and to the detailing of naval officers. He planned a naval expedition for the relief of Fort Pickens, Florida, which was officered and fitted out, and had sailed before the Secretary of the Navy got wind of it. This was the enterprise to which Lincoln supposed the above-mentioned document related when he signed it. On April 1 Seward had obtained Lincoln's signature to a second document. This ordered Lieutenant David D. Porter to proceed to the New York navy yard and prepare an expedition for the relief of Fort Pickens. At this very time Welles was fitting out at the New York yard an expedition for the relief of Fort Sumter, which was to be under the command of Gustavus V. Fox. Both Welles and Seward intended that the *Powhatan* should sail as one of the ships of their respective fleets. It therefore happened that the orders which Seward had obtained from the President and those of Welles respecting this vessel conflicted. The commandant of the New York yard was naturally confused. Since the President's orders were superior to those of the Secretary of the Navy, he gave Porter possession of the vessel. Welles was completely in the dark as to Porter's movements, until about the time that Porter's fleet sailed from New York for Fort Pickens on April 6. On receiving intelligence of them he, in company with Seward, went to the White House and asked an explanation of the diverting of the *Powhatan* from the Fort Sumter expedition, which, he said, would fail for lack of this ship. Lincoln yielded to Welles, and decided that Porter should turn the vessel over to Fox. An order to this effect signed by Seward was sent to Porter, but he had already sailed. A tug was procured, and the orders reached him before he got to sea. He declined to detach the *Powhatan* from his fleet, on the ground that he was acting under orders signed by the President, while the countermanding orders were signed by the President's subordinate, the Secretary of State. The *Powhatan,* therefore, proceeded to Fort Pickens.

[25] The Galaxy, X (1870), 624-626.

Welles and Fox always maintained that the sending of Porter's expedition was one of the main causes of the failure of Fox's.[26]

Porter cannot be freed from all blame for the part that he played in these strange proceedings. He was a man of mature years and long naval experience. The postscript of one of the aforementioned documents was in his handwriting. Knowing well the routine of the Department, he must have been aware of the irregularity of Seward's acts. He must have foreseen that they would likely cause confusion. One might suppose that he had some knowledge of the character of Barron, and of that officer's unfitness for the management of the navy during the crisis of the spring of 1861. On the other hand, it may be said in behalf of Porter, that he was acting in accordance with the orders of his superiors, the President and the Secretary of State; and that, under the extraordinary circumstances that then existed, irregularities were to be expected.[27] When he accepted the command of the Fort Pickens expedition, he was under orders to proceed to the West Coast and report for duty on the Coast Survey, a detail which he had sought. Welles did not forget the part that Porter played in Seward's machinations. That he did not permit it to prevent the advancement of that gallant and meritorious officer, is a tribute to his fairness.

Looking in retrospect, one can now see that during the first weeks of Welles's administration no matter deserved more consideration than the holding and defending of the Norfolk navy yard. It was one of the three principal navy yards in the United States, and contained numerous dwellings, sheds, storehouses and machine shops, large quantities of tools, machines, naval stores and provisions, and some two thousand pieces of artillery. Connected with the yard was a commodious dry dock of granite, and near it were twelve ships. One of these, the *Merrimac*, when equipped for sea, was worth $1,200,000. The total value of all this property was estimated by the Department at $9,760,000. The Norfolk yard was strategically situated for the use of either the Unionists or Confederates. To the latter, at the beginning of the war, its ordnance stores were worth far more than their value in money. These facts did not receive the consideration by the

[26] The Galaxy, X (1870), 627-637; XI (1871), 105-107; Official Records, ser. I, vol. 4, 228-241; Diary of Gideon Welles, I, 16-26.
[27] Soley, Admiral Porter, 101-102.

Secretary of the Navy and the President that they deserved. It is not here urged that they should have provided for the defense of this yard independent of the general policy of the administration. But certainly they should not have formulated their general policy independent of its effect upon the holding of the yard.

During the first weeks of his administration Lincoln's policy was to do nothing that might offend those Southern States that still remained in the Union. He was especially considerate of the feelings of the Virginians. While some slight measures for the defense of the Norfolk yard were taken late in March and early in April, 1861, not until about the time that the Old Dominion seceded from the Union were any vigor and decision respecting this establishment shown by the administration. On April 16, Welles ordered Commodore Hiram Paulding to proceed from Washington to Norfolk, and to consult with the commandant of the yard, Captain C. S. McCauley, about its defense and the protection of its ships. Paulding carried an order to McCauley that rang with true mettle, the first issued by the Department for several months, of which this may be said: " The vessels and stores under your charge," the order read, " you will defend at any hazard, repelling by force, if necessary, any and all attempts to seize them, whether by mob violence, authorized effort, or any assumed authority." During the next four days the Department showed considerable activity. Unfortunately its efforts were too late. McCauley and Paulding, who were in positions of authority, did not rise to the occasion. They were too old, too long schooled in routine, to accomplish great things in a sudden emergency. McCauley lacked energy and initiative, and he was largely under the influence of his disaffected officers, who were Southerners, and who did their utmost to deceive him as to the real situation of the yard. On April 20, fearing an attack on the ships, he ordered them to be scuttled. They were sinking when Paulding arrived from Washington with new orders. The two officers now decided not to attempt a defense, but to destroy all the public property, and to abandon the navy yard. Their work of destruction was hasty and ill executed, and much property fell into the hands of the Confederates.

Possession of the Norfolk navy yard with its valuable supplies was of great service to the South. Its cannon were used in fortifying the forts and batteries of the Confederacy on the Atlantic and Gulf coasts, and the Potomac, York, James, Rappahannock, and Mississippi rivers. The *Merrimac* was raised and converted into a terrible engine of war. Its dramatic contest with the *Monitor* made its name famous. The granite dry dock was little injured. Many of the workshops, with their valuable machinery, escaped harm. Admiral Porter said that, " but for the misfortune of losing, or we may say throwing away, the Norfolk navy yard, all the unarmed ports of the South would have easily fallen into our hands." The evacuation of Norfolk and the Norfolk navy yard was one of the greatest blunders of the war.[28]

The naval war with the Confederacy properly began on April 19, 1861, with the issuing by President Lincoln of a proclamation of the blockade of the coast of the Southern States from South Carolina to Texas. From this time the Department prosecuted its work with much industry and with considerable vigor. On July 4, when the members of the Thirty-seventh Congress met in special session, Welles was able to make a very creditable showing of his activities and achievements. Shortly after April 19, the commandants of the Boston, New York, and Philadelphia navy yards were authorized to equip all the public armed vessels that they could purchase or charter, and a flotilla, with its rendezvous at the Washington navy yard, was fitted out for the defense of the nation's capital and the Potomac River. On April 30 the commandants of the navy yards and the naval rendezvous were authorized to enlist seamen to serve for one year. In the latter part of April seven vessels were chartered. By July 4, 82 vessels, carrying upwards of 1100 guns, and manned by about 13,000 men, exclusive of marines and officers, were in commission. The East Indian, Mediterranean, Brazil, and African squadrons, with the exception of one ship in each of the two latter squadrons, had been recalled. The Department had contracted for 23 gunboats, of about 500 tons burden each, and had made preliminary arrangements for the construction of several larger and fleeter ships. It was also expediting the construction of eight sloops of war at the Northern navy yards.

On April 27 the President issued a proclamation extending the

[28] The Galaxy, X (1870), 112-119; Sen. Rept. 37 Cong. 2 sess., No. 37, 1-123; Official Records, ser. I, vol. 4, pp. 272-313; Sands, From Reefer to Rear-Admiral, 225-229; Porter, Naval History of the Civil War, 62; Parker, Recollections of a Naval Officer, 206-207; Diary of Gideon Welles, I, 41-53.

blockade so as to include the ports of North Carolina and Virginia. On April 30 foreigners were notified of the effective blockade of Hampton Roads, Virginia. The blockading vessels along the extensive seaboard of the Southern States were placed under two commands. Flag-Officer Silas H. Stringham was given the command of the squadron on the Atlantic coast; and Flag-Officer William Mervine, that on the Gulf coast. Stringham arrived at Hampton Roads with his flagship *Minnesota,* on May 13, and Mervine reached the Gulf on June 8. Previous to the arrival of the latter, the mouth of the Mississippi River and several Gulf ports had been blockaded. By July 4, Stringham's squadron consisted of 22 vessels, 296 guns, and 3300 men; and Mervine's of 21 vessels, 282 guns, and 3500 men. Colliers had been purchased, and were transporting coal to the two squadrons.[29]

The first notable service of the navy in the war was performed by the Potomac flotilla in April and May, 1861, in defending Washington, and in keeping open the Potomac for the passage of transports and supply ships. The Confederates tried to get possession of this river, fortify its banks and cut off communication between Washington and the Chesapeake. The first naval officer that was killed in the war, Commander J. H. Ward, lost his life while in command of this flotilla. The history of the Potomac flotilla and that of the Washington navy yard are inseparable. Before the military forts and batteries were erected on the heights surrounding Washington, the navy yard, situated within the city on the Eastern branch of the Potomac, was the principal defense of the capital. On or about April 22 almost every officer in this yard, including its commandant, Captain Franklin Buchanan, resigned their commissions in the navy. On this day Commander John A. Dahlgren, who was in charge of the department of ordnance of the yard, was ordered to succeed Buchanan, and during the next few months he performed with great industry and efficiency the arduous work that devolved upon him.

During the latter part of April, and the whole month of May, 1861, when it seemed that Washington would certainly fall into the hands of the Confederates before an effective force of troops from the North could reach the city, the President often visited the Washington navy yard and consulted with Dahlgren, for whom he had a high regard. The excitement, gloom, anxiety and

[29] Sen. Ex. Doc., 37 Cong. 1 sess., No. 1, 85-98.

alarm of those memorable days were never forgotten by the residents of the capital. For some time after the arrival of the first troops, the situation was little improved in the minds of the terror-stricken inhabitants, as may be seen from the words of Commander C. H. Davis, written on May 25, at his desk in the Navy Department to his wife: " We have had an exciting time this morning. Poor Ellsworth's funeral; an attack on the New Jersey regiment at the Chain Bridge by the Virginians; and the report of a fight at Sewall's Point. The alarm guns were fired for the first time, and war has actually begun. The Navy Department is well prepared with rifles and revolvers. The bells are now ringing, and it would seem that the alarm continued. The Commodore, Woodhull, and the clerk are loading the muskets (rifles) in the room where I am now writing." [80]

Directly after the battle of Bull Run, the fear, excitement and consternation in Washington was more intense than they had been during the first days of the war. A letter of Davis, written on July 23, shows the effect of the defeat upon the personnel of the Department: " Yesterday was a day of the deepest gloom. It was a day that recalled the scenes of history and historical painting, in novels and in the drama. Great excitement prevailed. Notwithstanding the rain, people stood about in groups and talked mysteriously, or listened to some straggler from the other side. Many countenances wore expression of alarm, all of anxiety. It was a long time before the clerks could get to work; they sat in listless apathy. Woodhull, who was among the most excited, burst out, while I was sitting at the desk writing, into expression of astonishment at what he called my coolness; though, as there was no danger immediately threatening us, there was no occasion for the exhibition of coolness. He was running around in the pouring rain as if set in motion by springs, and unable to keep still. Such was the alarm that the storm which hung the heavens in black was hailed with delight as an impediment to the march of the rebels, who, it was feared, would follow up their retreating foes and invade the capital. I shared of course in the alarm and depression; but after I had made up my mind to put on my uniform and go into the intrenchments in the event of an attack, I felt better, wrote all the morning and two hours in the evening." [81]

[80] Davis, Davis, 143-146.
[81] Davis, Davis, 151-152.

Part II

NAVAL OPERATIONS

President Lincoln has briefly described the work of the navy during the Civil War in most characteristic words, written on August 26, 1863, in response to an invitation to attend a mass-meeting of " unconditional Union men " to be held at Springfield, Illinois, the President's home town. Having referred to the achievements of the army at Antietam, Murfreesboro and Gettysburg, he paid his respects to its sister-service: " Nor must Uncle Sam's web-feet be forgotten. At all the watery margins they have been present. Not only on the deep sea, the broad bay, and the rapid river, but also up the narrow, muddy bayou, and wherever the ground was a little damp, they have been and made their tracks. Thanks to all." [32]

The principal work of the navy during the war was the blockading of the coast of the Southern states and the patrolling of their sounds, bayous and larger rivers. The length of the coast blockaded, measured from Alexandria, Virginia, to the Rio Grande, was 3549 miles. A large part of the coast presented a double shore. There were 189 harbors, openings to rivers, or indentations to be guarded. On the Mississippi River and its tributaries the gunboats traversed and patrolled 3615 miles; and on the sounds, bayous, rivers and inlets of the Atlantic and Gulf coasts, about 2000 miles. For the purposes of blockade and patrol the waters surrounding the Confederate states were divided into six divisions, and a squadron under the command of a flag-officer

[32] Nicolay and Hay, Complete Works of Lincoln, IX, 101.

or rear-admiral was assigned to each. The Potomac flotilla patrolled the waters of the Potomac and Rappahannock rivers. After 1862 it was chiefly employed in suppressing illicit commerce and unauthorized communications with the Confederates. In September, 1862, the original Atlantic and Gulf blockading squadrons were each divided. Two squadrons, the North Atlantic and South Atlantic, blockaded the Atlantic coast. The line of division between them was the boundary between North and South Carolina. The territory of the East Gulf squadron extended from Cape Canaveral to Pensacola; and that of the West Gulf squadron, from Pensacola to the Rio Grande. In 1864 the limits of the East Gulf squadron were extended so as to include the waters of Cuba and the Bahamas. The Mississippi flotilla held open for the Unionists the Mississippi River and its chief tributaries, and prevented the Confederates west of the river from trading or communicating with those east of it. In 1864 the waters traversed by the Mississippi flotilla were divided into ten naval districts, and a naval officer was placed in command of each of them. At the beginning of the war the blockading of the extensive coast of the Confederacy was deemed impossible by many, both at home and abroad. By the fall of 1861, however, it was an accomplished fact and it remained so throughout the war. Still, at no time was it wholly impossible for a Confederate privateer or a neutral adventurer to enter the Southern ports or escape therefrom.[33]

Next in importance to blockade duties, were the operations of the navy, alone or in co-operation with the army, against the batteries, forts and fortified towns on the seacoast and rivers of the Confederacy. The first important operations of this sort were the capture of Hatteras Inlet, North Carolina, by Commodore Silas H. Stringham and General B. F. Butler in August, 1861; the reduction of Forts Walker and Beauregard and the occupation of Port Royal, South Carolina, by Commodore S. F. Dupont and General Thomas W. Sherman in November, 1861; and the taking of Forts Henry and Donelson, in Kentucky, by Commodore A. H. Foote and General U. S. Grant in February, 1862. To the same class belong Farragut's memorable achievements at New Orleans, Vicksburg and Mobile; Porter's at Fort Fisher, Dupont and Dahlgren's at Charleston, and the perilous

[33] Ann. Rept. of Sec. of N., 1863, iii-iv; 1864, ix, xv.

and daring campaigns of Flusser and other gallant officers on the sounds and rivers of North Carolina. In reducing the fortified places on the Mississippi River and its tributaries, the services of the Mississippi flotilla were exceedingly valuable. Porter said that no vessels of the navy engaged in so many successful battles or made such a record for their commanding officers as did those on the Mississippi. During the first months of the war, the Potomac flotilla found employment in silencing the Confederate batteries which were planted on the banks of the Potomac River.

Many ships were sent in pursuit of the Confederate commerce-destroyers. On one occasion about thirty vessels were searching for a single ship of the Confederates, the *Tacony,* which is said to have been the only " rover " that attacked our navy at the entrance of our harbors. In the summer of 1862 a flying squadron, under the command of Acting Rear-Admiral Charles Wilkes, was established in the West Indies to capture the enemy's rovers and blockade-runners. The Confederate rovers or commerce-destroyers inflicted an enormous damage on American commerce and nearly drove it from the seas. The most destructive ships were the English-built vessels *Alabama, Florida, Georgia* and *Shenandoah.* The permitting of these vessels to sail by the British government was regarded by the United States as a breach of the laws of neutrality. The *Alabama,* Captain Raphael Semmes, destroyed some 60 vessels and $10,000,000 worth of property. She was finally sunk by the U. S. S. *Kearsarge,* Captain John A. Winslow, off Cherbourg, in June, 1864. The *Florida,* after having captured 21 vessels, was seized in the harbor of Bahia, in October, 1864.

During the war the expenditures of the navy were vastly increased, and were at the time wholly unprecedented. The net expenditures rose from $12,000,000 for the fiscal year 1861 to $123,000,000 for 1865. The largest annual appropriations for the navy were for the fiscal year 1863, and amounted to $144,000,000. The total expenditures for the navy during the war were $314,-000,000; the average annual expenditures were $73,000,000. The expenditures for the navy, however, were only 9.3 per cent of the total expenditures of the federal government. The total value of the vessels captured and destroyed by the navy was about $31,-500,000. Many of these belonged to neutrals and were captured while trying to run the blockade. The value of the captured vessels alone was placed at $24,500,000. The number of vessels captured and sent to the courts for adjudication was 1149; the number destroyed, 355; total, 1504. In 1868 the Navy Pension Fund, which is derived from one-half the proceeds arising from the sale of prizes, amounted to $14,000,000.[34]

The purchase and construction of vessels constituted a large source of expenditure. On March 4, 1861, the number of vessels in the navy, including receiving ships, vessels in ordinary, and ships both in and out of commission, was only 90. In December, 1864, when the navy was at or near its maximum strength, it contained 671 vessels. Their total tonnage was 510,396 tons, and they were armed with 4610 guns. From 1861 to 1866, 179 vessels were built and launched, and 497 were bought or transferred from some other executive department to the navy. These figures do not include the "stone fleet" of 78 vessels, which were purchased and sunk as obstacles to navigation. Still other ships were placed on the stocks, but they were not completed. The department purchased 313 steamers, at a cost of $18,000,000. The 179 ships that were constructed and completed during the war were all steam vessels. Fifty-five of them were built by the department at the Northern navy-yards, and 124 were constructed under contract. The cost of most of the vessels built during the war ranged from $75,000 to $650,000. The highest-priced vessel, the *Madawaska,* however, cost $1,673,000. The cost of the purchased vessels ranged, as a rule, from $10,000 to $60,000. The largest price, $595,000, was paid for the prize-ship *Tennessee.* The 671 vessels that comprised the fleet in December, 1864, were of the following classes: Screw steamers especially constructed for naval purposes, 113; paddle-wheel steamers especially constructed for naval purposes, 52; ironclad vessels, 71; steamers, chiefly purchased or captured, and fitted for naval purposes, 323; sailing vessels of all kinds, 112. Of the 671 vessels, 559 were steam vessels.[35]

The department purchased every available merchant steamer in the Northern ports that could be advantageously converted into a naval vessel and used on the blockade. Great pressure was brought to bear on the department to buy ships that were unfit for blockade duty. The purchased vessels are said to have repre-

---

[34] Sen. Ex. Doc., 45 Cong. 1 sess., No. 3, 156-157; Ann. Rept. of Sec. of N., 1865, xxx, xxxii; 1868, xxviii.

[35] Sen. Rept. 37 Cong. 2 sess., No. 37, 96-102; House Ex. Doc., 40 Cong. 2 sess., No. 280; Ann. Rept. of Sec. of N., 1864, xxii-xxiv; 1865, xii-xiii.

sented every style of marine architecture "from Captain Noah to Captain Cook." The best market for vessels was at New York, and many ships were obtained at that city. In the summer of 1861 Secretary Welles appointed a board, composed of a naval constructor, engineer and ordnance officer, to reside at New York, to visit all ships offered to the department and to determine their fitness and adaptability for naval purposes. The Secretary appointed Mr. George D. Morgan to act as the purchasing agent of the department. Morgan purchased the ships, guarded the interests of the public by investigating and certifying titles, and in general managed the mercantile and legal side of the transactions. He was a brother-in-law of Mrs. Gideon Welles, and was regarded by the Secretary as a man of great integrity, commercial experience and capacity for business.

A steam tug was placed at the disposal of Morgan and the board of inspection, and they proceeded daily for many weeks to inspect the vessels offered to the department in and near New York. By December 4, 1861, Morgan had purchased 90 vessels, at a cost of $3,500,000—a reduction of 25 per cent on the prices first asked by the owners. His commission was $2\frac{1}{2}$ per cent of the cost-price, and was paid by the seller. This was the rate and method of levying established by the New York Chamber of Commerce. His income for five months' work amounted to $70,000. Welles was severely criticised for nepotism in employing his brother-in-law; for paying him so large a commission; and for levying it on the seller, who, of course, raised his selling-price accordingly. In January, 1862, the Senate Naval Committee made a report adverse to Morgan's agency, declaring that the practice of levying commissions upon the selling-price of ships was reprehensible. It should be said, however, that the New York Chamber of Commerce had established this custom and had fixed the agent's commission at $2\frac{1}{2}$ per cent. That Morgan performed his work skilfully and honestly was not questioned. John Murray Forbes, who regarded Welles as an "honest old Democratic editor who knew but little of business," said in February, 1862, that Morgan's work was, "without being perfect, the best done of any that the government had yet done, always excepting Stanton's slaying of the Satanic." [36]

[36] Ann. Rept. of Sec. of N., 1861, 14-16; Sen. Rept., 37 Cong. 2 sess. No. 9; Sen. Doc., 37 Cong. 2 sess., No. 15; Hughes, Forbes, I, 230-231, 289-290; Congress Letters, XIII, 405; Diary of Gideon Welles, I, 487.

The method of purchasing vessels followed at some of the other Northern seaports was similar to that at New York. At Boston, during July and August, 1861, a commission composed of Commodore W. L. Hudson, the commandant of the Boston navy-yard; Mr. J. C. Delano, of New Bedford; and Mr. John Murray Forbes, of Boston, purchased merchant ships for the navy, fitted them for sea and selected some of their officers. Forbes, who was a most highly esteemed and successful merchant of Boston, showed great public spirit during the war, and rendered the Navy and War Departments invaluable aid. In April and May, 1861, he procured and fitted out the transports that carried the troops of his state to the relief of Washington, and he merited the title, which he won, of " Secretary of the Navy of Massachusetts." The members of the Boston commission, in sharp contrast to Morgan, made no charges for their services, and Forbes was inclined to believe that they even paid their traveling expenses. After the commission was dissolved, Forbes continued, when called upon, to serve the Navy Department. In January, 1862, he was directed by Secretary Welles to charter a vessel for three months or a longer period to go in pursuit of the Confederate commerce-destroyer *Sumter,* and to suggest proper men for commander and masters of the chartered vessel.[37]

The first vessels of the Mississippi flotilla were three Ohio River steamers, which were purchased at Cincinnati in May and June, 1861, by Commander John Rodgers, and were converted into gunboats. During 1861 and a part of 1862 the Mississippi flotilla was under the control of the War Department, although its vessels were commanded by naval officers. In September, 1861, Commodore A. H. Foote assumed command of the flotilla., In August Quartermaster-General Meigs of the War Department contracted with James B. Eades, the celebrated civil engineer, to build seven ironclad gunboats. Such were the energy and celerity with which Eades performed his work that two weeks after entering upon his contract he had 4000 men in his employ, and within 100 days he had completed his vessels, their aggregate tonnage being 5000 tons. On October 12, 1861, the first of these gunboats was launched, with her boilers and engines on board. She was named the *St. Louis* by Commodore Foote, and was the first completed ironclad in the United States. Before the war ended, more than

[37] Hughes, Forbes, I, 228-233, 292-293.

100 vessels were stationed on the Mississippi River and its tributaries.[38]

Many of the ships purchased for the navy were not adapted for naval purposes, and therefore wore out rapidly and soon needed extensive repairs. Some of the old ships of war could not be used in shallow waters. On the blockade, the navy needed many light-draft, heavily armed vessels; and before Congress met in July, 1861, the Navy Department had contracted for the construction of 23 gunboats, of the *Unadilla* type. Four months after the date of their contracts, several of these vessels were afloat, and were armed, manned and commissioned in time to participate in the first important naval operation of the war, the capture of Port Royal, in November, 1861. Next, the department built several larger ships, adapted to deep-sea navigation, such as the *Ossipee, Kearsarge,* and *Shenandoah.* As the war progressed, the naval service required vessels of various other types, the designing of which fell, in large part, to the Bureaus of Construction and Repair and Steam Engineering. The turreted monitors, after they had been tested in the memorable engagement between the *Monitor* and the *Merrimac* in March, 1862, were especially favored by the department, the press and public opinion. Various other kinds of ironclads were constructed. A " double-ender," with a bow and rudder at each end, was devised in order to obviate the necessity of turning the vessels in the narrow channels of the Southern rivers and inlets. Thirty-seven of these were built, some of iron and others of wood. Each year of the war saw produced in foreign shipyards blockade-runners of greater and greater speed. For the purpose of capturing these ships, and English commerce-destroyers in case of a war with the mother-country, the construction of seven fast cruisers of increased steam-power and of decreased armament was commenced in 1863. Two vessels of this type, fitted out with Isherwood's machinery, were completed after the close of the war, the *Wampanoag* and *Ammonoosuc.*

In the construction of vessels, both private and public enterprise were drawn upon by the department. All the public navy-yards and many private shipyards were pressed to their utmost capacity. There were but few eminent ship-builders or manufacturers of

[38] Hoppin, Admiral Foote, 164-165; Bennett, Steam Navy, 282-285; Boynton, Navy during the Great Rebellion, I, 502-504.

steam engines that were not in the employ of the government. Not a little rivalry and jealousy arose between public and private builders of ships and engines. The work of the Secretary of the Navy was severely criticised, and malignantly misrepresented. The department was accused of procrastination and needless delays. It was asserted that the hulls of its new vessels were defective, their engines worthless, and their speed far below the requirements of the navy. Isherwood's steam machinery was the subject of incessant attack. He was represented as a mechanical theorist and visionary, who loaded the naval ships with excessive and defective machinery. The critics of the department generally knew little of the magnitude, complexity and difficulties of its work, and were rarely impartial and discriminating in their criticisms. Several vessels were built by private enterprise with the avowed purpose of proving the faults alleged to exist in the practice of the department, but competitive tests between the vessels of private and of public construction showed the superiority of the latter. Mr. E. N. Dickerson, an engineer, and Mr. Paul S. Forbes, a responsible capitalist of New York City, were especially outspoken in their criticisms of the department. They were finally given an opportunity to prove their assertions by being permitted to build the machinery of the steamers *Algonquin* and *Idaho* after their own plans. On trial the vessels failed completely to substantiate the claims of Forbes and his engineer. The *Idaho* fell short of her required speed almost one-half. When Forbes refused to fulfill his contracts, the Secretary of the Navy declined to accept the vessels or to pay for them. Thereupon Forbes appealed to Congress, and that body forced the vessels upon the department.[39]

Another controversy, which caused much ill-feeling, arose over the introduction into the navy of mastless war vessels. The traditions and conservative instincts of the old navy were opposed to these ships. Not a few officers regarded them as " engineers' vessels " and as overloaded with machinery. The most important ships of this type developed by the Civil War were the monitors, or turreted ironclads, whose operations demonstrated the utility and practicability of armored vessels and of the turret system of mounting guns, and revolutionized modern naval warfare. In 1861 wooden screw-propelling steamships were the latest and most improved type of vessels in the American navy. In the European

[39] Congress Letters, XIV, 259-260; Bennett, Steam Navy, 514-531.

navies a few ironclads had been built and were building, but this type of vessel had hardly passed the experimental stage.

In introducing armored ships, the Confederates showed much enterprise. In May, 1861, S. R. Mallory, the Confederate Secretary of the Navy, wrote that "not only economy, but naval success, dictates the wisdom and expediency of fighting with iron against wood, without regard to first cost."[40] Early in 1862 Mallory had several ironclads nearing completion. The *Merrimac* was converted into an ironclad battery, and on March 8 made her famous raid upon the Unionist shipping at Hampton Roads, Virginia, capturing the *Congress* and sinking the *Cumberland.*

The Federal government proceeded with deliberation and caution. As early as March, 1861, the attention of the department was directed by a correspondent to the subject of ironclads. On July 4, 1861, Secretary Welles recommended the appointment of a board to report respecting "ironclad steamers or floating batteries." On August 4 Congress authorized the Secretary of the Navy to appoint a board consisting of three skilful naval officers "to investigate the plans and specifications that may be submitted for the construction or completing of iron- or steel-clad steamships or steam-batteries." Should the board report favorably, the Secretary of the Navy was authorized to cause one or more such vessels to be built. For their construction Congress appropriated $1,500,000.[41]

Welles at once appointed the Ironclad Board, choosing as members of it Commodores Joseph Smith and Hiram Paulding and Commander C. H. Davis. On September 16 the board made a conservative report, which, however, was favorable to the construction of ironclads. Its members confessed to having had no experience in this branch of naval architecture and but little knowledge of the subject. For the defense of coasts and harbors it conceived that ironclads would be formidable adjuncts to the fortifications on land, but it doubted whether these ships would prove to be valuable cruising vessels. Of the seventeen plans that were submitted to it, the board recommended that three be accepted, those of Bushnell and Company of New Haven, Merrick and Sons of Philadelphia, and John Ericsson of New York. The contracts were let and work upon the three vessels was com-

[40] Wilson, Ironclads in Action, I, 3.
[41] General Letters, LXIV, 43; U. S. Statutes at Large, XII, 286; House Ex. Doc., 38 Cong. 1 sess., No. 69.

menced in the fall of 1861. Each ironclad was of a different type, and all were completed in 1862. The *Galena,* owing to deficient armor, was a failure. The *New Ironsides* rendered good service until the end of the war. The third vessel was the *Monitor,* built after the plans of Ericsson.

Externally, the *Monitor* looked like a long oval raft with a single tower in the center, a " cheese-box on a raft." She had an extraordinary low free-board. Her extreme length was 172 feet; extreme breadth, 41 feet, 6 inches; depth of hold, 11 feet, 4 inches; mean draft, 10 feet, 6 inches; and height of turret, 9 feet. She had five layers of one-inch iron on her hull, and eight layers on her single steam-rotating turret, where were installed two 11-inch Dahlgren guns. She was built under the direction of Joseph Smith, chief of the Bureau of Yards and Docks, and president of the Ironclad Board. John Lenthall, chief of the Bureau of Construction and Repair, had no faith in Ericsson's plans, declaring that the *Monitor* would sink when she was launched. Many other naval officers had strong doubts of her seaworthiness. While she was building, the department was much ridiculed and abused for its novel experiment in naval architecture. She was sometimes referred to as " Ericsson's Folly." Welles, who was early convinced of her merits, was unmoved by the clamor. Credit for her construction is said to belong largely to the Secretary of the Navy, for appreciating her possibilities and for his action in influencing the board to approve the original plans; to her distinguished inventor, John Ericsson; to Chief Engineer A. C. Stimers, who superintended her construction; and to the Ironclad Board and especially its president, Rear-Admiral Joseph Smith. The opportune appearance of the *Monitor* at Hampton Roads and her dramatic fight with the *Merrimac* on March 9, 1862, are familiar to all students of history. The epoch-making character of this engagement in the annals of naval warfare, and the timeliness of her victory to the North, make the *Monitor* one of the most famous ships of the American navy.[42]

The success of Ericsson's vessel gave a great impetus to the

[42] Ann. Rept. of Sec. of N., 1861, 152-156; Bennett, Monitor and Navy under Steam, 70-93; Sen. Rept., 38 Cong. 2 sess., No. 142, pt. 3, p. 93; Porter, Naval History of the Civil War, 360-361; Bennett, Steam Navy, 281; Manuscript Papers of Gideon Welles; Diary of Gideon Welles, I, 214-215.

building of ironclads, and especially those of the monitor type. The newspapers which before the fight at Hampton Roads bitterly declaimed against the new ship now became its warmest partisans. A "monitor heresy" (in the view of some of the naval experts) swept over the country. A "monitor-ring" encouraged the craze. Both Welles and Fox were champions of the new type of ship. On March 31, 1862, Welles contracted with its distinguished inventor for six new monitors, to be built on a somewhat improved plan. On March 25 he recommended that $30,000,000 be appropriated for ironclads, ordnance and armor-plate. Already on February 13, Congress, in response to a recommendation in Welles's annual report for 1861, had appropriated $10,000,000 for ironclad steam gunboats. The opinion of many naval officers was by no means favorable to the monitors, although they were rated highly by Porter, Dahlgren and John Rodgers. The awkward appearance of these vessels, their restricted and uncomfortable quarters and the difficulties of navigating them contrasted unfavorably with the trim, capacious and manageable ships of the old types. They were regarded by some of the principal naval officers as deficient in offensive powers. A considerable difference of opinion respecting their merits arose between the Navy Department and Rear-Admiral S. F. Dupont, who in the first years of the war was in command of the South Atlantic blockading squadron. Welles and Fox were inclined to attribute Dupont's failure in his attack on Charleston in April, 1863, to his depreciation of the qualities of the monitors of his fleet, but the verdict of history seems to be that Dupont judged the worth of his vessels more accurately than did the department. The monitors were a transitional type of steamship.

The light-draft monitors are of unsavory memory, for their construction was the principal blunder of the Navy Department during the Civil War. . They were to draw but six feet of water and were designed by Ericsson to meet the needs of the navy for armored vessels capable of navigating shallow rivers and other inland waters. The construction of twenty of them was undertaken in 1863. The contracts were distributed among a dozen cities, from Portland, Maine, to St. Louis, Missouri. The department cut the red-tape by placing their construction in the hands of Chief Engineer A. C. Stimers, who was acting chief of the New York Bureau, and who in building the *Monitor* had convinced the department of his professional skill. While he was expected to advise with Ericsson, he was permitted to construct the vessels according to his own ideas, and to perform his work more or less independently of both Ericsson and the department. The ships began to arrive at completion in 1864 and at once revealed structural defects so serious as to destroy their usefulness. They were especially defective in draft and speed. They would barely float, and could not be risked in high seas. Their speed, which was to have been seven to nine knots an hour, was only three to four knots. Stimers was not alone implicated in their failure, although he was chiefly responsible for it. The department was to blame for exercising too little supervision and for intrusting its work to an incapable agent. The loss to the government may be estimated at $10,000,000.[43]

Since the science of naval architecture was in a transitional state, much experimenting necessarily had to be done during the war, and some failures were inevitable. The department tried various classes and sizes of ironclads, constructed of wood or of iron, propelled by one or by two screws. It thoroughly tested nearly every variety and type of engine, valve-gear, screw-propeller and boiler. It sent a chief engineer to Europe to collect information relating to steam engineering. Steam machinery of various sorts was designed by both the Bureau of Steam Engineering and by private manufactories. Nearly all the kinds of coal to be found in the seaboard states were made the subject of careful experiment, with a view to ascertaining their comparative value for naval purposes. A board of engineers experimented with petroleum as a substitute for coal on board naval steamers.

The supplying of the navy with ordnance, projectiles and ammunition was a work of considerable magnitude and was performed by the Bureau of Ordnance with great promptness and efficiency. In March, 1861, the navy possessed 2966 heavy guns and howitzers. By November 1, 1864, 4333 new guns had been added. The new guns were of a much larger caliber than the old, which were chiefly 8-inch and 10-inch guns and 32-pounders. Many of the new guns were manufactured after the Dahlgren, Fox or Parrott models. The Dahlgrens were 9-inch, 10-inch and 11-inch guns. The Fox 15-inch guns were introduced by Assistant Secre-

[43] Ann. Rept. of Sec. of N., 1865, xiii, xviii; Preble, Boston Navy-Yard, 431.

tary Fox, and were considered most ponderous and powerful.[44] The Parrott guns were rifled, and fired balls often weighing 100 or 150 pounds. Unfortunately they proved to be weak in the muzzle, and many of them burst with disastrous effect. Some of the Dahlgrens were also rifled, but most of the guns of the Civil War were smooth-bores. In 1863 some seven or eight firms were making guns for the Navy Department. The chief foundries were situated at Boston, South Boston, Providence, West Point, Reading and Pittsburgh. Naval officers were detailed to these private establishments to inspect materials and test the finished guns. Some notion of the difficulties of the department, as well as of its methods of business, may be gained from the following letter of Assistant Secretary Fox, dated November 22, 1862:

There are no big guns to spare. Parties cannot make guns who are not experienced. We have started a half dozen new foundries in New England the last year, and got only one good gun. Any man for a year past, and now, who wishes a contract for big guns can have it. No one has ever been refused. As to ironclads, it is the same. Every one is invited and has been, and no one capable of doing the work has been refused. So with marine engines. We will build a vessel for every party who will take an engine. Washington is reported to have said, " In peace prepare for war." We didn't, and here we are. It is no use to sacrifice anybody; we are caught unprepared, and must pay for it . . . We fired the 15-inch gun at nine inches of iron. It did not penetrate, but it shook the whole affair nearly to pieces. We are in the hands of the contractors, who are doing all they can, but it is far short of public expectation.[45]

The gun carriages were manufactured chiefly in the navy-yards. The " ordnance yard " at Washington employed about six hundred men, and performed many important duties. It furnished the standards that governed the manufacture of ordnance at all the yards and foundries. It tested guns at its experimental batteries, and safeguarded the navy against nostrums and would-be inventors and speculators; and it fabricated boat guns, gun carriages, fuses, primers, percussion caps, fireworks and ammunition. The principal ordnance depots were at New York and Boston. Depots were also maintained at the other Northern yards, and at Fortress Monroe, Baltimore and Mound City. Ordnance storeships were stationed at Port Royal, Key West, Pensacola and New Orleans. The Pacific squadron was supplied with ordnance at the Mare Island navy-yard.[46]

[44] Ann. Rept. of Sec. of N., 1863, pp. 840-845; 1864, pp. 970-975.
[45] Hughes, Forbes, I, 341.
[46] Ann. Rept. of Sec. of N., 1864, pp. 984-985.

The projectiles used in the Civil War were classified as smooth and rifled; and as shells, shot, shrapnel, grape and canister. The smooth projectiles were spherical in shape; and the rifled, elongated and of various forms and kinds. The Dahlgren, Parrott, Hotchkiss and Schenkl projectiles were the best-known types. From March, 1861, to October, 1863, 6,926,000 pounds of shrapnel, grape and canister were cast at the navy-yards, and 2,637,000 pounds of the same were purchased. During the same period the Bureau of Ordnance ordered for its use 2980 tons of gunpowder. This article was manufactured in the loyal states in sufficient quantities to meet the needs of the navy. Early in the war foreign nitre was exclusively used. Subsequently, however, nitre as good in strength as the imported article was manufactured by the New Haven Chemical Works. In 1864 a nitre depot was established at Malden, Massachusetts. Gunpowder magazines were situated near the Northern navy-yards, and at Baltimore and Fortress Monroe. The magazine at the latter place had a capacity of three thousand barrels. During the last two years of the war much attention was given to the subject of torpedoes.[47]

The ropewalk at the Boston navy-yard ran night and day and supplied the larger sizes of rope required by the navy. The smaller sizes were purchased from private manufacturers. The Washington navy-yard furnished a large part of the supply of anchors and cables. The equipping of ships with these and similar articles, and also with coal, fell to the Bureau of Equipment and Recruiting. It established a line of colliers, connecting with the blockading squadrons, Southern naval stations and several West Indian ports. Coaling depots were maintained at Havana, Guantanamo, Nicholas Mole, Cape Haytien, San Juan, St. Thomas, Pointe à Pitre and Curaçao. Outside of the West Indies the navy had coaling depots at Honolulu, Rio de Janeiro, St. Vincent, Fernando Po, St. Paul de Loando, Lisbon, Halifax, and St. John's in Newfoundland. Three colliers were captured by the Confederates, and during the last two years of the war 21 colliers were otherwise lost. A large part of the coal used by the navy was purchased by Commodore H. A. Adams, Sr., who was stationed for that purpose at Philadelphia. The naval vessels at no time experienced any serious inconvenience from

[47] Ann. Rept. of Sec. of N., 1863, pp. 847-848, 852.

want of coal. The consumption of this article in 1864 was about 500,000 tons.[48]

The work of purchasing and distributing supplies of food and clothing fell to the Bureau of Provisions and Clothing, whose efficient chief during the war was Paymaster Horatio Bridge. The economical management of this bureau is shown by the fact that the annual " clothing fund," which before the war amounted to about $570,000, was for 1864 less than four times this sum, although the number of men employed in the navy had increased sixfold and the average price of clothing had more than doubled. This bureau experienced many embarrassments in its work, owing to a lack of sufficient storage facilities and wharf accommodations in the several navy-yards. In 1863 Bridge obtained the permission of Congress to inaugurate a new system of supplying the navy with bread. Previously this essential article had been purchased of contractors and bakers and its quality was often poor. The flour was now purchased by the department, and the bread was baked under naval inspection. Under the new plan the bread cost less and its quality was much improved.

The employment in the navy of regular lines of supply steamers, with refrigerators on board, is said to have been an entirely novel undertaking. The initial step in providing these vessels was an order of Secretary Welles to Bridge, dated July 19, 1861, which read as follows:

You will proceed to New York and take the requisite means for placing on board the Steamer *Rhode Island* fresh beef, vegetables and other supplies necessary for crews of blockading vessels south of Cape Hatteras. Your arrangements will be made with reference to supplying all the vessels with fresh beef and vegetables on the outward trip of the *Rhode Island,* and on returning.

This ship was commanded by Lieutenant S. D. Trenchard. When the system was completed, two fast steamers ran regularly between Northern ports and the West Gulf squadron, and carried at each trip 25,000 to 35,000 pounds of fresh beef preserved in " capacious ice-houses," and 600 to 700 barrels of fresh vegetables. One large steamer, each, supplied the East Gulf and South Atlantic squadrons; and a small steamer, the North Atlantic squadron. These vessels obtained their supplies at New York, Boston and Philadelphia, and ran almost with the regularity of steam

[48] Ann. Rept. of Sec. of N., 1863, pp. 761-762; 1864, p. 909; 1899, p. 304.

packets. They also performed many incidental services, such as conveying mail, dispatches and passengers. They carried sutlers who sold various luxuries to the sailors. The supply steamers added greatly to the comfort and health of the officers and seamen of the blockading squadrons, and did much to brighten their monotonous and perilous life. A similar system was in operation on the Mississippi River.[49]

The facilities of the Bureau of Medicine and Surgery for caring for the sick and wounded of the navy were greatly increased. Early in the war the naval hospitals at Chelsea (Massachusetts) and New York City, the Naval Asylum at Philadelphia, and certain quarters placed at the service of the bureau in the St. Elizabeth Insane Asylum at Washington, afforded ample accommodations. These, however, soon became inadequate and additional quarters had to be rented. The hospitals at Chelsea and New York were enlarged. In 1863 a naval hospital was founded in Washington. It was located on Pennsylvania Avenue, near the navy-yard, on a site long owned by the government. The plain brick building that was erected here was not, however, ready for occupancy until 1866. In 1864 Congress appropriated $75,000 for an addition to the Naval Asylum at Philadelphia; but owing to the high prices asked for materials, the proposed improvement was not made during the war. A sum of money was also appropriated for a hospital at Portsmouth, New Hampshire. Unfortunately, the selection of a location became involved with the purchase of Seavey's Island and with certain political and private interests, and a hospital at this point was not erected. A naval hospital was established at the Mare Island navy-yard.

When the Confederates abandoned the naval hospital at Norfolk in the spring of 1862, they stripped it of its furniture and left it in a filthy condition; but otherwise it was not damaged. It was reoccupied by the Unionists, and by the end of 1862 it contained two hundred and fifty sick and wounded men. The Confederates burned the navy hospital at Pensacola. On the recapture of this place, a temporary building was made ready for naval patients. Temporary hospitals were also provided at Beaufort, Newbern and Port Royal. The marine hospital at Key West, under the control of the Treasury Department, afforded accommodations for the

---

[49] Ann. Rept. of Sec. of N., 1863, p. 1034; 1864, p. 1162; 1865, pp. 374-376; Bureau Letters, IV, 4; Maclay, Reminiscences of the Old Navy, 104-207.

sick sailors of the East Gulf squadron. At New Orleans a hospital of the War Department was placed at the service of the navy. Early in the war the Mississippi flotilla sent its sick and wounded to Mound City, Illinois, where a temporary hospital was established. In March, 1863, this was abandoned, and the hospital for the flotilla was located at Memphis. Ample accommodations were here found in the " Commercial Hotel." A hospital steamer was employed on the Mississippi River.

The number of cases on board the blockading and patrolling vessels treated during the war was 144,038; the number of deaths was 2532. The number of cases treated at hospitals and on board vessels in 1864 was 73,555. The number of naval men wounded in battle was 3266. Seventy-one men were supplied with artificial limbs. Most of the medicines used by the navy were prepared at the Naval Laboratory in New York City.[50]

The five Northern navy-yards were the great depots, manufactories and repair shops of the navy. Of these, the New York yard was by far the most important. Its location in the metropolis, where artisans, laborers and commodities of all sorts abounded, and its comparative nearness to the South, made it indispensable to the work of the navy. Here, in one year, one hundred and fifty-eight vessels were repaired, a much larger number than elsewhere. All the navy-yards were much improved, and their capacity for repairing vessels, storing supplies and performing naval work of various sorts was greatly increased. The artisans and laborers at the navy-yards increased more than fourfold. Toward the end of the war they numbered 16,880, and about an equal number of men were employed in private yards on work for the navy. The maximum number of men at the Boston yard was 3475. This establishment was enlarged by the purchase of additional ground. The docking facilities of the navy, which were quite inadequate, were improved by the construction of two floating dry docks, one for the New York yard and the other for the Philadelphia yard. Secretary Welles recommended the construction of several stone dry docks.[51]

In 1862 the Norfolk and Pensacola navy-yards were recovered by the Unionists, after the Confederates had destroyed most of

[50] Ann. Rept. of Bureau of Medicine and Surgery, 1862-1865; Ann. Rept. of Sec. of N., 1865; p. 387; 1866, p. 207; 1866, p. 302.

[51] Ann. Rept. of Sec. of N., 1865, xiii, xviii; Preble, Boston Navy-Yard, 43.

their buildings, stores, ordnance and machinery. The two yards were converted by the Unionists into naval depots and repair stations. At Pensacola but few improvements were made. Since the Norfolk yard was more strategically located, considerable progress was made in its restoration. The ruin that was here effected by the retreating Confederates is well depicted in the following account of Secretary of State Seward, who was a member of the party of Secretary Welles that visited Norfolk in May, 1862, shortly after its abandonment by the enemy:

We landed at what was the navy-yard and is now a mass of smoking ruins. Long rows of crumbling walls, and roofless, empty, charred brick buildings, piles of still smoking ashes, docks and wharves torn up by gunpowder, wrecks of vessels burned to the water's edge, cover many acres. A Massachusetts regiment was encamped among the ruins, and one man, with a Yankee readiness, had contrived to establish a blacksmith shop out of the fragments, and was driving a successful business, mending guns and shoeing horses. A huge gun, burst in the middle, was recognized as one which a ball from the *Cumberland* destroyed on board the *Merrimac,* and Captain Dahlgren found it one of his own make. The soldier who stood guard over it asked me if I remembered, about eighteen months ago, reading in the newspapers of a Boston shoemaker, cruelly beaten and tarred and feathered in Savannah for supposed "abolitionism." I told him I remembered printing it in the *Albany Journal.* " I am that shoemaker," said he. " I enlisted in the first Massachusetts regiment I could find; and I have got so far on my way back to Savannah, to see those gentlemen again."

Not quite everything was destroyed. Of the buildings, the officers' quarters alone remained intact. A large number of iron tanks in good condition, considerable mast and ship timber, several old and worthless guns, and some machinery were left by the Confederates. The dry dock, which they attempted to blow up, was not greatly injured. On May 20, 1862, Captain John W. Livingston was made the first commandant of the restored yard, and he at once began to put it in order. Considerable property which had been taken from the yard and concealed was restored to him by citizens of Norfolk. Those shops that were most needed were at once repaired, and in 1863 the dry dock was made ready for use.[52]

Several naval depots and stations were maintained in the Southern states for the convenience of the blockading and patrolling squadrons. Here were to be found machinery for repairing vessels, ordnance of all kinds, provisions, coal and naval stores. Toward

[52] Seward, Seward, 90-91; Lull, Norfolk Navy-Yard, 60-62.

the end of the war there were stations or depots at Memphis, New Orleans, Ship Island, Key West, Port Royal, Beaufort and Baltimore. One of the earliest naval operations, made with a view to obtaining a foothold for a naval station on the Atlantic coast of the seceding states, resulted in the capture of Port Royal, South Carolina, which became the chief station of the South Atlantic blockading squadron. At one time more than two hundred vessels were safely sheltered in its harbor. Key West, which during the war presented a very lively appearance, was a rendezvous for all vessels going to and coming from the Gulf. Here they were supplied with coal and provisions, large quantities of which were constantly arriving from the North. This port was also the seat of a prize court, which passed judgment upon all vessels captured in the Gulf.

In the spring of 1862 Commodore Foote established a naval depot at Cairo, Illinois, under the command of Commander A. M. Pennock. Later, Mound City, Illinois, became the most important naval station on the Western waters. Carondelet, near St. Louis, was also an important river port for the navy in that region. During the war the establishment of a permanent navy-yard in the West was much agitated and discussed. Welles recommended it in 1862, and frequently thereafter. Foote believed that the need of a navy-yard on the Mississippi was very great, and the Western members of Congress were naturally much interested in the project. Finally, in pursuance of a joint resolution of Congress of June 30, 1864, Welles appointed a commission, with Rear-Admiral C. H. Davis as senior member, to select a location for the proposed yard. After examining various sites the commission recommended that a navy-yard of construction be located at Carondelet, and that Mound City be continued as a naval station for equipping and repairing vessels. This recommendation was not satisfactory, and when the war came to an end the site for a permanent yard on the Western waters was still undetermined.[53]

The transformation of the wooden sailing navy into an iron steam navy, in the opinion of Secretary Welles, rendered necessary the establishment of a navy-yard adapted to the new vessels. He believed that a yard containing foundries, steam machinery and steam machine shops for the repair and construction of iron ships, ironclads and iron shafting was imperatively needed. The

[53] Sen. Ex. Doc., 38 Cong. 2 sess., No. 19.

essentials for such an establishment were an abundance of fresh water, sufficient to float heavy ships, security from attack by an enemy and nearness to supplies of iron and coal. In March, and again in June, 1862, Welles invited the attention of Congress to this subject. The city of Philadelphia was greatly interested in the recommendations of the Secretary of the Navy and offered to donate to the government League Island, located in the Delaware River near the mouth of the Schuylkill, and comprising some 900 acres. The citizens of New London, Connecticut, also discovered an eligible site for a navy-yard in the vicinity of their city. On July 15, 1862, Congress passed a joint resolution authorizing the Secretary of the Navy to accept the gift of League Island, provided that he could obtain a good title to it and that a board of officers (which he was directed to appoint) should recommend its acceptance. The resolution assigned to the board the further duty of ascertaining the fitness for a naval depot and a navy-yard of the waters adjacent to New London and of those of Narragansett Bay. Evidently this resolution was a compromise between conflicting interests. A board, consisting of six members, of which Rear-Admiral Silas H. Stringham was president, was appointed by Welles on August 12.

After more than two months' labor, the board in the fall of 1862 made a report in which it considered the respective advantages of League Island, New London and Narragansett Bay. Its members were unanimous in their rejection of Narragansett Bay. Four members gave their preference to New London and the remaining two to League Island. Notwithstanding the opinion of a majority of the board, Welles, in his annual report for 1862, said that he proposed to accept the gift of League Island, unless Congress should otherwise direct. He argued that an establishment at New London would merely add another navy-yard of the same character as the old ones, while the acceptance of League Island would lead to the abandonment of the Philadelphia yard and the founding of a new establishment adapted to the needs of a steam and iron navy. Among the members of Congress each site found strong supporters, and the wheels of legislation were locked. For several years, the continued recommendations of Welles in behalf of the acceptance of League Island, the reports of Assistant Secretary Fox on the subject and the expressed desire of President Lincoln that League Island be promptly obtained were insufficient to move

Congress to action. Welles, in the end, concluded not to accept League Island without Congressional sanction.[54]

In August, 1864, Chief Engineer J. W. King was sent abroad to examine the dock yards, engine factories, rolling mills and iron-clads of Great Britain and France, and to collect information on these subjects with a view to aiding the department in establishing a modern navy-yard. King visited many of the public and private establishments of these countries, finding them superior to our own, and made a valuable report on his trip of inspection.[55]

The Civil War effected profound changes in the personnel as well as in the matériel of the navy. The legislation of this period respecting naval officers was the most important since 1798, and it still remains the basis of the organization of the navy. Measures for the amelioration and improvement of the service, which had been agitated for many years, were now passed, and the navy was placed more nearly on a par with the army, which service, since the founding of the government, had been more highly regarded by Congress and the people. The navy now acquired great prestige and popularity, and the names of its chief officers, such as those of Farragut and Porter, became household words.

During the winter of 1860-1861 the naval officers were more or less confused and demoralized by the conflict of their principles, interests and allegiances, by the disaffection towards the Union of many Southern officers, and by the lukewarm policy of the government in failing to defend its naval property. The *esprit de corps* of the service was greatly weakened and many officers joined the seceding states. The exact number who withdrew from the service has not been determined. Secretary Welles placed the number of naval officers who " traitorously abandoned " the flag at 322. A document in the archives of the Navy Department gives the names of 422 officers of the line, ranking from acting midship-man to captain, who left the service during the three years from December 1, 1860, to December 1, 1863. Several of these officers, however, chiefly of the lower grades, were from the North. The document gives the names of 15 captains, 35 commanders, and 99 lieutenants.[56]

---

[54] Ann. Rept. of Sec. of N., 1862, p. 32; 1863, xvii; 1864, xxx; U. S. Statutes at Large, XII, 575-576; Diary of Gideon Welles, I, 185, 207, 222.

[55] Ann. Rept. of Sec. of N., 1864, p. 1216.

[56] Congress Letters, XIV, 73-78; Ann. Rept. of Sec. of N., 1865, xiii.

A chief engineer of the United States navy became the engineer-in-chief of the Confederate navy. The several grades of the Confederate navy, except the very lowest, were filled almost entirely by former officers of the United States navy, who took rank in the new service according to their previous rank in the old. Several of these officers acquired distinction in the Confederate navy. The Southerners of the Union navy at the beginning of the war could, with equal honor, have chosen to serve either their own state or the United States, but those officers who, while wearing the uniform and drawing the pay of the Federal government, played into the hands of the Confederacy and were unwilling to protect the public property, which they had taken an oath to defend, were traitors. That there were such officers at both the Pensacola and the Norfolk navy-yard when they surrendered cannot be doubted. Seventeen officers who were attached to the Norfolk yard were rightly dismissed from the navy. It is noteworthy that but few seamen and non-commissioned officers went with the South. Almost to a man the enlisted personnel remained faithful to the old flag.

Owing to resignations early in the war and to subsequent legislation, the number of officers in the higher grades of the regular navy was not as large in 1865 as in 1861. The *Naval Register* for January, 1861, contains the names of 514 captains, commanders and lieutenants, on the active list; while the *Register* for January, 1865, contains but 379 names between the grades of lieutenant and vice-admiral inclusive. A considerable increase was made in the numbers of most of the regular staff corps of the navy. From 1861 to 1865 the engineers increased from 192 to 474, the surgeons from 148 to 208, and the paymasters from 64 to 96. The chaplains, however, decreased from 24 to 21.[57] Many officers on the reserved and retired lists were assigned to duty at naval posts on shore.

The great need for additional officers was met largely by the appointment of volunteers. During the first months of the war considerable pressure was brought to bear upon the government and the department to establish privateering, but it was successfully resisted. Massachusetts was anxious and importunate to organize an auxiliary navy of her own. Her motives were not wholly patriotic, as one of her objects was the obtaining of lucrative employment for her men and capital. Ex-governor G. S. Boutwell, representing Governor John Andrew, came to Washing-

---

[57] Navy Registers, 1861 and 1866.

ton to make the necessary arrangements for a Massachusetts volunteer navy. This plan, as well as several others of a similar character, did not meet with the approval of Secretary Welles and was not adopted. Before Congress met in July, 1861, Welles had commissioned many volunteer officers. An act of July 24, providing for a temporary increase of the navy, legalized Welles's past appointments and established a naval volunteer corps. The total number of volunteer officers employed from 1861 to 1865 was about 7500. Near the close of the war there were in the navy, as volunteers, 2060 line officers, 1805 engineers, 370 paymasters and 245 surgeons. The highest rank attained by volunteer line officers was that of lieutenant-commander.[58]

The volunteers to the naval line came chiefly from the merchant service. A few civilians, who had formerly been in the navy and had resigned, hastened to offer their services to their country in its time of dire need. Of this class was Captain John S. Barnes, who on December 5, 1860, tendered his services to the department in case of a war. Many of the inexperienced officers acquitted themselves with credit, zeal and fidelity, but unfortunately not all of them were fitted for the naval service. This was especially true of the engineer corps. One of the acting engineers, for instance, was a village schoolmaster from the up-country of New Hampshire, whose knowledge of marine engineering had been gained from a picture of a condensing engine in a text-book on natural philosophy common in the schools of New England. He introduced into the service one of his favorite pupils, whose knowledge of engineering was, if possible, even more rudimentary.

Naval officers who are well fitted for the mild duties of peace may fall far short of the sterner requirements of war. In 1861, upon the outbreak of hostilities, the department determined, for the good of the country and the navy, to retire all those officers who were incapacitated by old age, ill health and the enervation incident to service in the old navy. In the upper grades there was much deadwood. The officers at the head of the list of commanders were sixty years old, and some of the lieutenants were between forty-eight and fifty years. The department therefore obtained the passage of the act of August 3, 1861, providing for a naval retired list, according to which incapacitated officers were to be either

[58] Manuscript Papers of Gideon Welles; U. S. Statutes at Large, XII, 272-273; Ann. Rept. of Sec. of N., 1865, xiii; Navy Register, 1865.

retired or discharged. Those who were retired were to be ineligible for promotion, and were to receive reduced pay, at rates fixed for the several grades. A naval board of commissioned officers, two-fifths of whose members were to be naval surgeons, was to select the incapacitated officers. The act also provided that officers might retire voluntarily after forty years' service. Secretary Welles at once appointed the retiring board, with Commodore George W. Storer as president, and Commander David G. Farragut as one of its members, which assembled at New York on October 18, 1861. The board found comparatively few officers incapacitated, and its work was not altogether satisfactory to the department. It virtually constituted itself a naval court, and felt itself bound by the rules of evidence governing such courts.[59]

On December 21, 1861, additional legislation respecting retirement was enacted. All officers were now to be retired at the age of sixty-two years, or after having been forty-five years in the naval service. It was also provided that the officers on the retired list might be assigned to shore-duty. After the passage of this law, little additional legislation on the retirement of naval officers was enacted for forty years. In 1863 the number of officers of the line on the retired list was 67, and in 1865, 85. In the latter year there were 45 officers on the reserved list established by the naval efficiency act of 1855. The two lists were kept separate.[60]

From the standpoint of the naval line officer, the most important naval legislation of the Civil War, or indeed the most important since the navy was founded, was the law of July 16, 1862, entitled "An Act to Establish and Equalize the Grade of Line Officers of the United States Navy." Legislation similar to that of this act was recommended by President Lincoln and Secretary Welles in their annual reports for 1861. The first section of the new law brought the navy the boon of higher grades, which it had long sought. For the first time in many years Congress definitely specified the number of naval officers and the number of grades. The active list of line officers was divided into nine grades. In addition to the old ranks of captain, commander, lieutenant, master and midshipman, four new ones were established: the rank of ensign between the ranks of midshipman and master, that of

---

[59] U. S. Statutes at Large, XII, 290-291; Ann. Rept. of Sec. of N., 1861, p. 18.

[60] U. S. Statutes at Large, XII, 329-330; Navy Registers, 1863 and 1865.

lieutenant-commander between the ranks of lieutenant and commander, and the ranks of commodore and rear-admiral above that
of captain. The number of officers established in each grade was
as follows: rear-admirals, 9; commodores, 18; captains, 36; commanders, 72; lieutenant-commanders, masters, lieutenants and
ensigns, each, 144. The number of midshipmen was not definitely
fixed, but it was made to depend chiefly upon the number of members of the House of Representatives.

The act of July 16, 1862, made due provision for the filling of
the new grades. It authorized the appointment of an advisory
board of naval officers, which was to scrutinize carefully the active
list and report those names that were deemed worthy of promotion.
The officers recommended by the board were to be promoted and
commissioned according to their seniority until the several grades,
with the exception of that of rear-admiral, were full. During
war, the nine rear-admirals were to be selected from those officers
who had distinguished themselves in their profession by their
courage, skill and genius. In peace, the rear-admirals were to be
chosen according to the method of promotion obtaining in the other
grades. The act further provided that a similar naval advisory
board on promotions should be appointed every four years. It
also established the relative rank of navy and army officers, and
provided the navy with a new pay-table. The latter fixed the
annual pay of a rear-admiral at sea at $5000, and of a captain at
$3500.[61]

On July 22, 1862, the Secretary of the Navy appointed the first
advisory board on promotions, which was composed of five naval
captains, of whom Captain William B. Shubrick was the senior
officer. It completed its work on August 6, and the officers whom
it recommended were at once promoted. Those officers whom it
passed over severely criticised its findings. They went to Congress for redress, and that body passed a bill for their relief, but
the President refused to sign it.

On April 21, 1864, the law of July 16, 1862, was somewhat modified. An act was then passed providing for an examining board
of three naval officers senior in rank to the officers whom it should
examine. All naval officers below the grade of commodore were
now required to pass both a mental and a physical examination
before each promotion, in order to test their professional qualifi-

[61] U. S. Statutes at Large, XII, 583-587.

cations. This act further provided that officers might be advanced in their own grade, not exceeding 30 numbers, for distinguished conduct in battle or extraordinary heroism. The present system of naval boards for the retirement and promotion of officers dates from these acts passed during the Civil War.[62]

During the war the rank of rear-admiral was not entirely filled. On December 1, 1862, the President nominated four naval captains to be rear-admirals on the active list—Farragut, Goldsborough, Dupont and Foote—with commissions dating July 16, 1862. Later, Davis, Dahlgren and Porter were promoted to this rank. In December, 1864, Congress established a still higher grade, that of vice-admiral, and provided that one rear-admiral should be promoted to it. The sea-pay of the new office was $7000 a year. The position was created for Farragut, and he was at once nominated and confirmed as vice-admiral.[63]

The Navy Department was conspicuously successful in selecting officers for the higher commands. Its good fortune in this respect, as compared with the bad success of the War Department, was commented upon by President Lincoln. He thought that the qualities of the officers of the navy must run more evenly, and that the task of selecting officers for the higher commands must be less difficult, than in the army.[64] The Navy Department did no experimenting corresponding to that of the War Department with McClellan, Halleck, Hooker and Pope. Before the end of 1862 the naval officers who acquired distinction had already received the highest posts in the gift of the department. Even at this early date the roll of great naval names could have been made out— Farragut, Porter, Dupont, Foote, Davis, Dahlgren and Lee. Secretary Welles had an intimate knowledge of the capabilities of his commanders, and the diary which he kept during the war abounds with his estimates of their qualities. He seems to have closely supervised the naval operations. The planning of the operations was of course a composite work, in which the naval officers largely shared. In the summer of 1861 the Commission of Conference served as a Board of Strategy. Fox was always fertile in suggestions. The honor of originating the New Orleans expedition

---

[62] Congress Letters, XIV, 115-116; Ann. Rept. of Sec. of N., 1862, 40-41; U. S. Statutes at Large, XIII, 53-54.

[63] U. S. Statutes at Large, XIII, 420.

[64] Diary of Gideon Welles, I, 440.

is claimed by Professor J. R. Soley for Porter, although Secretary Welles, writing after the war, gave Porter a less conspicuous part. In the naval expedition of the fall of 1861, which resulted in the capture of Port Royal, its commander, Commodore Dupont, was permitted to choose the point on the Atlantic coast to be attacked. In all co-operative movements with the army, much consultation took place between the officials and officers of the two services. Sometimes President Lincoln took a hand in the direction of the fleet.

During the war the standard of naval education was somewhat lowered by reason of the exigencies of the service and the poor accommodations of the Naval Academy, which was moved from Annapolis to Newport early in 1861. In July, 1864, Congress recognized the increased importance of steamships in the navy by authorizing the instruction at the Academy of " cadet engineers." The volunteer officers received elementary instruction in gunnery and seamanship at the navy-yards. Before entering the service they had to pass an examination in seamanship, navigation and gunnery. They had also to undergo an examination for promotion. In 1863 Lieutenant S. B. Luce made a report on the English apprentice system, in which he recommended a similar system for our navy; and in the following year Secretary Welles, who was very favorably disposed towards the sailormen of the navy, ordered the enlistment of a number of apprentices and the fitting out of the *Sabine* as a school-ship for them. The new system was organized by Lieutenant-Commander R. B. Lowry. Welles recommended that one-half of the midshipmen appointed to the Naval Academy should be selected from the apprentices.[65]

At the outbreak of the war numerous recruiting rendezvous were opened on the Atlantic coast and the Great Lakes for the enlistment of seamen, and within three months the number of seamen in the navy was doubled. In order to procure the necessary crews at the earliest moment, and also with a view to inducing the sailors engaged in the fisheries and coastwise trade to enter the navy, the term of enlistment was reduced from three years to one. The effect of this reduction was to call into the naval service at New York a large number of recent immigrants who were not adapted to a seafaring life. Complaints of their inefficiency compelled the curtailment of enlistments of this sort.

[65] Ann. Rept. of Sec. of N., 1864, xxxv.

Early in the war sailors entered the navy promptly, and the ships were seldom delayed more than three or four days for want of crews. In the spring and summer of 1864 the situation was quite different. In March, 35 vessels were waiting for their complements and the navy was in need of more than 10,000 seamen. In June the Secretary of the Navy wrote that " our squadrons are becoming almost paralyzed for defensive, offensive, or blockading purposes, and calls on the department from all quarters for men are constantly made." Because of her depleted crew the steamer *Water Witch* had recently been compelled to surrender to the Confederates. The laws discriminated in favor of the enlistment of soldiers, and many sailors entered the army in preference to the navy in order to receive the bounties given to the recruits of the land service. Enlistments in the navy received little local encouragement, since the accounts of communities against the " draft " were not credited by the recruiting of seamen for the navy. When the war came to an end in 1865 the total number of enlisted men in the navy was 51,500, an increase of about 44,000 over the number when the war began. The total number of men recruited during the war was 118,044.[66]

In 1861 the number of officers and privates in the marine corps was largely increased. Twenty commissioned officers left the corps on account of their sympathy with the South. An act of July 25, 1861, for the better organization of the marine corps, provided for 93 commissioned officers and 3074 non-commissioned officers and privates. At the close of the war the number of enlisted men was about 3650. Two new posts were established, one at Cairo, Illinois, and the other at the Mare Island navy-yard. The barracks at Boston and Portsmouth were rebuilt.[67]

Throughout the war Secretary Welles and his management of the Navy Department were severely criticised and denounced. His critics asserted that he was a friend of red tape, that he was an extravagant administrator and that he was entirely too slow and deliberate for the strenuous duties of war. It may be said briefly in reply that Welles often cut the red tape unmercifully, that no business of the war was more economically conducted than that of the Navy Department, and that, all things considered, he extem-

---

[66] Ann. Rept. of Sec. of N., 1865, xiii, 200; Congress Letters, XIII, 371-372, 381; XIV, 101, 127, 188.

[67] U. S. Statutes at Large, XII, 275; Collum, Marine Corps, 115.

porized a navy in a remarkably short time. It is true that the department made at least one egregious blunder, the building of the light-draft monitors. Some frauds were perpetrated upon it, and certain administrative abuses flourished. On February 6, 1863, Rear-Admiral Dahlgren, then chief of the Bureau of Ordnance, wrote that the " pressure of private interests is enormous and rascally "; and again on March 3, 1864, that Washington was " all alive with crowds making money on the war." Politics was still the bane of the navy-yards, and it was often responsible for the selection of negligent and faithless employees. Workmen were assessed for party purposes, and sometimes the chief officers of the yards had imposed upon them the " duty of tax-gatherers for electioneering purposes." In 1865 Welles issued orders to prevent such assessments. Some of the abuses relating to the purchase of naval supplies the Secretary of the Navy ascribed to the law which compelled him to award the naval contracts to the lowest bidder, no matter if they could not be honestly fulfilled. On several occasions he asked Congress to remedy the defective system of making contracts.[68]

In 1864 both the Secretary of the Navy and a committee of the Senate made extensive investigations into alleged abuses and malpractices connected with the navy-yards and naval contracts. Colonel H. S. Olcott, who was employed by Welles as a special commissioner to investigate the navy frauds, discovered in New York City a ring of dishonest contractors who, by collusions with the employees of the navy-yards, were able to supply poor articles in place of good ones and thus make large profits. A contractor by the name of Stover had in one year cleared $117,000 by substituting " horse fat, menhaden and other stinking fish oils " for " best winter-strained sperm oil " called for by his contract. At Philadelphia Olcott caused the arrest of 31 men, most of whom were employees of the Philadelphia yard, and among whom were a naval constructor and a first assistant engineer. He recovered large quantities of stolen copper, pitch, rosin and naval stores. " To say nothing of copper bath-tubs, brass filings, and other small things, the thieves had removed a steam engine bodily and sold it to a junk dealer." Welles's investigation led to the dismissal of the commandant, storekeeper and two masters of the Washington

[68] Ann. Rept. of Sec. of N., 1865, xxv-xxvi; Dahlgren, Dahlgren, 387, 443; Diary of Gideon Welles, I, 404, 507, 523.

navy-yard.   About $60,000 was restored to the government by
men who confessed their guilt.   Parties were tried and convicted,
and were fined to the amount of $75,000.   The Smith Brothers,
contractors for naval supplies at Boston, were fined $20,000 and
sentenced to two years' imprisonment.   Their case was carried
to President Lincoln by Senator Charles Sumner, who was convinced of the contractors' innocence.   Sumner wrote an opinion
based upon the evidence produced at their trial, in which he
showed that, according to the findings of the court, the government
had lost only $100 in transactions amounting to more than $1,200,-
000.   Guided by Sumner's opinion, Lincoln disapproved the judgment and sentence, and directed that the Smith Brothers be
released.   The loss of the department through frauds, as compared with its total expenditures, was slight.   This loss was probably much less than that of certain contractors for building ships,
whose bids were too low, and who after the war appealed to Congress for reimbursement.[69]

Welles's own words, which occur in his annual report for 1868,
may be taken as a just, concise and accurate statement of the
department's achievements during the Civil War, and they may be
appropriately quoted here, although they refer also to the later
work of the department.   Appearing shortly after his retirement
at the end of Johnson's administration, they constitute his vale-
dictory:

It has fallen to my lot to sustain a greater responsibility, and to have
had a much more eventful and varied, as well as a longer experience in
this department than any one of my predecessors.   While I claim no
exemption from error, it is a gratifying reflection that the duties entrusted
to me have been acceptably performed, and that the record which com-
memorates the services and achievements of our naval heroes, also bears
evidence, through a most important period of our country's history, of a
not unsuccessful administration of our naval affairs.

On this department, soon after I entered it, devolved the task of creating within a brief period a navy unequaled in some respects, and without
a parallel—of enforcing the most extensive blockade which was ever
established—of projecting and carrying forward to successful execution
immense naval expeditions—of causing our extensive rivers, almost
continental in their reach, to be actively patrolled—and finally, after four

---

[69] Rhodes, History of the United States, V, 221-224; Congress Letters,
XIV, 246-251; Sen. Rept., 38 Cong. 1 sess., No. 99; Annals of the War
(publ. by the Pa. Weekly Times), 717-723; Diary of Gideon Welles, I, 483,
511. 540.

years of embittered warfare, of retiring the immense naval armament which had been promptly called into existence, of disposing to the commercial marine the vessels procured from that service, and of re-establishing our squadrons abroad in the interest of peace.

The waste of war is always great, but much of the expenditure of the Navy Department, which is but a small per cent of the national war expenses, is invested in navy-yard improvements, which are worth to the government all they cost, and in naval vessels and ordnance, which have at all times an intrinsic value. When the fact of this large amount of property left on hand, of the return of millions to the treasury, of the magnitude of the war, of the vast operations of the navy, and of the depreciation of the currency, and the consequently enhanced prices with which those operations were conducted, are considered, the economical and faithful administration of the Navy Department will be admitted.[70]

---

[70] Ann. Rept. of Sec. of N., 1868, xxxiv.

CHAPTER EIGHT: A PERIOD OF DECLINE, 1865-1869

Part I

THE SECOND ADMINISTRATION OF GIDEON WELLES, 1865-1869. The ending of the Civil War and the beginning of Welles's second term in the department were almost coincident. In the spring of 1865 rumors that Welles would not remain in the cabinet were current in New England. He, however, continued in office during Lincoln's brief second administration and throughout the administration of Andrew Johnson, resigning on March 3, 1869. Of Lincoln's original cabinet, Secretary of State Seward was the only other member who held his post for eight years, he too serving until the end of Johnson's administration. Welles's second administration was marked chiefly by the withdrawal of the fleets from the duties of the war, the re-establishment of the foreign squadrons and the reduction of the naval matériel and personnel to a peace footing.

On June 1, 1866, Gustavus V. Fox retired from the position he had held in the department since July 31, 1861, and William Faxon, the chief clerk of the department, was promoted to the assistant secretaryship of the navy. On the retirement of Faxon at the close of Johnson's administration this office was discontinued, since Congress refused to appropriate for it. On May 26, 1866, Congress authorized the appointment of an additional Assistant Secretary of the Navy to serve for a period of six months. Fox was appointed to this new position, which was created for him and for a special purpose. On May 16 Congress had passed a resolution of greeting to the Emperor of Russia, congratulating him on his escape from assassination. President

Johnson selected Fox to carry a copy of the resolution to the Russian ruler; and, in order to add some dignity and pomp to his mission, a temporary assistant secretaryship of the navy was created for him. In June, 1866, he took passage at St. Johns, Newfoundland, on the *Miantonomoh,* the first American ironclad to cross the Atlantic, and proceeded to Cronstadt. He was welcomed with festivities and extraordinary courtesies and attentions not only at St. Petersburg, but at Moscow and other Russian cities. This successful mission made a fitting termination to his brilliant career in the Navy Department.[71]

When Faxon vacated the position of chief clerk of the department to become Assistant Secretary of the Navy, his place was taken by Mr. Edgar T. Welles, a son of the Secretary, who had been filling a clerkship in the Secretary's office. Since leaving the department in 1869, young Welles has achieved distinction in New York City as a man of affairs. The ending of the war caused little or no reduction in the regular clerical force of the department. The number of clerks and draftsmen in 1865 was 66; in 1866, 69; and in 1869, 62.[72] After several attempts had been made to establish permanently the office of solicitor and judge-advocate general of the navy, it was discontinued in 1870.

It is recollected that the Bureau of Navigation owed its origin largely to Rear-Admiral C. H. Davis, who designed it to be the scientific department of the navy. On April 28, 1865, the Office of Detail was placed in charge of the Bureau of Navigation. The resulting establishment was given the official title of the " Bureau of Navigation and Office of Detail." This was the first step towards the transforming of this bureau into a bureau of personnel. The incongruous union formed no part of Davis's plans. Indeed it proved fatal to them. In course of time the scientific work of the Navy Department fell to other bureaus, and the duties of an office of detail became the chief and characteristic part of the work of the Bureau of Navigation—a term that is now a misnomer. This transformation is one of the most significant steps in the evolution of our present navy system.

In 1863 Davis recommended the establishment of a hydrographic office to undertake a somewhat similar work to that per-

[71] U. S. Statutes at Large, XIV, 54, 355; Ann. Rept. of Sec. of N., 1866, 13-14; Loubat, Fox's Mission to Russia, 9-424.

[72] Navy Registers, 1865, 1866, 1869.

formed by Maury's Hydrographical Office. Finally, largely through his instrumentality, a law was passed in 1866 creating the "Hydrographic Office" and attaching it to the Bureau of Navigation.[73] The new office was quartered with the Nautical Almanac Office, in the Tayloe Building, in Washington. This latter office had been recently removed from Cambridge, Massachusetts, to the capital. For several years the growth of the Hydrographic Office was slow.

In 1866 Secretary Welles recommended the establishment of an additional bureau in the department, which was to have charge of all the duties of the Federal government relating to the enlisted force of the navy and the seamen of the merchant service. The creation of this bureau was a part of a comprehensive plan of Welles to elevate the character and status of the man-of-wars' men by giving them the privilege of retirement from the navy with pay, an extensive education on school-ships and at the Naval Academy, and a chance of promotion to the naval line.[74]

Both during and after the war attempts were made to establish in the Navy Department a board composed of naval line officers and vested with large advisory and directive powers; and several bills were introduced in Congress providing for a board of this character. The general and flexible grant of powers contained in these bills gave the proposed organization ample room to grow and expand. It was to occupy a position in the departmental hierarchy between the bureaus and the Secretary of the Navy. The establishment of a board of this sort met with much opposition. Certain civilians opposed it because it would diminish the civilian and increase the naval influence in the department. The Secretary of the Navy discovered in it an attempt to rule the navy by means of a clique, such as he had destroyed when he entered the department in 1861. The friends of the bureau system saw in it an undue subordination of the naval bureaus. The staff officers feared that the proposed board would bring about the complete supremacy of the line officers in naval administration.

The first measure providing for a naval board of the general character indicated above was introduced in the House by Henry Winter Davis, of Maryland, in 1864. It authorized the establish-

[73] Davis, Davis. 283.
[74] Ann. Rept. of Sec. of N., 1866, 33-36.

ment in the department of a " Board of Naval Administration."
Nothing came of this measure. In February, 1865, Davis offered
an amendment to the annual appropriation bill, providing for the
organization of a " Board of Admiralty." This was to consist
of the vice-admiral, one rear-admiral, one commodore, one
captain, one commander and one lieutenant-commander. Its presiding officer was to be either the Secretary of the Navy or the
senior officer of the board. It was to deliberate and to give advice
on naval organization and legislation, the construction, equipment
and armament of vessels, the navy-yards and other naval establishments, and the direction, organization and discipline of naval
forces in time of war. All plans for new ships, guns and engines
were to be submitted to it. The proposed board seems to have
been modelled on the British Board of Admiralty.

In 1867, 1868 and 1869 the Grimes Navy Bill was before Congress. This provided for a " Board of Naval Survey," which,
according to one of the later forms of the bill, was to consist of
three line officers not below the rank of rear-admiral. The members of the board were to be appointed by the President for a
term of four years. An officer not below the grade of commander
was to act as its secretary. The Bureaus of Medicine and Surgery
and Provisions and Clothing were to be abolished. The naval
staff considered the Grimes Bill inimical to their interests. It
passed the Senate on March 16, 1869, but it failed to become
a law.[75]

The first measures of naval retrenchment at the close of the
war were taken soon after the fall of Fort Fisher in January,
1865, in anticipation of the collapse of the Confederacy. In
February the commanding officers of the blockading squadrons
were ordered to send north all purchased vessels out of repair
and all unnecessary naval stores, and to use the greatest care in
decreasing their expenses. About May 1 orders were issued to
reduce the naval squadrons in domestic waters one-half; and
near the close of the month further reductions were directed to
be made, until the entire force of vessels in commission should not
exceed 100. Early in July the blockading squadrons were reduced
to 30 ships. On July 31 the Potomac flotilla, and on August 14

[75] Congressional Globe, 1863-1864, p. 1531; 1864-1865, pp. 601-602; 1869,
pp. 63-64, 86-87; Army and Navy Journal, II, 389, 393; IV, 475; V, 301, 329;
Clymer, Naval Staff Rank, 119-120, 157-170; Diary of Gideon Welles.

the Mississippi flotilla, were discontinued. Meantime, the two Atlantic and the two Gulf squadrons had been combined. In January, 1865, the vessels of the blockading squadrons numbered 471 and carried 2455 guns, in December they numbered 29 and carried 210 guns.[76]

During 1865 most of the vessels that had been purchased and some of those that had been built were sold. Many vessels, having been procured for special purposes, were not fit to become permanent acquisitions of the navy. By May 6, 1868, 429 vessels had been disposed of. In December of that year only 81 vessels were in commission; 125 vessels were either in ordinary or were in process of construction. Several ships which were on the stocks at the close of the war were finally launched, and others were never completed. Most of the ironclads were laid up in ordinary, chiefly at League Island, but also at Boston, New Orleans, Mound City and San Francisco. As the vessels were put out of commission, they deposited their ordnance and supplies at the several navy-yards, which were soon crowded to overflowing with naval stores of all sorts. These vast quantities of warlike materials were gradually exhausted by sale, use or decay. The ordnance was collected chiefly in the Northern navy-yards. Its most important depot was a gun-park at the New York yard, which had a capacity for 2000 cannon. The value of the ordnance and ordnance stores remaining on hand in 1868 was about $17,-000,000. Large quantities of unserviceable ordnance were sold.[77]

In the spring of 1865 the department took measures for the re-establishment of the foreign squadrons. A course of active cruising was ordered, so that the flag which had been so long withdrawn might be again exhibited in every important port where American commerce penetrated. For four years the commercial interests of the United States in foreign waters had been left without any protection, except such as a few isolated cruisers could give. The old method of hiring storehouses in foreign ports and of appointing storekeepers to take charge of them was now abandoned. These storekeepers had sometimes made their offices a means of traffic for their individual advantage. Their duties were now vested in the paymasters of the navy, and storeships took the place of storehouses. Changes were also made in

[76] Ann. Rept. of Sec. of N., 1865, ix-x.
[77] Ann. Rept. of Sec. of N., 1868, 71-72.

the number and distribution of the naval squadrons. The Mediterranean and African squadrons were supplanted by the European squadron, whose cruising grounds included the Mediterranean and the west coast of Africa. The Brazil squadron was renamed the South Atlantic squadron. The Pacific Ocean was divided between two squadrons. The cruising grounds of the Asiatic squadron were made to include the waters off the East African coast; and those of the former home squadron were divided between the North Atlantic and the Gulf squadrons.[78]

By October, 1866, the number of enlisted men in the navy had fallen to 13,600. One year later this number had been further reduced to 11,900. At the close of the war several rendezvous and recruiting stations were discontinued. In 1865 most of the volunteer officers were honorably discharged, and they returned peaceably to their homes and occupations. During the war a disposition was manifested to reward the most efficient volunteers by giving them permanent commissions in the regular navy. This step was recommended by Secretary Welles in his annual report for 1863. The same subject came up again after the war, and it was decided that in view of their faithful and meritorious conduct the volunteers should be rewarded. This decision was not favorably regarded by some of the regular officers, between whom and the volunteers considerable rivalry and jealousy existed. On July 25, 1866, an act was passed providing that five lieutenant-commanders, 20 lieutenants, 50 masters and 75 ensigns might be appointed to the line of the navy from those volunteer officers who had served not less than two years and who had been honorably discharged or were still in the service. The act further provided that a board of naval officers should examine the candidates and select those who were most meritorious in character, ability, professional competency and honorable service. Welles at once appointed the board, with Commodore S. P. Lee as senior member. It began its delicate and arduous task at Hartford, Connecticut, on September 5, 1867, and continued to sit at intervals for more than a year. The first names that it recommended were sent by President Johnson to the Senate in December, 1867; these were followed in 1868 by other names.[79]

[79] U. S. Statutes at Large, XIV, 222-223; Ann. Rept. of Sec. of N., 1866, 31, 151; 1867, 22-23, 117.

[78] Ann. Rept. of Sec. of N., 1866, pp. 12-22.

Positions for the fortunate volunteers were created in the lower ranks by increasing the total number of commissioned officers of the navy and by promoting the regular officers. The act of July 25, 1866, increased the number of rear-admirals from 9 to 10, commodores from 18 to 25, captains from 36 to 50, commanders from 72 to 90, lieutenant-commanders and lieutenants, each, from 144 to 180, and masters and ensigns, each, from 144 to 160. The regular officers were promoted to fill the additional numbers in the several grades in accordance with their merit. This act created also one additional rank, that of admiral. But a single officer was established in it. He was paid an annual salary of $10,000 and was permitted a secretary. Farragut was at once appointed to the new position, which was designed for him, and Porter succeeded Farragut as vice-admiral.[80]

The above act led to the rapid advancement of many young officers, even to the rank of lieutenant-commander. The naval staff did not fare as well as the line. After the war 50 additional paymasters were authorized and the naval constructors and the first and second assistant engineers were made commissioned officers. As no increases were made in the medical and engineer corps, the surgeons and the engineers felt that justice had not been done them. By the promotion of many young men of the line, the rank of their fellow-officers of the staff was relatively decreased. Rather than bear this indignity, some of the ablest engineers resigned from the navy. Of this class, Robert H. Thurston, the late director of Sibley College, Cornell University, was a conspicuous example. There were much strife and rivalry between the several corps for honors, preferment and increased pay.[81]

In 1866 the number of men in the marine corps was about 3600. By October, 1868, this number had been reduced to about 2700. As yet no new barracks had been erected in place of those destroyed by the Confederates at the Norfolk and Pensacola navy-yards. In 1869 the commandant of the marine corps was given the rank and pay of a brigadier-general of the army.[82]

The experiences of the war demonstrated that most of the navy-yards were too limited in area for the needs of the navy.

[80] U. S. Statutes at Large, XIV, 222-223.
[81] Bennett, Steam Navy, 607-608.
[82] U. S. Statutes at Large, XIV, 517.

In 1865 Welles said that none of them presented the requisite conveniences and facilities for fitting out in a rapid and efficient manner more than a single vessel at a time, and that with the exception of the yards at Mare Island and Norfolk not one of them had sufficient room to erect the works necessary for its present wants. He endeavored to increase the areas of the Northern yards, and small additions were made to those at Philadelphia, New York and Boston. In April, 1866, Congress appropriated $105,000 for the purchase of Seavey's island, near the Portsmouth navy-yard. This was at the rate of $1000 an acre, a much larger price than private individuals would have paid. In 1867 a navy board prepared plans for the island's improvement. During the same year the Bureau of Ordnance acquired from the Surgeon-General of the Navy 15 acres at Chelsea, Massachusetts, for a naval magazine. The attempts to establish a navy-yard on the Mississippi, to which reference has previously been made, failed. The naval station at Mound City, Illinois, however, was continued for several years after the war.

After the cessation of hostilities, Welles continued his agitation in behalf of the acceptance of League Island as a site for a navy-yard adapted to the needs of an iron navy. In 1865 he obtained permission from the city of Philadelphia to lay up in ordinary in the back channel of the island several of the ironclads. Finally, on February 18, 1867, an act was passed authorizing the Secretary of the Navy to accept League Island, provided a board of officers to be appointed by the President should recommend its acceptance. A board, of which Rear-Admiral C. H. Davis was president, was constituted, and it reported unanimously in favor of receiving the gift. Difficulties now arose respecting a title, but these were finally removed, and the island, which contains 923 acres, became the property of the United States in December, 1868.

The friends of New London, who had succeeded in delaying the acceptance of League Island, were rewarded for their perseverance. In the naval appropriation bill of March 2, 1867, under the suspicious heading, "Navy Yard at Washington," was a clause authorizing the Secretary of the Navy to accept a deed of gift, when offered by the State of Connecticut, of a tract of land near New London, with a water front of not less than one mile. This land became the property of the government on June

27, 1868. It was situated three miles north of New London, on the Connecticut River, and contained 80 acres.[83]

Before 1861 a tendency was manifested towards the extension of the bureau system of the Navy Department at Washington to the several navy-yards. The decentralization of administration in the central office led logically to decentralization in the branch establishments. The war seems to have increased this tendency. Each bureau came to exercise more and more control over the facilities for the performance of its work in the navy-yards. On July 1, 1868, Secretary Welles extended the bureau system to the several yards. He discontinued the naval storekeepers and directed them to turn over the stores and materials in their keeping to the local representatives of the several bureaus. The new system, it was believed, would fix the responsibility for the care of the naval stores upon those most interested in their preservation. It was not, however, adapted to secure unity and correlation in the work of the yards.[84]

Welles's experiences during the war led him to believe that the system of making naval purchases through navy agents whose total commissions were limited led to abuses, tended to corrupt the subordinate employees of the navy-yards, and discouraged and drove away honest dealers. In 1865 he discontinued the navy agents, and vested their duties in naval paymasters. The transfer of these places to naval officers caused quite a commotion among the politicians. The office of navy agent was first established in 1776.

Beginning with the fiscal year 1866, the naval expenditures fell off rapidly, but not as fast nor as much as one might have expected. When once the expenditures of a Federal bureau or department are greatly augmented, they never fall quite as far as the old level when the cause of the augmentation ceases to operate. When the war came to an end in the spring of 1865 the department had many contracts with private builders for vessels, engines, ordnance and various naval materials. Many of these had to be carried out. The construction of several ships which were upon the stocks was continued. At this time all prices were abnormally high owing to the depreciation of the currency. The

[83] Ann. Rept. of Sec. of N., 1866, xx; 1867, 18-20; 1868, xxvi; U. S. Statutes at Large, XIV, 396, 489.
[84] Ann. Rept. of Sec. of N., 1868, xxi; Preble, Boston Navy-Yard, 390.

net expenditures of the navy for the fiscal years from 1865 to
1869 were as follows: 1865, $123,000,000; 1866, $43,000,000;
1867, $31,000,000; 1868, $26,000,000; and 1869, $20,000,000.[85]
For a period of peace these expenditures were excessive. In
1867, however, Welles carried to the " surplus fund " $65,000,000.
This was derived from the unexpended balances of naval appropriations and from the sale of vessels and other naval property.

The expenditures of the navy appeared to be extraordinarily
high to the 44th Congress, which met in December, 1867. A
considerable divergence between the naval program of this body
and that of the Secretary of the Navy was soon found to exist.
Welles did not propose to reduce the enlisted force to its numbers
before the Civil War, but wished to keep it at about 15,000 men.
He would enlarge and improve the navy-yards, adapt them to the
needs of an iron navy, and equip them with machinery for the
repair and manufacture of hulls and engines. He would retain
the larger ships and the ironclads, and complete the vessels that
were upon the stocks. On the other hand, the naval program
of the 44th Congress called for a vigorous retrenchment. The
navy was to be reduced, as far as possible, to its old levels. This
Congress therefore fixed the number of the enlisted men at 8500.
It declined to make appropriations for the improvement of the
navy-yards or for the completion of the vessels building in them.
As a result of the new policy, the number of men employed in the
yards was reduced between November, 1867, and July, 1868, from
about 11,000 to about 6300, almost one-half.[86] In accordance
with the wishes of Congress, Welles reduced the naval estimates
of his annual report for 1867 more than $22,000,000. The abrupt-
ness with which this policy was decided upon caused severe
losses to the department. Uncompleted vessels decayed upon the
stocks, the engines that had been built for them were rendered
useless, and the ironclads and other naval property at the yards
greatly deteriorated in value for lack of proper care. This is by
no means the only instance when the navy has suffered from a
want of proper co-ordination and correlation of the work of the
executive and legislative departments of the Federal government.

The period 1865-1869 was a time of confusion in the naval
counsels. Wide differences of opinion upon the problems of

[85] Sen. Ex. Doc., 45 Cong., 1 sess., No. 3, 157.
[86] Congress Letters, XIV, 371-373, 382-393, 437.

naval construction existed. Chief-Engineer Isherwood and his
work were severely criticised by naval officers and other critics.
One of the service journals was outspoken and persevering in its
attacks on him. It is now clear that his critics were more or less
biased, and applied standards of judgment fast becoming obsolete.
In some respects Isherwood and his ships were in advance of
their time. Two of his fast cruisers, the *Wampanoag* and
Ammonoosuc, were commenced in 1863, but were not completed
until several years after the war. After the trial trip of the
Wampanoag, upon which she developed a speed of 17.75 knots
an hour, more than 21 years elapsed before her speed was
equaled by an American naval vessel, the steel cruiser *Charleston* in September, 1889. More than 11 years elapsed before her
speed was equaled by an ocean steamer, the *Arizona.* In 1869
the *Wampanoag* was condemned by a board of naval officers in
a report that is now said to be a " veritable curiosity of professional literature." She never went to sea again, but was permitted to decay at the wharves of the New York navy-yard and
the New London naval station. Finally in February, 1885, she
was sold for three per cent of her original cost.[87]

The scientific work of the navy, which was so important a
feature during the period 1842-1861, was in large part suspended
during the war. Many administrative duties on shore occasioned
by the war, however, fell to the naval officers. The number of
commissioned line officers, active and retired, employed on special
duty in January, 1865, was 92. Thirty-nine engineers were
employed in constructing ships and engines, and 14 were
attached to the Bureau of Steam Engineering. After the war
the scientific work of the navy partially revived. The Hydrographic Office was created, and the Naval Observatory entered
upon its golden era. In 1868 shore-duty as a legitimate employment for naval officers was recognized in a general order of the
department directing that a fixed period of sea-service should be
followed by a similar period of shore-duty and that the two periods
should alternate with each other throughout an officer's active
career. This order has been called the " first step in the decadence of the navy which followed the Civil War.[88]

[87] Bennett, Steam Navy, 553-583.
[88] Davis, Davis, 74.

The subjects of a naval code, rules and regulations for the navy, naval uniform, and assimilated or relative rank received from time to time the attention of the Secretary of the Navy. On July 17, 1862, admonished by the needs of the war, Congress established a new naval penal code. A joint resolution of Congress of March 3, 1863, provided for the appointment of a commissioner to codify the naval laws. Mr. Charles B. Sedgwick, who was selected to fill the new office, completed his work on March 1, 1864. His code consisted of 66 pages, and was very comprehensive. It embraced regulations respecting the organization of the Navy Department, the personnel and matériel of the navy, the Naval Academy, and miscellaneous topics. It, however, failed of adoption.[89] On October 18, 1865, Welles issued a new edition of the naval regulations, comprising 344 octavo pages. In 1862, 1864 and 1866, he issued new editions of the regulations on naval uniform. The regulations of 1866 contained 17 colored plates showing the required articles of dress.

During the administration of Secretary Welles the animosities and jealousies between the line and the staff officers respecting assimilated or relative rank flamed up with increased heat. Ill-feelings had arisen under the enforcement of the orders of the department granting assimilated rank to the surgeons, paymasters and engineers. The staff accused the line of reducing these orders to their lowest terms, and of being unable to discover occasions when they were applicable. On March 13, 1863, Welles issued an order that greatly intensified the feelings between the two classes of officers. He increased the assimilated rank of the surgeons, paymasters and engineers, adapting it to the new ranks of the line established by the act of July 16, 1862. He also specified the occasions when the officers of the line and of the staff should take precedence according to their assimilated rank: " In processions on shore, on courts-martial, summary courts, courts of enquiry, boards of survey, and all other boards." This order was a thorn in the flesh of the line, and they petitioned the Secretary of the Navy to revoke it. Its enforcement undoubtedly might at times produce confusion, for a surgeon on board of a ship might outrank the captain. In 1865 Welles appointed a

[89] U. S. Statutes at Large, XII, 600, 825; House Ex. Doc.. 38 Cong., 1 sess., No. 47.

board, with Vice-Admiral Farragut as president, to consider the rank and pay of the staff, but it accomplished no permanent results. After the war several bills were introduced in Congress giving the staff the recognition that it desired, but they failed of passage. The line was particularly determined to procure the rescinding of Welles's famous order of March 13, 1863, and in 1869 it succeeded.[90]

Part II

The Navy Department Under Grant and Hayes, 1869-1881.

The period 1869-1881 was a time of reaction, naval decline and wide-spread indifference to the needs of the navy. Tired of war and the instruments of war, the country turned its attention to industry and money-making and became apathetic in respect to naval affairs and the national defense. This feeling was naturally shared by Congress and the executive departments. A huge national debt and uncertain public finances admonished the Federal government to be economical in its expenditures. Fortunately, the nation remained at peace, and its unprogressive policy was by no means entirely bad, for when the expansion of the navy came in the last two decades of the nineteenth century advantage could be taken of the great progress made by the European navies in the 20 years succeeding the Civil War. Such was the rapid improvement in naval construction and armament that, had a navy been built in the seventies, it would have been in many respects obsolete in the nineties. The United States ran the risk of defeat in case of conflict, but with its usual good fortune succeeded in avoiding war. If the *Virginius* episode of 1873-1874 had developed into a Spanish-American war, which at one time seemed quite possible, its events would have doubtless been far different from those of the war of 1898 when the nation possessed a modern navy.

During the administrations of Grant and Hayes, party feelings ran high, and often determined the acts of Congress and the executive departments. Under Grant there were considerable politics and corruption in the civil service and extravagance in the administration of the Federal government, and the Navy Department did not escape these evils. Those who were in charge of

<hr />

[90] Clymer, Naval Staff Rank, 20; *Washington Chronicle*, November 16, 1869.

the government were properly blamed for its administrative and legislative abuses. To some extent, however, the evils from which Grant's administration suffered were an outgrowth of the Civil War and the early years of Reconstruction. They struck root during this time of commotion and came to baneful flower in the seventies.

For almost the whole of the period 1869-1881 the navy was administered by Secretaries George M. Robeson and Richard W. Thompson. With the exception of the first three and a half months, Robeson served throughout the whole of Grant's two terms. Thompson came in with Hayes in March, 1877, and resigned some two months before the end of his chief's administration in March, 1881. Robeson's predecessor, Adolph E. Borie, of Pennsylvania, and Thompson's successor, Nathan Goff, of West Virginia, were not in office long enough to have much influence upon the work of the department. The brief administration of Borie, extending from March 9 to June 25, 1869, is, however, noteworthy for the important part played in it by Vice-Admiral David D. Porter.

Borie was somewhat passed the meridian of life, and had no special liking or fitness for his task. He was one of the surprises of Grant's first cabinet, and owed his selection to his friendship with the President. Hugh McCulloch, who was Secretary of the Treasury under Johnson, wrote:

There was a good deal of astonishment at the nomination of Adolph E. Borie to be Secretary of the Navy. When it was understood that his name had been sent to the Senate, the inquiry everywhere was, " Who is Adolph E. Borie " ? Outside of Philadelphia, where he lived, he was unknown, and there he was known only as a citizen of wealth and good social standing. It was reported that only one senator had ever heard of him until his name was read by the secretary. To himself his appointment was as great a surprise as it was to the public. The place was undesired by him. He had no aptitude for the business he was called upon to perform, and he was glad to retire from public life after an experience, if such it could be called, of three months.[91]

On March 9, 1869, Borie took possession of the Navy Department, and in order to make the acquaintance of his chiefs and to gain some notion of the organization over which he was to preside he made the rounds of the bureaus. He was accompanied by

[91] McCulloch, Men and Measures, 350.

Vice-Admiral Porter, and, according to Rear-Admiral John A. Dahlgren, when they reached the Bureau of Ordnance of which Dahlgren was chief, Porter "stepping aside told me that Grant said he should run the machine as Borie's adviser." On March 12 Borie, under the direction of Grant, issued an order to the effect that "all matters relating to the navy coming under the cognizance of the different bureaus will be submitted to Vice-Admiral Porter before being transmitted to the Secretary of the Navy." [92] Porter was also given authority to transact the official business of the department. During Borie's administration many letters issuing from the Secretary's office were signed "David D. Porter, Vice-Admiral, by order of Secretary of Navy," or "For Secretary of Navy." Still other letters, which were signed by the Secretary, were prepared by the Vice-Admiral. For most purposes Porter was the Secretary of the Navy.

With the best of intentions, the Vice-Admiral ran the navy in a somewhat arbitrary and extravagant manner. Basing his act on a decision of the Attorney-General, he cancelled Welles's order of March 13, 1863, in respect to the relative or assimilated rank of staff officers, and added much fuel to a flame that never dies out. He organized boards to inspect the navy-yards and naval vessels, and to make recommendations thereon. He greatly increased the force of artisans and laborers at the navy-yards, and began the repair of numerous vessels—a much-needed work. Many of the steamers were provided with new rigging and were equipped with full sail-power, the use of sails instead of steam being a favorite notion of Porter. He inaugurated an administration of naval reform. Not content to make his reforms gradually, he attempted to introduce within a few weeks various changes in isolated matters, which he had long had at heart. While Gideon Welles issued only five general orders during the last two years of his administration, his successor during his short term issued 45. Porter was the principal author of Borie's orders, which covered a wide range of subjects, and varied somewhat in their usefulness. Professor J. R. Soley says that some of them were "rather fanciful, some of them were ill-timed, and some were distinctly harmful." [93]

[92] Dahlgren, Dahlgren, 642; Congressional Globe, 1870-1871, pp. 69-70.
[93] Soley, Admiral Porter, 458-460; Congressional Record, V, 1868.

Porter was not a successful administrator. His hand was too heavy for the finesse of a skilful and tactful executive. The qualities that win battles at sea are not always those which count for most in the Navy Department. The Vice-Admiral was too good a sailor to make a good landsman. As an administrator, he was often impatient, biased and impracticable. The following extract taken from the diary of Rear-Admiral Dahlgren shows the honest, plain-speaking, bluff, old sea-officer at work in the department: " Porter busy getting documents for the Secretary to sign. I told him I would not remain in the Bureau. Reasons, the report of the Committee. He damned the Committee, and said he would whip them; that I must not think of leaving." [94]

The Vice-Admiral's large exercise of authority naturally aroused much opposition, and on the coming of Robeson in July, 1870, his power and influence rapidly waned. The new Secretary was not willing to efface himself after the manner of the old. Porter soon wiped the dust of the Navy Department from his shoes. In 1876 he testified that he had not been inside the department four times in six years. His position was an anomalous one. While holding the highest rank in the navy, officers of inferior rank as bureau chiefs were much more influential than he. Isolated and neglected, he was forced to stand aloof from the main currents of naval administration. As had Farragut before him, he felt hurt that he was not more consulted and his services more largely utilized by the department.

While Porter from 1871 until his death in 1891 was well removed from the center of naval affairs, his connection with the business of the navy did not entirely cease. On November 16, 1870, Secretary Robeson addressed a letter to him for the purpose of stating more clearly his duties as admiral, to which office he had been promoted on the death of Farragut. Under Porter's supervision were now placed the inspection of ships in commission, of ironclads and wooden vessels laid up in ordinary, and of navy-yards and naval stations. Upon all of these matters the Admiral was directed to report regularly to the Secretary of the Navy. The trial of ships of war under sail and steam were also placed under his direction. In 1881 he was given supervision over the training of apprentices. For many years the Admiral

[94] Ammen, The Old and the New Navy, 461-462; Dahlgren, Dahlgren, 642.

made annual reports to the Secretary of the Navy. In these he discussed with great freedom and fullness the condition of the naval matériel and personnel. He plainly and fearlessly pointed out the lamentable state of the American fleet, and instituted comparisons between it and the navies of Europe showing its great inferiority to them. In the seventies, when the apathy and indifference of Congress and the people in respect to a naval armament were greatest, Porter vigorously and insistently declared the country's need of a new navy. His voice was as one crying in the wilderness.

Borie resigned his office on June 25, 1869, and on the same day George M. Robeson, of New Jersey, was commissioned by the President. As the Senate was not then in session, he was confirmed and recommissioned on December 8. He remained in the department until March 12, 1877, a little less than seven years and nine months. With the exception of Gideon Welles, he served longer than any other Secretary of the Navy. Richard W. Thompson, of Indiana, took charge of the department on March 13, 1877, and resigned his office on December 30, 1880. The careers of neither Robeson nor Thompson had been such as to specially fit them for their naval duties. Robeson was about 40 years of age when he become Secretary of the Navy, and Thompson was 69 years. Robeson came from New Jersey, and owning some land on the seacoast was at least familiar with the look of the sea. Thompson was an Indiana pioneer who had represented his state in its legislature as early as 1834. He enjoys the distinction of being the first fresh-water Secretary of the Navy, since all his predecessors had come from the seaboard states. Robeson was a member of the new school of Republican politicians, and Thompson was originally an old-line Whig. Their reputations and political services had been for the most part confined to their respective states, although Thompson is credited with drafting the national Republican platform of 1876. Robeson was attorney-general of New Jersey when called to the headship of the Navy Department. He had never served in the national legislature. Possibly it was for this reason that he proved so impatient of legislative control. Thompson was a Whig member of the House from Indiana in 1841-1843 and 1847-1849.

It was generally understood that Robeson owed his appointment to the influence upon Grant of Senator A. G. Cattell, of New Jersey. Robeson was a young man, high-strung and of excellent stock. He was a "hale fellow well met," true as steel to his friends, and fond of good living and the pomp of his position in the cabinet. In the Navy Department he was rather easy-going. He held the reins of administration too loosely, and had little aptitude for the details of the navy business. With an inborn desire to please he gave too ready an ear to his friends and the politicians of the capital. He had none of the qualities of a reformer, and was without the capacity to check departmental abuses. He, however, served the navy industriously and had its good at heart. He was much in advance of Congress in his efforts to increase and improve the fleet, and for this reason laid himself open to the charge of violating the law. His administration of the department was severely criticised, and he was made the subject of probably more cartoons than any other man of his time. He was reputed to be a "bad sailor," and they used to tell the story that the waving lines in the old carpet at the White House, presented by the Sultan of Turkey to the President, made him seasick. His knowledge of constitutional law suggested the *mot* attributed to Senator Matthew H. Carpenter that he was a "great constitutional lawyer among sailors, and a great sailor among constitutional lawyers." Hugh McCulloch wrote that the Secretary of the Navy was a "fine speaker and an able lawyer. Mr. Robeson was the most abused member of the cabinet, but the abuse to which he was subjected neither soured his temper nor injured his digestion. He was a hard worker, without being apt in business. If instead of being Secretary of the Navy, he had been Attorney-General, he would have won an enviable national reputation. Talented, genial, warm-hearted, he was and is a favorite wherever he is known." [95]

Secretary of the Navy Richard W. Thompson was somewhat old, slow-moving, conservative, and obedient to the strict and narrow interpretation of the law. He shared with his section of the Union its prejudices against the upbuilding of the navy and in favor of economy in naval expenditures. Since during Hayes's administration the navy in its decline touched its low-water mark,

---

[95] McCulloch, Men and Measures, 352.

it seems fitting that this shrewd and kindly old landsman should at this time have been called from his Hoosier home to preside over its destinies. The late Senator Hoar has left us in the following words an appreciative characterization of Thompson:

> I had great respect for him. He lived in the lifetime of every President of the United States, except Washington, and I believe saw every one of them, except Washington, unless it may be that he never saw Theodore Roosevelt. He was a very interesting character, a man of great common sense, public spirit, with a wonderful memory, and a rare fund of knowledge of the political history of the Northwest. Indeed he was an embodiment of the best quality of the people of the Ohio Territory, although born in Virginia. His great capacity was that of a politician. He made excellent stump speeches, managed political conventions with great shrewdness, and also with great integrity, and had great skill in constructing platforms. Colonel Thompson was a very valuable political adviser. It has never been the custom to select Secretaries of the Navy on account of any previously acquired knowledge of naval affairs, although the two heads of that Department appointed by Presidents McKinley and Roosevelt have conducted it with wonderful success in a very difficult time. A day or two after the inauguration, John Sherman, the new Secretary of the Treasury, gave a brilliant dinner party to the cabinet, at which I was a guest. The table was ornamented by a beautiful man-of-war made out of flowers. Just before the guests sat down to dinner a little adopted daughter of Secretary Sherman attached a pretty American flag to one of the masts. I asked Secretary Thompson across the table to which mast of a man-of-war the American flag should be attached. Thompson coughed and stammered a little, and said: "I think I shall refer the question to the Attorney-General." [96]

In managing the department neither Robeson nor Thompson were as forceful as Welles, and Borie was little more than a figure-head. The secretaries of Grant and Hayes failed to give the Navy Department the " executive touch." Under Welles, and especially during the Civil War, the influence of the navy on naval administration, relative to that of the secretariat, declined. During the war comparatively few naval officers were stationed in Washington. The masterful spirits were usually in command of vessels. With the ending of the war, and more particularly with the passing of Welles, the navy reasserted itself in the department. Under Borie it was all-powerful. Although checked under Robeson, it was still strong. The number of officers detailed to duty in the department was large. The chief of the Bureau of Navigation, who since 1865 had been also the head

[96] Hoar, Autobiography, II, 25-26.

of the Office of Detail, was an increasing power in naval administration. The head of this office occupies a strategic position
in the Navy Department. He, with the consent of the Secretary
of the Navy, moves and removes the officers and controls the
naval ships. In the naval firmament he is a star of the first magnitude and rivals the Secretary in brilliancy. Until after the
Spanish-American War, no other officer of the navy compared
with him in power, authority and consequence. Since among the
officers there is much rivalry to obtain good details of duty and
to escape bad ones, they are likely to blame the head of the
Office of Detail for their dissatisfaction over their orders. He
is therefore both feared and hated, and the visits to his office are
usually of an official character only. Since his duties were taken
from those of the secretariat, the power and influence of the
latter have greatly diminished. The Secretary of the Navy as
a positive force in naval administration has in recent years
greatly waned.

For seven years under Grant and Hayes the position of chief
of the Bureau of Navigation was efficiently, and to the best of
his ability impartially, filled by Rear-Admiral Daniel Ammen.
From 1869 to 1871 Ammen had been chief of the Bureau of Yards
and Docks. His successor in this latter position was Rear-
Admiral C. R. P. Rodgers, who filled it until 1874. In 1871
John Lenthall was succeeded by Isaiah Hanscom as chief of the
Bureau of Construction, who held this office until 1877. The
chiefs of the Bureau of Steam Engineering during the years
1869-1881 were Engineers in Chief James W. King, W. W. W.
Wood, and William H. Shock. Commodore William N. Jeffers
presided over the Bureau of Ordnance from 1873 until 1881.
The services of other chiefs of bureaus during this period were
not especially notable. In 1876 Charles G. McCawley succeeded
Jacob Zeilin as commandant of the marine corps.

During the administration of Grant and Hayes, but few changes
were made in the organization of the Navy Department, and
these were by way of the addition of new machinery. On the
discontinuance of the judge-advocate general of the navy in 1870,
his duties were vested in a naval solicitor, who was attached to
the Department of Justice. This arrangement lasted for ten
years. On June 8, 1880, a statute was passed authorizing the
President to appoint for a term of four years a judge-advocate

general of the navy from the officers of the navy or marine corps.[97] He was to have an office in the Navy Department, and was to receive the rank, pay and allowances of a captain of the navy or a colonel of the marine corps. His duties were to receive, revise and record the proceedings of all courts-martial, courts of enquiry and boards for the examination of officers for retirement and promotion. He was also to perform such other services as had been heretofore performed by the solicitor and naval judge-advocate. On June 8 President Hayes appointed Colonel William B. Remey, of the marine corps, to the new office, who served as Judge-Advocate General for twelve years.

In 1869 the chief signal office was organized and attached to the Bureau of Navigation. The principal duties of the chief signal officer of the navy were the preparation of signal books and codes and the instruction of young officers in signaling. In 1873 Secretary Robeson established in the same bureau the office of the superintendent of compasses, and gave it charge of the inspection and improvement of compasses and the determination of their deviation and variation. In 1870 or 1871 the board of inspection was organized to inspect the various vessels of the navy and to make reports upon their condition. In 1871 the board for the examination of officers for promotion and the board for the examination of officers for retirement, which had been organized by Secretary Welles, were consolidated.

In 1877 Professor Simon Newcomb, U. S. N., became superintendent of the Nautical Almanac Office, which since 1866 had been located in Washington, and for 20 years he filled this position with great ability and distinction. In his " Reminiscences of an Astronomer," Newcomb gives a most interesting account of the work and personnel of his office. On assuming his duties in 1877, he obtained more commodious quarters for the office, reduced the prices paid for computations, and removed two employees for inefficiency. One of these latter was a proof-reader, who occupied a high position in the Grand Army of the Republic and was " excellent in every respect except that of ability to perform his duty." Some of the most difficult and recondite of the mathematical studies of the office were made by Mr. George W. Hill, " who will easily rank as the greatest

[97] U. S. Statutes at Large, XXI, 164.

master of mathematical astronomy during the last quarter of the nineteenth century." Newcomb says that he never worked harder with a superior than he did " with Hon. R. W. Thompson, Secretary of the Navy, about 1880, to induce him to raise Mr. Hill's salary from $1200 to $1400. It goes without saying that Mr. Hill took even less interest in the matter than I did. He did not work for pay, but for the love of science. His little farm at Nyack Turnpike sufficed for his home, and supplied him necessities so long as he lived there, and all he asked in Washington was the means of going on with his work." [98]

On March 15, 1877, Secretary Thompson organized a board, consisting of the chiefs of the several bureaus of the department to reform the business of the bureaus and to correlate their work. The creation of this board is quite significant. For many years the Navy Department had developed by differentiating its functions. An attempt was now made by Thompson to unify its parts. The new board was to meet twice a week, and was to be presided over by the Secretary of the Navy. At its meetings the chiefs were to lay before it statements of the business of their bureaus, which were to be open for discussion. The board was also to consider the employment of men in the navy-yards. The new organization effected little, for the centrifugal forces of the department were too much for it. [99]

Throughout the period 1869-1881 attempts were made in Congress to create a permanent board of naval officers that should occupy a position in the administrative hierarchy between the chiefs of bureaus and the Secretary of the Navy. A considerable agitation for the creation of such a board was conducted in and out of the navy and the department. It is recollected that there was a similar agitation under Secretary Welles. The duties of the proposed board were not always clearly defined. It was to advise the Secretary of the Navy in professional matters, and especially in respect to the building, furnishing and equipping of the fleet. It was to review the action of the bureaus, and was to " harmonize and concentrate " their work. The line officers of the higher ranks, especially Farragut, Porter and Rowan, were chiefly interested in the project. Farragut thought that the

[98] Newcomb, Reminiscences, 214-233.
[99] General Orders and Circulars 1863 to 1887, p. 156.

board should be called the " Board of Admiralty," and should be composed of officers not below the grade of rear-admiral. Various bills were introduced in Congress embodying the views of the friends of the proposed organization. But whether it was called a board of admiralty, board of navy commissioners, board of survey, or board of assistants, it proved equally distasteful to the majority of the members of Congress. One measure, however, passed the Senate, but failed in the House. This was the famous Grimes Bill, which caused great commotion in the navy and the department in 1869. Secretary Robeson recognized that there was need of a board to correlate the action of the bureaus, but thought that it should be " wholly advisory, and without the power of interfering with the action of the Executive or his responsible representative." Secretary Thompson insisted that, if a board were created, it should be entirely responsible to himself. The secretaries did not favor the establishment of an organization that would encroach upon their powers. The staff officers were opposed to the proposed measures, since they regarded them as drawn in the interest of the line officers, who, they thought, were attempting to seize the reins of control in the department.[100]

It may be worth while to speculate upon the effects on the organization of the Navy Department of such a navy board as that contemplated by Farragut. Had it been established in 1869, it would in all probability have acquired by this time a position of commanding influence in the work of the department, if not one of dominant control. Composed of officers of the highest rank, and occupying a strategic position, it could hardly have been confined to the exercise of wholly advisory powers. Under the laws of departmental growth and of administrative absorption and accretion of powers, it must have gradually increased its duties and authority. The actual powers of the Secretary of the Navy would have been diminished, and the influence of the navy and especially of its chief officers in the department would have been augmented. The bureau chiefs could not have held their own against the new organization. The ear of the Secretary of

[100] Ann. Rept. of Sec. of N., 1869, 24-25; Congressional Globe, 1869-1870, p. 5329; Congressional Record, III, 217; IV, 2861, 3761; VII, 4467; House Miscl. Doc., 41 Cong., 2 sess., No. 33; House Ex. Doc., 41 Cong., 2 sess., No. 171; House Miscl. Doc., 44 Cong., 1 sess., No. 170, pt. 8, answers to circular letter.

the Navy must have gradually become inaccessible to all advice emanating from officers outside of the board. The department would have doubtless received what it has for a long time needed, a correlation and unification of its parts, and a larger element of permanence, continuity and technical knowledge at its apex.

During the period 1869-1881 the number of officers on duty in Washington increased rapidly. In January, 1869, the number of line officers of the active list employed at the capital was about 15. Fifteen years later, in January, 1884, this number had increased to 102; at the same time the staff officers in Washington numbered 59. These officers were employed at the Navy Department, Washington navy-yard, Hydrographic Office, Naval Observatory and "on special duty in Washington." The civil employees of the Navy Department at the capital also steadily increased. The Blue Books show that their number, exclusive of the employees at the Washington navy-yard, was 111 in 1869, and 222 in 1881—or exactly twice as many. The number of clerks increased during this period from 57 to 109. The number of regular employees of the eight bureaus changed but little. The increases occurred chiefly in the Secretary's office and the Hydrographic Office, and in the force of caretakers of the Navy Department building. The actual growth of the work of the department during 1869-1881 did not keep pace with the augmentation of the department's personnel.[101]

During the administration of Hayes the Navy Department occupied its new quarters, situated in the State, War and Navy Building in Washington, near the White House, on Pennsylvania avenue. This large structure is located on the site and grounds of the old buildings of the War and Navy Departments. It is a huge towering pile of granite, and is said to be honestly admired by the populace, but condemned by the architectural critics. It was designed by Mr. A. B. Mullett, when supervising architect of the treasury. Its style is that of the Italian Renaissance. Its four façades, which are substantially alike, surround a court, which is divided by a "center wing." The State Department building or south wing was first built, being commenced in 1871. The last wings were completed in 1888, when the whole building

---

[101] Navy Register, 1869 to 1881; Official Register of U. S., 1869 to 1881; House Ex. Doc., 48 Cong., 1 sess., No. 125, 19-21; Sen. Ex. Doc., 47 Cong., 1 sess., No. 17.

was for the most part finished. It covers four and one-half acres, contains two miles of corridors, and cost about $11,000,000.

The Navy Department occupies the east wing which faces the White House. On June 10, 1872, Congress appropriated $400,-000 to begin the construction of this wing, which was shortly commenced under the direction of the supervising architect of the treasury. After the expenditure of $923,000, it was stopped. On March 3, 1875, Congress placed the undertaking under the charge of the Secretary of War, and the work was resumed under the direction of a member of the engineer corps of the army. With the exception of the library of the department, the east wing was completed in the spring of 1879, and a year later the library was turned over to the Secretary of the Navy. The total cost of the east wing was $2,672,287. The only wood used was for the doors, floors, and interior furnishings. All other parts were constructed of stone, brick, concrete, plaster, iron, copper and glass. The length of the east wing is 341 feet, depth at the curtains 62 feet, and height from sidewalk 135 feet. The total number of rooms of all sorts is 173. There are seven floors—sub-basement, basement, first, second, third and fourth stories, and " cockloft." Two elevators afford easy communication. The library is finished and ceiled entirely in iron, and in a most artistic manner. The walls are of iron, inlaid with 32 marble panels. The green marble used in the construction of the panels is malachite, from the Alps; the yellow, sienna, from Italy; and the red, porphyry, from France. The conglomerate is from Lake Champlain. The floor is inlaid with Minton tiling. There are allegorical figures in the corners of the room representing " War and Peace," " Liberty," " Industry and Mechanics," " Literature, Arts and Commerce." [102]

The east wing was occupied by the Navy Department during 1878-1880. The Bureau of Steam Engineering was the first and the naval library the last to move to the new quarters. It was decided that the Navy Department should temporarily share its building with the War Department. On the afternoon of April 16, 1879, Thomas Lincoln Casey, lieutenant-colonel of the corps of engineers of the army, formally turned over the east wing to the Secretary of the Navy and the Secretary of the War, and

[102] Ann. Rept. of Sec. of War, 1876, p. 366; 1878, pp. 477-484; 1879, pp. 449-459; 1880, pp. 567-568; Description of Library for Visitors.

deposited its keys with them.   Casey furnished the Secretary of the Navy with twelve drawings and an explanatory memoir setting forth the arrangements respecting the supplies of water and gas, systems of heating and ventilation, telegraph service and sewerage.   A brief notice of the transfer of the building to the departments was given by the *Washington Star* of April 17, 1879:

Shortly after three o'clock yesterday afternoon Colonel Casey, superintendent of public buildings and grounds, conducted Secretaries Thompson and McCrary, and Chief Clerks Hogg and Crosby through the new wing of the new State, War and Navy Department building, and formally turned that portion of the building over to them.   The two Secretaries were much pleased with the new quarters they are to occupy, which are much more commodious and by far more elegant than those they now have.   Secretary Thompson says that perhaps his new room is a little too elegant and luxurious.[103]

---

[103] *Washington Star,* April 17, 1879.

CHAPTER NINE: BETWEEN TWO WARS, 1869-1897

Naval Ships and Congressional Investigations, 1869-1881.

The duties that fell to the navy during the peaceful administrations of Grant and Hayes were not specially important. Its vessels made the usual cruises in foreign waters for the protection of American property, commerce and citizens. A few of them were engaged now and then in making hydrographic surveys or in performing other scientific tasks. The fleet was regularly divided into the North Atlantic, South Atlantic, European, Pacific and Asiatic squadrons, and "vessels on special service," but at times the North Atlantic and Pacific squadrons were each divided into two divisions.

Twice during Grant's first administration a war with Spain seemed imminent. The war-scare of 1875, which has now been generally forgotten, soon subsided, but not until the department had concentrated a fleet at Port Royal, South Carolina, and had ordered home some of its ships from Europe and South America. The war-scare of 1873-1874, known as the *Virginius* episode, is probably familiar to most readers. A notion of the extent of the warlike preparations that were then made by the Navy Department may be obtained from a letter of Secretary Robeson to James A. Garfield, chairman of the House Committee on Appropriations. On December 8, 1873, Robeson wrote: " I have taken measures to put every available iron and wooden ship of our Navy in condition for immediate duty. I have ordered all the ships of the various squadrons within reach to rendezvous at Key West. I am enlisting men to supply and fill up the crews of all our vessels.

I have accumulated materials, provisions and supplies for their maintenance and support, and ordnance, ammunition and all the weapons of naval warfare for their use." [104]

Early in 1874 the differences between the two governments were settled by peaceful means, and the navy and the department settled down to that state of passivity and stagnation which generally characterized them at this time. The panic caused by the *Virginius* episode cost the department some $5,000,000, an expenditure for which no adequate return was received. The assemblage of a fleet, however, served to reveal the extreme weakness of the matériel of the navy. Rear Admiral Robley D. Evans says that the force which was collected at Key West in the winter of 1873-1874 " was the best, and indeed about all, we had. We had no stores, or storehouses to speak of at this so-called base of supplies, and if it had not been so serious it would have been laughable to see our condition. We remained several weeks, making faces at the Spaniards ninety miles away at Havana, while two modern vessels of war would have done us up in thirty minutes. As there was to be no war, the authorities in Washington allowed the foreign attachés to come and inspect us, and report our warlike condition to their different governments. We were dreadfully mortified over it all, but we were not to blame; we did the best we could with what Congress gave us." Several weeks were spent by the squadron in fleet maneuvers before its vessels separated. [105]

Owing to the *Virginius* episode the annual expenditures of the Navy Department during the period 1869-1881 reached their highest mark in the fiscal year 1874, when they amounted to $30,859,000. They were lowest in 1880, when they had fallen to $13,537,000. They were much higher under Grant than under Hayes. The annual average expenditures for the eight years 1870-1877 were $21,-709,000; and for the four years 1878-1881, $15,428,000. The total expenditures for the former period were $173,675,000; for the latter, $61,714,000; and for the twelve years, $235,389,000. By counting certain proceeds derived from the sale of vessels and certain payments of money made under Thompson, but really chargeable to Robeson, the minority of a committee of the House of Representatives friendly to Robeson calculated that the expenditures of the Navy Department from July 1, 1869, to June 30, 1877, were

---

[104] Congress Letters, U. S. Navy Dept. Arch., XV, 222.
[105] House Miscl. Doc., 45 C. 3 S., No. 21, 132; Evans, A Sailor's Log, 171.

$186,311,000. According to these figures, the annual expenditures during these eight years were $23,289,000. The chief items of expenditure were " for pay and support of the navy and marine corps," $73,700,000; " for construction and repair and steam engineering," $53,429,000; and " for yards and docks," $18,-714,000.[106]

The navy cost the country considerably more money during the eight years of Grant's administration than during the eight years 1884-1891 when the new navy was under construction. During the seventies Congress was indifferent to naval affairs, rather than parsimonious in its naval expenditures. It gave liberally for the maintenance of the navy, but almost nothing for the construction of new ships. It viewed with unconcern their increasing decay and obsoleteness. Questions of reconstruction, finance, and party success engrossed its attention. The Democratic party was especially committed to the policy of economy in the management of naval affairs. A Democratic House of Representatives, which first came into power in December, 1875, was largely responsible for the reduction in naval expenditures trat was made in the immediately succeeding years. The Democrats succeeded in discrediting Robeson's administration, and in creating a sentiment for reform and retrenchment in the management of the department. During 1877-1881 the navy touched its low-water mark. Indeed, probably less was done for the improvement of the fleet under Hayes than during any administration since that of Jefferson.

Many members of Congress believed that, owing to the large national debt, the country was not able to embark upon a program of naval construction. The opinion was common that the United States should not adopt the policy of building seagoing war vessels after the manner of the European nations, but should confine its construction to coastwise vessels of defense, to monitors, torpedoes and marine rams. This view was well expressed by Senator George S. Boutwell, of Massachusetts, the most seafaring state in the union. In February, 1877, he said in the Senate that he believed that the " time passed several years ago when it was for the interest of this country to make the least preparation for an open sea fight. Anybody who looks at the character and extent

[106] Sen. Ex. Doc., 45 C. 1 S., No. 3, 157; Ann. Rept. of Sec. of Treas., 1877 to 1881; House Rept., 45 C. 3 S., No. 112, 95-97, 109-111.

of this country, the number of its people, and the magnitude of our
influence as a nation, must see that an open sea fight would settle
nothing in any controversy that we might have with any power
upon the face of the globe; and to be expending money year after
year, whether one million a year or ten millions a year, or twenty
millions a year, with the idea that something is to be gained in
a naval contest, has no foundation in any generous conception of
public policy." He thought that it was not for the " interest of
this country to expend a dollar for naval appropriations directly,
except such as are necessary for coast defenses. To such perfection has the construction of torpedoes and steam-rams been carried
that there is not a navy on the face of the earth which could enter
a harbor that is protected by these modern inventions." If vessels
were to be built, he would construct those of about one thousand
tons each, capable of carrying from eight to ten guns and of out-
sailing the larger ships of war. However, " such is the pre-eminence
of this country to-day, so valuable is it a market for the products
of every nation on the globe, that we can command our rights by
withdrawing our diplomatic representatives from any country on
the face of the earth." [107]

Like Boutwell, many of the naval experts in Congress and some
of the secretaries of the navy pinned their faith to torpedoes,
marine rams, submarine batteries and smooth-water monitors;
the " monitor heresy " was still vigorously thriving. Even these
minor craft were not regarded as essential by the more rhetorical
and sentimental members of the House, for they were able to discover an adequate naval defense in the great moral force of the
American people, and in the intelligence, industry and ingenuity
of the most powerful nation on the face of the globe. Senator
John Sherman, of Ohio, once suggested that the Navy Department
might well be made a bureau of the War Department.[108] By no
means, however, were all the members of Congress opposed to
an offensive seagoing fleet, and especially during Hayes's
administration did sentiment in behalf of the reconstruction
of the navy increase. Indeed, the naval committees of Congress outran the Secretary of the Navy in recommendations for
the construction of new vessels. Neither Secretary Thompson
nor President Hayes took an aggressive stand on this question.

[107] Congressional Record, V, 1867.
[108] Congressional Globe, 1869-1870, p. 5329.

Hayes seemed to have almost forgotten that his country had a
navy. Grant, on the other hand, was more interested in naval
matters, and was somewhat inclined to improve the fleet.[109]

Robeson was more favorably disposed towards rebuilding and
modernizing the navy than Thompson, although his utterances
were not wholly consistent. In his first annual report he earnestly
urged the building of seagoing ironclads. In the midst of the
Virginius episode he said that " recent events have demonstrated
to all that the great immediate military necessity of this nation is
seaworthy war vessels, adequate to contend with those of other
nations, and well-armed and completely equipped for cruising or
fighting." On the other hand, in his last report he conceived that
we might " well dispense, for the present at least, with the heavy-
armored and unwieldy ironclads of European nations, and also
with the monster cannon necessary to penetrate them." [110] Robeson,
however, never balked at large naval expenditures, and he often
stretched the law in order to obtain money for the construction
of new ships. Thompson, on the other hand, made no clear-cut
recommendations in behalf of a new navy. His reports contain
long-winded discourses, in which he attempts to show that the
navy and the mercantile marine are mutually advantageous to
each other. From these, by proper industry, one may obtain the
notion that he wished to have some new ships added to the fleet,
sometime, when the public finances would permit it.

Not a few of the older naval officers pointed out to the proper
authorities the weakness of our naval defense. They instituted
comparisons showing that the American navy was yearly falling
farther and farther behind the European navies in type and
number of vessels, ordnance, and general condition of the whole
naval matériel. They made it clear that the large list of vessels
in the Navy Register was in reality a paper fleet, and that it would
be of little service in time of war. No one person did so much
to call attention to the actual state of the navy as Admiral Porter.
Never inclined to mince his words, he expressed his views with
great bluntness and vigor. In 1874 he declared in his annual
report to Secretary Robeson that " there is not a navy in the
world that is not in advance of us as regards ships and guns, and I,

[109] Richardson, Messages and Papers, VII, 40, 108, 196-197.
[110] Ann. Rept. of Sec. of N., 1869, p. 13; 1876, pp. 6-7; Sen. Miscl. Doc.,
43 C. 1 S., No. 40.

in common with older officers of the service, feel an anxiety on the subject which can only be appreciated by those who have to command fleets and take them into battle." Moreover, " if called upon at this time to command the naval forces of the United States, in case of hostilities, a position which it is my ambition and my right to fill, I should be put to my wit's end to succeed with such an incongruous set of vessels as we now possess. Prudence would probably recommend that they be shut up in port and no fleet operations attempted with them—sending the wooden vessels abroad singly to do all the damage possible until captured by the enemy ; our 50-gun frigates perhaps succumbing to a 2-gun clipper armed with 10-inch rifles, and our smaller cruisers driven off by merchant vessels carrying rifle guns of lesser caliber." Porter said that " it would be much better to have no navy at all than one like the present, half-armed and with only half-speed, unless we inform the world that our establishment is only intended for times of peace, and to protect the missionaries against the South Sea savages and eastern fanatics." Of all the vessels on the navy list he considers serviceable only 39 wooden ships of war and 6 monitors. " One such ship as the British ironclad *Invincible*," he declared, " ought to go through a fleet like ours and put the vessels *hors de combat* in a short time, for she could either run them down or destroy them at long range with her heavy rifled guns. We have no ordnance that would make any impression on such a ship at a distance of over six hundred yards, and no vessel of equal speed in our navy would be placed under her fire by a prudent commander." [111]

The period of 1869-1881 was one of differences of opinion among both naval amateurs and experts. This was in part doubtless inevitable, for a revolution, or several revolutions, were going on in naval science. The contests between wood and iron, and between iron and steel, as materials for the construction of ships ; between steam and wind as motive powers ; between armored and unarmored ships ; between ordnance and armor ; and between ships and torpedoes, were all still undecided. Robeson was much criticized for the kind of vessels that he built. But he doubtless followed the best light that he could obtain. The policy which the government should have pursued under Robeson and Thompson is precisely

[111] Ann. Rept. of Sec. of N., 1874, pp. 198-202.

the one which it later followed under Chandler and Whitney. It should have disposed of its worthless ships and of the huge quantities of old naval materials dating from the Civil War that encumbered the naval yards and stations. The running expenses of the navy under Robeson should have been reduced one-third, and this saving should have been expended for ships and guns of the most approved models. Had the government waited until the art of naval construction reached a static condition it would, even up to the present time, have constructed no new ships.

The total number of vessels in the navy in March, 1869, was 203; and in January, 1881, 139. This reduction, which was made almost entirely during 1869-1877, was caused by the loss of vessels at sea, by the sale of those that were obsolete or worthless for naval purposes, and by the breaking up of old ships for the uses of new. The number of vessels kept in commission was about fifty. Some notion of the character of these vessels may be obtained by considering the qualities of the flagships of the squadrons in 1876. They were all wooden, screw-propelled steamers with auxiliary sail-power. The *Franklin*, built in 1853, was a first-rate ship, with a tonnage of 3173 tons. The *Brooklyn, Hartford, Richmond* and *Pensacola* were second-raters and sister ships, dating from 1857 and having a tonnage of about 2000 tons. The *Tennessee*, which was of a later date, mounted twenty-three guns and had a tonnage of 2135 tons.

Congress authorized not a single vessel during the administration of Thompson, and only ten small craft during that of Robeson. In March, 1871, six hundred thousand dollars were appropriated towards the construction of two small iron-plated torpedo boats. These craft were completed in 1874, and were the first of their class in the American navy. The two boats, which were named the *Intrepid* and *Alarm,* were built experimentally and were only moderately successful. The *Alarm* was constructed from plans designed by Admiral Porter. Her dimensions were: Length, including a ram thirty feet long, 173 feet; breadth, 28 feet; and depth of hold below the spar deck, 13 feet. After modifications had been made in her machinery, the *Alarm* was considered well adapted in many respects for the service for which she was designed. In the seventies the science of torpedoes and torpedo-boats was in its infancy. Rear-Admiral Evans is of the opinion that most of the torpedoes manufactured at this time were

" good only for newspaper stories, or to scare timid people with." [112]

In 1873, in accordance with an act of Congress, the construction of eight small steam vessels-of-war was commenced. These, together with the two torpedo-boats, were the only vessels authorized by Congress during the years 1864-1881. Their total cost was less than one-half that of a modern battleship. Three of the eight ships ordered in 1873 had a tonnage of 541 tons each; four of 615 tons each; and one, the *Trenton,* of 2343 tons. The *Trenton* was a wooden frigate, and when completed was considered the finest ship in the navy. The other seven vessels were either iron or wooden gunboats. Of the eight ships, three were built by the department, and five by private builders. Two or three small vessels were purchased during Robeson's administration. [113]

Most of the vessels added to the navy during the Civil War were built under the stress of a great emergency and were not adapted for permanent acquisitions to the fleet. Unseasoned timbers, imperfect fittings and faulty machinery were often used in their construction. As a consequence they rapidly deteriorated. The keeping up of a navy of this sort inevitably absorbed large sums of money. Old patches were continually repatched. The repairs of the *Madawaska* (or *Tennessee*), within fifteen years after she was completed, almost equaled in cost the original value of the ship, $1,856,000. In 1883 the ninety-two best vessels of the navy had cost for repairs more than their original cost of construction. For many years old worthless hulks in ordinary stood rotting at the wharves or remained upon the stocks unfinished, until the expense of their maintenance exceeded several times their actual value. Robeson spent millions of dollars in repairing and rebuilding ships, and at the end of his administration had nothing to show for his work but an obsolete fleet in poor condition. Under him the two principal working bureaus of the Navy Department, Construction and Repair, and Steam Engineering, spent more than $6,000,000 a year. Under Thompson they spent about one-half of that sum. During the administration of the latter the condition of the fleet rapidly deteriorated. Moreover, Robeson could blink long stretches of authority, while Thompson refused to over-

[112] Hamersly, Naval Encyclopedia, 815; Evans, A Sailor's Log, 172-173.
[113] House Ex. Doc., 44 C. 1 S., No. 116.

look the plain letter of the law. Robeson, therefore, was able to add several new vessels to the fleet under the disguise of repairing old ones. In June, 1882, speaking of the navy under Thompson, Robeson said in a speech in the House of Representatives, of which body he was then a member, that $73,000,000 had been spent for the navy in the last five years and that not one ship had been launched, except the *Nipsic,* which he had finished, and not one new gun had been put afloat.[114]

Beginning in 1872 Robeson thoroughly overhauled fifteen or sixteen of the single-turreted monitors, dating from the Civil War. Some of their principal wooden parts were taken out and iron was substituted. This work went on in 1873 and 1874 under the added stimulus of the *Virginius* episode. A part of the $4,000,000 which Congress appropriated to meet the extraordinary expenses incurred at this time was used in the repairing of these ironclads. Robeson was much criticised for this expenditure as being a waste of money, but under the circumstances of the time it was proper and advisable. The repairs of these ironclads seem to have come within the law, notwithstanding that they were quite extensive.

Still more extensive were the " repairs " that Robeson made to certain old wooden ships. In this case his authority to perform the work is, to say the least, questionable. The " repairs " consisted of the construction of new ships under the guise of repairing old ones. Often it would have been more economical to have sold the old vessels, as it cost more to tear them up than their materials were worth. But under the circumstances such a disposition was wholly out of the question, for it involved the erasing of their names from the list of naval vessels, and these must be preserved at all hazards in order to maintain the fiction of making repairs. Robeson said that this method of repairing ships had been long followed by the department. The old historic ship *Constitution,* for instance, had several times been rebuilt in this way. Moreover, he conceived that it was to the navy's advantage, for in the end it obtained a new vessel, instead of an old one with innumerable patches. Granting this, it did, however, seem to be stretching the law almost to the breaking point, when the " repairing " of an old vessel, perchance at the time many miles away,

[114] Sen. Ex. Doc., 48 C. 1 S., No. 48; Congressional Record, XII, 5522.

was commenced by laying down a new ship of a somewhat different model from that of the old. Of course the great advantage of Robeson's system was that the navy acquired new vessels, notwithstanding Congress was unwilling to authorize them. To be repaired in this way Robeson selected a ship for each of the seven principal navy-yards: at Portsmouth, the *Marion;* Boston, the *Vandalia;* New York, the *Swatara;* Philadelphia, the *Quinnebaug;* Washington, the *Nipsic;* Norfolk, the *Galena;* and Mare Island, the *Mohican.* Several other vessels Robeson so thoroughly repaired that they lacked but little of being made into new ships. Of course this work was expensive. In the end you had a new ship, it is true, but one of an old and possibly obsolete model.[115]

On the recommendation of Robeson, Congress on June 23, 1874, authorized the Secretary of the Navy to use the balance of an appropriation for a floating dry dock, amounting to about $900,000, for the purpose of " completing the repairs " of four double-turreted monitors, *Miantonomoh, Monadnock, Terror,* and *Amphitrite.* These vessels, which were built during the Civil War, were considered very formidable ships and valuable for either coast defense or deep-sea navigation. The *Miantonomoh* had visited Europe, and the *Monadnock* had made the voyage to San Francisco by way of Cape Horn. Robeson decided to thoroughly " repair " them, putting into the new vessels but few materials of the old. The names of the latter, however, were to be carefully saved for the use of the new ships. Iron hulls were to be substituted for the old wooden ones. The new monitors were to be larger than the old, and were to be more heavily armored and to be fitted with better machinery. Robeson contracted with each of four private shipbuilders to build one of the new ships. He also concluded to " repair " the single-turreted monitor *Puritan,* the construction of which had been begun by John Ericsson in 1862, but had not been completed.

The Secretary of the Navy contracted with John Roach, a famous shipbuilder of Chester, Pennsylvania, to construct the new *Puritan* and *Miantonomoh.* To cut down the expense of building these two ships, he turned over to Roach the old *Puritan* and ten old monitors and steamships of little value. For the old iron in these vessels Roach allowed Robeson one and three-fourths

---

[115] Bennett, Steam Navy, 632-636, 647-648.

cents a pound. In a similar way the new *Amphitrite* and *Terror,* after swallowing up the original ships of these names, absorbed several other useless naval hulks. For this bartering of old ships, the Secretary of the Navy was severely criticised, and many members of Congress considered it illegal, since there was a law directing that the proceeds arising from the sale of old ships should be turned into the federal treasury. A legal disposition, however, did not serve the purpose of the Secretary, since thereby the navy would have lost the use of the old ship, the proceeds derived from its sale, and especially its name invaluable for keeping up the fiction of "making repairs." Robeson thought the end justified the means.

After its first appropriation of some $900,000 Congress refused to vote money for the reconstruction of the ironclads. Robeson, however, continued the work, as best he could, with money drawn from the appropriation for the "repair of ships." When Congress greatly decreased this appropriation the work on the five vessels came to a standstill. The Secretary of the Navy now resorted to a questionable expedient. On one of the very last days of his administration he contracted for the completion of four of the vessels on the condition that the government should not be bound to pay any money until Congress should appropriate it. The rescinding of these contracts, which were regarded as illegal, was one of the first acts of Secretary Thompson. Congress now proceeded to investigate Robeson's actions in respect to the five monitors, which for several years remained in an unfinished state in the yards of private builders at a heavy cost to the government for rent, and which were not completed until after Hayes's administration.[116]

Secretary Thompson, when new to his office, manifested a strong disposition to obey the letter of the law. Later, after he had felt the temper of Congress and had become aware of the exigencies of the naval service, he resorted to some of the expedients of his predecessor. In 1880 he drew upon the appropriation for the repair of ships in order to complete the construction of some of the "Robeson vessels" and to rebuild the *Lancaster.* Finally, even Congress sanctioned the expensive policy

---

[116] U. S. Statutes at Large, XVIII, 226; House Miscl. Doc., 45 C. 3 S., No. 21, 129-157; Bennett, Steam Navy, 628-629; Ann. Rept. of Sec. of N., 1877, pp. 28-30; House Rept., 45 C. 3 S., No. 112, 102-103.

of rebuilding old ships, although one of its investigating committees had condemned work of this sort for its extravagance. According to Robeson, he either built or effectively repaired forty-two ships. There was indeed real ground for his boast on the floor of the House in 1882 that " every ship that now floats bearing the American flag around the world, every ship that now carries a gun to respond to the demands of your government, was built, rebuilt or substantially repaired by me." For several years these " Robeson vessels " comprised almost the whole of the effective fleet of the United States.[117]

For building new ships under the guise of repairing them, for bartering old vessels on account of new, and for binding the government for the payment of money in excess of appropriations, Robeson was most severely criticised. By no means, however, did his critics stop at these alleged misdemeanors. He was accused of robbing the government in various ways, most especially by levying tolls on the contracts of the department for his personal use. It was said that he gave the navy contracts to favorites, that he maintained sinecures, and that he administered the navy-yards corruptly and inefficiently. He was charged with the illegal payment of old claims against the department and with various violations and evasions of the law ; with purchasing naval materials in excess of naval needs ; with great extravagance in the administration of the navy, and with manifold other frauds, errors, and abuses. For the last five years of his administration rumors of scandals in the Navy Department were current. These were zealously spread and amplified by the Democratic newspapers and the Democratic members of Congress. Whether true or false, they were eagerly pressed into partisan service.

Extensive investigations of Robeson and his administration were made by four committees of the House of Representatives: in 1872, 1876, 1878 and 1878-1879. The evidence taken, information ascertained and reports made by these committees consumed in printing 5675 octavo pages. The investigation of 1872 was made by a select committee, those of 1876 and 1878-1879 by the Naval Committee, and that of 1878 by the Committee on the Expenditures of the Navy Department. A majority of the members of the committees of 1876, 1878 and 1878-1879 were Demo-

[117] Congressional Record, 47 C. 1 S., XIII, 5693.

crats. By far the most extensive investigation was that of 1876. Its printed records contain 3745 pages. Seven sub-committees were appointed and the field of investigation was divided among them. The various navy-yards were visited and more than five hundred witnesses were examined. The hearings before this committee were for the most part not open to the public nor to the Secretary of the Navy.

The investigation of 1872 was undertaken by reason of a series of charges made against Robeson's conduct in office by the New York *Sun*. This newspaper accused him of robbery, theft, crookedness in awarding the naval contracts and other violations of law. It asserted that " this man is one of the greatest public robbers of the day," and that a " rough calculation shows that his robberies do not amount to less than $1,400,000." His frauds and robberies, said the *Sun,* are " almost innumerable." The editor of the accusing newspaper, Mr. Charles A. Dana, was invited by the. investigating committee to appear before it and prove his charges. He was permitted to bring his counsel, to summon and examine witnesses, and to call for papers and documents. Dana himself testified before the committee, but he " totally failed to produce a single witness, or any proof whatever, tending in the slightest degree to maintain the charges he had made, or affect in any manner the personal or official character of the Secretary." Both the Democratic and Republican members of the committee exonerated Robeson from all charges of corruption, fraud and dishonesty. Two members of the committee, however, were of the opinion that the Secretary of the Navy had violated the law, and one of the Republican members considered Robeson's administration of the navy discreditable.[118]

The majority report of the investigating committee of 1876, containing 161 printed pages, was signed by seven Democrats and in a very qualified way by one Republican. It is a highly partisan document and was doubtless prepared with a view to its effect on the presidential election of that year. By means of copious extracts from the evidence and the liberal employment of such words as " frauds," " jobs," " fat contracts," " corruption," " abuses," " errors " and " violations of law," the majority of the

[118] House Miscl. Doc., 42 C. 2 S., No. 201 ; House Rept., 42 C. 2 S., No. 80 ; New York Sun, Feb. 17 to March 11, 1872.

committee gave in the body of their report the impression that
Robeson was undoubtedly guilty of numerous crimes and misdemeanors. Yet, in conclusion, it merely submitted the rather
innocuous resolution that the evidence and the whole subject be
referred to the Committee on Judiciary "to examine and report
whether such violations of the law as are referred to herein constitute and are impeachable offenses under the Constitution, and if
so, then they shall report articles of impeachment against George
M. Robeson, Secretary of the Navy." The Committee on Judiciary, a majority of whose members belonged to the Democratic
party, allowed the matter to drop, and made no report to the
House. It is said, however, that this committee found Robeson
innocent of any criminal intent or corrupt motive. The minority
of the investigating committee, consisting of three Republicans,
presented a brief report, in which it replied to the arguments of
the majority. It recommended the adoption by the House of the
following resolution: "That in this investigation, no fraud, corruption, or wilful violation of the law has been shown or appears
to have been committed by Hon. George M. Robeson while in the
discharge of the duties of Secretary of the Navy; and we find no
reason to censure or find fault with his conduct in the administration of the Navy Department." [119]

The investigation of 1878 was an inquiry into the contracts,
accounts and expenditures of the department under Robeson.
The investigating committee endeavored to find out the amount
and the character of the department's indebtedness. It especially
investigated Robeson's dealings in respect to the double-turreted
monitors. The majority of its members, being Democrats, pronounced many of the acts of the Secretary of the Navy illegal;
and the minority of its members, being Republicans, upheld him.
The investigation of 1878-1879 in general covered the same subjects as those of 1876 and 1878. The Democratic majority of the
committee severely condemned the Secretary of the Navy and
the chiefs of the Bureaus of Steam Engineering, Construction and
Repair, and Provisions and Clothing. The Republican minority
reported that the "administration of the Navy Department by
George M. Robeson and his subordinates, as shown by the testi-

---

[119] House Miscl. Doc., 44 C. 1 S., No. 170; House Rept., 44 C. 1 S., No. 784.

mony taken, is free from fraud, corruption and wilful violation of law." [120]

The findings of the committees of 1876, 1878 and 1878-1879, since their members invariably voted in accordance with their party affiliations, cannot be relied upon. The reports of the minority may be said to cancel those of the majority. The arguments of the reports, and no little of the evidence, being often contradictory, biased and extravagant, is inconclusive. It is not easy to determine what these voluminous investigations prove or disprove in respect to George M. Robeson and his administration of the navy. A few facts, however, are well substantiated. The civil service of the navy-yards was badly demoralized by politics. In making appointments Robeson was exceedingly responsive to the politicians. In many cases where the authority of the Secretary of the Navy was questionable, Robeson resolved the doubt in his own favor. In order to cover the exercise of a doubtful power he greatly stretched the statutes. His administration of the department was weak and extravagant. In the purchase of naval materials there was a considerable leakage of money. Wastes of this sort doubtless often occur. They were certainly greater under Robeson than they would have been under a capable and painstaking executive. That he in any way profited by virtue of his office, the evidence failed to prove. Robeson's relations with a broker, who made a fortune by obtaining naval contracts for himself and his friends, looked very suspicious. A committee of Robeson's political enemies, however, sitting in secret and examining many witnesses, failed to prove that his relations with this broker were corrupt. Robeson did not succeed in correlating the work of the bureaus, in closely supervising them, or in running the department as an efficient machine.

While many men became doubtful of the integrity and honesty of purpose of the Secretary of the Navy, and others were wholly convinced that he was guilty of theft and corrupt practices, he never lost the confidence of his political friends. Shortly after he left the Navy Department the leading Republican citizens of New Jersey tendered him a public dinner as a mark of their " appreciation of his official career and personal worth, and as congratulatory upon the success he had attained in the eminent public station

[120] House Rept., 45 C. 2 S., No. 787 ; House Miscl. Doc., 45 C. 2 S., No. 63 ; House Rept., 45 C. 3 S., No. 112; House Miscl. Doc., 45 C. 3 S., No. 21.

which he had so worthily filled." Senator James G. Blaine was present on this occasion.[121] General Grant regarded Robeson as an intimate friend, and during his memorable tour of the world wrote many letters to his former cabinet officer. In 1878 and again in 1880 Robeson was elected to Congress from New Jersey. During his second term in the national legislature he was one of the most influential members of the House.

Robeson always regarded the investigations of his administration of the navy made by the Democratic committees of the House as inspired by gross partisanship and even personal malevolence. He was especially bitter towards W. C. Whitthorne, of Tennessee, for a time chairman of the House Naval Committee during the naval administrations of Robeson and Thompson. In 1882, in a fierce outburst of feeling, he attacked, on the floor of the House, the personal character of Whitthorne and defended his own management of the navy. Speaking of the period of his administration, he said: "Congressional investigation, with unlimited powers for personal or for party purposes, were then the regular order of the day. Reckless men, inspired with brutish instincts, were clothed with extraordinary powers to penetrate every man's private life and throw open the penetralia of his family circle to the unholy inspection of the vulgar and the malevolent. The Navy Department, of which I was then the head, sustained the full brunt of the fiercest assault. Passing the sphere of legitimate investigation, its tide was turned against myself individually—my father's grave was dishonored, my mother's dowry inquired into, my wife's estate investigated, my children's portions examined. The details of my household life and expenses were under this—how shall I characterize it—most brutal proceeding, held up for the examination of the world." [122]

Offices that were wholly or partly sinecures seem to have flourished under Robeson's administration of the Navy Department to a greater extent than was usual. In Florida twelve agents were employed to guard the growing timber of the navy. Their salaries ranged from $40 a month to $1000 a year. They resided from fifty to one hundred miles from the reservations of timber, which

[121] Daily State Gazette, Trenton, N. J., July 3, 1877.
[122] Congressional Record, XIII, 5694.

none of them had ever seen. Henry Clews, one of the agents, testified before a committee of Congress as follows:

Question. " Are you a timber agent in Florida ? "

Answer. " Yes, sir."

Question. " How far do you live from the timber you are expected to guard ? "

Answer. " I do not know anything about the public domains, and did not try to find out."

Question. " Did you ever see or visit the timber ? "

Answer. " No, sir."

Question. " Did you perform any service under that appointment ? "

Answer. " No, sir ; nothing but draw my pay."

Question. " What was your salary ? "

Answer. " Forty-one dollars a month."

Question. " What is the politics of these agents ? "

Answer. " They are Republicans," [123]

NAVAL STATIONS, OFFICERS AND SEAMEN, 1869-1881.

The investigation of the administration of Secretary Robeson made by the House Naval Committee in 1876 abundantly proved the baneful influence of politics upon the civil service of the navy-yards. It showed that immediately preceding important national or state elections hundreds of additional employees were temporarily employed at the yards. Work or so-called work was found for them until they had voted, and soon thereafter they were discharged. By the express command of Robeson, or the Navy Department at Washington, men were often employed against the wishes or recommendations of the commandants of the yards. The Secretary of the Navy sometimes abolished sinecures, but restored them in response to political pressure. It was common to assess the employees of the yards for political purposes. By virtue of his influence in the Navy Department at Washington the Congressman in whose district a navy-yard was situated exercised a large control in the appointment and retention of employees. Several yards were familiarly named for their controlling Congressman. For instance, the yard at Norfolk was

[123] Congressional Record, IV, 3259.

" Mr. Platt's yard " ; and that at Mare Island " Mr. Sargent's yard." Sargent supervised his naval bailiwick so closely that he procured for a friend an appointment to the insignificant office of " bumboatman," thereby compelling the sailors to purchase their luxuries from his appointee.[124]

The decentralization of the administration of the yards in 1868 by the extension to them of the bureau system increased the political and decreased the naval element in their management. It diminished the power of the commandant and correspondingly increased the power of the bureaus. Vice-Admiral Rowan said that the bureau system " pulled out all the teeth of the commandant " and made him a sort of head postmaster, whose duty was to pass orders between the department at Washington and its representatives in the yards. However, a navy board appointed in 1869 reported that the extension of the bureau system to the yards had resulted beneficially.[125]

During the period of 1869-1881 the condition of the houses, shops, sheds, wharves, docks and machinery of the several navy-yards generally deteriorated. This was especially true under Thompson when the appropriations were much reduced. The expenditures for yards and docks under Robeson amounted to $18,714,000, most of which sum was used for repairs and maintenance, and very little for permanent improvements. The old yards, with their antiquated buildings and appliances, like the old ships, absorbed large sums of money, and in the end had little to show for their outlay. In 1872 the construction of a first-class stone dry dock was commenced at the Mare Island yard, but in a year or two the appropriations for this object were so small that the work languished, and in 1881 the dock was still far from completion. A few valuable buildings were erected at this yard. In 1871 a million dollars were appropriated by Congress for a floating iron dry dock, but Robeson considered this sum insufficient to build the structure, and eventually most of the money was used in rebuilding the double-turreted monitors.

Some permanent works were erected at the League Island navy-yard, which for several years after its acquisition by Secretary Welles remained unimproved. A plan for its development

[124] House Miscl. Doc., 44 C. 1 S., No. 170, parts 1, 2, 3, 4, 6, 7, 8.
[125] Ann. Rept. 'of Sec. of N., 1869, pp. 211-221.

was prepared in 1872 by a board of civil engineers, which was appointed for that purpose. The removal of the public property of the old Philadelphia yard to League Island was begun in 1873, and completed in the winter of 1875-1876. During the removal some of the property was lost, destroyed or stolen, and in the sale of some of the old materials frauds were perpetrated upon the government. Several of the officers who had charge of this work were blamed for a lack of dispatch and executive capacity. The old Philadelphia yard was sold at public auction in December, 1875.[126]

For a long time the removal of the New York navy-yard and the sale of its site were agitated in and out of Congress. Its occupation of valuable grounds in Brooklyn was considered adverse to the interests of that city. By its removal a large tract of land advantageously situated within the limits of the city would be opened up for purposes of residence or trade. The yard was said to be a nuisance, and an impediment to the growth of Brooklyn. The metropolitan newspapers zealously advocated the project. In 1871 the Naval Committee of the House reported a bill providing for the sale of the yard. At first, Robeson and several leading naval officers favored the proposal. They argued that the present site was too small, was incapable of adequate defense and was too near the distractions of a large city. When it appeared, however, that some of the men who were foremost in the agitation were quite willing to discontinue the yard before a new site was obtained, or to give up altogether the notion of having a naval establishment in the vicinity of New York, the Navy Department reconsidered the question and threw its weight against a change. This final stand of Robeson together with the opposition of the chief of the Bureau of Yards and Docks was largely instrumental in preventing the removal or discontinuance of the New York establishment. The friends of the measure, however, succeeded in 1877 in obtaining from Congress an authorization for the conveyance of a certain part of the yard to the city of Brooklyn for a public market.[127]

[126] House Rept., 44 C. 1 S., No. 784, pp. 118-125, 182-183.

[127] Ann. Rept. of Sec. of N., 1869, pp. 18, 73; 1870, pp. 11, 72; 1872, p. 67; 1873, p. 60; 1874, pp. 20, 75; 1877, pp. 20-21; Congressional Globe, 1870-1871, pp. 1063-1067, 1087-1092.

New London continued to urge upon the government her claims for a share of the naval appropriations. In 1870 the department established a naval station upon the site near this city which Secretary Welles had acquired two years before. In 1875 a board of civil engineers reported an elaborate plan for a navy-yard at this point. Since the number of yards was already excessive, the plan was not carried out. In 1873 a board of civil engineers prepared a plan for the improvement and development of the Mare Island yard. Both the Navy Department and Congress were now recognizing the increased importance of the navy to the Pacific states and the need of adequate facilities on the west coast for the repair and equipment of vessels. In 1880 the Naval Committee of the House reported favorably a resolution providing for a navy-yard on the coast of Oregon or Washington.

During the period of 1869-1881 considerable differences of opinion were manifested respecting the general policy to be pursued toward the navy-yards. Congress was strongly disposed to take the view that their number was excessive and that some of them ought to be abandoned. Toward the end of Robeson's administration it began to reduce the appropriations for them. On the other hand, the Navy Department again and again advised the expenditure of more money upon the yards, the erection within them of many needed improvements, their extension by the purchase of additional grounds, and the adapting of some of them to the construction of iron ships. In the spring of 1869, when Admiral Porter was the leading spirit in the department, he appointed a board of line officers, with Rear-Admiral C. K. Stribling as president, to consider the needs of the navy-yards. This board made an elaborate report, containing numerous suggestions respecting the improvement and organization of the chief naval establishments. It found most of the yards entirely too small, and recommended the enlargement of several of them. It did not propose the closing of any of them.[128]

During the seventies a sentiment developed in Congress in favor of closing several of the yards. In 1876 Congress authorized the appointment of a board of five naval officers to examine fully the navy-yards and determine whether any of them could be dispensed with and abandoned. The board was composed of Admiral David

[128] Ann. Rept. of Sec. of N., 1869, pp. 211-221.

D. Porter, Vice-Admiral Stephen C. Rowan and Rear-Admiral Charles H. Davis, a naval constructor and a naval engineer. It recommended that the "navy-yard" at New London should be abandoned, and that the remaining navy-yards should be "not abandoned or dispensed with." Since the establishment at New London was merely a poor and indifferent naval station, the retrenchment advised was a very slight one. The board did not recommend a suspension of any of the activities of the Portsmouth or Boston yards. In case, however, such suspension was for any reason made, it suggested that the two yards should be provided with a sufficient number of officers and employees to render them ready for any emergency. In no case should the ropewalk at the Boston yard be shut down. It recommended the improvement of the establishments at New York, League Island, Norfolk, Washington, Pensacola and Mare Island. The board was really opposed to any retrenchment, but it was disposed to yield something to a contrary sentiment in Congress. In view of the naval policy which Congress pursued for the next twenty years, it doubtless would have been wise to have concentrated the work of the navy at some two or three of the yards. Moved by its instincts for economy, a private corporation under similar circumstances would certainly have consolidated its business and reduced its expenditures.[129]

During the seventies not much was done for the improvement of the naval stations. For a time a small sum of money was spent at New Orleans. From 1861 to 1865 Port Royal, S. C., was one of the most important depots of the navy. During the early seventies it was practically abandoned, but in the late seventies it was revived. In 1876 a navy board considered the establishment there of a naval station. The station at Mound City, Illinois, which had been maintained since the war, was discontinued in 1875. The rivalry between towns for naval favors was not now so great as formerly. Mount Desert, Me., and St. Marys River, Md., however, were thought by interested persons to possess eligible naval sites. In 1880 Secretary Thompson reported that he had taken steps toward the establishment of coaling stations on each side of the Isthmus of Panama, and that he had directed the establishment of a station of this sort on the bay of Pago

[129] U. S. Statutes at Large, XIX, 66; House Ex. Doc., 44 C. 2 S., No. 8.

Pago, Samoa Islands, in accordance with a right granted to the United States under the terms of a recent treaty with those islands. In 1879 the administration of Alaska was assumed by the Navy Department.[130]

In 1869 a torpedo station was established on Goat Island, in Newport Harbor, under the Sperintendence of the Bureau of Ordnance. This island, which contains twenty-four acres, was acquired by the Navy Department by transfer from the War Department in July, 1869. The purpose of the station was to instruct naval officers in the manufacture and use of torpedoes. Its establishment was largely the work of Admiral Porter, and is one of the permanent achievements of his bold and radical administration of the navy. On June 9, 1869, he ordered Commander E. O. Matthews to report for duty under the Bureau of Ordnance as instructor of the torpedo corps of the navy. In the summer of that year Matthews located the site of the school, and in September took possession of Goat Island and commenced the erection of the necessary buildings. An old frame house was converted into a temporary machine shop, and a laboratory and magazine were constructed. A competent chemist was appointed to take charge of the laboratory. In the spring of 1870 the *Nina* was attached to the new station. The first class reported for instruction on November 1 of that year, and consisted of nineteen members. For several years the officers of the navy were not disposed to attend the school. They disliked to resume the tasks and requirements of their school-boy days, nor did they take kindly to the manual work of fitting, laying out and firing torpedoes. But in course of time the school became quite popular. Under Robeson it gave instruction to 153 officers. The instructors were chiefly officers of the navy.[131]

Before and during the Civil War the experimental batteries of the Bureau of Ordnance, which were used in testing guns, gunpowders and fuses, and in fixing the ranges of guns, were located at the Washington navy-yard. Owing to the increasing commerce upon the eastern branch of the Potomac, over whose waters the guns were fired, and to the erection of new buildings near the

---

[130] Ann. Rept. of Sec. of N., 1880, pp. 25-26; Proceedings of U. S. Naval Institute, XVI, 2.

[131] Ann. Rept. of Sec. of N., 1869, p. 68; 1876, p. 113; Miscl. data, Bureau of Yards and Docks, 68-69; Hamersly, Naval Encyclopedia, 816.

navy-yard, these batteries had to be abandoned. The chief of the Bureau of Ordnance, after trying in vain to interest Congress and to obtain suitable grounds, erected an experimental battery in 1872 at Fort Madison near the Naval Academy at Annapolis. Here the proving-grounds of the navy remained for several years.[132]

Long before the Civil War naval magazines had been erected at Chelsea, Mass.; Fort Mifflin, Pa.; Ellis Island, N. Y.; and Fort Norfolk, Va. In 1873 a new site for the magazine of the Washington yard was purchased for $45,000. It contained ninety acres, and was situated on the Potomac about four miles from the yard. As early as 1846 St. Helena, lying opposite the Norfolk yard on the Elizabeth River, had been purchased for the storage of ordnance.[133]

During the fifteen years succeeding the Civil War the science of naval ordnance was being revolutionized. Rifles were displacing smooth-bores; breech-loaders, muzzle-loaders; and wrought-iron, cast-iron guns. The armament of ships was greatly increasing in power, and was getting the better of the armor. During this period the guns of the American navy fell far behind those of other nations. Some improvement, however, was made in the navy's small arms and light guns. Robeson reported that during his term of office a uniform system of breech-loading small arms had been introduced, and a supply of Gatling guns purchased. He said that he had endeavored to " lay the foundation of a general system of progress in our ordnance." In 1879 Hotch- kiss rifles were issued to some of the ships. The department was also making a slight improvement in its heavy guns. It was con- verting some of the old ante-bellum smooth-bores into rifles, and the old muzzle-loading Parrott's into breech-loaders. How weak the navy was in effective, up-to-date cannon may be seen from a report of a committee of the House made in 1880: " We have less than 250 guns afloat in our entire navy, and of these less than 40 are rifles (a few 8-inch, a few 100 pounds, and a few 60 pounds), all the rest are antiquated smooth-bores." The chief of the Bureau of Ordnance believed, however, that we had lost little or nothing by the delay in procuring new guns, and that " there

[132] Ann. Rept. of Sec. of N., 1872, p. 51.
[133] Miscl. data, Bureau of Yards and Docks, 18.

would be the same outcry of inefficiency if the navy were armed with the best breech-loader of five years' date "—such were the rapid advances being made in the art and science of naval armament. He also said that such cannon as the navy required could not be built by the steel manufacturers of the United States.[134]

The scientific work of the navy from 1869 to 1881, while not so brilliant as that of the period preceding the Civil War, was quite creditable. During the early seventies the personnel and work of the Hydrographic Office was gradually increased. Important hydrographical surveys were made in the Pacific Ocean and the West Indies and along the coasts and up the rivers of South America. Some deep-sea explorations in the Pacific were undertaken. During the first years of Robeson's administration the navy made several important surveys of canal routes across the Isthmus of Panama and Central America. Two Arctic expeditions were sent out under the direction of the Secretary of the Navy—the *Polaris* expedition in 1871, and the *Jeannette* expedition in 1879. The eighth decade of the nineteenth century was an important period in the history of the Naval Observatory. It was marked by the purchase of the largest telescope in the world, the discovery of the two satellites of Mars, and the observations of some notable solar eclipses and of the transit of Venus. In 1880 Congress decided to erect a new observatory on a new site.

In the early seventies the instruction of the naval engineers was made a permanent part of the work of the Naval Academy. In 1879 the department wisely decided, in view of the great changes taking place in naval architecture, to select each year from the most promising graduates of the academy a few students to pursue post-graduate work in naval construction at the best schools abroad, especially those at Greenwich, Paris and Glasgow. Cadet-Engineers F. T. Bowles and Richard Gatewood were the first graduates to avail themselves of this privilege. Bowles has attained great distinction in his profession, and has served as Chief of the Bureau of Construction and Repair. He resigned from the navy to accept a lucrative and responsible office with one of the great ship-building companies.

Throughout the administrations of Grant and Hayes members of Congress continually asserted that the number of naval officers

[134] Ann. Rept. of Sec. of N., 1876, p. 20; 1880, p. 79; House Rept., 46 C. 2 S., No. 169, p. 12.

was excessive, and they made frequent attempts to reduce it. In 1877 the active list and the retired list of the navy contained, respectively, 829 and 135 line officers, 594 and 107 staff officers, and 249 and 27 warrant officers. All told, the active list consisted of 1672 officers; the number of enlisted men at this time was 7012. That is, there was one officer for every 4.2 seamen— a greater ratio than obtained in either the British or French navy. Measured by its needs in time of peace; the navy undoubtedly contained an excess of shoulder straps.

In 1870, in accordance with the recommendations of Robeson, Congress made important reductions in several grades, while at the same time the number of lieutenants was considerably increased. In 1871 Robeson recommended that the grade of commodore be dispensed with, and that the offices of admiral and vice-admiral be permitted to lapse on the death of their present incumbents. Accordingly, Congress, in 1873, passed a law providing that vacancies in these two latter grades should not be filled. The office of vice-admiral lapsed on the death of Vice-Admiral Rowan in 1890, and that of admiral on the death of Admiral Porter in 1891.

The naval appropriation act of 1870 provided a new pay-table, which raised the pay of officers at sea about twenty-five per cent, but in general lowered their shore-pay. The admiral of the navy was now given an annual salary of $13,000. The sea-pay of the vice-admiral was fixed at $9000, a rear-admiral $6000, commodore $5000, captain $4500, commander $3500, and midshipman $1000. The chiefs of bureaus were given the pay of commodores on shore duty.[136] The pay of the officers and seamen of the navy in 1870 was about $2,500,000 more than in 1860. This was one, although by no means the chief, source of the large increase in the naval expenditures during Grant's administration as compared with those under Buchanan.

During the twenty years succeeding the Civil War the naval service did not offer an inviting career to the ambitious and energetic officer. It was never more dull and enervating than at this time. It presented all the dreary monotony and mechanical grind of a socialistic regime without any of the latter's promised

[135] Ann. Rept. of Sec. of N., 1871, p. 16; 1877, p. 7; Congressional Record, VII, 1952; VIII, 627.
[136] U. S. Statutes at Large, XVI, 330.

equity and elevation of ideals. Promotions from grade to grade
were exceedingly slow. The "naval hump," caused by the ad-
mission of so many young officers during and immediately after
the war, effectively blocked all below it. There were lieutenants
in 1869 who were still lietuenants in 1881, and the same condition
held in the grade of lieutenant commander. It was charged that
examinations for promotions were often a farce, and that incompetent men were passed without question. Politics contributed
its share in bringing about this unfortunate condition. By means
of acts of Congress officers who had been for years on the retired
list suddenly appeared in their old places again, and other officers
who had been dismissed from the navy by courts-martial were
restored to their former positions.[137]

Early in Grant's administration the smouldering quarrel between the line and the staff over questions of rank flamed out
again with increased heat. The principal cause of the renewal of
the controversy was the revocation by Porter and Borie of
Welles's order of March 13, 1863, fixing the rank of the staff.
This revocation followed a decision of Attorney-General E. R.
Hoar that Welles's order was in certain respects illegal. The
" degradation " in rank caused by the rescinding of the order was
considered very humiliating by the staff. It involved no loss of
pay, but it entailed the removal of stripes and other insignia of
rank from their uniforms, and the substitution of the marks of
the inferior grades. For instance, the fifteen surgeons who had
ranked as captains were reduced to the grade of commander.
Attempting to quiet the commotion Robeson, in November, 1869,
appointed a board to consider the subject. It consisted of the
eight chiefs of bureaus and of two additional officers, one of the
line and the other of the staff, and was presided over by Commodore Melancthon Smith. On January 24, 1870, a majority of
the board made a report fixing the " relative rank " of the several
grades of staff officers in accordance with a prescribed scale. It
should be said that the term " relative rank " had now come to
be used in place of the former term " assimilated rank." Robeson took the side of the line and made recommendations to Congress that were less liberal to the staff than those of the board.

The controversy was carried on in Congress as well as in the
department and the navy, and its members were copiously supplied

[137] International Review, March, 1879, pp. 280-281.

with literature on the mooted subject. Even before the rescinding of Welle's order the medical corps had gone to Congress to obtain desired legislation, and a bill had been introduced granting the naval surgeons " positive rank." This was a still higher grade of that impalpable and greatly coveted possession of the line, and the whole naval staff now set their hearts upon obtaining it. The House favored the cause of the staff and the Senate that of the line. The House passed a bill granting the staff " positive rank." The Senate stood out for merely increased " relative rank," which the line agreed to yield. The Senate won, and the staff was greatly grieved at the result. The flame of the unending controversy died down, but continued to smolder.[188]

In Robeson's administration until June 20, 1876, the number of seamen in the navy, as fixed by Congress, was 8500. In the winter of 1873-1874, owing to the difficulty with Spain over the *Virginius* affair, this number was temporarily raised to about 10,000. At the beginning of the fiscal year 1877, in accordance with an act of Congress, the number of the enlisted men of the navy was reduced to 7500. In 1878 the seamen in the navy proper did not greatly exceed 6000 men. The rest of the total quota were either boys, or else seamen employed in the Coast Survey, the Naval Academy or Fish Commission. The enlisted force of the navy probably had not been as low since the administration of Andrew Jackson. In May, 1879, Congress authorized the employment of 750 boys, increasing the total quota to 8250, at which figure it remained for several years. In 1874 Congress limited the number of privates in the marine corps to 1500.

Admiral Porter said that, owing to the introduction of steamships, the quality of the sailors of the American navy steadily declined from about the time of the Mexican War, and that " until 1846 we possessed, for the limited number of ships in our navy, the finest body of seamen in the world." He was of the opinion that the employment of sailors in coaling ship and hoisting out ashes caused a decadence in their character. Porter, who was a great lover of sailing vessels, probably exaggerated the influence of steamships upon the American sailor. The decline of the merchant marine, which, as everyone knows, was greatly accelerated

[188] Congressional Globe, 1870-1871, pp. 678, 1844; House Ex. Doc., 41 C. 2 S., No. 99; House Miscl. Doc., 41 C. 2 S., No. 33; speech of A. F. Stevens in the House, Jan. 23, 1871.

by the events of the Civil War, had much to do with the
impairment of the quality of the enlisted force of the navy. After
the war the department, in order to obtain recruits, was compelled to draw more and more from those seafaring waifs that
frequent the various ports of the world. Seamen of American
parentage or nationality were not to be had. In 1876 or 1877
the executive officer of an American sloop-of-war on the China
station prepared an analytical report of the crew of his vessel.
Of the 128 men on board, 47 were Americans, 21 Chinamen, 20
Irishmen, 9 Englishmen, and the rest Swedes, Danes, Germans,
Scotchmen, Greeks, Brazilians, French, Indians, Peruvians, Rus-
sians, Hawaiians, Welshmen and natives of the West Indies,
Azores, Jersey, Liberia, Newfoundland and Nova Scotia.
Twenty-two countries were represented. Admiral Porter is responsible for the story that during the seventies or thereabouts
an American sloop-of-war with a cosmopolitan crew was anchored
in the harbor of Villefranche. The crew represented nineteen
nationalities, and so little American was it in appearance that some
wag painted on board and hung in the gangway of the sloop the
words *" ici on parle Anglais,"* like the signs displayed in the
shops of Paris.[139]

The scarcity of good seamen led the department to undertake
again the training of young men for the naval service. The apprentice system had been tried several times, but had failed.
Secretary Welles's attempt, which was the last one, was abandoned
because the reduction by Congress of the number of the enlisted
force to 8500. The need of seamen was so great that it was impossible to include in this number any boys. It is said also that
the illusive hope of entering the Naval Academy that Welles
presented to the apprentices was injurious to the system. Admiral Porter again and again recommended the establishment of
a new apprentice system. Finally, in April, 1875, Secretary
Robeson ordered the enlistment of a limited number of apprentices. By October two hundred and sixty boys were under instruction, and training ships had been established at the New
York, Portsmouth and Mare Island navy-yards. In accordance
with the new system, the boys were first given preliminary instruction on ships in port, and later were sent to sea in training-

[139] Ann. Rept. of Sec. of N., 1870, p. 158; 1888, pp. 8-12; International
Review, 1879, p. 378.

ships and were taught seamanship, gunnery, and the practical arts of the naval craft. In 1880 the training squadron comprised some three or four vessels. In June of that year 1168 boys were in the naval service. In May, 1879, Congress recognized the new system by authorizing the enlistment of 750 boys. It proved quite successful, and is said to have met the most sanguine expectations of its friends. Its development was greatly furthered by Captain Stephen B. Luce, who for some years commanded the training squadron. For a time Admiral Porter exercised a general supervision over the apprentices.[140]

In December, 1880, a board of naval officers, of which Commodore Earl English was president, examined the naval station at New London, and also Coasters Harbor Island at Newport, with a view to locating a naval training station. Much to the regret of New London, the board chose the latter site. Coasters Harbor Island is situated near Newport, not far from the torpedo station on Goat Island, and contains ninety-five acres. On March 2, 1881, it was ceded to the United States by Rhode Island, and on August 26, 1882, Secretary of the Navy Chandler took formal possession of it. Captain Luce was the first commandant of the new station.[141]

By the end of the seventies several states had come to take a considerable interest in the training of seamen. Massachusetts had fitted out two ships for the instruction of boys in the arts of the sailor. New York had passed a law establishing a nautical school for the education and training of youths in the science and practice of navigation. To aid schools of this sort, Congress in June, 1874, passed the marine school bill. This authorized the Secretary of the Navy to furnish, under certain conditions, a vessel for the use of a nautical school at any one of the following ports: Boston, New York, Philadelphia, Baltimore, Norfolk and San Francisco. The vessel was to be equipped with all her apparel, charts, books and instruments of navigation. To be eligible to receive a ship a school must teach navigation, seamanship, marine engineering and all matters pertaining to the

[140] Ann. Rept. of Sec. of N., 1875, pp. 18, 85; 1880, 106-107; Hamersly, Naval Encyclopedia, 521-522.
[141] Congressional Record, XI, 1566; Miscl. data, Bureau of Yards and Docks, 66; R. I. Acts and Resolves, Jan., 1881, p. 101.

proper construction, equipment and sailing of vessels.[142] The President was authorized to detail naval officers as superintendents or instructors.

THE NAVY DEPARTMENT, 1881-1897.

With the Garfield-Arthur administration the navy and the department entered upon a new era. They now shook off the lethargy that fell over them soon after the Civil War. The public manifested a growing interest in the national marine. The politicians regarded it with increasing favor. Each of the two leading political parties came to advocate the building of new and larger ships, and, when once this work was under way, they vied with each other in carrying it forward. With the rehabilitation of the navy the current of naval affairs, both in the Navy Department and in Congress, deepened and widened. The navy assumed an importance that it had not known since the Civil War, and the naval committees of Congress became strong forces in national legislation and administration.

From 1881 to 1897 "the building of the new navy" was by far the most important work of the department. To this enterprise all other naval activities and interests yielded. It gives color, so to speak, to the naval history of this period. Questions relating to the naval personnel, it is true, were debated and agitated, and some attempts were made to settle them, but they were for the most part postponed. They were not so impersonal as were the questions relating to the matériel, and were therefore not so easy of solution. Then, too, the most pressing need of the navy was for modern vessels equipped with up-to-date guns and mechanisms. During these years the personnel and administrative machinery of the department were gradually increased, and the problems of naval administration more and more attracted the attention of the Secretaries of the Navy.

The increased work and importance of the Navy Department called for more efficient Secretaries than had been needed, or had been obtained, during the years of naval decadence. The Secretaries from 1881 to 1897 displayed a larger industry, more aptitude for naval affairs, and greater zeal for administrative reform

---

[142] U. S. Statutes at Large, XVIII, 121; Hamersly, Naval Encyclopedia, 521.

than did their immediate predecessors. Indeed, it would be difficult to find another period of equal length since the founding of the department when the navy was better managed—although perfection in its administration was by no means reached. During peace, with the possible exception of the years since 1898, at no time in our history have the naval executives had as good opportunities to distinguish themselves, whether in the building of new ships, the manufacture of warlike materials, or the improvement of naval administration, as during the period when the foundations of the new navy were being laid. This consideration, together with the fact that the term of office of the five Secretaries during the years 1881-1897 was longer than the average term, may account for their relatively successful administrations.

Since the founding of the department in 1798 those Secretaries of the Navy who have served for only some twelve or eighteen months have generally had little permanent or positive influence on naval administration. At least a year is necessary for a civilian to familiarize himself thoroughly with his duties and to acquire a working knowledge of the navy. The short-term Secretaries usually do little more than learn the routine of their office, render a few decisions at the bidding of their subordinates, and vex, through lack of knowledge or misplaced zeal, the already troubled waters of the navy. Of all the departments of the government the Navy Department is the most difficult for a lawyer and politician to administer. The navy has its own ways of thinking, standards of value, customs, traditions, prejudices and eccentricities. Of these a new Secretary is often wholly ignorant. Moreover, the Navy Department does a most complicated business relating to manufacturing of various sorts, naval architecture, steam engineering, scientific enterprises, naval education, the science and practice of war, naval and international law, diplomacy, medicine and surgery, finance and accounts, astronomy, and hydrography. In addition to knowing something about these subjects, which by no means exhaust the list, the Secretary of the Navy must have such knowledge of political affairs as will fit him for a seat in the cabinet among the President's political advisers. It is also likely that he will be encumbered with various formal duties of an official or social character. Indeed, his duties, both actual and potential, continually tend to become more numerous, complicated and technical.

Each of the five Presidents of the period 1881-1897 appointed
a single Secretary of the Navy. The administrations of the several
Naval Secretaries cover about the same period as those of their
respective chiefs. Garfield's Secretary, William H. Hunt, of
Louisiana, however, held office for several months under Arthur.
On April 17, 1882, Hunt was succeeded by William E. Chandler,
of New Hampshire. The Naval Secretary during Cleveland's
first administration, 1885-1889, was William C. Whitney, of New
York; and during his second, 1893-1897, Hilary A. Herbert, of
Alabama. Harrison's Secretary of the Navy was Benjamin F.
Tracy, of New York. He served for the period 1889-1893. Hunt,
Chandler and Tracy were Republicans, and Whitney and Herbert
Democrats. Chandler, Whitney and Tracy were Northerners,
and Hunt and Herbert, Southerners. Each of the five men had
been bred to the law. Only Herbert had served in Congress be-
fore entering the Navy Department.

Doubtless it is too soon to render a final judgment upon the
services and characters of these men. Each was greatly interested
in the reconstruction of the navy, and, no matter what his politics,
earnestly carried forward the shipbuilding program of his predecessor. Each made some change or reform in the administrative
machinery of the department. Mr. Charles H. Cramp, the shipbuilder, awards the palm of ability and efficiency to Whitney
and Tracy. Of the five Secretaries, Chandler and Whitney were
the most aggressive and positive, and the most ardent for naval
reform; they were men of courage, and were willing, if necessary,
to stem the tide of naval or political influence. Both were real
heads of the department, and exercised more power than any of
their predecessors since Gideon Welles. Chandler had had some
acquaintance with naval affairs and with federal administration.
For a short time, in 1865, he served as solicitor and judge-advocate of the navy, a position that he resigned to become Assistant
Secretary of the Treasury. He was industrious, accurate and self-
willed, and determined to rule in the department. Whitney,
on the other hand, was more tactful and adroit, although a most
direct and energetic man. He had had some experience in the
municipal administration of New York City.[143]

In 1885, when Whitney was entering upon his duties, he was
described as a " youthful looking and handsome man. He wears

[143] Army and Navy Journal, XX, 379; Buell, C. H. Cramp, 172-192.

glasses and his clothes fit ' like the paper on the wall.' No one has ever yet complained that Mr. Whitney equivocated. In this respect he resembles Ex-Secretary Chandler, who had the tact of making the bluntest, plainest and clearest statements in relation to matters in the Navy Department of any Secretary who has been in office since the war. Mr. Whitney is a good deal like Mr. Chandler in some other respects. He is quick, nervous and alert, and has the gift of instantly seeing the main point at issue, no matter how much it is covered up with a mass of details, and the courage to speak out his mind at once." [144] He was a most efficient Secretary, and was generally popular among the naval officers—a rare distinction. The " Prince of Secretaries," Rear-Admiral Evans has called him. So important was his administration that he has come to be popularly, though erroneously, regarded as the " Father of the New Navy."

Secretary Hunt was inclined to depend more upon his bureau chiefs for direction than were his two immediate successors. He was a native of Charleston, South Carolina, and was of Whig stock. His mother, whose family name was Gaillard, was of French extraction. He is described as being very much unlike an American in appearance, of " swarthy complexion, very marked features, and resembling much the races of Southern Europe. He is courtly—perhaps a little precise—in his manner, and he has always been considered a man of the greatest integrity." [145] He became Attorney-General of Louisiana in 1876, and Judge of the United States Court of Claims at Washington in 1878. Hunt will always be remembered as the Secretary of the Navy who initiated the movement for the construction of the new navy.

Tracy and Herbert were men of solid, rather than brilliant, parts. They performed their duties faithfully and efficiently, and without bluster. They were by profession lawyers. During the Civil War Tracy won the title of brigadier-general. He was severely wounded in the Wilderness campaign of Grant. In 1881-1882 he was Associate Justice of the New York Court of Appeals. Herbert saw service in the Confederate Army, where he rose to the rank of colonel. He also was wounded in the Wilderness campaign. He was a representative in Congress from 1877 to

---

[144] Army and Navy Journal, XXII, 958.
[145] Army and Navy Journal, XVIII, 687.

1892. At the time of his appointment he was one of the best qualified men in his party for the Naval Secretaryship, for he had taken a more prominent part in obtaining the legislation for the rebuilding of the navy than any other Democrat in the House. He was chairman of the House Committee on Naval Affairs in the 49th, 50th and 52d Congress, and was a prominent member of that committee in the 51st Congress when the Republicans were in control.

It is recollected that the office of Assistant Secretary of the Navy was established in 1861 at the outbreak of the Civil War, and that after it had been most acceptably filled by G. V. Fox and William Faxon, it was discontinued in 1869. In 1882 a movement for its re-establishment was started. In March of that year a bill providing for an Assistant Secretary of the Navy was introduced in Congress. At first it received the support of Secretary Hunt, but later he changed his opinion in respect to it. Secretary Chandler throughout his administration recommended the passage of some measure of this sort. He thought that one or more Assistant Secretaries were necessary in order to enforce the civilian control of the navy and to represent adequately popular ideas in the department, and he argued that the civilian element in the department should be strengthened to the extent that it would form a counterpoise to the predominating "naval" element. Senator Hale, of Maine, who for many years was the chief authority in the Senate on naval affairs, had often expressed the same view. For instance, in 1886 he said that the Navy Department needed a "further infusion of civilian or business experience and competency." One discovers in these opinions of Chandler and Hale an outcropping of the rivalry and antagonism that has always existed between the civilian and "naval" elements in respect to the management of the navy. The proposal to appoint an Assistant Secretary was not favorably regarded by the "naval" element.[146]

One of the clauses of an act of Congress approved on August 5, 1882, making appropriations for the civil establishments of the government, made provision for an Assistant Secretary of the Navy. He was to receive an annual salary of $3500. To obtain first-rate talent for so small a sum was difficult. Before Chandler

[146] Congress Letters, Navy Dept. Arch., XVII, 181; Congressional Record, XIII, 2297; XVII, 1122; Ann. Rept. of Sec. of N., 1883, p. 15.

was able to find such a man as he desired Congress, in March, 1883, repealed the provision creating the office. During the eighties various other attempts were made to provide the Secretary with an assistant. Finally, a provision for one was inserted in the bill of July 11, 1890, making appropriations for the civil establishments of the government. According to its terms, the new officer was to be appointed by the President from civil life, and was to receive an annual salary of $4500. This statute did not prescribe his duties. An act of March 3, 1891, assigned to him such duties "as may be prescribed by the Secretary of the Navy or required by law." [147]

On July 16, 1890, President Harrison appointed to the new office James Russell Soley, of Massachusetts. At the beginning of Cleveland's second administration, in 1893, Soley was succeeded by William McAdoo, of New Jersey, who served until his successor was appointed in 1897, early in the first administration of President McKinley. Both Soley and McAdoo possessed some admirable qualifications for the Assistant Secretaryship. Soley had what few civilian administrators ever obtain, an intimate knowledge of the military and administrative history of the navy and a familiarity with the habits of thought and action that exist in the naval service. From 1873 to 1882 he was head of the department of English studies, history and law at the Naval Academy, and from 1882 to 1890 he served as the librarian of the Navy Department in Washington. During the larger part of the latter period he was also superintendent of the Naval War Records Office, which he organized. From 1876 to 1890 he was professor in the navy, rising to the relative rank of commander. Soley had written several books treating of naval history, and he had lectured on international law at the Naval War College. McAdoo had formerly been associated with his chief, Secretary Herbert, as a member of the House Naval Committee, and had acquired some knowledge of naval affairs.

The "office of the Assistant Secretary" is attached to the Secretary's office, of which it constitutes a rather small part. The duties of the Assistant Secretary are not prescribed by law, but are fixed by the orders of the Secretary. They have, therefore, varied from time to time. In general they have consisted

[147] U. S. Statutes at Large, XXII, 243, 340, 550; XXVI, 254, 934.

of the odds and ends or detached parts of the naval business. They relate to miscellaneous matters, which, while by no means unimportant, are more or less subordinate to the main current of naval affairs. On the absence of his chief the Assistant Secretary acts as the Secretary of the Navy. He and the chief clerk of the department are the principal civilian advisers of the Secretary. Soley assisted Secretary Tracy in improving the methods of naval administration. McAdoo exercised a general supervision over vessels undergoing repairs, vessels under construction in the navy-yards, boards of survey and other naval boards, the departmental printing, the Office of Naval Intelligence, library of the department, Naval War Records Office, Naval War College, marine corps and naval militia.[148]

During 1881-1897 the Navy Department greatly increased its facilities for collecting and disseminating naval information of all sorts. On March 23, 1882, Secretary Hunt established the " Office of Intelligence " in the Bureau of Navigation for the purpose of " collecting and recording such naval information as may be useful to the department in time of war, as well as in peace." [149] One of the main duties of the new office was to collect information relating to foreign navies. That this was by no means a new idea is shown by the following extract taken from a letter of Secretary of the Navy Samuel L. Southard, dated January 26, 1827, to the American Minister to Great Britain. A similar letter was sent to the Ministers or representatives of the United States at St. Petersburg, Stockholm, Paris, Madrid, Lisbon, Algiers, Mexico, Guatemala, Bogota, Lima, Valparaiso, Buenos Ayres and Rio Janeiro:

It is an object of great interest with this department to have accurate information of everything connected with the naval force of other nations; and important benefits may result from your kindness and attention to my wishes on this subject. May I, therefore, beg the favor of you, from time to time, to communicate to me such information respecting the naval force of Great Britain, or other nations, as you may be able to procure without inconvenience; especially respecting the number, situation, use, and employment of their vessels, the number, character, etc., of their navy and dock yards; the number and mode of furnishing their seamen; the means of educating their officers; the amount and character of the expenditures; and, generally, anything which will enable this department completely to com-

---

[148] Army and Navy Journal, XXXIV, 579-580.
[149] General Orders of the Navy Department, No. 292.

prehend the extent and character of the naval means of the nation   Copies
of the annual detailed estimates for the service would be useful.[150]

The new office was soon called the "Office of Naval Intelligence," a term probably derived from the British "Department of Naval Intelligence." In 1883 its personnel consisted of Lieutenant T. B. M. Mason and nine junior officers. The agents of the office residing abroad are called naval attachés, and are connected with the American embassies or legations. The first American naval attaché, and for a time the only one, was Lieutenant-Commander French E. Chadwick, who performed his duties with great satisfaction to the department. In 1889 Secretary Tracy wrote that Chadwick's "extraordinary ability and judgement during six years of difficult service in England and on the Continent had a lasting influence upon the naval development of this country.[151] In 1896 there were three naval attachés, and they were assigned to European countries. Shortly after its organization the office began the publication of two series of valuable reports, one relating to naval operations in recent wars, and the other to general professional information. It soon made itself indispensable to the work of the department, the navy, and even the naval committees of Congress. It prepares reports on the shipbuilding programs of foreign countries, foreign naval statistics and news, recent developments in naval science and recent operations in naval wars.

A work in some respects similar to that of the Office of Naval Intelligence has for several years been conducted by the Library of the Navy Department and the Naval War Records Office. The chief purpose of each of these organizations is to render naval information accessible to the navy and the department. The library performs this function by collecting books relating to naval and kindred subjects. The bureaus and offices of the department also have libraries, but the main library is larger than all of these local libraries combined; and its contents, as a whole, are of a more general character. Its history begins with the collection of books which was made by the early Secretaries of the Navy. In 1820-1830 the Secretary's office and the Navy Commissioners' office were spending for books about two hundred dollars a year each. In the early eighties the books of the Secre-

[150] General Letters, Navy Dept. Arch., XVI, 14-15.
[151] Ann. Rept. of Sec. of N., 1889, p. 7.

tary's office and those of the bureaus that were of a more or less general character were deposited in the library-room of the new Navy Department Building, and they became the nucleus of the present library. The organization of the library may be dated with the appointment of Professor J. R. Soley, in 1882, to be librarian. The number of books increased from about 10,000 volumes in 1883, to about 30,000 volumes in 1896.

Soon after Soley became librarian he began to arrange the official records of the Union and confederate navies preparatory to their publication. This enterprise was heartily encouraged by Secretary Chandler, and elicited much interest on the part of historians and naval officers. Not much was done, however, until the latter part of 1884. On July 7 of that year Congress appropriated a small sum of money for the employment of a few clerks to copy and classify such naval documents as were available from the files of the department or could be obtained from other reliable sources. Professor Soley was made superintendent of the Naval War Records Office, as the new division which took charge of this work was called. He served until 1890, when he became Assistant Secretary of the Navy. He was succeeded by Lieut. Commander F. M. Wise, who, like Soley, also served as librarian of the department. Since the work of the records office and the library is somewhat similar, a single chief has always presided over both organizations. Several years elapsed before the appropriations for the new records office were large enough to insure rapid advancement of its work. In 1894 the first volume of the " Official Records of the Union and Confederate Navies in the War of the Rebellion " was published. This relates to the operations of the cruisers of the two belligerents during 1861 and 1862. Additional volumes of a somewhat similar character have appeared from time to time. In recent years the office has been ably conducted by Mr. Charles W. Stewart, a graduate of the Naval Academy of the class of 1882.[152]

On January 6, 1887, Secretary Whitney established the office oı naval inspector of electric lighting in the Bureau of Navigation, a name which was later changed to the office of inspector of electrical appliances. In 1889 it was transferred to the Bureau of Equipment. This office is quite small, and is always presided over

[152] Official Records, ser. I, vol. I, vii-xi.

by an officer of the navy. Its duties are to prepare detailed specifications for installing ships of war and naval stations with electrical appliances, and to inspect electrical materials and machinery before and after their installation.[153]

The Secretaries of the Navy have at different times tried to obtain legislation directing the transfer to the Navy Department of the several bureaus and offices of the Treasury Department whose duties are similar to those of the navy. They have argued that this work could be performed more economically and appropriately by the navy and its department, and that the inconveniences of detailing naval officers to duty in the Treasury Department should be avoided. Secretary Chandler, who was especially interested in increasing the duties and functions of the Navy Department, recommended that all national work on the ocean should be performed by the officers of the navy. He said that an " extension of the field of naval employment would strengthen and invigorate the service without any detriment to existing interests, while the fusion of all branches of nautical administration would secure concentration of purpose, unity of action, and broader and more substantial results." His plan involved the transfer to the Navy Department of the Light-House Service, Coast and Geodetic Survey, Revenue Marine Service, Life Saving Service, and all bureaus or offices of the Treasury Department whose duties related to the mercantile marine. He proposed to organize in the Navy Department a " bureau of mercantile marine," which should take charge of this branch of the national administration. One of its principal aims was to be the revival of the rapidly decaying American marine. So extensive a plan was doomed to fail. Such is the interest of individuals, classes and parties in the maintenance of the existing illogical distribution of duties among the several executive departments, that it is almost impossible to effect the redistribution of those duties in a logical manner.[154]

During the period 1881-1897, when the first vessels of the new navy were built, the work of the Bureaus of Construction and Repair, Steam Engineering, Ordnance, and Equipment—the four manufacturing bureaus—greatly increased in magnitude and importance, and became more highly specialized, technical, detailed

[153] Ann. Rept. of Sec. of N., 1887, p. 157.

[154] Ann. Rept. of Sec. of N., 1883, pp. 32-42; 1884, pp. 46-49.

and complicated. These bureaus manage large manufactories, design complicated ships, guns and machinery, and inspect the manufacture of ordnance, steel, gun-forgings, armor-plate, engines and naval supplies. The character of their work is " civil " rather than " naval." They conduct a manufacturing, engineering and mechanical business. It has been remarked that the point of view of line officers who serve in these bureaus for a long time is likely to become assimilated to that of the civilian or the mechanical engineer. Such line officers may even become deficient as naval executives on shipboard, and may in a measure lose their taste for the sea and a purely naval life. Their outlook on their profession, however, is greatly broadened, and they come to realize adequately that the mechanical and engineering sciences more and more condition modern naval warfare. Naval routine and traditions appear to them less significant.

The two naval constructors who had charge of the Bureau of Construction and Repair when the first vessels of the new navy were built were Chief Constructor Theodore D. Wilson, 1882-1893, and Rear-Admiral Philip Hichborn, 1893-1901. Engineer-in-Chief Charles H. Loring, 1884-1887, and Rear-Admiral George W. Melville, 1887-1903, presided over the Bureau of Steam Engineering during this important period. Several illustrious officers served in the Bureau of Equipment. Its chief from 1884 to 1889 was Commodore Winfield Scott Schley, from 1889 to 1893 Commodore George Dewey, and from 1893 to 1897 Commodore French E. Chadwick. The manufacture of the new ordnance of the navy was conducted by three efficient chiefs of the Bureau of Ordnance—Commodores Montgomery Sicard, 1881-1890; William M. Folger, 1890-1893; and William T. Sampson, 1893-1897. Several of these chiefs served for more than a single term of four years. Wilson held office for eleven, Hichborn for eight, and Melville for sixteen years. These three men played a most prominent part in designing the hulls and engines of the new fleet and in overseeing their construction. Melville, whose heroic achievements in the Arctic seas won for him an especial distinction, also showed capacity for extraordinary effort as Chief of the Bureau of Steam Engineering. In 1887 he personally prepared the general designs of the machinery of five of the new vessels then under construction.[155]

---

[155] Hamersly, Record of Living Officers of Navy, 1898, p. 301.

From 1881 to 1897 the two chiefs of the Bureau of Navigation were Commodore James G. Walker, 1881-1889, and Rear-Admiral Francis M. Ramsay, 1889-1897, each of whom held office for two terms. They exercised large powers, not only in superintending the naval personnel and directing the movements of the fleet, but also in the general administration of the navy. Even in building the new ships the energy and judgment of Walker was much relied upon by Secretary Whitney. He has been called the " ablest and most forceful man of his time in the navy." [156] During these years the influence of the Chief of the Bureau of Navigation probably reached its culmination. His rooms adjoin those of the head of the department, to whom he therefore has easy access, and whose ear he can gain and keep to the exclusion of his less fortunate colleagues. He is more frequently in conference with the Secretary than the other chiefs. He is in position to give the Secretary his naval point of view, and perhaps his prejudices and biased information. Since at this time he virtually detailed all the inferior officers of the line and had a large and often a determining influence in detailing those of command rank, he could make or break an officer by giving or refusing him an important command. Walker and Ramsay were the most unpopular officers in the naval service. They were charged with being autocratic chiefs, and with belonging to a naval clique.

In order to curb the power of the Chief of the Bureau of Navigation and abolish all grounds for suspicions of favoritism, Secretary Chandler in October, 1884, vested the power of assigning officers to duty in a small board of bureau chiefs. This plan seems not to have worked well. In May, 1885, Secretary Whitney restored to the Chief of the Bureau of Navigation, for the most part, the duties which Chandler had taken from him. [157]

Since 1881 the business of the naval committees in Congress has greatly grown in volume and importance, and appointments to them have come to be highly prized. They are among the chief " working committees " of Congress, and are powerful factors in determining the naval policy of the country. Their decision upon the numbers and types of vessels in the shipbuilding program of each year is usually final. Their views upon any measure which

[156] Buell, C. H. Cramp, 181.
[157] General Orders of the Navy Department, Nos. 322, 337; Army and Navy Journal, XXII, 225.

the department wishes to have enacted into law must be reckoned with, for their opposition to it will prevent its passage. Their members may acquire a considerable knowledge of naval affairs, especially if they are granted a long period of service. The chairmen of these committees often acquire an extensive knowledge of the navy. During the first years of the new navy the most expert and influential chairmen were Hilary A. Herbert and Charles A Boutwell of the House, and Eugene Hale of the Senate.

Throughout the period 1881-1897 much adverse criticism of the organization of the Navy Department, and especially of the system of naval bureaus, was made by Secretaries of the Navy, naval officers, members of Congress, and the newspapers. A part of this criticism was intelligent and a part was decidedly otherwise. Some of it was temperate and judicious, and some extravagant, partisan and rhetorical. Much of it was of a more or less general character, and was based upon an imperfect knowledge of the facts. As illustrating in considerable degree the rhetorical, partisan and extravagant criticism of the department, the following extract from President Cleveland's first message dated December 8, 1885, may be quoted:

I deem it my duty to especially direct the attention of Congress to the close of the report of the Secretary of the Navy, in which the humiliating weakness of the present organization of his department is exhibited and the startling abuses and waste of its present methods are exposed. The conviction is forced upon us, with the certainty of mathematical demonstration, that before we proceed further in the restoration of a navy we need a thoroughly reorganized Navy Department. The fact that within seventeen years more than $75,000,000 have been spent in the construction, repair, equipment, and armament of vessels, and the further fact that instead of an effective and creditable fleet we have only the discontent and apprehension of a nation undefended by war vessels, added to the disclosures now made, do not permit us to doubt that every attempt to revive our navy has thus far, for the most part, been misdirected, and all our efforts in that direction have been little better than blind gropings and expensive, aimless follies.

Unquestionably, if we are content with the maintenance of a Navy Department simply as a shabby ornament to the government, a constant watchfulness may prevent some of the scandal and abuse which have found their way into our present organization, and its incurable waste may be reduced to the minimum. But if we desire to build ships for present usefulness, instead of naval reminders of the days that are past, we must have a department organized for the work, supplied with all the talent and ingenuity our country affords, prepared to take advantage of the experience of other nations, systematized so that all effort shall unite and lead in one direction, and fully imbued with the conviction that war vessels, though new, are useless unless they combine all that the ingenuity of man has up to this day brought forth relating to their construction.[158]

The most reliable and definite criticism of the bureau system was made by the Secretaries of the Navy and the naval committees. The principal defects in the departmental organization which they discovered may be divided into two classes: (1) those relating to the division of responsibility, and (2) those relating to the division of labor. The former class will be first considered. It was maintained that the division of responsibility or executive power in the Navy Department, and likewise in the navy-yards, was excessive. There were too many bureaus. Each of them was more or less independent of the other. Each magnified its own work, was jealous of its own powers, and was impatient of restraint. The bureaus were like so many little navy departments occupying towards the Secretary of the Navy the same relation that the several departments of the government occupy towards the President. The excessive division of authority at Washington caused a like division of powers in the navy-yards, with results especially direful. Each bureau at Washington had in each yard its own representatives, employees and equipment. It was said that in the pursuit of special ends the general ends were lost sight of. The department lacking proper correlating, co-ordinating or unifying organs. The only instrumentality of this sort was the Secretary of the Navy. In actual practice, often ignorant of the details and technicalities of the business of the navy, he fell far short of the needs of the department. He did not have the expert knowledge, time or inclination to correlate properly the work of the several bureaus and offices, and direct their activities as a unit.

The evils of the excessive division of responsibility were said to be especially manifest in the building, equipping and arming of ships. This work, the critics pointed out, was shared by four bureaus, Construction and Repair, Steam Engineering, Equipment, and Ordnance. Since a modern ship was a unit and did not fall into four well-defined and mutually exclusive parts, the duties of these bureaus often overlapped; they interfered and conflicted with each other. As a result the Secretary of the Navy was again and again called upon to settle disputes between con-

---

[158] Richardson, Messages and Papers, VIII, 351.

tending authorities. Each bureau attended carefully to its own work, but no one attended to combining their several activities into an organized, homogeneous and effective whole. Each bureau might perform its work perfectly from its own standpoint, while in the end the finished product might be a decided failure. The critics gave examples of this. For instance, after the *Omaha* had been commissioned and was ready for sea, it was discovered that, as a result of the bureaus working independently, her space had been so appropriated that coal-room had been left for no more than four days' steaming.[159]

Several remedies for the excessive division of responsibility and executive power were proposed. The most obvious one, of course was the uniting of two or more bureaus. With the zeal of an official new to his office, Secretary Whitney, in his annual report for 1885, recommended a sweeping reorganization of the Navy Department. The authorship of Whitney's recommendations, as well as of the criticism upon which they were based, has been attributed to Professor J. R. Soley. Whitney believed that the work of the department fell logically into three parts, and he proposed to divide the departmental duties among three bureaus: The bureau of " personnel," of " material and construction," and of " finance and accounts." A chief was to preside over each. The new organization would reduce the number of bureaus from eight to three. The work of each bureau was to be divided according to its subject matter. For instance, under the " bureau of material and construction " there were to be erected the divisions of " construction," " engineering," " equipment," and " ordnance." Whitney's plan consolidated responsibility, but did not greatly change the existing division of labor in the department. It was entirely too revolutionary to have any prospects of being enacted into law.[160]

Whitney was shortly moved to modify his plan by increasing the number of bureaus to five. Early in 1886 a bill embodying his later recommendations was introduced in the House. It provided for five naval bureaus: " Navigation," " ordnance," " medicine and surgery," " material, construction and repair," and " supplies and accounts." It changed the existing organization chiefly by

[159] Ann. Rept. of Sec. of N., 1885, xxvii-xli; Congressional Record, XVII, 5833.
[160] Ann. Rept. of Sec. of N., 1885, xxviii, xli.

consolidating three of the four shipbuilding bureaus. The bill was favorably reported by the House Committee on Naval Affairs. The House divided on party lines. The Republicans opposed the measure partly on its demerits, but also doubtless for the reason that its passage would seem to justify Cleveland and Whitney's severe arraignment of the Republican management of the department. Representative Charles A. Boutelle, of Maine, who led the opposition to the bill, succeeded in making out a rather strong case against it, and in preventing its reaching a vote.[161]

The recommendations of several other Secretaries of the Navy were less thoroughgoing than those of Whitney, and were confined to the shipbuilding bureaus. In his annual report for 1883 Secretary Chandler, in accordance with the views of a naval board that had considered the subject, recommended the uniting of the Bureaus of Construction and Repair and Steam Engineering. In his annual report for 1894 Secretary Herbert favored the consolidation of the several bureaus having to do with the building, arming and equipping of ships. Admiral Porter was of the opinion that a reduction in the number of the shipbuilding bureaus would be advantageous. In 1886 he said that " there should be a single Bureau of Construction, Steam Engineering, and Repair under one head." The opposition to the consolidation of the bureaus was very strong, and was sufficient to prevent favorable action upon any of the foregoing recommendations. The respective interests of the line and the staff were involved in the proposed changes. The engineers feared that the union of the Bureau of Steam Engineering with one of the other bureaus would deprive them of a representative in the Navy Department. The employees under the existing system viewed with alarm the introduction of a new system that might result in a reduction of the number of offices or in some other change adverse to their interests. The concentration of large powers in the hands of the chief of the proposed " bureau of ships " was considered dangerous. Many held that the existing number of bureaus was not excessive.[162]

Another proposed remedy for the excessive division of responsibility was the establishment within the Navy Department of a special correlating and unifying organ. A naval board, com-

[161] House Rept., 49 C. 1 S., No. 1469.
[162] Ann. Rept. of Sec. of N., 1883, p. 27; 1880, p. 67; 1894, p. 14.

posed largely or entirely of line officers, was to be vested with
more or less power to direct the work of the department. For
many years the creation of a board of this sort had been the line
officers' favorite panacea for the ills of naval administration.
Admiral Porter was especially partial to a " board of control,"
which was to consist of three line officers not below the grade of
captain, and of one additional line officer of the grade of captain
to act as secretary of the board. " Under the direction of the
Secretary of the Navy, the board should have the general management of the naval service." The Secretaries of the Navy have
generally been unwilling to give such an organization affirmative
duties of administration and control. Secretary Whitney favored
the establishment of a " board of control," consisting of five bureau
chiefs and three additional naval officers, but he wished to vest in
it merely advisory powers. A board of this sort would not have
been an effective correlating force. The Secretaries during the
period 1881-1897 were jealous of their powers, and naturally opposed any measure calculated to increase greatly the influence and
control of naval officers within the department.[163]

Unable to obtain from Congress legislation affecting the consolidation of the bureaus, and unwilling to establish a special board
to correlate and unify the work of the department, the Secretaries
of the Navy resorted to other means to bring about the same end.
In 1889 Secretary Tracy organized the Construction Board, consisting of the chiefs of the five bureaus, Construction and Repair,
Steam Enginering, Equipment, Ordnance, and Yards and Docks,
and gave it a general supervision over the designing, constructing
and equipping of new ships. In this manner the several chiefs
of the shipbuilding bureaus were brought together for consultation. The board was to agree upon the general plan of a ship
before its construction was commenced. It was held responsible
for all delays, and for failures in correlating the work of shipbuilding. Each bureau stood for its respective specialty, but the
board stood for the ship as a whole, and was responsible for the
success and efficiency of the completed vessel.[164]

After a thorough consideration of the subject Secretary Herbert on October 2, 1894, issued an order designed to still further

[163] Ann. Rept. of Sec. of N., 1885, xl; 1886, pp. 66-67; House Rept., 49 C.
1 S., No. 1469.
[164] Ann. Rept. of Sec. of N., 1889, p. 39.

correlate and unify the work of the shipbuilding bureaus. This he effected in the main by giving to the Bureau of Construction and Repair a certain pre-eminence. He made it responsible for the design, structural strength and stability of new vessels. It was to be responsible also for changes made in the construction of a ship after its design had been approved. Full and accurate knowledge of every change in the plans of the ships was concentrated in this bureau. The effect of Herbert's order was very beneficial.[165]

The second class of criticisms against the bureau system related to the division of labor, which, it was asserted, was both illogical and excessive. While the bureau system had fostered the growth of these evils, it was not wholly responsible for them. The Secretary of the Navy had permitted the bureaus to take on duties in a haphazard manner, until several or all of them were doing the same kinds of work. Often their duties were most heterogeneous, and were apparently assigned on no ascertainable principle. For the excessive division of labor at the navy-yards the bureau system was largely responsible. The Secretaries of the Navy proceeded to remedy these defects, as far as they were able, by executive orders.

Early in his administration Secretary Whitney turned his attention to the methods of the department of purchasing stores and supplies and of keeping accounts. He made some interesting discoveries respecting the division of the work of making open purchases. For the fiscal year 1885 $138,000 was " spent by the seven bureaus, each acting independently of the other, for coal bought, not in one lot, but at 166 several open purchases (this does not include coal bought by ships on foreign stations) ; 299 different open purchases of stationery were made by eight different bureaus; $121,315.66 was spent for lumber and hardware by six bureaus in 499 separate open purchases. Seven bureaus spent $46,000 for oils and paints in 269 separate purchases ; 117 different open purchases of iron and steel were made at an expense of $41,524.48 ; $68,881.59 was spent for hemp and cordage in 45 different open purchases. Eight bureaus supply stationery to ships ; three bureaus supply ships with lamps and lanterns. To the same ship one bureau supplies electric lights and the light for

---

[165] Ann. Rept. of Sec. of N., 1894, p. 15.

general illuminating purposes; another supplies electric search lights; and a third oil and light for the engine and fire rooms." [166]

Whitney also discovered that little responsibility for the care and disposition of the stores and supplies of the navy-yards existed, and that such property had accumulated far beyond the needs of the service. A remarkable hoarding of materials had taken place. Since neither the laws nor the system of naval administration offered any inducement to a bureau to sell its surplus stores or to turn them over to some other bureau that needed them, unnecessary stores of all kinds had accumulated in the navy-yards to the value of more than $20,000,000. About one-fifth of these were obsolete and useless, "only entailing expense for keepers and constant care to preserve them in condition." A navy board that investigated the subject brought to light some curious facts. It reported that "at the eight navy-yards there have accumulated altogether of augurs and bits, 46,566, of which 25,274 have been lying for several years at closed yards, where no work has or is likely to be done. Twenty-nine thousand five hundred and forty-two gross of screws are on hand, 10,896 gross lying at closed yards. There are 146,385 files in stock, 42,142 of them lying at closed yards. There are 11,813 paint brushes in stock; 2246 of these in the stores at closed yards. All of these tools are serviceable, mostly new." [167]

To assist him in obtaining information and deciding upon methods of reform, Whitney appointed several navy boards. One of these, which was presided over by Captain R. W. Meade, made an inventory of all the stores and materials at the yards. After thoroughly considering the subject, Whitney concluded to concentrate the work of making purchases and keeping accounts in one bureau, that of Provisions and Clothing. He began this reform in 1886, but it proceeded slowly. The advocates of the old system, under which each bureau at Washington and its representatives in the several navy-yards made their own purchases and kept their own accounts, were emphatic in their opposition to the new plan. Whitney had taken only the initial steps when his administration came to an end.

The perfecting of the new system and the putting of it into practical operation fell to Secretary Tracy. Its main features

[166] Ann. Rept. of Sec. of N., 1885, xxx.
[167] Ann. Rept. of Sec. of N., 1886, pp. 4-5.

were the establishment at each yard of a general storekeeper, who was charged with the purchase and custody of all the stores of the yard, and was responsible to the Bureau of Provisions and Clothing; the making of this bureau the purchasing agent for the whole navy; and the opening in this bureau of one set of accounts, both of stock and purchases, designed to show the exact condition of the naval appropriations and expenditures. The business, which formerly had been handled by seven or eight bureaus, was now to be transacted by the Bureau of Provisions and Clothing. This bureau was divided into two divisions: the "division of purchase and supplies," which was charged with the making of all naval purchases; and the "division of audit and accounts," which served as the bookkeeper of the navy. The chief of this bureau was now the Paymaster-General of the navy. The store-keepers in the navy-yards and the paymasters on board the naval ships, who acted as his agents, were members of the naval pay corps.[168] In 1892 the Bureau of Provisions and Clothing was given a name which more accurately described its new duties. It became the Bureau of Supplies and Accounts.

The new system was further developed by Secretary Herbert, who, like Whitney and Tracy, pronounced it a decided improvement over the old one. By concentrating the work of making purchases, various economies were effected. The hoarding of supplies was in large part prevented. Responsibility was increased and made more definite. The accounting and bookkeeping of the department were simplified, and became intelligible. The open purchases of the navy were greatly decreased. The new system, however, had its disadvantages. The purchasing agents at times lacked an intimate knowledge of the purchased articles. Long delays in making purchases sometimes occurred. From the point of view of the consumer of materials, the new system was more cumbersome than the old.

The reform begun by Whitney in making the Bureau of Provisions and Clothing the financial bureau of the Navy Department was continued by Tracy, who transformed the Bureau of Navigation into a bureau of personnel and the Bureau of Equipment and Recruiting into a bureau of equipment. It is recollected that the Bureau of Navigation had been created as the scientific

[168] Ann. Rept. of Sec. of N., 1892, pp. 53-56.

bureau of the department, and had therefore been given charge of the Naval Observatory, Nautical Almanac Office and Hydrographic Office. In 1865 the Office of Detail had been joined to the Bureau of Navigation, and since that time one officer had presided over both. To this bureau had fallen the duties of supplying ships with compasses, chronometers, navigating instruments and other articles of equipment. Its functions were most diverse and illogical. By an order dated June 25, 1889, Tracy rearranged the duties of the Bureaus of Navigation and Equipment and Recruiting. Under the latter were now placed the Naval Observatory and Nautical Almanac Office. A like disposition would have been made of the Hydrographic Office, but a law prevented, and Tracy had to content himself with asking Congress to repeal the law. The Bureau of Equipment and Recruiting was also given all the duties of the Bureau of Navigation relating to equipment, and the latter received all the duties of the former relating to recruiting. By the same order the Bureau of Navigation absorbed the Office of Detail. This order also specified that the Naval Academy, Naval Intelligence Office, Library of the Navy Department and Naval War Records Office should be attached to the Bureau of Navigation. Its duties were now fairly homogeneous, and it might have been appropriately named the " bureau of personnel and detail." In 1889 Tracy changed the name of the Bureau of Equipment and Recruiting to the Bureau of Equipment.[169]

A further simplification of the work of the Navy Department was effected by the concentration of some of its factories. For many years the fabrication of various articles of equipment had been conducted at the several navy-yards, but principally at the Boston and Washington yards. The chief products of the former were ropes and sails, and of the latter anchors, chains and galleys. The factories for these articles were concentrated by Secretary Whitney at the Boston yard. Here were to be made ropes, sails, anchors, chains, galleys, rigging, cordage, hammocks, canvas, awnings, tarpaulins and other articles of equipment. Under Whitney's orders the Washington yard confined its manufacturing to the making of ordnance. It ceased to perform many of the usual duties of a navy-yard, and became, as it was henceforth called, the " Naval Gun Factory."

[169] Ann. Rept. of Sec. of N., 1889, pp. 37-40.

The redistribution of duties among the bureaus and the addition of new offices relatively increased the work of the Bureaus of Navigation and Supplies and Accounts and the Office of the Secretary of the Navy. The chief increases in the personnel of the department from 1881 to 1897 were made in these three administrative divisions. The number of regular employees of the Navy Department in Washington, exclusive of the caretakers of the Navy Department building, on July 1, 1881, was 151; and on July 1, 1897, 293. Rather singularly the number of the employees in the four shipbuilding bureaus was but slightly increased. In 1893 an Assistant Chief of the Bureau of Navigation, and in 1894 an Assistant Chief of the Bureau of Supplies and Accounts was authorized. The former was to be of a rank not below that of commander, and the latter was to be chosen from the pay corps.

In 1883 the passage of the Pendleton civil service act placed the appointments of employees of the Navy Department in Washington receiving an annual salary of $720 or upwards, except twenty-one of them, under civil service rules. All merely clerical offices were put within the "classified service." Positions in this service could be filled only through the Civil Service Commission from a list of eligible applicants, whose merits had been satisfactorily tested by an appropriate examination. Under the rules prescribed in 1883 the Navy Department on the occurrence of a vacancy notified the Commission, which at once certified to the department the four applicants on the eligible list whose grades were highest; and from these the department selected one to fill the vacancy.[170] In course of time the Commission established several lists of eligibles corresponding to the classes of positions in the department. In 1894 President Cleveland placed the watchmen and messengers within the classified service, and in 1896 he classified many of the laborers. By the end of his second administration all the civilian positions of the Navy Department in Washington, with the exception of those of the Secretary of the Navy, the Assistant Secretary of the Navy, the private secretary of the Secretary, and a few laborers, were under the merit system. In 1896 Cleveland extended the civil service rules so as to include many of the employees of the navy-yards.

[170] First Ann. Rept. of Civil Serv. Comm., 24, 45-51, 68.

CHAPTER TEN: THE NEW NAVY, 1881-1897

The Need for Modern, Agressive Ships

Before the beginning of Garfield's administration on March 4, 1881, a strong sentiment in favor of a new navy was manifested in Congress. The naval appropriation bill of 1877, as it passed the House, provided for a commission of nine members to formulate a progressive naval policy and to decide upon a shipbuilding program, but this provision was struck out by the Senate. In 1878 the House Committee on Naval Affairs under the able leadership of Benjamin W. Harris, of Massachusetts, pointed out with much detail the lamentable weakness of the American fleet in comparison with European fleets, and recommended that " immediate and adequate measures be taken for the formation of a new and formidable navy." In 1880 the same committee fully set forth the inefficiency of the several units composing the American fleet, and recommended the disposal of the old ships and obsolete materials and the establishment of a permanent construction fund for the building of new ships. Early in 1881 a measure which made provision for such a fund passed the House, but failed in the Senate for want of time for its proper consideration. During Hayes's administration some of the leading members of the two principal political parties warmly advocated the improvement of the navy.[171]

Shortly after his inauguration President Garfield showed considerable interest in the building of a fleet of modern war vessels.

[171] Congressional Record, V, 1866; XIII, 111, 2960; House Rept., 45 C. 2 S., No. 662, 26; House Rept., 46 C. 2 S., No. 169.

He believed that in this work his naval Secretary would find a great opportunity to distinguish himself. The act which has come to be regarded as the first step in the construction of the new navy was taken by Secretary Hunt on June 29, 1881, when he appointed the "First Naval Advisory Board," the chief purpose of which was to advise the Secretary of the Navy upon the technical problems involved in the building of new ships. It was to report upon the "number of vessels that should now be built," their class, size and displacement, the materials and methods of their construction, and their engines, armament and equipment. Upon these and similar technical questions a wide difference of opinion existed at this time among naval officers. Hunt wished to resolve these differences, to determine upon a specific ship-building program, and to fortify his recommendations to Congress by a unanimity of naval advice.

The "First Naval Advisory Board" was composed of one rear-admiral, one commodore, one captain, three commanders, three lieutenants, three engineers and three naval constructors. Of its fifteen members, nine were of the line, and six of the staff of the navy. A majority of its members had not reached the higher ranks of the service. Hunt believed that those officers who were to command and manage the new ships, and perhaps fight them, should have the largest share in determining their character. He probably feared that the recommendations of older men might prove too conservative, or possibly reactionary. According to Hunt all the members of the board were officers of "recognized ability, experience and attainments." Its president, Rear Admiral John Rodgers, was one of the best-equipped officers in the service. Commanders R. D. Evans and A. S. Crowninshield, whose names are now familiar, were also members. The engineers were represented by Isherwood, Loring and Manning; and the naval constructors, by Lenthall, Wilson and Hichborn. Isherwood and Lenthall were veteran members of their corps, and had rendered conspicuous service as chiefs of bureaus during the Civil War.

The board held its sessions in Washington from July 11 to November 7, 1881, on which latter date it reported to Secretary Hunt. As its members failed to agree at all points, majority and minority reports were submitted. These showed the usual cleavage of opinion between the line and the staff. The majority report was signed by all the officers of the line and two of the staff. The minority report was signed by the four remaining officers of the staff—the three naval constructors and Chief Engineer Isherwood. The majority of the board recommended the construction of 68 vessels at a total cost of $29,607,000—the value of some four or five battleships of recent date. In respect to types of construction, the 68 ships were to be distributed as follows: 18 steel unarmored cruisers, 20 wooden unarmored cruisers, 5 steel rams, 5 torpedo gunboats and 20 torpedo boats. The largest and fastest vessels were the steel unarmored cruisers. Two of these were to be first-rate steel, double-decked, unarmored cruisers, each having a displacement of about 5873 tons, an average sea-speed of 15 knots, and a battery of 5 8-inch and 21 6-inch guns; the cost of each was to be $1,780,000. Of the remaining 16 steel unarmored cruisers, six were to have a speed of 14 knots, and ten a speed of 13 knots. The majority did not recommend the construction of ironclads, although it recognized that such vessels would be needed in time of war. It recommended that all the ships should have full sail power, and that the " fifteen-, fourteen-, and thirteen-knot classes of vessels should be ship-rigged, and the ten-knot class of vessels barquentine-rigged." It proposed to build the ten-knot vessels of live-oak and yellow pine, and all the larger vessels of steel. The proposal in respect to steel was so radical that the majority felt called upon to give their reasons for favoring the use of this material.

The minority disagreed with the majority upon various minor technicalities of naval construction. Some more important differences related to the construction of ironclads and the use of steel for the larger ships. The minority expressed the decided opinion that a " modern navy must consist essentially of powerful ironclads; and the constant tendency in their design has been to approximate them more and more to machines, and to depart farther and farther from ships of the unarmored types." On this subject it was more progressive than the majority. The report of the minority respecting the use of steel, however, exhibited it in a less favorable light. It dissented from the views of the majority on this subject on the grounds that steel would cost more than iron, that for shipbuilding it was but little better than iron, and that it could not be made in the United States until a manufactory was erected. These reports show very clearly the backwardness and rudimentary state of naval construction in this

country in 1881. From them one can reckon how far we have
advanced in this art during the last thirty years. The differences
in construction between the best ship recommended by the board
and a battleship of recent date are truly remarkable.[172]

Secretary Hunt made the report of the First Naval Advisory
Board a part of his annual report for 1881, and he recommended
the views of the majority as being " entitled to the entire approba-
tion of Congress." For the first time the subject of the new navy
was assigned a place in the annual reports of the Secretary of
the Navy. Hunt gave it precedence over all other subjects. In
the opening paragraph of his report, he vigorously set forth the
naval needs of the country: " The condition of the navy imperatively demands the prompt and earnest attention of Congress.
Unless some action be had in its behalf it must soon dwindle into
insignificance. From such a state it would be difficult to revive
it into efficiency without dangerous delay and enormous expense.
Emergencies may at any moment arise which would render its aid
indispensable to the protection of the lives and property of our
citizens abroad and at home, and even to our existence as a
nation."

Hunt closed a glowing appeal to Congress to come to the rescue
of a languishing and neglected navy in the following words:
" Whether it be as a means of self-protection to the long line of
cities and harbors upon our coasts, or to guard our commerce on
the high seas; or to insure our citizens sojourning in foreign lands
and their property and persons against outrage; or to take and
keep our proper place among nations; or to maintain the sentiment of patriotism connected with our navy, and with the memories of its departed heroes; or to reap the advantages of the
researches and labors of its officers in the further progress of
advanced science; it becomes the duty of Congress to see to it that
the navy of the United States should not be left to perish through
inanition, but should be restored to a condition of usefulness in
which it may upon occasion be so expanded as to become the ready
means of protection at home or of active and aggressive warfare
in the ports and waters of an enemy."

With these words of Hunt, President Arthur was in complete
agreement. In his first annual message, that of December, 1881,

[172] Ann. Rept. of Sec. of N., 1881, pp. 27-81.

he strongly urged upon Congress his " conviction that every consideration of national safety, economy and honor imperatively demands a thorough rehabilitation of our navy "; and he recommended liberal appropriations for the reconstruction of the fleet. Arthur's emphatic words are in striking contrast to the perfunctory references to the navy of President Hayes.[173]

In January, 1882, the House Committee on Naval Affairs, having before it for its instruction its own previous reports on the state of the navy and the recommendations of Secretary Hunt and the First Naval Advisory Board, again took up the subject of building a modern fleet. It called before it the leading officers of the navy and certain manufacturers of iron and steel, and obtained their advice upon the best modes of constructing ships of war and the kinds of materials and armament best adapted for naval purposes. On February 15 a conference, which was held in the office of Secretary Hunt, discussed the same subjects. The Secretary of the Navy, members of the two naval committees, members of the First Naval Advisory Board, and some of the leading naval officers were present. Hunt presided and the greatest interest and harmony prevailed.[174] Important addresses were made by Chairman Harris of the House Naval Committee, Admiral Porter, Rear-Admiral John Rodgers, and Chief Engineer Isherwood.

On March 8 Harris reported a bill to the House, which provided for the construction of fifteen of the vessels recommended by the First Naval Advisory Board: Two 15-knot ships, four 14-knot ships, one steel ram, and eight torpedo boats. The total cost of the fifteen vessels was estimated at $10,000,000. The House Naval Committee, " without hesitation or doubt," recommended the use of steel in their construction. The bill further provided for a temporary board of advice and survey, which was to advise the Secretary of the Navy in regard to all technical matters relating to the construction of the new ships.[175]

Harris was unable to bring his measure to a discussion or a vote, and he therefore dropped it. His next move was to graft some of its features on the naval appropriation bill. On July 1

---

[173] Ann. Rept. of Sec. of N., 1881, 3-6; Richardson, Messages and Papers, VIII, 51.

[174] House Rept., 47 C. 1 S., No. 653.

[175] Congressional Record, XIII, 1719; House Rept., 47 C. 1 S., No. 653.

he proposed to amend the latter by inserting in it a provision for the construction of five new ships. After consulting with the leaders of his party and more accurately ascertaining the sentiment of the House respecting the improvement of the navy, he reduced his proposal to two new ships. An amendment to this effect was accordingly inserted in the bill. The provision of his measure of March 8 providing for a board of advice and survey was also included in it. The naval appropriation bill, containing these provisions, became a law on August 5, 1882.[176]

As respects naval legislation, this epoch-making act is the dividing-line between the old steam navy and the new navy. It is a turning-point in the history of American naval construction. It provided for two new steam cruising vessels of war of the highest attainable speed. The larger of the two cruisers was to have a displacement of from 5000 to 6000 tons; and the smaller from 4300 to 4700 tons. They were to be built of steel of domestic manufacture, and were to be equiped with " full sail power and full steam power." The Secretary of the Navy was authorized to appoint a Naval Advisory Board consisting of seven members— five naval officers and two civilians—to advise and assist the Secretary in building and arming the new ships. In case the board deemed it advisable, the Secretary was to use " interior deflective steel armor." The board was authorized to report on the wisdom and expediency of completing the construction of the five monitors —*Miantonomoh, Monadnock, Puritan, Amphitrite* and *Terror*— which had been commenced by Secretary Robeson and had been stopped in 1877. For the building of the new ships and the " repairing " of the old the act appropriated $3,350,000. It also contained most noteworthy provisions in respect to a limitation of the cost of repairs, and in respect to the navy yards and the personnel of the navy. These will be considered in their appropriate connections.[177]

Soon after the passage of the act of August 5, 1882, Secretary Chandler advertised for plans for the two cruisers, and in the fall of 1882 he selected the members of the " Second Naval Advisory Board." Only one of the members chosen, Lieutenant Edward W. Very, had served on the advisory board appointed by Hunt. Commodore R. W. Shufeldt was the president of the new

---

[176] Congressional Record, XIII, 5569, 5647.
[177] U. S. Statutes at Large, XXII, 291-293.

board. Chandler with difficulty found two civilians of " established reputation and standing as experts in naval or marine construction," such was the low state of these arts in this country. He finally chose Mr. Henry Steers, a ship architect, and Mr. Miers Coryell, a marine engineer. The board was organized on November 13, 1882. Its secretary was Assistant Naval Constructor Francis T. Bowles, who had recently returned from the Royal Naval College in England, where he had received advanced instruction in naval architecture. It at once took up the work of providing a shipbuilding program for 1883. On November 21 it recommended that two 13-knot ships, one steel ram, and one dispatch boat be constructed, and that the five monitors be completed. It was opposed to the building of as large a vessel as the first cruiser authorized by the act of August 5. Chandler agreed with the conclusions of the board, and Congress decided to follow most of them.[178]

On March 3, 1883, Congress appropriated $1,300,000 towards the construction of four new vessels: the smaller steel cruiser authorized by the act of August 5, 1882, two additional steel cruisers of from 2500 to 3000 tons displacement, and one dispatch boat. The building of the larger cruiser authorized at the previous session of Congress was abandoned. One million dollars was appropriated for the completion of the five monitors. On July 3, 1883, contracts for the construction of the four new vessels were awarded to John Roach, of New York City, a noted shipbuilder in his day, and he soon commenced work upon the vessels. The first keel of the new navy, that of the dispatch boat *Dolphin,* was laid on October 15, 1883, at Chester, Pennsylvania, and this ship was launched on April 12, 1884. She was designed for a displacement of 1500 tons, a sea-speed of 15 knots, and an armament of one 6-inch breech-loading rifled gun and of secondary batteries. The largest of the four vessels was the *Chicago.* She was to have a displacement of 4500 tons and a speed of 14 knots. Each of the two other cruisers, the *Atlanta* and *Boston,* were to have a displacement of 3000 tons, and a sea-speed of 13 knots. When completed the total cost of these four vessels was $4,269,000, considerably less than the present cost of a first-class battleship.[179]

[178] Ann. Rept. of Sec. of N., 1882, pp. 22-23, 154-155; House Ex. Doc., 47 C. 2 S., No. 28.
[179] U. S. Statutes at Large, XXII, 476-477.

Measured by recent achievements in naval construction, these first vessels of the new navy appear small, weak, slow-moving and ineffective. At the time, they represented three main types of unarmored warships. It was recognized that they were not adapted for heavy offensive warfare, but chiefly for "general national service upon the high seas." Naturally, in the unsettled state of naval science then existing, a considerable difference of opinion arose as to whether the best types had been chosen. After the work of construction was begun the ships were severely criticised. Admiral Porter maintained that they were too small, and were deficient in sail power. Much fault was found with their sheathing, machinery, speed, and construction. These censures so unsettled the public confidence in the new vessels and in the judgment of the Navy Department, that Secretary Chandler felt called upon to reply to them, and the Senate Naval Committee made a special investigation of the designs of the new ships. The committee approved of the work of the Secretary and his subordinates, and reported that "nothing has appeared to show that the confidence of the Navy Department and of the Advisory Board in the success of these vessels is misplaced." [180]

Secretary Whitney's sharp criticism of the designs and construction of the new ships was not calculated to restore public confidence. He declared that the *Dolphin* was a pleasure boat rather than a ship of war, and he considered the other three vessels defective in construction and deficient in speed. He said that the Department had acted hastily in preparing the designs and in making the contracts. On the completion of the *Dolphin* early in 1885, Whitney at first refused to accept her because of defects in her construction and her failure to develop the stipulated steam-power. Long negotiations between the Department and her builder, John Roach, ensued. Finally Whitney accepted the *Dolphin* conditionally. While involved in his dispute with the Secretary of the Navy, Roach failed in business and made an assignment. The Department thereupon took over the construction of the ships *Chicago, Boston,* and *Atlanta,* and after long delays completed them. While Whitney's criticisms were based upon obvious defects, they nevertheless seem quite excessive in the light of the excellent services the first four vessels of the new navy have rendered, both in peace and in war. The friends of

[180] Ann. Rept. of Sec. of N., 1884, pp. 2-8.

Roach blamed the Secretary of the Navy for the shipbuilder's failure in business.[181]

The shipbuilding program for 1884, according to the recommendations of Secretary Chandler and the Second Naval Advisory Board, called for the construction of seven additional unarmored cruisers at a cost of about $7,450,000. The Senate passed a bill authorizing the construction of several new ships, but the House, under the leadership of Samuel J. Randall, of Pennsylvania, opposed this measure and all others increasing the fleet. No additions to the navy were made in 1884. With this exception, new ships were authorized every year from 1882 to 1897. An act passed on March 3, 1885, provided for the construction of four additional vessels. The new heading, " Increase of the Navy," became a regular feature of the annual naval appropriation bill.

The amount of new tonnage authorized each year varied considerably. The new tonnage provided for under Chandler amounted to 23,076 tons; under Whitney, to 67,183 tons; under Tracy, to 70,831 tons; and under Herbert, to 67,984 tons. Under Chandler, 1882-1885, the authorizations consisted of five unarmored cruisers and three gunboats; under Whitney, 1885-1889, of two battleships of the second class, one armored cruiser, one armored harbor-defense vessel, nine unarmored cruisers, four gunboats, one practice vessel, one ram, one dynamite-gun cruiser, and one torpedo boat; under Tracy, 1889-1893, of four first-class battleships, one armored cruiser, two unarmored cruisers, one torpedo boat, one submarine torpedo boat, and three gunboats; and under Herbert, 1893-1897, of five first-class battleships, 19 torpedo boats, one submarine boat, six gunboats, and one training ship. After much discussion of the merits of the monitors, the five ships of this class, whose construction had been commenced by Robeson, were in 1886 and 1887 ordered to be completed. Counting these five monitors, the total number of ships in the new navy on March 4, 1897, completed, under construction, or authorized, was 78.

A study of the types of these vessels reveals some well-marked developments in naval construction during the years 1882-1897. The first armored vessels were authorized under Whitney in 1886. These were the second-class battleships, *Maine* and *Texas,* and the

[181] Ann. Rept. of Sec. of N., 1885, XIX-XXV.

armored cruiser *New York*. The displacement of the *Texas* was 6315 tons. Under Tracy in 1889 the first first-class battleships, the *Indiana, Massachusetts* and *Oregon,* were ordered. The displacement of each of these ships was 10,288 tons. The largest battleship of the date of 1896, the *Wisconsin,* had a displacement of 11,653 tons. The displacement of the *Chicago,* the largest vessel authorized in 1883, was 5000 tons. The speed of the unarmored cruisers of the date of 1883 was from 15 to 18 knots; and of 1889-1890, from 19 to 23 knots. Under Herbert the construction of torpedo boats was for the first time commenced in earnest. Some of these attained a speed of 30 knots. The first submarine was ordered in 1893. In 1895 a submarine of the Holland type was contracted for. Armored harbor-defense vessels, or monitors and gunboats, types dating from the period of the Civil War, maintained a place in the new navy. The developments in naval construction from 1883 to 1897 in the United States were from small to large ships, from unarmored to armored vessels, and from ships of moderate to ships of high speed. The number of types of vessels increased. As the ships became larger, their armament became more powerful, and their cost of construction greater. The cost of the *Massachusetts,* including her armament, was $6,047,000.[182]

The general policy of the Department was to build the new vessels at private shipyards. Of the 73 new vessels authorized from 1882 to 1897, only four were constructed at the navy yards. These were the second-class battleships *Maine* and *Texas* and the two protected cruisers *Cincinnati* and *Raleigh*. Each of the two methods of construction has its advantages and disadvantages. The evidence seems to show that vessels can be built cheaper at the private yards, but that better vessels are constructed at the government yards. The policy of employing private builders encourages the shipbuilding industry and tends to increase and strengthen the mercantile marine. On the other hand, it weakens the navy yards, and renders them less able to perform their work in time of war.

The next contracts after the first ones, those of 1883, were not let until 1887. Whitney insisted that ample time should be allowed for fully preparing all the plans and specifications. Among the new contractors were William Cramp and Sons, of Philadelphia, and the Union Iron Works of San Francisco, two of the

---

[182] Sen. Doc., 58 C. 2 S., No. 100, 439-441.

most famous and efficient builders of the new navy. Of the three first battleships, the Cramps built the *Indiana* and *Massachusetts,* and the Union Iron Works the *Oregon.* These three vessels, together with the battleship *Iowa* authorized in 1892, were the nucleus of the "battleship fleet," and were the chief reliance of the navy during the war of 1898. They especially distinguished themselves at the battle of Santiago. The memorable cruise of the *Oregon* from the Pacific around Cape Horn to the Atlantic coast will not soon be forgotten.

Some information contained in an address of the great shipbuilder, Charles H. Cramp, shows plainly the wonderful advance in naval construction made between the war of 1861-1865 and that of 1898. The first vessel that the Cramps built for the navy was the *New Ironsides,* completed in 1862; and the last before the Spanish-American War was the battleship *Iowa.* Each ship represented the most advanced type of its day. The *New Ironsides* had one machine—her main engine—involving two steam cylinders; the *Iowa* had 71 machines involving 137 steam cylinders. The guns of the *New Ironsides* were worked, the ammunition hoisted, the ship steered, the engines started and reversed, and the boats lowered, by hand. The ship was lighted by oil lamps, and ventilated, when at all, by natural air currents. In the *Iowa* it "may almost be said that nothing is done by hand except the opening and closing of throttles and pressing of electric buttons. Her guns are loaded, trained, and fired, her ammunition hoisted, her turrets turned, her torpedoes—mechanisms in themselves—are tubed and ejected, the ship steered, her boats hoisted out and in, the interior lighted and ventilated, the great searchlight operated, and even orders transmitted from bridge or conning-tower to all parts, by mechanical appliances." [183]

In building the first vessels of the new navy, not a few difficulties and embarrassments were encountered in obtaining suitable materials. During the Civil War the United States had constructed her own ships, armor and guns, and they were of the most-approved types of that period. Since 1865 great advances had been made in the construction of ships and armament, and with these this country had not kept pace, since she had permitted her navy to decay. Among the most important improvements, were the substitution of steel for wrought-iron armor, and

[183] C. H. Cramp, Necessity of Experience to Efficiency, 3-5.

of steel, built-up, breech-loading rifles for cast-iron, muzzle-loading, smooth-bore guns. In 1883 steel forgings for the engine shafts and large guns, modern armor-plate, and the best machine and rapid-fire guns were not manufactured in the United States. The fabrication of high-grade mild-steel plates was a new and undeveloped industry in this country.

At the very beginning of the work of rebuilding the fleet, it was recognized that the United States must not be dependent upon foreign countries for any of the materials of naval construction, and most especially for gun-forgings and armor-plate. Secretary Chandler early recommended that steps be taken to domesticate the manufacture of forgings and armor. In April, 1883, the Gun Foundry Board, consisting of army and navy officers, was appointed. Its president was Rear-Admiral Edward Simpson. It thoroughly investigated the manufacture of heavy ordnance for the army and the navy, and made an elaborate report in February, 1884. It visited the factories of arms in England, France and Russia, and would have inspected Krupp's establishment in Germany, could it have obtained permission. The board recommended that the government of the United States should encourage domestic manufacturers to establish foundries for the making of steel gun-forgings, and that the government itself should establish two gun factories, one for the army and the other for the navy. The private foundries were to supply the public factories with the required gun-forgings. The board further recommended that the naval factory should be located at the Washington navy yard. Meantime, while these questions were being agitated and decided, Secretary Chandler imported from England both gun-forgings and armor-plate.[184]

Soon after entering the Department, Secretary Whitney took up the subject of domesticating the manufacture of these essential articles, and as a preliminary step he stopped their importation. In 1886 the subject was reported upon by the Endicott Board on Fortifications and Other Defences composed of army and navy officers, and by two special committees of Congress, one of the House and the other of the Senate. The board and the committees made reports which greatly elucidated the problems involved. They agreed that substantial encouragement should be given to

[184] Ann. Rept. of Sec. of N., 1884, pp. 255-382.

domestic manufacturers. This was to take the form of binding the government to purchase large quantities of gun-forgings and armor-plate—some $35,000,000 worth. Congress naturally hesitated to authorize so large an expenditure of money. Meanwhile, Whitney undertook to interest the steel manufacturers in the subject. In the summer of 1886 he consolidated in one advertisement all the requirements for gun-forgings and armor-plate for the ships of war then authorized, stipulating that these articles should be of domestic manufacture and should be delivered within two and one-half years, a time deemed sufficient to erect the necessary manufactories and to fabricate the articles. He opened up correspondence with the principal steel-makers of the United States. As a result of his efforts, he received bids from four companies to supply all or a part of the required forgings and armor; and in April, 1887, he contracted with the Bethlehem Iron Company, of South Bethlehem, Pennsylvania, to furnish all the requirements of the vessels then authorized, for the sum of $4,462,000. Congress had already, on March 3, seconded Whitney's efforts by appropriating $4,000,000 for armor-plate and gun-steel of domestic manufacture. The fabrication of the articles in the United States was thus assured.[185]

During this same period Whitney effected the establishment of a naval gun factory under the management of the Navy Department. For this purpose Congress, on August 3, 1886, appropriated $1,000,000. In the same year Whitney transferred the Washington navy yard, the site chosen for the factory, to the Bureau of Ordnance, which was to have charge of the new establishment. In the spring of 1887 the conversion of the old forge and anchor shop of this yard into a gun shop for the manufacture of 6-inch and 8-inch guns was begun. The construction of a large new gun shop was soon undertaken, and modern tools and machinery were installed. Year by year the Naval Gun Factory has added to its facilities until it has become one of the best and largest manufactories of heavy naval guns in the world. Within five years after its establishment it was making cannon with calibers varying from 4 to 13 inches. In 1882 there was not one high-powered gun in the navy, and only 87 guns that were worth retaining. In December, 1896, Secretary Herbert reported

[185] Ann. Rept. of Sec. of N., 1887, IV, 475.

that 196 cannon were under construction, and that during the past four years 213 cannon had been completed. The guns which were being built were rifled, built-up, forged-steel guns. They consisted of several parts, which were assembled and machined into one solid mass of steel.[186]

The domestication of the manufacture of gun-forgings and armor-plate and the founding of the Naval Gun Factory were among the most noteworthy achievements of Whitney's administration. A third event of a similar sort was the establishment in the United States of a manufactory of Hotchkiss arms. The Hotchkiss Ordnance Company of Paris made machine and rapid-fire guns of the most-approved types. The Navy Department had been importing these guns for the secondary batteries of its ships. On Whitney's refusing to buy them unless they were made in the United States, the Hotchkiss company saw fit to erect a branch manufactory in this country.[187] The only foreign articles which the Secretary of the Navy was willing to import were drawings and designs of the latest ships and machinery. He resisted a strong influence in Congress to give to English builders a part of the work of constructing our marine engines. For his domestication of these various naval industries he deserves unstinted praise.

Whitney's contract with the Bethlehem Iron Company called for the first delivery of armor by February, 1890. The work of installing the necessary machinery proved more difficult than was anticipated, and the first substantial deliveries were not made until 1892. Embarrassed by these delays, Secretary Tracy made efforts to obtain a second source of supply, and in November, 1890, he entered into a contract with Carnegie, Phipps and Company, steel manufacturers of Pittsburgh, for 5900 tons of armor-plate. The second company pushed its work most vigorously, and by December, 1891, it had delivered 150 tons of nickel-steel armor. Meantime, a second source of gun-forgings, the Midvale Steel Company of Philadelphia, had been established. It made its first delivery in September, 1890.[188]

During Tracy's administration the Navy Department exhibited much enterprise in testing various kinds of armor. In the history

---

[186] Ann. Rept. of Sec. of N., 1882, p. 7; 1887, p. 235; 1896, p. 25.
[187] Ann. Rept. of Sec. of N., 1887, IV-V.
[188] Ann. Rept. of Sec. of N., 1890, pp. 18-19; 1891, pp. 10-11.

of the development of this article, some of these tests are justly famous. In 1890, at the Annapolis proving-grounds, three kinds of armor were tried, the English compound armor, Le Creusot all-steel armor, and a sample of nickel-steel armor of French manufacture. The superiority of the plates made of nickel-steel was most conclusively demonstrated, and the Department at once decided to use this armor in preference to all other kinds. Congress rose to the occasion and immediately appropriated $1,000,000 for the purchase of steel. " The Annapolis trials of 1890," according to Secretary Tracy, " may be said to have stripped off, in five shots, half the protection of the armored fleet of Great Britain, and of most of the fleets of the world.[189]

In the same year, 1890, some other interesting tests of armor were made at Annapolis. These showed that a surface-hardened steel-plate possessed a remarkable resistance to perforation. The process of hardening the surface of the steel was named from its inventor the " Harvey process," and armor so treated came to be known as " Harveyed " armor. From 1890 to 1892 the Department was testing and improving this armor, and by the end of 1892 it had demonstrated that the Harveyed nickel-steel plates were superior to all others. The Harvey process, or one similar thereto, was adopted by all the great naval powers. The trials and developments of armor-plate made by the Department from 1889 to 1893 were among the signal events of Tracy's administration, and in respect to the science of armor, they placed the United States in the foremost ranks among the naval powers.[190]

In 1889 the navy had no automobile torpedoes. Tracy introduced them by contracting for 100 18-inch Whitehead automobile torpedoes, the most successful torpedoes in use, and he domesticated their manufacture. Tracy also introduced into the navy heavy rapid-fire guns of 4-inch, 5-inch and 6-inch calibers. During his administration the Department began the manufacture of a smokeless gunpowder of a better variety than any hitherto made, and also of certain high explosives which could be safely used in shells fired from high-powered guns. These improved articles were developed at the Naval Torpedo Station at Newport. Tracy also began the fabrication of gun-cotton in large quantities, and he

[189] Ann. Rept. of Sec. of N., 1890, p. 19; 1891, p. 11; 1892, p. 15.
[190] Ann. Rept. of Sec. of N., 1891, pp. 11-13; 1892, pp. 16-19.

domesticated the manufacture of armor-piercing projectiles, a most important industry.[191]

The Department's manufactories of guns, ammunition, explosives and projectiles were in charge of the Bureau of Ordance. This bureau also inspected articles of a similar sort made by private firms—torpedoes, rapid-fire and machine guns, gun-carriages, gunpowder, shot, shells and projectiles. The principal private manufactories of these articles were located in the New England and Middle States. The principal public establishments were the gun factory at Washington, the torpedo station and the torpedo school at Newport, and the naval proving-grounds at Annapolis and Indianhead. In 1890 and 1891 the bureau purchased new proving-grounds, which were at once ample in area and convenient to the Naval Gun Factory at Washington. They were situated 26 miles below Washington, on the Potomac, at Indianhead, Maryland, and contained 881 acres. The new grounds were rapidly improved, and were made ready for the testing of guns, fuses, projectiles and gunpowders. In 1892 the old proving-grounds at Annapolis were abandoned for the new site. During the same year the Bureau of Ordnance acquired 315 acres of land at Lake Denmark, New Jersey, for a naval gunpowder depot. In 1896 a tract of land was obtained near Portsmouth, Virginia, for the Saint Julien naval magazine, and 25 acres were added to the site of the naval magazine at Fort Mifflin, Pennsylvania. [192] The work of the Bureau of Ordance was greatly increased by the rebuilding of the fleet and by the remarkable improvements being made in the science of naval ordnance. Since its establishment this has been one of the most efficient of the naval bureaus, and has been served by most able and expert officers.

By the latter part of Tracy's administration most of the embarrassments caused by the inexperience of the United States in modern naval construction and by the necessity of establishing new naval industries had been removed, and the reconstruction of the navy was greatly accelerated. The slowness with which the work at first proceeded is plainly shown by the dates of the commissioning of the first four vessels, authorized in 1882 and 1883.

The *Dolphin* was commissioned in December, 1885, *Atlanta* in 1886, *Boston* in 1887, and *Chicago* in April, 1889. Under Chand-

[191] Ann. Rept. of Sec. of N., 1891, p. 15; 1892, p. 6.
[192] Miscl. data, Bureau of Yards and Docks, 35, 46, 52, 83.

ler, no new vessels were commissioned. Under Whitney three vessels of an aggregate tonnage of 7863 tons were commissioned, under Tracy 19 vessels of 54,832 tons, and under Herbert 22 vessels of 177,184 tons.

As the new ships were added to the navy, the old ones disappeared from it. A very important provision of the act of August 5, 1882, forbade the repairing of any ship, the expense of which exceeded 30 per cent of the cost of a new ship of the same size and of like materials. The permissible cost of repairs was shortly reduced to 20, and later to 10 per cent. The act of 1882 also provided that a board of naval officers should regularly inspect the ships of the navy and condemn those that were unfit for service. This act put an end to the expensive policy of repairing or rebuilding old and worthless vessels of obsolete types. In 1882 two inspection boards condemned 44 ships, almost one-third of the entire number borne upon the Navy List at that time, and recommended that they should be broken up or sold. In 1893, of the old wooden ships, only nine remained in active service. Secretary Herbert believed that all of these would be retired within the next three years, except the *Hartford* and *Kearsarge,* which were specially exempted for sentimental or patriotic reasons from the operation of the clause limiting the cost of repairs. In 1896 several of the old vessels were still used as training, school, or receiving ships, or by the naval militia.

An occasion illustrative of the disposition of the worn-out hulks of the navy, was the opening of bids at the Navy Department in Washington on September 24, 1883, received in response to an advertisement for the sale of 21 old ships. The total cost of these relics of a bygone age was $15,380,000. They sold for $308,273. Most of them antedated the Civil War. One of them was the 74-gun ship *New Orleans,* whose construction had been commenced at Sacketts Harbor during the War of 1812. For many years she had remained upon the stocks, and was now rotten and almost worthless for any purpose. She was sheltered by a ship-house, which, having been injured by a gale of wind, was, in 1879, pronounced valueless. In anticipation of a possible war with Great Britain, in which neither the *New Orleans* nor the ship-house could have been of any appreciable service, they were carefully guarded for 68 years at a cost to the Department of some $50,000—a fine illustration of the inertia and waste of governments. The

New Orleans sold for $427. Another of these old ships was the *Ohio,* built in 1820. We are informed that on the occasion of the opening of the bids, the Secretary's office had the "appearance of an auction shop. The majority of those present were the bidders themselves, though a naval officer occasionally strolled in to see what some favorite old hulk was selling for, and a dozen or so newspaper men loitered around on the desks and window-sills, taking notes as each bid was opened and read aloud by Chief Clerk Hogg. Fully two hours was occupied in opening and recording the proposals. The prices offered exceeded what was expected. Mr. Chandler stood behind his desk apparently occupied with business, but when a bid was read that reached much above the appraised value, he would glance around at the bidders, and by a nod of the head signify his assent." [193]

The building of the new navy had no large effect upon the annual naval appropriations until 1888, when they reached their high-water mark during Whitney's administration, $26,000,000. For 1881, when no new vessels were being built, the sum appropriated was $14,000,000. By 1887 it had advanced to $16,000,000. From 1889 to 1891, it varied from $20,000,000 to $24,000,000. In 1892, it reached its highest point during the periods 1881-1897, $32,000,000. The financial depression may in part account for the fall to $22,000,000 in 1894. In 1897 it had risen to $31,000,000. The average sum carried by the naval appropriation bills from 1881 to 1897 was $21,000,000, a strikingly small figure when one recollects that the annual naval expenditures during Robeson's administration, 1869-1877, exceeded it. [194]

Under Secretary Tracy the fixing of a shipbuilding program for a term of years assumed importance. According to one of his recommendations the future navy should consist of 100 vessels—20 battleships, 20 coast-defense vessels, and 60 cruisers. To bring the fleet up to this point would necessitate the annual expenditure of $9,000,000 for fifteen years. The McCann Policy Board which Tracy appointed in July, 1889, recommended the expenditure of more than twice that amount. Its program called for 18 first-class, 12 second-class, and 5 third-class battleships, 10 rams, 9 thin-armored cruisers, 15 protected cruisers, 15 torpedo cruisers, 8 minor vessels, and 100 torpedo boats. It estimated that these

[193] Army and Navy Journal, XXI, 177.
[194] Congressional Record, XXVIII, 4567.

192 vessels would cost $282,000,000. Its recommendations were regarded as extravagant by both the Secretary of the Navy and Congress.[195]

NAVAL ESTABLISHMENTS, OFFICERS AND SEAMEN, 1881-1897.

The noteworthy act of August 5, 1882, contained some important legislation respecting navy yards.[196] It provided that, in case the money which it appropriated should prove insufficient for the maintenance of all the yards, the Secretary of the Navy should close those which could be best dispensed with; and it authorized the appointment of a commission of three men—one line officer, one staff officer, and one civilian—to report upon the navy yards and determine whether any of them should be sold. At this time the United States owned nine navy yards situated at the following places on the Atlantic, Gulf and Pacific coasts: Portsmouth, Boston, New London, New York, League Island, Washington, Norfolk, Pensacola and Mare Island. Naval stations were maintained at Newport, Annapolis, Port Royal, Key West, New Orleans and Sacketts Harbor. The total cost of the improvements, repairs and sites of the nine navy yards from 1798 to 1882 was $54,000,000. About the year 1882 the annual expenditures of the navy yards were $4,500,000. On November 16, 1882, the total number of officers employed at them (excluding the New London yard which at this time was wholly undeveloped) was 326; enlisted men and marines, 2501; civilian employees, 4462; total number of men of all classes, 7289. At this time no vessels were being constructed, and only seven were being repaired. Secretary Chandler firmly believed that more capital was invested in the yards, more money was annually spent for their maintenance, and more men were employed in them than were required by the existing or prospective wants of the naval service. He therefore determined to make such reductions in their number and the cost of their maintenance as the circumstances seemed to warrant.[197]

On October 9, Chandler appointed the commission authorized by the act of August 5, 1882. Its members were Commodore S. B.

---

[195] Sen. Ex. Doc., 51 C. 1 S., No. 43.
[196] U. S. Statutes at Large, XXII, 289-290.
[197] Ann. Rept. of Sec. of N., 1882, 10-12.

Luce, president, Chief Engineer C. H. Loring, and A. B. Mullett, sometime supervising architect of the treasury. The report of this commission laid the foundations for the policy respecting navy yards that was pursued for the next fifteen years. It visited the chief establishments of the navy, and made a thorough investigation of their condition. It recommended that the establishments at New York, Norfolk and Mare Island be retained as first-class yards; that those at Pensacola, League Island and New London should be closed, and that the Washington yard should be used for manufacturing purposes only. The members of the commission differed as to the proper disposition to be made of the establishments at Portsmouth and Boston. Two members recommended the closing of the Portsmouth yard. Only one member was in favor of continuing the Boston yard in full operation.[198]

In 1883 Chandler put in force many of the recommendations of the commission. He doubtless would have gone farther than he did, had he had the support of his chiefs of bureaus. He closed the Pensacola, League Island and New London yards. At the Boston yard, he discontinued the construction and repair of ships, but continued the ropewalk and manufactory of sails. He reduced considerably the operations of the Portsmouth yard, but permitted there the repairing of wooden ships. He decreased the total number of men employed at the several yards by about 1000.

In respect to the reformation of the administration of the yards, Chandler was less successful in enforcing the views of the Luce commission, which recommended a " reorganization and concentration of the mechanical departments in every navy yard, so that there shall be but one shop in each for the performance of the same class of work." It is recollected that the shops, property and employees of the yards had been divided among the naval bureaus. Each bureau at Washington had in each yard its own representatives, employees and storehouses, and even its own power-station. A navy yard was described at this time as consisting of a " number of separate and comparatively independent establishments, little principalities as it were, each owing allegiance to its own sovereign, the chief of the bureau to which it belongs." Chandler said that the principal defects in the administration of the yards arose from the excessive division of labor, responsibility

[198] Ann. Rept. of Sec. of N., 1883, pp. 15, 107.

and executive power, and from the combination under one management of a manufactory of ships and naval supplies and a " military post." These could be remedied by concentrating the construction, repair and equipment of ships under one technical head, and by separating this work from that of the " military post." The changes recommended by the Luce commission had his hearty support, and he issued orders putting them into operation, but the opposition of his bureau chiefs and other persons interested in the maintenance of the old system prevented his orders from being carried out. Convinced that he could not reform the yards without the assistance of Congress, he asked that body to pass the needed legislation, but failed to obtain it. The yards continued to suffer from an excessive decentralization of their administration.[199]

In concentrating the work and management of the yards, Whitney was a little more successful than Chandler. He introduced or reintroduced the system of general storekeepers, to which reference has already been made in a previous chapter. This went far towards centralizing the making of purchases, the keeping of accounts, and the care and preservation of stores. Whitney continued this policy of concentration by making the Boston yard a manufactory of articles of equipment, and the Washington yard a naval gun factory.

The reforms of the navy yards effected by Tracy and Herbert were along different lines from those of Chandler and Whitney. The influence of politics and favoritism in the selection of the employees of the yards had been the bane of their administration since the days of Andrew Jackson. At times these sinister powers were extraordinarily potent, as for instance, under Toucey in 1857-1861 and Robeson in 1869-1877. At other times they appeared to subside somewhat, but they were always in no small degree operative. During the presidential campaign of 1888 more than 1000 men were temporarily employed at the New York navy yard for political purposes.[200] Under Tracy the repair and construction of the ships of the new navy assumed much importance. Since these vessels were complicated mechanisms, intelligent and skilful artisans were needed even to repair

[199] Ann. Rept. of Sec. of N., 1883, pp. 17, 107; 1884, pp. 16-19; Congressional Record, XVII, 5833-5834.

[200] Fourteenth Rept. of U. S. Civil Service Commission, 180.

them. In the days of the old navy, a political appointee, who could perchance bore and mortise in wood, might be of some service. But under the new conditions some technical skill was required of the workmen. Political bosses could no longer be permitted to name the employees of the yards.

As a preliminary to the introduction of a system of selection based upon merit, Tracy in April, 1891, dismissed all the foremen of the yards. To assist him in filling the vacancies he had thus created, he appointed a board of practical men for each yard. These boards chose for foremen the very best mechanics, after they had proved their abilities by practical tests. Next, Tracy established in each yard an employment board composed of the heads of departments and their assistants. Its duty was to classify all applicants for positions according to their trades. When the head of one of the mechanical departments of a yard desired to fill vacancies, he made a requisition on the employment board, which sent him a list of names taken in the order in which the men had applied. On receiving these names, the head of the department gave the men a trial, and selected for permanent employment those who proved capable.[201]

Tracy put the new system into operation in the face of much opposition from the politicians, and from others who were interested in maintaining the old system. The presidential campaign of 1892 was the first in many years, in which the navy yards had not been manipulated for partisan purposes. It is said that no workmen were employed during this year otherwise than in accordance with Tracy's rules. The commandant at New York was of the opinion that the new system of appointment effected a reduction of 25 per cent in the cost of the work of his yard. Secretary Herbert continued Tracy's system and improved it. Plausible complaints, however, were made from time to time that Herbert did not operate it fairly. He maintained that these were groundless. Herbert, however, conceived that an equal division of the employees of the yards between the Democrats and the Republicans would be advantageous, and he permitted Tracy's rules to be operated so as to bring about gradually a rough equalization between the two parties. Probably under both Tracy and Herbert politics and favoritism played some part in manipulating the rules.

[201] Ann. Rept. of Sec. of N., 1891, pp. 49-51.

The spirit of the old system still survived. A long step towards the establishment of a fair and just system, however, had been taken. Another extension of the principles of civil service was made by President Cleveland, when on May 6, 1896, he placed all the clerks, messengers and watchmen of the navy yards within the classified service, and directed that in the future all appointments to these offices should be made through the Civil Service Commission.[202]

The improvement of the navy yards and dry docks from 1881 to 1897 by no means kept pace with the construction of new ships. The condition of those yards which Chandler closed inevitably became worse. During Whitney and Tracy's administration modern tools and machinery adapted to the construction and repair of the new ships were installed at Norfolk, New York and Mare Island. Much pressure was brought to bear to obtain the fitting out of other yards in the same manner, but it was successfully resisted. Under Tracy and Herbert the expenditures for yards and docks were considerably increased, and in view of the large number of modern vessels of war that were being placed in commission a still more liberal policy could have been followed with advantage to the navy. In 1889 a navy board recommended a scheme of development for the League Island yard involving the expenditure of $14,000,000, and about the same time another board proposed to expend $8,000,000 in improving the New York yard. The Navy Department, although favorable to the adoption of a more liberal policy in respect to these establishments, did not accept the extensive plans of the boards.[203]

Between 1889 and 1897 several new docks, considerably larger than the old ones, were completed. The new docks, however, were generally too small to accommodate the larger battleships, and in 1897 the docking facilities for these vessels were entirely inadequate. Two new graving docks, one of concrete and the other of wood, were constructed at the New York yard; the former was completed in 1890, and the latter in 1897. The dimensions of the wood dock were as follows: Length, 669 feet; breadth, 151 feet; and depth over sill, 29 feet. At the time of its completion it was the largest dock in the United States. In 1889

[202] Ann. Rept. of Sec. of N., 1892, pp. 49-53; 1893, pp. 51-52; 1894, pp. 38-39; 1896, pp. 45-48.
[203] Ann. Rept. of Sec. of N., 1889, p. 28.

a wood graving dock for the Norfolk yard was completed, and in 1891 a new wood and concrete dock was ready for use at League Island. The granite dock which was begun at Mare Island in 1872 was not finished until 1891. Its cost was $2,772,000. In 1883 37 acres of land was purchased for $5000 for the naval station at Port Royal, South Carolina, and a large timber dry dock was completed there in 1895. It was, however, barely commodious enough to admit the new battleship *Indiana,* which was repaired at Port Royal in March, 1896, the first vessel of her class to be docked in the United States.[204]

With the development of the commerce of the United States in the Pacific Ocean and with the growth of Washington and Oregon, the sentiment in Congress in favor of the establishment of a dry dock and navy yard on the Northwest Coast increased. The Pacific squadron had considerable need for a repair shop in this region, the most northerly ports of which are some 1000 miles from the Mare Island navy yard near San Francisco. In 1888 Congress authorized the appointment of a commission to select a site for a navy yard and docks on the Northwest Coast. It was duly organized, with Captain A. T. Mahan, the well-known naval historian and strategist, as its president. It visited various sites on the coast of Washington and Oregon, and in September, 1889, made an elaborate report, in which it decided in favor of Port Turner on Puget Sound. The commission said, however, that a suitable site might be found on Lake Washington, a body of water lying back of Seattle, provided a navigable canal could be constructed connecting the lake with the sound.[205]

The Department was not satisfied with this report. Moreover, those who were interested in other sites wished to reopen the subject. Congress therefore authorized the appointment of a second commission. This was chosen by President Harrison on September 6, 1890. It was composed, according to law, of two naval officers, two army officers, and two civilians. Its president was Captain T. O. Selfridge, and its two civilian members were Ex-Senator T. C. Platt, of New York, and Ex-Secretary of the Navy R. W. Thompson, of Indiana. After paying a visit to the Northwest Coast, this commission came to the same conclusion

[204] Congressional Record, XXVIII, 3254; XXXIX, 3497.
[205] Ann. Rept. of Sec. of N., 1889, pp. 30-31.

as the former one, and recommended that the proposed dockyard be located at Point Turner in the estuary of Port Orchard on Puget Sound. In March, 1891, the Department detailed Lieutenant A. B. Wyckoff to select and purchase a body of land on Port Orchard, not exceeding 200 acres. Wyckoff chose a tract consisting of 191 acres, which he bought for $10,312. He was made the first commandant of the " Puget Sound Naval Station." In 1892 the construction of a large dry dock of wood and masonry, 650 feet in length, was commenced, and in 1896 it was completed at a cost of $633,000.[206]

The closing of the Pensacola yard by Chandler in 1883 again opened the question as to the proper site of a navy yard on the Gulf coast. New Orleans was not slow to present her claims and qualifications. At various times since the acquisition of Louisiana in 1803, the Navy Department had maintained a naval station at or near that city. Some years before the Civil War, the Department had come into the possession of a naval reservation, containing 23 acres, and located at Algiers opposite New Orleans on the Mississippi. In the eighties it maintained here a small naval station. In 1888 Congress authorized the appointment of a commission to report " as to the most desirable location on or near the coast of the Gulf of Mexico and the south Atlantic coast for navy yards and dry docks." The president of the commission was Commodore W. P. McCann. After visiting Key West, Tampa, Pensacola, Mount Vernon, Mobile and New Orleans, it made a report in the fall of 1889, in which it recommended the establishment of a navy yard at Algiers. The claims of this location were now pressed unremittingly on Congress by New Orleans and Louisiana. The people of Florida, and especially of Pensacola, were naturally much dissatisfied with this report.[207]

Congress, doubtless glad of an opportunity to postpone its final decision, concluded to reopen the question of locating a yard in the South, and authorized the appointment of a second commission. This was selected by President Harrison on November 22, 1890. Its president was Captain F. M. Bunce. After going over the same ground the Bunce commission came to the same conclusions as its predecessor, and recommended Algiers. Congress appar-

---

[206] Sen. Ex. Doc., 51 C. 2 S., No. 24; Ann. Rept. of Sec. of N., 1890, p. 36; 1892, p. 105.

[207] Ann. Rept. of Sec. of N., 1889, p. 29.

ently was not particularly desirous of establishing a dockyard at this point. It did, however, appropriate some money to enlarge the site of the naval reservation. In October, 1894, the Department purchased 47 acres of land adjoining its holdings at Algiers. In 1895 the chief of the Bureau of Yards and Docks asked for an appropriation of $100,000 with which to commence the construction of a dry dock at the New Orleans naval station, estimated to cost $1,250,000, but nothing more was done at this time towards making the proposed improvement.[208]

Secretary Chandler manifested considerable interest in the establishment of foreign coaling stations, but neither he nor his immediate successors were able to increase their number. In 1883 the navy had coaling stations at Honolulu, Tutuila in the Samoan Islands, and Pichilingue in Lower California, and the *Monongahela*, which had a capacity for 1000 tons of coal, was being fitted as a storeship for Callao, Peru. Chandler recommended that these coaling stations be placed upon a firm basis, and that additional stations be established in Haytí, Curaçao, Brazil, the Straits of Magellan, Central America, the Isthmus of Panama, Madagascar, Liberia, the island of Fernando Po and Korea, but nothing came of his recommendation. In 1889, however, Congress appropriated $100,000 to establish permanently a naval station on the shores of the bay of Pago Pago, Tutuila. In the summer of that year Rear-Admiral L. A. Kimberly, in pursuance of orders from the Department, made a careful survey of the harbor of Pago Pago, and selected a tract containing 121 acres as a site for a naval station. In 1891 and 1892 the Department, aided by the American consul at Apia, purchased the land. The negotiations were quite tedious, since the titles to the land were held, in accordance with the customs of Samoa, by families and not by individuals.[209]

Until after the Spanish-American War of 1898, the naval establishments outside of the States were few and unimportant. As we have seen, there were but few foreign coaling stations. Marine barracks were established at Sitka, Alaska, in 1891-1892, and a naval hospital at Yokohama in 1872.

During the period of naval decadence following the Civil War the naval hospital service suffered exceedingly. Its buildings,

---

[208] House Ex. Doc., 52 C. 1 S., No. 79; Ann. Rept. of Sec. of N., 1895, p. 79.
[209] Ann. Rept. of Sec. of N., 1883, p. 32; 1893, pp. 101-103.

which were of an antiquated style, became worn and dilapidated. Their appliances and interior fittings were not adapted to the needs of modern surgery and sanitary science. In 1874 Congress appropriated only $5000 for their repair and improvement. This had to suffice for seven large hospitals, two smaller ones, a large building at New York used for a naval laboratory, and the various grounds connected with these establishments. With the revival of interest in the navy, the condition of the naval medical service slowly improved. Some of the larger hospitals were thoroughly renovated, and fitted out in accordance with the latest improvements in medical science. New surgical appliances were introduced. In 1896 all the hospitals were supplied with complete outfits of bacteriological and chemical supplies and with aseptic operating rooms and furniture. In 1887 a hospital was erected at Widow's Island, Maine, for the treatment of infectious diseases. Before it was ready for use improvements in the treatment of this class of diseases and in the construction of ships rendered it obsolete. In 1894 the Bureau of Medicine and Surgery recommended that it be sold.[210]

In 1883 the Bureau of Medicine and Surgery founded in Washington the Museum of Hygiene. Its primary purpose was to collect information relating to the " hygiene of civil life, private life, and naval life." It made a large collection of articles, plans and appliances illustrative of hygiene and sanitation, and brought together in its library many books dealing with these and kindred subjects. Soon after it was founded it established an important experimental laboratory for the investigation of chemical, physiological, biological and bacteriological problems, and it has made some valuable investigations for the Navy Department. In 1894 the museum was removed to permanent quarters in the Old Naval Observatory, in northwest Washington.

In 1893 Secretary Herbert established at the naval laboratory in New York a department of medical and professional instruction for the assistant surgeons of the navy. Its purpose was to familiarize these young men with their new duties immediately after their entrance into the service. The instructors of the school were drawn from the surgeons of the naval hospital, naval laboratory and medical examining board at New York. The course of instruction, which was to continue for a period of not less

[210] Ann. Rept. of Sec. of N., 1894, p. 633; 1896, pp. 568, 576.

than three months, embraced various subjects relating to the physical, medical and surgical sciences, and to the routine and professional duties of naval surgeons. The establishment of this
school was in keeping with the general movement which was now
in progress to provide the navy with a more highly trained and
efficient personnel.[211]

A most noteworthy event in naval education was the founding of
the Naval War College in 1884. Some years previous, the establishment of a post-graduate school for naval officers had been
advocated in the PROCEEDINGS of the United States Naval Institute, a high-class professional and technical quarterly published
by the officers of the American navy, by Lieutenant-Commander
C. F. Goodrich who had presented in its pages an outline of the
studies which he thought ought to be pursued at the proposed
school. Secretary Chandler became interested in the subject, and
on May 3, 1884, he directed a naval board, consisting of Commodore S. B. Luce, Commander W. T. Sampson, and Lieutenant-
Commander C. F. Goodrich, to prepare an advanced course of
studies for naval officers. On June 13 the board made a report
in which it recommended in most emphatic terms the establishment
of a post-graduate school of the navy. It also outlined a course
of instruction in the science and art of naval warfare and in
international law and history. After a consideration of the advantages offered by Washington, Annapolis, New York, Newport and Boston as a site for the school, it recommended Newport,
chiefly for the reason that the torpedo school was located there,
but also because the Department possessed at Newport proper
buildings and grounds.

On October 6, 1884, Chandler, by a general order, established
the Naval War College at Newport, Rhode Island. He placed the
school under the general direction of the Bureau of Navigation,
and assigned for its use the principal building on Coasters Harbor
Island. According to Chandler's order, the president of the college was to be a naval officer not below the grade of commander,
who was to be assisted in the performance of his duties by a
faculty. The president and the members of the faculty were to
constitute an academic board, over which the president was to
preside. The board was to meet regularly once a month, and also

[211] Ann. Rept. of Sec. of N., 1893, p. 565.

on the call of the president, and it was to prepare a course of instruction. Commodore Stephen B. Luce was designated as the first president of the new college.[212]

Soon after the college was established Captain A. T. Mahan was ordered to prepare to give instruction in naval history and naval tactics, and Professor J. R. Soley was selected to conduct the courses in international law, and Paymaster R. W. Allen those in naval law and administration. The first session of the school was held in September, 1885, but it was not a complete success. Of the three instructors above mentioned, Professor Soley only was able to be present. President Luce invited several other naval officers to deliver courses of lectures, but they could not comply with his request, since the Department neglected to assign them to duty at the school. The only regular instructors at the first session were Professor Soley and Lieutenant Tasker H. Bliss, of the army.[213] For some years a strong opposition or indifference to the college was manifested among the naval officers, many of whom did not sympathize with its aims and purposes, believing that the only necessary post-graduate school of the navy was the quarter-deck of a ship. Congress was not inclined to favor an institution founded without its consent by executive decree. In 1886 the House Naval Committee made a report adverse to the school. The first years of the Naval War College were unpropitious, and not until Secretary Herbert's administration was its future assured.

During its critical period the college was ably served by Presidents S. B. Luce, A. T. Mahan and H. C. Taylor, and Professor J. R. Soley. Its sessions were held in the summer or fall. Instruction was given largely by lectures. In January, 1889, the college was united with the torpedo station on Goat Island, and its management became somewhat complicated. In 1894 the war college, naval training station, torpedo school and torpedo station, all located at Newport, were consolidated under one command. In 1890 and 1891 the school was closed. In September, 1892, chiefly through the efforts of Assistant Secretary of the Navy Soley, it was reopened. It now occupied a part of a new building, which had been erected for the war college and the torpedo school

<hr />

[212] PROCEEDINGS of U. S. Naval Inst., V, 316, 323-344; Sen. Ex. Doc., 48 C. 2 S., No. 68; General Orders of Navy Dept., No. 325.

[213] Ann. Rept. of Sec. of N., 1885, pp. 96-103.

on Coasters Harbor Island at a cost of $100,000. This was a handsome structure of granite, 210 feet long and 48 feet broad.

Under Herbert the scope of the college's work was considerably broadened. In 1894 a permanent staff of officers began the study of problems relating to coast defense, naval strategy and international law. Previous to this time the assignment of the members of the faculty to duty at Newport had been temporary. The college now came to emphasize the solution of war problems. It began to perform some of the duties of a " general staff " of the navy. It prepared war plans, war charts and other data relating to the solution of strategical and tactical questions. This valuable information was either filed at the Office of Naval Intelligence in Washington, or in the archives of the college at Newport. For the elucidation of various disputed points in naval science, war games or exercises were employed. The work of the college was favorably commented upon by foreign naval experts.[214]

During the period 1881-1897 the naval personnel underwent no transformation or improvement similar to that of the fleet. The stagnation which began soon after the Civil War continued to exist. Many circumstances rendered the service discouraging to the officers. Their pay and emoluments remained stationary. The age at which they reached the higher ranks advanced. The rate of promotion decreased. In regard to these subjects, every corps in the navy was dissatisfied. Bills of all sorts in behalf of this or that corps were introduced in Congress. Organizations of officers were formed to further desired legislation. The differences between the line and the staff, and especially between the line and the engineers, became more acute. Since it was a period of peace, few opportunities for important service at sea were presented to the officers. The paucity of ships in commission relating to the number of officers in the navy tended to lower the importance of sea-service, and to elevate shore-duty at its expense. The all-absorbing work of rebuilding the fleet had the same tendency. Service on board the obsolete and antiquated hulks of the old navy was not attractive. The junior line officers had especial causes for discouragement. Their promotions were few. Their duties aboard ship were often petty and irksome, and, according to their notion, degrading. This condition resulted by reason of

[214] Ann. Rept. of Sec. of N., 1894, p. 28; 1895, XLI.

the excessive number of line officers assigned to ships at this time. On shore the junior officers were often given mere routine, clerical and nominal duties, better fitted for school-boys than for ambitious, energetic sailor-men. They complained without avail of the smothering, stunting processes to which their intellects were subjected.[215]

There was, however, a brighter side to the naval service during these years. The reconstruction of the fleet afforded many interesting tasks to an ever-increasing number of officers. There were materials of all sorts to be inspected, questions of naval construction and naval policy to be determined, and new administrative duties in the Department and the navy yards to be performed. From 1890 to 1897 many new ships were placed in commission, and service on board of them was most desirable and attractive. These well-equipped vessels, perfect in every detail, the equal of the ships of European navies, aroused the pride of officers and seamen and renewed their professional zeal. They were the harbingers of promised improvements in the naval personnel. Under the régime of the new navy, the officers took additional interest in the literature of their profession, which was now rapidly growing. This was fostered by the work or publications of the Naval Intelligence Office, Naval War Records Office, Naval War College and Library of the Navy Department. The circulation of service periodicals was expanding. The officers of the navy contributed many valuable and highly creditable articles to their professional organ, the PROCEEDINGS of the United States Naval Institute. Their desire to prepare themselves for the increasing and more exacting demands of their profession may be seen in their founding of the Naval War College. In the eighties fleet drills were inaugurated, and under Secretary Tracy the Squadron of Evolution was organized. This latter carried out programs of fleet exercises and maneuvers, of target and small-arms practice, of landing drills and engagements and of torpedo attacks.

The remarkable improvements in the naval arts and sciences, and more specifically the important advances in naval construction and armament, gave a decided impetus to the development of specialties in the naval profession. For many years the division

---

[215] PROCEEDINGS of U. S. Naval Inst., V, 349; IX, 155; XVI, 482; Army and Navy Journal, XXVII, 813, XXVIII, 326-327.

of naval officers into line officers, naval constructors, surgeons, paymasters, chaplains, civil engineers and steam engineers had existed. The tendency of the new conditions was to specialize the work of the line officers. To the general professional knowledge required of an executive on shipboard, they added the special knowledge of some small department of naval science. Among the officers of the line there now arose torpedoists, artillerists, strategists, naval administrators, electrical experts, steam engineers, ordnance experts of various kinds, compass experts, nautical surveyors and hydrographers. Of course not all the officers acquired a specialty, but the tendency was to do so. Most of these specialties are of a mechanical or engineering character. Indeed, naval science tends to become, in large part, a branch of applied mechanics and engineering. The modern vessel of war is a floating machine, and requires a new type of officer and seaman.

The act of August 5, 1882, was by far the most important measure relating to naval officers that was passed by Congress during the period 1881-1897. When Chandler became Secretary of the Navy in 1882, the disproportion between the number of ships in commission, 31, and the number of officers in the navy, 1817, was absurdly great. That is, there were 59 officers to each ship, or one to every five seamen. Almost one-half of the officers were assigned to duties on shore. Since the number of graduates of the Naval Academy was in excess of the number of vacancies in the service, the number of line officers was gradually increasing. The act of August 5, 1882, both reduced the number of officers in the navy and limited the number of appointments that could be made from the graduates of the academy. It provided that no promotions should be made in the principal staff corps until the medical corps should be reduced 10, the pay corps 30, and the engineer corps 100 numbers; and that only one-half the vacancies above the grade of midshipman should be filled by promotion until there was effected a reduction of 4 rear-admirals, 15 commodores, 5 captains, 5 commanders, 6 lieutenant-commanders, 30 lieutenants, 25 masters and 25 ensigns. This law effected, by a gradual process, a total reduction of 255 officers. It further provided that no appointments to the navy of graduates of the Naval Academy should be made, except to fill vacancies.[216]

[216] Ann. Rept. of Sec. of N., 1882, pp. 7-9; Proceedings of U. S. Naval Inst., V, 360; IX, 155; Army and Navy Journal, XX, 192; U. S. Statutes at Large, XXII, 285-287.

The enactment of this measure was vigorously opposed by the officers of the navy. It, however, had the cordial support of Secretary Chandler and Ex-Secretary Robeson, the latter having charge of it in the House, where it elicited a lengthy and heated discussion. The Senate made but few changes in it, although several senators tried to have it modified in the interest of the officers adversely affected. While the measure reduced somewhat the expenditures for the naval personnel, whether upon the whole it was salutary is doubtful. For several years it lowered the rate of promotion, and it increased the age at which the line officers arrived at command rank. It also worked an injustice to those cadets who, having finished their studies at the academy, were serving their two years at sea when the measure was passed; in respect to these young men it was retroactive. The error had been made, long before 1882, in admitting students to the Naval Academy in excess of the navy's needs.

The act of August 5, 1882, also attempted to remedy the abuses connected with the assignment of officers to shore-duty. Not one of the least of the evils that accompanied the decline of the navy was the impetus that it gave to the production of " landgoing " officers. To these sailor-men of the desk and office, as Captain Mahan has pointed out, the revolving-chair becomes more attractive than the quarter-deck.

From 1883 to 1897 various bills were introduced in Congress with a view to bettering the condition of the naval personnel. These dealt chiefly with the pay, rank, number and promotion of the officers of the several corps. Some of them attempted to reconcile differences and remove inequalities existing between the corps. The engineers especially were dissatisfied, and various bills designed to increase their number or to grant them positive rank were urged upon the attention of Congress. The most important measures, however, were those whose purpose was to increase the number of promotions of the line officers and to bring them to command ranks at earlier ages. In 1891 Secretary Tracy appointed a board of naval officers to " examine into and report upon the present condition of stagnation in the promotion of line officers, and to recommend such measures as it might deem desirable on the subject with a view to the increased efficiency of the navy." Captain R. L. Pythian was the president of this board. Its report was especially valuable for its discussion of the causes of the existing stagnation in naval promotions. The remedies which it proposed aroused much opposition. Under Secretary Herbert the growing evils in the condition of the naval personnel received increased attention, and he gave them much consideration. In 1894 a joint commission composed of the members of the two naval committees of Congress considered the complaints of the officers of the navy. All these efforts largely failed because of the lack of unanimity of opinion among the naval officers, and of the jealousy and strife between the different corps. Not until after the Spanish-American War was any important remedial legislation passed.[217]

At sea the period 1881-1897 afforded the naval officers but few opportunities to achieve distinction. In the affair with Chile of 1891-1892, caused by an attack of the Chilean rabble upon some seamen of the U. S. S. *Baltimore,* who went ashore at Valparaiso, Captain W. S. Schley and Commander Robley D. Evans attained considerable prominence. The preparations of the Navy Department for a war with this South American republic were much greater than were generally known. Emergency orders for extra work were given to the various navy yards, the merchant steamer *Ohio* was chartered for use as a floating machine shop, orders for materials of war were placed with private establishments, plans of operations in the South Pacific Ocean were mapped out, and an informal " Naval Strategy Board " composed of the Assistant Secretary of the Navy, Captain A. T. Mahan and the officers of the Office of Naval Intelligence began the consideration of strategical problems.[218] After this affair had been peacefully settled, Commander R. D. Evans was placed in command of a small fleet, and was ordered to cruise in and about Bering Sea for the purpose of carrying out the convention of à *modus vivendi* with Great Britain respecting the capture of seals. From 1892 to 1894 this undertaking was a rather important one.

During the administration of President Arthur, several Arctic expeditions of the navy once more exhibited the enterprise, fortitude and heroism of the American naval officer. On March 3, 1881, Congress appropriated $175,000 for the prosecution of a search for the ship *Jeannette,* which had sailed for the Arctic

---

[217] Ann. Rept. of Sec. of N., 1891, pp. 38-43; 1893, 41-43; Sen. Miscl. Doc., 53 C. 2 S., No. 98.

[218] Army and Navy Journal, XXIX, 326, 396-397.

regions in the summer of 1879 under the command of Lieutenant-Commander George W. DeLong, and which was reported to be lost. On March 14 Secretary Hunt organized the Search Expedition Board, of which Rear-Admiral John Rodgers was president. It was instrumental in fitting out two relief expeditions, which sailed during the summer of 1881. One of these, under the command of Lieutenant Robert M. Berry, searched for the *Jeannette* in the region of Siberia, Alaska and the Bering Sea; and the other, commanded by Commander George H. Wadleigh, visited Greenland, Iceland and the northern coasts of Norway. Wadleigh obtained no information concerning the missing ship, since it had never been within the region of his search. Berry, however, after losing his vessel and undergoing considerable hardships, effected a union with a part of the survivors of the *Jeannette* under Chief Engineer Melville. In 1882 a search for the missing officers and men of the *Jeannette* was prosecuted by Lieutenants Giles B. Harber and W. H. Schuetze, and in 1883-1884 these officers recovered the bodies of DeLong and his companions. In the spring of 1884 a relief expedition, under the command of Commander W. S. Schley, was sent to the Arctic regions to search for Lieutenant A. W. Greeley and his party of the ill-fated Lady Franklin Bay Expedition, and Schley succeeded in rescuing Greeley and several surviving companions. Such was their great extremity when found that they could have lived but a few hours longer. The dramatic success of Schley's expedition has made it memorable in the annals of Arctic exploration.[219]

During the administration of Tracy and Herbert, when many new ships were placed in commission, the need of seamen became urgent. Congress, however, was slow to increase their number, and the Department found it difficult to fully man the fleet. The authorized number of enlisted men and boys in the navy from 1881 to March 3, 1893, was 8250; and for the next three years, 9000. On June 10, 1896, the number was increased to 10,000; and on March 3, 1897, to 11,750.[220] The marine corps increased from about 1900 men in 1883 to about 2600 men in 1896.

In 1891 a school of application for the marine corps was established at the Washington Marine Barracks. It gave professional

[219] Ann. Rept. of Sec. of N., 1881, pp. 6-10; 1882, pp. 18-19; 1883, p. 22; 1884, pp. 21-26.
[220] Congressional Record, XXXVIII, 2721.

instruction to the commissioned and uncommissioned officers and the enlisted men of the corps. Its establishment was in line with the general policy of the Navy Department of developing a more highly-trained and efficient personnel.

The new sailless ships of the navy, with their complicated steam and electrical machinery and their modern high-powered guns, demanded a new type of seaman—the sailor-mechanic. While a first-class seaman must now know the duties of the old-time sailor, he is also required to be, according to his position on shipboard, a mechanic, an artillerist, a torpedoist, an electrician, or a signal-man. He must have not only the habit of the sea, but also the habit of the ship's machinery. He must understand " battleship-seamanship." The intricate and complicated mechanisms of the new ships require a higher grade of intelligence in the crew than did the simple sails and guns of the old navy. Better morals and a better education, a more careful and a more highly specialized training are demanded. An admiral of the English navy is the authority for the statement that a " seaman of to-day must know as much as a lieutenant of forty years ago."

Under the new conditions the training of seamen became a subject of great importance. It was much discussed in the professional periodicals and service journals, was treated of in prize essays, and was thoroughly considered by the Navy Department. In regard to the proper methods of training seamen, a difference of opinion among naval officers naturally arose. The principal point at issue was the relative amount of time and attention that should be paid to the seamanship of sailing ships and the seamanship of battleships, to the handling of sails and the handling of machinery. The older and more conservative officers were likely to insist, as one of them did, that " as a mere method of training, nothing has yet been devised so good as cruising on board a sailing ship. It quickens the observation, stimulates the mind to the solution of new problems, and produces a habit of self-reliance in a well-developed physique. To pass a weather reef-earing in a gale of wind, with the topsail shaking and tugging and the ship rolling deeply, is an experience from which one emerges, for the first time, with a confidence in his powers that makes him practically twice the man he was before." Rear-Admiral Luce, one of the ablest of the older officers, said that the loss of the " school of the topman," consequent upon the want of a square-rig, would breed a force of "deckhands" instead of "sailors"; and Admiral Porter agreed with him.[221]

On the other hand the younger officers of the navy were inclined to emphasize the importance of changing the training of man-of-war's men to meet the new conditions resulting from the transformation of the wooden sailing ship into a sailless floating battery of iron and steel. Lieutenant Richard Wainwright, one of the most brilliant and progressive of the younger men, conceived that Rear-Admiral Luce's "school of the topman" was not the only means to enure a sailor to danger. "He may confront it in boats under oars and sail, in bad weather and through surf. The ship of war must be allowed to follow out its lines of highest development, and the seamen must be trained to suit the development of the machine." Ensign A. P. Niblack said that the "handling and fighting of a ship's armament is the true modern bases of the education and training of our men. We give too much importance to the paint-pot, holy-stone, active-topman type of man." [222] This issue in the navy over the proper training of seamen reminds one of the discussions in civil life over the proper college cirriculum, in which the conservatives insist upon making Greek, Latin, mathematics and philosophy the backbone of the course, and the liberals maintain that these studies must yield a prominent place to the modern languages and literatures and physical sciences. From the standpoint of the liberals, the question involved in both controversies is whether modern education should be adapted to modern needs.

The system of training for apprentices that was developed in the navy during the 20 years following its establishment in 1875, was, in the main, based on the ideas of the conservative officers. It provided for: (1) A preliminary course at the Naval Training Station at Newport in the rudiments of the sailor's calling; (2) one year's service in a cruising training ship; (3) service on board a man-of-war in the general duties of his calling, until the apprentice reached his majority; and (4) technical and special courses for enlisted seamen at the Naval Gun Factory at Washington and the Naval Torpedo Station at Newport. Boys upon entrance into

[221] American Journal of Social Science, XXXIII, 33; PROCEEDINGS of U. S. Naval Inst., XVI, 370-377, 410-411; Army and Navy Journal, XXVIII, 124.

[222] Army and Navy Journal, XXVIII, 124-125; PROCEEDINGS of U. S. Naval Inst., XVII, 32.

the naval service were to be between the ages of 14 and 17, and of
sound frame and robust constitution.   At Newport they were
instructed in reading, writing, arithmetic, geography and history,
and more especially in the arts of the sailor, such as knotting and
splicing, heaving the log and the lead, reading the compass, reefing
and furling sails, steering, rowing, sailing and signaling.   They
were also trained in the use of small arms, swords, pistols, rifles
and great guns.   After a six months' preliminary course, they
were drafted into the cruising training ships and sent to sea to
learn the usages of sea-life and the practical duties of a sailor.
At the end of this course, which lasted for a year, they were
shipped upon regular men-of-war.   Upon becoming of age, their
apprenticeship came to an end, and they were permitted to enlist
as seamen.   The most skilful of those who re-enlisted were sent
to the Naval Gun Factory, where they were given a 17 weeks'
course in the elementary use of tools and in the work of the carpenter's shop, coppersmithery, erecting-shop for guns, blacksmith
shop, machine shop and laboratory.   On the completion of their
instruction here the most proficient seamen were sent to the Naval
Torpedo Station for a second course of 17 weeks, and were taught
the art of diving, the elementary principles of electricity and the
manufacture and use of torpedoes.[223]

One of the drawbacks of the apprentice system was its failure
to instil in the apprentices a love of the sea or of the naval service.
Upon reaching their majority, considerably more than one-half
of the young men refused to re-enlist.   Lieutenant W. F. Fullam
said that 90 per cent of the apprentices left the navy.   It should
be said, however, that before leaving they gave the naval several
years of valuable service, and that the apprentice system raised
the standard of intelligence and morality of the enlisted men and
increased the relative number of native Americans in the navy.
In 1889, of the enlisted men of the navy, the foreign-born numbered 4278, and the native-born 3668; in 1896, the foreign-born
numbered 4400, and the native-born 5133.   In the former year the
enlisted force contained natives of 57 countries.   More than 11
per cent were born in Ireland.   Every continent and many islands
of the sea, and such remote countries as Syria, Iceland, Finland,
Uruguay, Roumania, Tasmania, St. Helena and Turkey were
represented.[224]

[223] American Journal of Social Science, 29-38.

[224] Army and Navy Journal, XXVIII, 326-327; Congressional Record,
XXI, 3156-3157; Sen. Doc., 54 C. 1 S., No. 252.

During Secretary Whitney's administration an active interest in the establishment of a naval reserve, or a naval militia, was taken by various cities on the Atlantic and Pacific coasts and on the Great Lakes. The idea was by no means a new one. Indeed, in 1805 President Jefferson consulted his Secretary of the Navy, Robert Smith, on a " plan of a regular naval militia to be composed of all our seafaring citizens, to enable us to man a fleet speedily by supplying voluntary enlistments by calls on the militia "; and he drafted a bill providing for an organization of this sort.[225] One of the first steps in the movement that finally resulted in the establishment of a naval militia was taken on February 17, 1887, when Senator W. C. Whitthorne of Tennessee introduced a bill in the Senate to " create a naval reserve of auxiliary cruisers, officers and men from the mercantile marine of the United States." In 1888 Whitthorne was sponsor for other bills on the same subject. His plan, in general, followed those of foreign naval reserves. In 1887 the Navy Department prepared a scheme of organization for a naval militia, and Secretary Whitney in his annual report for that year favored the establishment of a naval militia on the plan of the land militia or national guard.

The states now took up the subject, and acted more promptly than the national government. On May 17, 1888, the governor of Massachusetts approved an act establishing a naval battalion to be attached to the volunteer militia of that state. This was the pioneer measure. One of the leaders of the movement in Massachusetts was Lieutenant John C. Soley, a retired officer of the navy and a resident of Boston. He and several friends, a number of whom, like himself, were yachtsmen, prepared the measure that became a law. Massachusetts did not complete her organization until March 25, 1890. In 1889 New York, Pennsylvania and Rhode Island passed laws similar to that of Massachusetts, and in 1890 these four organizations were perfected. In that year the Massachusetts battalion was drilled on board the receiving ship *Wabash,* and the New York battalion on board the receiving ship *Minnesota.*[226]

The year 1891 was a most important one in the growth of the movement. On March 2 Congress appropriated $25,000 for arms and equipment for the naval militia, and in June the Navy Depart-

---

[225] Ford, Jefferson, VIII, 381, 403.
[226] Laws and regulations relating to the naval militia, 5-6; Outing (magazine), XXII, 334, 436.

ment issued regulations governing the disbursement of this fund. Additional naval battalions were organized in California, North Carolina and Texas; and the initial steps towards the formation of organizations in Maryland and Pennsylvania were taken. In July the naval battalions of Massachusetts, New York and Rhode Island were drilled on board the Squadron of Evolution, under the command of Commodore J. G. Walker. On October 1, 1891, the total number of men in the naval militia of the six states that had perfected their organizations was 1149. In 1896 the number of states having organizations had increased to 14, and the total number of men to 3339. During the summer of that year, six naval militia officers attended lectures at the Naval War College, and 19 were instructed at the Naval Torpedo School. Many of the officers of the militia were ex-graduates of ex-students of the Naval Academy. On August 3, 1894, Congress passed an " act for the encouragement of the naval militia," which authorized the Secretary of the Navy to loan to each state having an organization one of the old vessels of the navy, together with her apparel, charts, books and instruments of navigation, for the purpose of promoting drills and instruction.[227]

Whitthorne's bill of February 17, 1887, provided for a naval reserve of auxiliary vessels, officers and seamen. The laws of the states respecting the naval militia made no provision for auxiliary vessels. The federal government, in a fashion, now made such provision. An act of March 3, 1891, granted a subsidy for carrying the mails to such American vessels as held themselves in readiness for naval service in time of war and as had adapted their construction to the purposes of war. In 1892 an American register was granted to certain foreign-built ships, and it was stipulated that under certain conditions these vessels might be used for naval purposes. In 1896 Congress appropriated $400,000 towards providing the auxiliary cruisers with armaments. At this time the " auxiliary navy " consisted of 29 vessels. Of these the largest were the *New York, Paris, St. Louis* and *St. Paul,* ships that rendered most effective service in the Spanish-American War.[228]

[227] Laws and regulations relating to the naval militia; Ann. Rept. of Sec. of N., 1896, p. 20; U. S. Statutes at Large, XXVIII, 219.

[228] U. S. Statutes at Large, XXVI, 830-832; XXVII, 27-28; XXIX, 363; Congressional Record, XXVIII, 4458-4459.

CHAPTER ELEVEN: THE SPANISH-AMERICAN WAR, 1898

Part I

The Navy Department, 1897-1911

The Spanish-American War was the principal event in the history of the navy and the Navy Department during the period 1897-1911, and by reason of its epoch-making results it has been the chief factor in shaping the recent naval policy of the United States. The war gave an impetus to every naval activity. It accelerated the building of ships, the increase of officers and seamen, the improvement of the navy yards and the establishment of naval stations, coaling depots, magazines and hospitals. It left its mark upon the organization of the Navy Department and of the naval service. Its effect upon the amalgamation of the line and the engineers and upon the provision of adequate educational facilities for naval officers was far-reaching. Since the war the improvement in the materiel and the personnel of the navy has gone on hand in hand. As a result of the brilliant victories of Dewey and Sampson, which greatly popularized the navy, large sums of money have been freely granted for naval purposes.

For a little more than half of the decade 1897-1907, the Secretary of the Navy was John D. Long, of Massachusetts. Entering the department in March, 1897, as the New England member of McKinley's cabinet, he served through McKinley's two administrations and a part of the first administration of Roosevelt. He had had a varied political career as a member of the Massachusetts legislature, governor of his state and one of its representatives in Congress. Secretary Long was conservative, steady-going and of a judicial temperament. In his love of books, gift of diction, integrity of character and ethical view-point, he was a typical New Englander. He had published a translation of the Æneid and a volume of after-dinner speeches, and, soon after his resignation from the secretaryship in 1902, he issued a book on the " New American Navy." His habits were exceedingly democratic, and, in Massachusetts where he was familiarly known as " Governor Long," he was popular with all classes. His appearance was plain, but striking; and is still vividly recalled by the employees of the department. He was short and stout, with broad, stocky shoulders, topped with an enormous head. He came promptly and early to office, and usually carried with him a green bag well stuffed with documents and papers. His rusty silk hat and cheap suit of ready-made clothes contrasted oddly with the dress of his polished and well-groomed colleague in the State Department, the late John Hay. In a novel published some years ago, one of the characters, " Mr. William Shortley, commonly called Billy Shortlegs," was modelled after Mr. Long. Shortley was " very popular, well up in classics, and stands a good chance of being governor some day." He was a " short man, with a corpulent body and a large, open face; but he was a born orator of a certain type. Rounded and polished, mellow and musical, his sentences rolled from his mouth in liquid cadence and perfect balance. Sir Hugh put him down as his ideal after-dinner speaker. He made his points, clearly, neatly, and with occasional vigor that was always surprising." [229]

On May 1, 1902, Secretary Long was succeeded by W. H. Moody, of Massachusetts, and after a little more than two years of service, Moody, on July 1, 1904, yielded his position to Paul Morton, of Illinois. One year later Morton resigned, and Charles J. Bonaparte, of Maryland, became Secretary of the Navy. On December 17, 1906, Bonaparte gave way to Victor H. Metcalf, of California, who, on December 1, 1908, was succeeded by Truman H. Newberry, of Michigan, Roosevelt's fifth and last Secretary of the Navy. President Taft's choice for the naval office was George von L. Meyer, of Massachusetts. Moody's career in the House of Representatives, where he served in the 54th, 55th, 56th and 57th Congresses, recommended him as a man of

[229] Hoar, Autobiography, I, 299.

ability and integrity. Following the precedent established by two of his predecessors in the department, Thompson and Woodbury, Moody became a justice of the Supreme Court. Morton's success in administering railroads and manufacturing industries seems to have been his principal recommendation for the secretaryship. The choice of a man of affairs to be Secretary of the Navy was in a way a return to an earlier practice, which obtained before 1818, when the rule of the lawyers and statesmen in the department began. Morton was the second incumbent of the secretaryship to hail from an inland state, and Newberry the third. Bonaparte was an intimate friend of President Roosevelt, whom he somewhat resembles in character. Both are independent in temper, zealous for reform, fearless in initiative and strenuous for their ideals. Metcalf is the first man from the Pacific Coast to become Secretary of the Navy. He had been a member of Congress and Secretary of the Department of Commerce and Labor. Long, Moody, Bonaparte and Metcalf were bred to the law. Newberry and Meyer were capitalists and men of affairs.

Secretary Long's Assistant Secretary of the Navy for a little more than a year of his administration was Theodore Roosevelt, of New York, a most picturesque and masterful personality. He served from April, 1897, until May, 1898. In the Navy Department Roosevelt displayed his well-known qualities of omniscience, quickness on the trigger, self-confidence and indefatigable industry. Early in his life he became interested in the navy, and at the age of twenty-four published a history of the Naval War of 1813. He brought to the assistant-secretaryship a considerable first-hand knowledge of naval history and naval affairs. During his brief term in the department, he greatly magnified his office, and made himself felt as an influential factor in naval administration. Possessed with unusual powers for acquiring information, he left the department with a rather extensive knowledge of the navy, and certainly with decided opinions in respect to it. As President of the United States, these have stood him in good stead. In his first message to Congress not less than one hundred specific points connected with the navy were raised and discussed. His judgment of naval affairs was not infrequently better informed than that of his secretaries of the navy, several of whom were wholly unacquainted with their duties on first entering upon them.[230] Indeed,

[230] United Service, ser. 3, V, 291; Army and Navy Journal, XXXIX, 61.

outside of the naval officers, few men in official life had a more intimate knowledge of the navy and its wants than President Roosevelt. Its rapid enlargement formed a most important part of his policy of rampant nationalism. Roosevelt is one of the very few presidents who have been strong, positive factors in the administration of the navy.

Secretary Long's book, the New American Navy, contains a vivid characterization by the author of his chief civilian assistant in the Navy Department:

" Mr. Roosevelt was an interesting personality as Assistant Secretary of the Navy, as, indeed, he is in any capacity. There were several candidates for the place, which President McKinley allowed me to fill. In May, 1897, on the retirement of Mr. McAdoo, an excellent official under the previous administration, who had consented to hold over till that time, I selected Mr. Roosevelt, who had had, and indeed has had to this day, a hearty interest in the navy. His activity was characteristic. He was zealous in the work of putting the navy in condition for the apprehended struggle. His ardor sometimes went faster than the President or the department approved. Just before the war, when the Spanish battle-fleet was on its way here, he as well as some naval officers, regarding that as a cause of war, approved of sending a squadron to meet it without waiting for a more formal declaration of war. He worked indefatigably, frequently incorporating his views in memoranda which he would place every morning on my desk. Most of his suggestions had, however, as far as was applicable, been already adopted by the various bureaus, the chiefs of which were straining every nerve and leaving nothing not done. When I suggested to him that some future historian reading his memoranda, if they were put on record, would get the impression that the bureaus were inefficient, he accepted the suggestion with the generous good nature which is so marked in him. Indeed, nothing could be pleasanter than our relations. He was heart and soul in his work. His typewriters had no rest. He, like most of us, lacks the rare knack of brevity. He was especially stimulating to the younger officers, who gathered about him and made his office as busy as a hive. He was especially helpful in the purchasing of ships and in every line where he could push on the work of preparation for war. Almost as soon, however, as it was declared, he resigned his assistant secretaryship of the navy to accept the lieutenant-colonelcy of the Rough Rider regiment in the army. Together with many of his friends, I urged him strenuously to remain in the navy, arguing that he would there make a signal reputation, and that to go into the army would be only to fight mosquitos on the Florida sands or fret in camp at Chickamauga. How right he was in his prognosis and how wrong we were in ours, the result has shown. He took the straight course to fame, to the governorship of New York and to the presidency of the United States. He has the dash of Henry of Navarre without any of his vices.[231]

On May 11, 1898, Charles H. Allen, of Massachusetts, Roosevelt's successor, became Assistant Secretary of the Navy. He brought to his task a thorough training in business and an aptness for administrative work. On April 21, 1900, Allen resigned to become governor of Porto Rico, and was succeeded by Frank W Hackett, of Washington, D. C. Hackett was born in Portsmouth, New Hampshire, and during the Civil War was a member of the naval pay corps. He served until December 16, 1901, when Judge Charles H. Darling, of Vermont, became Assistant Secretary of the Navy. Darling was a decisive man, with a judicial temper and a sound judgment. On November 1, 1905, he was succeeded by Truman H. Newberry, of Michigan. Newberry had seen service in the navy during the Spanish-American War. He was succeeded on December 1, 1908, by Herbert L. Satterlee, of New York, who served until the end of Roosevelt's administration. President Taft's Assistant Secretary of the Navy was Beekman Winthrop, of Massachusetts.

The war of 1898 and the rapid expansion of the navy succeeding greatly increased the work of the naval bureaus. Secretary Long on more than one occasion testified to the professional skill, valuable counsel and painstaking labors of his bureau chiefs, and he said that the importance of their services during the war was too little known and that they, as well as the commanders of ships, ought to be rewarded for conspicuous merit. The chiefs of the several bureaus during the war of 1898 were as follows: Bureau of Navigation, Commodore A. S. Crowninshield; Bureau of Equipment, Commodore Royal B. Bradford; Bureau of Ordnance, Commodore Charles O'Neill; Bureau of Yards and Docks, Commodore M. T. Endicott; Bureau of Construction and Repair, Commodore Philip Hichborn; Bureau of Steam Engineering, Commodore George W. Melville; Bureau of Supplies and Accounts, Commodore Edwin Stewart; and Bureau of Medicine and Surgery, Commodore William K. Van Reypen. The head of the Marine Corps was Colonel-Commandant Charles Haywood.

Endicott, who was appointed chief of the Bureau of Yards and Docks on the recommendation of Secretary Long, was a civil engineer of the navy. Previous to his appointment, this position

[231] Long, New American Navy, II, 173-175.

had been filled by a line officer, who of course had no expert knowledge of civil engineering. Information of this sort is highly valuable to the chief of this bureau, since he is principally engaged in the improving of navy yards and naval stations and in the construction of buildings and docks. In 1901 F. T. Bowles, a brilliant young naval constructor, succeeded Rear Admiral Hichborn as chief of the Bureau of Construction and Repair, a position of great importance. In 1903 Rear Admiral Melville, who had been chief of the Bureau of Steam Engineering since 1887, was succeeded by Chief Engineer C. W. Rae. In 1902 Rear Admiral C. H. Taylor took the place of Rear Admiral Crowninshield as head of the Bureau of Navigation. Various other changes in the headships of the bureaus have been made from time to time. An assistant to the chief of the Bureau of Ordnance was authorized in 1898.

By all odds the most important addition made to the administrative machinery of the Navy Department for many years was that of the General Board, which was established in 1900. An account of this organization, however, is appropriately preceded by a brief description of a temporary board of a somewhat similar character, which was organized to assist the Secretary of the Navy in conducting the war with Spain. The " Naval War Board " or " Naval Strategy Board " was created in the spring of 1898, with the following membership: Rear Admiral Montgomery Sicard, Commodore A. S. Crowninshield, who was at that time chief of the Bureau of Navigation, Captain A. S. Barker and Assistant Secretary of the Navy Theodore Roosevelt, chairman *ex officio*. In May Captain A. T. Mahan (retired) became a member of the board, and Captain Barker and Assistant Secretary Roosevelt severed their connection with it. At one time an army officer reported as a member. During the greater part of the war it consisted of Sicard, Crowninshield and Mahan, the two last-named officers being its most active members. It was closely connected with the Bureau of Navigation. The board was dissolved in the fall of 1898, shortly after the war had been concluded.

The principal duties of the Naval War Board were to collect military information, to prepare strategical plans of war, to advise the Secretary of the Navy in regard to questions of naval strategy and policy, and to assist him in conducting the naval war. It

gathered information respecting the movements, resources, conditions and plans of the Spanish naval forces. Its two principal
agents abroad were Ensigns W. H. Buck and H. H. Ward. These
officers travelled under assumed names and characters, representing themselves as Englishmen. In reporting the movements
of Admiral Cervera's fleet, Ward visited Cadiz, Gibraltar, the
Madeiras, St. Thomas and Porto Rico, and several times narrowly
escaped detection. Buck followed the course of Admiral Camara's
fleet through the Mediterranean, going as far east as Port Said.
On the retrograde movement of Camara, he returned to Algiers.
These two officers had many thrilling experiences, and exhibited
much cleverness and sagacity in executing their difficult and delicate missions. The Naval War Board performed its part in the
war with signal success and distinction, and to the great satisfaction of Secretary Long, who said that it did not make a single
error, and that its deliberations were distinguished by wise judgment, comprehensive forethought and a competency to every contingency.[232]

Shortly after the Naval War Board was dissolved, a movement for the establishment of a somewhat similar organization
was set on foot. It was argued that a permanent war board
would do away with the necessity of extemporizing a temporary
administrative organ in case of another naval war. The friends
of the movement, however, laid most stress upon the need of an
organization within the department for the performance of a
number of highly-important naval duties, which properly fell to
none of the several bureaus and offices, and which therefore were
not well done. Among these duties were the preparation of plans
for war, the study of strategical problems, the collection of military information, the co-ordination of the work of the bureaus,
and the advising of the Secretary of the Navy. Some of the
critics of the movement saw in it merely another attempt of the
line officers of the higher ranks to gain control over naval administration, and they asserted that the proposed duties of the new
board were already adequately performed by the Naval War College, Naval Intelligence Office, Bureau of Navigation, Office of
the Secretary of the Navy, or some other administrative division

---

[232] House Doc., 55C. 3S., No. 3, 33-34; Army and Navy Journal, XXXV,
669, 703, 771, 1079.

of the department. They thought that they discovered in Admiral Dewey's "general board" or "general staff" the reappearance of Admiral Farragut's "board of admiralty," or of Admiral Porter's "board of control." The arguments now used, however, were somewhat different from the old ones. Formerly, the need of a unifying and advising power in the department was emphasized, while now the need of some organization to prepare plans of war and other military information was chiefly dwelt upon.

The name generally given to the proposed board was the "general staff," or the "naval general staff." Several years before the war of 1898, the need, or alleged need, of our navy for an organization of this sort had been pointed out by some of the naval officers. European practice, they said, had clearly established the great value of a general staff. The "military general staff" originated in Sweden when Gustavus Adolphus made his army the model of the civilized world. Thence it found its way into Prussia under the Great Elector. In Germany it had had a natural growth and development for two hundred and fifty years. The present German general staff contains some eight hundred officers, and its organization is quite complicated. The grafting of this institution upon the American navy was not contemplated. What was proposed was the introduction of a highly-modified form of the German or European general staff.[233]

In the winter of 1899-1900 Captain Henry C. Taylor, who had given much consideration to the subject of naval administration, submitted to Secretary Long a memorandum setting forth the duties and organization of a general staff and the needs of the navy for such an institution. Long did not wholly agree with Taylor, and he was opposed to the establishment of a general staff upon the plan suggested by its friends. He could not see his way clear to do more than to organize a general navy board, which he effected by an order of the department, dated March 13, 1900. The General Board was to be composed of the following officers: the Admiral of the Navy, who was to act as president, the chief of the Bureau of Navigation, who was to preside in the absence of the president, the chief intelligence officer and his principal assistant, the president of the Naval War College and his principal assistant, and three other naval officers of or above

[233] United Service, ser. 3, V, 2.

the grade of lieutenant commander. The chief of the Bureau of Navigation was to be the custodian of the plans of campaign and of other military information prepared by the board. The duties of the new organization were not specified in detail. Its purpose was " to insure efficient preparation of the fleet in case of war and for the naval defense of the coast." It was to meet at least once a month, and two of its sessions each year were to extend over a period of not less than one week each, during which time it was to meet daily. Five members were to form a quorum.[234]

On April 16, 1901, the provision respecting membership was modified,[235] and the board was made to consist of the following officers: Admiral George Dewey, president; the chief of the Bureau of Navigation, the chief intelligence officer, the president of the Naval War College, and such other officers of or above the grade of lieutenant commander as the department may designate. In April, 1902, the board comprised eleven members; and in April, 1904, thirteen. On the latter date four additional officers were on duty with the board, and two officers were engaged under its direction in the study of target practice. Counting its members and its assistants, the board at this time consisted of nineteen officers.

The Regulations for the Government of the Navy issued in 1905 again changed the membership of the board, which was made to consist of the four officers specifically enumerated above, and of such additional officers above the grade of commander as may be necessary to maintain the total membership at seven. An officer above the grade of lieutenant was to act as secretary, and was to record the proceedings of the board and have charge and custody of its files and correspondence. When the exigencies of the service permitted, the department was to order to appear before the board, upon its request, officers of special experience or fitness whose knowledge and suggestions might be of assistance in its deliberations. Such officers might take part in the discussions, but they could not act as members. The regulations for 1905 specified with considerable detail the duties of the board.

[234] Long, New American Navy, I, 123-124; General Orders of Navy Dept., No. 544.
[235] General Orders of Navy Dept., No. 43.

It was to devise measures and plans for the effective preparation
and maintenance of the fleet for war, and was to advise the Secretary of the Navy as to the disposition and distribution of the
fleet and as to the re-enforcements of ships, officers, seamen and
marines. It was to prepare and revise plans of naval campaigns,
and was to consider the number and types of ships proper for the
fleet, and the number and rank of the officers and the number and
ratings of the enlisted men. It was to advise the Secretary of the
Navy concerning the location and arrangements of coaling depots,
naval stations and depots of ordnance and supplies. It was to
undertake the co-ordinating of the work of the Naval War College, Office of Naval Intelligence and Board of Inspection and
Survey, and it was to consider and report upon naval operations,
maneuvers, tactics, organization and training. Finally, it was to
perform such additional duties as might be prescribed from time
to time by a competent authority.[236]

Since its organization in 1900, some of the ablest officers of the
navy have served on the General Board. It has prosecuted its
work with vigor and success, and has collected much military information, prepared plans of war, constructed shipbuilding programs and advised the Secretary of the Navy upon professional
subjects. It has largely extended the sphere of its powers and
influence. According to Assistant Secretary Darling, the General
Board, in 1904, was in practice the most influential and the most
controlling force in the navy. Although it had no authority to
issue orders, nevertheless, on a proposition fairly within its jurisdiction, it outweighed the judgment of any bureau. Both Secretary Long and Assistant Secretary Darling were of the opinion
that it was encroaching on what they considered the field of civil
administration. Darling's view may be obtained from his testi-
mony before the House Committee on Naval Affairs, given in
April, 1904:

I think the board has done some good work and is a good institution,
but I would restrict rather than extend its powers and authority. The
board has taken up a great many things that it ought not to. It has taken
up the question of title to land—work that could be done in any law
office, and which has no more military or tactical significance than the
administration of a law office. It has undertaken the purchase of land.
It has attempted to administer navy yards. It has undertaken to locate

<hr>

[236] Regulations for the Government of the Navy, 1905, pp. 12, 19.

storehouses, machine shops, and other buildings within naval reservations. These questions are entirely without military significance. It has undertaken to inform the department what legislation was needed. It has devoted much time and attention to the reorganization of the Navy Department, as well the civilian as the military side. It has prepared and circulated much literature advocating a general staff. In short, it has already invaded the province of civil administration and planted there the standard of conquest.[237]

The advocates of a naval general staff were by no means willing to accept the General Board as a substitute for the more powerful organization, and they conducted a lively propaganda in its behalf. Nominally, the General Board had only advisory powers. The general staff, however, was to possess affirmative powers of administration and was to exercise more or less control over the bureaus. The directive force of the navy was to become naval or military, as is the case with European navies. As a matter of policy, these facts were not always put to the forefront, but sometimes they were clearly stated. Secretary Moody favored the organization of a naval general staff, and in his annual report for 1903 President Roosevelt warmly advocated it. As a step towards its introduction, it was proposed to obtain legislation legalizing or incorporating the General Board. With this in view a strong fight was made by the friends of the movement in the spring of 1904. Important hearings upon the proposed legislation were held before the House Committee on Naval Affairs. Among others, Secretary Moody and Admiral Dewey spoke in its behalf. Assistant Secretary of the Navy Darling vigorously opposed it. His exceedingly able argument went far towards causing the committee to drop the measure. The fight for a naval general staff has been merely postponed. The sentiment in favor of it among the older line officers of the navy is very powerful. Moreover, the army has obtained an organization of this sort, and the navy naturally feels that its claims and needs are as well founded as those of its sister-service.[238]

It is plain that the organization of a general staff involves some fundamental questions of naval administration. Not the least of

[237] Hearings before House Com. on Naval Aff., April, 1904, pp. 927-935; Long, New American Navy, II, 183-185.

[238] Ann. Rept. of Sec. of N., 1905, pp. 3-6; Ann. Rept. of Bureau of Nav., 1905, pp. 4-6; Ann. Mess. of Pres., 1903; Hearings before House Com. on Naval Aff., April, 1904, pp. 909-991.

these is the proper division of duties and powers between the civil and naval elements of the Navy Department. Without attempting to discuss this subject, a few observations on it may be ventured. That the military should be subordinate to the civil function is one of the unwritten laws of our government. The secretaries of the army and navy must therefore be civilians. Now, the selection of a civilian Secretary of the Navy involves the anomaly of placing an amateur or novice in naval affairs over a body of professional and expert naval men. Such a system has its obvious defects. It weakens the Navy Department at its apex. The secretariat fails to become an adequate correlating and unifying force. Unnecessary friction arises between the secretary, more or less ignorant of his duties, and his naval chiefs. The technical naval men have never welcomed the exercise of positive powers of direction and control by untechnical civilians. Undoubtedly naval affairs would be vastly better conducted could the Secretary of the Navy bring to his work a hand practised in naval administration, the knowledge and assurance which come from long experience in the navy or the department, and the full understanding of one who is familiar with the customs, traditions and prejudices of naval officers and with their habits of thought and action.

On the other hand, the present system possesses certain counter-balancing advantages. A civilian secretary provides the department with one of its greatest needs, a judicial and impartial mind that has no service prejudices. A naval officer as secretary could hardly keep a level keel amid the animosities and diverse interests of conflicting naval corps. A civilian secretary is more likely than a naval one to understand the temper of Congress, to work in harmony with it and to obtain the necessary means for conducting the navy. Moreover, the present system gives assurance that the civilian point of view shall have due weight in the department, where the naval point of view is adequately represented by the bureau chiefs. In a very real sense the Secretary of the Navy is a minister of the people sent to the department to represent their opinions and prejudices in the naval counsels. He mediates between the people and the navy.

In the practice of the Navy Department many unwritten laws, customs and usages have grown up. An accurate knowledge of them is difficult to obtain. Moreover, they differ somewhat under different administrations. In the official communication of bureau with bureau, or the secretary's office with the bureaus, custom and the orders of the department have definitely fixed the procedure. Thus, a uniform method of briefing, indexing and referring of letters and documents is followed. A sort of code of official routine has been evolved which methodizes and facilitates the business of the department. The routine of business within the bureaus is also fixed. Owing to the necessity for a division of labor, most of the bureaus fall into divisions which are unknown to the law. For instance, the " office of detail " still constitutes a well-defined division of the Bureau of Navigation. As its name indicates, the Bureau of Supplies and Accounts is composed of a division of supplies and a division of accounts. In the Bureau of Construction and Repair there is a division of drafting. The office of the Secretary of the Navy may be divided into the division of the Secretary of the Navy, the division of the Assistant Secretary, the division of the Disbursing Officer, and the division of the Chief Clerk. The latter officer is a most important one, having charge of the correspondence of the secretary's office, the expenditure of the contingent funds, and the civilian personnel of the department.

The duties of the Secretary of the Navy, and also his relations to the chiefs of bureaus, to the President and to Congress, are for the most part not determined by law, but fixed and sanctioned by precedents, customs and forgotten orders of the President. The practice of making an annual report is unknown to the law and did not exist in the early history of the department. The first annual report appeared in December, 1823. It is an invariable rule that a senator or representative who calls to see the Secretary of the Navy shall be admitted to him. There are many unwritten customs respecting naval legislation. The two naval committees of Congress practically decide the amount of the annual appropriations for the navy, the uses to which this money shall be applied and the numbers and types of new ships. In reaching conclusions, they are assisted by the Secretary of the Navy, the chiefs of bureaus and the members of the General Board, who are called before the committees to explain their estimates and recommendations and to give all sorts of naval information. The Secretary of the Navy is the servant of Congress as well as of the President. Conferences on naval problems are often held between

the President and the members of the naval committees. It is
scarcely too much to say that the Secretary of the Navy, the chiefs
of naval bureaus, the members of the General Board, the President
of the United States, the Speaker of the House and the leading
members of the two naval committees, constitute a grand committee on naval legislation, whose members, by conference or otherwise, resolve differences, compromise conflicting interests, bring
the legislature and executive to an understanding and reach an approximate agreement upon naval legislation.

Among the few duties of the Secretary of the Navy that are
prescribed by statute are the preparing of estimates of the annual
appropriations, and the reporting annually of the expenditures
of the department, contracts for supplies, and the vessels and
naval materials that have been sold. The laws sometimes authorize the Secretary of the Navy to perform some special duties,
such as the appointment of a board of naval officers, the making of a specified contract, or the locating of a naval station.
At the department, the chief duties of the secretary are the recep-
tion of visitors bound on public or private errands, the conferring
with the principal officers of the department and the navy, the
conducting of his official correspondence, and the signing of his
name to numerous official letters and documents, such as naval
contracts, orders for the payment of money, orders to officers and
naval commissions. If he is a lawyer, he may spend considerable
time in reading the proceedings of courts-martial. He acts as
the governor or balance-wheel of the department, and may be
called upon to settle the disputes which arise between the naval
bureaus. Ordinarily, the administrative machinery runs of its own
momentum, without unnecessary friction, and the secretary may
absent himself from his office for considerable periods of time
without much inconvenience to the department. Of the great
mass of correspondence of the department, the secretary sees
nothing. Only the most important papers come to him. A month
or more may elapse between the visits to him of some of the chiefs
of bureaus. On the other hand, the chief of the Bureau of Navigation consults with him almost daily. The bureaus are semi-inde-
pendent principalities, whose obligations to their suzerain, the secretariat, are rather slight.

The duties of the Assistant Secretary of the Navy are fixed
principally by the orders of the secretary, and only slightly by law

and custom. They vary considerably with different administrations. They were somewhat limited by Secretary Long in April, 1897, but they were much increased during and after the war with Spain. The regulations for the government of the navy issued in 1900 assigned to the assistant secretary cognizance and general supervision of all matters relating to the "Islands of Guam and Tutuila and the United States naval stations in island possessions and elsewhere beyond the continental limits of the United States; vessels in building at navy-yards; repairs to vessels, ships fitting for sea; tugs and other boats for service at navy yards; the Marine Corps and applications of enlisted men thereof for discharge; the Naval Militia; the Naval War College; the Library and War Records Office; reports of boards of survey; surveys and appraisals afloat and ashore; the loaning of flags belonging to the navy." In December, 1901, the Naval War College was placed under the direction of the Bureau of Navigation. In the fall of 1905 the duties of the assistant secretary were considerably modified by Secretary Bonaparte. He was now relieved of much of his strictly routine work. He was required to make personal inspections of ships and naval stations, and to examine into the fitness of all candidates for commissions in those branches of the navy that are recruited from civil life.[239]

In February, 1899, Congress provided for the regular establishment of the Office of Naval Intelligence.[240] This office had previously existed only by authority of the orders of the Navy Department. Some of its clerks were detailed from the bureaus, and others were paid out of the appropriations for the "increase of the navy." Congress now authorized the office to employ five clerks, a translator, a draftsman and a laborer. The office was organized into six divisions, as follows: "Naval attachés," "ships," "ordnance," "personnel," "communications" and "steam engineering," each of which was to be presided over by an officer of the navy. In 1899 four naval attachés reported to the office. Three of these were attached to the American embassies or legations in Europe, and one to our legations at Tokyo and Peking. The work of the Naval Intelligence Office has greatly increased since the war with Spain. The head of the office is called the "chief intelligence officer."

[239] Ann. Rept. of Sec. of N., 1900, p. 67; 1905, p. 16.
[240] U. S. Statutes at Large, XXX, 874; Ann. Rept. of Sec. of N., 1899, pp. 464-466.

During recent years, the Navy Department, if we may rely upon the judgment of its secretaries, has continued to suffer from an excessive division of responsibility and executive power. It is recollected that this evil was chiefly manifested in the shipbuilding bureaus. Among their chiefs, considerable ill feeling was often aroused over conflicts of authority. According to Secretary Long, their relations were sometimes so strained that ordinary courtesy was impaired. Long frequently recommended the consolidation of the Bureaus of Construction and Repair, Steam Engineering, and Equipment. This change was not considered advisable or advantageous by many officers of high rank and conspicuous ability and by many members of the naval committees. Little attention was therefore paid to the secretary's recommendation. In his annual report for 1905 Secretary Bonaparte submitted some observations on the organization of the Navy Department. He conceived that the system of autonomous bureaus was in theory open to very serious objections, and was attended in practice with some measure of friction, circumlocution and delay. He suggested that the department might be organized into four bureaus, dealing respectively with " men," " ships," " armament " and " supplies." This suggestion is similar to one made by Secretary Whitney in 1885.[241] In his annual report for 1906 Bonaparte elaborated his plan of departmental organization. He now proposed that the head of one of the four bureaus should be the Secretary of the Navy, of another the assistant secretary and of each of the two remaining bureaus an officer of flag rank. Despairing of aid from Congress, Secretary Newberry began to reform the department by executive order shortly before his term of office came to an end. Secretary Meyer followed the same method. In 1909 he appointed four aides, one each, respectively, for " operations," " personnel," " materiel " and " inspections," to advise him in their respective fields and to co-ordinate the work of the bureaus. In the following year he abolished the Bureau of Equipment, and later he undertook to improve the business methods of the department.

The rapid increase in the number of civilian employees of the Navy Department in Washington during recent years is wholly

[241] Congressional Record, XXXV, 5393; Long, New American Navy, I, 117; Ann. Rept. of Sec. of N., 1905, pp. 3-4.

unprecedented. The number in 1897 was 282; in 1905, 608.[242]
With unimportant exceptions the personnel of every bureau and
office was increased. The Navy Department building was too
small to accommodate the additional force, and great inconveniences were suffered from the overflowing of its rooms. In 1903
the "Naval Annex" was established in the Mills building, situated conveniently near the Navy Department building. This furnished quarters for the Naval Intelligence Office, Hydrographic
Office, General Board, office of the admiral, office of the Marine
Corps, Naval Pay Office, Board of Inspection and Survey, Naval
Examining Board, Naval Retiring Board, Board of Medical Examiners, and Medical Dispensary.

Secretary Long was an ardent friend of civil service reform.
At the navy yards he continued and extended the system of appointment devised by Tracy and improved by Herbert. To Long
fell the distinction of placing under the labor-rules the office of
ship-keeper, the last position in the yards to remain in the hands
of the spoilsmen. He also directed that appointments in the navy
to the offices of civil engineer, assistant paymaster and professor
of mathematics should be made after competitive examinations.
In 1902 examinations were prescribed for paymasters' clerks and
naval pharmacists.

On March 26, 1897, Long issued regulations governing promotions in the Navy Department, which were prepared by the Civil
Service Commission in consultation with the Secretary of the Navy
and in conformity to certain amendments to the civil service rules
promulgated by President Cleveland on May 6, 1896. These regulations provided for the filling of vacancies in the higher grades
of the department by promoting employees from the lower grades.
The promoting authorities were to be guided chiefly by certain
"records of efficiency," which were to show the character of the
services rendered by each employee. In determining his efficiency,
the character, quantity and quality of his work and his office habits
were to be considered. These records were to be placed in custody
of a "board of promotion." It was thought that this plan would
largely do away with scholastic tests for promotion, and the exercise of political pressure, favoritism and personal influence. It
does not appear, however, that in practice the new system has

[242] Official Register of U. S., 1897 and 1905.

greatly changed the old methods. The Navy Department does not offer an attractive opening to ambitious and capable young men. Their opportunities for advancement are less than in some of the other departments or in civil life. As a result, resignations are frequently tendered by the most useful and wide-awake clerks, and the clerical force of the department lacks stability. Secretary Bonaparte proposed to remedy this defect by establishing a clerical corps of the navy, the members of which were to enjoy the privileges of relative rank and the right of retirement on the same basis as obtains in the other non-combatant corps of the service.[243]

[243] Fourteenth Rept. of Civil Service Comm., 166-169; Ann. Rept. of Sec. of N., 1905, pp. 8-9.

CHAPTER ELEVEN: THE SPANISH-AMERICAN WAR, 1898

Part II

THE NAVY IN THE SPANISH-AMERICAN WAR, 1898

The larger features and the more important dates of the Spanish-American War will be readily recalled. The first precautionary measures of the department were taken in January, 1898, in view of the critical condition of affairs then existing in Cuba. The blowing up of the *Maine* on February 15 was followed by the appointment of a board of inquiry, of which Rear Admiral Montgomery Sicard was president. On March 9, Congress appropriated $50,000,000 for the national defence. From this time until April 25, when war was declared, the department was incessantly busy preparing for the coming struggle.

The two principal theaters of naval operations were the coast of Cuba and Manila Bay. Since the operations in the Atlantic were chiefly within the West Indies, Key West assumed much importance as a naval base. In Asiatic waters there was a single squadron under Rear Admiral George Dewey. Early in the war the vessels in the Atlantic comprised three fleets: the blockading squadron, commanded by Rear Admiral W. T. Sampson; the flying squadron, commanded by Commodore W. S. Schley; and the northern patrol squadron, commanded by Commodore J. A. Howell. Later, these three squadrons were united under the command of Sampson. The principal events of the war were the destruction of Admiral Montojo's fleet by Commodore Dewey on May 1; the blockade of the Cuban coast throughout the war; the battle of Santiago on July 3, and the operations against Porto Rico in July and August. The ending of hostilities may be dated with the signing of the peace protocol on August 12, 1898.

The work of buying ships was in charge of the Assistant Secretary of the Navy. Between March 16 and August 12 one

445

hundred and two vessels of all sorts were bought, at a cost of $21,431,000. Before their purchase these vessels were thoroughly inspected by boards of naval officers in order to ascertain whether they were fit for the navy. Many of them were inspected by the New York board, which was appointed on March 12, and of which Captain Frederick Rodgers was president. The most expensive ships and the first to be bought were the *New Orleans* and *Albany,* two protected cruisers, constructed at Elswick, England. The cost of the former was $1,429,000, and of the latter $1,205,000. They were purchased on March 16 from the Brazilian government. The *Albany,* not being completed at the outbreak of hostilities, was in accordance with the laws of neutrality retained in England until after the close of the war. The *New Orleans* rendered valuable service in Cuban waters. The gun-boat *Topeka* was purchased from the Thames Iron Works, in England; the torpedo boat *Somers,* from the Schichau Iron Works, of Elbing, Germany; and the torpedo boat *Manly* from Mr. Charles R. Flint, of New York. The rest of the purchased vessels were merchantmen. Five large ships, the *City of Pekin, St. Paul, St. Louis, New York* and *Paris* were chartered. The government paid for the *St. Paul* a rental of $2500 a day. Two yachts were loaned to the department without charge, and the city of Philadelphia rented her ice-boat for the nominal sum of one dollar. Fifteen revenue cutters, four lighthouses tenders, and two vessels of the Fish Commission were placed temporarily in charge of the department. Altogether 131 ships were added to the navy in one way or another. The maximum fighting force of the regular navy consisted of 73 vessels, and of the auxiliary navy of 123 vessels. Of the 73 ships in the regular navy, 14 had belonged to the old navy, including several old monitors which had not seen service for many years. The strength of the fleet for fighting purposes lay largely in seven ships: the first-class battleships *Indiana, Massachusetts, Oregon* and *Iowa,* the second-class battleship *Texas,* and the two armored cruisers *Brooklyn* and *New York.* These seven vessels, with the possible exception of the coast-defence monitors, comprised at this time our entire sea-going armored fleet.[244]

[244] Ann. Rept. of Sec. of N., 1898, pp. 21-24; Long, New American Navy, I, 150-153.

Nearly five million dollars were expended in preparing the auxiliary vessels for service. The fitting out and repairing of the ships of the regular navy also entailed much work. These tasks fell chiefly to the Bureaus of Construction and Repair and Steam Engineering. Their shops at the five principal navy yards—New York, Norfolk, Mare Island, Boston and League Island—were exceedingly busy throughout the war. The force employed at these yards by the Bureau of Construction and Repair increased from 2200 men in January to more than 6000 men in the summer of 1898. Private shipyards also aided in repairing and converting ships. The purchased merchantmen were strengthened to bear the shock of gun-fire; unnecessary woodwork was taken out, batteries were installed, steam machinery was renewed or repaired, articles of equipment were supplied, and the vessels were freshly docked and painted. Every available ship in ordinary was prepared for service. Some of the old single-turreted monitors of an ancient date were fitted with new boilers by cutting the old ones into pieces and passing them out through the smoke-pipe openings and passing in the sections of the new in the same way. The ship *Vulcan* was made into a floating repair shop, carrying forges, furnaces, machine tools, skilled mechanics and a large outfit of stores, and proved to be exceedingly useful in making repairs on the blockade. For the vessels operating in Cuban waters, Key West was a most important repair station. Many inconveniences, however, were experienced here for want of proper machinery, shops and outfits of tools. The deliveries of needed articles at this point were slow and uncertain.[245]

The Bureau of Equipment furnished the vessels with coal, fresh water, rigging, canvas, galleys, boat supplies, anchors, chains, ground tackle, hawsers, cordage, binnacles, compasses, sextants, chronometers, charts, sails and hammocks. The number of employees of this bureau at the Boston yard, where many articles of equipment were manufactured, was doubled. The number of charts issued by the Hydrographic Office increased six-fold. To meet the demand for new flags and signals, the force in the flag-making department at the New York yard was increased from twelve to eighty persons.

Among the most important tasks of the Bureau of Equipment was the supplying of the fleets with coal and fresh water. Before

[245] Ann. Rept. of Sec. of N., 1898, pp. 34-35, 40, 514-515, 611-614.

the outbreak of hostilities, this bureau endeavored to procure coaling stations in the West Indies, especially in the vicinity of the passages of the Antilles. Such attempts of course could not succeed at so inopportune a time. Recognizing the importance of Key West and the Dry Tortugas as bases of operations, the bureau early contracted for the installation of modern coaling plants at these places, but they were not ready for use when the struggle ended. When the war began there was at Key West but one coal shed, with a capacity of 3000 tons, and before additional provision could be made, the war was well under way. Eventually, all the available space at Key West was covered with coal sheds. Their total capacity, however, was only 9000 tons, not sufficient to fill the bunkers of one of Sampson's largest vessels. Unfortunately, owing to their large drafts, these vessels could not enter Key West harbor or approach within six miles of the coaling wharf, and therefore had to be coaled from lighters or colliers.

Before the war commenced the Bureau of Equipment asked and obtained many offers to supply coal and to transport it to the West Indies. When the crucial moment came, all except one firm refused to adhere to their proposals, owing to the supposed risk of transporting coal to the scene of hostilities. In desperate straits, the bureau was compelled to purchase steamers, convert them into colliers and provide them with crews and officers taken from the navy. The owners of suitable vessels, knowing the necessities of the government, forced it to pay exorbitant prices. Early in April six ships were purchased for $1,247,000, and they were rapidly fitted out and were dispatched to the fleet with cargoes of coal. When the first great emergency was passed additional colliers, mostly foreign vessels, were obtained at fair prices. Recovering from its fright, the private coaling fleet on the Atlantic was employed in carrying coal to the shore stations. At one time 40,000 tons of coal were afloat at Hampton Roads, ready to sail at a moment's notice to any point desired. The fleet of colliers on the Atlantic belonging to the Navy Department in the summer of 1898 consisted of fifteen vessels, with a total capacity of 50,000 tons. Two colliers were purchased on the Pacific coast and sent with coal to Dewey's fleet at Manila. During the entire war no ship suffered the slightest delay from want of coal.[246]

[246] Ann. Rept. of Sec. of N., 1898, pp. 26-27, 270-271.

A much more difficult task of the Bureau of Equipment was the providing of the fleet off the Cuban coast with adequate supplies of fresh water. Some of the boilers of the ships on blockade duty before Santiago were injured for want of this article, and gave Sampson much concern. The distillers on shipboard were generally too small to supply all the needs of the ships. Before the outbreak of the war the Bureau of Equipment contracted for a distiller to be erected at Key West, capable of making 45,000 gallons of fresh water a day, but the contractor failed to complete it until long after the specified time. When finally it was ready for use its capacity was only 25,000 gallons a day, and owing to its imperfect construction frequent repairs were found to be necessary. An evaporating and distilling plant, with a capacity of 50,000 to 60,000 gallons a day, was installed on board the *Iris*, but it was not completed in time to be of service during the war. It was first used in supplying the army at Camp Wikoff on Long Island. The bureau bought considerable water, for some of which it was compelled to pay exorbitant prices.[247]

When it became apparent that a war with Spain was inevitable, the Bureau of Ordnance placed orders with private manufacturers for large quantities of gunpowder, projectiles, fixed ammunition, small arms and guns for secondary batteries. The manufacturers showed every disposition to meet the requirements of the bureau, nor did they in any instance take advantage of its unusual needs. When necessary, they greatly increased the output of their factories and ran them without intermission. During the war one hundred and thirty-five vessels received batteries and complete outfits of ordnance. Five hundred and seventy-six guns were placed on board the vessels of the auxiliary navy. Seventy-five auxiliary torpedo boats were fitted out, and many gun-cotton mines and mining outfits were manufactured. The ordnance shops of the Navy Department worked night and day. The naval gun factory was equal to every demand made upon it. Indeed, the resources of the department and of private manufacturers for ordnance, ammunition and projectiles were but lightly taxed by the brief conflict with Spain.[248]

The plan for purchasing supplies that was inaugurated by Secretary Whitney in 1886 was thoroughly tested by the war, and its

---

[247] Ann. Rept. of Sec. of N., 1898, pp. 41, 271-272.
[248] Ann. Rept. of Sec. of N., 1898, pp. 31, 463.

efficiency was fully proved. The Bureau of Supplies and Accounts during the period of active operations furnished 193 ships with naval stores. Early in March the bureau established a base of supplies at Key West and commenced making shipments thereto. Here and at several of the navy yards large quantities of provisions, clothing and other articles were collected. The bureau maintained at Key West a three months' supply of stores for 8000 men; at New York a three months' supply for 9000 men; and at Norfolk and Mare Island, each, a three months' supply for 4000 men. New York was the chief market for naval stores, and the New York navy yard was the chief receiving and distributing depot of the navy. To meet the needs of the greatly enlarged personnel of the navy, the bureau manufactured more than a million garments. The prices paid during the war were on the average no higher than those paid during peace.

Early in April the commander-in-chief of the Asiatic station was directed to fill his ships with stores and to buy a collier and supply ship, and within forty-eight hours after receiving his orders, he had purchased the *Nashan* and *Zafiro*. The former he loaded with coal and the latter with provisions. When war was declared, he was in possession of supplies sufficient to last for five months. Early in May the *City of Pekin* was dispatched from San Francisco with three months' provisions for the Asiatic fleet and a large consignment of miscellaneous stores. In June a refrigerating ship, laden with 600,000 pounds of fresh meats and a like quantity of fresh vegetables, was sent from San Francisco to Manila. Sampson's first refrigerating ship was the *Supply*, which on May 7 sailed for the fleet off Cuba loaded with fresh meats, vegetables, fruits, ice and other supplies. Subsequently, two other ships, the *Celtic* and *Glacier*, were fitted out with refrigerators, and were used to carry supplies to the naval vessels in the West Indies.

Another task that fell to the Bureau of Provisions and Clothing was the caring for prisoners. On receiving information that 1720 Spanish prisoners from Admiral Cervera's fleet were to be quartered on Seavey's Island in Portsmouth harbor, New Hampshire, and were expected to arrive there within two or three days, the bureau at once assembled all necessary provisions at the island, and when the Spaniards arrived, all was in readiness. A wholesome dinner was served to the prisoners, and each man was furnished with a mattress, hammock, two blankets and such clothing as he needed.[249]

Immediately after the destruction of the *Maine,* the Bureau of Medicine and Surgery made preparations to meet every contingency. The naval hospitals were equipped to their full capacity for the accommodation of patients, and the naval laboratory at New York made preparations to issue supplies on short notice. Medical and surgical outfits suitable for the auxiliary vessels were purchased, assembled and boxed, ready for shipment whenever and wherever needed. In no instance did any vessel have to wait for its medical stores. Forty-two assistant surgeons were appointed, and nineteen assistant and passed assistant surgeons were mustered into service with the state militia. In sixteen days the merchantman *Creole* was converted into the hospital ship *Solace,* and fitted out with modern medical appliances, a well-lighted operating room, a steam disinfecting plant, an ice machine, a steam laundry plant, cold storage rooms and an elevator for taking patients from the operating room and upper deck to the wards below. The *Solace* accommodated 200 patients, either in berths, swinging cots or staterooms. She was supplied with fresh water by means of distillers and evaporators. Her medical officers inaugurated a complete system of antiseptic surgery at sea—the first ever established. The wounded at the battle of Santiago, both American and Spanish, were taken on board the *Solace,* and transported to the naval hospital at Norfolk. Temporary hospitals were erected at Seavey's Island to accommodate the sick Spanish prisoners. Several young women volunteered their services as nurses, and were assigned to duty at the naval hospitals at New York and Norfolk. A permanent naval hospital corps was organized in accordance with an act of Congress approved on June 17, 1898.[250]

The supplying of the new ships with officers and seamen fell to the Bureau of Navigation. In all 813 officers received temporary appointments. Of these, 456 were line officers, varying in rank from commander to naval cadet. Two hundred and sixty-three officers entered the service from the naval militia. Two hundred and twenty-five officers on the retired list of the navy were assigned such duties as their age or physical condition permitted. Many more men applied for service than were needed. Examin-

[249] Ann. Rept. of Sec. of N., 1898, pp. 665-666.
[250] Ann. Rept. of Sec. of N., 1898, pp. 769-773.

ing boards were appointed to ascertain the professional knowledge of the applicants. The volunteer officers were assigned to
duty in the Auxiliary Naval Force and the Coast Signal Service,
and on board the small cruising ships, such as the *Yankee, Dixie*
and *Prairie*. A few of them saw duty in West Indian waters,
but many of them did not leave the coast of the United States.
Naturally they were deficient in professional experience and training, but they were zealous and attentive to duty. Immediately
after the signing of the peace protocol most of the volunteer
officers were discharged; a few, however, still remained in service
in 1899. During the war forty-three second lieutenants received
commissions in the marine corps.[251]

Prior to the outbreak of hostilities the number of enlisted men
allowed by law was 12,500. On August 15, when the enlisted
force reached its maximum, it numbered 24,123 men. On March
28 a circular letter was issued by the Navy Department calling
for enlistments for one year, and on this basis 9767 men entered
the service. Three thousand eight hundred and thirty-two men
were obtained from the naval militia. Thousands of men applied
for enlistment, whose services were not needed. For the fiscal
year ending June 30, 1898, 63,135 applicants were rejected. Many
of the recruits were landsmen, perchance clerks, lawyers, or professional men, and not seamen in any sense, and totally unfit for
their new calling. By June 30, 1899, the enlisted force had been
reduced to 14,501 men. During the war the marines were increased by some 2100 men.[252]

Two large and important organizations, the Auxiliary Naval
Force and the Coast Signal Service, were established early in the
war, and were discontinued at its close. The Auxiliary Naval
Force, organized for the purpose of defending the coast of the
United States, constituted the "second line of defence." It
guarded and patrolled the coast and protected the submarine
mines, and served to give the people of the Atlantic Gulf and
Pacific states a feeling of safety. The commencement of this
organization may be dated with the order of the Navy Department to Commander Horace Elmer to prepare with all possible
dispatch a plan for a "mosquito fleet," in "general accordance
with the methods prepared by the Naval War College." Elmer,

---

[251] Ann. Rept. of Sec. of N., 1898, pp. 29-30, 132.
[252] Ann. Rept. of Sec. of N., 1898, pp. 23, 320, 827; 1899, pp. 19, 404.

who established his headquarters at New York, was assisted in his work, which was most complicated and arduous, by the officers and clerical force of the New York navy yard, by the New York naval militia and by the New York board on auxiliary vessels. When war was declared on April 25 many details of a plan of organization had been worked out. At this critical moment Commander Elmer died, and was succeeded by Rear Admiral Henry Erben (retired), who proceeded to put into operation the plan of his predecessor. During the first month of his work he was considerably hampered by the delay of Congress in passing legislation providing for an auxiliary force. A measure which met the views of the department had been drafted in the first week of April. Finally, on May 26 a joint resolution of Congress was passed authorizing the organization of the United States Auxiliary Naval Force, and appropriating $3,000,000 for the purchase or hire of vessels.[253] Erben was at once made chief of the new organization. The officers and enlisted men of the force were paid from the regular appropriation for the " pay of the navy."

On July 9 Erben was succeeded by Captain John R. Bartlett (retired), the chief intelligence officer, who had charge of the force until it was discontinued, and on the same day the headquarters were removed from New York to the Office of Naval Intelligence in the Navy Department at Washington. The Auxiliary Naval Force was under the general supervision of the Assistant Secretary of the Navy. Early in July its staff consisted of two lieutenants, two naval constructors, six chief engineers, two pay officers and three surgeons. It was recruited almost entirely from the state naval militia, from which source about 1400 men, exclusive of officers, were derived. A few men came from the merchant service. To facilitate the work of the force, the coast of the United States was divided into nine districts (six on the Atlantic, two on the Gulf and one on the Pacific coast), and a naval officer was placed in charge of them. The vessels of the force, forty-one in number, were distributed among the districts, and were stationed at the important ports and strategic points. Twenty-three vessels were employed in patrolling mine-fields and in maintaining the quarantine regulations. Some of them cruised from port to port, or went to sea for target practice. Ten of the vessels were old monitors, which had been in ordinary for many

[253] U. S. Statutes at Large, XXX, 744-745.

years. The officers of the force furnished their own uniforms and side arms, and the enlisted men came into the service uniformed, armed and equipped. The officers and men of a given district were generally selected from the naval militia of the adjoining states, since their knowledge of local waters and of local conditions gave them a special aptitude for patrol duty near home.[254]

The Coast Signal Service, like the Naval Auxiliary Force, was organized to assist in the defence of the coast. Before a war with Spain was anticipated, Secretary Long on October 18, 1897, appointed a board, of which Commander John Schouler was president, to consider the establishment of " coast signal stations for naval defence." On October 27 this board reported a plan for a coast signal service, but no further action was taken on the subject by the department at that time. On March 15, 1898, Secretary Long, moved by the prospects of a war, ordered Captain C. F. Goodrich, president of the Naval War College, to make and report with dispatch a preliminary plan for the establishment of a coast signal service on the Atlantic and Gulf coasts. Goodrich made a report which closely followed the recommendations of the Schouler board, and on April 9 the department ordered him to establish a coast-line system of signal stations in accordance with the plan contained in his report and in consultation with the Naval War Board. Goodrich fixed his headquarters at New York on board the U. S. S. *New Hampshire,* the armory of the First Naval Battalion of New York. On April 23 he was relieved by Captain Theodore F. Kane (retired), and on May 9 Kane was succeeded by Captain John R. Bartlett, who served until the service was discontinued. Bartlett transferred the headquarters to the Naval Intelligence Office in Washington, and conducted his work under the general supervision of the Bureau of Navigation.

For the purposes of this service, the coast from Maine to Texas was divided into eight districts, and thirty-six signal stations, officered and manned entirely by men drawn from the naval militia, were established. The stations were in telegraphic or telephonic communication with the central office in Washington, and were connected with the lines of the Life Saving Service on the beach. The light-house keepers and the observers of the U. S. Weather Bureau along the coast were also brought into the

[254] Ann. Rept. of Sec. of N., 1898, pp. 19-20, 105-137, 143.

system. Altogether there were in the service 210 naval militiamen, 1443 men of the Life Saving Service, 850 light-house keepers and 33 observers of the Weather Bureau; a total of 2526 men. These observers were stationed on the Atlantic and Gulf coasts, and were continually on the lookout for the vessels of the enemy and suspicious craft of all sorts, as well as for American vessels, the movements of which they watched. While no Spanish ships came within the range of their observations, they several times made important reports of the vessels of our own fleet, and announced the arrival of the *Oregon* from her famous cruise around Cape Horn. The knowledge that was gained in establishing the system will be of much value in case of another war.[255]

In its efforts to mobilize rapidly a naval force the department was much hampered by its want of jurisdiction over the naval militia of the states, which were of course organized under state laws. Officers and enlisted men were mustered into the several divisions of the federal service from the militia as they were needed. On the outbreak of the war, the number of men in these state organizations was rapidly increased, and many militiamen were disappointed in not being called into the federal service. All told, the naval militia furnished the navy 4316 men. Of these, 2600 men served in the regular navy, and the rest in the Auxiliary Naval Force or the Coast Signal Service. The militiamen of a state were often assigned to widely different duties. Those of only one state, Michigan, were kept together, being assigned to duty on board the U. S. S. *Yosemite*. While the officers and seamen from the state organizations were zealous and patriotic and rapidly acquired experience and efficiency they naturally were less competent than the regularly-trained officers and seasoned man-of-wars' men.[256] After the war many attempts were made to obtain the establishment of a permanent national naval reserve, but they all failed.

[255] Ann. Rept. of Sec. of N., 1898, pp. 20, 386.
[256] Ann. Rept. of Sec. of N., 1898, pp. 137-149.

CHAPTER TWELVE: THE NAVY MOVES AHEAD, 1897-1911

Part I

PERSONNEL

For several years immediately preceding the war with Spain, the navy and the department gave much consideration to the naval personnel, the condition of which had become very unsatisfactory, and many attempts were made to obtain remedial legislation of various sorts. There was not a corps in the navy that did not believe that it suffered from some hardship. The especial grievance of the line officers was the infrequency of promotions. Some of the lieutenants had spent more than 20 years in their grade, and in 1898 a few officers were still lieutenants who had entered the navy as midshipmen during or immediately after the Civil War. Several lieutenants were between 40 and 50 years of age. This long service in the lower ranks worked an injustice to the officers, and was detrimental to the navy since it unfitted the officers for command ranks. Men who had spent the best years of their lives in subordinate stations, occupied often with trifling and routine tasks, were not likely to have the executive habit, initiative, decision and resourcefulness, when having passed the meridian of life they became captains, commodores and rear admirals. Moreover, the existing system rushed the officers through the upper grades so rapidly that they were able to acquire but little experience in them.

The causes of the dearth of promotions in the nineties were both chronic and acute. Owing to the small number of officers in the higher grades as compared with the large number in the lower, the normal operation of a system of promotions based on seniority results in the slow movement of the officers from rank to rank in the lower grades, and the arrival of an officer at the command ranks late in his naval career—far later than the good of the navy requires. This was the chronic cause of the stagnation of promotions. The acute cause dated from the Civil War. Under a system of promotion by seniority, if at any time the movement from grade to grade is abnormally accelerated, then at some subsequent period it will be unduly retarded. During and immediately after the Civil War, the number of promotions was greatly increased, and many young men were rapidly advanced. By 1890 this had resulted in placing in the higher ranks many officers who were still some years below the retiring age of 62 years, and who blocked the movement of all below them. Moreover, since an unusually large number of officers entered the navy about the time of the Civil War, considerable inequalities in rank arose when these men began to reach the higher grades. The officers of the date of the Civil War were sufficient in number to fill all the grades above, and part of, the lieutenant's grade. It seemed unfair to lieutenants of the date of 1861-1865 to see their fellow-officers of the same date filling the positions of commodore and rear admiral.

By 1897 the differences between the line officers and the engineers engaged the attention of the department even more than the evils of infrequent promotions. The origin of this controversy dates from the establishment of the engineer corps in 1842. Differences in the origin, history and traditions of the corps naturally led to jealousies and misunderstandings. Moreover, the development of steam power, machinery and engineering on board naval ships had for half a century gradually and continually enhanced the importance of the engineer corps, which had correspondingly increased in importance, risen in rank and in the education of its officers, and grown in dignity and consideration. In some respects, however, the enhancement of the position of the engineers did not appear to them commensurate with the importance they had attained in the economy of modern ships. In 1897 the chief controversy between them and the line related to their demand for certain rights and privileges which were enjoyed by the line and which the line was unwilling to share with them. Speaking generally, one may say that the engineers were asking for an increase of numbers, positive rank, " naval " titles, greater recognition, and absolute command over their own divisions aboard ship.

In the first year of Secretary Long's administration, the strife between the line and the engineers became a matter of much importance and solicitude, and both the Navy Department and Congress determined to make another attempt to restore harmony. The civilian engineers espoused the cause of their professional brethren within the navy, and demanded that they be given a higher standing and recognition. Long decided to refer the questions at issue to a board of experienced men. Accordingly, on November 4, 1898, he appointed the Naval Personnel Board, consisting of Assistant Secretary of the Navy Roosevelt, president, and nine naval officers, five of the line and four of the staff, and directed it to "consider the matter of a reorganization of the personnel of the navy," and to embody its conclusions in a report and a bill. The principal representatives of the line were Captains A. S. Crowninshield, W. T. Sampson and R. D. Evans; and of the staff, Engineer in Chief G. W. Melville and Chief Engineer Charles W. Rae. The board held sessions and deliberated over its problems for some four weeks. At one of its first meetings Engineer in Chief Melville submitted a proposition in behalf of the engineers conceding most of their demands. This was rejected. Captain Evans then proposed a plan which involved the abolition of the engineer corps and the amalgamation of the engineers with the line officers. Mr. Ira N. Hollis, professor of engineering in Harvard University and a graduate of the Naval Academy, had suggested this solution in the summer of 1897, and Assistant Secretary Roosevelt had become its able champion. Animated by a strong desire to promote the harmony of the navy, the board finally agreed to recommend the amalgamation of the two corps, notwithstanding some of the members had misgivings respecting the efficacy of this remedy.

The report of the board was written by Roosevelt, who spiritedly advocated the amalgamation of the two corps. One argument for it he based upon an analogy between the conditions of the naval service 250 years ago and those of to-day. The two principal corps of officers on board the naval ships of the seventeenth century were those of the sailormen and the sea-soldiers. The sailormen, who had charge of the motive power and sailed the ship, may be said to correspond to the engineers of to-day. The sea-soldiers, who fought the ship, had duties analogous to those of the modern line officers. Just as the sailormen and the sea-soldiers were finally merged into one naval corps, a similar merger or amalgamation must take place between the engineers and the line. Another argument of Roosevelt was based upon the similarity of the duties of the two corps. The work of both classes of officers on shipboard, he said, was now largely of an engineering character, and for its proper performance it required officers possessed of a considerable knowledge of engineering. "Every officer on a modern war vessel in reality has to be an engineer whether he wants to or not. Everything on such a vessel goes by machinery, and every officer, whether dealing with the turrets or the engine room, has to do with engineers' work. There is no longer any reason for having a separate body of engineers responsible for only a part of the machinery. What is needed is one homogeneous body, all of whose members are trained for the efficient performance of the duties of the modern line officer. The midshipmen will be grounded in all these duties at Annapolis, and will be perfected likewise in all of them by actual work after graduation. We are not making a revolution; we are merely recognizing and giving shape to an evolution, which has come slowly but surely and naturally, and we propose to reorganize the navy along the lines indicated by the course of evolution itself."

The Naval Personnel Board also recommended a plan for increasing the number of promotions in the navy, according to which the weak and incapacitated officers of the lower grades were to be selected for retirement by a naval board, each member of which was to take an oath to act without prejudice and impartiality. The Assistant Secretary of the Navy vigorously condemned the system of promotion by seniority. He said that it made the "promotion of an officer dependent not upon the zealous performance of his duties but upon the possession of a good stomach and of an easy nature; while a positive premium is put upon the man who never ventures to take a risk, and who therefore never does anything great." Several minor reforms were also proposed. The board embodied its recommendations in a bill, which Secretary Long on January 12, 1898, after suggesting a few slight modifications, transmitted to Congress, earnestly recommending its passage. In the spring of 1898 the House Committee on Naval Affairs thoroughly considered the amalgamation of the two corps, holding lengthy hearings on the subject and calling before it Assistant Secretary Roosevelt and many leading naval officers. On May 19 it reported a bill, based upon the recommendations of the board, but containing some new provisions. Owing to the distractions of the war with Spain, consideration of this measure was postponed. In January, 1899, the naval personnel bill was again taken up by Congress, and after being debated, amended and passed by both Houses, was signed by President McKinley on March 3, 1899.[257]

The Naval Personnel Act contained the most important legislation concerning the officers of the navy that had been passed since the Civil War. Its most noteworthy provisions related to the amalgamation of the line officers and the engineers, naval pay and rank, the number of officers, the flow of promotions, the enlistment and retirement of seamen, the establishment of a corps of warrant machinists, and the marine corps. The first section of the act was the most important one, and the most far-reaching in its effect upon the navy. It provided that the " officers constituting the engineer corps of the navy be, and are hereby transferred to the line of the navy, and shall be commissioned accordingly." The engineers were divided into three classes; those above the rank of commander, who were to have shore-duty only; the older officers below this rank, who were given the option of assuming line or retaining engineering duties; and the younger officers, who were to perform line duties. All engineers who were assigned to line duties had first to qualify for them by passing an appropriate examination. One hundred warrant machinists, who were to take the place of the engineers in the engine rooms, were authorized. To make room in the line for the engineers, its numbers in the various grades were considerably increased.

One of the most popular provisions of the act was that which increased the pay of officers, and which tended to neutralize the opposition to amalgamation. The pay and allowances of the officers of the line, the medical corps, and the pay corps were made to correspond to the pay and allowance of the army officers of corresponding ranks. The sea-pay of the first nine rear admirals was

[257] Sen. Doc., 55C. 2S., No. 116; House Doc., 55C. 2S., No. 1375; Long, New American Navy, I, 81-88; Army and Navy Journal, XXXIV, 952, 962; Atlantic Monthly, LXXX, 318-319; Congressional Record, XXXII, 658, 1974.

fixed at $7500; of the second nine rear admirals, $5500; of a captain, $3500; and of a lieutenant, $1800. All officers below the rank of rear admiral were allowed "longevity pay," that is, an increase of pay of ten per cent for each five years of service. In order to discourage shore-duty, the pay of officers on shore was placed 15 per cent below the pay of those at sea. The act also gave positive rank to all staff officers who by statute were given relative rank. The number of naval constructors was increased to 40, and this corps was given positive rank. The number of officers in the marine corps was considerably increased, and its enlisted force was raised to 6000 men. The grade of commodore was abolished. The length of the term of enlistment of all seamen was made four years.

The Naval Personnel Act also contained a provision for accelerating the flow of promotions. The Secretary of the Navy was authorized to keep a list of "applicants for voluntary retirement." In case the number of vacancies for each year in certain specified grades did not equal certain specified numbers, the President was authorized to select from the list of applicants the requisite number of officers and retire them. If it should happen that the specified number of vacancies could not be created in this way, the Secretary of the Navy was empowered to convene a board, which was to select the required number of officers for retirement. All officers who were thus retired either voluntarily or involuntarily were granted three-fourths of the pay of the next higher grade, a provision which was popular with the officers, but which did not meet the sanction of Secretary Long, who believed that it placed a premium on retirement.[253]

Respecting the advisability of amalgamation, the officers of the navy were by no means a unit. Some of the older officers, who strongly opposed amalgamation, argued that it was contrary to the prevailing tendency of the times, specialization, and that it would make the line officer a jack-of-all-trades. Moreover, according to them, there was needed on board the naval ships a thoroughly trained corps of engineers, and its place could not be taken by a corps of warrant machinists.

The passage of the act proved to be one thing, and its enforcement quite another. In its passage the engineers seem to have

[253] Long, New American Navy, I, 86; U. S. Statutes at Large, XXX, 1004-1009.

scored, but the line has for the most part interpreted it. The act apparently contemplated the assignment of young officers to line and engineering duties indiscriminately. In practice, however, only a few of them were given the duties of engineers. As a result, there arose a lamentable dearth of officers of engineering experience. The young officers of the line did not seriously take up the study or practice of their new duties. The chief of the Bureau of Steam Engineering in his annual report for 1905 said that the " situation is critical and something must be done." He recommended the assigning of engineering duties to the young line officers, and the establishment of a corps of engineering specialists within the line. There was at this time considerable sentiment in the navy favorable to the revival of the engineer corps. Secretary Bonaparte, however, was of the opinion that by a thoroughgoing and persevering enforcement of the Naval Personnel Act a satisfactory engineering service at sea might be provided, and that a reversal of the policy of amalgamation would cause "embarrassment and an impairment of confidence in the department, both within and without the service." [259] By 1910, if we may judge from the reports of the Secretary of the Navy and of the chief of the Bureau of Steam Engineering, the new system was working satisfactorily. The Secretary reported that the line officers compared favorably as operating engineers with the officers of the old engineer corps. A body of engineering experts drawn from the line was receiving training in a school of post-graduate work in marine engineering, at Annapolis.[260]

Notwithstanding the provisions of the Naval Personnel Act respecting the retirement of officers, they still reach the flag or command ranks late in their naval careers. In recent years the chiefs of the Bureau of Navigation have given much attention to this evil, and have proposed various remedies. In 1904 Secretary Morton, following the bureau's suggestions, recommended that captains be retired at 60 years of age and commanders at 55 years, and that the age of retirement for captains be gradually reduced to 55 and that of commanders to 50 years. By this means the flow of promotions would be accelerated and officers

[259] Army and Navy Journal, XXXIX, 286; Ann. Rept. of Sec. of N., 1905, pp. 6-8; Ann. Rept. of Chief of Bureau of Steam Engineering, 1905, pp. 31-34.

[260] Ann. Rept. of Sec. of N., 1910, pp. 26, 489.

would be brought to the command ranks at earlier ages. Secretary Bonaparte, however, was opposed to this plan, believing that an officer's fitness for command diminishes little between his fortieth and sixtieth year. In place of it, he recommended a quite novel and radical measure, according to which every officer after serving five years in any grade should be either promoted, dropped or retired. A personnel board, of which Assistant Secretary Newberry was president, was appointed by Bonaparte in August, 1906. It recommended the adoption of a system of promotion fixing more or less definitely the time the officers should spend in each grade, and eliminating from the navy all officers in excess of the required numbers for each grade. President Roosevelt has always been inclined to attack the problem chiefly from "below." He would increase the number of promotions by advancing the fit officers of the lower grades and removing from the service the unfit. That is, he would introduce the system of promotion by selection.[261] The subjects of promotion, rank and amalgamation are still under discussion. In 1911 the department favored a method of promotion that would bring officers to flag rank at an earlier age, the creation of the ranks of admiral and vice admiral, and the amalgamation of the construction corps and the pay corps with the line.[262]

The rapid growth of the commissioned fleet since 1898 has necessitated considerable increases in the number of officers in every naval corps, except those of chaplain and professor of mathematics. Secretary Bonaparte, indeed, has recommended an increase in the number of chaplains. The enlargement of the naval personnel, however, has by no means kept pace with the needs of the service, and for several years the navy has been crippled for want of officers. In 1902 President Roosevelt said that a thousand additional officers were required. In 1904 the chief of the Bureau of Navigation showed that, in order to man adequately the ships already built and building, the number of line officers would need to be doubled. His estimate called for 2078 line officers from the grade of midshipman to that of captain.[263] In 1911 the number of line officers on the active list from

[261] Ann. Rept. of 'Sec. of N., 1904, pp. 8-9; 1905, pp. 4-6; Ann. Message of President, 1905.
[262] Ann. Rept. of Sec. of N., 1911, pp. 47-49.
[263] Ann. Message of President, 1902; Ann. Rept. of Sec. of N., 1904, p. 473.

midshipman-at-sea to admiral was 1629; on the retired list, 434.
In order to meet the future demands of the navy for officers,
Congress has greatly increased the number of midshipmen at the
Naval Academy. This number rose from 280 in 1899, to 879 in
1906. The yearly appointment of 12 ensigns from the warrant
officers of the navy is now permitted.

To the request of the Navy Department for more officers, Congress at times replied that the deficiency could be considerably
reduced by sending more of them to sea. To this the department
rejoined that additional officers were required on shore as well as
on board the naval vessels, and that one reason for the high efficiency of the American navy was the training which its officers
received in the administrative posts of the navy yards and the
department. Congress was inclined to exaggerate the number of
officers employed on shore and the evils of shore-duty. In January, 1901, the chief of the Bureau of Navigation reported that
76 per cent of the younger, and 40 to 50 per cent of the older
officers were at sea. The tendency during the decade 1897-1907
was to exalt the chief function of the naval officer, the command
of ships. President Roosevelt, who would discourage long details to shore-duty, said in his first annual message that the
" officers and men alike should be kept as much as possible on
blue water, for it is there only they can learn their duties as they
should be learned." [264]

During the last decade the educational facilities of the navy have
been greatly improved. For many years the Naval Academy at
Annapolis was neglected. Finally some of its buildings became
so dilapidated and insecure that they were a disgrace to the
nation. In 1898 Congress made a liberal appropriation for new
buildings, in 1900 it authorized the reconstruction of the academy
at a cost of $8,000,000, and later it raised this sum to $10,000,000.
By 1907 the work of reconstruction was nearing completion. In
1897 a postgraduate course in naval construction was established
at the academy, but two years later this was discontinued, and
the members of this corps were sent to the Massachusetts Institute of Technology for advanced technical instruction. In 1902
Secretary Long gave orders for the establishment at Annapolis
of a postgraduate course in engineering for the purpose of

[264] Congressional Record, XXXIII, 5224, 5267; XXXIV, 1355, 2130; Ann.
Message of President, 1901.

instructing the junior line officers in engineering duties, which, under the Naval Personnel Act, they were to assume on shipboard. In May, 1903, the school of application of the marine corps was transferred from the marine barracks at Washington to the Naval Academy at Annapolis. In 1902 the school for naval surgeons was located in Washington, and greatly strengthened, and a little later a school for the assistant paymasters of the navy was established.

In recent years the training of officers at sea in fleet maneuvers and practical drills of various kinds has been much extended and improved, and to enhance the value of these exercises a policy of concentration of the fleets has been followed. In the winter of 1904-1905 the European and South Atlantic squadrons were consolidated with the North Atlantic squadron, and early in 1907 the Pacific and Asiatic squadrons were brought together under one command. In that year the Atlantic fleet consisted of 43 vessels and was divided into four squadrons. The Pacific fleet, which was made up of three squadrons and the first and fourth torpedo flotillas, contained 35 vessels. In 1910 the Asiatic squadron was reestablished.

In 1911 the marine corps contained 322 commissioned officers on the active list, ranking from major general to second lieutenant, and 62 officers on the retired list. From 1898 to 1910 the enlisted personnel increased from 2600 men to 9267.[265] The commandant in 1911 was Major General W. P. Biddle. He was assisted in administering the corps by 21 officers, belonging to the adjutant and inspector's department, quartermaster's department and paymaster's department. The headquarters of the marine corps are at Washington, D. C. Marine barracks are maintained near the chief navy yards in the United States and at Annapolis, Port Royal, New Orleans and Sitka, and in Porto Rico, Hawaii, Guam and the Philippines. Marines are stationed in Cuba and Panama and at Peking. In 1910 the advanced base school of the marine corps was established at New London, Connecticut. A school for officers is maintained at Port Royal, South Carolina. While recognizing the efficient service of the corps in the past, many naval officers have from time to time favored its abolition,

[265] Navy List, July, 1905; Jan., 1912; Ann. Rept. of Sec. of N., 1910, p. 813.

a step which is urged in order to render the organization of the navy more homogeneous.

The number of seamen to be trained, and their need of a better and more highly specialized training, have grown with the growth of the fleet and the development of naval construction. In 1898 the authorized strength of the enlisted force of the navy was fixed at 13,750; in 1899, at 20,000; in 1901, at 25,050; in 1902, at 28,000; in 1903, at 31,000; in 1904, at 34,000; in 1905, at 37,000; in 1907, at 38,500; in 1909, at 42,000 and in 1911, at 44,000.[266] To enlist and train these seamen for the naval service has been a task of considerable magnitude. Owing to the small number of professional seamen in the United States and the difficulties in the way of procuring landsmen, the mere enlisting of the requisite numbers has taken much work and time. In 1905 recruiting was conducted at the various receiving ships at coast ports, at permanent recruiting stations at Boston, New York, Buffalo, Philadelphia, Baltimore, Chicago and San Francisco, and by four recruiting parties in the field which covered practically the entire continental limits of the United States. The whole country was scoured for recruits. Only about one-third of the men who presented themselves for enlistment were able to pass the prescribed examination. The total number of men enlisted in 1911 was 14,756. During the last few years the navy has suffered greatly from want of seamen. In 1902 President Roosevelt wrote that "serious trouble threatens us if we cannot do better than we are now doing as regards securing the services of a sufficient number of the highest type of sailormen, of sea mechanics." In December, 1906, the navy was about 4500 men short of its authorized strength.[267]

The facilities for training seamen and landsmen in the naval arts have been greatly enlarged. Important improvements have been made in the naval training station at Newport, notably by the erection of barracks for the accommodation of 2000 recruits. In April, 1896, Congress passed an act establishing a training station for the Pacific coast on the island of Yerba Buena in the harbor of San Francisco, and on April 12, 1898, 140 acres of land was

---

[266] Congressional Record, XXXVIII, 2721; U. S. Statutes at Large, XXXIII, 1092; XXXV, 753; XXXVI, 1266.

[267] Ann. Rept. of Chief of Bureau of Navigation, 1905, pp. 15-16; Ann. Message of President, 1902.

acquired for that purpose by transfer from the War Department. This has been improved by grading and the erection of barracks, officers' quarters and other necessary buildings, and accommodations for 600 apprentices have been provided. In 1902 the establishment of a training station on the Great Lakes was determined upon, and accordingly on April 27, 1904, Congress appropriated $250,000, and directed that a board of three members should select a site. After viewing various proposed locations, the board chose a site at Lake Bluff, on Lake Michigan, a few miles north of Chicago. Most extensive improvements have been made there, and they are now nearing completion.

Soon after the war with Spain the policy of enlisting and training landsmen was inaugurated, since in no other way could the ever-increasing demand for recruits be met. In the fiscal year 1901, 4198 landsmen were enlisted, chiefly in the Mississippi valley and to the eastward thereof. The landsmen are given a training similar to that of the apprentices, and in 1901 seven training vessels were thus employed. Port Royal, South Carolina, was first assigned as the training station for landsmen, but it was soon abandoned and Norfolk was selected. The ships *Richmond* and *Franklin,* with accommodations for 1000 men were attached to the station. On the Pacific coast the landsmen are trained at the San Francisco training station. Until 1904 the training systems for boys and landsmen were distinct from each other, but in December of that year, in accordance with the recommendations of the Bureau of Navigation, they were united, and the training ships were retired from service. After the seamen apprentices, whether boys or landsmen, receive four months' instruction at one of the training stations, and after they pass an appropriate examination at the end of this course, they are rated as ordinary seamen and transferred to the regular cruising vessels of the navy. The new system needs fewer officers and sailors for its operation, since none are required for training ships, and it secures for the regular navy the services of the apprentice seamen in a comparatively short time after their enlistment. As a method of training apprentices it is probably less effective than the old system, but it causes a saving of officers and seamen, a consideration that led to its adoption.[268]

[268] Ann. Rept. of Chief of Bureau of Navigation, 1905, pp. 12-13.

In recent years the special training of seamen in gunnery has been greatly improved. For the seamen-gunner class of the navy, a four months' course of instruction in constructing and mounting guns and in lathe and machine work is given at the Naval Gun Factory at Washington, and a six months' course in torpedoes, submarine mines and diving, at the Naval Torpedo Station at Newport. For several years gun captains were trained on board the *Amphitrite*. Special training is provided for the crews of the submarine boats. Since the war of 1898 training in gunnery and target practice has been a special feature of the work of the cruising ships. President Roosevelt insisted that these most essential drills should not be neglected. Small-arm target ranges and target galleries have been established on shore at all training stations, at various naval stations and navy yards and near the receiving ships. In his annual message for 1904 the President said that the markmanship of the navy had improved in a remarkable degree.

In 1898 a school for the training and instruction of the enlisted men in electricity was established at the Boston yard, and during the succeeding year similar schools were started at the New York and Mare Island yards. In 1900 the Boston school was discontinued. The course of instruction at the New York and Mare Island schools covers a period of five months, and is pursued either by professional electricians or by men who have had experience in handling electrical apparatus aboard ship. Instruction is given in electrical science, the handling of electrical machinery, and wireless telegraphy. During 1905 120 men completed the electrical courses. About 1902 an artificers' school for the instruction of carpenters' mates, shipwrights, blacksmiths, coppersmiths, painters and ship-fitters was established at the Norfolk yard, and was placed under the supervision of a commissioned officer of the navy, who was assisted by warrant officers and the leading mechanics of the Norfolk yard. The course of instruction covered a period of three months. Schools for petty officers belonging to other than the artificers' branch of the service are maintained at the Newport training station and at the New York navy yard. Schools for yeomen have been established at the New York and Mare Island yards. Under Secretary Long a training school for firemen was organized on board the U. S. S. *Cincinnati*, and a school for the training of bandsmen has been recently opened.

These various schools and means of instruction have greatly enhanced the efficiency of the sailorman. They have specialized his training to meet new naval needs, and have enabled him to use and understand the complicated machinery with which ships are now fitted. He is coming to know less and less about sails, and more and more about machines. The old training in "marlinspike seamanship" is yielding to a new training which follows the lines of recent naval developments. The bluff, jolly, illiterate, profane and picturesque man-of-war's men of the old school is disappearing. The newcomers are men of better morals, more booklearning, and more specialized skill, though less indigenous to the sea and more likely to abandon a seafaring life. An excellent class of seamen is being obtained from the interior of the United States, and the number of citizen-sailors is increasing. When Secretary Long entered the Navy Department in 1897, almost 25 per cent of the enlisted force were foreigners. In 1904 only 9 per cent were foreigners, 11 per cent were naturalized citizens, and 80 per cent were natives of this country. The introduction into the navy of men from the interior states, who have little or no knowledge of the trials and hardships of a seafaring life, has doubtless increased the number of deserters. The percentage of desertions for the fiscal year 1904 was 15.6.[269]

The large increases in the number of officers and seamen in the navy during the last decade has necessitated a large increase in the "pay of the navy." The appropriations under this head for 1898 amounted to $8,235,385, and 1911, to $35,000,000. This was an increase in 13 years of more than 300 per cent. During the period 1881-1897, when the first vessels of the new navy were constructed, the average sum carried by the annual naval appropriation bills was $21,000,000. The naval appropriation bill for 1897 carried, in round numbers, $31,000,000; for 1901, $61,000,000; for 1905, $98,000,000; and for 1910, when they reached their maximum, $137,000,000. That is, the naval appropriations more than trebled in eight years and more than quadrupled in 13. Than annual appropriations for the navy during the Civil War were $73,000,000. The appropriations for the repair and improvement of navy yards and docks increased from $1,515,000 in 1897 to $8,714,000 in 1901. The estimates of the department

[269] Long, New American Navy, I, 92; Ann. Rept. of Sec. of N., 1904, p. 499.

for these purposes for 1903 amounted to $21,566,000. For 1906 these appropriations were only $3,140,000. The appropriations for new ships, including the cost of hull, machinery, armor, armament and equipment, increased from $11,479,000 in 1897, to $32,177,000 in 1905. The total appropriations for new ships for 1906, including deficiencies, amounted to the remarkable sum of $55,356,000. The naval appropriations for 1912 were $129,000,000.[270]

[270] U. S. Statutes at Large, XXIX, 648-649; XXXIII, pt. 1, 1092; Congressional Record, XXXVIII, 2079; XXXIX, 2567, 2580; Ann. Rept. of Sec. of N., 1904, p. 54; 1905, pp. 48-49; 1910, p. 57.; 1912, p. 157; Proc. of U. S. Naval Inst., XXVIII, 56; House Rept., 56C. 1S. and 2S., No. 905, 26, table; Congressional Record, XXXIX, 3484-3485, 3490.

CHAPTER TWELVE: THE NAVY MOVES AHEAD.
1897-1911

Part II

MATÉRIEL

The building of ships has been greatly accelerated since 1897. The rate at which keels were laid down before that date now seems exceedingly slow. With the exception of Great Britain, the United States has in recent years increased her fleet faster than any other naval power. When the ships that have been authorized are completed, the American navy, in efficiency, will be exceeded only by that of Great Britain; and in number of ships and tonnage, only by the navies of Great Britain and France. New vessels have been authorized each year since the Spanish-American War, with the exception of 1901. Counting ships built, building and authorized, the navy in 1897 consisted of 141 vessels; and in 1910, of 371 vessels. Of the latter, there were fit for service 308 vessels; under construction, 31; authorized, but their construction not yet commenced, 20; and unfit for sea service, 12. The armored fleet of the navy, its real dependence in time of war, has been remarkably strengthened. In 1897 it consisted of 20 vessels: 9 first-class battleships, 2 second-class battleships, 2 armored cruisers, 1 armored ram and 6 harbor-defence monitors. In 1910 it consisted of 58 vessels: 35 first-class battleships, 1 second-class battleship, 12 armored cruisers and 10 harbor-defence monitors. To the unarmored fleet there have been added since 1897, nine protected cruisers, and a large number of torpedo-boats, torpedo-boat destroyers, submarine torpedo-boats and subsidiary vessels. The later armored ships are much larger than the earlier ones. The displacement of the first-class battleship *Indiana,* authorized in 1890, was 10,225 tons; that of the *Minnesota,* authorized in 1903, 16,000 tons; and that of the *Nevada,* authorized in 1911, 27,000 tons. The displacement of the *Brooklyn,* one of the first armored cruisers, is 8150 tons; while that of the *Tennessee* is 14,500 tons. The cost of a battleship, including her armament, of the date 1904 was about $8,000,000 and of 1911 somewhat more.

The speed of the more recent ships is greater than that of the first vessels of the New Navy. A notion of the size, strength and armament of the later battleships of the navy may be obtained from some figures respecting the *Nebraska,* a 15,000-ton ship commissioned in 1907. This ship has a water-line length of 435 feet; her beam is 76 feet 2½ inches, and her maximum draft 26 feet. Her complement consists of 41 officers, 675 enlisted men and 60 marines. Her twin reciprocating engines are designed to generate 19,000 horse-power and to give a speed of 19 knots. Her main battery consists of 12-inch and 8-inch guns, and her secondary battery of 6-inch, 3-inch, 3-pounders and 1-pounders. Her torpedo armament is exceedingly powerful, consisting of four 21-inch torpedoes driven by turbine engines. The total weight of her armor is 3690 tons. Two of the new 27,000-ton battleships are to be 565 feet long and 95 feet beam, and each of them is to carry ten 14-inch guns.[271]

The Navy Department has continued to follow the policy of building its ships under contract with private shipbuilders, although considerable opinion favorable to constructing vessels in the government yards exists. Now and then ships are built in the yards, but their cost always exceeds that of sister-ships constructed by private builders. In 1905 31 vessels were being constructed by 12 shipbuilding companies. Six different companies were constructing battleships. Cramp and Sons, of Philadelphia, and the Union Iron Works, of San Francisco, have had the largest part in building the new fleet. In 1903 it was said that one-half the larger ships of the navy had been constructed by the Cramps. Other leading shipbuilding firms are situated at Bath, Maine; Quincy, Massachusetts; Camden, New Jersey; Newport News, Virginia; and Seattle, Washington. During the fiscal year 1905 the Bureau of Construction and

[271] Scientific American, Aug. 4, 1906, p. 82; Dec. 22, 1907, p. 462; July 13, 1907, p. 22.

Repair inspected 154,000,000 pounds of steel; and the Bureau of Steam Engineering, 50,000,000 pounds of engineering materials. The steel was furnished by 65, and the engineering materials by 318 companies. At the same time other private establishments were manufacturing large quantities of materials for the Bureaus of Ordnance and Equipment. Each bureau inspects its own materials.[272]

To meet the navy's increasing demand for armor, the Bethlehem and Carnegie companies greatly enlarged their plants. In 1903 the Navy Department obtained a third source of supply in the Midvale Steel Company, of Philadelphia. The prices paid for armor in 1903 and 1904 ranged from $400 to $420 a ton, exclusive of royalties. The first armor of the New Navy was contracted for at the rates of $574 and $605 a ton. In 1893 it was costing $646 and $671 a ton. In 1897 Congress came to the conclusion that the Bethlehem and Carnegie companies were not competing with each other, and were forcing up prices. On March 3, 1897, a law was passed limiting the average price to be paid by the department for armor at $300 a ton; and on July 19 another law was enacted authorizing the Secretary of the Navy, in case he could not obtain armor at that price, to begin the establishment of a public armor factory, and to appoint a naval board to advise him on the subject. The Carnegie and Bethlehem companies declined to submit bids on the ground that armor could not be made at the price established by Congress. On August 5, 1897, Secretary Long appointed the Armor Factory Board, of which Commodore J. A. Howell was president. This board held sessions from August to December, 1897, and made a report in which it estimated the cost of establishing a factory at $3,748,000. Secretary Long was not favorable to the proposed enterprise, and the war with Spain caused the government to come to terms with the armor makers. In May, 1898, Congress raised the maximum price to $400 a ton, and contracts were let to the Carnegie and Bethlehem companies to furnish all the armor that was then needed.

In 1899 Congress again reduced the price of armor to $300 a ton, and the Navy Department again failed to find bidders. In 1900 Congress, displaying much confidence in the Secretary

[272] Ann. Rept. of Chief of Bureau of Construction and Repair, 1905, pp. 13-16; Ann. Rept. of Chief of Bureau of Steam Engineering, 1905, p. 28.

of the Navy, authorized him to contract for armor at any price which in his judgment was reasonable and equitable, and in case of failure to purchase, to begin the construction of an armor factory, for which purpose $4,000,000 was appropriated. Secretary Long did not find it necessary to avail himself of the latter alternative, for he succeeded in making contracts on reasonable and equitable terms, agreeing to pay for Harveyized armor $411.20 a ton, and for Krupp armor $456 a ton. The long series of difficulties of the department over the purchase of armor now came to an end.[273]

Since 1897 many important and permanent improvements have been made in the establishments under the Bureau of Ordnance. From 1897 to 1902 the volume of the work at the Naval Gun Factory increased almost threefold, and since 1902 it has been further augmented. In 1905 this factory employed 3929 workers of all sorts, including officers, clerks, mechanics and laborers. Even by running continuously, day and night, it has been unable to manufacture all of the large guns required by the navy. Contracts have been let to the Bethlehem and Midvale companies for the completed guns and gun-mounts for some of the new ships. The Army Gun Factory at Watervliet, New York, also furnishes guns for the navy.

The largest gun ever built at the Naval Gun Factory was a 14-inch breech-loading, rifled cannon. The standard gun, which is made of nickel steel, is the 12-inch cannon, and is 46.1 feet in length and weighs 62.5 tons. When mounted its total weight is 108 tons. Its projectile weighs 870 pounds, and its maximum charge of smokeless gunpowder 400 pounds. The muzzle velocity of its projectile is 2800 feet a second, and its maximum range is about 12 miles. Its fighting range is from 5000 to 6000 yards, at which distance its projectile will penetrate about 14 inches of steel. It is a built-up gun, as are all the guns of the navy, being composed of nine sections, exclusive of its breech mechanism.[274]

The war of 1898 revealed the defects and needs of the naval magazines, and since its close the facilities for the storage and

---

[273] House Doc., 55C. 2S., No. 95; Congressional Record, XXXI, 934; XXXII, 2190-2191; Long, New American Navy, I, 49-52; Ann. Rept. of Chief of Bureau of Ordnance, 1905, pp. 45-47.

[274] Vandegrift and Bassett, Washington Navy Yard, 22.

manufacture of ammunition and explosives have been much extended and improved. Many new buildings have been erected, and the sites of the magazines have been enlarged by the purchase of additional grounds. About 1898 11 acres were added to the site of the naval magazine at Fort Mifflin, Pennsylvania. In 1900 the grounds of the St. Juliens Creek naval magazine, near Norfolk, were increased by the addition of 25 acres. In 1900 Iona Island, situated seven miles below West Point, New York, was acquired for a naval magazine convenient to the New York navy yard. It contains 116 acres of land, and cost $160,000. In 1902 79 acres adjoining the gunpowder depot at Lake Denmark, New Jersey, were obtained. Sites for magazines have been acquired at Hingham, Massachusetts, and Ostrich Bay, Washington. The magazine at Hingham is to supersede that at Chelsea, and is to serve the Portsmouth and Boston yards. The magazine at Ostrich Bay will furnish ammunition to the vessels that frequent Puget Sound. A naval magazine for the Philippine Islands has been constructed. In 1899 "Cedar Grove," near Norfolk, was purchased as a rendezvous for torpedo-boats. In 1901 1200 acres were added to the Naval Proving Grounds at Indianhead, Maryland. A smokeless powder factory has been erected there, and in other ways the establishment at this place has been developed. The Naval Torpedo Station and the Rose Island magazine near Newport have been much improved.[275]

Soon after wireless telegraphy was invented, the Bureau of Equipment made a study of it with a view to introducing it into the navy, and in 1901 Commander F. M. Barber (retired), residing in Paris, was ordered to report upon foreign wireless appliances. In 1903 the establishment of shore stations and the installation of wireless apparatus on shipboard was begun, and by 1905 48 vessels and 36 shore stations were either equipped or were being equipped. The shore stations were situated on the Atlantic, Gulf and Pacific coasts, at San Juan, Guantanamo, and Colon, and in the Philippines. Since 1905 many improvements in the equipment and installation of wireless apparatus have been made.

The beginning of aviation in the navy may be dated with a successful flight made in a Curtiss biplane in November, 1910,

[275] Miscl. Data, Bureau of Yards and Docks, 35, 46, 50, 52, 81. 83.

from the deck of the U. S. S. *Birmingham* at Hampton Roads. In December the Secretary of the Navy recommended the appropriation of $25,000 to carry on experiments in the development of aviation for naval purposes, and Congress in March of the following year made the appropriation. With the money thus supplied three flying machines were purchased and an aerodrome established at Annapolis. Some initial flights over Chesapeake Bay and the neighboring country have been made by Lieutenant John Rodgers, U. S. N.[276]

During the '80's and early '90's the improvement of the navy yards, docks and naval stations did not keep pace with the reconstruction of the fleet. In his first annual report Secretary Long devoted much space to setting forth the urgent need of the navy for adequate docking facilities and for the establishment at the principal navy yards of well-equipped repair shops, and referred to the desirability of concentrating the power stations of each yard. In the summer of 1897 he appointed a board to consider the construction of new docks. The estimates for the improvement of the several navy yards submitted by their commandants in 1897 called for the expenditure of more than $8,000,000.[277] The deficiencies of the navy yards were especially felt during the war with Spain, and Congress was moved to take some initial steps toward improving their facilities for the docking and repairing of ships.

By 1899 the improvement of the yards and docks began to be vigorously prosecuted. The establishments at Portsmouth, Boston, League Island and Pensacola, which had been for the most part closed since 1883, were reopened, and the expenditures at these yards were greatly increased. The development of the League Island yard was for the first time begun in earnest, and in 1901 the appropriation for its improvement amounted to almost a million dollars. The grounds of the Washington and the Norfolk yards were enlarged. Two new navy yards were established, one at Charleston, South Carolina, and the other at the naval station on Puget Sound, thus increasing the number of navy yards in the United States to ten.

The improvements recently made at these ten establishments have been numerous and important. Various shops and build-

---

[276] Ann. Rept. of Sec. of N., 1910, p. 23; 1911, p. 58.
[277] Ann. Rept. of Sec. of N., 1897, pp. 12-18.

ings have been erected, and much machinery has been installed for the repair of hulls and engines. Among the improvements are new water and drainage systems, paved streets, new wharves and quay walls, electric lighting of buildings and streets, and the installation of telephones and railway connections. In 1905 the consolidation of the power stations at the several yards was begun. The New York yard has been fitted out for the construction of battleships; and with little additional expense the Portsmouth, Boston, Norfolk and Mare Island yards might be similarly equipped. At these five establishments are located the principal repair shops of the navy. In 1902 the Bureau of Construction and Repair employed more than 5000 workmen and expended about $16,000,000 at the principal navy yards in the United States. From 1897 to 1905 the number of employees of the navy yards and naval stations, including officers, seamen, clerks, mechanics and laborers, at home and in our colonial possessions, increased from less than 7000 to more than 24,000.[278]

The organization and economy of the navy yards have continued to elicit differences of opinion both in and out of the navy. Various boards have from time to time given advice, and more than one Secretary of the Navy has attempted reforms. Early in 1909, after a board, of which Rear Admiral C. F. Goodrich was president, had considered the subject and made recommendations, Secretary Newberry put into operation a plan for reorganizing the yards. All the mechanical departments, all the laborers of the yard, the care of buildings and grounds, and all civil engineering work were placed under the direction of a manager, and a single pay-roll for the manufacturing department was created. Under the new plan the manager was able to reorganize the manufacturing and repair work, to consolidate the power plants, to reduce the number of ships, and to distribute more economically the machinery and tools. The commandant was left nominally in control, but with little real supervision over the manager. Secretary Meyer did not wholly approve of Newberry's reforms, taking the view that they deprived line officers of an opportunity to obtain experience in shop and navy yard work, and on July 1, 1909, he placed the work of repairing the machinery of ships under the direction of line officers.[279]

[278] Sen. Doc., 57C. 2S., No. 110, Official Register of U. S., 1897, 1905.
[279] Army and Navy Journal, XLVI, p. 580; Ann. Rept. of Sec. of N., p. 12.

Another reform recently attempted is the reduction of the number of navy yards and naval stations. Shortly before Secretary Newberry went out of office he issued an order closing certain southern yards, but this was suspended by his successor on the ground that it was illegal and unwise. Later however Secretary Meyer recommended that the navy yards at New Orleans and Pensacola and the naval stations at San Juan, Port Royal, New London and Sacketts Harbor be abandoned. In 1911 the subject of navy yards and naval stations was considered by a joint army and navy board, which reported in favor of a considerable reduction in their number. Owing to the interests of politicians and their constituents in the maintenance of naval establishments, it has so far been impossible to settle this question by an appeal to military needs and principles.[280]

The improvement of the docking facilities of the navy began with the appointment by Secretary Long on August 7, 1897, of a navy board, with Commodore F. M. Bunce as senior officer, to consider the subject. One of its members visited the dockyards of the European navies, and made a report on them. The board recommended the construction of six large graving, and three steel floating dry docks, and reported that docks were urgently needed at Boston, New York, Norfolk, Port Royal, New Orleans and Mare Island.[281] Admonished by the war with Spain, Congress made its first authorizations on May 4, 1898, when it provided for the construction of four graving-docks of timber, one each for the Portsmouth, Boston, League Island and Mare Island yards; and of a floating steel dock for the New Orleans naval station. Later, Congress decided to build the graving-docks of granite and concrete, since docks built of masonry last longer, need fewer repairs and are more serviceable than those constructed of timber. These four docks are larger than any previously constructed in the United States. They vary little in size, the one at League Island being 753 feet long, 140 feet wide, and 31 feet deep.

Soon after the close of the Spanish-American War, Congress authorized the construction of three additional graving-docks, of granite and concrete, to be built one each at the Charleston, Norfolk and New York navy yards. In 1901 a steel floating

[280] Ann. Rept. of Sec. of N., 1909, p. 16; 1910, pp. 32, 35; 1911, p. 22.
[281] Ann. Rept. of Sec. of N., 1897, p. 13; Sen. Doc., 55C. 2S., No. 107

dock was purchased from the Spanish government for $195,000, and was removed from Havana to the Pensacola navy yard. A floating steel dock for the New Orleans station was built by the Maryland Steel Company, at Sparrows Point, near Baltimore. In 1905 the same company, at a cost of $1,125,000, completed the steel floating dock Dewey, intended for the naval station at Cavite, Philippine Islands. Under the command of Commander H. H. Hosley it was successfully towed from its place of construction to the Philippines by way of the Mediterranean Sea, a distance of 13,000 miles. In 1907 the construction of a dry dock at Puget Sound, and in 1908 one at Pearl Harbor, Hawaii, were authorized. The docking facilities of the navy are now vastly improved over those of 1897, when there were only three docks capable of receiving battleships, and one of these, the Port Royal dock, was too small to permit the entrance of a battleship fitted with bilge keels. In that year, when the large dock at New York was out of repair, the Navy Department found it necessary to send the *Indiana* to Halifax, Nova Scotia, to have her bottom scraped and cleaned. At the present time such a mortifying necessity could scarcely arise.[282]

During the decade 1897-1907 considerable improvements were made at the various naval stations in the United States. The Navy Department increased its holdings of land at Newport, Annapolis, Port Royal, the Dry Tortugas, Key West and New Orleans. In 1898 and 1899 41 additional acres of land were acquired at Port Royal, and in 1901 the department decided that that place, owing to its inconvenient location and its shallow harbor, was not fitted for a naval station, and that a better site could be found near Charleston. A naval board which considered the subject recommended a location six miles above Charleston on the west bank of the Cooper River, and later more than a thousand acres were purchased there, extensive improvements made, and a large granite graving-dock constructed. Port Royal is now but little more than a coaling station.[283]

The need of greater and better coaling facilities became urgent during the war of 1898. In June of that year Secretary Long appointed a board, of which Rear Admiral George E. Belknap

---

[282] Long, New American Navy, I, 113.
[283] Ann. Rept. of Sec. of N., 1901, p. 144.

(retired) was president, to report on the location of coaling
depots at the navy yards and naval stations in the United States.
After visiting various sites, this board made a lengthy report,
in which it recommended the establishment of coaling pockets
and modern coaling facilities at nine ports on the Atlantic seaboard. During the war steps were taken for the installation of
modern coaling plants at Key West and the Dry Tortugas. On
May 4, 1898, Congress appropriated $250,000 for the establish-
ment of suitable coaling depots, and at its next session it gave
$400,000 more for the same purpose. Improved facilities for
coaling are now provided at the principal yards and stations
in the United States and several depots for coal have been established at other points on the coast. At Frenchmans Bay, Maine,
there is a 10,000-ton coaling depot, and a stand-pipe which will
hold 250,000 gallons of fresh water. A new coaling plant on
Narragansett Bay has a capacity of 40,000 tons, and one at New
London of 10,000 tons. The facilities for coaling have been
greatly increased at the Dry Tortugas and Key West, and a new
coaling plant has been installed at New Orleans. On the Pacific
coast, in addition to the coaling depots at the Mare Island and
Puget Sound navy yards, there are coaling facilities at San
Diego, California City Point, and Pichilinque Bay in Mexico.
There is a coaling station at Sitka, Alaska. The establishment of
a small station at Dutch Harbor, Alaska, and a large one at
Kiska Bay, Aleutian Islands, has been considered by the department.[284]

Several important naval stations and coaling depots have been
established in our island possessions, and the location of others
is contemplated. After the war with Spain a naval station was
maintained at Havana until it was abandoned in 1903. According to the terms of the Platt Amendment and of the Cuban
Constitution of 1902, Cuba agreed to lease lands to the United
States for coaling or naval stations. In 1903 she carried out
this agreement by granting to the United States, for a yearly
rental of $2000, complete jurisdiction and control over certain
lands at Guantanamo on the eastern part of the southern coast
of the island and containing 18,530 acres and a smaller tract
at Bahia Honda on the western part of the northern coast.[285]

[284] Ann. Rept. of Sec. of N., 1898, pp. 177-191; 1899, pp. 25-26; Proc. of
U. S. Naval Inst., XXX, 568-570.
[285] Ann. Rept. of Sec. of N., 1903, pp. 14-15.

Surveys of the Guantanamo reservation and some initial improvements upon it have been recently made, including the construction of a dry dock at a cost of $1,400,000. Plans for a coaling station at Bahia Honda have been prepared.

The principal naval station in the Philippine Islands is located at Olongapo, Luzon, on Subig Bay, whose mouth is 30 miles north of Manila Bay. The naval base of the Spanish was at Cavite on Manila Bay, but they had recognized the superior advantages of Subig Bay, and had commenced there the construction of a naval station. Two naval boards, together with Admiral Dewey, reported in favor of establishing a naval base at Olongapo, and in 1905 Congress appropriated $862,000 for the improvement of the site there, which contains about 30,000 acres. In 1909 a joint army and navy board, instructed by the events of the Russian-Japanese War, reported against the establishment of an extensive station at Olongapo, and in favor of the selection of Pearl Harbor, Hawaii, as the American naval base in the Pacific. The building up of a station at the latter place is now under way. Among other improvements a dry dock to cost $2,000,000 has been authorized. After the war with Spain, the Cavite station served as a base for the naval vessels in the Philippines, although it was deficient in many particulars. Here were located repair shops, storehouses, officers' quarters, barracks, coaling depot, and until recently a naval hospital. In 1905 more than 3000 employees, including officers, clerks, mechanics and laborers, were employed at Cavite.[286] Depots for coal and supplies were established at Isabela de Basilan, Cebu and Polloc.

The United States has a naval and coaling station at Yokohama, Japan. The Hawaiian naval station situated near Honolulu comprises some 700 or 800 acres of land, and has a coaling plant with a capacity for 30,000 tons. This will be superseded by the Pearl Harbor station. United States naval stations are located at the islands of Tutuila and Guam, where facilities have been provided and other improvements made. The senior naval officers at these islands not only act as the commandants of their stations, but they are also charged with the duties and responsibilities of military governors, in which capacity they exercise plenary powers. Their reports deal with the health, schools,

[286] Official Register of U. S., 1905.

roads, occupations and government of their respective islands. Two small naval stations are maintained in Porto Rico, one at San Juan, and the other at Culebra to the eastward of the main island.

The acquisition of tropical territories and the recent increase in the number of officers and enlisted men of the navy has greatly added to the work of the medical corps, which is now called upon to treat various tropical diseases abounding in our island possessions. In 1899 a temporary naval hospital was established at Cavite. In 1905 a permanent naval hospital for the Philippines was completed at Canacao, where the Spanish had begun the erection of a hospital. It is about a mile from Cavite, situated on a narrow sandy peninsula, and is freely swept by refreshing breezes from Manila Bay. Other naval hospitals in the Pacific are maintained at Yokohama, Sitka, Honlulu, Guam and Tutuila. At the two latter islands the care of sick natives falls in large part upon the naval surgeons. At Guam the patients, whether natives or sailormen, are treated at the Maria Scroeder Hospital, established by our government. The naval hospital at Tutuila, we are told, was a few years ago " far from what it should be. It was a trader's store, over 30 years old, rotten in every part, leaking, and infested with vermin." The hospital for the natives was in a separate building. " It is a thatched-roofed native hut, and answers its purpose well." [287] In January, 1904, a hospital for the San Juan naval station was established at Puerta de Fiera.

In the United States new naval hospitals have been constructed at Washington and Annapolis. With the exception of these two and those at New York, Mare Island and Canacao, the hospitals of the navy are said to be " ill arranged for administration, as well as for the care and treatment of the sick, are defective in design, lacking in many essentials of proper construction, obsolete in type, inadequate in capacity, and require remodeling to adapt them to the demands of modern medical and surgical practice." [288] These old buildings are much inferior to the better class of civilian establishments. In 1905 a new naval supply depot was being erected at New York. Medical depots are also maintained at Mare Island and Cavite. In 1902 the school for

[287] Ann. Rept. of Surgeon General of U. S. Navy, 1905, p. 101.
[288] Ann. Rept. of Surgeon General of U. S. Navy, 1905, p. 15.

naval surgeons at the old depot or " naval laboratory " at New York was moved to Washington, and combined with the Naval Museum of Hygiene. At first the new establishment was known as the " Naval Museum of Hygiene and Medical School," but later its name was changed to the " Naval Medical School." The course of instruction at the school was enlarged and improved, and adapted not only to the needs of the recruits to the surgical corps, but to the older surgeons as well. In 1902 a training school for the members of the naval hospital corps was established at the Norfolk naval hospital.

SECRETARIES OF THE NAVY
AND THEIR TENURE OF OFFICE*

BENJAMIN STODDART	June 18, 1798—March 31, 1801
ROBERT SMITH	July 27, 1801—March 7, 1809
PAUL HAMILTON	May 15, 1809—December 31, 1812
WILLIAM JONES	January 19, 1813—December 1, 1814
B. W. CROWNINSHIELD	January 16, 1815—September 30, 1818
SMITH THOMPSON	January 1, 1819—August 31, 1823
SAMUEL SOUTHARD	September 16, 1823—March 3, 1829
JOHN BRANCH	March 9, 1829—May 12, 1831
LEVI WOODBURY	May 23, 1831—June 30, 1834
MAHLON DICKERSON	July 1, 1834—June 30, 1838
JAMES K. PAULDING	July 1, 1838—March 3, 1841
GEORGE E. BADGER	March 6, 1841—September 11, 1841
ABEL P. UPSHUR	October 11, 1841—July 23, 1843
DAVID HENSHAW	July 24, 1843—February 18, 1844
THOMAS W. GILMER	February 19, 1844—February 28, 1844
JOHN Y. MASON	March 26, 1844—March 10, 1845
GEORGE BANCROFT	March 11, 1845—September 9, 1846
JOHN Y. MASON	September 10, 1846—March 7, 1849
WILLIAM B. PRESTON	March 8, 1849—July 23, 1850
WILLIAM A. GRAHAM	August 2, 1850—July 25, 1852
JOHN P. KENNEDY	July 26, 1852—March 7, 1853
JAMES C. DOBBIN	March 8, 1853—March 6, 1857
ISAAC TOUCEY	March 7, 1857—March 6, 1861
GIDEON WELLES	March 7, 1861—March 3, 1869
ADOLPH E. BORIE	March 9, 1869—June 25, 1869

*George Cabot was nominated as the first Secretary of the Navy on May 1, 1798. His nomination was confirmed by the Senate, but he declined to accept the appointment.

GEORGE M. ROBESON	June 26, 1869—March 12, 1877
RICHARD W. THOMPSON	March 13, 1877—December 20, 1880
NATHAN GOFF, JR.	January 7, 1881—March 6, 1881
WILLIAM H. HUNT	March 7, 1881—April 16, 1882
WILLIAM E. CHANDLER	April 17, 1882—March 6, 1885
WILLIAM C. WHITNEY	March 7, 1885—March 5, 1889
BENJAMIN F. TRACY	March 6, 1889—March 6, 1893
HILARY A. HERBERT	March 7, 1893—March 5, 1897
JOHN D. LONG	March 6, 1897—April 30, 1902
WILLIAM H. MOODY	May 1, 1902—June 30, 1904
PAUL MORTON	July 1, 1904—June 30, 1905
CHARLES J. BONAPARTE	July 1, 1905—December 16, 1906
VICTOR H. METCALF	December 17, 1906—November 30, 1908
TRUMAN H. NEWBERRY	December 1, 1908—March 5, 1909
GEORGE VON L. MEYER	March 6, 1909—March 4, 1913
JOSEPHUS DANIELS	March 5, 1913—March 4, 1921

CHARLES OSCAR PAULLIN, historian and nautical expert, contributed extensively to the written history of the United States Navy during his lifetime. He was born in Jamestown, Ohio, about 1870, and died in Washington, D.C. in 1944. Unmarried, Dr. Paullin was long a member of the Cosmos Club of Washington. He was awarded a BS degree at Union Christian College, Merom, Indiana, in 1893; did graduate work at Johns Hopkins and the Catholic University of America and took his PhD degree at the University of Chicago in 1904.

From 1896 to 1900, Dr. Paullin worked with the Hydrographic Office, U. S. Navy Department. He was a member of the Carnegie Institute staff in Washington from 1910 to 1936, and during those years he lectured on diplomatic and naval history at Johns Hopkins and George Washington Universities. He was a member of several historical and naval associations, including the U. S. Naval Institute, and served as trustee for the Naval Historical Foundation. A complete listing of his written works appears in the front pages of this book.